BARRON'S
STUDENTS' #1 CHOICE

PASS KEY
TO THE
LSAT
LAW SCHOOL ADMISSION TEST

Jerry Bobrow, Ph.D.
Founder
Bobrow Test Preparation Services

Programs at major universities, colleges, and law schools throughout California. Lecturer, consultant, author of more than 30 nationally known test preparation books. Bobrow Test Preparation Services instructs over 2,000 LSAT test takers each year.

Revised by Bernard V. Zandy, M.S.

Contributing Authors and Consultants

William A. Covino, Ph.D.

Brian N. Siegel, J.D.

Merritt L. Weisinger, J.D.

David A. Kay, M.S.

Pitt Gilmore, B.A.

Daniel C. Spencer, M.S.

Allan Casson, Ph.D.

Bernard V. Zandy, M.S.

Keith R. Strange, M.P.A.

Jean Eggenschwiler, M.A.

Seventh Edition
BARRON'S EDUCATIONAL SERIES, INC.

Dedicated to the memory of Jerry Bobrow

All inquiries should be addressed to:
Barron's Educational Series, Inc.
250 Wireless Boulevard
Hauppauge, New York 11788
www.barronseduc.com

Library of Congress Control Number: 2009927251

ISBN-13: 978-0-7641-4083-9
ISBN-10: 0-7641-4083-3

PRINTED IN UNITED STATES OF AMERICA
9 8 7 6 5 4

CONTENTS

Chapter 3   Analytical Reasoning   106

PREFACE

The LSAT is a difficult exam and we want to give you every possible advantage!
In this book, *Barron's Pass Key to the LSAT,* the compact version of Barron's best-selling *LSAT,* we have gathered the expertise and materials developed in more than 30 years of successful LSAT, GMAT, GRE, CSET, NTE, CBEST, ACT, ELM, RICA, and SAT preparation courses that are currently offered at more than 25 universities, colleges, and law schools.

So how are we going to give you every possible advantage?
By thoroughly analyzing each of the sections of the LSAT and reviewing the thinking processes and the skills necessary for top performance, this text aims at complete preparation. It is up to date with the most recent forms of the latest test. The staff of writers and consultants includes specialists in problem solving, reading, writing, logic, law, and test psychology. All these authors and consultants have been teaching prelaw students in LSAT preparation programs for many years.

An introductory section will acquaint you with the format of the LSAT. Then, a series of insightful chapters on the most recent sections of the test will carefully analyze each question type, pinpoint specific test-taking strategies, and give additional practice. Three full-length practice tests will allow you to get the feel of the real thing while you begin applying new skills and techniques. Your answer sheet will resemble the machine-graded LSAT answer sheet, and an analysis chart will enable you to assess your strengths and weaknesses. The answers to each practice test are fully explained.

Will this be effective?
Complete analysis, thorough instruction, extensive practice, up-to-date examples, and the most successful overall systems of objective test taking are described in detail in this book to give you invaluable insight into the LSAT. The test-taking strategies and approaches we've included have been proven effective for over 2,000,000 graduate and undergraduate students and teachers whom we've assisted in preparing for these important exams. If you're short of time, *Barron's Pass Key to the LSAT* is what you need.

All right, let's get down to business and start with a brief overview of How to Prepare.

PREPARING FOR THE LSAT: A FIVE-STEP APPROACH

Preparing to take the LSAT is no easy task; it takes a well thought-out, focused study plan. This plan should follow these five basic steps:

1. Awareness
2. Knowing the Basic Skills
3. Understanding the Thinking Processes
4. Applying Strategies and Techniques
5. Practice, Practice, Practice

STEP ONE: AWARENESS

Before taking the LSAT, you should know everything possible about the test from the length of each section to the specific types of questions. Be an expert on the structure and construction of the exam.

The LSAT consists of five 35-minute multiple-choice sections. Four sections count toward your LSAT score; one experimental section is a repeat of the other sections and does not count toward your score. An unscored essay is also included. The types of questions are: Logical Reasoning (two sections), Analytical Reasoning (one section), and Reading Comprehension (one section).

Logical Reasoning—two sections that include short passages, statements, arguments, or discussions, each followed by 1 question (sometimes 2) asking about the reasoning involved. Each section contains between 24 and 26 questions. This question type requires good reading and reasoning skills and accounts for 50 percent of your LSAT score. You will have two sections of Logical Reasoning, about 50 of the 100 questions that count toward your score. A course in formal logic is not necessary but could be helpful, as would any course that requires critical reading and reasoning.

Analytical Reasoning—one section that includes four sets of conditions, statements, or rules. You are required to see the relationships among the items being described and discussed. Constructing a simple display or diagram using the information given is an important part of attacking this question type. Each set is followed by 5 to 7 questions for a total of 22 to 24 questions. This section appears to be the most difficult for most test takers, but it also appears to be the most preparable.

Reading Comprehension—one section that includes three fairly sophisticated passages or sets, each containing from 400 to 500 words. A fourth set called comparative reading was introduced in June 2007. It contains two similar passages of about 250 words each. Each of the four reading comprehension sets will have 5 to 8 questions, for a total of about 26 to 28 questions for the section. The passages can be from the fields of science, philosophy, economy, history, law, and so on, but the questions must be answered from the actual passages given, not from your general or specific knowledge of a subject.

These sections total from 96 to 104 questions and are scaled to a scoring range of 120–180 with an average score about 150 or 151. Approximately 60 percent correct is necessary to obtain an average score. There is no penalty for guessing on the LSAT, so never leave a question without at least taking a guess.

Unscored Essay—the multiple-choice sections of the LSAT are followed by a 35-minute unscored essay. This essay is written on special sheets of lined paper. Scratch paper is given so that you can organize your essay before writing. A copy of your essay is sent to each law school to which you apply. The law schools may use the essay in a number of ways—as a tiebreaker between two applicants, as a measure for admittance, and so on. Test takers who have not seen a sample topic are often worried about the essay topic. You should review a few sample topics and try writing a few essays. The topics typically involve a selection that needs to be made between two people, items, techniques, places, and so on.

There is no right or wrong answer. Simply make your selection and support it by using the criteria and information given.

STEP TWO: KNOWING THE BASIC SKILLS

You should know the basic skills necessary to do well on the LSAT. Because the LSAT is designed to measure skills necessary to do well your first year in law school (and not what kind of an attorney you are going to be), it is important to focus your study and some review on these skills. These skills include reading comprehension skills, critical reading skills, analytical skills, and reasoning skills. Notice that the test is reading and reasoning based.

STEP THREE: UNDERSTANDING THE THINKING PROCESSES

The LSAT, unlike many other standardized exams, is not content oriented, but is reasoning oriented. Therefore, it is vital to understand the thinking processes involved in obtaining the correct/credited response. You should not memorize information, but focus your preparation on understanding the reasoning involved. Carefully analyzing each question type, the credited response, and the common mistakes will help you understand the thinking processes. You should understand that the correct answer to each question is facing you on the page and that the incorrect answers are called "distracters." An incorrect answer that looks good or is close is often called an "attractive distracter." Learn to avoid the attractive distracters by analyzing the choices and understanding the thinking processes.

STEP FOUR: APPLYING STRATEGIES AND TECHNIQUES

There are many strategies and techniques that you can and should learn before taking your LSAT. The general strategies include how and when to skip problems, eliminate answers, and circle important words. The specific strategies should include how to draw diagrams or simple displays for Analytical Reasoning, how to actively read Reading Comprehension passages and how to preread questions and focus on Logical Reasoning questions. You should also be very familiar with the many types of questions you could be asked in each section. You should take the test only after reviewing and practicing many specific strategies for the question types.

STEP FIVE: PRACTICE, PRACTICE, PRACTICE

As with other standardized exams, becoming a proficient LSAT test taker takes lots of practice. This practice helps you get acclimated to working under time pressure as well as dealing with the fatigue factor. When you practice, try to replicate testing conditions. Don't use scratch paper, do your work in the test booklet, and transfer your answers to an answer sheet. Don't practice on a large tabletop, as in most cases you will be taking your test in a classroom with fairly small desktops. When you practice, you should give yourself only 30 minutes to complete a section, even though the time allotted is actually 35 minutes. Shorting yourself on time will force you to work faster and should increase your speed. Another reason for extended practice is to identify the types of mistakes you make when you're tired, that is, dealing with the fatigue factor. Practice taking three 35-minute sections (giving yourself 30 minutes for each section) back to back to back with only about a 5 second break between each one. Then, take a short break of about 10 minutes and try another two sections. When you complete your practice tests, carefully analyze each section and watch for any consistent types of errors. On your next practice session, focus on eliminating those errors.

The LSAT is an important, difficult exam, but you can prepare for it, and you owe it to yourself to be prepared. Read and review this book carefully. You'll be glad you did.

Good Luck!!!
Jerry Bobrow, Ph.D.

Jerry Bobrow, Ph.D., is the author of *Barron's LSAT* and many other national best-selling preparation books. The founder of Bobrow Test Preparation Services, Dr. Bobrow taught and directed programs for most of the California State Universities for more than 30 years.

ACKNOWLEDGMENTS

I gratefully acknowledge the following sources for granting permission to use materials from their publications:

Pages 64, 319: Dr. Albert Upton, *Design for Thinking,* Stanford University Press, Stanford, California.

Pages 233–234: George E. Riggs, publisher; news articles and editorials from *The Herald News,* Fontana, California.

Pages 257–258, 265–267, 297–298, 368–369, 425–426, 448: Dean Seymour Greitzer, Law Reviews from Glendale University College of Law.

Pages 259–260: June Axinn and Mark J. Stern, *Social Welfare: A History of the American Response to Need,* Allyn and Bacon, Pearson Education, Needham Heights, MA, 2001, pages 237–238.

Pages 260–261: William A. Kelso, *Poverty and the Underclass: Changing Perceptions of the Poor in America,* New York University Press, 1994, pages 31–32.

Pages 262–263: Peter Heather, *The Goths: The Peoples of Europe Series,* Blackwell, Oxford, England, 1996, pages 3–4.

Page 302: C. Vann Woodward, *The Future of the Past.* New York: Oxford University Press, 1991.

Pages 304–305: Joseph E. LeDoux, "Emotion, Memory and the Brain," *Scientific American,* June 1994. All rights reserved.

Pages 370–371: Mark Willner et al., *Let's Review: Global History and Geography,* 3rd Ed., Barron's Educational Series, Inc., Hauppauge, N.Y., 2000.

Pages 372–373 John Kenneth Galbraith, *American Capitalism.* Sentry edition. Boston: Houghton Mifflin, 1962.

Pages 391–392: Law Reviews from the University of California at Los Angeles (UCLA) Law School—Comment, "United States Tax Treaty Policy Toward Developing Countries: The China Example," 35 UCLA L. Rev. 369 (1987).

Page 393: Jacinto Quirarte, *Mexican American Artists,* University of Texas Press, Austin, TX, 1973.

Pages 393–394: Shifra M. Goldman, *Contemporary Mexican Painting in a Time of Change,* University of New Mexico Press, Albuquerque, NM, 1995, page 8.

Pages 395–396: Robert A. Nisbet, *The Present Age: Progress and Anarchy in Modern America.* New York: Harper & Row, 1988. Reprinted by permission of HarperCollins.

Pages 398–399: P. James E. Peebles, David N. Schramm, Edwin L. Turner and Richard G. Kron, "The Evolution of the Universe," *Scientific American,* October 1994.

Pages 452–453: William Fleming, *Arts and Ideas,* Holt, Rinehart and Winston, New York, 1968, page 520.

Pages 453–454: From de la Croix Tansey, Kirkpatrick. *Gardner's Art Through the Ages,* 7E. © 1980 Wadsworth, a part of Cengage Learning, Inc. Reproduced by permission, www.cengage.com/permissions

Pages 456–457: Gabrielle I. Edwards, *Biology the Easy Way,* 3rd Ed., © 2000 by Barron's Educational Series, Inc., Hauppauge, N.Y.

(Note: Some of the Law Reviews have been edited, including changes in names, places, and dates.)

My thanks to James Zinger, President, Hypmovation, for the use of excerpts from his writings; to Jean Eggenschwiler, writer and editor, for her contributions; to Joy Mondragon, for her assistance in assembling the manuscript; to Lynn Turner, Dana Lind, Brenda Clodfelter, and Jennifer Johnson for typing the manuscript; and to Linda Turner for manuscript editing and final preparation.

And finally thanks to my wife, Susan Bobrow, for critical analysis and moral support; and to my three children, Jennifer, Adam, and Jonathan, for their many years of providing comic relief.

A special thank you to the contributors and consultants:
Allan Casson, Ph.D., Former Chairman, Department of English, University of Southern California (USC)

William A. Covino, Ph.D., Former Chairman, Department of English, Florida Atlantic University, Florida; Provost, Stanislaus State University, California

Pitt Gilmore, B.A., Editor, Educational Administrator, Bobrow Test Preparation Services; UCLA

David A. Kay, M.S., Former Chairman, Math Department, Moorpark College, California

Brian N. Siegel, J.D., Bar Review Specialist, Author/Legal Study Aids

Daniel C. Spencer, M.S., Management Services Officer, University of California at Los Angeles (UCLA)

Keith R. Strange, M.P.A., Educational Administrator, Junipero Serra High School, California

Merrit L. Weisinger, J.D., Attorney at Law, Lecturer, Weisinger and Associates

Bernard V. Zandy, M.S., Professor, Math Department, Fullerton College, California

PART ONE

INTRODUCTION

Getting Acquainted with the Test

INTRODUCTION
TO THE LSAT

ANSWERS TO SOME COMMONLY ASKED QUESTIONS

What does the LSAT measure?

The LSAT is designed to measure a range of mental abilities related to the study of law; therefore, it is used by most law schools to evaluate their applicants.

Will any special knowledge of the law raise my score on the LSAT?

The LSAT is designed so that candidates from a particular academic background are given no advantage. The questions measure reading comprehension, logical reasoning, and analytical reasoning, drawing from a variety of verbal and analytical material.

Does a high score on the LSAT predict success in law school or in the practice of law?

Success on the LSAT demonstrates your ability to read with understanding and to reason clearly under pressure; surely these strengths are important to both the study and the practice of law, as is the ability to write well, measured by the LSAT Writing Sample. To say that success on the LSAT *predicts* success in law school may overstate the case, however, because success in law school also involves skills that are not measured by the LSAT.

When is the LSAT administered?

The regular administration of the test occurs nationwide four times each year, around the beginning of the fall, winter, spring, and summer seasons. Except for the summer month, the test is usually administered on a Saturday morning from 8:30 A.M. to about 1:00 P.M. For the past few years, the *summer exam* has been given on a Monday afternoon. Dates are announced annually by the Law School Admission Council (LSAC) in Newtown, Pennsylvania.

What if I cannot take the test on a Saturday?

Some special arrangements are possible: Check the Law School Admission Services (LSAS) General Information Booklet in your registration packet. Those who must take the exam at a time when the regular administration occurs on Saturday, but who cannot participate on Saturday for religious reasons, may arrange for a special Monday administration.

How early should I register?

Regular registration closes about one month before the exam date. Late registration is available up to about three weeks prior to the exam date. There is an additional fee for late registration.

How do I register for the LSAT?

You can register for the LSAT three different ways: online, by telephone, or by mail. **To register online**, use: *www.LSAC.org*. **To register by telephone**, call (215) 968-1001. (Be sure to complete the worksheet in the *LSAT & LSDAS Registration/Information Book* before calling.) **To register by mail**, complete the appropriate sections in the *LSAT & LSDAS Registration/Information Book* and mail with payment to Law Services in the preaddressed return envelope.

The LSAC encourages you to register online and take advantage of the benefits available. The benefits listed by the LSAC include:

"Faster test score delivery via e-mail
Access to real-time test center availability for LSAT registration
Fast, easy test date and center changes
Printable LSAT ticket
Electronic test disclosure material
Fast additional law school report orders
Up-to-date file status
Instantly accessible LSDAS documents
Faster processing for publication, video, and software orders
Forum preregistration—saves time at the forums
No snail-mail"

Is walk-in registration available?

No. The LSAC will not permit walk-ins on the day of the test. Be sure to read carefully the *LSAT & LSDAS Registration/Information Book* section on registering to take the LSAT.

What is the LSDAS?

The LSDAS (Law School Data Assembly Service) compiles a report about each subscribing applicant. The report contains LSAT results, a summary of the applicant's academic work, and copies of college transcripts. A report is sent to each law school that the applicant designates. Thus, if you register for the LSDAS, you will not need to mail a separate transcript to each of your prospective law schools. **Reminder:** You should review information about the Candidate Referral Service in your *LSAT & LSDAS Registration/Information Book.*

How is the LSAT used?

Your LSAT score is one common denominator by which a law school compares you to other applicants. Other factors also determine your acceptance to law school: a law school may consider your personal qualities, grade-point average, extracurricular achievements, and letters of recommendation. Requirements for admission vary widely from school to school, so you are wise to contact the law school of your choice for specific information.

How do I obtain registration forms and registration information?

The registration forms covering the LSAT and LSDAS are available in the *LSAT & LSDAS Registration/Information Book.* Copies of the book are available at the admissions offices of most law schools, and testing offices at most undergraduate universities and colleges. You may also obtain the book and more information by writing to Law Services, Box 2000, 661 Penn Street, Newtown, PA 18940-0998; by Internet, using *www.LSAC.org;* by fax, at (215) 968-1119; by e-mail, at Lsacinfor@LSAC.org; or by telephone, at (215) 968-1001.

What is the structure of the LSAT?

The LSAT contains five 35-minute multiple-choice sections followed by a 35-minute Writing Sample. The Writing Sample does not count as part of your LSAT score. The common question types that do count toward your score are Logical Reasoning (two sections), Analytical Reasoning (one section), and Reading Comprehension (one section). In addition to these four sections, one experimental or pretest section will appear. This experimental or pretest section, which will probably be a repeat of one of the common question types, will not count in your score.

How is the LSAT scored?

The score for the objective portion of the test ranges from 120 to 180, and there is no penalty for wrong answers. The Writing Sample is unscored, but copies are sent to the law schools of your choice for evaluation.

What about question structure and value?

All LSAT questions, apart from the Writing Sample, are multiple-choice with five choices. All questions within a section are of equal value, regardless of difficulty.

Should I guess?

There is no penalty for guessing on the LSAT. Therefore, before you move on to the next question, at least take a guess. You should fill in guess answers for those you have left blank or did not get to, before time is called for that section. If you can eliminate one or more choices as incorrect, your chances for a correct guess increase.

How often can I take the LSAT?

You may take the LSAT more than once if you wish. But keep in mind that any report sent to you or to law schools will contain scores for any exams taken over the past five or so years, along with an average score for those exams. The law school receiving your scores will decide which score is the best estimate of your ability; many law schools rely on the average score as a reliable figure. Normally, you may not take the test more than three times in a two-year period.

Is it possible to cancel my LSAT scores?

You may cancel your score at the test center or within six calendar days after taking the test.

How early should I arrive at the test center and what should I bring?

Arrive at the test center 20 to 30 minutes before the time designated on your admission ticket. Bring three or four sharpened No. 2 pencils, an eraser, and a noiseless watch (no alarm, calculator, or beeping), as well as your LSAT Admission Ticket and proper identification as described in the *LSAT & LSDAS Registration/Information Book*. **Note:** You may use only a No. 2 pencil or a highlighter pen to underline passages in the test book. Ink or ballpoint pens are not permitted.

Are there accommodations for persons with disabilities?

Persons with documented disabilities may have special accommodations available. Candidates who need accommodations are urged to register and submit all required documentation well in advance of the registration deadlines.

Can I prepare for the LSAT?

Yes. Reading skills and test-taking strategies should be the focus of your preparation for the test as a whole. Success on the more specialized analytical sections of the test depends on your thorough familiarity with the types of problems you are likely to encounter and the reasoning process involved. For maximum preparation, work through this book and practice the strategies and techniques outlined in each section.

BASIC FORMAT OF THE LSAT AND SCORING

THE *ORDER* OF THE FOLLOWING MULTIPLE-CHOICE SECTIONS *WILL* VARY. The Experimental Section is not necessarily the last section.

Section	Number of Questions	Minutes
I. Logical Reasoning	24–26	35
II. Analytical Reasoning	22–24 (4 sets)	35
III. Reading Comprehension	26–28 (4 passages)	35
IV. Logical Reasoning	24–26	35
V. Experimental Section	varies	35
Writing Sample	1 essay	35
TOTALS	118–132 questions (only 96–104 count toward your score)	210 minutes or 3 hours 30 minutes

The LSAT is scored on a 120 to 180 scale.

The following simple chart will give you a very general approximation of the LSAT scoring system. It shows the approximate percentage of right answers necessary on the LSAT to be in a certain score range.

Approximate % of Right Answers	Approximate Score Range
Between 75% and 100%	160–180
Between 50% and 75%	145–159
Between 25% and 50%	130–144
Between 0% and 25%	120–129

Note that this chart is meant to give you an *approximate* score range.

A CLOSER LOOK AT THE TIMING—WHAT IT REALLY MEANS

Although the LSAT comprises five 35-minute multiple-choice sections and a 35-minute unscored essay, it is important to understand the timing breakdown and what it means. The test is actually broken down as follows:

105 min. { Section I 35 mins.
Section II 35 mins.
Section III 35 mins.

Short break—usually 10–15 minutes

70 min. { Section IV 35 mins.
Section V 35 mins.

35 min. { Writing Sample (Essay)—35 mins.

Notice that you are given three multiple-choice sections with no breaks in between. When they say "stop" at the end of 35 minutes they will immediately say something like, "Turn to the next section, make sure that you are in the right section, ready, begin." So, in essence, you are working three sections back to back to back. This means that when you practice you should be sure to practice testing for 1 hour and 45 minutes without a break.

After the short break, when you may get up, get a drink, and go to the restroom, you are back for two more back-to-back multiple-choice sections.

For the final 35-minute writing sample you will be given scratch paper to do your prewriting or outlining.

Keep in mind that there will be some time taken before the exam and after the exam for clerical-type paperwork—distributing and picking up paperwork, filling out test forms, and so on.

IMPORTANT REMINDERS

- At least half of your test will contain Logical Reasoning questions; prepare accordingly. Make sure that you are good at Logical Reasoning!
- The experimental or pretest section will usually repeat other sections and can appear in different places on the exam. At the time of the exam, you will not know which section is experimental. Take the test as if all of the sections count.
- Scoring will be from 120 to 180. This is the score, and the percentile rank that goes with it is what the law schools look at and are referring to in their discussions.
- All questions in a section are of equal value, so do not get stuck on any one question. The scores are determined by totaling all of your right answers on the test and then scaling.
- Answer all the easy questions first; then come back and answer the tougher questions. Don't be afraid to skip a question, but always at least take a guess.
- There is NO PENALTY for guessing, so at least take a guess before you move to the next question.
- The 35-minute Writing Sample will not be scored, but copies will be forwarded to the law schools to which you apply. Scratch paper will be provided for the Writing Sample only.
- Keep in mind that regardless of the format of your exam, two sections of Logical Reasoning, one section of Analytical Reasoning, and one section of Reading Comprehension always count toward your score.

SOME WORDS TO THE WISE

ASK A FEW QUESTIONS

Before you actually start your study plan there are four basic questions that you should ask the law schools to which you are applying:

1. Considering my GPA and other qualifications, what score do you think I need to get into your law school?
2. When do you need to get my score reports? Or, When should I take the test to meet your deadlines?
3. What do you do if I take the LSAT more than once? Remember that when the law school receives your score report it will see a score for each time you've taken the test *and* an average of the scores. It is up to the law schools and their governing bodies as to what score(s) they will consider. Try to do your best on the first try and take the LSAT only once, if possible.
4. What do you do with my Writing Sample? Is it used as a tiebreaker? Do you score it yourself? Is it just another piece of the process?

Knowing the answers to most of these questions before you start your study will help you understand what is expected and will help you get mentally ready for the task ahead.

AN EFFECTIVE STUDY PROGRAM

A THREE-WEEK LSAT STUDY PLAN

Many students don't even bother to read the LSAT bulletin, let alone do any thorough preparation for the test. You, however, should begin your LSAT preparation by reading the LSAT bulletin (book) carefully; information about how to obtain one is on page 3. The bulletin is filled with information about registration and score reporting. Also provided with the registration book is an "official" practice test. You should also send for copies of old exams (good practice) and check online for more materials.

With the preliminaries out of the way, begin working through this book. Because it is geared to an intensive three-week study plan, your study time must be well focused and well planned. This study time should be free from distractions. If you plan your study time wisely, you will find the techniques, strategies, practice, and analyses in this book invaluable to your LSAT preparation.

Most people can keep up with the following study sequence by devoting about 10 to 12 hours a week. It is most important that you review and practice *daily,* for about an hour or two each day. Don't "save up" your practice for one long session each week. Shorter, regular practice sessions will allow you to assimilate skills and strategies more effectively and efficiently.

Always spend some extra time reviewing "why" you made your mistakes. Watch for repeated or consistent errors. These errors are often the easiest to correct. As you review, focus on the thinking process involved in reaching the credited response, and note specifically where you made the error.

If you have reviewed an explanation, and still do not understand where you made an error, mark the problem in your book and go on. Return to review this problem later, after you have had an opportunity to review other problems that use similar thinking processes. Don't get stuck on reviewing one problem.

When reviewing answers, don't just look at the ones you got wrong. Instead, be aware of not only "what" questions you're getting right, but also "how" you are getting them right. Positive habits need to be reinforced.

Week 1

- Read the section "Answers to Some Commonly Asked Questions" (p. 3).
- Read carefully "Before You Begin" (p. 11), paying special attention to the "One-Check, Two-Check System" and the "Elimination Strategy." Applying these techniques confidently should make quite a difference in your test taking.
- Read carefully the chapters on Reading Comprehension, Logical Reasoning, Analytical Reasoning, and the Writing Sample.
- Spend some extra time reviewing the chapter on Logical Reasoning. Remember: Logical Reasoning will comprise two of the four scored sections of your exam.
- Review the chapter on Reading Comprehension. Do the Reading Comprehension problems in the chapter, the ones in the LSAT sample test, and those in Model Test One (p. 297). Correct and analyze your performance.

Note: Do not time yourself on these practice tests. Your task at present is to familiarize yourself with strategies and techniques, a task that is best done slowly, working back and forth between the introductory chapter and the practice problems. You may get an uncomfortable number of problems wrong at this stage, but, instead of being discouraged, you should attempt to understand clearly the reasons for your errors. Such understanding will become a plus in the future.

- Review the chapter on the Writing Sample, and write an essay about one of the given topics. Ask a friend with good writing skills to read your essay and offer constructive criticism.
- Review the chapter on Logical Reasoning. Do the Logical Reasoning problems in the chapter, those in the LSAT practice test, and the ones in Model Test One (pp. 313 and 327). Correct and analyze your performance.

Week 2

- Review the chapter on Analytical Reasoning. Do the Analytical Reasoning problems in the chapter, those in the LSAT practice test, and those in Model Test One (pp. 308 and 322). Correct and analyze your performance.
  Note: At this point you have introduced yourself to the whole test, and have tried some effective strategies. Now you should begin timing each of your practice tests.
- Do the Reading Comprehension problems in Model Test Two (pp. 368 and 391), and the Logical Reasoning problems in Model Test Two (pp. 359 and 383). Correct and analyze your performance.
- Do the Analytical Reasoning problems in Model Test Two (p. 378). Correct and analyze your performance.
- Write another essay about one of the topics given in the Writing Sample chapter, and have a friend read and respond to your effort.

Week 3

- Early in the week, do all of Model Test Three in one setting. For each section, time yourself, then correct and analyze your performance. Again, have a friend read and respond to your efforts on the Writing Sample.
  Note: This long practice testing will familiarize you with some of the difficulties you will encounter on the actual test—maintaining focus and concentration, dealing with fatigue, pacing, etc. It will also help you build your endurance. Remember, as you analyze your mistakes, to watch for repeated errors. Sometimes these are the easiest to eliminate. For extra practice, you could also use the full-length practice test offered by the Law Services at *www.LSAC.org*.
- Review carefully all of the Logical Reasoning problems in the sample test in the LSAT bulletin, Chapter 1, and any others you have completed in the model tests in this book.

- A few days before your exam, review some of the problems you have already completed—focus on the thinking processes. You may wish to reread chapters that gave you the most difficulty.
- Finally, carefully read the review of test-taking strategies at the end of the book (p. 287). It will recap the highlights of the book, and supply a variety of tips for putting yourself into an effective state of mind before the LSAT.

BEFORE YOU BEGIN

THE MAIN FOCUS

Understanding the Thinking Processes

One of the key factors in your success on the LSAT is your mastery of the LSAT "thinking processes." There is no question that this will take lots of time working practice problems, but it will also take a carefully focused analysis of that practice.

As you read each introductory chapter, keep in mind the thinking process involved as it is explained. You are not trying to learn or memorize any actual problem; rather, you are trying to learn the process behind solving each problem type so that you will be able to apply that process to new problems.

Notice that each section is designed to analyze this thinking process and to help you understand what the test maker had in mind when constructing the question. Learn to understand the reasoning behind the construction of each question.

If you focus on this reasoning as you prepare, the techniques carefully explained in each chapter will be easier to apply and will become even more effective. Remember that it is the mastery of this thinking process within the time constraints that will yield success on the LSAT.

SOME GENERAL STRATEGIES

The One-Check, Two-Check System

Many people score lower than they should on the LSAT simply because they do not get to many of the easier problems. They puzzle over difficult questions and use up the time that could be spent answering easy ones. In fact, the easy questions are worth exactly the same as the difficult ones, so it makes sense not to do the hard problems until you have answered all the easy ones.

To maximize your correct answers by focusing on the easier problems, use the following system:

1. Attempt the first question. If it is answerable quickly and easily, work the problem, circle the answer in the question booklet, and then mark that answer on the answer sheet. The mark on the answer sheet should be a complete mark, not merely a dot, because you may not be given time at the end of the test to darken marks.

2. If a question seems impossible, place two checks ($\checkmark\ \checkmark$) on or next to the question number in the question booklet and mark the answer you guess on the answer sheet. Again, the mark on the answer sheet should be a complete mark, not merely a dot.

3. If you're in the midst of a question that seems to be taking too much time, or if you immediately spot that a question is answerable but time-consuming (that is, it will require more than two minutes to answer), place one check ($\checkmark$) next to the question number, mark an answer you guess on the answer sheet, and continue with the next question.

   NOTE THAT NO QUESTIONS ARE LEFT BLANK. AN ANSWER CHOICE IS *ALWAYS* FILLED IN BEFORE LEAVING THAT QUESTION.

4. When all the problems in a section have been attempted in this manner, there may still be time left. If so, return to the single-check ($\checkmark$) questions, working as many as possible, changing each guessed answer to a worked-out answer, if necessary.

5. If time remains after all the single-check ($\checkmark$) questions are completed, you can choose between

   a. attempting those "impossible" double-check ($\checkmark\checkmark$) questions (sometimes a question later on in the test may trigger one's memory to allow once-impossible questions to be solved);

   or

   b. spending time checking and reworking the easier questions to eliminate any careless errors.

6. Remember: use *all* the allotted time as effectively as possible.

You should use this system as you work through the practice tests in this book; such practice will allow you to make "one-check, two-check" judgments quickly when you actually take the LSAT. As our extensive research has shown, use of this system results in less wasted time on the LSAT.

The Elimination Strategy

Faced with five answer choices, you will work more efficiently and effectively if you *eliminate unreasonable or irrelevant answers immediately.* In most cases, two or three choices in every set will stand out as obviously incorrect. Many test takers don't perceive this because they painstakingly analyze every choice, even the obviously ridiculous ones.

Consider the following Logical Reasoning problem:

> **According to the theory of aerodynamics, the bumblebee is unable to fly. This is because the size, weight, and shape of its body in relationship to the total wingspan make flying impossible. The bumblebee, being ignorant of this "scientific truth," flies anyway.**

The author's statement would be strengthened by pointing out that

(A) the theory of aerodynamics may be readily tested
(B) the bumblebee does not actually fly but glides instead
(C) bumblebees cannot fly in strong winds
(D) bumblebees are ignorant of other things but can't do all of them
(E) nothing is impossible

A student who does not immediately eliminate the unreasonable choices here, and instead tries to analyze every choice, will find herself becoming confused and anxious as she tries to decide how even silly choices might be correct. Her thinking goes something like this: "I wonder if bumblebees do glide; I've never looked that closely—maybe the test has me on this one . . . come to think of it, I've never seen a bumblebee in a strong wind; (C) is tricky, but it just might be right . . . I can't understand (D); it seems irrelevant but that just might be a trick . . ."

On and on she goes, becoming more and more uncertain.

Using the elimination strategy, a confident test taker proceeds as follows:

?(A) Possible choice.
~~(B)~~ Ridiculous. Both false and irrelevant. Cross it out.
~~(C)~~ Another ridiculous, irrelevant one. Cross it out.
~~(D)~~ Incomprehensible! Eliminate it.
?(E) Too *general* to be the best choice.

This test taker, aware that most answer choices can be easily eliminated, does so without complicating the process by considering unreasonable possibilities.

To summarize the elimination strategy:

- Look for unreasonable or incorrect answer choices first. Expect to find at least two or three of these with every problem.
- When a choice seems wrong, cross it out in your test booklet *immediately,* so that you will not be tempted to reconsider it.

Eliminating choices in this fashion will lead you to correct answers more quickly, and will increase your overall confidence.

Anticipating an Answer

For some question types, it is helpful to have an idea about what a possible credited answer choice could look like. This is called anticipating an answer, or anticipation. For example, you may read a logical reasoning question and already have a good idea of what is being assumed before you read the choices. In this case, you could go in looking for "your" answer.

Marking in the Test Booklet

Many test takers don't take full advantage of opportunities to mark key words and draw diagrams in the test booklet. Remember that, in the Reading Comprehension and Logical Reasoning sections, *marking key words and phrases will significantly increase your comprehension and lead you to a correct answer.* Marking also helps to keep you focused and alert. In the Analytical Reasoning section, *drawing diagrams is absolutely essential.*

Further, more specific hints about marking are given in the introductory chapters that follow. The important general point to stress here is that active, successful test taking entails marking and drawing, and that passive, weak test takers make little use of this technique.

Guessing

Because there is no penalty for guessing, you should *never leave a question without taking a guess.* And because there is no penalty for guessing, when you have about 3 minutes left, place your finger on where you are on your answer sheet (or make a light mark in your question booklet); then take your favorite letter and fill in the remaining answers on your answer sheet for that section. That is, if there are 26 questions in a section, you should fill in 26 answers. Once you have taken your ending guesses, go back and continue working where you left off and change your answers on the answer sheet. That way, if the proctor says "Stop, time is up!" you will at least have gotten all your guesses in.

PITFALLS—WHAT TO WATCH OUT FOR

The Common Mistake—The Misread

The most common mistake for many test takers is the MISREAD. The MISREAD occurs when you read the question incorrectly. For example, "Which of the following *must* be true?" is often read as "Which of the following *could* be true?" and "All of the following must be true EXCEPT" often loses the word "except."

If you MISREAD the question, you will be looking for the wrong answer.

To help eliminate the MISREAD, always underline or circle what you are looking for in the question. This will also help you focus on the main point of the question.

By the way, the MISREAD also occurs while reading answer choices. You may wish to underline or circle key words in the answers to help you avoid the MISREAD.

Distracters and "Attractive Distracters"

When the test makers put together the LSAT they spend a great deal of time and effort not only making sure that "credited response" is the best answer given, but also that the wrong answer choices (distracters) are good possibilities.

Distracters, as the word indicates, are meant to distract you away from the right answer. Some distracters are easily eliminated as they are just "wrong"—they are irrelevant, contradict something, or bring in items that are not addressed. Some distracters are too general, too specific or narrow, or use a word or words that miss the mark or point of the question. Some distracters are very close to the best or right answer. We refer to the wrong answers that are close as "attractive distracters." The choice looked good but was wrong. When you have narrowed your choices down to two, let's say (A) or (B), keep in mind that one is probably an "attractive distracter."

As you prepare for the LSAT it is important that you focus on the difference (in some cases a very fine difference) between the correct answer and the attractive distracter(s). When you analyze your practice tests, focus on what constitutes a right answer and on spotting the differences.

ANALYZING YOUR LSAT SCORE: A BROAD RANGE SCORE APPROXIMATOR

The chart that follows is designed to give you a general approximation of the number of questions you need to get right to fall into a general score range and percentile rank on your LSAT. It should help you see if you are in the "ballpark" of the score you need. This range approximator is *not* designed to give you an exact score or to predict your LSAT score. The actual LSAT will have questions that are similar to the ones encountered in this book, but some questions may be either easier or more difficult. The variance in difficulty levels and testing conditions can affect your score range.

OBTAINING YOUR APPROXIMATE SCORE RANGE

Although the LSAT uses a very precise formula to convert raw scores to scaled scores, for the purpose of this broad range approximation simply total the number of questions you answered correctly. Next, divide the total number of correct answers by the total number of questions on the sample test. This will give you the percent correct. Now look at the following chart to see the approximate percent you need to get right to get into your score range. Remember, on the actual test one of the sections is experimental and, therefore, doesn't count toward your score.

Approximate Scaled Score Range	Approx. % of Correct Answers Necessary	Approx. Score Percentile for 94–95 Test Takers (Est. % below)
171–180	95 and up	99–99.9%
161–170	80–94%	88–98%
151–160	65–79%	53–85%
141–150	45–64%	17–48%
131–140	30–44%	3–15%
121–130	20–29%	0–2%

On the actual LSAT, the percent of correct answers to get certain scores will vary slightly from test to test, depending on the number of problems and the level of difficulty of that particular exam.

An average score is approximately 151.

If you are not in the range that you wish to achieve, check the approximate percent of correct answers that you need to achieve that range. Carefully analyze the types of errors you are making and continue practicing and analyzing. Remember, in trying to approximate a score range, you must take the complete sample test under strict time and test conditions.

New Security Regulations

A complete list of test center regulations is available in the LSAC *Information Book* and online at *www.LSAC.org.* Below we highlight some of the most significant changes made:

- *Items permitted in the test room.* Tests takers may bring into the room **only** a clear plastic ziplock bag, maximum size one gallon (3.79 liter), which must be stored under the chair and may be accessed **only** during the break. The ziplock bag may contain only the following items: LSAT Admission Ticket stub; valid ID; wallet; keys; hygiene products; #2 or HB pencils, highlighter, erasers, pencil sharpener (**no mechanical pencils**); tissues; beverage in plastic container or juice box (20 oz./591 ml maximum size) and snack for break only.
- *Items permitted on the desktop.* Test takers may only have tissues, ID, pencils, erasers, a pencil sharpener, highlighter, and analog (nondigital) wristwatch. **No electronic timing devices are permitted.** This is a change from previous testing years.
- *Prohibited items.* Candidates are **not** permitted to bring into the testing room the following items: weapons or firearms, ear plugs, books, backpacks, handbags, papers of any kind, calculators, rulers, **timers**, listening devices, cellular phones, recording or photographic devices, pagers, beepers, headsets, and/or other electronic devices. Prohibited items may not be used during the break. **Bringing prohibited items into the test room may result in the confiscation of such items by the test supervisor, a warning, dismissal from the test center, and/or cancellation of a test score by LSAC. In addition, they may be referred to the LSAC Misconduct/Irregularities in the Admission Process Subcommittee or the Questioned Score Review Board.** LSAC and LSAT testing staff are not responsible for test takers' belongings.
- *Hats/hoods.* No hats or hoods are allowed (except items of religious apparel).
- *Handbags, backpacks, briefcases.* No handbags, backpacks, briefcases or other bags—except the ziplock bag described above—are allowed in the test room.
- *Cancellation/Complaint deadlines.* Test taker complaints and cancellation requests must be received at LSAC within six (6) days of the test date. (This is a change from previous years.)

If candidates need further clarification or information, please contact LSAC at 215.968.1001 or send an e-mail to *LSACINFO@LSAC.org.*

PART TWO

ANALYSIS

Understanding the Sections and the Key Strategies

1

A BRIEF REASONING REVIEW (AND WARM-UP)

Before analyzing LSAT question types, let's review a few basics of logical and analytical reasoning. Keep in mind that formal logic is not necessary for this test. The LSAT won't ask whether you know the definition of a *universal syllogism,* for example.

These next few pages should get you to start thinking about some of the reasoning involved in LSAT Logical and Analytical Reasoning questions. The formal principles of logic (which are not required by the test) can be very complex and this short discussion is a simple illustration of a few of the basic concepts that should be helpful.

DEDUCTIVE AND INDUCTIVE REASONING

Although logical reasoning may take many forms, basically, it is either deductive or inductive.

Deductive reasoning goes from general to specific. A deduction, or deductive reasoning, can be demonstrated by a simple syllogism as follows:

Major Premise: A person cannot be a world traveler unless he or she has been out of the country.
Minor Premise: Bob has never been out of the country.
Conclusion: Bob is not a world traveler.

Notice that the major premise is followed by a particular instance, or minor premise, which is followed by a conclusion. The conclusion is only as valid as the major and minor premises. Therefore, a conclusion may be logical, but not necessarily true. Piano student A might reason, for example, that, if she spends four hours practicing the piano each week, while piano student B spends only one hour practicing the piano each week, then student A will be the better piano player. Student A is basing her conclusion on the hidden premise that the amount of practice is directly proportional to her improvement and becoming a better piano player. Although the conclusion is logically based, in actuality, she may find that student B is a better piano player because the major premise is incorrect; so the conclusion is invalid.

Inductive reasoning goes from specific to general. That is, inductive reasoning moves from a particular situation or fact to a generalization or conclusion. You might reason, for example, that because four hundred people are killed each year in boating accidents, boating is a dangerous activity. This conclusion is based on induction, moving from specific facts to a generalization. Notice that the larger the number of specific facts, the more valid the generalization or conclusion. If forty thousand people are killed each year in boating accidents, then the conclusion that boating is a dangerous activity becomes a more valid conclusion. An even more valid conclusion could be drawn as follows: If forty thousand people are killed worldwide each year in boating accidents, and twenty thousand of those occur in the small isolated Lake Tibar, then boating in Lake Tibar is probably very dangerous.

These simple examples of deductive and inductive reasoning are meant to give you some idea of how to examine the validity of generalizations or conclusions in Logical Reasoning questions. Is the conclusion warranted by the facts? Do the facts support the conclusion? Are the generalizations valid?

SOME TYPES OF REASONING

Four of the basic types of reasoning and inference include:

1. Reasoning from Signs or Symbols

You might reason that, because a woman wears expensive jewelry, she is wealthy. Your reasoning would be even stronger if she also drove an expensive car. Since these are signs of wealth, your reasoning might appear valid. But the jewelry and car may be borrowed, so your reasoning might not be valid. The more signs or symbols you have that are good indicators to support your inference or conclusion, the better your chance of a valid conclusion.

2. Cause–Effect Reasoning

You might reason that a healthy diet causes people to live longer. To reasonably make this assumption, you would need concrete evidence to support it. The reasoning that your essays were published by a major publisher because you started using a computer might be difficult to prove. Would this cause–effect reasoning be reasonable? Of course not.

3. Reasoning by Analogy

You might reason that, since your friend purchased a treadmill for exercising and lost ten pounds, you should also purchase one. To follow this line of reasoning, you must consider whether your needs are similar to your friend's needs. Do you want to lose weight? Do you have room for a treadmill? Establishing a solid basis for comparison with sufficient similarities is necessary to make reasoning by analogy valid.

4. Reasoning from Statistics

You might reason that, since nine out of the ten dentists surveyed recommended Popsodent toothpaste, it is the best toothpaste on the market. The strength of the reasoning will depend upon the validity of the facts and the authority behind them. Would the reasoning be more apt to be valid if 99 out of 100 dentists recommended Popsodent? Could you reason that, if nine out of the ten dentists surveyed recommended Popsodent toothpaste, most people buy Popsodent toothpaste? Since only ten dentists were surveyed, could you really make any strong conclusions? Probably not. From this survey of ten dentists, could you make a valid conclusion about *most* people? I don't think so. Since statistics are subject to interpretation, watch them carefully.

LOGICAL FALLACIES

Now let's take a quick look at some logical fallacies. These typical errors in logic come from problems in reasoning or connecting ideas. Some common errors include:

Argument Ad Hominem: This argument is based on name-calling or attacking a person either directly or indirectly. The attempt here is to avoid discussing the issue.

The candidate shouldn't be elected because his parents were convicted of tax evasion.

Sam would be a fine choice for principal if he didn't provide a bad example by sometimes eating fast food at lunch.

Bandwagon/Celebrity Appeal: This argument implies that the reader should agree with a premise because a celebrity or a majority agrees with it.

Our president said that it is the best plan.

Almost everyone agrees with the decision to change the speed limit.

Begging the Question: When a conclusion is presented as part of a premise, the writer is *begging the question.*

We must act immediately to stop violence on our campus.

The writer presumes that there is violence on the campus.

Circular Reasoning: The use of a statement to support itself is *circular reasoning.* The writer employs this type of reasoning by restating the original problem.

The witness's testimony was truthful because he said he was telling the truth.

Either/Or Reasoning or Oversimplification: This logical fallacy occurs when the writer assumes that there can be only one cause or one solution to a problem.

The only way to stop smokers is to outlaw cigarettes.

False Analogy: Comparing two objects or ideas that have too few similarities to establish a basis for a good comparison leads to a *false analogy*.

Ted will be an outstanding coach because he was a good player.

Non Sequitur: When the writer reaches a conclusion that does not follow or is not warranted by the evidence offered, he has committed a *non sequitur*.

Since crosswalks are designed for the safety of walkers, I don't need to watch for oncoming traffic before using the crosswalk.

In some ways, all logical fallacies are non sequiturs—they don't follow.

Post Hoc; Ergo Propter Hoc: The writer draws a conclusion based only on the assumption that the time sequence is sufficient proof for a particular deduction.

Janis drives the sporty, turbocharged Mach SKM and has a lot of dates. So, if you drive the Mach SKM, then you will be irresistible to the opposite sex.

Since President Reagan was in office during the hostage crisis, it must have been his fault.

The words "Post Hoc; Ergo Propter Hoc" mean "after this; therefore, because of it."

Slippery Slope/Unfounded Generalization: The writer assumes that because one minor fact is true, then, despite any further proof, a larger premise must also be true. When a conclusion is made on the basis of too little information, it is said to be *unfounded*.

School board member Heller voted for teacher pay raises at the last meeting; therefore, she will always vote for teacher pay raises.

Three math students were caught cheating on a test; therefore, all the math students cheated.

Don't worry about remembering the names of these logical fallacies, just understand *why* the reasoning is faulty.

CONDITIONAL STATEMENTS (IF–THEN)

Finally, let's take a quick look at conditional statements. *If–then statements* are called "conditional statements" or "conditionals." The part of the statement following *if* is called the hypothesis, and the part immediately following *then* is called the conclusion. For example:

If it is Saturday, then Andy plays tennis.

Hypothesis: *It is Saturday.*

Conclusion: *Andy plays tennis.*

If the hypothesis is true, then the conclusion must be true.

Some statements that are conditionals are not written in *if–then* form but could be easier to understand logically if they were. For example:

Cats have quick reflexes.

If–then form: *If it is a cat, then it has quick reflexes.*

Hypothesis: *It is a cat.*

Conclusion: *It has quick reflexes.*

When a statement is put into *if–then* form, it often becomes easier to reason from. So, in this case, use "If it is a cat, then it has quick reflexes" as the original conditional.

If you exchange the *if* (hypothesis) and the *then* (conclusion) in a conditional statement, you get the **converse** of the original conditional. For example:

Original conditional: *If it is a cat, then it has quick reflexes.*

Converse: *If it has quick reflexes, then it is a cat.*

The converse is not necessarily true because other animals have quick reflexes. So, the **converse of a true statement is not necessarily true.**

If you take the opposite (negative) of each of the parts of a conditional statement, then you get the **inverse** of the original conditional. For example:

Original conditional: *If it is a cat, then it has quick reflexes.*

Inverse: *If it is not a cat, then it does not have quick reflexes.*

The inverse is not necessarily true because other animals have quick reflexes. So, the **inverse of a true statement is not necessarily true.**

If you exchange and negate the parts of a conditional statement you get the **contrapositive** (that is, take both the converse and inverse of a conditional statement). For example:

Original conditional: *If it is a cat, then it has quick reflexes.*

Contrapositive: *If it does not have quick reflexes, then it is not a cat.*

The contrapositive of a true statement is always true. Keep this in mind as you work logical and analytical reasoning problems.

Let's take one more look using our first example:

Original conditional: *If it is Saturday, then Andy plays tennis.*
(This is a true statement.)

Converse: *If Andy plays tennis, then it is Saturday.*
(This is not necessarily true. Andy could also play tennis on other days.)

Inverse: *If it is not Saturday, then Andy does not play tennis.*
(This is not necessarily true. Andy could also play tennis on other days.)

Contrapositive: *If Andy does not play tennis, then it is not Saturday.*
(This must be true.)

2

LOGICAL REASONING

INTRODUCTION TO QUESTION TYPE

The LSAT will contain *two* Logical Reasoning sections that will count toward your score. The unscored experimental section could also be Logical Reasoning. Each Logical Reasoning section is 35 minutes in length and contains from 24 to 26 questions. *Since approximately half of your exam consists of Logical Reasoning questions, you should spend additional time reviewing, understanding, and practicing this question type.*

Logical Reasoning questions, which require you to apply your reading and reasoning skills, measure your aptitude for understanding, analyzing, utilizing, and criticizing various short passages and types of arguments. Your ability to reason logically and critically is tested by questions that require you to do the following:

- Recognize a point.
- Follow a chain of reasoning.
- Draw conclusions.
- Infer missing material.
- Apply principles from an argument.
- Identify methods.
- Evaluate arguments.
- Differentiate between fact and opinion.
- Analyze evidence.
- Assess claims critically.

Let's take a closer look:

First, let's check the approximate percentages of problem types.

LOGICAL REASONING QUESTIONS

Types	Approx. Frequency
Author's Main Point or Main Idea (Example of)	10–15%
Author Information or Author's Purpose	1–2%
Form of Argumentation (Vulnerable to criticism)	10–15%
Strengthening or Weakening Author's Statement or Conclusion (Undermines, supports)	20–25%
Author's Assumptions, Presuppositions, Underlying Principles (Justifies)	15–20%
Inferences and Implications	3–5%
Deductions	5–8%
Parallel Reasoning or Similarity of Logic	8–10%
Argument Exchange	5–8%
Syllogistic Reasoning	1–2%
Conclusions	5–10%
Logical Flaws	8–10%
Situation Analysis	*
Passage Completion	2–3%
Word Reference	**

*Appeared in recent bulletins
**Appeared infrequently in earlier exams

Now, let's preview the common question stems.

SAMPLE LOGICAL REASONING QUESTION STEMS

- The statements above, if true, must support which one of the following?
- Each of the following, if true, strengthens the argument EXCEPT:
- Megan and Channen disagree over whether . . .
- Which one of the following, if true, most weakens the editorial's argument?
- The conclusion of the argument follows logically if which one of the following is assumed?
- The reasoning in the letter to the editor is vulnerable to criticism in that it
- Which one of the following, if true, would most seriously undermine the claim that the explanation given above is the only one available?
- Which one of the following, if true, most helps to resolve the apparent discrepancy described above?
- Which of the following is an assumption on which the author's argument relies?
- Which one of the following most accurately describes a flaw in the argument's reasoning?

- The pattern of reasoning in which one of the following arguments is most similar to the pattern of reasoning in the argument above?
- If the educator's statements are true, then which one of the following must be true?
- Which one of the following most accurately expresses the main conclusion of the editorialist's argument?

And finally, let's take a quick overview of the key strategies.

OVERVIEW OF THE THREE (3) KEY STRATEGIES
YOUR ACTIONS AND . . . REACTIONS

Actions	Reactions
1. Read the question first	Mark the key word or words, circle or underline the reference points for the question (conclusion, first sentence) and tip word for the question (strengthens, weakens, assumes, flaw, main point)
2. Read the passage actively	Mark the main point and conclusion, focus on the logic of the argument or statement
3. Look for key words in choices	Spot and mark the essence of the choice, know what each choice means and how the choices differ

Logical reasoning questions may take many forms. In analyzing these forms, consider their basic component parts:

1. A *passage*, *argument*, or *discussion*
   followed by
2. A *question* based upon the preceding text
   followed by
3. The five *answer choices* (A, B, C, D, and E)

The following discussion offers some tips for each of these parts.

THE APPROACH

THE BASIC COMPONENTS

1. The Passage, Argument, or Discussion

For the passage, read *actively;* that is, as you read you should mark the important parts with circles, exclamation points, etc., directly on the page of your question booklet. Reading actively helps you stay involved in the passage, it keeps you an active participant in the testing process, and it helps you note and highlight the important points mentioned, should you need to refer to the passage.

As you read you should also note the major issue being discussed, along with the few supporting points, if any.

2. The Question

For the question, it is often very helpful to *preread actively;* that is, to read the question first, *before* reading the passage. That way you have an idea of what to look for as you read the passage. This is an effective technique only if the question is short. If the question is as long as (or longer than) the passage, this technique may not be helpful. Use your judgment.

As you read the question, note the key words and *circle* them, in the same manner as you mark the passage. Also note the *reference* of the question. Is it positive or negative? Is it asking what would strengthen the author's argument or what would weaken the author's argument? Is it asking what the author would agree or disagree with? Is it asking what the author believes, or what his critics would believe? Finally, be aware that questions often refer to *unstated* ideas: assumptions (a supposition or a truth taken for granted); implications/inferences (what would logically follow from a previous statement); and conclusions (the necessary consequence or result of the ideas in the passage). Assumptions and implications/inferences are usually not directly mentioned in the passage. Conclusions may or may not be mentioned. You must arrive at all three through logical thinking.

3. The Choices

For the choices, note that you must select the *best* of the five alternatives. Therefore, there may not be a perfect choice. There may also be two good choices. You are to pick the best of the five. Therefore, the elimination strategy (p. 12) is an effective way to approach the answer choices. Eliminate choices that are irrelevant (have nothing to do with the particular topic or issue), off-topic, or not addressed by the passage. Note that often a choice will be incorrect simply because one word in that choice is off-topic. Learn to look for and mark these off-topic key words.

Finally, be very careful as you read the passage, question, and choices, to watch for words that have very special meanings. The following words, for instance, are frequently used:

except   some   all   none   only   one
few   no   could   must   each

These types of words will often be the key to finding the best answer. Therefore, make sure to underline or circle them in your reading.

ANALYZING QUESTION CATEGORIES

The following sections give detailed examples of the most common types of Logical Reasoning questions, complete with important techniques and strategies. You should not try to memorize the different categories presented here, but rather use them as an aid in identifying strategies needed and in practicing techniques.

Author's Main Point or Main Idea

A very common Logical Reasoning question type will ask you to identify or understand the main point or main idea of the passage. This is also a common question type in the Reading Comprehension section.

As you read the short passage, focus on what the author is trying to say—the major issue. Each paragraph usually contains only one main idea, often stated in the first sentence.

Let's analyze the following passage:

EXAMPLE
1

> **Law Professor: As the legal profession becomes more special-ized and complex, clerical assistance must become more spe-cialized as well. One legal secretary might be an expert in bankruptcy law, another an expert in criminal justice.**
>
> Which one of the following is the main point of the passage?
>
> (A) A legal secretary may understand subjects other than law.
> (B) A legal secretary should have special training in a particular branch of law.
> (C) A legal secretary must be an expert in several types of law.
> (D) Attorneys will hire only secretaries without legal experience so they can be trained on the job.
> (E) Attorneys will still need legal secretaries with a very general background.

Analysis

The first sentence of the passage, a general statement about increasing specialization in the legal profession, states the main idea. It is followed by a more specific statement, which gives you additional information.

To help you focus on the main point, you may wish to use the following technique when practicing this question type. As you finish reading each paragraph, try to mentally summarize the paragraph in a few words. For example, after reading the sample above, you might summarize it by saying to yourself, "Legal secretaries should specialize in different types of law."

Next, note whether the paragraph states a particular attitude toward the subject. Typically the author will either approve or disapprove of the main point, or remain neutral. In the Example 1 passage, the author takes no position pro or con, but delivers the additional information in a matter-of-fact way.

The correct answer is (B). In this case, the main point is that legal secretaries must become more specialized, and the correct answer emphasizes "special training." Notice also that the correct answer here refers as well to the second sentence, which contains additional information about particular branches of law.

(A) is irrelevant. Although particular types of law are mentioned, subjects other than law are not. Note that this statement may certainly be true for some legal secretaries, but receives no support from the paragraph. (C) contradicts information in the passage; the passage discusses legal secretaries who specialize in one type of law, not several. (D) and (E) are not addressed in the passage. The passage does not discuss attorneys' hiring requirements or the need for legal secretaries with a very general background.

Remember, when asked for a main point, be sure to differentiate the main point from secondary or minor points.

EXAMPLE 2

The belief that positive thinking is the key to success can lead to laziness. It encourages some people to engage in slipshod work, in the hope that an optimistic mental attitude will take the place of hard, careful, dedicated work.

Which one of the following is the main idea of this passage?

    (A) Laziness is always the result of positive thinking.
    (B) Laziness is practiced by successful people.
    (C) Laziness is only permissible after one has completed a hard day's work.
    (D) Laziness may result from a reliance on positive thinking.
    (E) Laziness may result from an assortment of mental attitudes.

Analysis

The correct answer is (D), which restates the opening statement that "positive thinking . . . can lead to laziness." However, the paragraph does not say that laziness is always the result; therefore (A) is incorrect. (B) is unreasonable and is contradicted by the paragraph. (C) is irrelevant; the paragraph does not discuss when laziness is permissible. (E) brings in an assortment of mental attitudes that are not addressed.

EXAMPLE

3   Few people understand poetry, and few prefer to read it. Although English professors speak in glowing terms about the greatness of Pope's *Rape of the Lock* and Tennyson's *Ulysses,* it seems that only other professors share their enthusiasm. To appreciate the greatness of difficult poetry, readers must exercise great patience and concentration, and must tolerate the unusual, compressed language of rhythm and rhyme; with so many urgent issues demanding our attention almost every hour of the day, choosing to figure out a poem seems an unlikely possibility.

In the passage above, the writer makes which one of the following arguments?

(A) English professors pay lip service to great poetry, but, in fact, rarely read it for pleasure.

(B) Even English professors may not really understand difficult poetry.

(C) Few laypeople will spend the time necessary to read difficult poetry.

(D) Simple poetry may continue to be popular, but only English teachers now read difficult poetry.

(E) To read difficult poetry requires patience, concentration, and tolerance.

Analysis

The correct answer is (C). The passage does not suggest that the English professors' enthusiasm is insincere (A) nor that they may fail to understand difficult poems (B). It argues that only English professors have the skills, time, and interest in poetry to deal with its difficulties, that laypeople are now unlikely to do so (C). The passage does not allude to simple poetry. (E) is tempting at first, but the argument of the passage is that understanding or appreciating poetry requires these skills, not simply reading it, so (C) is the best of the five choices.

Author Information or Author's Purpose

Another common Logical Reasoning question refers to a reading passage or paragraph and asks you to understand some things about the author. You may be asked to interpret what the author is trying to accomplish by this statement, or to predict the action and feeling of the author on similar or unrelated subject matter (tell whether the author would agree or disagree with some idea).

To answer this type of question, first look for the values and attitudes of the author. (Ask yourself, "Where is the author coming from?") Second, watch for word connotation: the author's choice of words can be very important. Third, decide the author's purpose and point of view, but don't OVERREAD. Keep within the context of the passage. Sometimes it will be advantageous to skim some of the questions (not the answer choices) before reading the short passage, so that you will know what to expect.

Remember while reading to mark the passage and look for *who, what, when, where, why,* and *how.* (See the section on "Active Reading" that begins on page 233).

EXAMPLE

1   **Recent studies show that the general public is unaware of most new legislation and doesn't understand 99% of the remaining legislation. This is mainly because of the public's inattention and lack of interest.**

The author of this argument would most likely be

(A) in favor in new legislation
(B) against new legislation
(C) advocating public participation in legislation
(D) advocating the simplifying of the language of new legislation
(E) advocating more interesting legislation

Analysis

The correct answer is (C). The statement does not imply that an increase or decrease in legislation would change the public awareness; therefore (A) and (B) are incorrect. (C) follows in the tenor of the argument because the author's purpose appears to be centered around involvement. He points out that the general public is unaware because of inattention and lack of interest. (D) would be possible, *but* the author is not focusing his criticism on the complex wording of legislation and does not mention it as a reason for unawareness. Remember (1) *whom* the author is talking about—the general public, (2) *what* he mentions—their unawareness of most new legislation, and (3) *why* they are unaware—because of inattention and lack of interest. The author is not advocating more interesting legislation (E).

EXAMPLE

2   **Writing Teacher: There are advantages and disadvantages to clear, simple writing. Sentences that are easy to understand are processed more quickly and efficiently by readers; those who can express themselves in simple terms are rarely misunderstood. However, prose that is crystal clear often lacks both complexity and imagination. Whether one chooses a style that is simple and clear or complex and unusual often depends upon the tolerance of one's readers.**

The purpose of the writing teacher who makes this statement to a class is probably to

(A) encourage students to write more simply
(B) encourage students to imitate in their own pure style the points the teacher is making about pure style
(C) encourage students to be more imaginative in their writing
(D) remind students of the importance of the audience to a piece of writing
(E) urge students to combine simplicity and complexity, clarity and imagination in all their writing

Analysis

The correct answer is (D). The passage points out the disadvantages and advantages of both simple and complex prose and concludes with the reminder that the readers will determine which is appropriate The passage does not favor one style over another as in (A) and (C), nor does it say that all writing should be both simple and complex (E). It argues for a style suitable to the audience.

Form of Argumentation

In this type of question, you are asked to decide what type of argument, logic, or reasoning the author is using (example, exaggeration, deduction, induction, etc.).

To answer this type of question, carefully follow the author's line of reasoning while focusing on his or her intent or purpose. Notice how the author starts and finishes the argument. Consider what the author has concluded or proved, or what point has been made or argued. Watch "if" and "how" specific points or examples are used in relation to more general statements.

EXAMPLE

1   **Once again, refer to the argument used earlier concerning legislation.**

Recent studies show that the general public is unaware of most new legislation and doesn't understand 99% of the remaining legislation. This is mainly because of the public's inattention and lack of interest.

To make the point, the author of this statement

(A) gives a general statement followed by supporting facts
(B) argues by pointing out the effects and then the cause
(C) uses specific examples to disprove an argument
(D) infers an outcome and then attempts to support that outcome

(E) assumes the conclusion is true and uses circular reasoning to state the premise

Analysis

The correct answer is (B). The author starts by making specific points about the general public. It is "unaware of most new legislation and doesn't understand 99% of the remaining legislation." This is followed by a statement of the cause: "This is mainly because of the public's inattention and lack of interest."

EXAMPLE 2

Editorial: **In the twelfth century, people used the abacus (a simple device made of beads strung on wire) to perform complex calculations. Today we use electronic calculators, and the abacus has become obsolete. In fifty or one hundred years, the calculator will be as quaint and outmoded as the abacus. Every invention of man, every breakthrough of science will, if we wait long enough, be out of date and used no longer.**

Which one of the following is a questionable technique used in the argument in this passage?

(A) It ignores the fact that the abacus is still in use in Asia.
(B) It generalizes from a single instance of obsolescence.
(C) It makes a prediction without specifying exactly when the prediction will come true.
(D) It mistakes a minor premise for a major premise and so deduces erroneously.
(E) It considers only scientific advances, but some inventions are not related to science.

Analysis

The correct answer is (B). The question calls for a questionable technique. The error here is the hasty generalization, based on a single instance of obsolescence. (A), (C), and (E) may be true but they do not point to a technique of argument. (D) is irrelevant and not true of this argument, which is not a syllogism.

Strengthening or Weakening the Author's Statement or Conclusion

This question type is very common on the LSAT. Here you are given a short reading passage or paragraph followed by the question "Which of the following would strengthen the author's statement the most?" or "Which of the following would most weaken the author's statement?" (Both of these questions may be asked. There are many possible varieties of this question type: "least likely to weaken," "strongest criticism of," and so on).

You may find it helpful to preread, or read the question before reading the short paragraph. Focus on the major point of the statement and "how" or "if" it is supported. Be aware of the strength of the statement or argument. Is it a harsh criticism of a certain system? Is it a mildly persuasive paragraph? What point is the author trying to make in supporting this cause?

Remember to always read actively, marking key words or phrases.

EXAMPLE
1

Psychiatrists and laypeople agree that the best sort of adjustment is founded upon an acceptance of reality, rather than an escape from it.

Which one of the following would probably most weaken the author's point?

(A) Psychiatrists and laypeople do not often agree.
(B) Reality is difficult to define.
(C) Escaping reality has worked for many.
(D) Accepting reality is often traumatic.
(E) Psychiatrists' definition of reality and laypeople's definition of reality are different.

Analysis

The correct answer is (C). If escaping reality has worked for many, then it becomes more difficult to defend the acceptance of reality theory. (A) would probably strengthen the point being made. (B) could strengthen or weaken the point. (D) and (E) are irrelevant.

EXAMPLE
2

The likelihood of America's exhausting her natural resources is growing less. All kinds of waste are being reworked and new uses are constantly being found for almost everything. We are getting more use out of our goods and are making many new by-products out of what was formerly thrown away. It is, therefore, unnecessary to continue to ban logging in national parks, nature reserves, or areas inhabited by endangered species of animals.

Which one of the following most seriously undermines the conclusion of this argument?

(A) The increasing amount of recycled material made available each year is equal to one-tenth of the increasing amount of natural material consumed annually.
(B) Recent studies have shown that the number of endangered animals throughout the world fluctuates

sharply and is chiefly determined by changes in weather conditions.

(C) The logging industry contributes huge sums of money to the political campaigns in states where it has a financial interest.

(D) The techniques that make recycling possible are constantly improved so that more is reclaimed for lower costs each year.

(E) Political contributions by the recycling industry are now greater than those of the logging or animal protection interests.

Analysis

The correct answer is (A). First, remember to circle the words <u>undermines</u> and <u>conclusion</u> to help you focus on what you're looking for. Now let's look at the choices. (D) would support rather than undermine the conclusion. (B), (C), and (E) neither support nor weaken the argument, though with more information (C) and (E) might be relevant. If the recycled materials are equal to only one-tenth of the natural materials lost each year, the argument is seriously injured.

EXAMPLE

3   Some scientists have proposed that, over two hundred million years ago, one giant land mass—rather than various continents and islands—covered one-third of the earth. Long before there was any human life, and over vast periods of time, islands and continents drifted apart. Australia was the first to separate, while South America and Africa were late in splitting apart. Some islands, of course, were formed by volcanoes and were never part of the great land mass.

All the following would support the author's claim EXCEPT:

(A) Many of the plants of the South American rain forests are markedly similar to those of the African rain forest.

(B) Australia has more animals that are not found on any other continent than have several of the much larger continents.

(C) Volcanic islands like Hawaii have ecosystems very different from those of continental lands with the same average temperature.

(D) The plants of similar conditions in South America have less in common with those of Australia than with those of Asia, Africa, or Europe.

(E) The primitive languages of Australia are unlike those of Africa, which resemble those of South America.

Analysis

The correct answer is (E). If Australia was the first continent to separate, it would follow that its flora and fauna would develop in isolation over a longer period of time. Similarly, we may expect the plants and animals of South America and Africa that separated later to be more alike. (A), (B), and (D) support these ideas. That the separately developed islands are different is also in accord with the passage. However, the languages of all the continents would have developed in isolation, since man did not evolve until after the break-up of the land mass and it is surprising that African and South American languages are similar. Human likeness or difference are irrelevant to the claims of the passage.

EXAMPLE 4

Columnist: In America, a baseball game should be described as a series of solo performances: at any given moment, attention is focused on one player and one play. On the other hand, soccer involves all of the team most of the time: each player interacts with others constantly, so that no single individual seems responsible for success or failure. It is because spectators prefer concentrating on individual personalities that baseball remains a much more popular spectator sport than soccer.

Which one of the following, if true, can best be used to undermine the conclusion of this argument?

(A) Soccer is more popular with spectators in France than baseball.

(B) Among the ten most televised sports in America, by far the most watched is football, and the least watched are tennis and bowling.

(C) Many people watch only the baseball teams of the city in which they live and for whom they root.

(D) Compared to football and basketball, baseball games are much cheaper to attend.

(E) In some sections of the United States, soccer leagues for children under fifteen are more popular than Little League baseball.

Analysis

The correct answer is (B). The weakness of this argument is not its claim that baseball is more popular than soccer with spectators in America. This is true from the passage. The weakness is its claim that the reason for baseball's greater popularity is that it is an individual performance rather than a team sport. (B) cites a team sport that is more watched than baseball and two solo performance sports that are not very popular. (A) makes a good point, but the passage is concerned with spectators "in America." Even if

(C) is true, it may be that these people watch the teams to see individual performances. (D) is true, but not as powerful a criticism as (B). (E) does not necessarily deal with spectators; popularity could refer to the number of participants.

Author Assumptions, Presuppositions, Underlying Principles

This is another very common question type in the Logical Reasoning section. Here you are again given a short reading passage or paragraph followed by questions asking about the author's possible assumptions, presuppositions, or underlying principles.

To answer this question type, you may wish to first read the question actively. Make a careful note of what part of the paragraph the question refers to. Is the question asking about the conclusion of the passage? (Which of the following assumptions must be made for the author to reasonably arrive at the stated conclusion?) Or about the opening statement? Or about the complete paragraph? (The complete paragraph may be only one or two sentences.)

Keep in mind that assumptions and presuppositions are things taken for granted, or supposed as facts. In the same sense, an underlying principle is the basis for the original statement. It is necessary for the conclusion to be logical. There may be a number of assumptions possible, but in most cases you are looking for the major assumption, not a minor one. In some cases the major assumption will be evident; you will know what the author is assuming before you even get to the answer choices. In other cases, the assumptions are more subtle, and the answer choices will be helpful by stating them for you.

EXAMPLE

1   **Use the statement in Example 1 on page 34:**

Psychiatrists and laypeople agree that the best sort of adjustment is founded upon acceptance of reality, rather than an escape from it.

The author of this statement assumes that

    (A) there is only one sort of adjustment
    (B) escaping reality is possible
    (C) psychiatrists and laypeople disagree on most things
    (D) psychiatrists never escape reality
    (E) laypeople need many sorts of adjustments

Analysis

The correct answer is (B). In stating "rather than an escape from it [reality]," the author is assuming that escaping reality is possible.

**EXAMPLE
2**
It has been said that a weed is a flower whose virtue has not yet been discovered. As if to prove this point, a homeowner who was tired of constantly maintaining a pretty lawn and shrubbery decided to let weeds run wild in his yard. The result, so far, has been an array of lively shapes and colors. If everyone in the neighborhood would follow this leader, we could save time, effort, money, and water, and soon have one of the most unusual neighborhoods in the city.

Which one of the following is a basic assumption on which this argument depends?

(A) The neighborhood values convenience more than maintaining an attractive environment.

(B) All the other yards will look like the first homeowner's if the weeds are allowed to run wild.

(C) Allowing the weeds to take over will save money spent on maintaining a lawn.

(D) Other neighborhoods in the city will not follow the example of this neighborhood.

(E) The loss of jobs or revenue to gardeners and garden supply businesses is not so important as the time and money that will be saved.

Analysis

The correct answer is (A). Although all five of the propositions here may well be true, it is (A) that is the basic assumption of the argument. No one who highly values an attractive lawn and yard will want to let weeds take over, so for the argument to have any validity, its speaker must assume that an audience willing to allow the gain in convenience outweighs the loss in appearance of the neighborhood.

**EXAMPLE
3**
Political Analyst: Four of the candidates for reelection in this state had been named among those who had more than 100 overdrafts on the House Bank. Of these four, two were Democrats, one was a Republican and one an Independent. One other Republican incumbent candidate had bounced over 50 checks. All of the Democrats favored increased federal spending on education and increased government regulation of firearms, while the Republicans opposed these measures. Of the five incumbents, only the Independent candidate was reelected.

Which one of the following is the most likely principle upon which the majority of voters cast their votes in the elections?

(A) The voters opposed any candidate who had more than 49 overdrafts on the House Bank.

(B) The voters opposed any candidates who favored increased federal spending.

(C) The voters opposed reelection of any members of the two major parties who bounced 50 or more checks.

(D) The voters opposed any candidate who favored increased firearms control.

(E) The voters opposed any candidate who opposed firearms legislation.

Analysis

The correct answer is (C). Since the Independent also bounced more than 100 checks, that cannot be the reason for the defeat of the other four candidates. Since we do not know how the Independent candidate stands on spending for education or on firearms regulation, the only factor to explain his victory is his not belonging to one of the two major parties.

EXAMPLE 4

Social Worker: Time and again studies have shown that 85 percent of the young adults sent to special juvenile prison farms lead productive lives when they are released. On the other hand, 85 percent of young adults of the same age who are sent to prisons for adults later return to prisons. The bad influence of the older inmates is permanent. We must expand the number of special juvenile prison farms so that all young adults convicted of crimes can be sent to a penal institution that will not maim them for life.

Which one of the following principles most helps to justify this argument?

(A) It is more expensive to house adult prisoners in prisons than to house young adults on prison farms.

(B) Young adults exposed to bad role models will imitate these models.

(C) Some young adults who are sent to prison farms later become criminals who are sent to prisons for adults.

(D) Some of the young adults who are sent to prisons for adults become productive members of society and never return to prison.

(E) Young adults who have been sent to prison farms on two occasions are more likely to return to prison than young adults who have been sent to prison farms only once.

Analysis

The correct answer is (B). This principle is the basis of the argument to prevent young adults from being exposed to adult felons. If the hope of penologists is to reintegrate young adults into society, these young adults must be kept away from bad models they are likely to imitate. (C) and (D) may be true, but they do not justify the argument. (A) is a practical matter, not a principle to justify the case. (E) would not justify the argument, and might, in fact, be used against it.

EXAMPLE
5   Drunken drivers in our state kill or maim people every day. I understand that only one out of 500 drunken drivers on the highway is flagged down by the police. Also, 50 percent of these arrests are made on four holiday weekends when the policing of highways is greatly increased. With these odds, I can afford to drink heavily and drive, as long as I am careful not to do so on holiday weekends.

Which one of the following is a necessary premise for the speaker's conclusion in the paragraph above?

(A) The odds against being arrested from drunken driving are greater on weekends than on weekdays.

(B) Fear of arrest is a good reason not to drink and drive.

(C) All that drunken drivers need to fear is being arrested.

(D) The chances of being arrested for drunken driving are greatest on four holiday weekends.

(E) The penalties for drunken driving are often incommensurate with the dangers to the public.

Analysis

The correct answer is (C). The speaker of this passage notes that drunk driving can kill and maim, but his concern is solely with the chances of his being arrested. His conclusion is based on the assumption that no other consequence of drunk driving need trouble him. (A), (B), (D), and (E) are not untrue, but they are not the underlying principle in the speaker's conclusion.

Inferences and Implications

In this very common question type you are asked to "read between the lines." Inferences and implications are not expressed in words in the passage, but may be fairly understood from the passage. If you draw or infer something from a passage, it is called an <u>inference</u>. From the author's point of view, if he or she imparts or implies something, it is called an <u>implication</u>. For the purposes of your exam, you should not be concerned with the differences in the terms, but in understanding what unstated information is in the passage. As you read the passage, focus on the main idea, what the author is suggesting but not actually saying, and what information you can be drawing.

As you approach the choices in inference and implication questions, look for the most direct answer that is not explicitly stated. That is the one that most directly ties back into the passage. Remember that your inference is NOT directly stated in the passage, but is implied by the passage.

EXAMPLE 1

> Since 1890, the federal government and the individual states have passed a number of laws against corrupt political practices. But today many feel that political corruption is a regular occurrence, and deeply distrust their public leaders.

> Each of the following can be reasonably inferred from the passage EXCEPT:

> (A) Corrupt political practices have been going on for many years.
> (B) The laws against corrupt political practices have not been effective.
> (C) The federal government and the individual states are against corrupt political practices.
> (D) Many public leaders may be distrusted even though they are not corrupt.
> (E) Leaders in private industry are also involved in corrupt political practices.

Analysis

The correct answer is (E). Since the passage does not address leaders in private industry, you could not reasonably make an inference regarding their practices. Though (A), (B), (C), and (D) are not stated, all of them are reasonable inferences from the passage.

EXAMPLE 2

> Teacher: The ability to recognize grammar and usage errors in the writing of others is not the same as the ability to see such errors in one's own writing.

> The author of this statement implies that

> (A) a writer may not be aware of his own errors
> (B) grammar and usage errors are difficult to correct
> (C) grammar and usage errors are very common
> (D) one often has many abilities
> (E) recognizing grammar and usage errors and writing correctly use two different abilities

Analysis

The correct answer is (A). The author's statement points out that recognizing errors in others' work involves a different ability than recognizing errors in one's own work. Since these abilities are different, writers may not possess both abilities and therefore may not be aware of their own errors. (B) is irrelevant because its focus is "difficulty to correct," which is not addressed. (C) and (D) are incorrect because they are too general, addressing items that are not specific to the statement. (E), which is a common mistake, simply restates information in the statement.

EXAMPLE

3   A poll of journalists who were involved in the Senate campaign revealed that 80 percent believed Senator Smith's campaign was damaged by press reports about his record during his last six years in office. His opponent, the recently narrowly elected Senator Jones, believes he was benefited by press coverage of his campaign. Journalists believe the election was covered without bias, and the Senator was defeated because of his record, not, as he insists, because of unfair press coverage. Ninety percent of the voters who supported Senator Smith believe the press was unfair in this election, while 85 percent of the voters who supported Senator Jones thought the coverage free of any bias.

Which one of the following can be inferred from this passage?

(A) The press coverage of the Senate election was free from bias.

(B) Senator Smith lost the election because the press reported his record accurately.

(C) The public's view of the objectivity of the press is likely to be influenced by the election results.

(D) The election was close because of different perceptions of the bias of the press.

(E) Journalists are probably the best judges of bias in political campaign reportage.

Analysis

The correct answer is (C). We cannot be sure whether or not the reporting of the press was biased since the election was close and the pros and cons are nearly equal. The press cannot be counted on to be objective, so (A), (B), and (E) are not reasonable inferences. The large percentage of each candidate's supporters, whose views of the press coincide with the success or defeat of their candidates, strongly support the inference of (C). Whether or not (D) is true, we cannot tell.

Deductions

You may be asked to deduce information from a passage. Deductions are arrived at or attained from general premises—drawing information to a specific piece of information—from general laws to specific cases. In a deduction, if the general premises are true, then the deduction is necessarily true.

To answer this question type you may wish to first actively read the question. Focus on the general premises to see where they lead. As you continue reading, try to follow the logic as it narrows the possibilities of what must be true.

EXAMPLE

1   Years ago, a nationwide poll concluded that there are more televisions than there are bathtubs in American homes. No doubt that fact remains today, especially in light of the growing popularity of home computers. Now, in addition to owning televisions for entertainment, more and more families are purchasing TV monitors for use with a personal computer. We can safely guess that there are still many more people staring at a picture tube than singing in the shower.

Which one of the following statements can be deduced from this passage?

(A) Personal computers probably cost less than installing a shower or a bathtub.

(B) People can wash themselves without a tub or shower, but they cannot watch television unless they own a television set.

(C) TV monitors will work with personal computers in place of regular computer monitors.

(D) As many computers are sold today as television sets a few years ago.

(E) More television monitors are now used with personal computers than are used to watch commercial television broadcasts.

Analysis

The correct answer is (C). Though (A) and (B) may well be true, they are not deductions that we can make from the information in the passage. But (C) can be deduced since, "more and more families are purchasing TV monitors for use with a personal computer." TV monitors must work with these computers. Otherwise, people would not buy them for that purpose. (D) and (E) may or may not be true, but they are not deductions from the passage, simply additional information.

EXAMPLE 2

Scientist: Antifreeze lowers the melting point of any liquid to which it is added so that the liquid will not freeze in cold weather. It is commonly used to maintain the cooling system in automobile radiators. Of course, the weather may become so cold that even antifreeze is not effective, but such a severe climatic condition rarely occurs in well-traveled places.

Which one of the following can be deduced from the passage?

(A) Well-traveled places have means of transportation other than automobiles.

(B) Antifreeze does not lower the melting point of certain liquids in extreme conditions.

(C) Severe climatic conditions rarely occur.

(D) It is not often that many travelers who use antifreeze have their cooling systems freeze.

(E) Antifreeze raises the melting point of some liquids.

Analysis

The correct answer is (D). Since severe climatic conditions rarely occur in well-traveled places, it is necessarily true that "It is not often that many travelers who use antifreeze have their cooling systems freeze." (A) mentions other means of transportation, which is not addressed in the passage. (B) refers to "certain" liquids, which again are not addressed. You cannot deduce that "severe climatic conditions rarely occur" (C), because the passage alludes to only well-traveled places. (E) discusses raising the melting point, which is irrelevant to the passage.

EXAMPLE 3

Sociologists have noted that children today are less "childish" than ever; when they are still very young, perhaps only six or seven years old, children are already mimicking adult fashions and leading relatively independent lives. Dressed in designer jeans, an elementary school child is likely to spend much of every day fending for herself, taking charge of her own life while waiting for her working parents to arrive home. Children become less dependent on adults for their day-to-day decisions.

From the passage above, since children are less dependent on adults for their day-to-day decisions, it must be true that

(A) children need more supervision

(B) children are growing up faster

(C) children should be completely independent

(D) parents should not leave children home alone

(E) parents need to spend more "quality time" with their children

Analysis

The correct answer is (B). Since children today are "less childish than ever," and since they are "less dependent on adults for their day-to-day decisions," they must be "growing up" faster. Although (A), (D), and (E) are probably true, they are not necessarily true and therefore cannot be deduced from the passage.

Parallel Reasoning or Similarity of Logic

In this type you will be given a statement or statements and asked to select the statements that most nearly parallel the originals or use similar logic. First, you should decide whether the original statement is valid. (But don't take too much time on this first step because some of the others may tip you off to the correct choice.) If the statement is valid, your choice must be a valid statement. If the statement is invalid, your choice must be an invalid one. Your choice must preserve the same relationship or comparison.

Second, the direction of connections is important—general to specific (deduction), specific to general (induction), quality to thing, thing to quality, and so on.

Third, the tone of the argument should be the same. If the original has a negative slant, has a positive slant, or changes from negative to positive, then so must your choice.

Fourth, the structure and order of each element is important. Remember: Corresponding elements should be in the same order as the original.

It may be helpful to substitute letters for complex terms or phrases, to simplify confusing situations and help you avoid getting lost in the wording. Direction and order are usually more easily followed by letter substitution.

Remember: Don't correct or alter the original; just reproduce the reasoning.

EXAMPLE

1   Alex said, "All lemons I have tasted are sour; therefore all lemons are sour."

Which one of the following most closely parallels the logic of the above statement?

(A) I have eaten pickles four times and I got sick each time; therefore, if I eat another pickle, I will get sick.

(B) My income has increased each year for the past four years; therefore, it will increase again next year.

(C) I sped to work every day last week and I did not get a ticket; therefore, they do not give tickets for speeding around here any more.

(D) All flormids are green. This moncle is red; therefore, it is not a flormid.

(E) Every teacher I had in school was mean; therefore, all teachers are mean.

Analysis

The correct answer is (E). First, the logic of the original is faulty; therefore, the correct choice must also be faulty, eliminating (D). Next, notice the direction of connections: generalization from a *few* experiences → generalization about *all* similar experiences. (A) and (B) each project the result of a few past experiences to only ONE similar experience. (C) starts from a few experiences, but finishes with a result that implies a change in a specific area. You could assume that "they" used to give tickets here.

EXAMPLE
2

Some serious novelists prefer scientific studies to literary studies. All science fiction writers are more interested in science than in literature. Therefore, some serious novelists are science fiction writers.

Which one of the following is most closely parallel to the flawed reasoning in the argument above?

(A) All trees have leaves. Some cactuses have leaves. Therefore, all trees are cactuses.

(B) All orchestras include violins and all chamber groups include violins. Therefore, some chamber groups are orchestras.

(C) Some animals sleep through the winter and some animals sleep through the summer. Therefore, all animals sleep through either the summer or the winter.

(D) All hotels have restaurants. Some shopping malls have restaurants. Therefore, some shopping malls are hotels.

(E) Some sweaters in this store are made of cotton. All shirts in this store are made of cotton. Therefore, all the wearing apparel in this store is made of cotton.

Analysis

The correct answer is (D). The stem asserts that all science fiction writers prefer science to literature and so do some serious novelists. It then concludes that some serious novelists must be science fiction writers. The "some serious novelists" who prefer science do not have to be science fiction writers, though they share a preference with them. The stem would have to say only science fiction writers prefer science to make this conclusion certain. The two terms used in the stem are "all" and "some," so we can exclude (B) and (C), which use "all" and "all" and "some" and "some." (D), though it gives the "some" term first and the "all" term second, is parallel to the passage.

EXAMPLE

3

(with a slight twist)

Why do you want to stop smoking?

Which one of the following most closely parallels the reasoning of this question?

    (A) Why do you want to go to Italy?
    (B) When will you decide on the offer?
    (C) Will you ever play cards again?
    (D) When do you want to learn to play tennis?
    (E) Which desk do you like better?

Analysis

    The correct answer is (C). This response is the only one that implies that the *action has already taken place,* as in the original question. To stop smoking, one must have been smoking *before.* To stop playing cards, one must have been playing cards *before.* (A) appears to be the closest, but this is only true regarding sentence structure, not reasoning. (B) and (D) are asking about future plans without implying anything about past actions. (D) does imply past lack of action. (E) merely asks for a comparison.

Argument Exchange

    In this question type, two or more speakers are exchanging arguments or merely discussing a situation. You will then be asked to choose the statement that most strengthens or weakens either argument. Or you may be asked to find the inconsistency or flaw in an argument, or to identify the form of argument. In some instances you will be asked to interpret what one speaker might have thought the other meant by his response.

    To answer these questions, you should first evaluate the strength and completeness of the statements. Are they general or specific? Do they use absolutes? Are they consistent?

    Second, evaluate the relationship between responses. What kind of response did the first statement elicit from the second speaker?

    Third, evaluate the intentions of the author in making his remarks. What was his purpose?

EXAMPLE

1

Tom: It is impossible to hit off the Yankee pitcher Turley.
Jim: You're just saying that because he struck you out three times yesterday.

Which one of the following would strengthen Tom's argument most?

    (A) Tom is a good hitter.
    (B) Turley pitched a no-hitter yesterday.
    (C) Tom has not struck out three times in a game all season.

    (D) Tom has not struck out all season.

    (E) Turley has not given up a hit to Jim or Tom all season.

Analysis

The correct answer is (B). Tom's is a general statement about Turley's relationship to all hitters. All choices except (B) mention only Tom or Jim, not hitters in general.

EXAMPLE 2

Sid: **The recent popularity of hot-air ballooning and bungee-jumping are instances of the latest quest for new types of adventure in the modern world.**

Phil: **That's ridiculous! Certainly these brightly colored floating globes of air are not modern inventions; rather, they recall the spectacle of county fairs and carnivals from the turn of the century.**

Sid: **Well, bungee-jumping wasn't around at the turn of the century.**

Phil's best counter to Sid's last statement would be

    (A) But bungee-jumping is used in fairs and carnivals.

    (B) No, bungee-jumping is merely a newer version of a Polynesian ritual hundreds of years old.

    (C) You do know that bungee-jumping is more dangerous than hot-air ballooning.

    (D) Yes, but hot-air ballooning is more popular than bungee-jumping.

    (E) No, but lots of other inventions are adventurous.

Analysis

The correct answer is (B). Sid's point is that these modern adventures are with modern inventions. His last statement is trying to say that bungee-jumping is modern. Phil's best counter would be to point out that bungee-jumping is not new.

EXAMPLE 3

Al: **To be a good parent, one must be patient.**

Bill: **That's not so. It takes much more than patience to be a good parent.**

Bill has understood Al's statement to mean that

    (A) if a person is a good parent, he or she will be patient ·

    (B) if a person is patient, he or she will make a good parent

    (C) some patient people make good parents

(D) some good parents are patient
(E) a person cannot be a good parent unless he or she is patient

Analysis

The correct answer is (B). This is a problem in grasping an understanding of necessary and sufficient conditions. Al states that if one is a good parent then one is patient. Patience is necessary to be a good parent. However, Bill's response shows that he (Bill) has inferred that Al considers patience to be sufficient to be a good parent, not just a necessary condition. (B) reflects Bill's mistaken inference. (A) is incorrect because it accurately describes Al's statement. (C) and (D) are incorrect because Al's statement concerns "any" or "all" persons and not "some." (E) is incorrect because it is equivalent to (A) and thus accurately describes Al's statement.

Syllogistic Reasoning

Syllogistic reasoning is a slightly more formal type of reasoning. It deals with an argument that has two premises and a conclusion. This type of question gives you short propositions (premises) and asks you to draw conclusions, valid or invalid. You may be expected to evaluate assumptions—information that is or is not assumed.

First, if possible, simplify the propositions to assist your understanding.

Second, draw diagrams (Venn diagrams; see p. 159 in Chapter 3), if possible.

Third, replace phrases or words with letters to help yourself follow the logic.

EXAMPLE
1   **All couples who have children are happy.**
All couples either have children or are happy.

Assuming the above to be true, which one of the following CANNOT be true?

(A) All couples are happy.
(B) Some couples who are happy have children.
(C) Some couples who have children are not happy.
(D) Some couples have happy children.
(E) Children of happy couples are happy.

Analysis

The correct answer is (C). If all couples who have children are happy, and if all couples who don't have children are happy, then all couples are happy. Simplifying the two statements to "all couples are happy" makes this question much more direct and easier to handle. Thus (C) is false, since it contradicts the first statement; we have no information about children.

EXAMPLE

2

All As are Bs.
Some Cs are As.

Which one of the following is warranted based upon the above?

(A) All Bs are As.
(B) Some Cs are Bs.
(C) All Bs are Cs.
(D) No Bs are As.
(E) All Cs are Bs.

Analysis

The correct choice is **(B)**. Here is a diagram of the original information:

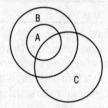

With this diagram, the following is evident:

(A) "All Bs are As" is false.
(B) "Some Cs are Bs" is true.
(C) "All Bs are Cs" is false.
(D) "No Bs are As" is false. If all As are Bs, then some Bs must be As.
(E) "All Cs are Bs" is false.

EXAMPLE

3

In this question, the second premise shows up in the actual question.

If the Dodgers do not finally win a championship for their fans this season, the team's manager will definitely not return to guide the club next year.

It follows logically from the statement above that, if the Dodgers win a championship this season, then next year the team's manager

(A) will definitely not return
(B) will probably not return

(C) will probably return
(D) will definitely return
(E) may or may not return

Analysis

The correct answer is (E). The passage states, "if the Dodgers do not win the championship [condition A], then the manager will not return [condition B]. Thus we have if A then B. The question then asks, what follows if they *do* win the championship [a negation of condition A]? If A implies B, the negation of A [if the Dodgers do win the championship] does *not* imply the negation of B [the manager will return]. Hence, condition A or not A (win or lose) may be the case; the manager may or may not return. (C) is possible, but he may also not return. All we know for sure is that if he loses, he positively won't return.

Conclusions

Here you will be given a list of conditionals, statements, or a short paragraph, and asked to follow the logic to reach a valid conclusion.

In this type, you will first want to underline key terms to eliminate looking at excess wording.

Second, mark the direction of each statement. Where does it start and end? What connection is it making?

Third, look for the "kicker" statement. That's the one that starts the chain reaction; it gives you the information to work with other statements.

If there is no "kicker" statement, carefully check how the information given in one statement is relative to the information given in the next statement. This relationship may be enough to help you understand the reasoning.

In checking the validity of a conclusion, you should be looking for a key statement that leads you as directly as possible to that conclusion. Sometimes, if the choices don't start with the word "therefore," you may wish to insert the word "therefore" before the answer choices to help you see which one follows logically.

EXAMPLE

1   Senator Jones will vote for the Pork bill if he is reelected. If the Pork bill passes, then Senator Jones was not reelected. Senator Jones was reelected.

Which one of the following can be concluded from these statements?

(A) Senator Jones assisted in the passage of the Pork bill.
(B) The passage of the Pork bill carried Senator Jones to victory.
(C) Senator Jones voted against the Pork bill, but it passed anyway.

(D) The Pork bill didn't pass, even though Senator Jones voted for it.

(E) The Pork bill was defeated by a large majority.

Analysis

The correct answer is (D). Notice that the "kicker" statement that started the chain reaction is "Senator Jones was reelected." From this, we know that he voted for the Pork bill. But the Pork bill could not have passed; otherwise, he could not have been reelected.

**EXAMPLE
2**   Meteorology may qualify as a science, but there is a great deal of guesswork involved as well. Even with increased knowledge about wind currents and weather patterns, and the most sophisticated equipment, forecasters' predictions are often wrong. Even the movement of a phenomenon as prominent as a hurricane cannot be determined very far in advance.

Which one of the following is the best conclusion to the passage?

(A) Therefore, we should be especially skeptical of weather predictions for the distant future.

(B) Therefore, we cannot control the weather, but we can predict it.

(C) Therefore, even though we cannot accurately predict the weather now, it will be possible in the near future.

(D) Therefore, since we cannot predict the weather, our aim should be to control it.

(E) Therefore, meteorology is a worthless science.

Analysis

The correct answer is (A). The passage points out that, although we can to some extent predict the weather, we are often wrong. This leads us to the conclusion that we cannot predict far in advance. (A) is the best answer. (B) and (D) do not follow since the passage does not mention controlling the weather. (C) does not follow since the passage does not address our gaining additional knowledge or more sophisticated equipment to help us in the future. The passage does not condemn meteorology, so (E) can be eliminated.

Logical Flaws

This common question type gives you a passage, statement, or argument, and asks you to find, understand, analyze, or name the type of flaw in the reasoning.

As you watch for logical flaws, notice that some are very evident especially if the passage or argument seems nonsensical. Others are very subtle, and need a second look. If you don't spot the flaw immediately upon reading the passage, let the choices help. Remember, the choices are showing you some possibilities.

Also, reading the question first will stop you from trying to make complete sense from a nonsensical passage, or trying to follow the logic or reasoning when, by design of the question, it does not follow. You see that the question itself warned you that there was a flaw in the reasoning.

EXAMPLE
1

The new American revolution is an electronic one. Advances in sophisticated circuitry have yielded more gadgets than anyone could have imagined only a few years ago: calculators as small as a wristwatch and automobile dashboards full of digital readouts are two of the many products that have enhanced the quality of life. But we may become so dependent on solid-state circuits to do our thinking that we may forget how to do it ourselves. Certain birds living on islands where there were no predators have, in time, lost their ability to fly. We may just as easily lose the ability to perform even the simplest mathematical calculation without the aid of an electronic gadget.

Which one of the following best describes the flaw in the reasoning in this passage?

(A) It assumes that a temporal sequence implies a causal relation.
(B) It generalizes from one instance to every other instance of the same type.
(C) It draws an analogy between two very different situations.
(D) It wrongly assumes that no new and better electronic devices will be invented.
(E) It assumes that what happens in America also happens in the rest of the world.

Analysis
The correct answer is (C). The flaw in the reasoning here is the comparison of two wholly unlike situations. The analogy compares men and birds and compares an event in the evolutionary history of certain birds that happened under unique circumstances over vast periods of time to what is supposed to be similar situations in the modern world, but which has in fact no real similarity.

EXAMPLE
2

With the continued water shortage in our area, the Water Department has had to restrict the use of water during daylight hours and to increase the cost of water to consumers. An average water bill has risen twenty-four dollars a year for three years in a row. Three years from now, our water costs will be astronomical.

A major flaw in the reasoning is that it

(A) relies upon figures that are imprecise to support a conclusion

(B) fails to indicate exactly how high expenses will be in three years

(C) assumes the conditions of the past three years will continue

(D) overlooks the possibility that conservation methods may improve in the next five years

(E) ignores the likelihood of the high cost driving down the water usage

Analysis

The correct answer is (C). To follow the author's line of reasoning, the author must assume that "the conditions of the past three years will continue." This assumption is flawed since the conditions could change. The conclusion is therefore based on a faulty assumption.

EXAMPLE
3

School Principal: In 2004 and 2005, when the limit on class size in grades 6, 7, and 8 was 25, our middle school students had an average reading score of 79 and an average math score of 75 in the state tests administered at the end of grade 8. But, in 2006 and 2007, when the limit on class size was raised to 28, our middle school students had average scores of 75 in the state reading tests and 75 in the state math tests. The increase in class size limitations has brought about the decline in state test scores.

Which one of the following is a major flaw in the reasoning in this passage?

(A) The author believes that test scores are accurate.

(B) The author fails to realize that some students' math test scores have not declined, though the average has.

(C) The author regards scores in math tests more important than scores in reading.

(D) The author assumes class size has caused the variation in test scores.

(E) The author does not know whether or not class size actually increased.

Analysis

The correct answer is (D). Since the class size limitations were increased and only the reading scores decreased, the author came to the conclusion that class size limitations caused the decline. But the math scores did not decrease, which would lead one to believe other factors are involved in the scores' decline. Also, because there were different class size limitations does not mean the sizes of the classes were different. The author's reasoning is flawed by his assumption that class size caused the variation. (E) is a fact, but is not the flaw in the author's reasoning.

Situation Analysis

This question-type requires you to select the situation, from the ones given, that most appropriately illustrates a principle expressed by the analysis of the situation in the passage.

To answer this question type, you should focus on the analysis and how it applies to the situation. After reading the situation, you may wish to read the analysis twice before proceeding to the question and the choices.

EXAMPLE
1   **Situation: In order to discourage the use of tobacco products, the state imposes a 50-cent tax on each package of cigarettes. It employs the revenues generated by the cigarette tax to fund television advertisements whose purpose is to deter teenagers from smoking.**

Analysis: The objective of both is to reduce smoking, and the success of the first may help to achieve the objective of the second.

The analysis provided for the situation above would be most appropriate in which one of the following situations?

(A) In order to reduce the number of cars on the five major highways into the city, the transportation board sets aside one lane in each direction for the exclusive use of cars carrying two or more passengers. To keep these lanes moving at higher speeds, taxis and buses are not allowed to use them.

(B) In order to stem the rising crime rate, the city council approves a budget that spends $600 million to increase the size of the police force. To avoid a tax increase, the money for the additional officer is provided by reducing the funding of gang prevention and neighborhood watch programs.

(C) In an effort to get rid of the rodents that have been feeding on the grain stored in his barn, Mr. McDonald buys five cats to live in the barn. To keep the cats warm and inside the barn, he carefully repairs all of the holes in the doors and walls where the wood has weathered.

(D) In order to reduce its liability insurance rates, the Ace Car Rental Agency no longer allows drivers under the age of twenty-one or over the age of seventy-five to drive its trucks and cars. To make up for the lost revenues, it offers lower rates on weekend rentals.

(E) To reduce the air pollution caused by automobile emissions, the city establishes bicycle lanes on many of the roads from the suburbs to the downtown working areas. To provide space for the bicycle lanes without the expense of widening the roads, the number of car lanes is reduced by one in all of the highways with multiple lanes.

Analysis

The correct answer is (C). As the increased taxes and the television advertising both contribute to the reduction of smoking, so the use of cats to prey on the grain-eating rodents, and the repairs to the barn that will keep the cats in and keep rodents out will both contribute to the preservation of the grain. In (A), the restriction may or may not reduce the number of cars on the highways. By denying buses and taxis the use of the faster lanes, the city may actually increase the number of cars on the highways. There is no certainty that either of the two steps will work, and the success of the one will not contribute to the success of the other. In (B), the reduction of funds that support gang prevention and neighborhood watch programs will probably result in an increase in crime, rather then encourage its reduction. Though it is possible that the reduction of weekend rental rates (D) may make up for lost revenues, the two objectives are not closely related, and success in the one will not contribute to success in the other. In (E), if the automobiles must spend more time on the road because of increased congestion that results from the loss of a driving lane, air pollution will not be reduced.

EXAMPLE
2

Situation: In order to increase its advertising revenues, radio station WJBW changes its format from all news to the rap and salsa music that is popular with the younger listeners that advertisers prefer. To accommodate the revised format, the station reduces the time for commercial messages from 16 to 12 minutes each hour.

Analysis: The success of the first objective is undermined by meeting the requirements of the second.

The analysis provided for the situation above would be most appropriate in which one of the following situations?

(A) In order to improve profitability, Fox Produce Company raises only a popular yellow tomato that sells at a higher price than the red. It uses the profits from sales to expand the greenhouses in which it develops seedlings of the yellow tomato.

(B) The aquarium raises its fees in order to finance the construction of a wing to exhibit tropical jellyfish. In order to educate the public, its new Web site is devoted to information about jellyfish of the world's oceans.

(C) In order to increase her disposable income, Mrs. Scudder gives used clothing, books, and furniture to the church thrift shop for which she receives both federal and state income tax deductions. She uses the money she saves on her taxes to buy tax-free bond mutual funds.

(D) In order to increase its profits, a cable television company raises its fees to customers and adds an additional channel of nature programs. To make room for the new station, the company eliminates a popular classic movie channel, as well as a Spanish language station, and a successful all-news channel.

(E) In order to increase the value of their stock holdings, members of the Key Investment Club contribute at least $500 each month, to buy additional shares in the stock portfolio of the club. In order to diversify its holdings, the club invests only in stocks that it does not already own.

Analysis

The correct answer is (D). Though not an ideal answer, this is clearly the best of the five choices. In the original situation, the number of advertising minutes are reduced, and so the advertising revenues are likely to decline. In (D), though the station will increase revenues by raising its fees, the reduction in the number of channels and the elimination of two popular ones will probably lead to customer defections, and the plan to increase profits will be undermined. In (A), the use of the profits to increase the availability of seedlings will contribute to, rather than injure, the success of the first objective. In (B), there is no reason to believe that information on the Internet will have an effect one way or the other on the aquarium's ability to finance new construction. In (C), both the tax deductions and the mutual funds will contribute to the disposable income that is sought. In (E), it is impossible to say how the choice of stocks that are not already in the portfolio will affect the value of the holdings. It is possible, but not certain, that previously owned stocks would be better investments, so we cannot be sure how the second factor will affect the first.

Passage Completion

This question type requires you to choose a phrase or sentence that best completes the passage.

It is initially important that you preserve the meaning of the passage, completing or maintaining the same thought. Unity (same subject) and coherence (order of thoughts) should be carefully noted. Second, it is important that the words you choose fit stylistically, use the same vocabulary, and are from the same context. Many times you will be able to eliminate some choices that "just don't sound good."

EXAMPLE
1

> English, with its insatiable and omnivorous appetite for imported food, has eaten until it has become linguistically unbuttoned. And the glutton has cloaked his paunch with the pride of the gourmet. We would not imply that a large vocabulary is bad, but rather that it is self-destructive if uncontrolled by _____.

Which one of the following is the best completion according to the context of this passage?

    (A) a smattering of slang
    (B) a fine sense of distinction
    (C) the removal of all but Anglo-Saxon derivatives
    (D) a professor who knows the limits of good usage
    (E) an unbuttoned tongue

Analysis

The correct answer is (B). The passage describes the English language itself; therefore, references to individuals, (D) and (E), are inappropriate. They do not maintain the same general level of thought. Since the author does not condemn a large and distinguished vocabulary, (A) and (C), which do, are both poor choices. (B) preserves the meaning of the passage and fits stylistically.

EXAMPLE
2

> In a reversal of past trends, last year more lawyers left courtroom practice to go into the teaching of law than vice versa. Since courtroom practice on average yields a much higher annual income, this shift discredits the theory that _____.

Which one of the following best completes the last sentence in the passage above?

    (A) incomes in the teaching of law will at some future time match those of courtroom practice

(B) the change in profession by those lawyers who are likely to increase their incomes can be predicted in advance

(C) more lawyers have remained in the teaching of law in the past few years than previously was the case

(D) lawyers under 40 years of age are more likely to change professions for financial rather than other reasons

(E) lawyers are likely to move into those professions in which the income is highest

Analysis

The correct answer is (E). The passage argues a connection between lawyers, profession changes, and income. Any answer choice that does not address those items cannot be a logical conclusion. (E) addresses the three key items and offers a conclusion that is logically consistent with the apparent change from higher to lower paying professions. (A) is irrelevant because the passage does not address the "future." (B) is irrelevant because the passage does not address "prediction." (C) is irrelevant because the passage does not address "remained" in a profession, only changing. (D) is irrelevant because the passage does not address the "age" of lawyers.

Word Reference

Here a word, or group of words, is taken out of context, and you are asked either what the word or words mean or what they refer to. In this type of question, first consider the passage as a whole, then carefully examine the key word or words surrounding the selected ones.

EXAMPLE

English, with its insatiable and omnivorous appetite for imported food, has eaten until it has become linguistically unbuttoned. And the glutton has cloaked his paunch with the pride of the gourmet. We would not imply that a large vocabulary is bad, but rather that it is self-destructive if uncontrolled by a fine sense of distinction.

As used here, the word "glutton" refers to

(A) an English language with a lack of Anglo-Saxon derivation

(B) one who never stops talking about foreign food

(C) an English language bursting with pride

(D) one who is bilingual

(E) an English language bursting with derivatives from foreign languages

Analysis

The correct answer is (E). The passage, as a whole, is commenting on the English language, and (E) is the only choice that equates "glutton" with the subject of the passage.

IN CONCLUSION

As you have seen, Logical Reasoning includes a potpourri of problem types all requiring common sense and reasonableness in the answers. You should take care in underlining what is being asked so that you do not (for example) accidentally look for the valid conclusion when the invalid one is asked for. Because of the nature of the Logical Reasoning problems, it is very easy to get tangled in a problem and lose your original thought, spending too much time on the question. If you feel that you have become trapped or stuck, take a guess and come back later if you have time. Remember that you must work within the context of the question, so do not bring in outside experiences or otherwise complicate a problem. The Logical Reasoning question is looking not for training in formal logic, but just for common sense and reasonableness.

Remember: Logical Reasoning accounts for 50 percent of your LSAT score.

REVIEW OF SOME GENERAL STRATEGIES FOR LOGICAL REASONING

THE PASSAGE
Read *actively,* circling key words.
Note major issue and supporting points.

THE QUESTION
Preread (before reading the passage) *actively*.
Note its reference.
Watch out for *unstated* ideas:
assumptions, implications/inferences, and sometimes conclusions.

ANSWER CHOICES
Sometimes there may not be a *perfect* answer; thus choose the *best* of the five choices.
Use the elimination strategy.
Note that "wrong" words in a choice make that choice incorrect.
Watch for those off-topic key words.

ANSWER SHEET
EXTRA PRACTICE: LOGICAL REASONING

1. Ⓐ Ⓑ Ⓒ Ⓓ Ⓔ
2. Ⓐ Ⓑ Ⓒ Ⓓ Ⓔ
3. Ⓐ Ⓑ Ⓒ Ⓓ Ⓔ
4. Ⓐ Ⓑ Ⓒ Ⓓ Ⓔ
5. Ⓐ Ⓑ Ⓒ Ⓓ Ⓔ
6. Ⓐ Ⓑ Ⓒ Ⓓ Ⓔ
7. Ⓐ Ⓑ Ⓒ Ⓓ Ⓔ
8. Ⓐ Ⓑ Ⓒ Ⓓ Ⓔ
9. Ⓐ Ⓑ Ⓒ Ⓓ Ⓔ
10. Ⓐ Ⓑ Ⓒ Ⓓ Ⓔ
11. Ⓐ Ⓑ Ⓒ Ⓓ Ⓔ
12. Ⓐ Ⓑ Ⓒ Ⓓ Ⓔ
13. Ⓐ Ⓑ Ⓒ Ⓓ Ⓔ
14. Ⓐ Ⓑ Ⓒ Ⓓ Ⓔ
15. Ⓐ Ⓑ Ⓒ Ⓓ Ⓔ
16. Ⓐ Ⓑ Ⓒ Ⓓ Ⓔ
17. Ⓐ Ⓑ Ⓒ Ⓓ Ⓔ
18. Ⓐ Ⓑ Ⓒ Ⓓ Ⓔ
19. Ⓐ Ⓑ Ⓒ Ⓓ Ⓔ
20. Ⓐ Ⓑ Ⓒ Ⓓ Ⓔ
21. Ⓐ Ⓑ Ⓒ Ⓓ Ⓔ
22. Ⓐ Ⓑ Ⓒ Ⓓ Ⓔ
23. Ⓐ Ⓑ Ⓒ Ⓓ Ⓔ
24. Ⓐ Ⓑ Ⓒ Ⓓ Ⓔ
25. Ⓐ Ⓑ Ⓒ Ⓓ Ⓔ
26. Ⓐ Ⓑ Ⓒ Ⓓ Ⓔ
27. Ⓐ Ⓑ Ⓒ Ⓓ Ⓔ
28. Ⓐ Ⓑ Ⓒ Ⓓ Ⓔ
29. Ⓐ Ⓑ Ⓒ Ⓓ Ⓔ

30. Ⓐ Ⓑ Ⓒ Ⓓ Ⓔ
31. Ⓐ Ⓑ Ⓒ Ⓓ Ⓔ
32. Ⓐ Ⓑ Ⓒ Ⓓ Ⓔ
33. Ⓐ Ⓑ Ⓒ Ⓓ Ⓔ
34. Ⓐ Ⓑ Ⓒ Ⓓ Ⓔ
35. Ⓐ Ⓑ Ⓒ Ⓓ Ⓔ
36. Ⓐ Ⓑ Ⓒ Ⓓ Ⓔ
37. Ⓐ Ⓑ Ⓒ Ⓓ Ⓔ
38. Ⓐ Ⓑ Ⓒ Ⓓ Ⓔ
39. Ⓐ Ⓑ Ⓒ Ⓓ Ⓔ
40. Ⓐ Ⓑ Ⓒ Ⓓ Ⓔ
41. Ⓐ Ⓑ Ⓒ Ⓓ Ⓔ
42. Ⓐ Ⓑ Ⓒ Ⓓ Ⓔ
43. Ⓐ Ⓑ Ⓒ Ⓓ Ⓔ
44. Ⓐ Ⓑ Ⓒ Ⓓ Ⓔ
45. Ⓐ Ⓑ Ⓒ Ⓓ Ⓔ
46. Ⓐ Ⓑ Ⓒ Ⓓ Ⓔ
47. Ⓐ Ⓑ Ⓒ Ⓓ Ⓔ
48. Ⓐ Ⓑ Ⓒ Ⓓ Ⓔ
49. Ⓐ Ⓑ Ⓒ Ⓓ Ⓔ
50. Ⓐ Ⓑ Ⓒ Ⓓ Ⓔ
51. Ⓐ Ⓑ Ⓒ Ⓓ Ⓔ
52. Ⓐ Ⓑ Ⓒ Ⓓ Ⓔ
53. Ⓐ Ⓑ Ⓒ Ⓓ Ⓔ
54. Ⓐ Ⓑ Ⓒ Ⓓ Ⓔ
55. Ⓐ Ⓑ Ⓒ Ⓓ Ⓔ
56. Ⓐ Ⓑ Ⓒ Ⓓ Ⓔ
57. Ⓐ Ⓑ Ⓒ Ⓓ Ⓔ
58. Ⓐ Ⓑ Ⓒ Ⓓ Ⓔ

59. Ⓐ Ⓑ Ⓒ Ⓓ Ⓔ
60. Ⓐ Ⓑ Ⓒ Ⓓ Ⓔ
61. Ⓐ Ⓑ Ⓒ Ⓓ Ⓔ
62. Ⓐ Ⓑ Ⓒ Ⓓ Ⓔ
63. Ⓐ Ⓑ Ⓒ Ⓓ Ⓔ
64. Ⓐ Ⓑ Ⓒ Ⓓ Ⓔ
65. Ⓐ Ⓑ Ⓒ Ⓓ Ⓔ
66. Ⓐ Ⓑ Ⓒ Ⓓ Ⓔ
67. Ⓐ Ⓑ Ⓒ Ⓓ Ⓔ
68. Ⓐ Ⓑ Ⓒ Ⓓ Ⓔ
69. Ⓐ Ⓑ Ⓒ Ⓓ Ⓔ
70. Ⓐ Ⓑ Ⓒ Ⓓ Ⓔ
71. Ⓐ Ⓑ Ⓒ Ⓓ Ⓔ
72. Ⓐ Ⓑ Ⓒ Ⓓ Ⓔ
73. Ⓐ Ⓑ Ⓒ Ⓓ Ⓔ
74. Ⓐ Ⓑ Ⓒ Ⓓ Ⓔ
75. Ⓐ Ⓑ Ⓒ Ⓓ Ⓔ
76. Ⓐ Ⓑ Ⓒ Ⓓ Ⓔ
77. Ⓐ Ⓑ Ⓒ Ⓓ Ⓔ
78. Ⓐ Ⓑ Ⓒ Ⓓ Ⓔ
79. Ⓐ Ⓑ Ⓒ Ⓓ Ⓔ
80. Ⓐ Ⓑ Ⓒ Ⓓ Ⓔ
81. Ⓐ Ⓑ Ⓒ Ⓓ Ⓔ
82. Ⓐ Ⓑ Ⓒ Ⓓ Ⓔ
83. Ⓐ Ⓑ Ⓒ Ⓓ Ⓔ
84. Ⓐ Ⓑ Ⓒ Ⓓ Ⓔ
85. Ⓐ Ⓑ Ⓒ Ⓓ Ⓔ
86. Ⓐ Ⓑ Ⓒ Ⓓ Ⓔ

To remove, cut along dotted rule.

EXTRA PRACTICE: LOGICAL REASONING

Directions: In this section you will be given brief statements or passages and be required to evaluate the reasoning involved. In some instances, more than one choice will appear to be a possible answer. You are to choose the *best* answer. Use common sense and reasonableness in making your selection; then mark the correct answer.

Questions 1–3

Robots have the ability to exhibit programmed behavior. Their performance can range from the simplest activity to the most complex group of activities. They not only can build other robots, but also can rebuild themselves. Physically they can resemble humans, yet mentally they cannot. Even the most highly advanced robot does not have the capacity to be creative, have emotions, or think independently.

1. From the passage above, which one of the following must be true?

   (A) Robots could eventually take over the world.
   (B) The most complex group of activities involves being creative.
   (C) A robot should last forever.
   (D) Emotions, creativity, and independent thought can be written as programs.
   (E) Building other robots involves independent thinking.

2. The author of this passage would agree that

   (A) robots would eventually be impossible to control
   (B) in the near future, robots will be able to think independently
   (C) robots have reached their peak of development

   (D) there are dangers in robots that think for themselves
   (E) there are some tasks that are better done by robots than by humans

3. The author's assertions would be weakened by pointing out that

   (A) humans exhibit programmed behavior for the first few years of life
   (B) robots' behavior is not always predictable
   (C) building other robots requires independent training
   (D) internal feeling is not always exhibited
   (E) the most complex group of activities necessitates independent thinking

4. The management of Trans-Caribbean Airways has announced that the airline's bonus mileage program will be discontinued on July 1. A survey conducted on weekdays in February on the Miami to Port-of-Spain route asked passengers to rate in order of importance: low fares, on-time performance, prompt baggage handling, quality in-flight refreshments, and bonus mileage. More than 95 percent of the respondents put low fares and on-time performance either first or second, whereas less than 1 percent placed the bonus mileage program above fourth. Since bonus

mileage is not important to Trans-Caribbean passengers, management has decided to eliminate it.

The decision of the management is based on all the following assumptions EXCEPT:

(A) that because the bonus mileage program was not the passengers' first or second concern, it is not important to them
(B) that the passengers on the Miami to Port-of-Spain route reflect the opinion of other passengers of Trans-Caribbean Airways
(C) that the passengers flying in February are representative of the airline's passengers throughout the year
(D) that other airlines will not attract Trans-Caribbean customers by offering attractive mileage bonus plans
(E) that the number of passengers who failed to complete the survey is statistically insignificant

5. *Botanist:* No plant in the botanical gardens blossoms twice in the same month. All of the plants in the botanical gardens that blossom in January are grown from either bulbs or tubers. None of the plants that blossom in January will flower again later in the year.

If the statements above are true, which one of the following must also be true?

(A) No plant in the botanical garden grown from a bulb will blossom in October.
(B) No plants in the botanical garden blossom twice in the year if they blossom first in January.

(C) None of the plants in the botanical gardens that blossom in June are grown from tubers.
(D) All of the plants in the botanical gardens grown from bulbs or tubers that did not blossom in January will flower later in the year.
(E) All plants in the botanical gardens grown from bulbs or tubers flower in January.

6. The simplest conceivable situation in which one human being may communicate with another is one in which structurally complementary communicants have been conditioned to associate the same words with the same things.

The sentence that would best complete this thought is:

(A) Therefore, dictionaries are of little value to foreigners.
(B) Therefore, man cannot communicate effectively with animals.
(C) Therefore, communication is a matter of relation.
(D) Therefore, communication is simplest following a common experience.
(E) Therefore, communication is dependent on complementary structures.

7. In a nationwide survey, four out of five dentists questioned recommended sugarless gum for their patients who chew gum.

Which one of the following would most weaken the above endorsement for sugarless gum?

(A) Only five dentists were questioned.
(B) The dentists were not paid for their endorsements.
(C) Only one of the dentists questioned chewed sugarless gum.
(D) Patients do not do what their dentists tell them to do.
(E) Sugarless gum costs much more than regular gum.

8. In Tom and Angie's class, everyone likes drawing or painting or both, but Angie does not like painting.

Which one of the following statements cannot be true?

(A) Angie likes drawing.
(B) Tom likes drawing and painting.
(C) Everyone in the class who does not like drawing likes painting.
(D) No one in the class likes painting.
(E) Tom dislikes drawing and painting.

9. *Mark:* The big test is tomorrow and I didn't study. I suppose I'll just have to cheat. I know it is wrong, but I have to get a good grade on the test.
Amy: I don't think that's a good idea. Just go to the teacher, tell the truth, and maybe you can get a postponement.

Amy attacks Mark's argument by

(A) attacking his reasoning
(B) applying personal pressure
(C) implying that good triumphs over evil
(D) presenting another alternative
(E) suggesting a positive approach

Questions 10–11

The microwave oven has become a standard appliance in many kitchens, mainly because it offers a fast way of cooking food. Yet, some homeowners believe that the ovens are still not completely safe. Microwaves, therefore, should not be standard appliances until they are more carefully researched and tested.

10. Which one of the following, if true, would most weaken the conclusion of the passage above?

(A) Homeowners often purchase items despite knowing they may be unsafe.
(B) Those homeowners in doubt about microwave safety ought not to purchase microwaves.
(C) Research and testing of home appliances seldom reveal safety hazards.
(D) Microwaves are not as dangerous as steam irons, which are used in almost every home.
(E) Homeowners often purchase items that they do not need.

11. Which one of the following, if true, would most strengthen the conclusion of the passage above?

(A) Homeowners often doubt the advertised safety of all new appliances.
(B) Speed of food preparation is not the only concern of today's homeowner.
(C) Modern homeowners have more free time than ever before.
(D) Food preparation has become almost a science, with more complicated and involved recipes.
(E) Many microwave ovens have been found to leak radioactive elements.

12. Cats that eat Vitagatto Cat Food each day will have sleek coats and excellent night vision. Since Jane feeds her cats only white tuna or poached chicken breasts, they cannot have excellent night vision. Therefore, they should be kept indoors at night to prevent injuries.

    Which one of the following contains a reasoning error most similar to that in the argument above?

    (A) Older houses in Canary Park sell for about $100,000, if the kitchen and bathrooms have been modernized. Arthur has put new fixtures in the bathrooms of his Canary Park house, but has not changed the kitchen. Therefore, the house will sell for less than $100,000.
    (B) Plants that have never been exposed to fungicides are especially susceptible to mildew. Since Jarmilla never uses any chemicals in her garden, her plants are liable to be subject to mildew in wet or cloudy weather.
    (C) Restaurants in Arlmont that buy their baked goods from Vonder's Bakery do brisk business at breakfast. Since Tamale Tom's restaurant does all its own baking, it will not have many breakfast customers, and should not open until lunchtime.
    (D) Students who take the law exam preparation class offered by the English department receive scores above the national average. Sally has taken a more expensive and more time-consuming course from a private tutor. She will, therefore, receive a very high score, and be accepted at Yale.

    (E) Police in Allentown solve most of the robberies that take place in daylight hours, but more than half of the robberies that take place after 6 P.M. are unsolved. Since the Borden Furniture Company was robbed at midnight, the thieves will probably not be caught.

13. According to a count of the men and women listed in the Glenarm Telephone Directory, there are 10,000 more men than women in this city of only 100,000. But according to the last census report, the population of Glenarm is 55 percent female.

    All of the following can be used to explain this discrepancy EXCEPT:

    (A) not all phone users list their names in the directory
    (B) married couples are more likely to use the husband's than the wife's name in the directory
    (C) the census report has been faulted for undercounting the minority population of large cities
    (D) the phone book count may be misled by initials or names that are not gender specific
    (E) there are many more females under 14 than males

14. Given that this rock is white in color, it must be quartz.

    The foregoing conclusion can be properly drawn if it is true that

    (A) only quartz rocks are white in color
    (B) quartz rocks are generally white in color
    (C) other white rocks have proved to be quartz

(D) few other types of rocks are white in color

(E) all quartz rocks are white in color

Questions 15–16

"Even the smallest restaurant in Paris serves better breads than the best restaurants in New York," the visiting chef said. He was complaining about the quality of the bread available in America. "I was trained in France," he added, "so I understand bread-making. But in America, there are hardly any good bakers. You can tell just by looking at the roll baskets. In every restaurant I have visited in New York, the roll baskets are still full on every table at the end of the meal."

15. The chef's conclusions depends on all of the following assumptions EXCEPT:

   (A) if the bread is good, all of it will be consumed

   (B) the quality of a restaurant can be determined by the quality of its breads

   (C) all good bakers are professionals

   (D) the norm for good bread-making is France

   (E) restaurants do not replenish roll baskets

16. All of the following are errors in the reasoning of the speaker in the passage above EXCEPT:

   (A) the argument takes as fact what is unproven personal opinion

   (B) the argument assumes that New York restaurants represent American baking

   (C) the speaker claims complete knowledge of a large number of small restaurants in Paris

(D) the speaker claims that he knows how to bake bread

(E) the examples the speaker cites of good and bad bread makers are vague and unspecific

Questions 17–18

Some American auto factories are beginning to resemble their Japanese counterparts. In many Japanese factories, the workers enjoy the same status and privileges as their bosses. Everyone works in harmony, and there is much less of the tension and anger that results when one group dominates another.

17. With which one of the following would the author of the above passage most likely agree?

   (A) American work environments ought to emulate Japanese auto factories.

   (B) Japanese automobiles are better built than American automobiles.

   (C) Tension in the workplace enhances worker productivity.

   (D) Japanese culture differs so much from American culture that it precludes any overlap of styles.

   (E) Striving for managerial status induces worker productivity.

18. The argument gives logically relevant support for which one of the following conclusions?

   (A) Some American auto factories are experiencing changes in their work environments.

   (B) American auto workers envy their Japanese counterparts.

   (C) There is no tension or anger in Japanese factories.

(D) Decrease in tension leads to higher productivity.

(E) There is no tension or anger in American factories that follow Japanese models.

19. When we approach land, we usually sight birds. The lookout has just sighted birds.

Which one of the following represents the most logical conclusion based upon the foregoing statements?

(A) The conjecture that we are approaching land is strengthened.

(B) Land is closer than it was before the sighting of the birds.

(C) We are approaching land.

(D) We may or may not be approaching land.

(E) We may not be approaching land.

20. The presence of the gas Nexon is a necessary condition, but not a sufficient condition, for the existence of life on the planet Plex.

On the basis of the foregoing, which of the following would also be true?

(A) If life exists on Plex, then only the gas Nexon is present.

(B) If life exists on Plex, then the gas Nexon may or may not be present.

(C) If life exists on Plex, then the gas Nexon is present.

(D) If no life exists on Plex, Nexon cannot be present.

(E) If no life exists on Plex, Nexon is the only gas present.

21. The absence of the liquid Flennel is a sufficient condition for the cessation of life on the planet Fluke, but it is not a necessary condition.

On the basis of the foregoing, which of the following would also be true?

(A) If life on Fluke ceased to exist, there would have to have been an absence of the liquid Flennel.

(B) If all liquid Flennel were removed from Fluke, life there would surely perish.

(C) If all liquid Flennel were removed from Fluke, life there might or might not cease.

(D) If all liquid Flennel were removed from Fluke, the cessation of life would depend upon other conditions.

(E) Life on Fluke cannot cease so long as Flennel is present.

22. The gas rates in Edina are low only for the first 30 therms used each month; the next 30 cost twice as much, and all gas over 60 therms costs four times as much as the first 30. The city has very cold winters and warm summers. To heat an average-size two-bedroom home in the winter by gas is prohibitively expensive, but not as costly as electric heating. Consequently

All of the following are logical conclusions to this passage EXCEPT:

(A) most homeowners use oil heating

(B) many homes are kept at temperatures below 70 degrees in the winter

(C) the consumption of gas is lower in the winter than in the summer

(D) electric cooling is more common than electric heating

(E) many homes have wood burning stoves and fireplaces

23. *Dog Trainer:* If the poodle was reared at Prince Charming Kennels, then it is a purebred.

The foregoing statement can be deduced logically from which one of the following statements?

(A) Every purebred poodle is reared at Prince Charming Kennels or at another AKC approved kennel.

(B) The poodle in question was bred at either Prince Charming Kennels or at another AKC approved kennel.

(C) The poodle in question either is a purebred or looks remarkably like a purebred.

(D) The majority of poodles reared at Prince Charming Kennels are purebred.

(E) There are no dogs reared at Prince Charming Kennels that are not purebred.

24. There is no reason to eliminate the possibility of an oil field existing beneath the Great Salt Lake. Therefore, we must undertake the exploration of the Salt Lake's bottom.

The foregoing argument assumes which one of the following?

(A) Exploration of the Salt Lake's bottom has not been previously proposed.

(B) An oil field located beneath the lake would be easy to identify.

(C) The Great Salt Lake is the only large inland body of water beneath which an oil field may lie.

(D) The quest for oil is a sufficient motive to undertake exploration of the Salt Lake's bottom.

(E) An oil field exists beneath the Great Salt Lake.

Questions 25–26

My course of study had led me to believe that all mental and moral feelings and qualities, whether of a good or of a bad kind, were the results of association; that we love one thing, and hate another, take pleasure in one sort of action or contemplation, and pain in another sort, through the clinging of pleasurable or painful ideas to those things, from the effect of education or of experience. As a corollary from this, I was convinced, that the object of education should be to form the strongest possible associations of the salutary class; associations of pleasure with all things beneficial to the great whole. It now seemed to me, on retrospect, that my teachers had occupied themselves but superficially with the means of forming and keeping up these salutary associations. They seemed to have trusted altogether to the old familiar instruments, praise and blame, reward and punishment. I did not doubt that by these means, begun early, and applied unremittingly, intense associations of pain and pleasure, especially of pain, might be created, and might produce desires and aversions capable of lasting undiminished to the end of life. But there must always be something artificial and casual in associations thus produced.

25. By "salutary" the author means

(A) "the strongest possible associations"

(B) ideas that "salute" one's mind

(C) capable of giving pain

(D) promoting some good purpose
(E) those earning a middle-class income or better

26. All of the following questions are answered in the passage EXCEPT:

(A) Is there any sort of thinking that is not associational?
(B) Is schooling the only cause of our lifelong "desires and aversions"?
(C) What else besides education causes these associations?
(D) What do teachers praise and what do they blame?
(E) How long would the desires and aversions last?

---

27. The San Diego Chargers practice expertly for long hours every day and keep a written log of their errors.

The above statement is an example of which one of the following assumptions?

(A) Practice makes perfect.
(B) To err is human.
(C) People make mistakes; that's why they put erasers on pencils.
(D) Practice is what you know, and it will help to make clear what now you do not know.
(E) Writing is a mode of learning.

28. Pine trees may be taller than any other tree. Pines are never shorter than the shortest palms, and some palms may exceed the height of some pines. Peppertrees are always taller than palm trees. Peach trees are shorter than peppertrees but not shorter than all palms.

Given the foregoing, which one of the following would be true?

(A) Peach trees may be shorter than pine trees.
(B) Peppertrees may be shorter than some peach trees.
(C) Every pine is taller than every palm.
(D) A particular palm could not be taller than a particular pine.
(E) Now and then a peach tree may be taller than a pepper.

29. Most popular paperback novels are of low intellectual quality; therefore *Splendor Behind the Billboard*, an unpopular paperback novel, is probably of high intellectual quality.

The foregoing argument is most like which one of the following?

(A) Most locusts inhabit arid places; therefore, locusts are probably found in all deserts.
(B) Most acts of criminal violence have declined in number during the past few years; therefore, law enforcement during this period has improved.
(C) Most people who stop drinking gain weight; therefore, if Carl does not cease drinking, he will probably not gain weight.
(D) Most nations run by autocratic governments do not permit a free press; therefore the country of Endorff, which is run by an autocratic government, probably does not have a free press.
(E) Most new motor homes are equipped with air conditioning; therefore, Jim's new motor home may not be equipped with air conditioning.

Questions 30–31

Jane states, "All mammals have hair. This creature possesses no hair. Therefore, it is not a mammal."

30. Which one of the following most closely parallels the logic of Jane's statement?

    (A) All reptiles have scales. This creature possesses scales. Therefore, it is a reptile.
    (B) All physics tests are difficult. This is not a physics test. Therefore, it is not difficult.
    (C) All American cars are poorly constructed. Every car sold by Fred was poorly constructed. Therefore, Fred sells only American cars.
    (D) All mammals do not have hair. This creature possesses hair. Therefore, it may be a mammal.
    (E) All lubricants smell. This liquid does not have an odor. Therefore, it is not a lubricant.

31. Which one of the following, if true, would most weaken Jane's argument?

    (A) Animals other than mammals have hair.
    (B) Some mammals do not have hair.
    (C) Mammals have more hair than nonmammals.
    (D) One could remove the hair from a mammal.
    (E) Reptiles may have hair.

Questions 32–33

A recent study of Hodgkin's disease in young adults has examined a large number of sets of twins, half of them identical and half nonidentical. Identical twins have the same genetic makeup, but like any other siblings nonidentical twins share only about 50 percent of their genetic material. In the study of twins with Hodgkin's disease, the researchers found that the chances of the second of a set of identical twins also developing the disease was 100 times higher than in the case of the sibling of a nonidentical twin, or of any other average individual. The number of cases where both identical twins were affected was, however, not a very large proportion of the identical twin pairs.

32. Based on the information in this passage, we can infer all of the following EXCEPT:

    (A) genetic inheritance is one factor in determining the susceptibility to Hodgkin's disease
    (B) if one twin of a set of nonidentical twins develops Hodgkin's disease, the chances of the second twin developing Hodgkin's disease are no greater than that of a person who is not a twin
    (C) Hodgkin's disease is more likely to appear first in a twin who is one of a pair of identical twins than one of a pair of nonidentical twins
    (D) genetics alone is not sufficient to cause Hodgkin's disease
    (E) the chances of the second of a pair of identical twins whose twin has developed Hodgkin's disease also developing the disease are not very high

33. For which reason of the following are studies of identical twins likely to be valuable to medical research?

    (A) Identical twins are usually raised in the same environments.
    (B) Researchers using identical twins can discern differences more easily.
    (C) Identical twins may differ psychologically, but not physically.
    (D) Identical twins may reveal information related to genetics.
    (E) It is easier to arrange medical examinations at the same hospital for identical twins than for unrelated persons.

34. The frog population in the lake each year is determined by the number of two avian predators: egrets and blue herons. The weather has little effect on the egret population, but the number of herons varies according to the rainfall in the area. Therefore, a greatly changing frog population in the lake three years in a row will probably occur when the annual rainfall fluctuates widely for three years.

    Of the following arguments, which one most closely resembles this paragraph in the pattern of its reasoning?

    (A) The annual profit or loss of Acme Desk Company depends chiefly on the number of new office buildings in the city and on the stability of the mortgage rates. In a year when mortgage rates fluctuate, the building rate is also likely to fluctuate.
    (B) The parking lot at the university is filled to capacity on nights when the business school holds classes at the same hours as the extension college. If there are classes at the business school and no classes at the extension college, or classes at the extension college and no classes at the business school, the parking lots are three-quarters full.
    (C) The restaurant can sell a beef and cheese pizza for a one dollar profit if the price of cheese remains at less than two dollars per pound and the price of beef at less than one dollar per pound. For the last six months, cheese has sold at $1.95 per pound. Since the pizzas have failed to earn a profit of one dollar in this period, the price of beef must have risen to above one dollar per pound.
    (D) Farmers in the valley can legally purchase federal water at a reduced rate only if they raise cotton or if their farms are no larger than 960 acres. Several of the farmers who continue to purchase federal water at the reduced rate are raising only alfalfa. Therefore, their farms must be larger than 960 acres.
    (E) A cake will not collapse in the oven if the eggs have been brought to room temperature before mixing or if the sugar syrup is at a temperature above 140 degrees. The cake must have collapsed because the eggs were too cold or the sugar was not hot enough.

35. *Editorial:* Scientific studies have shown that second-hand tobacco smoke in the workplace greatly increases the number of workers who take more than fifteen days of sick-leave and the number of workers who suffer serious respiratory ailments. It has also been shown that the number of workers who die of lung cancer is twice as high in workplaces that permit smoking than

in workplaces that do not. Therefore, the state must pass laws that require all companies to forbid smoking in the workplace.

Which one of the following is the underlying principle in this argument?

(A) Every individual has a responsibility for the well-being of every other individual with whom he or she comes into daily contact.

(B) Employers who do not take care of the health of their workers risk increasing losses from absenteeism each year.

(C) States must be permitted to outlaw any dangerous substances or implements.

(D) States must be responsible for the safety of the workplace of all businesses in their jurisdiction.

(E) Workers must be permitted to make their own decisions about their workplace.

36. For the post-election festivities, no athlete was invited to the White House unless he or she was more than 35 years old. No one older than 35 was both an athlete and invited to the White House.

Which one of the following conclusions can be logically drawn from the statements above?

(A) No one but athletes were invited to the White House.

(B) No athlete was invited to the White House.

(C) Only persons older than 35 were invited to the White House.

(D) No one over 35 was invited to the White House.

(E) Some athletes over 35 were invited to the White House.

37. At the Brightman Diet Center, 20 men and women who wished to lose ten pounds undertook a program that included an hour of exercise and a limit of 200 calories for breakfast and lunch each day. A second group of 20 men and women, similar in age and weight to the first group, exercised for only half an hour and ate up to 500 calories for breakfast and lunch each day. Surprisingly, at the end of three weeks, all 20 who had exercised less and consumed more calories at breakfast and lunch had lost more weight than members of the other group.

Which one of the following best explains these unexpected results?

(A) Some of those who lost more weight exercised longer than the half hour.

(B) Forty people is too small a sample to produce any meaningful statistics.

(C) The exercise of some of the members of those who lost more weight was more vigorous than that of members of the other group.

(D) Those in the group that ate 500 calories for breakfast and lunch chose foods lower in fat and cholesterol than those in the other group.

(E) The group that had eaten more and exercised less during the day ate fewer calories at dinner than those in the other group.

38. Of the 8,000 American victims of isochemic optic neuropathy, most are over 60. The condition occurs suddenly and normally in only one eye. Its cause is unknown, though doctors agree that an interruption of the blood flow to the optic nerve is a major factor. Untreated, most people recover full vision in six months. The most common treatment, an operation called optic nerve decompression surgery, has proven to be less effective than no treatment at all. Fewer regain their sight after the operation, and those who do require nine months to do so.

The conclusions of this paragraph would be most useful in support of an argument for

(A) increasing federal supervision of surgical procedures
(B) reducing the cost of surgical procedures
(C) reducing the number of surgical procedures
(D) expanding federal oversight of cosmetic surgery
(E) funding a study of isochemic optic neuropathy in men and women under 40

39. No one who is a member of the tennis team will smoke cigarettes. No first-rate athlete smokes cigarettes. Therefore, only first-rate athletes will become members of the tennis team.

The reasoning here is in error since the conclusion does not allow for the possibility of

(A) a nonsmoker on the tennis team who is a second-rate athlete
(B) a first-rate athlete who doesn't play tennis

(C) an ex-smoker who is a first-rate athlete
(D) a nonsmoker who is not a first-rate athlete
(E) a smoker who is a first-rate tennis player

40. The sale of clothing featuring characters from children's television programs such as *Hannah Montana* or *SpongeBob Square Pants* has increased enormously in the last five years. The number of children who watch television must also have increased greatly in the same period.

Which one of the following would fail to support this conclusion and at the same time explain the rise in clothing sales?

(A) The relaxation of trade barriers has substantially reduced the cost of Asian-made clothes in the last five years.
(B) Five years ago, the most popular children's television program, Sesame Street, was seen on educational television stations.
(C) In many areas, the three most popular children's television programs are carried on both cable and network television stations.
(D) There are now several stations, such as the Disney Channel or Nickelodeon, which intend most or all of their programs for a young or very young audience.
(E) Television programs directed at children have been increasingly attacked in the last five years for excessive violence.

41. Alfred Thomason, one of the ten brokers in the mortgage department of Kean and Landers, will certainly write more than $5 million in mortgages this year. Last year the department's sales totaled more than $50 million and this year's totals will be just as high.

Which one of the following contains the same kind of reasoning error as this passage?

(A) Jacobson expects the dahlias he exhibits in this year's flower show will win a prize. His dahlias failed to win in last year's exhibition, but he believes that the cause was a jealous judge who is not on this year's panel.

(B) The debate squad is expected to win the state tournament in May. They have won all nine of their debates this year, including a large tournament in Memphis competing against most of the teams highly regarded in the state competition.

(C) The Vasquez family plans to drive from Boston to Scottsdale in four days. Last winter the drive took six days, but they were delayed by bad weather in New England, Pennsylvania, and New Mexico.

(D) South Texas State's Edward Meany will represent his college in a two-day tournament for top golfers from 30 different colleges in the state. Since the team from South Texas State easily won the state intercollegiate golf championship, Meany should have no trouble winning this tournament.

(E) Seeded first in the NCAA championships in Atlanta, Laura Lomax should breeze through the tournament. She already has won the two tournaments she has entered, and has a 38-match winning streak.

42. Although it is subject to the variations of currencies and interest rates, the Asian influx is now a major factor in the Australian real estate market. Although many Australians are nervous about the waves of Asian immigration, their economy welcomes the purchase of Australian properties by investors from Asia who have no residential rights. Foreigners are permitted to purchase up to half of the units of a condominium, provided they do so before the condo is first occupied. They can also purchase real estate in areas designated as "integrated tourism resorts," though few exist at present. The average purchase price paid by foreign investors is 80 percent more than the average paid by Australian residents. The United States is still the largest foreign investor, and Singapore recently has replaced Britain in second place.

From which one of the following can we infer that Australian regulations of foreign investments in real estate are not determined by a policy designed to exclude Asians?

(A) Asians make purchases chiefly of the more expensive dwelling units.

(B) Asians pay higher average purchase prices than Australians.

(C) The largest foreign investor is the United States.

(D) Traditional ties to Great Britain are no longer important to many Australians.

(E) Asians can purchase property in "integrated tourism resorts."

43. Thirty-eight percent of people in America drink unfluoridated water and, as a result, have 25 percent more cavities. Early opponents of fluoridation, like the John Birch Society, claimed it was a demonic communist scheme to poison America. More recent opponents invoke the fear of cancer, though years of scientific studies have continued to declare fluoridation safe. Almost every dental and medical organization has endorsed the process, but cities as large as Los Angeles are still without it, though its yearly cost is about 50 cents per person.

The claim that fluoridation is a communist plot is cited here because

(A) it gives historic breadth to the argument

(B) it exemplifies the eccentricity of the opposition

(C) it is what the argument is attempting to refute

(D) it supports the assumption that fluoridation is dangerous

(E) it supports the conclusion of the argument

44. The sickle-cell trait is usually regarded as a characteristic of black Africans. As a single gene, it confers a resistance to malaria, but if the gene is inherited from two parents, it may lead to a dangerous form of anemia. That trait, however, is not a unique characteristic of black Africans but appears wherever malaria has been common. The gene occurs as often in areas of Greece and of southern Asia as it does in central Africa. A genetic grouping by how well they digest milk would separate Arabs and northern Europeans from southern Europeans, native Americans, and some Africans. Most Europeans, black Africans, and east Asians have a gene that determines how they inherit fingerprint patterns, but Mongolians and the Australian aborigines do not. We have the notion that race is important because the surface is what we see. We now have the means to look beneath the skin.

This paragraph is probably part of a longer article that seeks to show

(A) the importance of genetic inheritance in the incidence of disease

(B) the difficulty of finding a scientific definition of race

(C) the decline of parasitic diseases like malaria in the wake of the discovery of their causes

(D) that most of the genes in a member of one race are likely to be unique to that race

(E) the genetic determination of the higher incidence of certain diseases in different racial groups

Questions 45–46

Auto accident victims in this state can sue for both their medical costs and for "pain and suffering" awards. Because the "pain and suffering" awards can be very large, often when the medical expenses are high, victims have an incentive to inflate their medical needs and medical costs in order to receive a higher total payment. For the victims of automobile accidents of equivalent seriousness, medical costs in this state are 30 percent higher than in all four of the neighboring states that have no-fault insurance programs and do make "pain and suffering" awards. Motorists in this state pay more than $300 more for the same insurance coverage of motorists in the four adjoining states. A no-fault insurance system eliminating the lawsuits for "pain and suffering" and fairly compensating victims for medical costs would save the insured drivers of the state medical costs of nearly $1 billion.

45. This argument depends on all of the following assumptions EXCEPT:

(A) juries assume a higher medical cost signifies greater pain and suffering
(B) accident victims may falsify the extent of their injuries
(C) doctors and lawyers have no incentives to keep costs low
(D) accident victims should not be rewarded for "pain and suffering"
(E) the medical costs of automobile accidents exceed their legal costs

46. Which one of the following, if true, would weaken the persuasiveness of this argument?

(A) The per-vehicle accident rate in this state is 4 percent higher than in the four neighboring states.
(B) The average motorist in this state drives fewer miles than the average motorist in two of the four neighboring states.
(C) There are more state patrolmen per driver in this state than in any other in the region.
(D) Medical costs in the four neighboring states are 20 percent lower than in this state.
(E) Though the sales tax rate is lower, the income tax is higher in this state than in any other in the region.

47. In order for Agri-Cola Corporation to show a profit this year, it must again sell $10 million worth of soft drinks in the United States and an equal amount overseas. Though sales in this country will certainly be equal to last year's, market unrest in Asia and South America will limit this year's overseas sales to at least $2 million less than last year's. It is, therefore, impossible that the company can show a profit this year.

The conclusion of this paragraph is correct if which one of the following is assumed?

(A) Last year's overseas sales were more than $10 million .
(B) This year's expenses on overseas sales can be reduced so that profits will increase.
(C) This year's sales of domestic soft drinks may surpass last year's.
(D) The margin of profit on this year's sales will not be higher than last year's.
(E) Both this year and last, sales in the overseas markets are more profitable than sales in the domestic market.

Questions 48–49

Ecologist: It is true that the solution of the problem of global warming will require important changes in the way we use fossil fuels over the long term and that the free market must play an important role in making these changes possible. But these facts should not make us forget how crucial near-term limits on the emissions of "greenhouse gases" are to motivate these changes. When the issue was the limitation of ozone-reducing substances, it was short-term emissions limits that quickly brought the needed technologies to the marketplace. These technologies were not available until the international community had adopted specific limits on ozone-depleting substances.

48. By which one of the following means does the author of this passage make his case?

(A) making a careful distinction between two key terms

(B) questioning the accuracy of the evidence given to support the opposition's case

(C) using an appropriate analogy

(D) using the literal meaning of a word that could be construed as metaphoric

(E) using premises that are contradictory

49. The author's case would be weakened if it could be shown that

(A) the immediate economic consequences of reducing the emission of greenhouse gases will be catastrophic in both the industrialized world and developing countries

(B) there has been virtually no research to develop a technology to deal with global warming

(C) the long-term limits on greenhouse gas emissions may not be adopted for at least 25 years

(D) many multinational corporations are reluctant to abide by any international agreements to limit the use of oil and oil-based products

(E) many scientists are skeptical about the effect of fossil fuel use on global warming

50. *Robert:* Cattle are turning up dead all over the place with their eyes removed with surgical precision. Strange lights have been seen in the sky on the night before the bodies were discovered, and no human culprits have ever been found. It must be extraterrestrial invaders.

June: Maybe it's some weird cult. Or a college student prank. I don't know all the facts of the story, and I have no certain explanation myself, but I am sure that it's not likely to be aliens who want to collect eyes from cattle.

June responds to Robert's explanation by

(A) demonstrating that his conclusion is inconsistent with the evidence that is advanced in its support

(B) questioning the accuracy of the evidence on which his argument depends

(C) providing evidence that contradicts his conclusion

(D) refusing to deal with the logic of his argument

(E) offering counterexplanations equally supported by the evidence

51. If people would use cloth towels and napkins instead of paper, less paper would be manufactured. So we should replace paper napkins and towels with cloth, and the forests of the world will not be consumed so rapidly.

This argument depends on which one of the following assumptions?

(A) The pace at which the forests are being consumed should be reduced.

(B) Washing cloth towels and napkins will consume resources less valuable than forests.

(C) The cost of paper napkins and towels may be less than that of cloth.

(D) The economic advantages of using cloth napkins and towels outweigh those of using paper.

(E) People are rarely willing to give up a convenience for an advantage that is not immediately perceptible.

52. The average number of fatal cases of influenza in the winter months in the Boston area is likely to decline noticeably if 50 percent of the population over the age of fifty is inoculated in October or November. If the government program that supplies information about influenza and makes free shots widely available is discontinued to save money, the number of men and women over age fifty who have been inoculated before the flu season begins this year will sharply decrease.

If the statements are true, which one of the following is the conclusion most likely to follow from the statements above?

(A) Programs that contribute to the health of the community should not be dependent on public funding.

(B) The severity and frequency of influenza outbreaks in the winter months can vary widely from year to year.

(C) The number of influenza fatalities this winter will probably increase.

(D) The number of fatal cases of influenza will sharply increase this year.

(E) The number of fatal cases in men and women less than fifty years old is likely to remain unchanged.

53. *Transit Official:* In order to increase the number of riders and improve its financial position, the Central Transit Company has purchased new air-conditioned buses for its routes from the west side and the east side to the city center. The routes from the north side and the south side continue to use the older buses, which are not air-conditioned. In the six spring and summer months since the new buses were put into service, the ridership on the west side and east side routes has increased. Therefore, the purchase of the new buses was a wise expenditure.

Which one of the following, if true, most calls into question the conclusion of this passage?

(A) The ridership on the bus routes from the north and south has increased more than that on the east and west routes in the spring and summer.

(B) The increased ridership on the north and south routes normally falls off in the fall and winter.

(C) The price of fares on all the city bus routes was increased early in the spring, though the increase was a very small one.

(D) There are more buses on the north and south routes to the city center than on the east and west routes.

(E) If more commuters in the city take the buses to work than drive their own cars, the traffic congestion problem in the downtown area will be solved.

54. *Mayor:* If the stadium improvement bond measure on the November ballot is passed by the electorate, the city will be able to host a New Year's Day bowl game. This assures huge tourist revenues for the businesses of the city, and so the electorate will certainly approve the bond measure.

Which one of the following assumptions, if true, will verify the argument that the measure will pass?

(A) Any bond measure that does not bring revenues to the city will not be approved in November.

(B) Any bond measure that would prevent the city's hosting a New Year's Day bowl game will not be approved this November.

(C) No bond measure that does not bring large revenues to the businesses of city will be defeated in the November election.

(D) No bond measure that brings large revenues to the city's businesses will be defeated in November.

(E) Next year's tourist revenues will be twice as large as this year's.

55. There were no arrests for currency smuggling at Logan International Airport this month. Therefore, illegal currencies are no longer being smuggled into the United States.

The flawed reasoning of the above is like that of all of the following EXCEPT:

(A) The termite inspections revealed no sign of the insects in any of the even-numbered houses on Third Avenue. Therefore, there are no termites in the houses on Third Avenue.

(B) The Save-A-Lot Stores are selling boneless chicken breasts for 99 cents a pound. Therefore, all of the supermarkets in the city will have chicken breasts on sale.

(C) There are no weeds in the flower gardens of Silverlake Park. Therefore, the gardens must have been weeded earlier in the week.

(D) The head of the accounting department has been found guilty of tax evasion. Therefore, tax fraud must be widespread among employees of the company.

(E) The captain of the high school cross-country team has agreed to participate in the 10-kilometer run this weekend. Therefore, all of the cross-country team will run in this race.

56. *State Legislator:* The law requiring motorcyclists to wear protective helmets should be enacted immediately. The individual's loss of a freedom of choice is trivial when set beside the suffering and the costs to the state of head injuries that are the result of not wearing safety helmets.

Which one of the following, if true, weakens this argument?

(A) With the recent reductions in the speed limit, the number of motorcycle accidents has been sharply reduced.

(B) Cyclists complain that helmets obscure their vision when they are worn under normal driving conditions.

(C) Highway patrolmen report that most of the motorcyclists that they arrest for speeding are wearing helmets.

(D) The state's expense for the long-term care of people who suffer severe head injuries in highway accidents is less than $1 million monthly.

(E) The fees for the registration of motorcycles in this state have increased every year for the past five years.

57. *Professor:* Did you study for this exam?

Student: Yes. And I spent at least two hours on the endocrine system alone.

Professor: And you reviewed the circulatory system?

Student: I read that chapter three times.

Professor: You aren't being honest here. If you'd studied, you wouldn't have confused such basic facts as the functions of the left and right ventricles.

The professor's reasoning is flawed for each of the following reasons EXCEPT:

(A) it does not consider the possibility that lack of concentration can cause poor retention

(B) it assumes the study regimen mentioned by the student would be effective

(C) it assumes that basic facts are easy to remember

(D) it connects repeated reading with retention

(E) it ignores the possibility that the student may have been ill or tired during the exam, causing poor performance

58. People who dream in color are creative. Conrad is a creative person. Therefore, Conrad must dream in color.

The pattern of reasoning in the argument above is flawed most similarly to which of the following arguments?

(A) Ants leave scent trails for other ants to follow to food. Food scent trails are common among social insects. Therefore, all social insects leave scent trails.

(B) Redwood is extremely weather resistant. Cedar is less resistant but less expensive. Therefore, cedar is the choice of most builders.

(C) Plumbers and electricians often belong to unions. Sally wants to become an electrician. Therefore, Sally will probably join a union.

(D) Oak trees provide acorns as food for wildlife. Wildlife has many food sources. Therefore, oak trees are not necessary as a wildlife food source.

(E) Corn is not a good plant to grow in containers. Maize is not a good plant to grow in containers. Therefore, maize is corn.

Questions 59–60

Park visitor advisory: Chigger activity in the park is high. According to a popular misconception, chiggers burrow under one's skin, but they don't. They bite and hold on, exuding an enzyme that liquefies the skin so they can sip it up. The longer they stay attached and exude the enzyme, the more severe a person's reaction is likely to be. Chiggers, so small they can't be seen on the body without magnification, perch on the tops of weeds and other plants, particularly tall plants, and jump onto a person or animal coming close to them. They then often migrate to areas such as the ankles, waist, underarms, and groin because they are relatively weak and need something such as socks or a waistband to push against in order to bite into the skin. Preventive measures include spraying with an insect repellant and showering immediately upon returning from outside to dislodge the insects. If showering is not possible, a brisk rubdown with a rough towel is somewhat effective. Prophylactic measures after bites include application of an anti-itch medication and complete avoidance of scratching the bite, which causes more severe itching and may cause infection. The effects of chigger bites may last up to two weeks or more.

Parks and Recreation Supervisor

59. Which of the following assumptions is most likely being made by the Parks and Recreation Supervisor?

(A) Visitors to the park will invariably be bitten by chiggers but with varying levels of discomfort.

(B) Prophylactic measures are generally only marginally effective.

(C) Visitors to the park would like to avoid being bitten by chiggers.

(D) Showering will remove all chiggers on the body.

(E) Tight clothing will lessen the severity of chigger bites.

60. According to the information supplied by the supervisor, which of the following people would be LEAST likely to be affected by chigger bites?

(A) Before going into the woods, Sheila sprays herself with insect repellant and then showers.

(B) Consuela picks blackberries in the woods and towels herself off when she reaches her cabin.

(C) George stays on the woodland paths, except for a strenuous climb up a rock face. He showers when he returns to his room.

(D) Dimitri makes sure to spray insect repellant at waist, ankles, and wrists before taking his dirt bike up Thunder Mountain through the brush.

(E) During her walk through the forest, Connie briskly towels herself off and applies insect repellent.

61. There are now almost three million undocumented immigrants living in the United States. They are taking jobs that legal citizens should have and using services that cost federal tax dollars to which they don't contribute. Consequently, these undocumented immigrants must be identified and deported immediately.

Which of the following, if true, would most call into question the speaker's conclusion?

(A) There are actually 3.2 million undocumented immigrants living in the United States.

(B) Undocumented immigrants do pay taxes in the form of local sales taxes on their purchases.

(C) Undocumented immigrants come primarily from Central and South America, important areas for the production of raw materials crucial to the United States.

(D) The jobs taken by undocumented immigrants are largely those low-paid positions U.S. workers refuse to take.

(E) New laws would need to be passed in order to grant amnesty to undocumented immigrants.

62. The Woodward family, in reviewing their electricity cost for the month of August, discovered the following facts: The electric company's average charge per kilowatt hour throughout their area was the same as it was in July. The Woodwards' total kilowatt usage in August was higher than it was in July, but their total expenditure for August's electricity was less than their expenditure in July.

Of the following, which fact, if true, would most likely explain the difference between the July and August electricity charges?

(A) The Woodwards had to repair their air conditioner during July.

(B) The Woodwards' August electricity usage was more often at off-peak, lower-rate times than it was in July.

(C) The electric company began buying electricity from a different, lower-cost source in August.

(D) During August, the Woodwards lowered the temperature setting on their hot water heater and hung their clothes outside to dry rather than using the electric dryer.

(E) In July, the Woodwards were away on vacation for two weeks.

63. *Pete:* Although it's a mistake to equate the life of a spotted owl and the life of a human, I agree with the ecoterrorists' concerns for the planet. It's undeniable that burning down buildings can stop overbuilding in natural environments, and embedding spikes in trees to harm loggers and their equipment can slow down clear-cutting operations.
Anne: Then you think the ends can justify the means.

Anne's response indicates she has most likely misunderstood Pete to believe which one of the following?

(A) Spotted owls are not as important as other endangered species.

(B) Spikes in trees unacceptably endanger human life and arson unnecessarily endangers human possessions.

(C) Environmentalists share the concerns of ecoterrorists in that they realize drastic measures must be taken to save the planet.

(D) Human life must take precedence over the lives of other animals.

(E) The need to stem the danger to the planet makes spiking trees acceptable.

64. In the United States, pharmaceutical plant research is hailed by most scientists as holding promise for important medical breakthroughs.

Ninety percent of doctors actively promote the research. But the majority of people do not know enough about the process to make an informed decision on the necessity of protecting the rain forests in which most of the promising plants are discovered. Fewer than two out of a hundred can speak knowledgeably about the basics of the subject. Politicians in rain forest countries tend to denounce the research, stressing the economic needs of their citizens over the nebulous promise of new medicines.

If the information given above is true, which one of the following must also be true?

(A) No politician in a rain forest country is among those who can speak knowledgeably about pharmaceutical plant research.

(B) Ten percent of doctors do not actively promote pharmaceutical plant research.

(C) Ninety-eight percent of people oppose pharmaceutical plant research.

(D) Most doctors are well informed about pharmaceutical plant research.

(E) Some doctors oppose pharmaceutical plant research.

65. Although the regulation that airline pilots be provided nine hours of rest in a twenty-four-hour period seems reasonable and prudent, serious safety concerns remain due to pilot fatigue. The nine hours of rest may be on paper only because schedule delays often mean the pilot is in the airport hours before a flight, and the time traveling to and checking into a hotel is counted as part of the rest time.

The argumentative technique used in the argument above is most accurately described by which one of the following?

(A) setting up a hypothesis and then giving examples to both support and refute it

(B) citing specific information that calls a conclusion into question

(C) contrasting the details of two opposing points of view

(D) presenting an analogy between assumed and actual facts

(E) comparing the general attitude of the public with the more informed attitude of a regulatory body

66. The penny coin ought to be discontinued. People no longer want pennies taking space in pockets and purses, and the coins no longer serve any viable function in today's economy. There is no longer anything that can be purchased with a penny.

Of the following, which statement, if true, most strongly calls into question the above argument?

(A) The citizenry would not approve rounding up the sales tax to the nearest nickel, which would be necessary if the penny were eliminated.

(B) Pennies can be easily exchanged for other coins or bills.

(C) The elimination of the penny coin would immediately make coin collectors' penny mint sets more valuable.

(D) Penny candy has historically been widely available.

(E) Pennies cost the U.S. Mint more to make than they are worth.

67. *Janice:* Continued building on coastal
    shorelines is nothing but a recipe
    for disaster. The threat of hurricane
    destruction of homes and
    businesses is ever present, and
    erosion caused by construction
    activities is extremely destructive to
    the natural coastal environment.
    Both state and federal government
    should take more decisive steps to
    stop U.S. coastal development.
    Wayne: People have a right to their
    property, the use of it, and any
    benefit they may derive from its
    ownership. Such rights should
    never be abridged by government
    without a compelling reason.

Which one of the following best
summarizes the point under discussion
by Janice and Wayne?

(A) whether hurricane destruction and
    erosion constitute a compelling
    reason to ban coastal development
(B) the need for a ban on coastal
    development due to damage to
    property and the environment
    versus the property rights of
    individuals
(C) the possibility of a government
    buyout of existing private coastal
    property versus the grandfathering
    in of rights for existing property
    owners
(D) the need for a ban on coastal
    development based on the
    compelling reasons of loss of shore
    bird habitat and beach areas due to
    erosion
(E) whether the benefits derived from
    coastal property ownership offset
    the damage caused to the
    environment

68. State auto emission testing is less
    effective against air pollution than

generally thought. Not all states require
such testing before license renewal,
and those that do may be more or less
stringent in their checking procedures,
allowing local garages, whose priorities
may be earning the fee, not controlling
emissions, to do the testing. It is clear
that approximately 12 percent of
vehicles, those that are older or
malfunctioning, produce over
50 percent of emission pollution.

Of the following, which one is most
strongly supported by the information
above?

(A) Consistent auto emission checking
    by all states would result in less
    emission pollution.
(B) Half of auto emission pollution is
    caused by 50 percent of older and
    malfunctioning vehicles.
(C) The general thought concerning the
    effectiveness of emission testing is
    irrelevant to a constructive handling
    of the problem.
(D) If checking stations themselves
    were regulated, making sure they
    efficiently enforced appropriate
    auto emission standards, the
    problem would be eliminated.
(E) A stringent federal program to
    identify and repair or delicense
    vehicles with unacceptable
    emission levels would most likely
    lower emission pollution.

69. The venomous brown recluse spider,
    as its name indicates, is not regularly
    seen because of its reclusive habits.
    Outdoors it may be discovered under
    stones and rocks, but it is more likely
    to inhabit indoor areas, particularly
    dark closet or drawer corners or any
    quiet and unused cranny. It is,
    however, also often seen in bathtubs.

Which one of the following, if true, LEAST explains the fact that brown recluse spiders are found in bathtubs?

(A) Although the brown recluse spider inhabits many indoor areas, it is most easily spotted in contrast to the often light-colored field of the bathroom fixtures.

(B) The insects upon which the brown recluse spider preys are likely to inhabit the moist areas of a bathroom.

(C) Since the brown recluse spider prefers to inhabit indoor areas, it can bite humans when they step into the tub, sometimes causing ulcerative sores that are slow to heal.

(D) The brown recluse spider is unable to negotiate the slick surface of bathroom fixtures.

(E) Since these spiders prefer to inhabit indoor areas, they are statistically likely to sometimes appear in bathtubs.

70. A research study on corporate behavior concludes that without the threat of government intervention, only a third as many recalls of dangerous products would occur as there are at present. Based on interoffice memos concerning products eventually recalled, the research finds that prior to recalling a product, company employees cite the possibility of government sanctions in two-thirds of the correspondence.

Based on the information above, the reasoning upon which the conclusion of the research study is based is likely to be flawed for all of the following reasons EXCEPT:

(A) the study makes the assumption that companies should recall dangerous products on their own, without the impetus of government intervention or sanctions

(B) interoffice memos may be sent and received by low-level employees who have little or no input into the decision-making process of a company

(C) of all the recalled products studied, those that are dangerous may constitute only a small percentage of the whole

(D) citing the possibility of government sanctions does not necessarily make such sanctions a consideration in making the decision whether to recall or not

(E) the mention of the possibility of government sanctions in two-thirds of the correspondence does not necessarily equate to a reduction of two-thirds of recalled products

71. *Political analyst:* Contributions to political campaigns carry with them not only the possibility but the near certainty of conflicts of interest for politicians elected to office. When a politician votes on issues that will have an impact on the business interests of wealthy, generous constituents, it is highly likely that the politician's vote will be influenced. But needed as it is, pending campaign contribution reform legislation is in for a rocky road because the very politicians who benefit from campaign donations would have to vote to discontinue them.

Upon which of the following assumptions does the political analyst's argument most depend?

(A) Public and private good are inevitably at odds with one another when conflicts of interest arise in the political arena.

(B) Campaign contribution reform will be voted down by politicians in power because it is antithetical to their interests.

(C) Politicians, because they rely on contributions to their campaigns in order to be elected, would be ineffective champions for any sort of reform legislation while they are in office.

(D) Campaign contributors will make their points of view on legislation known to the politicians to whom they contributed.

(E) Those who receive campaign contributions are likely to adopt points of view reflecting those of the majority of their contributors.

72. Advertising and conducting closeout sales of summer merchandise should be banned until September. It's still hot in August, and people are still going on vacations, so they need the merchandise available to them.

Of the following principles, which one, if valid, most provides justification for the reasoning above.

(A) If closeout sales are advertised, they always take place.

(B) If closeout sales take place, they have not only been advertised, they are also successful.

(C) When one merchant has closeout sales of summer merchandise, all other merchants have closeout sales of summer merchandise.

(D) After a closeout sale of summer merchandise, no summer merchandise remains for sale until the following year.

(E) Advertising of closeout sales is regulated by law, and merchants may not falsely depict what is for sale, its price, and how long the sale will continue.

73. Sales of SUVs (sports utility vehicles), which use twice the gas that compact cars do for the same mileage, have not decreased even in periods of high gas prices. Automobile manufacturers have continued to produce these vehicles at an escalating rate and without any new fuel-efficient features. So the lowering of gas consumption is not a concern among purchasers and owners of these vehicles.

Which one of the following, if true, most weakens the argument above?

(A) In periods of high gas prices, owners of SUVs drive them twenty-five percent fewer miles than they do when gas prices fall.

(B) Fuel-efficient features were incorporated in the design of SUVs when they were first produced.

(C) SUV owners support the fact that manufacturers have designed many fuel-efficient features to use in these vehicles as soon as government regulations mandate them.

(D) The sales of SUVs in Europe have sharply declined compared to sales in the United States.

(E) SUV owners generally purchase the same lower octane fuel as do drivers of compact cars.

74. The dry heat of the southwestern United States has long been touted as an excellent environment for alleviating respiratory problems such as asthma and emphysema. But with the growing

air pollution problems in southwestern cities, retirees with such conditions should not plan for the Southwest as their retirement home.

Which one of the following is an assumption that the speaker above must make in order to appropriately draw his or her conclusion?

(A) Air pollution problems in the Southwest are as bad as or worse than those problems in other urban areas of the country.

(B) Retirees plan for housing and move to new areas when they stop working.

(C) The effect of air pollution on respiratory ailments offsets the benefit of dry heat for these ailments.

(D) Although respiratory problems have many causes, air pollution is certainly one of them.

(E) Air pollution problems in the Southwest reduce the dryness of the heat, causing it to be ineffective in alleviating respiratory problems.

75. Thirty minutes of exercise several times a week and, for those who are overweight, a reduction in weight of as little as 7 percent, can be effective in preventing or delaying the onset of adult type II diabetes. Therefore, if you are sedentary and obese, your chances of having this disease are higher than if you are thinner and active.

If the statements above are true, which one of the following must also be true?

(A) If you reduce your weight by 7 percent, your chances of remaining free of type II diabetes are enhanced.

(B) If you are not overweight, if you exercise, and if you don't have type II diabetes, your weight and exercise may be playing a role in your freedom from the disease.

(C) Thirty minutes of exercise several times a week and a reduction of weight by 7 percent will likely lengthen your life span.

(D) If you have type II diabetes, the addition of exercise and the careful attention to diet will make it more likely that your disease can be eliminated.

(E) If you do not have type II diabetes, you have controlled your weight and engaged in some exercise.

76. *Defense lawyer:* The releasing of computer viruses is a form of vandalism. That the vandalism is electronic does not change the fact that, like spray painting a wall or knocking down a mailbox, it is the destruction of property. So punishment for releasing computer viruses should be no harsher than for other types of vandalism.

Of the following, which most accurately describes the defense lawyer's argument?

(A) It draws a conclusion based on semantic differences in disparate points of view.

(B) It uses a metaphor to point out substantive variations in definition.

(C) It moves from a specific identification to general description.

(D) It proposes that seemingly unrelated events are members of the same larger category.

(E) It defines a principle and then posits an exception to that principle.

77. *Politician:* The Three Strikes Law is a failure! Imprisoning a person for life after he or she commits a third felony has filled our prisons with hundreds of people serving life sentences for trivial offenses and strained state budgets, while the crime rate continues to rise.

Each of the following, if true, supports the politician's claim EXCEPT:

(A) Serious crimes, defined as those that have resulted in the perpetrator being sentenced to life in prison, have risen 13 percent in the last year.

(B) Prisoners are now being housed four to a cell, and the state is being sued by the federal government for violating prisoners' civil rights.

(C) More time in prison has increased educational opportunities with many prisoners acquiring college degrees at the taxpayers' expense.

(D) Violence in prisons is on the rise as more prisoners with three strikes are switched to maximum security prisons with hardened criminals.

(E) Penalties for misdemeanors have also increased.

78. *Civil libertarian:* Many employers try to justify their prying into their employees' e-mails by pointing out that the equipment on which the e-mails are created, sent and/or received is owned by the company. Additionally, the companies believe that monitoring employees' e-mails encourages employees to be more conscientious and hardworking and respectful of company property. All of these arguments are clearly false and are intended to obscure the fact that the companies in question are invading the privacy of their workers.

Which one of the following is a questionable technique used in the argument above?

(A) Making a generalization based on limited evidence.

(B) Questioning the employers' motives rather than examining their reasons for those arguments.

(C) Attempting to hold the companies in question to a much higher standard than is common to other businesses.

(D) Seeking to exculpate the workers by attacking the employers.

(E) Justifying the employees' actions on the basis that the actions are necessary for the continued health of these businesses.

79. If all well-executed architecture inspires lofty thoughts, and the Genesee Opera House is a well-executed example of architecture, then it follows that the Genesee Opera House inspires lofty thoughts. But the Genesee Opera House does not inspire lofty thoughts. So either the Genesee Opera House is not an example of well-executed architecture, or not all well-executed examples of architecture inspire lofty thoughts.

Which one of the arguments below has the same pattern of reasoning as the reasoning illustrated above?

(A) Poetry has the capacity to invoke emotions. "A Sunset Song" is a poem. Therefore "A Sunset Song" invokes emotions.

(B) If all penicillins have the capacity to destroy disease-causing bacteria and Zencillin B is a penicillin, then Zencillin B has the capacity to destroy disease-causing bacteria. But Zencillin B does not destroy bacteria. So either Zencillin B is not penicillin, or not all penicillins have the capacity to destroy bacteria.

(C) If all trucks carrying propane have to use the overpass to cross the Little Eagle River and the vehicle crossed the Little Eagle River by using the overpass, then the vehicle is a truck. But the vehicle is not a truck. So either it did not cross the river, or it was not carrying propane.

(D) If all the butchers at the major supermarkets are union members, and John is a butcher, then it follows that John is a union member. But John is anti-union. So either John is not a butcher at a major supermarket, or he is lying about his hatred of the union.

(E) If all scouts are obliged to take the Cub Scout Oath and Kyle wishes to become a Cub Scout, Kyle will be obliged to take the Cub Scout Oath. But Kyle has yet to take the Cub Scout Oath. So either Kyle is opposed to taking the oath, or he is opposed to becoming a Cub Scout.

80. The cliff-dwellers of Arajaput live an average of 89 years, fifteen years longer than their low-land countrymen. This is due to the cleansing and life-enhancing effects of their yogurt, which is a staple of the Arajaput diet. Now that yogurt, created from the same cultures that have granted long life to generations of Arajaputians, is available here in the States.

Which one of the following, if true, most seriously weakens the claim that their eating yogurt is responsible for the longer lives of Arajaputians as compared to their low-land countrymen?

(A) Diseases have ravaged Arajaput in the last fifteen years, killing off people both in the mountains and the plains.

(B) The largest cause of death in the cliff dwellers of Arajaput is cholera, a disease notably absent in many other parts of the country.

(C) Due to the high altitude, few mountain-dwelling Arajaputians get malaria, the second largest mortality factor elsewhere in the country.

(D) The Arajaputians have not fought a war in this century.

(E) Cuozo, a country remarkably like Arajaput, has a population with even longer life spans.

81. Illiteracy has long been acknowledged as one of the leading causes of crime. Scientists studying hundreds of career criminals at a series of prisons throughout the Southwest discovered that over half of those studied could neither read nor write. These findings form the basis for the governor's appeal to raise taxes to support primary education.

Which one of the following reasons, if true, most strengthens the governor's conclusion to appeal to the electorate to support primary education?

(A) The criminals studied committed more vicious crimes and more of them than any of their counterparts in prison.

(B) Particularly violent crimes are harder to obtain convictions for and thus cost the taxpayers more money to prosecute.

(C) Many criminals reported that negative experiences motivated early criminal acts.

(D) Prison classes are instrumental in preparing inmates for a successful return to society.

(E) Adult literacy is causally related to a strong elementary education.

82. Albert Goodman, a long-time student of the stock market, has recently published a study that claims to be able to predict when a rise in the market will occur. Goodman's study notes that substantial rises in the stock market for the last fifty years have occurred in years in which an American League team was victorious in the World Series. So, he argues, since an American League team won the Series this year, the prudent investor can count on substantial returns.

Which one of the following accurately describes the flaw in Goodman's reasoning?

(A) The argument fails to state just how much money the average investor made during these times of stock market increases.

(B) The argument's conclusion is simply a restatement of one of its premises.

(C) The argument implies that, just because one event happened before another event, the first event caused the second.

(D) The argument goes on to say that depressions often occur when the National League wins.

(E) Baseball is no longer the most popular sport in America, which has greatly reduced the power of the World Series outcomes to predict trends in the stock market.

83. Throughout history, most generals in wartime have resisted transferring their

military units to other generals who requested such transfers. These refusals have occurred even when the general who received the request for additional troops was in a relatively safe area and sometimes even when the requesting general's position was being attacked.

Each of the reasons below, if true, supports the decision of the general with the stronger force not to share his forces with the requesting generals EXCEPT:

(A) War is unpredictable, and situations can change in an instant.

(B) Generals with the largest armies are typically promoted faster than those commanding smaller armies.

(C) Moving troops from one place to another often unnecessarily exposes them to attack.

(D) Many of the greatest generals have waged successful campaigns with forces inferior to those of their adversaries.

(E) Transportation is always difficult in wartime because of destruction of roads and rail lines.

84. *Pundit:* The end of the recent recession has signaled the end of the truce between labor and management in many industries. Fearful of forcing already strapped businesses into insolvency, unions postponed wage demands and avoided strikes. With better times on the way, you can be sure that unions will be vigorous in demanding an increased share of corporate profits.

The action taken by the unions is most supported by which one of the following ideas?

(A) To combat recession, nothing is more important than teamwork.
(B) Unions never ask for something that a company doesn't have to give.
(C) In times of economic stress, unreasonable demands by unions could destroy the companies and thereby cost union members their jobs.
(D) Unions and management are, by their very natures, always at odds.
(E) To secure and retain their positions, union leaders must oppose management whenever they can.

85. Every angler in the Big Liar's Club exaggerates the size of every fish he or she catches. To hear a member talk, one would think that only large, record-sized fish are caught by club members. Yet some fish that are caught by club members are actually quite small despite how they are described by the anglers who catch them.

For the statement that some fish caught by the members are small to be true, which one of the following has to be assumed?

(A) Every fish the angler catches is actually quite small.
(B) The only fish in the sample discussed are small fish.
(C) The anglers catch various sizes of fish.
(D) Exaggerating the size of the fish they catch is something that most anglers do.
(E) The size of the fish is unimportant given that all sizes are subject to the same degree of exaggeration.

86. Athletes are often encouraged to eat higher amounts of protein than would be indicated by their bodyweights in order to help build muscles broken down in strenuous workouts. But recent studies prove that any protein ingested that exceeds the body's maintenance needs is simply excreted. Therefore, athletes can safely ingest a normal amount of protein for their bodyweights without worrying about any extraordinary needs their vigorous lifestyle may impose on them.

Which one of the following statements, if true, would most seriously weaken the argument that athletes need not ingest larger amounts of protein than is normal for their body weights?

(A) Athletes are generally larger than non-athletic people, so they need more protein.
(B) A thick steak is extremely satisfying for many athletes.
(C) The dangers of excess protein intake are more substantial and long lasting than were previously thought.
(D) These most recent studies were all funded by the beef industry.
(E) Vigorous lifestyles break down more muscle tissue than can be rebuilt by normal protein intake.

ANSWER KEY

1. C		23. E		45. E		66. A	
2. E		24. D		46. D		67. B	
3. E		25. D		47. D		68. E	
4. D		26. D		48. C		69. C	
5. B		27. D		49. B		70. A	
6. D		28. A		50. E		71. D	
7. A		29. C		51. A		72. D	
8. E		30. E		52. C		73. A	
9. D		31. B		53. A		74. C	
10. C		32. C		54. D		75. B	
11. E		33. D		55. C		76. D	
12. C		34. C		56. B		77. E	
13. C		35. D		57. C		78. B	
14. A		36. B		58. E		79. B	
15. B		37. E		59. C		80. C	
16. D		38. C		60. C		81. E	
17. A		39. A		61. D		82. C	
18. A		40. A		62. B		83. D	
19. A		41. D		63. E		84. C	
20. C		42. C		64. B		85. C	
21. B		43. B		65. B		86. E	
22. C		44. B					

ANSWER EXPLANATIONS

1. **C**   The passage states that robots not only can build other robots but also can rebuild themselves; therefore, they should last forever. (B) is probably true, but (C) must be true. According to the passage, (A) and (E) are not implied, and (D) is probably not true.

2. **E**   There are tasks that robots can do better than humans. Any task in which not being able to think independently or not having emotions would be advantageous might be better done by robots. Tasks that require exposure to dangerous chemicals or radioactivity are also suitable for robots.

3. **E**   The author states that the robot can do the most complex group of activities, but "does not have the capacity to . . . think independently." If the most complex group of activities necessitates independent thinking, then the author's assertions are in *direct* contradiction. (C) would be a good choice if it mentioned independent thinking, not training, as training is not mentioned in the passage.

4. **D**   All of the four other answers are clearly assumptions that can be inferred from the details of the paragraph. Choice (D) may or may not be true, but unlike the other choices, there is nothing in the paragraph that suports it, since there is no reference to the policies of other airlines.

5. **B**   Since none of the January blossoming plants will flower again later in the year, no plants that first blossom in January will flower twice in the year. (A), (C), and (E) may be untrue, because we are not told that all the bulbs and tubers in the garden blossom in January; we are told only that all the plants that blossom in January are from bulbs or tubers. (D) need not be true since some bulbs may not flower every year.

6. **D**   (A) and (B) are irrelevant, and (C) and (E) are not as effective as (D) because they are just restatements of the thought, rather than a clarification.

7. **A**   The phrase "four out of five" implies 80% of a large sample (nationwide). If only five dentists were in the sample, the reliability would certainly be in question. (B) would strengthen the endorsement, while (D) and (E) are irrelevant. (C) could weaken it, but not nearly as much.

8. **E**   (A) must be true by the first statement because everybody in the class likes drawing or painting or both, so if Angie does not like painting, she must like drawing. This same logic holds for (C). "Everyone in the class who does not like drawing," must like painting. And (D), it is possible that no one in the class likes painting. But (E) cannot be true if everyone likes drawing or painting or both.

9. **D**   (A) is incorrect since there is no attack on Mark's reasoning. (B) is incorrect because personal pressure is not implied. (C) is incorrect since it is hearsay. (E) is incorrect, since who is to say what a "positive" approach is? (E) could have been the correct choice if (D) were not a possibility.

10. **C**   The conclusion of the passage is that, because of safety concerns, more research and testing ought to be done before microwaves become standard household appliances. If, however, research and testing are ineffective means of discerning

safety problems, then research and testing would be irrelevant. This criticism seriously weakens the conclusion.

11. **E** If many microwave ovens have been found to leak radioactive elements, then the conclusion—that microwaves should not be standard appliances until they are more carefully researched and tested—is further strengthened because more safety concerns needed to be addressed.

12. **C** The pattern of reasoning here is since X follows from Y, if Y is absent, there will be no X. In choice (C), buying from the bakery (Y) results in good breakfast business (X). But the restaurant that does not buy from the bakery (Y is absent) will have poor breakfast business (X). In the original, the first step is an action (eating Vitagatto), whereas in choice (B), it is inaction that has a consequence.

13. **C** Choices (A), (B), (D), and (E) are all reasonable ways of explaining the discrepancies. If the census report did undercount, we would still need to know if it undercounted one gender more than the other.

14. **A** The conclusion can be properly drawn only if the condition, "*being white*," is sufficient to rule out all but quartz. (A) allows the conclusion, "*must* be quartz," to be reached.

15. **B** Though this chef probably believes that the restaurants of Paris are superior, the passage passes judgment only on the breads, not on the restaurants of New York. It does assume that good bread will be eaten, that lacking French training there are hardly any good bakers in America, and that if the bread is good the roll basket will be empty. But it may have been refilled three times.

16. **D** The chef's claim to know how to bake bread is, no doubt, just, but the four other answers point to weaknesses to be seen in the passage. The speaker asserts American incompetence on the basis of flimsy evidence, and the assumption that American food can be judged on the basis of some New York restaurants generalizes about the small restaurants in Paris and is not specific about restaurants in New York or Paris.

17. **A** The tone of the passage is positive: workers "enjoy" the same status; "harmony"; less "tension and anger." One can therefore conclude that the author approves of the work environment of the Japanese auto factory for the workers' well-being, and any resemblance of American factories to those of the Japanese ought to be encouraged. Note that there is no indication at all regarding the quality of the goods produced (B).

18. **A** Only (A) is logically supported by the passage. There is no direct support regarding worker envy for (B). There may be less tension and anger in Japanese auto factories; however, to conclude that there is no tension or anger is not logically sound. Nothing in the passage describes the relation of tension to productivity (D).

19. **A** When we approach land, we usually sight birds. The lookout has just sighted birds. The question is not which possible answer statement is true or false but which statement represents the most logical conclusion based on a set of conditions. The set of conditions is an opinion or theory based on a presumption of what usually happens—not every time, just usually. Answer (A), the

conjecture (opinion or theory) that we are approaching land is strengthened, is a logical conclusion. The statements that land is closer or we are approaching land, as in answers (B) and (C), are absolutes and are negated by the word "usually" in the original set of conditions. Answer (D), we may or may not be approaching land, and answer (E), we may not be approaching land, do not support the logical progression of thought expressed in the original statement (opinion or theory) and contradict the stated theory.

20. **C** (A) is not true, since Nexon is not a sufficient condition for life; that is, Nexon alone is not enough. (B) is not true because Nexon must be present if there is life (necessary condition). (C) is true; Nexon must be present (it is a necessary condition). (C) does not suggest the absence of things other than Nexon and, therefore, does not contradict the original statement. (D) is untrue since Nexon alone is not a sufficient condition.

21. **B** (A) need not be true, because the absence of Flennel is not a necessary condition; that is, there can be other conditions that result in the end of life. (C) is not true, because the absence of Flennel is sufficient to end life (one cannot say life may "not cease"). (B) is true, given the absence of Flennel is sufficient to end life. Both (D) and (E) are untrue. Absence of Flennel is sufficient cause (D) but there might be other causes as well (E).

22. **C** Choices (A), (B), (D), and (E) are all logical conclusions. Since electric heat is very expensive and the winters are very cold but the summers

are merely warm, choice (D) makes sense. But even with high costs, we expect gas consumption to be higher in the very cold winters.

23. **E** The statement presented can be logically made only if being reared at Prince Charming Kennels assures that a poodle is purebred. (E) provides such assurance. (A) does not state that only purebreds are reared and, therefore, does not assure that any given poodle from the kennels is pure.

24. **D** (A) may be eliminated because the argument does not rule out a possible previous proposal. (B) may be eliminated as no suggestion of easy identification or the necessity of easy identification is presupposed. (C) may be eliminated because the argument is independent of any comparison between the Great Salt Lake and any other body of water. (E) can be eliminated because the argument presents the weaker claim of the *possibility* of oil. (D) allows, if true, the *possibility* of oil to be sufficient cause for exploration.

25. **D** The context suggests that salutary associations are positive ones, and the phrase *associations of pleasure* immediately following the first mention of *salutary* certifies (D) as the best choice.

26. **D** (A) is answered in the first sentence, as are (B) and (C). In the first sentence we are told that all thinking is associational, and in the second, that both education and experience promote accusations. Nowhere, however, does the author mention just what teachers blame and praise.

27. **D** Only this choice addresses both parts of the statement, which implies that expert practice helps iden-

tify errors. (B) and (C) stress error only; (A) stresses practice only; and (E) stresses writing only.

28. **A** Refer to the following diagram:

On the basis of the foregoing diagram, (B), (C), (D), and (E) are false.

29. **C** The structure of the given argument may be simplified:
Most are popular and low.
Splendor is not popular and high (not low).
(C) parallels this structure:
Most who stop do gain.
Carl does not stop and will not gain.

30. **E** The statement given can be simplified:
All <u>have</u> <u>hair</u> (mammal).
<u>This</u> does <u>not</u> have <u>hair</u>.
<u>It</u> is <u>not</u> (mammal).

Only (E) can be reduced to this same form:
All <u>have</u> <u>smell</u> (lubricants).
<u>This</u> does <u>not</u> have <u>smell</u>.
<u>It</u> is <u>not</u> (lubricant).

31. **B** (A) has no bearing because the argument is concerned only with mammals. (C) is not relevant; the argument does not address the amount of hair. (E) is likewise outside the argument's subject. (D) is a possible answer because the claim is that the absence of hair indicates a nonmammal. However, (B) is a better choice. (D) is a possibility— "One *could* remove." (B) points out that, without any other intervention, there *are* creatures with no hair that are also mammals.

32. **C** If the chances of a person with the same genetic makeup as someone who has developed the disease are 100 times higher than someone with different genes, genetic material must play some role. But if the proportion of people who do develop the disease is very small, genetics cannot be the only cause. The study supports (B) and (E), but gives no information on whether the disease is more likely to affect one identical twin than one nonidentical twin.

33. **D** Because they share the same genetic makeup, identical twins are especially useful in medical studies of the role of genes.

34. **C** The pattern of reasoning here is that X is caused by changes in either Y or Z. If Y is unchanged, and X happens, it must have been caused by Z. In (C), X is the rise in pizza costs, the steady Y is the cost of cheese, and the causative Z is the price of beef.

35. **D** Since the argument concerns state laws to be passed, the best choices must be those that refer to the responsibility of the state, (C) and (D). Of the two, (D) is clearly the more specific and directly relevant to the situation described in the paragraph.

36. **B** The first proposition states that if an athlete and invited, then over 35. The second proposition states that if over 35, then not both an athlete and invited. The propositions contradict each other. Therefore, no person can be both an athlete and invited.

37. **E** The most plausible answer here is that the group that lost more weight ate less at dinner. Presumably, members of the other group were much hungrier because they had

exercised so much more and had less to eat at lunch, and so they ate more at dinner. (A) and (C) will not work if applied only to "some" of the group.

38. **C**   If this surgical procedure does more harm than good, it would be wise not to perform it at all. This would reduce by one the number of needless surgical procedures.

39. **A**   The passage insists that the tennis team will be composed only of first-rate athletes and nonsmokers. But there is no reason given to prevent a nonsmoker who is not a first-rate athlete from being on the team. Presumably he or she made up for lack of great natural ability with more practice.

40. **A**   If the prices have gone down, the clothing sales might well increase, and television watching would be irrelevant. Options (B), (C), (D), and (E) have no information to explain the rise in sales apart from television.

41. **D**   The error in the reasoning is the assumption that what was true of a group (the mortgage sales department) can predict something specific about a single member of that group (Thomason's presumed sales). The correct parallel is in (D), where the individual's performance (Meany's winning the golf championship) is based on the accomplishment of a group (the South Texas State golf team).

42. **C**   If the largest foreign investor is the United States and the third largest is Britain, it appears that the rules are not intended to exclude Asians, since the same rules apply even more extensively to Europeans and Americans.

43. **B**   The author, whose position is clearly in favor of fluoridation, refers to

the "demonic scheme" to suggest the irrationality of the opposition. Choice (C) is careless. The argument is not trying to refute the notion of a communist plot.

44. **B**   Only the first example (sickle-cell trait) is related to disease. The second concerns the response to lactose, and the third to fingerprints. What all three have in common is that they cannot be predicted by race, and the passage is part of a consideration of the difficulty of providing a scientific definition of race.

45. **E**   Options (A), (B), (C), and (D) assumptions in the passage, but there is nothing here to support the idea that either medical or legal costs are greater.

46. **D**   If all medical costs in the other states are much lower, the fact that the medical costs of automobile accident victims are also lower would be explained, and the argument that "pain and suffering" awards lead to higher medical costs would be weakened.

47. **D**   Most of the paragraph is concerned with the sales figures. Only in the last sentence does the subject of profit arise, and we are never told exactly how sales relate to profit. To assume that there can be no profit with this decline in sales, we must also assume that the profit margin will not be higher.

48. **C**   The author makes his point by using an analogy. That is, he argues that the passage of limits on ozone-depleting gases resulted in the rapid development of affordable technologies to deal with the problem, and suggests that unless short-term limits on greenhouse gases are enacted, there will be no urgency to develop the necessary technologies.

49. **B** If there has been no research to develop a technology to deal with global warming, the enactment of short-term limits would not bring the needed technologies to the marketplace. Choice (A) deals with an "immediate economic consequence" but the issue is short- and long-term limits, not immediate ones.

50. **E** The suggestions of a cult or college prank are alternate explanations that are supported by the evidence as well as the alien-invader notion. Though the evidence is questionable, the response here does not quarrel with its accuracy.

51. **A** The best choice should be related directly to the claim that "forests will not be consumed so rapidly." Choice (B) is the next best choice, but we cannot know if the speaker is concerned with ecology in general or simply with the preservation of forests. Choices (C) and (D) may be true, but they are not required assumptions for this argument. The speaker may be willing to spend more money to save the forests.

52. **C** Although the writer would probably agree with the ideas of choices (A), (B), and (C), the most logical conclusion from the information in the passage is choice (C). If the number of fatalities increases when less than 50 percent of the older population has been inoculated, and the number of the inoculated declines, the number of fatalities should increase. Since we do not know how many (50 percent or more?) were inoculated last year, and only that fewer will be inoculated this year, we cannot be sure that "fatalities will increase sharply," choice (D).

53. **A** Since the ridership on the route served by the older buses that are not air-conditioned increased, the larger number of commuters on the other routes may not be due to the new vehicles.

54. **D** If no bond measure that will bring in large revenues will lose, the argument must be true. The verifying statement can also be expressed with positives instead of the two negatives. Both choices (A) and (B) could be true without assuring the passage of the stadium bond, since bills that do bring profits could also be defeated. Similarly, choice (C) could be true, without assuring the success of the stadium bond. Choice (E) is not relevant.

55. **C** The flawed reasoning is a hasty generalization based on a single fact: If Logan Airport is crime-free, so are all other airports in the United States. Choices (A), (B), (D), and (E) have the same kind of errant reasoning. Choice (C) presents an observed effect and its probable cause.

56. **B** The right answer should undermine the case for using safety helmets. If, as choice (B) claims, the cyclist's vision is impaired, accidents are more likely. Choices (A) and (E) do not bear directly enough on the benefits of wearing or not wearing a helmet, whereas choice (D) strengthens the argument.

57. **C** The professor accuses the student of being less than honest about the study time mentioned and so is assuming that the two hours spent on the review of the endocrine system and the rereading of the chapter on the circulatory system three times would have been effective (B), which is not necessarily the case. Consequently, the professor is saying, the student must be less than honest about the study time. But the

student's study time and methods may not have been effective through poor concentration (A), lack of retention perhaps during the rereading (D), or physical problems during the exam itself (E) and may not be dishonest at all. The passage assumes only that the "basic facts" could have been learned in the study time that the student had specified; there is no evidence to suggest, however, that the professor considers the learning of basic facts to be easy.

58. **E** The argument is in this form: A (people who dream in color) are B (creative). C (Conrad) is B (creative). Therefore, C (Conrad) is A (one who dreams in color). The final statement logically doesn't follow because the first statement doesn't say *only* people who dream in color are creative. The only answer that follows this pattern is (E). A (corn) is B (not good in containers). C (maize) is B (not good in containers). Therefore, C (maize) is A (corn). This question is made more difficult by the fact that in reality maize actually is corn. But that doesn't change the flawed reasoning. Any other plant could have been substituted for maize in the pattern of this argument, producing a statement such as "tomatoes are corn." No other answer exhibits this flawed pattern of logic. Answer (C) is incorrect because Sally is not now an electrician, and there's nothing that suggests she will be, only that she wants to be.

59. **C** The only assumption made by the Parks and Recreation Supervisor is that visitors to the park would like to avoid being bitten. If the supervisor didn't make such an assumption,

there would be no reason to write the advisory in the first place.

60. **C** Although George doesn't do all that he could to avoid bites, what he does is the most likely to be effective. By staying on the paths, he avoids the weeds and other plants that are likely to harbor chiggers. And climbing the rock face is unlikely to put him in harm's way from the insects because a rock face would not tend to have heavy plant growth. By showering when he returns, he's likely to dislodge any stray chiggers that might have gotten on his body. Sheila (A) showers after applying repellant, rendering it ineffective. Consuela (B), by venturing into a blackberry patch will probably have picked up chiggers, and toweling alone may not rid her of them. Dimitri (D) sprays only a few areas of his body and is going through heavy brush, where insects are likely to be. Connie (E) may be applying countermeasures too late into her walk.

61. **D** The fact that the immigrants are taking jobs that U.S. citizens won't take calls into question the speaker's statement that the immigrants are taking jobs away from legal citizens. It doesn't approach the speaker's contention that the immigrants use federal tax dollars for services, but it calls the conclusion into question more than does any other choice given. (B) is not correct because it mentions local taxes, not the federal taxes the speaker cites.

62. **B** Only this fact could explain the seeming inconsistency presented. The Woodwards used *more* kilowatt hours in August than in July, but they were charged *less* for those hours. The information given makes

it clear that the electric company didn't lower their *average* rate. It remained the same as July's, so the company's buying cheaper electricity (C) isn't relevant. Neither is the fact that the Woodwards tried to conserve electricity in August. Since they used more hours in August than in July, they obviously weren't successful in that endeavor.

63. **E** Pete clearly says that he agrees with the *concerns* of the ecoterrorists. But he also suggests that the life of the spotted owl and the life of a human shouldn't be equated; in other words, methods used to save the planet should *not* endanger people (he doesn't comment on whether harming human possessions is unacceptable). The fact that Pete recognizes the effectiveness of the ecoterrorists' methods doesn't mean that he agrees with them. But Anne mistakenly believes that Pete agrees with the *methods* of the ecoterrorists, not only their *concerns.*

64. **B** If 90 percent of doctors actively promote pharmaceutical plant research, then it can be assumed that 10 percent do not. But it doesn't follow that those who don't actively promote the research are opposed to it (E). It also can't be known from the facts given that all politicians in rain forest countries are ignorant about the subject (A) or that 98 percent of people oppose the research (C) (they simply aren't knowledgeable about it). And even though 90 percent of doctors actively promote the research, it doesn't necessarily follow that they are well informed about it (D).

65. **B** The argument uses specific information (schedule delays, travel and check-in time) to call into question

the conclusion that the allowance of nine hours of rest in a twenty-four-hour period is reasonable and prudent. By this argumentative technique, the speaker suggests that pilots may not be getting the nine hours of rest they are thought to get. Although the argument does deal with a possible discrepancy between assumed and actual facts, it doesn't use an analogy (D).

66. **A** If the citizenry would not approve the rounding up of sales tax to the next nickel, then local government would have a real dilemma. They would lose money if the amount were rounded down, and they would be unable to collect their present sales tax if pennies were eliminated and consequently would lose needed funds. Of the answers given, this problem would most strongly call the elimination of the penny coin into question. The other answer choices either support (mildly or strongly) the argument (choices B and E) or are irrelevant (choices C and D).

67. **B** Janice promotes a ban on coastal development. Wayne, however, raises the question of property rights of individuals in this matter. All the other choices go too far, given the discussion presented. The conversation might go on to discuss whether Janice's points constitute a compelling reason for the ban (A), but it doesn't do so as presented. A government buyout or grandfathering in of rights (C) might be options discussed as the conversation progresses, but they aren't here. The specific damage of lost shore bird habitat and beach areas aren't discussed (D), only erosion damage in general. And, although

you might surmise that Wayne may contend that property rights offset the damage (E), he doesn't actually make that point.

68. **E** The passage states that not all states have emission testing. A first step in controlling the emission problem, then, would be to have testing on a national (federal) level. The fact that the testing program would be "stringent," that is, rigorous and exacting, indicates that it may be more effective than existing state programs. In addition, the choice suggests that these measures would "probably" be effective, not absolutely. Choice (A) isn't the best answer because there is no indication of the level of effectiveness of the state programs. Checking can be consistently bad as well as good, in which case the problem would not be reduced. The general view of emission testing is not irrelevant (C), although it may be incorrect, as public opinion can be important in the passing of laws and the functioning of government. Choice (D) overstates the effect when it says the problem would definitely be "eliminated."

69. **C** For choice (C) to explain why the spiders are found in bathtubs, it would have to be assumed that they intentionally lie there awaiting a chance to bite humans, which is illogical considering that, first, the spiders prefer isolated, dark, unused areas and, second, that they would somehow consider humans prey, which is not likely considering their size. All other choices give possible reasons for the phenomenon, although (E) does so fairly weakly. Choice (D) does explain the presence of the spiders, as they may

fall into the tub and be unable to climb back out.

70. **A** According to the information, the study makes no ethical judgment on what the companies should or should not do; it simply reports, based on this research, on what is done. But given these facts, the other choices all indicate a likely flaw in the study's reasoning. The actual decision makers may not agree with the memo writers (B); the study seems to confuse dangerous recalled products with all recalled products (C); the awareness of possible sanctions doesn't automatically make them factors in the decision (D); and the assumption that mention of sanctions in two-thirds of the correspondence equates to a two-thirds reduction of dangerous products (or even of all recalled products) is illogical (E).

71. **D** If contributors don't somehow make their points of view known to the politicians, it would be difficult for those points of view to be influential at voting time. Although the discussion does seem to suggest that public and private good may sometimes be in conflict, it doesn't assume that it would be "inevitably" so (A). Nor does the analyst imply that campaign contribution reform will necessarily be "voted down" (B), only that it will face challenges (a "rocky road"). Choice (C) mentions reform legislation in general, which isn't under discussion here. There is an assumption by the analyst that politicians may adopt the view of "wealthy, generous contributors," but choice (E) mentions the "majority" of contributors. The wealthy and generous donors may not be in the majority. Their number,

as opposed to, say, donors of small sums, isn't mentioned.

72. **D** Although there are several logical problems with the reasoning in the passage, and no choice fully justifies its reasoning, choice (D) at least in part justifies it. If people actually still need summer merchandise in August, and if no summer merchandise remains after a sale, then an argument might be made that no such closeout sales should be allowed until September. No other choice indicates that no summer merchandise remains for consumers to buy in August.

73. **A** Only this choice definitely suggests that the SUV owners are concerned about the lowering of gas consumption, at least to some extent and at least during periods of high gas prices, and weakens the argument that they are unconcerned. The fact that fuel-efficient features were originally incorporated in these vehicles is irrelevant, as the SUVs are now high gas users. Choice (C) is also irrelevant; these owners may simply not want their vehicles banned and so support features that will still allow them to drive them. Because the conclusion about SUV owners' unconcern is not restricted to only U.S. drivers, choice (D) may seem to be a good answer, because it indicates a drop in sales in Europe. But the choice doesn't say why the drop in sales has occurred. Perhaps it's just a cultural change in preference. The purchase of lower octane fuel (E) doesn't necessarily have to do with the concern about amount of gas consumption, only with the cost of that consumption, and nothing indicates that these vehicles would need higher octane fuel in any case.

74. **C** If dry heat alleviates respiratory problems, and this speaker now recommends against the Southwest as a retirement destination for retirees with respiratory problems because of the air pollution, the speaker must make the assumption that the pollution substantially offsets the benefits of dry heat. Choice (D) is incorrect because air pollution is not listed as a *cause* of respiratory problems such as asthma or emphysema (although it perhaps could be), and such an assumption is not necessary to the argument, which addresses itself to those who already *have* respiratory difficulties. Choices (A), (B), and (E) are not assumptions that the speaker must make. Choice (A) deals with comparing pollution problems with those in other areas. Choice (B) deals with retirees' plans, and Choice (E) deals with the reduction of dryness of the heat.

75. **B** Choice (B) is the only choice that must be true if the statements are true. Note that the choice says that weight and exercise "may" be playing a role, which is true given the fact that we know they are effective in preventing or delaying the onset of the disease. The choice would not necessarily be true if it said they "are" definitely playing a role because other factors may be involved in the disease (say, genetic factors or simply your age). Choice E is incorrect for this same reason. Choice (A) is not necessarily true because it discusses weight alone, and the original statements speak only of the combination of exercise and weight reduction. Choice (C) is incorrect because you may die from other causes and life span would

not be affected. Choice (D) introduces the elimination of the disease, which isn't discussed in the original statements, only the onset of the disease.

76. **D** The lawyer's argument proposes that seemingly unrelated events—the releasing of computer viruses, the spray painting of a wall, and the knocking over of a mailbox—are part of a larger category, vandalism. The argument doesn't deal with "disparate points of view" (A), a metaphor (B), a general description (C), or an exception to a principle (E). The argument goes on to draw a conclusion based on the fact that the events are part of one larger category, but even though choice (D) may not be a complete description of the lawyer's argument, it remains the best of the choices given.

77. **E** The argument says nothing about misdemeanors. (A) and (B) support the contention that prisons are more crowded now than ever, and (A) also supports the idea that crime rates are rising. Prisoners whose sentences allow them to stay in prison long enough to earn college degrees are an additional burden on state budgets, particularly because their severe sentences preclude them from returning as useful members of the society that educated them. (D) suggests that those imprisoned for trivial offenses might become the victims of more ruthless criminals.

78. **B** The argument does make a generalization (A) but does not provide us with any information as to the breadth of the evidence on which it is based. There is nothing in the argument that would suggest either (C) or (D). (E) is false because the argument deals with the actions of the employers, not those of the employees.

79. **B** (A) lacks the form of the original. The argument says that "all well-executed architecture has the capacity to inspire lofty thoughts." None of the other choices has a clause that mirrors that.

80. **C** To weaken a claim, you are obliged to weaken the premises on which the claim is built. (C) offers an alternative reason that the mountain people do not die as early as their low-land countrymen. (A) does not specify in which part of the country the diseases raged, and B does not mention which parts of the country did not experience cholera. (D) applies to the whole country, while (E) is totally irrelevant. We're talking about Arajaput—not another country.

81. **E** The governor proposes giving money to support primary education, which will in turn fight adult illiteracy, which is a major cause of crime. (A) is an irrelevant comparison. (B) is appealing because it shows how money can be saved, but the major issue is not saving money but rather combating crime by reducing illiteracy. (C) is too vague. The negative experiences could have happened anywhere and at any time, not just at school. Also, negative experiences are not directly related to illiteracy. The argument is about preventing crime, not rehabilitating criminals, ruling out (D).

82. **C** That which is correlative is not necessarily causative. (B) implies that the argument is a circular one, which it is not. (A), (D), and (E) are irrelevant.

83. **D** All of the others offer reasons for a general *not* to share his forces with

other generals. (D) suggests that large forces are not an absolute necessity for a successful campaign and that a smaller force that emerges victorious over its larger foes may actually enhance a general's reputation.

84. **C** The unions acted in a way that is really out of character for unions, and did so because of the threat that the recession posed to the welfare of their members. While (D) is probably true, it doesn't explain why the union acted in the way it did. (B) does not seem supported by fact and the word *never* makes it an absolute. (A) is unresponsive to the question, and (E) is unsupported by the pundit's statement.

85. **C** The statement says that some fish caught are actually quite small despite the descriptions given to them. For that to be true, there have to be small fish in the set of fish that are caught (along with fish of other sizes).

86. **E** The fact that athletes are larger than others (A) is immaterial; after all, the argument clearly states that protein intake should be relative to body size. (B) is also irrelevant. (C) is tempting but leaves us still with the problem of what excess intake is. The fact that the beef industry underwrote these studies would more likely strengthen the argument against excess protein intake than weaken it, since the beef industry might have a vested interest in increasing the amount of beef (a rich source of protein) consumed. But (E) suggests that more protein than normal for a given bodyweight may be requested by an athlete's lifestyle.

3

ANALYTICAL REASONING

INTRODUCTION TO QUESTION TYPE

The Analytical Reasoning section is designed to measure your ability to analyze, understand, and draw conclusions from a group of conditions and relationships. This section is 35 minutes long and contains from 22 to 24 questions (usually four sets of conditions, statements, or rules). Each set is followed by five to seven questions.

The Analytical Reasoning type of question first appeared officially on the LSAT in June 1982, but a similar form of Analytical Reasoning had been used on the Graduate Record Exam since 1977. It was removed from the GRE in 2003.

Analytical Reasoning situations can take many forms, but you should be aware of some general things before reviewing the problem types. Remember, even though Analytical Reasoning is the most difficult section for most students, it is also the most preparable.

Let's take a closer look:

First, let's check the approximate percentages of analytical reasoning displays.

ANALYTICAL REASONING DISPLAYS

Types	Approx. Frequency
The Position Organizer (linear)	40–50%
The Position Organizer (Non-linear)	4–7%
The Position Organizer with Diagram Provided	*
The Group Organizer	20–25%
The Group Organizer (with several conditional statements)	20–25%
The Group Organizer (Venn diagrams/grouping arrows)	**
The Table Organizer (information table)	8–12%
The Table Organizer (elimination grid)	2–3%
The Spatial Organizer	4–5%
The General Organizer (simply pulling out information)	**
The General Organizer with Diagram Provided	**

*Appeared in recent bulletins
**Appeared infrequently in earlier tests

Now, let's preview the common question stems.

SAMPLE ANALYTICAL REASONING QUESTION STEMS

- Which one of the following is an acceptable order of students from first to last?
- Which one of the following is a complete and accurate list of athletes who could have been on the team?
- Which one of the following CANNOT be a complete and accurate list of the films shown?
- Which one of the following could be a complete and accurate matching of the clubs and their members?
- If two films in French are shown on the first day of the festival, which one of the following must be true?
- If the fall semester offers a history class, then which one of the following could be true?
- If Tim is faster than Sal, and Bill is not the third fastest, then which one of the following must be true?
- If J is taller than B, then the shortest member is …
- If Taylor is selected first, then any of the following could be selected sixth EXCEPT:
- Which one of the following must be false?
- Which one of the following must be true?
- Which one of the following could be true?
- Which one of the following CANNOT be true?
- Which one of the following bands marches earlier than ninth?
- Which one of the following pairs of jugglers CANNOT juggle together?

And finally, let's take a quick overview of the key strategies.

OVERVIEW OF THE THREE (3) KEY STRATEGIES
YOUR ACTIONS AND . . . REACTIONS

Actions	Reactions
1. Start a Set Confidently	Read the conditions carefully Mark the conditions
2. Draw Your Organizer (Keep it simple)	Look for key items Draw and place information Reason from the conditions Look at some questions for help
3. Answer the Questions (Anticipate some of the question stems)	Read the questions carefully Work with the choices given Eliminate answer choices

WHEN YOU START A SET, FOCUS ON:

Reading the Conditions

1. Read each statement carefully and actively, marking important words.
2. As you read, learn to flow with the information given, looking for relationships between items.
3. Remember that making simple charts, diagrams, or simply displaying information is essential on most sets, so read the conditions as though they are describing a display or diagram.
4. If you wish to read through all of the conditions of a set before starting a diagram, begin your diagram on the second reading.
5. If no diagram seems apparent or conducive to the information given, look at a few questions. Sometimes the questions can give you some good hints on how to display the information.

Marking the Conditions

1. Because you will probably be drawing some sort of diagram or display, place a check mark next to each statement or condition as you read it or use it in the diagram. This will help you avoid skipping a statement or condition as you work back and forth in setting up your diagram.
2. Put a star or an asterisk next to big, general, and important statements. Sometimes these statements will affect a group, category, or placement. (Examples are, "No two people of the same sex are sitting in adjacent seats," and "All of the members of a department cannot take the same day off." Two other examples might include: "At least two graduate students must be on the team," and "People with pets with them must stay in hotel room 1 or 8.")
3. Put a star or an asterisk by statements that are difficult to understand. Try to rephrase these statements to yourself for better understanding.

WHEN YOU START DRAWING YOUR DISPLAY, FOCUS ON:

Finding Key Items

1. Look for a simple way to display the information. Don't complicate the issue.
2. Look for the setup, frame, or framework. Sometimes this is given in the first statement, but in other cases you may need to read a number of conditions before constructing the type of drawing that will be most effective.
3. If you discover the frame or framework, fill in as much of the diagram as possible, but do not spend a great deal of time trying to complete it. This may not be possible or necessary to answer the questions.
4. Be aware that you may have to redraw all or part of your diagram several times (typically, a few times for each set) as different conditional information is given for specific questions.

5. If a framework is not given, see if the information can be grouped by similarities or differences.

6. As you read each statement, look for concrete information that you can enter into your chart or that you can simply display. (For example, "Tom sits in seat 4," or "Cheryl coaches swimming.")

Drawing and Placing Information

1. Locate off to the side any information that you cannot place directly into your chart. (Whatever you can't put in, goes out; for example, "Jill will not sit next to Helen," or "A biology book must be next to a science book.")

2. Some very important statements may not fit into your chart. Remember to put a star or an asterisk by these big, general, and important statements.

3. If some statements are not immediately placeable in your chart (and they are not the big, general statements), you may have to return to them for later placing, after you have placed other statements. Remember to mark such statements with an arrow or some other symbol so you don't forget to return to them.

4. As you place information, use question marks (?) to mark information that is variable or could be placed in a number of different places in the diagram.

5. Underline and abbreviate or write out column headings and labels. Don't use single letters as they may be confused with the actual items (If you use "m" for males, it could be confused with an "m" for Manuel, one of the males).

6. If, as is true in many cases, no standard type of chart will apply to the problem, be aware that you can merely pull out information in a simple display or through simple notes. Remember to flow with the information given, looking for relationships between items.

Reasoning from the Conditions

1. No formal logic is required.

2. Apply evidence in both directions. For instance, if a statement tells you that a condition must be true, consider whether this means that certain other conditions must not be true. (For example: "All blue cars are fast" tells you that a slow car is *not* blue.)

3. Notice what information is used, and what is left to use. (For example, "Bob, Carl, Don, Ed, and Fred are riding the school bus home. Don, Ed, and Fred are sitting in seats one, two, and three, respectively." You should realize that Bob and Carl are left to be placed.)

4. Watch for actions and the subsequent reactions in initial conditions or from information given in the questions. (For example, "Dale, Ralph, and Art cannot be on the same team. Dale is on Team A." Your action is that Dale is on Team A, your immediate reaction is that Ralph and Art cannot be on Team A.)

5. Watch the number of items, places, and people (males to females, adults to children, etc.) you are working with. Sometimes these numbers are the basis for correct answers, and they can even tip off how to construct a diagram.

6. If the diagram you construct shows positions or specific dates or other limits, watch for items that will force you off the end or out of the limits. (For example, "There are five houses in a row on the north side of the street numbered 1, 2, 3, 4, 5 consecutively. There is one yellow house that is between two blue houses." Therefore, the yellow house cannot be in place 1 or 5, because there would be no room for a blue house. It would be forced off the end or out of bounds.)

WHEN YOU START ANSWERING THE QUESTIONS, FOCUS ON:

Reading the Questions

1. Read the questions actively, marking the important words. You should first always circle what you are looking for (Which of the following must be true? All of the following are possible except . . .).

2. Notice and underline any *actions* given to you in a question (If <u>Bob is selected</u> for the team, who else must be selected?). Watch for any subsequent *reactions* (If Bob is selected, Tom can't be selected).

3. Keep in mind that any information given to you in a specific question (Usually starting with the words "If . . . ," "Assume . . . ," "Suppose . . . ," "Given the fact that . . . ," and so on.) can be used only for that question and not for any other questions.

4. Don't take any information from one question to another question. That is, if you get an answer on one question, don't use that information (answer) in any other questions.

Working with the Answer Choices

1. Using the elimination strategy mentioned in the introduction can be invaluable here. Watch for rule breakers, that is, statements that contradict initial conditions. If the conditions state "X cannot sit next to Y" then any answer choice with X sitting next to Y can be eliminated (unless of course, the initial condition was changed in the question for that particular question).

2. Watch for certain types of wrong answers known as *distracters*. Since *"could be"* and *"must be"* are often confused, a *"could be true"* answer choice is a great distracter (*attractive distracter*) for a question that asks what *must be true*.

Understand the distinction between *must be* and *could be*:

Must Be	**Could Be**
No exceptions	May be, but doesn't
All the time	necessarily have to be
Always	

3. If a question looks like it's going to be difficult or time-consuming, you may wish to **scan the answer choices.** When you scan, **look for winners, losers, workers, and question marks**:

Winners—right answers that jump at you or are easy to spot (circle the answer in your question booklet, mark it on your answer sheet, and move on)

Losers—answers that you can eliminate instantly or very easily (cross out the answer choice and move on)

Workers—answer choices that can be fairly easily worked out to determine if they are right or wrong (go on and work this one)

Question Marks—answer choices that you either can't work or don't know what to do with (put a question mark ? and move on)

AND A FINAL REMINDER: KEEP THE DRAWING SIMPLE; DON'T COMPLICATE YOUR THINKING.

The following sections provide some detailed examples of typical problem types and useful ways of organizing the information given. These examples are intended to give you insight into some efficient methods of organizing by presenting a variety of displays or organizers—charts, tables, grids, diagrams, and so on. Some of these terms may be used interchangeably, but don't get hung up on the names of the different types. You should practice enough to be comfortable with many different types of basic displays and variations and be able to adjust your display as needed. Remember, different students may prefer different types of displays or organizers. Use what is effective and efficient for you!

THE APPROACH

ANALYZING THE TYPES OF DISPLAYS

Here are some key symbols you should use on the most common types of organizers.

KEY SYMBOLS	
Symbols	**Meaning**
In position organizers	
AB	A is to the left of and next to B.
A B	A is next to B on either side.
AB	A is **not** next to B.
A B	B is to the right of A.
A □ B	A is to the left of B with one space in between.

KEY SYMBOLS (Continued)

Symbols	Meaning
A ⬚ B	There is one space between A and B.
A ? B	A is to the left of B, but there could be spaces between them.
B ⬚C A⬚	A is to the right of B and next to C.
⬚ 1	Space 1 is empty.
A̶ 2	A cannot be in space 2.
B 3	B is in space 3.
B ———	B is taller than A and C.
C (↑↓)	C is shorter than B but could be taller, shorter, or the same height as A.
A ———	

In group organizers

x–y or ⬚xy⬚	x is in the same group as y.
x ⤙ y or x̶y̶	x is **not** in the same group as y.
x → y	If x is in the group, y must also be in the group.
y̶ → x̶	Logically, if y is not in the group, then x cannot be either.
N̶	N cannot be in the reading group.
<u>Reading</u> <u>Writing</u>	
O	O is in the writing group.
A → B and B → C , A → C	If A is in the group, then so is B, and if B is in the group, then so is C; therefore, if A is in the group, then so is C.

The Position Organizer (Linear)

This display is used for a problem set that can be organized in a straight line. This linear display is often the simplest to set up and tends to be very common on the LSAT. These problem sets can come in a variety of forms. In constructing this type of organizer, you should follow these steps:

1. Look for a frame or framework (often given in a statement preceding the conditions or in the first condition).
2. Look for key words to help you set up the frame, such as

   sequence order first last before after taller shorter in a row

   The words used in the problem set will often lead you to setting up your organizer either horizontally or vertically.

3. Look for concrete information (that is, specific information to fill in the positions or information that shows restrictions or connections). Have techniques and symbols for showing restrictions (B cannot be next to A—BA) and connections (C is adjacent to D—CD) before you take the test.
4. List the items, people, or letters that will be used to fill in the positions, and mark the relationships and/or restrictions between them.
5. Watch for and mark large, general, important statements (statements that cover a group or category). Remember to place a small check mark next to each statement as you read it, and an asterisk next to general statements.
6. Fill in as many of the positions as possible, but don't be concerned if you can't fill in any immediately; the questions themselves may give you information to fill in the positions. (For example, if X sits in position 4, then which of the following sits in position 6?)
7. Watch for situations that push you out of bounds (for example, if Bill sits between Alice and Jan, then Bill cannot sit on either end—that would push Alice or Jan out of bounds).
8. Also watch for situations that lock you into certain positions. For example, consider this situation: There are seven seats in a row numbered 1 to 7 consecutively, and there are four boys and three girls to fill the seats. A statement like "no boys sit in adjacent seats" would lock you into certain positions, because you would immediately know that the boys must be in positions 1, 3, 5, and 7.
9. If you can't fill in any positions from the initial conditions, read some of the questions to get a feel for how much you should know and have filled in.

Keep in mind, whatever won't go in the chart immediately, goes out to the side for possible placement later (whatever won't go in, goes out).

EXAMPLE

Seven poker players—Arlo, Biff, Chuckie, Dixie, Eunice, Fong, and Glenn—will play at the final table in a Texas Hold-Em tournament. They will sit in a straight line next to each other on one side of the table with seats numbered in order 1 through 7 from left to right. The following conditions apply:

Chuckie sits to the right of Biff and next to Glenn.
Dixie sits to the left of Biff and next to Arlo.
Eunice's seat has a lower number than both Fong's seat and Arlo's seat.

Analysis—The setup
You should first number from 1 through 7.

1 2 3 4 5 6 7

Next, you should build a visual display that will show you the relationships.

"Chuckie sits to the right of Biff and next to Glenn." The display could start with:

B   G C

Notice that G and C are next to each other and could swap places.

"Dixie sits to the left of Biff and next to Arlo." Adding this information gives:

A D   B   G C

Notice that D and A are next to each other and could swap places.

"Eunice's seat has a lower number than both Fong's seat and Arlo's seat." Adding this information gives:

E   A D   B   G C

| — F →

1 2 3 4 5 6 7
E

Notice that E must sit in seat 1 and that spaces are left between some players because F still needs to be placed.

Question 1

If Arlo sits next to Biff, then each of the following could be true
EXCEPT:

(A) Biff sits in seat 4.
(B) Chuckie sits in seat 6.
(C) Dixie sits in seat 4.
(D) Fong sits in seat 2.
(E) Glenn sits in seat 5.

Analysis

The correct answer is C. If Arlo sits next to Biff, then Dixie must sit in seat 2 or 3, depending on where Fong sits. The display would look like this:

```
              F           F           F

         E        D  A  B    C  G
```

Notice that Fong could sit in seat 2, 5, or 7.

If you use an elimination approach, remember you are looking for "could be true
EXCEPT."

Choice (A), "Biff sits in seat 4," could be true: E, D, A, B, F, C, G. Eliminate (A).
Choice (B), "Chuckie sits in seat 6," could be true: E, D, A, B, G, C, F. Eliminate (B).
Choice (C), "Dixie sits in seat 4," can't be true; she must sit in seat 2 or 3. Stop here;
   you've found the EXCEPTION. Record your answer.

For your information:

Choice (D), "Fong sits in seat 2," could be true: E, F, D, A, B, C, G. Eliminate (D).
Choice (E), "Glenn sits in seat 5," could be true: E, D, A, B, G, C, F. Eliminate (E).

Note that once you have found the answer that could not be true, the EXCEPTION, you
could stop, record your answer, and move on to the next question.

Question 2

If Fong sits next to Biff, then which one of the following seats could be occupied by
Arlo?

(A) Seat 1
(B) Seat 2
(C) Seat 4
(D) Seat 5
(E) Seat 6

Analysis

The correct answer is B. If Fong sits next to Biff, you would have the following display:

$$F \quad F$$
$$E \quad \widehat{A \, D} \quad B \quad \widehat{C \, G}$$

Notice that Arlo must sit in seats 2 or 3. Therefore, choice (B) is correct.

Question 3

Which one of the following players could sit in seat 3?

(A) Arlo
(B) Biff
(C) Chuckie
(D) Eunice
(E) Fong

Analysis

The correct answer is A. Using the original display, you can see that either Arlo or Dixie could sit in seat 3.

$$E \quad \widehat{A \, D} \quad B \quad \widehat{G \, C}$$
$$| - F \rightarrow$$

Notice that Biff, choice (B), could sit only in seat 4 or 5. Chuckie, choice (C), could sit only in seat 5, 6, or 7. Eunice, choice (D), must sit in seat 1. Fong, choice (E), could sit only in seat 2, 4, 5, or 7.

Question 4

Which one of the following could be a list of people sitting in seats 5, 6, and 7, respectively?

(A) Chuckie, Fong, Glenn
(B) Chuckie, Glenn, Fong
(C) Dixie, Biff, Chuckie
(D) Dixie, Biff, Glenn
(E) Glenn, Fong, Chuckie

Analysis

The correct answer is B. (A) and (E) are not correct, since Fong cannot sit in seat 6, between Chuckie and Glenn. (C) and (D) are not correct, since Dixie cannot sit in seat 5, only seat 2, 3, or 4. And Biff cannot sit in seat 6 because there wouldn't be seats to the right of Biff for Chuckie and Glenn. (B) is possible.

Question 5

If Arlo sits in seat 4, then for exactly how many of the seven players are the seating positions determined?

(A) two
(B) three
(C) four
(D) five
(E) seven

Analysis

The correct answer is D. If Arlo sits in seat 4, then Biff must sit in seat 5, Dixie in seat 3, Fong in seat 2, and Eunice in seat 1. The only seat positions not determined are seats 6 and 7, which are occupied by Chuckie and Glenn (or Glenn and Chuckie).

The arrangement would look like this:

$$1 \quad 2 \quad 3 \quad 4 \quad 5 \quad 6 \quad 7$$

$$E \quad F \quad D \quad A \quad B \quad \overset{\frown}{C \quad G}$$

So five positions are determined.

When a question gives you a placement, such as Arlo sits in seat 4, immediately go to the display and make the placement.

Question 6

Which one of the following must be false?

(A) Arlo sits next to Biff.
(B) Biff sits next to Chuckie.
(C) Eunice sits next to Dixie.
(D) Fong sits next to Biff.
(E) Glenn sits next to Arlo.

Analysis

The correct answer is E. Note that you are looking for "must be false." Using the original display, you can determine that Biff sits between Arlo and Glenn; therefore, they cannot sit next to each other.

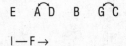

You could eliminate the other choices as follows:

Choice (A), "Arlo sits next to Biff," could be true, since Arlo and Dixie could swap places. Eliminate (A).

Choices (B), "Biff sits next to Chuckie," could be true, since Glenn and Chuckie could swap places. Eliminate (B).

Choice (C), "Eunice sits next to Dixie," could be true, since Arlo and Dixie could swap places. Eliminate (C).

Choice (D), "Fong sits next to Biff," could be true. A careful look at the display will make this evident. Eliminate (D).

Question 7

If there are exactly three seats between Arlo and Fong, then for exactly how many of the seven players are the seating positions determined?

(A) one
(B) three
(C) four
(D) five
(E) seven

Analysis

The correct answer is D. If there are exactly three seats between Arlo and Fong, the display would look like this:

$$1 \quad 2 \quad 3 \quad 4 \quad 5 \quad 6 \quad 7$$

$$E \quad D \quad A \quad B \quad C \quad G \quad F$$

Notice that the only way there could be three seats between Arlo and Fong is if Arlo is in seat 3 and Fong is in seat 7. Only the positions of Chuckie and Glenn in seats 5 and 6 are not determined.

Question 8

Which one of the following players could sit in one of exactly two different seats?

(A) Arlo
(B) Biff
(C) Dixie
(D) Fong
(E) Glenn

Analysis

The correct answer is B. From the display you can see that three or four players sit to the left of Biff and two or three players sit to the right of Biff; so Biff can sit in either seat 4 or 5.

E $\widehat{A D}$ B $\widehat{G C}$

$| \!-\! F \rightarrow$

(A) is not correct, since Arlo can sit in seat 2, 3, or 4. (C) is not correct, since Dixie can sit in seat 2, 3, or 4. (D) is not correct, since Fong can sit in seat 2, 4, 5, or 7. (E) is not correct, since Glenn can sit in seat 5, 6, or 7.

EXAMPLE

In a parking lot, seven company automobiles are lined up in a row in seven adjacent parking spots.

There are two vans, which are both adjacent to the same sports car.
There is one station wagon.
There are two limousines, which are never parked adjacent to each other.
One of the sports cars is always on one end.

Analysis—The setup

From this information, you could have made the following display:

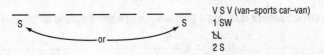

Question 1

If the station wagon is on one end, then one of the sports cars must be in the

(A) 2nd spot
(B) 3rd spot
(C) 4th spot
(D) 5th spot
(E) 7th spot

Analysis

The correct answer is C. In this question, two charts are possible:

S						SW
___	___	___	___	___	___	___

and

SW						S
___	___	___	___	___	___	___

Now notice that for *both* of the vans to be adjacent to the same sports car, there must be another sports car, and they must always be in the order V S V. Thus, the only way to place V S V in either of the above diagrams so that two limousines are never adjacent is to place V, S, and V in spots 3, 4, and 5, as follows:

S		V	S	V		SW
___	___	___	___	___	___	___

or

SW		V	S	V		S
___	___	___	___	___	___	___

Thus, the limousines will not be adjacent if one of the sports cars is in the 4th spot.

Question 2

If one of the vans is on one end, then the station wagon must be

(A) only in the 4th spot
(B) either in the 2nd or the 6th spot
(C) only in the 3rd spot
(D) either in the 3rd or the 5th spot
(E) only in the 6th spot

Analysis

The correct answer is D. Again there are two possible diagrams for this question:

V	S	V				S
___	___	___	___	___	___	___

and

S				V	S	V
___	___	___	___	___	___	___

Now notice that, in order that the limousines not be adjacent, the station wagon must be in either the 5th spot or the 3rd spot.

Question 3

If a limousine is in the 7th spot, then the station wagon could be in

(A) the 2nd spot
(B) the 3rd spot
(C) the 6th spot
(D) either the 2nd or 6th spot
(E) either the 2nd, 3rd, or 6th spot

Analysis

The correct answer is E. If a limousine is in the 7th spot, then a sports car, to be on an end, must be in the 1st spot:

S						L
_	_	_	_	_	_	_

Notice that the station wagon could now be in the 6th spot:

		V	S	V	L	
S	L	V	S	V	SW	L

or else in either the 2nd or the 3rd spot:

	L	SW				
S	SW	L	V	S	V	L

So the station wagon could be in either the 2nd, the 3rd, or the 6th spot.

Question 4

If one of the sports cars is in the 2nd spot, then the station wagon

- (A) could be in the 5th spot
- (B) could be in the 6th spot
- (C) must be in the 5th spot
- (D) must be in the 6th spot
- (E) must be in the 3rd spot

Analysis

The correct answer is C. If one of the sports cars is in the 2nd spot, the other sports car must be in the 7th spot:

V	S	V				S
_	_	_	_	_	_	_

Thus, in order for the limousines not to be adjacent, the station wagon must be in the 5th spot.

Question 5

If both sports cars are adjacent to a van, the station wagon must be in

- (A) the 2nd spot
- (B) the 4th spot
- (C) the 6th spot
- (D) either the 2nd or 4th spot
- (E) either the 2nd or 6th spot

Analysis

The correct answer is E. Two diagrams are necessary for this problem. If both sports cars are adjacent to a van, your diagrams will be:

S	V	S	V			

and

		V	S	V	S

Thus, in order for the limousines not to be adjacent, the station wagon must be in either the 2nd spot or the 6th spot.

Question 6

If an eighth car (a limousine) is added, and another parking spot is also added, then in order not to violate any of the original statements EXCEPT the number of limousines

(A) a limousine must be parked in the 2nd spot
(B) the station wagon must be parked in the 2nd spot
(C) the station wagon must be parked in the 6th spot
(D) a limousine must be parked on one end
(E) a limousine cannot be parked on either end

Analysis

The correct answer is D. If another limousine is added along with an eighth parking spot, all the original statements can be obeyed ONLY if a limousine is parked on one end. For example:

S	L	V	S	V	L	SW	L

EXAMPLE

A graphic artist is designing a modern type style for the alphabet. This type style is based on artistic design and relative sizes of the letters. At this point, the relative sizes among the letters that the artist has designed are as follows:

A is taller than B but shorter than C.
B is shorter than D but taller than E.
F is shorter than A but taller than B.
G is taller than D but shorter than F.
H is shorter than B.

Analysis—The setup

From the information given, a simple display may be constructed using the following steps:

The first statement reads, "A is taller than B but shorter than C." Using a position chart where the top is the tallest and the bottom is the shortest, you have:

C

A

B

The first part of the second statement reads, "B is shorter than D. . . ." Notice that D can be *anywhere* taller than B, so a "range" for D has to be drawn:

Adding the second part of the second statement gives "B is shorter than D but taller than E." Since B is taller than E, E will be placed under B:

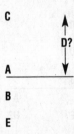

The third statement reads, "F is shorter than A but taller than B." Therefore F must fit between A and B:

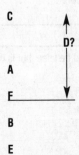

According to the fourth statement, "G is taller than D but shorter than F." Therefore G is above D, but since it's below F, both G and D must fit between F and B:

C

A

F

G

D

B

E

The fifth statement reads, "H is shorter than B," so H must have a possible range anywhere under B:

C

A

F

G

D

B̲ _____

E   H?

Note that H is in a variable position.

Question 1

Which one of the following could be false, but is not necessarily false?

(A) E is shorter than D.
(B) C is taller than E.
(C) D is taller than F.
(D) H is taller than E.
(E) E is shorter than A.

Analysis

The correct answer is D. H may be taller than E, or it may be shorter than E. This is the only part of the chart that isn't definitely resolved.

Question 2

Which one of the following could be true?

(A) D is taller than most of the others.
(B) A is the tallest.
(C) H is the shortest.
(D) D is not shorter than G.
(E) H is taller than F.

Analysis

The correct answer is C. Answer (A) is incorrect since D is only taller than three of the other seven. Answer (B) is incorrect since C is the tallest. Answer (D) is incorrect since D *is* shorter than G. Answer (E) is incorrect since H is shorter than F. The only height relationship that is not determined is that between H and E. Therefore, answer (C) is the only answer choice that could be true.

Question 3

Which one of the following must be true?

(A) F is taller than D.
(B) H is the shortest of all.
(C) H is taller than D.
(D) E is the shortest of all.
(E) E is taller than H.

Analysis

The correct answer is A. Inspection of the chart reveals that F is taller than D. It also reveals that H cannot be taller than D and that H or E *could* be the shortest of all, since H is in a relatively variable position.

Question 4

If Q is added to the group and Q is taller than B but shorter than G, then Q must be

(A) taller than F
(B) shorter than D
(C) between D and F
(D) taller than only three of the others
(E) shorter than at least three of the others

Analysis

The correct answer is E. Answer (A) is incorrect since F would be taller than Q. Answers (B) and (C) are incorrect since Q could be shorter or taller than D. Answer (D) is incorrect since Q could be taller than three or four of the others, depending on the relative heights of Q and D. Answer (E) is correct since Q is shorter than four or five of the others.

Note that Q and H are in variable positions.

Question 5

If Q and Z are both added to the group, and both are taller than H, then

(A) H is the shortest of all
(B) E is the shortest of all
(C) C is the tallest of all
(D) either Q or Z is the tallest of all
(E) either H or E is the shortest of all

Analysis

The correct answer is E. If Q and Z are added to the group and positioned taller than H, then H or E will remain the shortest, answer (E). Because it is not known which of the two (H or E) is shortest, answers (A) and (B) are incorrect. Refer to the original display that shows that C is the tallest. With the addition of Q and Z, all that is known about them is that they do not have any limits placed on their height. It is not known if Q, Z, or C may be the tallest; therefore, answers (C) and (D) are incorrect.

EXAMPLE

The Rockford Tennis Club is composed of seven tournament players. Four of these players are women—Carol, Denise, Evelyn, and Gneisha. Three of these players are men—Abel, Ben, and Fritz. Each became a member of the club in a different year starting in 2000 and going through 2006. The following conditions apply:

> Denise became a member before Evelyn.
> Gneisha became a member after Fritz.

Abel and Ben became members before Carol.
Fritz and Gneisha became members after Evelyn.
None of the women became members in consecutive years.

Analysis—The setup

From the information given, you can set up the following list of years and relationship between the players:

		Earlier	Women	Men
2000		↑	C	A
2001		D	D	B
2002		A ? B	E	F
2003		C E	G	
2004				
2005		F		
2006				
		↓		
		Later		

You may wish to scan the conditions before you begin. Let's build the setup from the start.

From the initial information first list the years involved. Next, sort and list the men and women. Finally, apply the conditions.

"Denise became a member before Evelyn."

D

E

Notice the space between D and E because players could be in between.

"Gneisha became a member after Fritz."

D

E

F

G

Since a later condition states "Fritz and Gneisha became member after Evelyn," scanning the conditions helped make the display above.

Finally, "Abel and Ben became members before Carol."

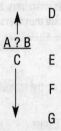

The final statement needs to be starred. It is an important statement. Since there are four women and seven years involved, and "None of the women became members in consecutive years," then the women must have joined the club in the even years—2000, 2002, 2004, 2006. Mark this in the chart.

Now taking a second look at the information as displayed and using some reasoning should help you place some of the members.

Denise must have become a member in 2000, since she is the first women member. Evelyn must have become a member in 2002, since Carol became a member after the two men (Abel and Ben), and Gneisha became a member after Evelyn. So your final working display should look like this:

		Earlier		Women	Men
	2000	D		C	A
A or B	2001		D	D	B
	2002	E	A ? B	E	F
F, A, or B	2003	C	E	G	
G or C	2004				
F, A, or B	2005		F		
G or C	2006				
		Later	G		

You could simplify the display with arrows, and you could circle the women in the middle display.

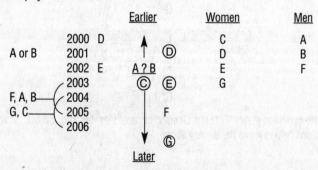

You may wish to list the years vertically at the bottom of the page of your test booklet in case you want to grid the scenario for each question as follows:

		Q1	Q2	Q3	Q4	Q5	Q6
	2000 D						
A or B	2001						
	2002 E						
	2003						
F, A, B	2004						
G, C	2005						
	2006						

In this particular set, only two questions (questions 2 and 6) actually require that you identify a specific member in a specific year, so it's probably easier simply to list the years only next to each of those two problems.

Question 1

Which one of the following must be true?

(A) Carol became a member before Gneisha.
(B) Fritz became a member before Carol.
(C) Denise became a member before Carol.
(D) Gneisha became a member before Fritz.
(E) Ben became a member before Gneisha.

Analysis

The correct answer is C. Let's work through the choices and eliminate.

Choice (A), "Carol became a member before Gneisha," is possible, but we're looking for "must."

Choice (B), "Fritz became a member before Carol," is possible.

Choice (C), Denise became a member before Carol. Must be true, since Denise is in 2000. STOP! You have the right answer. No need to look at the rest.

For your information, here are the other two choices.

Choice (D), "Gneisha became a member before Fritz," is not possible.

Choice (E), "Ben became a member before Gneisha," is possible.

Question 2

Which one of the following became a member in 2002?

(A) Abel
(B) Carol
(C) Denise

(D) Evelyn
(E) Gneisha

Analysis

The correct answer is D. Since we've filled in as much of the display as possible, we already knew that Evelyn became a member in 2002. Notice the way this question is asked—no conditions or information is given with the question. It tells you that you should have been able to deduce this from the initial conditions. It should have been in your original display. If you missed this information when setting up your display, this question alerts you to it.

Question 3

Suppose the original condition that Gneisha became a member after Fritz is replaced with Gneisha became a member the year before or the year after Fritz. If all the other conditions remain in effect and if Ben became a member in 2003, then which one of the following must be true?

(A) Abel became a member in 2001, and Carol became a member in 2004.

(B) Evelyn became a member in 2002, and Gneisha became a member in 2006.

(C) Abel became a member in 2001, and Fritz became a member in 2005.

(D) Fritz became a member in 2005, and Carol became a member in 2006.

(E) Denise became a member in 2002, and Gneisha became a member in 2004.

Analysis

The correct answer is C. For this question, you will need to go into the years chart as follows:

	2000	D
A or B	2001	A
	2002	E
	2003	B
A, B, F ——	2004	
G, C ————	2005	F
	2006	

Since Ben is in 2003, Abel must be in 2001. Fritz must be in 2005, since that is the only remaining place for men.

(A), (B), and (D) could be true, while (E) is false. (C) *must* be true. A typical wrong answer to a "must be" question is a "could be" answer.

Note that any change, replacement, or deletion of an original condition in a question applies only to that question.

Question 4

Which one of the following is a complete and accurate list of members who could have joined the club in 2004?

(A) Carol
(B) Denise, Evelyn
(C) Carol, Gneisha
(D) Carol, Denise, Gneisha
(E) Carol, Evelyn, Gneisha

Analysis

The correct answer is C. Since Denise and Evelyn are in 2000 and 2002, respectively, they could not join in 2004. Eliminate (B), (D), and (E). (A) is accurate, but not complete, since Gneisha could also join in 2004. On this type of question, be sure to look at all the choices. Remember, some answers might be accurate, but not complete.

Question 5

Which one of the following is a possible order of players becoming members of the club from 2000 through 2006?

(A) Denise, Abel, Evelyn, Carol, Fritz, Gneisha, Ben
(B) Evelyn, Ben, Denise, Fritz, Carol, Abel, Gneisha
(C) Denise, Abel, Evelyn, Fritz, Carol, Ben, Gneisha
(D) Carol, Fritz, Ben, Evelyn, Gneisha, Abel, Denise
(E) Denise, Ben, Evelyn, Abel, Carol, Fritz, Gneisha

Analysis

The correct answer is E. Eliminate (B) and (D), since Denise must be first. Next eliminate (A), since a man (Ben) cannot be in 2006. Finally, eliminate (C) because Ben became a member before Carol.

Question 6

If Fritz became a member in 2003, then which one of the following must be true?

(A) Gneisha became a member in 2004.
(B) Carol became a member in 2004.
(C) Ben became a member in 2005.
(D) Evelyn became a member in 2006.
(E) Abel became a member in 2005.

Analysis

The correct answer is A. For this question, you will need to go into the years chart as follows:

	2000	D
A or B	2001	
	2002	E
	2003	F
G, C	2004	G
	2005	A or B
	2006	C

Notice that if Fritz became a member in 2003, then either Abel or Ben became members in 2005. Carol became a member after Abel and Ben, so she must be in 2006. If Carol became a member in 2006, then Gneisha became a member in 2004.

EXAMPLE

Alice, Bobby, Carole, Dwight, and Elva were playing a game with marbles. When the game ended, Alice wrote down the following information:

Carole has more marbles than Alice and Bobby together.
Alice's total is the same as the total of Dwight and Elva together.
Alice has more marbles than Bobby.
Bobby has more marbles than Elva.
Everyone has at least one marble.

Analysis—The setup

From the information given, you can set up the following relationships:

$$C > A + B$$
$$A = D + E$$
$$A > B$$
$$B > E$$

Then you can construct the following diagram (Note: This chart is more easily realized by starting with the last condition and working up.):

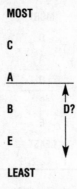

Question 1

Who ended the game with the most marbles?

(A) Alice
(B) Bobby
(C) Carole
(D) Dwight
(E) Elva

Analysis
The correct answer is C. Using the relationships you can see that Carole has more
marbles than Alice and Bobby together. Because Alice has more marbles than Dwight,
Elva, or Bobby each have alone, Carole must have most of all.

Question 2

If Dwight has more marbles than Bobby, who ended the game with the least
marbles?

(A) Alice
(B) Bobby
(C) Carole
(D) Dwight
(E) Elva

Analysis

The correct answer is E. If Dwight has more marbles than Bobby, then Elva must have the least number of marbles. The arrangement would be as follows:

MOST

C

A

—

D

—

B

E

LEAST

Question 3

Which one of the following is a possible order of children going from most marbles to least?

(A) Alice, Bobby, Carole, Dwight, Elva
(B) Carole, Alice, Bobby, Elva, Dwight
(C) Carole, Bobby, Alice, Dwight, Elva
(D) Dwight, Carole, Alice, Bobby, Elva
(E) Carole, Alice, Elva, Bobby, Dwight

Analysis

The correct answer is B. From the original chart, we can see that Carole must have most of all, followed by Alice. Because Bobby has more marbles than Elva, only answer (B) can be a possible correct order.

Question 4

Which one of the following must be true?

(A) Elva has more marbles than Dwight.
(B) Dwight has fewer marbles than Bobby.
(C) Alice has more marbles than Elva.
(D) Dwight and Bobby have the same number of marbles.
(E) Elva and Dwight have the same number of marbles.

Analysis

The correct answer is C. Only (C) *must* be true. In (A) and (E) Elva *could* have more marbles than Dwight, but not necessarily. She could have less *or the same*. Notice the possible range of placement for Dwight on the original chart. Again, in (B) and (D) Dwight's placement is uncertain: Dwight could have fewer, *the same,* or more marbles than Bobby.

Question 5

If Elva has 3 marbles and everyone has a different number of marbles, which one of the following could NOT be the number of marbles that Alice could have?

(A) 5
(B) 6
(C) 7
(D) 8
(E) 9

Analysis

The correct answer is B. Using the relationships you can see that if Elva has 3 marbles, then Dwight can have any number *but* 3. Because Alice's total equals Dwight's and Elva's total together, Alice cannot have 3 + 3, or 6.

The Position Organizer (Non-linear)

EXAMPLE

John, Phil, George, and Herman sit around a square table with eight chairs, which are equally distributed.

Bob, Carmen, Ted, and Alyssa join them at the table.

The two women (Carmen and Alyssa) cannot sit next to each other.

John and Herman are seated on either side of George and are next to him.

Ted is seated next to Herman.

Carmen is seated next to John, but not directly across from George.

John is directly across from Alyssa.

Analysis—The setup

Note that the statement preceding the six conditions immediately suggests that you draw a square table with two spaces on each side. The first piece of concrete information is condition 3, which tells you to seat John, George, and Herman in that order. Next, seat Ted next to Herman (#4), seat Carmen next to John (#5), and seat Alyssa across from John (#6). Note that Carmen and Alyssa are not sitting next to each other (#2), and that Phil and Bob are in *variable* positions on either side of Alyssa. The resulting chart is as follows:

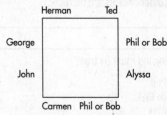

Question 1

Which men could switch positions without contradicting the seating arrangement?

(A) George and Herman
(B) John and George
(C) Phil and Ted
(D) Bob and Phil
(E) Bob and George

Analysis

The correct answer is D. As the chart points out, only Bob and Phil are in variable positions and, thus, interchangeable.

Question 2

Which one of the following must be false?

(A) George is not next to Ted.
(B) Alyssa is not next to Carmen.
(C) Herman is next to Carmen.
(D) George is across from Phil.
(E) Bob is not next to Phil.

Analysis

The correct answer is C. Working from the answer choices and inspecting the chart, you see that (C) *must* be false in any case, and that (D) *may* be false, depending upon where Phil is seated.

Question 3

Which one of the following could be true?

(A) Herman sits next to Carmen.
(B) Herman sits next to John.
(C) Ted sits next to Phil.
(D) John sits next to Phil.
(E) George sits next to Alyssa.

Analysis

The correct answer is C. From the diagram you can see that Phil could be in the seat next to Ted. None of the other choices are possible.

Question 4

Which one of the following must be true?

(A) Ted sits next to Phil.
(B) Alyssa sits next to Phil.

(C) George sits next to Carmen.
(D) Ted sits next to Bob.
(E) Bob sits next to John.

Analysis
The correct answer is B. Since the two seats next to Alyssa are taken by Phil and Bob, then Alyssa must sit next to Phil.

Question 5

If Arnold were now to take Ted's seat, then Arnold

(A) must now be next to Bob
(B) must be next to Alyssa
(C) must be across from Bob
(D) is either next to or across from Phil
(E) is either next to or across from George

Analysis
The correct answer is D. If Arnold takes Ted's seat, then either he is seated next to Phil, or else Phil is seated across from him.

The Position Organizer with the Diagram Provided

On occasion, the position chart or diagram will be provided. That is, instead of, or along with, a description of the set up, an actual diagram is given. Use the following steps if a chart or diagram is given:

1. Either redraw the chart or diagram or mark the diagram dark enough so you can understand your notes but also so you can erase without losing information.
2. Follow the same procedures you would use in filling in or completing the position chart.

Nine guests—A, B, C, D, E, F, G, H, I—attend a formal dinner party. Ten chairs are arranged around the rectangular dining room table as follows:

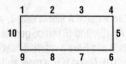

Seat 1 is directly across from seat 9.
Seat 2 is directly across from seat 8.
Seat 3 is directly across from seat 7.
Seat 4 is directly across from seat 6.

Seats 5 and 10 are at the ends of the table and are directly
across from each other.

A, B, C, and D are females.

E, F, G, H, and I are males.

A and E are a married couple.

B and F are a married couple.

C and G are engaged to each other.

Each married couple always sits next to his or her spouse
on one side of the table.

Members of the same sex never sit in adjacent seats.

Guests in end seats 5 and 10 are considered adjacent to
seats on each side of them.

If G is in seat 10, then C is not in seat 5.

I is never in seat 6.

A is always in seat 1.

Analysis—The setup

From the initial conditions, the diagram and markings would look like this:

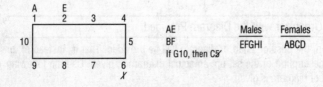

Question 1

Which one of the following could sit in seat 10?

(A) A
(B) C
(C) D
(D) F
(E) H

Analysis

The correct answer is E. Since guest A sits in seat 1, a male must sit in seat 10 if it is not empty. This eliminates (A), (B), and (C) since guests A, C, and D are females (A is in seat 1 anyway). Since guests B and F are a married couple, they must sit next to each other on a side. This eliminates (D). Guest H is a male and could sit in seat 10.

Question 2

Which one of the following is a complete and accurate list of guests who could sit in seat 3?

(A) A, B, C, D, E, F, G
(B) B, C, D, E, F
(C) B, C, D, E
(D) B, C, D
(E) B, C

Analysis

The correct answer is D. Since guest E is in seat 2, only a female could sit in seat 3. Since guest A is in seat 1, the remaining females are guests B, C, and D.

Question 3

If seat 9 is empty and G sits in seat 10, which one of the following could sit in seat 5?

(A) B
(B) D
(C) C
(D) H
(E) I

Analysis

The correct answer is B. From the information given in the question and the initial conditions, the diagram should look like this:

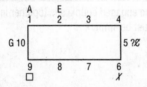

It can now be determined that seat 3 is a female, seat 4 is a male, and seat 5 is a female. You may have added to your diagram so it would now look like this:

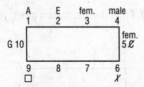

Seat 5 cannot be guest B, since guest B cannot be on the end. Guest H and I are males so (D) and (E) are eliminated. Since guest G is in seat 10, then guest C cannot be in seat 5 (from initial conditions), so only guest D is left.

Question 4

If C sits in seat 5, and F sits in seat 4, which one of the following could be the arrangement of seats from 1 to 10 respectively?

	1,	2,	3,	4,	5,	6,	7,	8,	9,	10
(A)	A,	B,	E,	F,	C,	G,	__,	I,	D,	H
(B)	A,	E,	B,	G,	C,	F,	D,	H,	__,	I
(C)	A,	E,	B,	F,	C,	I,	D,	__,	G,	H
(D)	A,	E,	B,	F,	C,	H,	D,	I,	__,	G
(E)	A,	E,	B,	F,	C,	G,	D,	H,	__,	I

Analysis

The correct answer is E. From the information given, the diagram should look like this:

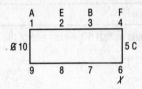

You could eliminate (A) because guest B cannot be in seat 2. Since guest F is in seat 4, guest B is in seat 3. This eliminates (B). (C) can be eliminated since male guests G and H cannot be seated next to each other. Since guest C is in seat 5, guest G cannot be in seat 10, so (D) is eliminated. (E) is a possible arrangement.

Question 5

If D sits in seat 5, and the engaged couple sits together in seats 7 and 8, which one of the following seats must be empty?

(A) 3
(B) 4
(C) 6
(D) 9
(E) 10

Analysis

The correct answer is D. From the information given, your chart should now look like this:

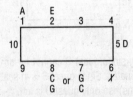

You should also be able to fill in seats 3 and 4 and determine that seats 6 and 10, if not empty, must be males. Your diagram should now have this information:

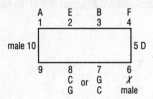

Since only male guests H and I are not seated, guest H must be in seat 6 and guest I in seat 10. This leaves seat 9 empty. In any other arrangement, two males are next to each other. (This also forces C into 7 and G into 8.)

Question 6

Which one of the following is a complete and accurate list of guests who could sit in seat 5?

(A) C
(B) D
(C) C, D
(D) B, C, D
(E) C, D, G

Analysis
The correct answer is C. First eliminate (D) since guest B must be on a side. If guest G is in seat 5, then the diagram would look like this:

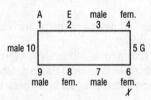

This requires two males to be next to each other, so seat 5 must be a female, either guest C or D.

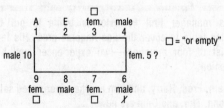

Question 7

If a female sits directly across from A, which one of the following must be true?

(A) Seat 3 is empty.
(B) Seat 4 is empty.
(C) Seat 6 is a female.
(D) Seat 7 is a female.
(E) Seat 8 is a male.

Analysis

The correct answer is E. If a female sits across from guest A, your diagram would now have the following information:

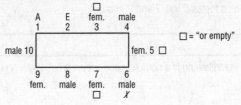

Since seat 3, 5, or 7 could be empty, only (E), a male is in seat 8, must be true.

The Group Organizer

One of the many types of displays is the group organizer. This is a problem set in which different items, names, or products can be placed in distinct categories, which may contain different numbers of items. In constructing this organizer, you should follow these steps:

1. Group or align items into general categories (remember you group items by similarities and differences).
2. Draw connections according to relationships between specific items. Your markings should indicate whether items always go together (x—y), never go together (x ⤬ y), are conditional (if x goes then y goes; x →y), and so on.

After you've drawn your chart, remember to take information forward and backward (what can and can't happen) and to watch for actions and subsequent reactions.

EXAMPLE

Sales manager Phil Forrester is trying to put together a sales team to cover the Los Angeles area. His team will consist of four members—two experienced and two new salesmen.

Sam, Fred, Harry, and Kim are the experienced salesmen.
John, Tim, and Dom are new.
Sam and Fred do not work together.

Tim and Sam refuse to work together.
Harry and Dom cannot work together.

Analysis—The setup

When drawing a group organizer and making connections, always prefer fewer connections to many connections. In this case, drawing connections between the workers who can work together will result in a complicated system of intersecting lines. Connecting those who *do not* or *cannot* work together results in a simple, clear chart:

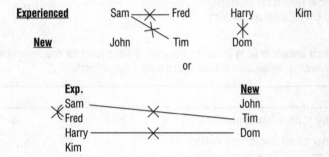

Each group organizer encourages you to use information in both directions, recognizing that, because connected workers *cannot* work together, unconnected workers *can* work together.

Notice that the conditions gave initial information about those who cannot work together, helping you to formulate the most efficient method of connecting the diagram. If the conditions had stated that some salesmen always work together and some never work together, you would have used a different type of marking to denote each type of connection. Also notice that the labels or headings should be written out or abbreviated *and* underlined.

Question 1

If Sam is made part of the team, the following must be the other members:

(A) John, Tim, Dom
(B) John, Dom, Kim
(C) Tim, Harry, Kim
(D) Dom, John, Fred
(E) John, Dom, Harry

Analysis

The correct answer is B. The team must consist of two experienced and two new salesmen. Sam is experienced, so the rest of the team must include one experienced and two new salesmen. (C) should be eliminated both because it contains two experienced salesmen and because Sam does not work with Tim; also eliminate (A) because it includes Tim. Eliminate (D) because Sam does not work with Fred, and eliminate (E) because Dom does not work with Harry.

Question 2

If Sam is not chosen as part of the sales team and Tim is, then which one of the following must be true?

(A) Dom and Harry are on the team.
(B) Kim and John are on the team.
(C) Harry and Fred are on the team.
(D) John or Dom is not on the team.
(E) Fred or Kim is not on the team.

Analysis

The correct answer is D. With Tim on the team, there is room for one other new salesman. Therefore, *either* John *or* Dom is on the team, but not both.

Question 3

Which one of the following must be true?

(A) Fred and Sam always work together.
(B) Kim and Dom never work together.
(C) Kim and Fred always work together.
(D) If John works, then Kim doesn't work.
(E) If Sam works, then Dom works.

Analysis

The correct answer is E. The key word in this question is *must,* which excludes possible but not necessary combinations. (A) is false, as the chart reveals. (B) is false because they *could* work together if Harry does not work. (C) is false because Kim and Fred do not have to work together. You could have the team of Kim, Sam, John, and Dom. This also eliminates (D). (E) must be true since Sam and Tim never work together; Sam must always work with Dom and John.

Question 4

If Dom is chosen as part of the sales team but John is not, then the other three members must be

(A) Fred, Tim, and Harry
(B) Fred, Tim, and Kim
(C) Harry, John, and Tim
(D) Tim, Dom, and Kim
(E) Sam, Fred, and Harry

Analysis

The correct answer is B. If Dom is chosen as part of the team and John is not, then Tim must be the other inexperienced member. So, if Dom and Tim both are chosen, then Sam and Harry are not chosen. The team now consists of Dom, Tim, Fred, and Kim.

Question 5

Which one of the following must be true?

(A) If Harry works, then John works.
(B) If Kim works, then John works.
(C) If John works, then Dom works.
(D) If Dom works, then John works.
(E) If John works, then Kim works.

Analysis

The correct answer is A. Since Harry will not work with Dom, then John must be one of the other inexperienced members in the group when Harry works. The other combinations (Kim and John, John and Dom) do not always work together.

EXAMPLE

Seven students—John, Kim, Len, Molly, Neil, Owen, and Pam—will be assigned to three study stations—reading, writing, and math. Students are assigned to the stations under the following conditions:

> Each student must be assigned to exactly one station.
> Each station must have at least one student, but cannot have more than three students.
> Kim and Len are always assigned to the same station.
> Len and Molly are never assigned to the same station.
> Pam is assigned to the reading station.
> If John is assigned to math, then Kim is assigned to reading.
> Neil is never assigned to writing.
> Owen is never assigned to math.

Analysis—The setup

Your first step should be to set up the placement categories—reading, writing, and math. Be sure to underline the categories.

Reading   Writing   Math

From the condition "Each station must have at least one student, but cannot have more than three students," you could add the following:

	Reading	Writing	Math
?	_____	_____	_____
?	_____	_____	_____

Next, you could put information off to the side from the conditions "Kim and Len are always assigned to the same station" and "Len and Molly are never assigned to the same station."

	Reading	Writing	Math	
				KL
?	_____	_____	_____	
?	_____	_____	~~LM~~	

The statement "Pam is assigned to the reading station" gives you a quick placement as follows:

	Reading	Writing	Math	
	P	_____	_____	KL
?	_____	_____	_____	
?	_____	_____	_____	~~LM~~

The conditional statement "If John is assigned to math, then Kim is assigned to reading" should be marked as follows:

K   J

	Reading	Writing	Math	
	P	_____	_____	KL
?	_____	_____	_____	
?	_____	_____	_____	~~LM~~

Notice that the arrow is pointing from J to K.

Finally, "Neil is never assigned to writing" and "Owen is never assigned to math" can be marked as follows:

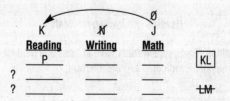

Ø

K   N̸   J

	Reading	Writing	Math	
	P	_____	_____	KL
?	_____	_____	_____	
?	_____	_____	_____	~~LM~~

Question 1

Which one of the following is a complete and accurate list of the students who could be assigned to reading?

(A) JKL
(B) LMO
(C) KLMN
(D) JKLMOP
(E) JKLMNOP

Analysis

The correct answer is E. Since Pam is assigned to reading, you could eliminate any answer that does not include P. Choices (A) , (B), and (C) should be eliminated. Now take a careful look at the difference between (D) and (E). The difference is that choice (E) contains N, and since there is no reason that N could not be assigned to reading, (E) is the correct answer.

Question 2

Which one of the following is an acceptable assignment of students to stations?

(A) Reading: PKLN; Writing: MO; Math: J
(B) Reading: KLN; Writing: PO; Math: JM
(C) Reading: PJN; Writing: MO; Math: KL
(D) Reading: PMO; Writing: JN; Math: KL
(E) Reading: PN; Writing: MO; Math: JKL

Analysis

The correct answer is C. Since the question asks you for "an acceptable assignment," you should look for unacceptable assignments (rule breakers) and eliminate them. (A) can be eliminated because there can't be four students in reading. (B) can be eliminated because P is in writing and must be in reading. (D) can be eliminated because N cannot be in writing. (E) can be eliminated since "If John is assigned to math, then Kim is assigned to reading," so J and K cannot both be in math.

Question 3

Which one of the following is a pair of students who could be assigned to math?

(A) OM
(B) JL
(C) JK
(D) JN
(E) LM

Analysis

The correct answer is D. Since the question asks "who could be assigned to math," you should again look for those who couldn't (rule breakers). (A) can be eliminated because O cannot be in math. (B) can be eliminated because if J is in math, K must be in reading, so L must then be in reading. And because if J is in math, K must be in reading, so (C) can be eliminated. (E) can be eliminated because L and M cannot be assigned to the same station.

Question 4

If John is assigned to math, then which one of the following must be true?

(A) Molly is assigned to reading.
(B) Neil is assigned to writing.
(C) Molly and Owen are assigned to writing.
(D) Neil is assigned to Math and Owen is assigned to writing.
(E) Neil is assigned to Math and Len is assigned to writing.

Analysis

The correct answer is D. Once John is assigned to math, Kim and Len are assigned to reading and the display will look like this:

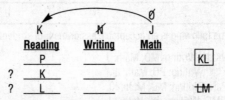

Therefore Neil must be in math and Owen must be in writing.
Notice that (C) could be true, but doesn't necessarily have to be true.

Question 5

If Neil is assigned to reading, then which one of the following could be true?

(A) John is assigned to math.
(B) Kim is assigned to reading.
(C) Molly is assigned to the same station as Kim.
(D) John is assigned to reading.
(E) Len is assigned to writing and Molly is assigned to reading.

Analysis

The correct answer is D. Once again, you should probably be looking for what can't be true and eliminate. If you place Neil in reading, the display would look like this:

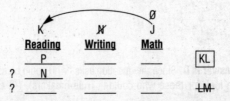

Now, since there are two students in reading, neither K nor L can be in reading and therefore J can't be in math. You can eliminate (A) and (B). You can eliminate (C); because K and L must be together, and M cannot be with L, so M could never be with K. If L is assigned to writing, then K is assigned to writing. If M is assigned to reading, then O must be assigned to writing (O can't be in math and reading already has three), and then J is assigned to math. But if J is assigned to math, K must be in reading; therefore, eliminate (E).

EXAMPLE

Six piano players—Moss, Nance, Odell, Parish, Quayle, Reed—are auditioning for a musical. Each pianist may choose to play one selection from one of four different composers—Berlin, Cohan, Gershwin, or Lennon. Exactly twice as many pianists choose a selection from Cohan as choose a selection from Berlin. The following conditions apply:

Moss and Nance choose selections from the same composer.

Odell chooses a selection from Berlin.

Parish and Quayle choose selections from different composers.

Quayle and Reed choose selections from different composers.

Analysis—The setup

From the information given, a simple display may be constructed. Since the first sentence mentions "six piano players" and the second sentence mentions one selection each, you might set up the following:

Pianists

Mo	Nan	Od	Par	Qu	Re

Next, pay special attention to the numerical relationship between the selections. "Exactly twice as many pianists choose a selection from Cohan as choose a selection from Berlin" is a key statement. Here's what it means: If exactly one pianist chooses a selection from Berlin, then exactly two choose a selection from Cohan. The remaining three would have to choose selections from Gershwin or Lennon. If exactly two pianists choose a selection from Berlin, then exactly four choose a selection from Cohan and none chooses a selection from Gershwin or Lennon (remember, only six pianists). Three pianists could not choose a selection from Berlin because then six would have to choose a selection from Cohan, and that would be too many pianists (remember, only six pianists). The small important chart that you should put to the side of your original display should look like this:

Composers

Berlin	1	2
Cohan	2	4
Gershwin	?	0
Lennon	?	0

These are the only two possible number of selections from Berlin and Cohan.

Now a closer look at the remaining conditions will help you mark the display as follows:

"Moss and Nance choose selections from the same composer."

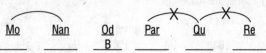

"Odell chooses a selection from Berlin."

Mo	Nan	Od	Par	Qu	Re
		B			

"Parish and Quayle choose selections from different composers."

Mo	Nan	Od	Par	Qu	Re
		B			

"Quayle and Reed choose selections from different composers."

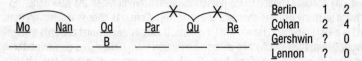

Simply from the initial conditions, the final display and chart would look like this:

Mo	Nan	Od	Par	Qu	Re
		B			

Berlin	1	2
Cohan	2	4
Gershwin	?	0
Lennon	?	0

Question 1

If Moss chooses a selection from Gershwin, then which one of the following must be true?
(A) Parish chooses a selection from Gershwin.
(B) Odell chooses a selection from Cohan.
(C) Quayle chooses a selection from Berlin
(D) Nance chooses a selection from Gershwin.
(E) Reed chooses a selection from Berlin.

Analysis
The correct answer is D. If Moss chooses a selection from Gershwin, then the first thing you should notice is that Nance must also choose a selection from Gershwin. At this point, scan your answers looking for Nance. Choice D is "Nance chooses a selection from Gershwin." Take it and don't worry about the other choices since this must be true. Go for the things you know.

Question 2

Which one of the following is a possible list of the pianist choices?

(A) Berlin: Moss, Nance, Odell
    Cohan: Parish, Quayle
    Gershwin: Reed
(B) Berlin: Odell
    Cohan: Nance, Parish
    Gershwin: Moss, Quayle
    Lennon: Reed
(C) Berlin: Odell
    Cohan: Parish, Quayle
    Gershwin: Moss, Nance
    Lennon: Reed
(D) Berlin: Parish, Reed
    Cohan: Odell, Moss, Nance, Quayle
(E) Berlin: Odell
    Cohan: Parish, Reed
    Gershwin: Moss, Nance, Quayle

Analysis
The correct answer is E. Remember, the only two possible number of selections from Berlin and Cohan is 1 and 2 or 2 and 4. Now go through the choices using the elimination strategy.

Choice (A) has too many Berlins, and Parish and Quayle can't choose from the same composer. Eliminate (A).
Choice (B) has the right numbers, but Moss and Nance must choose the same composer. Eliminate (B).

Choice (C) has the right numbers, but Parish and Quayle can't choose from the same composer. Eliminate (C).

Choice (D) doesn't have Odell choosing a selection from Berlin. Eliminate (D).

Choice (E) has the right numbers and doesn't break any of the conditions.

Question 3

If Nance chooses a selection from Cohan and no one chooses a selection from Lennon, then which one of the following CANNOT be true?

(A) Moss chooses a selection from Cohan.
(B) Parish chooses a selection from Cohan.
(C) Quayle chooses a selection from Berlin.
(D) Reed chooses a selection from Gershwin.
(E) Odell chooses a selection from Berlin.

Analysis

The correct answer is D. If Nance chooses a selection from Cohan, then with the help of a little reasoning the display should look like this:

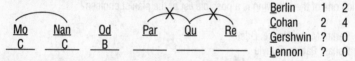

Berlin	1	2
Cohan	2	4
Gershwin	?	0
Lennon	?	0

Now, since no pianist chooses Lennon, Gershwin must have either three spots or no spots, but the three spots cannot be Par, Qu, and/or Re because that would leave either Par and Qu or Qu and Re having a selection from the same composer, which would break a rule. At this point you may have realized that, in this case, none of the pianists could choose Gershwin, so the answer is D. For your information, the filled-in display must be:

Mo	Nan	Od	Par	Qu	Re
C	C	B	C	B	C

Berlin	1	2
Cohan	2	4
Gershwin	?	0
Lennon	?	0

Remember, this question asks for what CANNOT be true.

Question 4

Which one of the following CANNOT be true?

(A) At least one selection is chosen from each composer.
(B) At least two selections are chosen from two composers.
(C) No selection is chosen from Gershwin.
(D) No selection is chosen from Cohan.
(E) Three selections can be chosen from one composer.

Analysis

The correct answer is D. This question is also asking for what CANNOT be true. Looking at the chart on the right, you know that either two or four selections are from Cohan. (D) cannot be true.

Question 5

Which one of the following could choose a selection from Berlin?

(A) Moss
(B) Nance
(C) Parish
(D) Quayle
(E) Reed

Analysis

The correct answer is D. If another pianist chooses Berlin, since Odell already chooses Berlin, there must be two selections from Berlin. Since you have two selections from Berlin, you must have four selections from Cohan, and the completed chart would have to be:

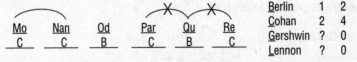

Berlin	1	2
Cohan	2	4
Gershwin	?	0
Lennon	?	0

So aside from Odell, Quayle is the only other pianist who can choose a selection from Berlin.

Question 6

Which one of the following pairs of pianists must choose a selection from the same composer?

(A) Odell and Reed
(B) Nance and Parish
(C) Parish and Reed
(D) Odell and Quayle
(E) Moss and Quayle

Analysis

The correct answer is C. You could work through the choices and eliminate as follows:

Choice (A): Odell and Reed cannot choose from the same composer because they would both have to choose from Berlin. If you have two from Berlin, you must have four from Cohan. But the four Cohans would have to include Parish and Quayle, who cannot choose from the same composer. Eliminate (A).

Choice (B): Nance and Parish could choose from the same composer, but they don't have to. Eliminate (B).

Choice (C): Parish and Reed have to choose from the same composer, which can be seen in the following charts.

Choice (D): Odell and Quayle could choose from the same composer (Berlin), but they don't have to. Eliminate (D).

Choice (E): Moss and Quayle could choose from the same composer, but they don't have to. Eliminate (E).

The choices can be more easily examined using the following information and charts.

Since you must have either one or two Berlins and either two or four Cohans, the possible completed group organizers are:

With one Berlin:

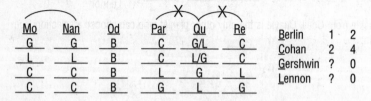

Mo	Nan	Od	Par	Qu	Re
G	G	B	C	G/L	C
L	L	B	C	L/G	C
C	C	B	L	G	L
C	C	B	G	L	G

Berlin	1	2
Cohan	2	4
Gershwin	?	0
Lennon	?	0

With two Berlins:

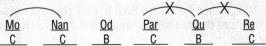

Mo	Nan	Od	Par	Qu	Re
C	C	B	C	B	C

In each chart, Parish and Reed must choose a selection by the same composer.

Question 7

Which one of the following is a complete and accurate list of the pianists who could choose a selection from Cohan?

(A) Moss
(B) Moss, Nance
(C) Nance, Parish, Reed
(D) Moss, Nance, Parish, Quayle
(E) Moss, Nance, Parish, Reed

Analysis

The correct answer is E. If you realize that there must be four pianists who choose Cohan, you could immediately eliminate (A), (B), and (C). Then you could simply check (D) and (E). Otherwise, you could work through all the choices and eliminate as follows:

Choice (A): If Moss could choose Cohan, so could Nance. Also notice that there must be four possible pianists who choose Cohan. Eliminate (A).

Choice (B): Moss and Nance could both choose a selection from Cohan. This is accurate but not complete. Cohan must be chosen by two more pianists when two of the pianists choose Berlin. Eliminate (B).

Choice (C): If Nance could choose Cohan, so could Moss. Also notice that there must be four possible pianists who choose Cohan. Eliminate (C).

Choice (D): Quayle cannot choose a selection from Cohan. Since there are either two or four chosen from Cohan, the three possible arrangements for Cohan are:

Mo	Nan	Od	Par	Qu	Re			
		B	C		C	Berlin	1	2
C	C	B				Cohan	2	4
C	C	B	C	B	C	Gershwin	?	0
						Lennon	?	0

Eliminate (D).

Choice (E): Moss, Nance, Parish, and Reed is a complete and accurate list of the pianists who could choose a selection from Cohan. This is evident from the group organizer above.

Remember, on a question that asks for a "complete and accurate" list, you must look at all the choices. An answer could be accurate but not complete.

The Group Organizer (With several conditional statements)

Some group organizers lean heavily on a list of conditional statements (if–then statements) such as "If A is in the forest, then so is B." (Conditional statements are reviewed in Chapter 1.) It can also be used with statements that show relationships between sets or groups of sets, such as "All A's are B's." When putting together this type of group organizer, you should follow these steps:

1. When if–then statements are involved, mark them carefully, making sure that the arrow is going from the if to the then (if A then B should be noted as A → B).
2. Remember that whenever "If A then B" is true, then "If not B then not A" must also be true (this can be written $\not B \to \not A$). An example would be: If bluejays are in the forest, then so are sparrows. This statement also tells you that, if sparrows are not in the forest, neither are bluejays. This second statement is called the *contrapositive* of the first statement. Make sure that you understand the original statement and the contrapositive. And remember, if the original statement is true, then the contrapositive must also be true.
3. Combine rules or make connections whenever possible. For example, A → B and B → C means that A → B → C.

EXAMPLE

A landscape designer wishes to use roses of different colors in a large planter. Seven colors of roses are available for selection: lavender, orange, pink, red, tan, white, and yellow. Only certain color combinations will be used based on the following conditions:

If lavender is used, then so is tan.
If red is used, then yellow is not used.
If orange, tan, or both are used, then so is red.
If pink is not used, then neither is lavender.
If white is not used, then yellow is used.

Analysis—The setup

From the information given, a simple group organizer could be constructed as follows:

	Used		Not
	L →T		
	R	→	Y
	O/T →R		
			P →L
	Y	←	W

Notice that the group headings are underlined and that the arrows are pointing in one direction. "If–then" statements should be represented by arrows pointing from the "if" to the "then."

Now let's take a closer look at the following conditions and their contrapositives. Read each pair of statements carefully to make sure you understand the reasoning involved. Keep in mind that the contrapositive to an if–then statement is true.

"If lavender is used, then so is tan." Therefore, if tan is not used, then lavender is not used.

"If red is used, then yellow is not used." Therefore, if yellow is used, then red is not used.

"If orange, tan, or both are used, then so is red." Therefore, if red is not used, then neither orange nor tan is used.

"If pink is not used, then neither is lavender." Therefore, if lavender is used, then pink is used.

"If white is not used, then yellow is used." Therefore, if yellow is not used, then white is used.

Don't let this additional information confuse you. A careful look at the reasoning involved should help you understand the following explanations. It should also give you some insight into this type of problem set.

Using this chart or display should make answering the questions much easier.

Question 1

If lavender is used, what is the least number of colors that can be used?

(A) 2
(B) 3
(C) 4

(D) 5
(E) 6

Analysis

The correct answer is D. If L is used, then so is T. If T is used, then so is R. If R is used, then Y is not. If Y is not used, then W is used. Since L is used, so must P. Therefore, Y cannot be used and O doesn't have to be used. Five is the correct answer. The following summarizes the results.

Used	Not
L	Y
T	O?
R	
W	
P	

Question 2

If tan is not used, which one of the following must be true?

(A) Pink is not used.
(B) Either lavender or red is used.
(C) Orange and red are the only two colors used.
(D) Either white or yellow or both are used.
(E) Both red and yellow are used.

Analysis

The correct answer is D. If T is not used, then neither is L. Since L is not used, P may or may not be used; therefore, answer (A) is incorrect. Since R may or may not be used, answer (B) is incorrect. Since R does not have to be used, answers (C) and (E) are incorrect. It is not possible for both W and Y not to be used; therefore, answer (D) is correct.

	Used		Not
			T
			L
		P?	
		R?	
Either	Y		W
or	W		Y
or	W, Y		

Question 3

Which one of the following sets of colors CANNOT be a complete set of colors used?

(A) orange, pink, red, and white
(B) yellow only

(C) lavender, red, tan, and white
(D) red and white
(E) pink, red, tan, and white

Analysis

The correct answer is C. Only answer choice (C) fails to meet the conditions. If P were not used, then L would not be used. Since L is used, so must P. All the other choices are possible.

Question 4

If exactly two colors are used, which of the following CANNOT be those two colors?

(A) red and white
(B) pink and white
(C) white and yellow
(D) orange and red
(E) pink and yellow

Analysis

The correct answer is D. If R is used, then Y is not used. If Y is not used, then W must be used. Therefore, if R is used, then so must W, and choice (D) is only O and R.

Question 5

If white is not used, then which one of the following must be true?

(A) Tan must be used.
(B) Pink must be used.
(C) Pink cannot be used.
(D) Yellow must be used.
(E) Yellow cannot be used.

Analysis

The correct answer is D. If W is not used, then Y must be used. T can't be used because then R would have to be used and then Y couldn't be used (eliminate A). Eliminate choices (B) and (C) since either *could* be true. Choice (E) cannot be true since Y must be used.

The Group Organizer (Venn diagrams/grouping arrows)

Another type of less commonly used group organizer is Venn diagrams/grouping arrows (also mentioned in Chapter 2: Logical Reasoning). This type of diagram can be useful when information is given that shows relationships between sets or groups of sets. Keep in mind that:

1. Venn diagrams should be used only in *very simple situations* involving small numbers of items.

2. Grouping arrows seem to be *more effective and simpler* to work with, especially in complex situations.

Some very basic Venn diagrams and grouping arrows look like this:

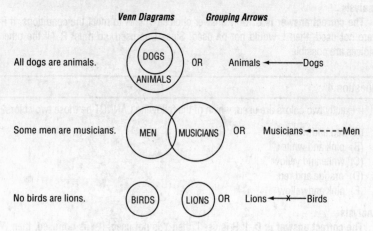

	Venn Diagrams	*Grouping Arrows*
All dogs are animals.	DOGS / ANIMALS OR	Animals ◄———— Dogs
Some men are musicians.	MEN MUSICIANS OR	Musicians ◄- - - - -Men
No birds are lions.	BIRDS LIONS OR	Lions ◄—×— Birds

In diagramming more than two groups, you may find it helpful to draw the most general or largest category before drawing any of the others.

EXAMPLE

A pharmacist has labeled certain pills—A, B, C, D, and E—by the categories they fall into. Some of the categories overlap as follows:

(1) All As are Bs.
(2) All Bs are Cs.
(3) Some, but not all, Ds are As.
(4) All Ds are Bs.
(5) No Es are Cs.

Analysis—The setup

From statement 1 we may draw a Venn diagram or grouping arrows as follows:

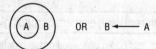

A B   OR   B ◄——— A

From statement 2 our diagrams or grouping arrows grow to look like this:

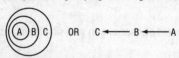

A B C   OR   C ◄——— B ◄——— A

Now statements 3 and 4 add another circle in the Venn diagram (note that we need the fourth statement in order to "contain" the D circle within the B circle) or another element to the grouping arrows as follows:

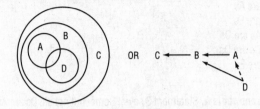

And, finally, from statement 5 we get:

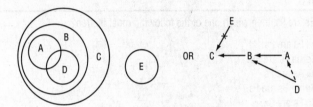

Now it will be relatively simple to answer the questions simply by referring to our final Venn Diagram or grouping arrows.

Remember that Venn diagrams can become unwieldy, while grouping arrows are usually much simpler to display and easier to use.

Question 1

Which one of the following must be true?

(A) All Cs are As.
(B) Some Es are Bs.
(C) All As are Ds.
(D) No Bs are Es.
(E) Some Es are As.

Analysis

The correct answer is D. From the grouping arrows or Venn Diagram, you can see that Bs and Es do not connect, so no Bs are Es must be true. Notice that (A) is false, all As are Cs, but not all Cs are As. Choice (B) is false because the Es are separate from the Bs. Choice (C) could be true, but doesn't have to be true. Choice (E) is false since no As are Es, no Es are As.

Question 2

Which one of the following must be false?

(A) All Ds are As.
(B) No As are Es.
(C) Some As are Ds.
(D) Some Cs are Ds.
(E) No Bs are Es.

Analysis

The correct answer is A. Statement 3 says, "Some, but not all, Ds are As." The other four answer choices are incorrect since each is a true statement.

Question 3

If all Es are Fs, then which one of the following must be true?

(A) All Fs are Es.
(B) Some Fs are Es.
(C) All As are Fs.
(D) Some Bs are Fs.
(E) No Fs are Cs.

Analysis

The correct answer is B. Note that this problem requires us to add another circle to our Venn diagram, as follows:

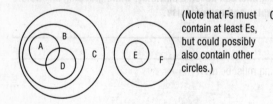

(Note that Fs must contain at least Es, but could possibly also contain other circles.)

OR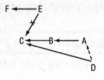

Question 4

If some Gs are As, then which one of the following must be true?

(A) Some Gs are Ds.
(B) All Ds are Gs.
(C) All Bs are Gs.
(D) Some Es are Gs.
(E) Some Gs are Cs.

Analysis

The correct answer is E. This problem, too, requires us to add to our original Venn diagram. If some Gs are As, our Venn diagram must *at least* contain some Gs in the A circle (x notes location of some Gs):

but it *could* also look like this:

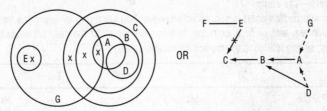

The Table Organizer (Information table)

The table organizer is helpful for spotting information and making deductions quickly. This is a problem set that sets up in a row and column format. In this way, you can have categories in both the rows and columns at the same time—for example, days of the week and workers, or students and grades received. When putting together a table organizer, you should follow these steps:

1. Carefully decide on the type of framework, categories, or labels. You may need to read all of the statements or conditions before deciding how to arrange the information.
2. If you have selected a good way of showing the information—proper labels, categories, and so on—the information should fit in fairly easily and be easy to understand and interpret.
3. Be sure to note variable positions or possibilities in your information chart (for example, Bob can work on Mondays or Tuesdays).

EXAMPLE

In order to open a new furniture store the following week, Mr. Worble hired a painter, a carpet layer, an electrician, and a carpenter. In scheduling the workmen, he had to consider the following conditions:

The painter is available only on Tuesday morning, Wednesday afternoon, and all day Friday.

The carpet layer is available only on Monday, Wednesday, and Friday mornings.

The electrician is available only on Tuesday morning and Friday afternoon.

The carpenter is available only on Monday morning, Tuesday all day, and Wednesday afternoon.

> Unless otherwise stated, each workman must work alone in the store.
>
> Unless otherwise stated, each workman is able to complete his own job in half a day.

Analysis—The setup

An information chart is suggested whenever you are trying to determine the points at which two sets of facts coincide. In this case, we chart the daily schedule of each worker, simply following the explicit information given.

	M	T	W	T	F
Painter		Morning	Afternoon		All day
Carpet layer	Morning		Morning		Morning
Electrician		Morning			Afternoon
Carpenter	Morning	All day	Afternoon		

Although we have written out "morning," "afternoon," and "all day," you may wish to abbreviate such terms. Another possible chart might look like this:

	Mon.	Tue.	Wed.	Th.	Fri.
A.M.	CL C	P E C	CL		CL P
P.M.		C	P C		P E

Question 1

If the carpenter and the electrician must work on the same day to coordinate their efforts, but cannot work at the same time, who of the following will NOT be able to start work until Wednesday, at the earliest?

(A) painter
(B) carpet layer
(C) electrician
(D) carpenter
(E) carpet layer and electrician

Analysis

The correct answer is A. The carpet layer may work on Monday, and the carpenter and the electrician *must* work Tuesday (the only day they are available together). In this case, the painter (A) may not begin until Wednesday.

Question 2

If the painter needs the whole day on Friday to complete his job, the

(A) carpenter must work on Thursday
(B) electrician and carpet layer must work on the same day
(C) total job cannot be completed in one week
(D) electrician must work on Tuesday
(E) carpet layer and carpenter must work on the same day

Analysis

The correct answer is D. If the painter works for the entire day on Friday, then none of the other workers can work on Friday. This means that both the carpet layer and the electrician must work on a day other than Friday. The carpet layer can work either Monday morning or Wednesday morning. The only other day the electrician can work is Tuesday morning (see the first setup). When checking the possible answers, this would make (D) the correct answer. (A) is incorrect because no one works on Thursday. (B) is incorrect because now the carpet layer and the electrician can no longer work on the same day, Friday. There are many possibilities for the carpenter and carpet layer to work between Monday morning and Wednesday. So (C) is incorrect, the job can be finished in one week, and (E) is incorrect, they do not have to work on the same day.

Question 3

Mr. Worble is expecting a supply of furniture on Thursday morning. Which one of the following must be true?

(A) The carpenter will be the only one finished before the merchandise arrives.
(B) Before the merchandise arrives, the painter will be finished, but the electrician will have to work Wednesday night.
(C) The carpet layer, the carpenter, and the electrician will be the only ones finished before the merchandise arrives.
(D) The carpet layer will have to work on the Tuesday before the merchandise arrives.
(E) All of the workers could have their jobs completed before the merchandise arrives.

Analysis

The correct answer is E. One possible plan is this: The carpet layer works Monday morning, the electrician works Tuesday morning, the carpenter works Tuesday afternoon, and the painter works Wednesday afternoon.

Question 4

If the store must be closed Monday and Tuesday and no worker may enter on those days, then, for all the work to be completed by the end of the week,

(A) the carpet layer must work Friday morning
(B) the painter must work Friday morning
(C) the painter must work Wednesday afternoon
(D) the painter must work Friday afternoon
(E) the carpet layer must work Friday afternoon

Analysis
The correct answer is B. If the store must be closed on Monday and Tuesday, then the carpenter must work Wednesday afternoon, and the electrician must work Friday afternoon, as these workers have no other available days to work. Since the painter cannot work Wednesday afternoon (the carpenter is already working then), he must work Friday morning. This leaves the carpet layer Wednesday morning to complete his work.

Question 5

If the store must be painted before any of the other work may begin, then, for all the work to be completed, all the following are true EXCEPT:

(A) the carpenter may work Tuesday or Wednesday afternoon
(B) the electrician must work Friday afternoon
(C) the carpet layer must work Wednesday or Friday morning
(D) the electrician and the carpet layer may work the same day
(E) the painter and the electrician may work the same day

Analysis
The correct answer is E. If the store must be painted first, then the painter could do his work Tuesday morning. All of the choices then are true, except (E). The painter and electrician may not work the same day, because if it's Tuesday, then they both would work in the morning, which is not allowed. The only other day they could both work is Friday, but that wouldn't allow all the work to be completed if the painter first works Friday morning.

The Table Organizer (Elimination grid)

This type of chart will assist you in eliminating many possibilities, thus narrowing your answer choices and simplifying the reasoning process. To set up an elimination grid you should:

1. Decide on the column and row headings.
2. Mark X's in squares or situations that are not possible. You may use Y's and N's for yes and no.
3. Place check marks or fill in squares or situations that are possible.

4. Fill in any items that you can deduce or "eliminate" with the grid (for example, if Ann receives an A, she cannot receive a B, C, or D).

EXAMPLE

> Two boys (Tom and Sal) and two girls (Lisa and Molly) each receive a different one of four different passing grades (A,B,C,D) on an exam.
>
> (1) Both boys receive lower grades than Lisa.
> (2) Sal did not get a B.
> (3) Tom got a B.
> (4) Molly did not get an A.

Analysis—The setup

Although a chart is not necessary to answer question 1, you could have constructed the following using the information given in the statements:

First, since both boys received lower grades than Lisa, we know that Lisa could not have gotten the C or D, and that neither of the boys could have gotten the A. Thus, your chart will look like this:

	A	B	C	D
Tom	X			
Sal	X			
Lisa			X	X
Molly				

From statements 2 and 3, we can fill in that Tom received the B (and thus the others didn't):

	A	B	C	D
Tom	X	✓	X	X
Sal	X	X		
Lisa		X	X	X
Molly		X		

Statement 4 allows us to indicate on our chart that Molly didn't get an A. Thus, we can see from our chart that Lisa *must* have gotten the A:

	A	B	C	D
Tom	X	✓	X	X
Sal	X	X		
Lisa	✓	X	X	X
Molly	X	X		

Notice that we could have deduced that even without statement 4, as there was no other grade Lisa could possibly receive.

Now we know that Lisa received the A, and Tom received the B. But we cannot deduce Sal's or Molly's grade. Be aware that, on many problems like this, you will have to proceed to the questions with an incomplete chart.

Question 1

Which statement(s) may be deduced from only one of the other statements?

(A) statement 1
(B) statement 2
(C) statement 3
(D) statement 4
(E) statements 1 and 3

Analysis
The correct answer is B. Statement 2 may be deduced from statement 3. If Tom got the B, it must be true that Sal did not get the B.

Question 2

If Molly received the lowest grade, then Sal must have received

(A) the A
(B) the B
(C) the C
(D) the D
(E) either the A or the B

Analysis
The correct answer is C. Using the chart, if Molly received the lowest grade (D), then Sal must have gotten the C. Note that by elimination on the grid, the only possibilities for Sal and Molly were Cs and Ds.

Question 3

Which one of the following is a complete and accurate list of the grades that Sal could have received?

(A) A
(B) A, C
(C) B, D
(D) C, D
(E) B, C, D

Analysis
The correct answer is D. From our chart we can easily see that Sal could have received either the C or the D.

Question 4

Which one of the following is a complete and accurate list of the grades that Molly could NOT have received?

(A) A
(B) B
(C) B, C
(D) C, D
(E) A, B

Analysis

The correct answer is E. From our chart we can easily see that Molly could not have received either the A or the B. We could also have determined this from statements 3 and 4.

Question 5

If Sal received the D, then Molly received

(A) the A
(B) the B
(C) the C
(D) the D
(E) either the A or the D

Analysis

The correct answer is C. From our chart we can easily see that, if Sal received the D, then Molly must have received the C.

Question 6

If the grades that Sal and Lisa received were reversed, then which one of the original statements would no longer be true?

(A) statement 1
(B) statement 2
(C) statement 3
(D) statement 4
(E) statements 2 and 3

Analysis

The correct answer is A. If Sal and Lisa reversed their grades, then

Sal would get the A.
Tom would get the B.
Lisa received either the C or the D.
Molly received either the C or the D.

Therefore, only statement 1 ("Both boys receive lower grades than Lisa") would no longer be true.

EXAMPLE

The Intermediate League board of directors is composed of exactly four members—Beals, Dunphy, Franks, and Mellon. Beals and Dunphy are the senior directors, whereas Franks and Mellon are the new directors. At the off-season meeting, the directors must consider three proposed changes to the league rules. The changes to be voted on are these: fee increases, fewer players on a team, and a longer season. The following conditions apply:

Each proposed change must have three votes to pass.

None of the changes has a unanimous vote, either for or against.

Exactly three directors vote for the fee increases.

Both of the senior directors vote against fewer players on a team.

Both new directors vote against a longer season.

Beals and Mellon vote for fee increases.

Analysis—The setup

In setting up this chart, you should list the directors across the top and the proposed changes along the side (or vice versa). Mark the senior directors and the new directors.

	Senior		New	
	B	D	F	M
Fees				
Players				
Season				

Next, quickly fill in as much information as possible. Use Y for "for" and N for "against."

	Senior		New	
	B	D	F	M
3 for Fees	Y			Y
Players	N	N		
Season			N	N

Since "None of the changes has a unanimous vote," you can add the following notations to the chart:

	Senior		New	
	B	D	F	M
3 for Fees	Y			Y
Players	N	N		
Season			N	N

X stands for "not the same"

←not NN

↑
not NN

Question 1

Which one of the following statements could be true?

(A) One director votes for all the changes.
(B) One director votes against all the changes.
(C) Two directors vote for all the changes.
(D) Two directors vote against all the changes.
(E) Three directors vote against all the changes.

Analysis
The correct answer is B. Notice that you are looking for what "could be true." Using the chart, you can quickly eliminate (A) and (C), since each director votes against at least one change. (D) and (E) can be eliminated, since there are three votes for the fee increase. Either Franks or Dunphy could vote against all the changes, but not both. So only one director could vote against all the changes.

Question 2

Which one of the following statements must be true?

(A) The fee increase change does not pass.
(B) The fewer player change passes.
(C) The longer season change and the fewer player change pass.
(D) The fee increase change and the longer season change pass.
(E) The fee increase change passes.

Analysis
The correct answer is E. Using the chart, since the fewer player change and the longer season change each have at least two against votes, then neither of them could pass. The only change that passes is the fee increase, since one of the conditions stipulates that there are exactly three votes for that change.

Question 3

If Dunphy votes for the fee increase and against the longer season, then which one of the following must be true?

(A) Beals votes for the longer season.
(B) Franks votes for the fee increase.
(C) Mellon votes for fewer players.
(D) Franks votes against all the changes.
(E) Mellon votes for all the changes.

Analysis

The correct answer is A. Filling in the Dunphy votes and using some reasoning gives the following chart:

	Senior		New	
	B	D	F	M
3 for Fees	Y	Y	N	Y
Players	N	N			←not NN
Season	Y	N	N	N

Since Dunphy votes for fee increases, Franks must vote against fee increases. Since Dunphy votes against a longer season, Beals must vote for a longer season.

Question 4

If the new directors vote the same on only one change, and the senior directors vote the same on only two changes, then which one of the following must vote for a longer season?

(A) Beals
(B) Dunphy
(C) Franks
(D) Mellon
(E) Beals or Dunphy

Analysis

The correct answer is E. If the new directors vote the same on only one change, it must be the longer season, so they must vote differently on fewer players and fee increases. Since Mellon votes for fee increases, Franks must vote against fee increases. Since three directors must vote for fee increases, Dunphy must vote for them. Since the senior directors vote the same on only two changes, they must vote differently on the longer season. So either Beals or Dunphy must vote for a longer season. The following shows how the chart is completed:

	Senior		New	
	B	D	F	M
3 for Fees	Y	Y	N	Y
Players	N	N			← YN or NY
Season			N	N

↑
YN or NY

Question 5

Which one of the following is a complete and accurate list of directors who could possibly vote for a longer season?

(A) Beals
(B) Dunphy
(C) Beals, Dunphy
(D) Beals, Franks
(E) Beals, Dunphy, Mellon

Analysis
The correct answer is C. Using the chart, you can see that only Beals or Dunphy could possibly vote for a longer season. Choices A and B are accurate, but not complete.

	Senior		New	
	B	D	F	M
3 for Fees	Y	✕		Y
Players	N	N			← not NN
Season			N	N

↑
not NN

Question 6

Which one of the following is a possible vote outcome on the fee increase?

(A) Beals: for   Dunphy: for   Franks: for   Mellon: for
(B) Beals: for   Dunphy: for   Franks: for   Mellon: against
(C) Beals: for   Dunphy: against   Franks: against   Mellon: for
(D) Beals: for   Dunphy: for   Franks: against   Mellon: for
(E) Beals: against Dunphy: for   Franks: for   Mellon: for

Analysis
The correct answer is D. Using the chart you can easily eliminate choices (A), can't pass unanimously; (B), Mellon is against; (C), need three votes for; and (E), Beals is for.

The Spatial Organizer

The spatial organizer is used when a problem set describes the relative positions of different items to each other. These items with relative positions may simply have connections between them, or overlapping areas. When putting together a spatial organizer, you should follow these steps:

1. Look for key words to tip off the type of "simple map" you should be drawing.
2. As you place the objects, islands, cities, and so on, watch for relative positions.
3. Placements of items will sometimes be relative to a central location or other placements.
4. In some instances, you may be placing houses, cities, objects, or people in general areas, limited areas, or zones—north, south, east, west, northeast, southwest, and so on.
5. Sometimes the items will be placed directly north (due north), directly southeast, and so on.
6. Watch for limited areas or zones, as opposed to exact locations. This takes careful reading, reasoning, and placement.
7. Place question marks next to items that are movable (this is, not stuck in one spot).
8. If appropriate, mark connections from one item to the next.
9. If appropriate, mark overlapping areas.
10. Watch for items, areas, or connections that have special restrictions—a connecting bridge that only goes in one direction, an island that can only be visited once, or a route that only goes to certain places.

EXAMPLE

LSAT Airlines flies to and from exactly eight cities—A, B, C, D, E, F, G, and H—using exactly five flight paths—1, 2, 3, 4, and 5. The flight paths are described as follows:

Flight Path 1: Connects cities A and C with its only stop in city G

Flight Path 2: Connects cities A and H with its only stop in city F

Flight Path 3: Connects cities D and H with its only stop in city B

Flight Path 4: Connects cities A and E with its only stop in city D

Flight Path 5: Connects cities D and G with its only stop in city F

A direct connection is a flight between two cities that does not require a stop. An indirect connection is a flight between two cities that requires at least one stop.

Analysis—The Setup

From the flight path descriptions, the following diagrams can be drawn:

Flight Path 1:   A – G – C
Flight Path 2:   A – F – H
Flight Path 3:   D – B – H
Flight Path 4:   A – D – E
Flight Path 5:   G – F – D

Combining these diagrams gives the following complete map:

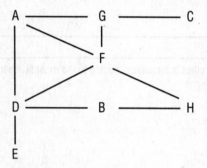

Combine diagrams whenever possible to get a complete picture of what you have to work with and the relative positions of each item.

Question 1

Without stopping in city A, what is the fewest number of stops required to travel between cities C and E?

(A) 1
(B) 2
(C) 3
(D) 4
(E) 5

Analysis

The correct answer is C. Notice that you are looking for the fewest number of stops required, *without stopping at city A*. By carefully following the map you can see that to get from city C to city E requires at least three stops—cities G, F, and D.

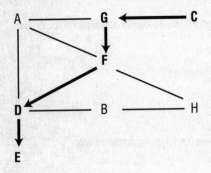

Question 2

Which one of the following cities is directly connected to the most number of cities?

(A) City A
(B) City B
(C) City C
(D) City D
(E) City E

Analysis

The correct answer is D. Make sure that you underline "directly connected to the most." From the original completed map you can see that city D is directly connected to four other cities. City A is directly connected to three other cities. City B is directly connected to two other cities. Cities C and E are directly connected to only one other city.

Question 3

Using only Flight Paths 2, 4, and 5, which of the following is a complete and accurate list of the other cities that can be reached from city A by taking an indirect connection and making exactly one stop?

(A) D, F
(B) E, G, H
(C) C, D, F, H
(D) B, C, E, G, H
(E) D, E, F, G, H

Analysis

The correct answer is E. Using only Flight Paths 2, 4, and 5 gives the following map:

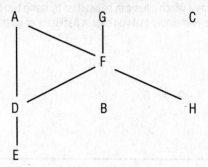

Starting from city A:

City D can be reached by making one stop at city F.
City E can be reached by making one stop at city D.
City F can be reached by making one stop at city D.
City G can be reached by making one stop at city F.
City H can be reached by making one stop at city F.

Question 4

Which one of the following is a complete and accurate list of the flight paths that must be used to travel from city C to city H?

(A) 1
(B) 1, 2
(C) 1, 2, 3, 4
(D) 1, 3, 4
(E) 2, 3

Analysis

The correct answer is A. From the original completed map, you can see that only Flight Path 1 must be used. Flight Paths 2, 3, and 4 could be used, but they do not have to be used. Flight Path 1 must be used, since it is the only flight path that flies to city C.

Question 5

How many other cities can be reached from city F after using an indirect connection, making exactly two stops and not going through the same city twice?

(A) 2
(B) 3
(C) 4
(D) 5
(E) 6

Analysis

The correct answer is E. By using the original diagram, follow the flight paths from City F and methodically determine which cities can be reached by using two stops and which ones cannot be reached. Remember that you cannot backtrack or go through the same city twice.

City B: F – A – D – B
City C: F – A – G – C
City D: F – H – B –D   or   F – G – A – D
City E: F – A – D – E
City G: F – D – A – G
City H: F – D – B – H

Question 6

If no city is stopped at more than once, then which one of the following is a possible order of cities stopped at when traveling from city G to city E?

(A) H, F, A, D, B
(B) F, C, H, B, D
(C) A, F, D, A, D
(D) A, F, H, B, D
(E) F, A, H, B, D

Analysis

The correct answer is D. Since the question is asking for a "possible" order, using the original map you could eliminate choices that are not possible as follows:

Eliminate (A) because cities G and H do not connect directly.
Eliminate (B) because cities F and C do not connect directly.
Eliminate (C) because cities A and D are stopped at more than once.
Eliminate (E) because cities A and H do not connect directly.

Question 7

If the airline adds a new flight path, Flight Path 6, connecting cities C and E and stopping only at city H, then which one of the following must be true?

(A) City H can only be reached by exactly two direct connections.
(B) City E can only be reached by exactly two direct connections.
(C) City H cannot be reached by an indirect connection.
(D) City G cannot be reached by an indirect connection.
(E) City C can only be reached by exactly one direct connection.

Analysis

The correct answer is B. First, add the new information and redraw the map as follows:

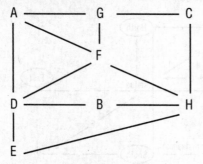

Now using this new map, review each of the choices.

Eliminate (A) because city H can be reached by three direct connections.
(B) is correct because city E is directly connected to cities D and H.

You could stop here and mark your answer.

(C) could be eliminated because city H can be reached by many indirect connections (for example, A to F to H, or D to B to H).
(D) could be eliminated because city G can be reached by many indirect connections (for example, A to F to G, or D to F to G).
(E) could be eliminated because city C can be reached by two direct connections, one from city H and one from city G.

EXAMPLE

Six cabins—A, B, C, D, E, and F—were constructed on a small flat area in the mountains. The focal point of the area was a statue that was constructed years before the cabins were constructed.

Cabin A is directly north of the statue.
Cabin C is directly west of the statue.
Cabin D is south of Cabin C.
Cabin E is west of Cabin A.
The statue is directly southeast of Cabin B and directly northwest of Cabin F.

Analysis—The setup

From the information given, a simple display may be constructed as follows (possible ranges are denoted with arrows):

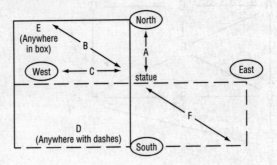

Or an even simpler map (if you can remember the zones) is possible:

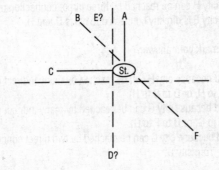

Question 1

Which one of the following must be true?

(A) Cabin B is east of Cabin C.
(B) Cabin B is west of Cabin C.
(C) Cabin F is west of Cabin E.
(D) Cabin D is south of Cabin B.
(E) Cabin D is east of Cabin A.

Analysis

The correct answer is D. Statements (A), (B), and (E) *could* be true, but do not necessarily have to be true. (C) is false. Only (D) must be true.

Question 2

Which one of the following must be false?

(A) Cabin A is north of Cabin E.
(B) Cabin C is east of Cabin E.

(C) Cabin B is south of Cabin F.
(D) Cabin D is north of Cabin F.
(E) Cabin D is east of Cabin E.

Analysis

The correct answer is C. Choices (A), (B), (D), and (E) *could* be true, but (C) *must* be false.

Question 3

How many cabins must be west of Cabin A?

(A) 0
(B) 1
(C) 2
(D) 3
(E) 4

Analysis

The correct answer is D. Cabins E, B, and C must be west of A. Cabin D does not have to be west of Cabin A.

Question 4

What is the maximum number of cabins you could encounter traveling directly east from Cabin C?

(A) 0
(B) 1
(C) 2
(D) 3
(E) 4

Analysis

The correct answer is B. Traveling directly east from Cabin C, you could encounter Cabin E.

Question 5

If another cabin, Cabin G, is constructed directly north of Cabin F, then all of the following must be true EXCEPT:

(A) Cabin A is west of Cabin G
(B) Cabin G is east of Cabin C
(C) Cabin D is south of Cabin G
(D) Cabin G is east of Cabin A
(E) Cabin B is west of Cabin G

Analysis

The correct answer is C. Adding Cabin G to the display results in:

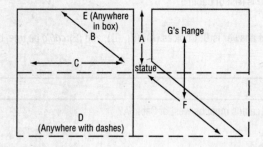

Statements (A), (B), (D), and (E) must be true. Statement (C) could be true, but does not necessarily have to be true.

Question 6

If Cabins H and J are constructed so that H is directly east of J, and H is directly north of A, then which one of the following must be true?

(A) Cabin H is north of Cabin B.
(B) Cabin C is west of Cabin J.
(C) Cabin H is south of Cabin D.
(D) Cabin E is south of Cabin H.
(E) Cabin F is east of Cabin J.

Analysis

The correct answer is E. Adding Cabins H and J to the display results in:

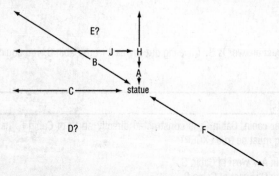

From the display, Cabin F must be east of Cabin J. Choices (A), (B), and (D) could be true, but do not necessarily have to be true. Choice (C) must be false.

Question 7

If Cabin M is constructed west of Cabin A, which one of the following is a possible order of cabins a traveler could encounter while traveling directly northwest from F?

(A) BEDM
(B) DMBE
(C) MDEBC
(D) DMCBE
(E) MDABE

Analysis

The correct answer is B. Adding Cabin M to the display results in:

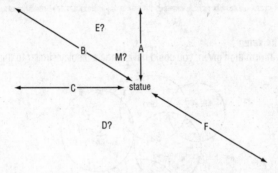

From the display, you could possibly encounter DMBE while traveling northwest from F.

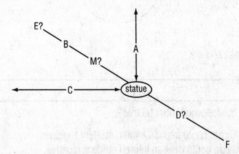

EXAMPLE

Five school playground aides—Alice, Bert, Carrie, Diego, and Emma—are each given one circular area to supervise. Because some of the areas are used more often than others, the areas overlap as follows:

Alice's area overlaps part of Bert's area.
Bert's area overlaps part of Emma's area.
Emma's area overlaps part of Alice's area.

> Part of Alice's and Bert's overlapping area is also over-
> lapped by part of Emma's area.
>
> Carrie's area overlaps part of Bert's area, but no one else's
> area.
>
> Diego's area overlaps part of Emma's area, but no one
> else's area.

The playground aides must follow these rules:

> An aide can only treat a student who is injured in the aide's
> area.
>
> No more than two aides can ever treat an injured student.
>
> An injured student cannot be taken out of the aide's area.

Analysis—The setup

From the information given, you could have made a display similar to this:

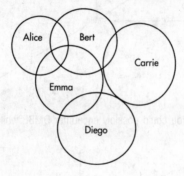

Check the overlaps carefully.

Question 1

Which one of the following must be true?

(A) Alice and Carrie could treat an injured student together.
(B) Bert and Diego could treat an injured student together.
(C) Emma could treat an injured student with Carrie.
(D) Alice and Bert could treat an injured student together.
(E) Diego and Alice could treat an injured student together.

Analysis

The correct answer is D. Since Alice and Bert's areas overlap, they could treat an injured student together. You could have eliminated each of the other choices because they don't overlap.

Question 2

If a student is injured in Emma's area, which one of the following is a complete and accurate list of the aides who could possibly treat the student?

(A) Emma
(B) Alice, Bert
(C) Alice, Bert, Emma
(D) Bert, Diego, Emma
(E) Alice, Bert, Diego, Emma

Analysis

The correct answer is E. Since Emma's area is overlapped by Alice, Bert, and Diego's areas, they could also treat the student if the student happened to be in the overlap.

Question 3

If a student is injured in Bert's area, which one of the following CANNOT be true?

(A) Bert must treat the student by himself.
(B) Alice could treat the student.
(C) Alice and Emma could treat the student together.
(D) Diego cannot treat the student.
(E) Carrie could treat the student.

Analysis

The correct answer is A. Since part of Bert's area is overlapped by other areas, Bert would not have to treat the student by himself or treat the student at all. It would depend on where in Bert's area the student was injured. The answer is false and, therefore, the correct answer. Answer (B) is incorrect since Alice's area overlaps Bert's area. Alice could treat the student by herself (or with Bert) if the student was injured in the area overlapped by Alice and Bert. Answer (C) is incorrect since the intersection of Alice's area and Emma's area also intersects Bert's area. If the student was injured in the intersection of Bert's, Alice's, and Emma's areas, then Alice and Emma could treat the student. Answer (D) is incorrect since Diego's area does not intersect Bert's area; therefore, statement (D) is true. Answer (E) is incorrect since Carrie's area intersects Bert's area, and thus Carrie could treat the student, either alone or with Bert, if the student was injured in the intersection of Carrie's area and Bert's area.

Question 4

If a student is injured in Bert's area, how many different possible combinations of one or two aides could treat the student?

(A) 3
(B) 4
(C) 5
(D) 7
(E) 8

Analysis

The correct answer is E. The possibilities are: (1) Bert; (2) Alice; (3) Emma; (4) Carrie; (5) Bert and Alice; (6) Bert and Emma; (7) Bert and Carrie; (8) Alice and Emma.

The General Organizer (Simply pulling out information)

In most cases, you will be able to construct some sort of organized display, but on a rare occasion no chart or diagram may appear to fit the situation. If this is the case, then:

1. Simply pull out or note whatever information seems important to you.
2. Mark any relationships between the items you have pulled out.
3. Go on to the questions.

EXAMPLE

Tongo is a sport similar to racquetball, except in each game three players oppose each other. Sandy, Arnie, and Betsy are the only entrants in a tongo tournament. Sandy is a left-handed tongo player, while Arnie and Betsy are right-handed tongo players. The players must compete in the tournament according to the following rules:

The winner of each game receives 5 points; the second place finisher gets 3 points; and the third place finisher gets 1 point.

There are no tie games.

The one player with the most game points at the end of the tournament is the grand winner.

If, at the end of the tournament, two or more players have the same total number of points, there will be a playoff.

Analysis—The setup

You probably found that this set of conditions was not conducive to constructing any standard chart. As soon as this was evident, you should have simply pulled out information as follows:

L—Sandy	1st—5 pts.
R—Arnie	2nd—3 pts.
R—Betsy	3rd—1 pt.

Question 1

Which one of the following must be true?

(A) Betsy plays only right-handed opponents
(B) Arnie never plays a right-handed opponent.
(C) Arnie plays just right-handed opponents.
(D) Sandy never plays right-handed opponents.
(E) Sandy always plays right-handed opponents.

Analysis

The correct answer is E. Since Sandy is the only left-handed player, then she must play only right-handed opponents.

Question 2

If, after three games, both right-handed players have each scored 9 points, which one of the following could be true?

(A) One of the right-handed players finished first twice.
(B) At least one of the right-handed players finished second three times.
(C) Both right-handed players each finished first, second, and third.
(D) The left-handed player finished first twice.
(E) The left-handed player was ahead after three games.

Analysis

The correct answer is C. Only (C) may be true. (A) is blatantly false, since two first-place wins would result in 10 points. (B) is incorrect because, if one player finished second in all three games, then there is no way a second player could score exactly 9 points in three games. (D) and (E) are incorrect since there must be 27 points scored during the three games with each player scoring 9 points.

Question 3

Which one of the following must be true?

(A) A player with no first-place game points cannot win the tournament.
(B) A player with only second-place game points can win the tournament.
(C) A player with no first-place game points can win the tournament.
(D) A player with no third-place game points must win the tournament.
(E) A player with no second-place game points cannot come in second.

Analysis

The correct answer is A. Only (A) is true. With no first-place game points, the most a player could score per game is 3 points. The best that that player could hope for would be that the other two players would split first place and third place on all the games. But even then, the other two players would average 3 points per game. At best a playoff would be necessary, and the player without a first-place finish would thus lose the tournament. (D) and (E) are false by example.

Question 4

If, after three games, Arnie has 11 points, Betsy has 9 points, and Sandy has 7 points, which one of the following must be false?

(A) After four games, there is a three-way tie.
(B) After four games, Betsy is alone in first place.
(C) After four games, Betsy is alone in third place.

(D) After four games, Sandy is alone in first place.

(E) After four games, Sandy is alone in third place.

Analysis

The correct answer is D. The only statement that could not be true is (D). Since the most Sandy could score after four games would be 12 points, Betsy and/or Arnie will at least tie her for first place.

Question 5

If, just before the last game, it is discovered that the left-handed player has finished first in every even-numbered game, then

(A) Sandy must win the tournament

(B) Sandy cannot win the tournament

(C) Arnie may win the tournament

(D) Betsy can't win the tournament

(E) Betsy must win the tournament

Analysis

The correct answer is C. Even though Sandy may have scored 5 points in every even-numbered game, she may not necessarily win the tournament. For instance, if, say, Arnie scores 5 points in every odd-numbered game, and if the tournament consists of an odd number of games, then Arnie will win the tournament. Sandy *can* win the tournament, but not necessarily *must* win the tournament. Betsy, also, could possibly win the tournament, if she scores first-place wins in every odd-numbered game.

The General Organizer with Diagram Provided

EXAMPLE

A puzzle in a local newspaper gave a series of numerals in the following four four-letter sequences:

A B C D

D E H G

F B A K

H C F J

The rules for answering questions about the puzzle are as follows:

Each row represents a sequence, and some sequences could be the same.

Any letter that occurs in more than one sequence represents the same numeral in each of those sequences.

The numerals 6, 7, 8, and 9 are each represented once in each of the four sequences—no other numerals are represented.

**The first letter of any sequence can represent only 6 or 7.
The last letter of any sequence cannot be 6.**

Analysis—The setup

Since the display is already given, you should simply pull out information from the conditions and mark in or make notes as follows:

$$6/7 \quad \cancel{8}$$
$$A\ B\ C\ D \qquad 6, 7, 8, 9$$
$$D\ E\ H\ G$$
$$F\ B\ A\ K$$
$$H\ C\ F\ J$$

You may have deduced some additional information from the conditions given. If you haven't, read a few questions to get a sense of what you need to know.

Question 1

What numeral is represented by A?

(A) 6
(B) 7
(C) 8
(D) 9
(E) 6 or 7

Analysis

The correct answer is A. This particular question is asking you something that you should have been able to deduce from the initial conditions. So, in this case, you can actually put your answer into the display. Otherwise, you cannot take information from one question and use it in another question. Since A is in column 1, it must represent 6 or 7. Since D is in column 1, it must represent 6 or 7, but because D is in column 4, it cannot be 6. So D is 7. Since A and D are in row 1, and D is 7, A must represent 6.
Your display should now look like this:

$$6/7 \quad \cancel{8}$$
$$A^6\ B\ C\ D^7 \qquad 6, 7, 8, 9$$
$$D^7\ E\ H\ G$$
$$F\ B\ A^6\ K$$
$$H\ C\ F\ J$$

Notice that if A is 6 in row 1, then it is also 6 in row 3. Since D is 7 in row 1, it is 7 in row 2. Notice that you could have also figured out the value for F at this point.

Question 2

What numeral is represented by D?

(A) 6
(B) 7
(C) 8
(D) 9
(E) 6 or 7

Analysis

The correct answer is B. Since D is in column 1, it must represent 6 or 7, but because D is in column 4, it cannot be 6. So D must represent 7. You already knew this from finding A in the previous problem.

Question 3

Which one of the following is a possible order of the numerals for the last sequence?

(A) 6 7 8 9
(B) 8 6 7 9
(C) 7 9 6 8
(D) 7 8 6 9
(E) 6 8 7 9

Analysis

The correct answer is E. From the display, since A is 6 (in row 3), F must represent 7. In the last row, if F is 7, H must be 6. The only sequences possible for HCFJ are 6, 8, 7, 9 or 6, 9, 7, 8.

IN CONCLUSION

You have just worked through some of the basic types of displays that you may encounter on the LSAT. Be aware that there are *many other possible displays and modifications of the displays presented.* In the following practice tests, as you work through some of the other possible displays, carefully review the explanations of each to assist you in understanding these other types.

Remember that the exact type of display you make is not of critical importance. What is important is that you can get the necessary information from your display, and that it is simple to understand. Do not spend a great deal of time trying to make an elaborate display; a simple one will usually serve the purpose.

AN ALTERNATIVE GENERAL APPROACH

Some students, regardless of how much they review, analyze, and practice, cannot seem to finish the Analytical Reasoning section. They simply cannot work fast enough or make displays or rough diagrams quickly enough to see relationships and maintain a high level of correct answers. If you find that you consistently have a problem getting to or into the fourth set, you may wish to try this alternative approach: Focus your time on only three of the four sets. That is, try to set up and do well on the three sets and the questions that follow, and simply guess at the questions to the remaining set. You can skip one of the four sets and still receive a good score. The idea is to significantly raise your percentage of correct answers on the questions you *are* attempting. Remember, this is an alternative approach that you may wish to try if you are having a real problem getting to all four sets and maintaining a good level of correct answers. In using this method, you may wish to decide which set of questions you are going to skip after you have read the conditions and realize that the set is going to be problematic and difficult to complete.

ANSWER SHEET
EXTRA PRACTICE: ANALYTICAL REASONING

To remove, cut along dotted rule.

1. Ⓐ Ⓑ Ⓒ Ⓓ Ⓔ
2. Ⓐ Ⓑ Ⓒ Ⓓ Ⓔ
3. Ⓐ Ⓑ Ⓒ Ⓓ Ⓔ
4. Ⓐ Ⓑ Ⓒ Ⓓ Ⓔ
5. Ⓐ Ⓑ Ⓒ Ⓓ Ⓔ
6. Ⓐ Ⓑ Ⓒ Ⓓ Ⓔ
7. Ⓐ Ⓑ Ⓒ Ⓓ Ⓔ
8. Ⓐ Ⓑ Ⓒ Ⓓ Ⓔ
9. Ⓐ Ⓑ Ⓒ Ⓓ Ⓔ
10. Ⓐ Ⓑ Ⓒ Ⓓ Ⓔ
11. Ⓐ Ⓑ Ⓒ Ⓓ Ⓔ
12. Ⓐ Ⓑ Ⓒ Ⓓ Ⓔ
13. Ⓐ Ⓑ Ⓒ Ⓓ Ⓔ
14. Ⓐ Ⓑ Ⓒ Ⓓ Ⓔ
15. Ⓐ Ⓑ Ⓒ Ⓓ Ⓔ
16. Ⓐ Ⓑ Ⓒ Ⓓ Ⓔ
17. Ⓐ Ⓑ Ⓒ Ⓓ Ⓔ
18. Ⓐ Ⓑ Ⓒ Ⓓ Ⓔ
19. Ⓐ Ⓑ Ⓒ Ⓓ Ⓔ
20. Ⓐ Ⓑ Ⓒ Ⓓ Ⓔ
21. Ⓐ Ⓑ Ⓒ Ⓓ Ⓔ
22. Ⓐ Ⓑ Ⓒ Ⓓ Ⓔ
23. Ⓐ Ⓑ Ⓒ Ⓓ Ⓔ
24. Ⓐ Ⓑ Ⓒ Ⓓ Ⓔ
25. Ⓐ Ⓑ Ⓒ Ⓓ Ⓔ
26. Ⓐ Ⓑ Ⓒ Ⓓ Ⓔ
27. Ⓐ Ⓑ Ⓒ Ⓓ Ⓔ
28. Ⓐ Ⓑ Ⓒ Ⓓ Ⓔ

29. Ⓐ Ⓑ Ⓒ Ⓓ Ⓔ
30. Ⓐ Ⓑ Ⓒ Ⓓ Ⓔ
31. Ⓐ Ⓑ Ⓒ Ⓓ Ⓔ
32. Ⓐ Ⓑ Ⓒ Ⓓ Ⓔ
33. Ⓐ Ⓑ Ⓒ Ⓓ Ⓔ
34. Ⓐ Ⓑ Ⓒ Ⓓ Ⓔ
35. Ⓐ Ⓑ Ⓒ Ⓓ Ⓔ
36. Ⓐ Ⓑ Ⓒ Ⓓ Ⓔ
37. Ⓐ Ⓑ Ⓒ Ⓓ Ⓔ
38. Ⓐ Ⓑ Ⓒ Ⓓ Ⓔ
39. Ⓐ Ⓑ Ⓒ Ⓓ Ⓔ
40. Ⓐ Ⓑ Ⓒ Ⓓ Ⓔ
41. Ⓐ Ⓑ Ⓒ Ⓓ Ⓔ
42. Ⓐ Ⓑ Ⓒ Ⓓ Ⓔ
43. Ⓐ Ⓑ Ⓒ Ⓓ Ⓔ
44. Ⓐ Ⓑ Ⓒ Ⓓ Ⓔ
45. Ⓐ Ⓑ Ⓒ Ⓓ Ⓔ
46. Ⓐ Ⓑ Ⓒ Ⓓ Ⓔ
47. Ⓐ Ⓑ Ⓒ Ⓓ Ⓔ
48. Ⓐ Ⓑ Ⓒ Ⓓ Ⓔ
49. Ⓐ Ⓑ Ⓒ Ⓓ Ⓔ
50. Ⓐ Ⓑ Ⓒ Ⓓ Ⓔ
51. Ⓐ Ⓑ Ⓒ Ⓓ Ⓔ
52. Ⓐ Ⓑ Ⓒ Ⓓ Ⓔ
53. Ⓐ Ⓑ Ⓒ Ⓓ Ⓔ
54. Ⓐ Ⓑ Ⓒ Ⓓ Ⓔ
55. Ⓐ Ⓑ Ⓒ Ⓓ Ⓔ
56. Ⓐ Ⓑ Ⓒ Ⓓ Ⓔ

57. Ⓐ Ⓑ Ⓒ Ⓓ Ⓔ
58. Ⓐ Ⓑ Ⓒ Ⓓ Ⓔ
59. Ⓐ Ⓑ Ⓒ Ⓓ Ⓔ
60. Ⓐ Ⓑ Ⓒ Ⓓ Ⓔ
61. Ⓐ Ⓑ Ⓒ Ⓓ Ⓔ
62. Ⓐ Ⓑ Ⓒ Ⓓ Ⓔ
63. Ⓐ Ⓑ Ⓒ Ⓓ Ⓔ
64. Ⓐ Ⓑ Ⓒ Ⓓ Ⓔ
65. Ⓐ Ⓑ Ⓒ Ⓓ Ⓔ
66. Ⓐ Ⓑ Ⓒ Ⓓ Ⓔ
67. Ⓐ Ⓑ Ⓒ Ⓓ Ⓔ
68. Ⓐ Ⓑ Ⓒ Ⓓ Ⓔ
69. Ⓐ Ⓑ Ⓒ Ⓓ Ⓔ
70. Ⓐ Ⓑ Ⓒ Ⓓ Ⓔ
71. Ⓐ Ⓑ Ⓒ Ⓓ Ⓔ
72. Ⓐ Ⓑ Ⓒ Ⓓ Ⓔ
73. Ⓐ Ⓑ Ⓒ Ⓓ Ⓔ
74. Ⓐ Ⓑ Ⓒ Ⓓ Ⓔ
75. Ⓐ Ⓑ Ⓒ Ⓓ Ⓔ
76. Ⓐ Ⓑ Ⓒ Ⓓ Ⓔ
77. Ⓐ Ⓑ Ⓒ Ⓓ Ⓔ
78. Ⓐ Ⓑ Ⓒ Ⓓ Ⓔ
79. Ⓐ Ⓑ Ⓒ Ⓓ Ⓔ
80. Ⓐ Ⓑ Ⓒ Ⓓ Ⓔ
81. Ⓐ Ⓑ Ⓒ Ⓓ Ⓔ
82. Ⓐ Ⓑ Ⓒ Ⓓ Ⓔ
83. Ⓐ Ⓑ Ⓒ Ⓓ Ⓔ
84. Ⓐ Ⓑ Ⓒ Ⓓ Ⓔ

85. Ⓐ Ⓑ Ⓒ Ⓓ Ⓔ
86. Ⓐ Ⓑ Ⓒ Ⓓ Ⓔ
87. Ⓐ Ⓑ Ⓒ Ⓓ Ⓔ
88. Ⓐ Ⓑ Ⓒ Ⓓ Ⓔ
89. Ⓐ Ⓑ Ⓒ Ⓓ Ⓔ
90. Ⓐ Ⓑ Ⓒ Ⓓ Ⓔ
91. Ⓐ Ⓑ Ⓒ Ⓓ Ⓔ
92. Ⓐ Ⓑ Ⓒ Ⓓ Ⓔ
93. Ⓐ Ⓑ Ⓒ Ⓓ Ⓔ
94. Ⓐ Ⓑ Ⓒ Ⓓ Ⓔ
95. Ⓐ Ⓑ Ⓒ Ⓓ Ⓔ
96. Ⓐ Ⓑ Ⓒ Ⓓ Ⓔ
97. Ⓐ Ⓑ Ⓒ Ⓓ Ⓔ
98. Ⓐ Ⓑ Ⓒ Ⓓ Ⓔ
99. Ⓐ Ⓑ Ⓒ Ⓓ Ⓔ
100. Ⓐ Ⓑ Ⓒ Ⓓ Ⓔ
101. Ⓐ Ⓑ Ⓒ Ⓓ Ⓔ
102. Ⓐ Ⓑ Ⓒ Ⓓ Ⓔ
103. Ⓐ Ⓑ Ⓒ Ⓓ Ⓔ
104. Ⓐ Ⓑ Ⓒ Ⓓ Ⓔ
105. Ⓐ Ⓑ Ⓒ Ⓓ Ⓔ
106. Ⓐ Ⓑ Ⓒ Ⓓ Ⓔ
107. Ⓐ Ⓑ Ⓒ Ⓓ Ⓔ
108. Ⓐ Ⓑ Ⓒ Ⓓ Ⓔ
109. Ⓐ Ⓑ Ⓒ Ⓓ Ⓔ

EXTRA PRACTICE: ANALYTICAL REASONING

Directions: In this section you will be given a group of questions based on a specific set of conditions. Drawing a simple diagram may be helpful in answering some of the questions. You are to choose the best answer and mark the corresponding space on your answer sheet.

Questions 1–4

There are four books standing next to each other on a shelf. The books are in order from left to right. The colors of the books are red, yellow, blue, and orange, but the placement of these books has not been determined. The following is known about the placement of the books:

The red book is between the yellow and blue books.
The blue book is between the orange and red books.
The orange book is not fourth.

1. If the orange book could be fourth, then which one of the following can be deduced?

   (A) The red book is fourth.
   (B) The blue book is not third.
   (C) The red book is next to the orange book.
   (D) The blue book is next to the yellow book.
   (E) The yellow book is not second.

2. If a white book is added to the shelf, and the fourth book is not necessarily an orange book, then which one of the following is a possible order of the books?

   (A) yellow, red, orange, blue, white
   (B) white, yellow, blue, red, orange
   (C) yellow, red, blue, white, orange
   (D) orange, blue, red, yellow, white
   (E) blue, red, yellow, orange, white

3. Which one of the following pairs are next to each other on the shelf?

   (A) yellow and blue
   (B) blue and orange
   (C) yellow and orange
   (D) red and orange
   (E) No books are next to each other on the shelf.

4. If a green book were placed just to the left of the blue book, what position would it be in (counting from the left)?

   (A) first
   (B) second
   (C) third
   (D) fourth
   (E) fifth

Questions 5–13

A head counselor is choosing people to go on a hiking trip. The head counselor must choose from among three adult counselors (A, B, C) and nine campers (boys D, E, F, G, H, and girls J, K, L, M).

At least two adult counselors must go on the hike.
Camper D will not go without friends E and F.
Campers J and L will not hike together.
Camper M will not hike with counselor C.
There can never be more boy campers than girl campers.

5. If camper D is chosen for the hike

(A) camper L must be chosen
(B) camper J cannot be chosen
(C) camper L cannot be chosen
(D) camper G cannot be chosen
(E) camper H must be chosen

6. If camper K is NOT chosen for the hike

(A) camper G cannot be chosen
(B) camper H cannot be chosen
(C) camper E cannot be chosen
(D) camper D cannot be chosen
(E) camper L cannot be chosen

7. If camper D is chosen for the hike, which one of the following CANNOT be true?

(A) Camper H goes on the hike.
(B) Camper K goes on the hike.
(C) Counselor A goes on the hike.
(D) Counselor B goes on the hike.
(E) Camper M goes on the hike.

8. An acceptable combination of campers and counselors is

(A) ABCDEFJKM
(B) ABDEFJLM
(C) ABGHJKM
(D) ACDEFJK
(E) ACEFGKLM

9. If counselor A is NOT chosen for the hike, then

(A) camper D must be chosen
(B) camper D cannot be chosen
(C) camper J must be chosen
(D) camper L cannot be chosen
(E) camper F cannot be chosen

10. If counselor A is NOT chosen for the hike, then which one of the following must be true?

(A) If camper E is chosen, camper K must be chosen.
(B) If camper F is chosen, camper K must be chosen.
(C) Camper J cannot be chosen.
(D) Camper D cannot be chosen.
(E) If camper L is chosen, camper F must be chosen.

11. If camper D is chosen for the hike, which one of the following could represent the other hikers?

(A) ACEFJKM
(B) ABGHKML
(C) ABEFJKM
(D) ABFGJKL
(E) ACEFGKLM

12. What is the largest number of hikers that can go on the hike?

(A) 5
(B) 6
(C) 7
(D) 8
(E) 9

13. Which one of the following must be true?

(A) Campers K and M never hike together.
(B) Campers E and G never hike together.
(C) Campers D and G never hike together.
(D) Campers J and M never hike together.
(E) Campers D and M never hike together.

Questions 14–19

There are exactly six people waiting in line to buy tickets for a play. The names of the six people are Alexis, Brady, Hal, Len, Phyllis, and Sandy, not necessarily in that order. Their placement in line is governed by the following set of conditions:

   One person stands in each place in line, no people are side by side.
   Alexis is in front of Brady with more than one person separating them.
   Sandy is either the second, fourth, or sixth person in line.
   Phyllis is in front of Hal with exactly one person separating them.

14. If Brady is the next person in line behind Phyllis, then who could be the fifth person in line?

(A) Alexis
(B) Hal
(C) Len
(D) Phyllis
(E) Sandy

15. If Len is the second person in line, then which one of the following must be true?

(A) Alexis is the first person in line.
(B) Brady is the sixth person in line.
(C) Hal is the sixth person in line.
(D) Phyllis is the fifth person in line.
(E) Sandy is the fourth person in line.

16. Which person CANNOT be the person immediately in front of Sandy?

(A) Alexis
(B) Brady
(C) Hal
(D) Len
(E) Phyllis

17. Which of the following could be a list of the names of the people ordered from first in line to last in line?

(A) Len, Sandy, Alexis, Phyllis, Brady, Hal
(B) Phyllis, Alexis, Hal, Sandy, Brady, Len
(C) Alexis, Len, Sandy, Hal, Brady, Phyllis
(D) Phyllis, Hal, Alexis, Len, Brady, Sandy
(E) Brady, Sandy, Hal, Len, Phyllis, Alexis

18. If Sandy is the next person in line behind Phyllis, then who must be the third person in line?

(A) Alexis
(B) Brady
(C) Len
(D) Phyllis
(E) Sandy

19. Which one of the following is NOT a true statement?

(A) Alexis cannot be the third person in line.
(B) If Phyllis is the second person in line, then there is only one possible order of the six people in line.
(C) If Hal is the sixth person in line, then there is only one possible order of the six people in line.
(D) If Phyllis is the first person in line, then Len may be either the fourth, fifth, or sixth person in line.
(E) If Sandy is the sixth person in line, then Len must be either the second or fourth person in line.

Questions 20–26

The last names of six card players are Axelrod, Benton, Carlton, Dexter, Elliott, and Fellows. Three of the card players are male, and three are female. The six card players have formed three teams of two players each, comprised of one female and one male player. In an upcoming tournament, each team will play in one of exactly three rounds: first (earliest), second, and third (latest). The following conditions will apply for team composition and round of play:

Elliott will not play in the first or third rounds.

Dexter will not play in a later round than Axelrod.

Fellows, who is female, will play in a later round than Carlton, who is male.

20. If Elliott is female and Axelrod plays in an earlier round than Carlton, then which one of the following must be true?

(A) Axelrod is male.
(B) Benton is male.
(C) Carlton plays in the third round.
(D) Dexter is female.
(E) Fellows plays in the second round.

21. If Fellows plays in round 2, then which one of the following players could play in the round immediately following Dexter's round and be the same gender as Dexter?

(A) Axelrod
(B) Benton
(C) Carlton
(D) Elliott
(E) Fellows

22. Which one of the following is a complete and accurate list of the players, any one of whom could be female and playing in round 3?

(A) Axelrod, Benton, Carlton, and Fellows
(B) Alexrod, Benton, Dexter, and Fellows
(C) Axelrod, Dexter, and Fellows
(D) Benton and Dexter
(E) Elliott and Fellows

23. If Fellows plays in round 2, then which of the following could be two of the three female players?

(A) Axelrod and Benton
(B) Axelrod and Carlton
(C) Benton and Carlton
(D) Benton and Elliott
(E) Carlton and Dexter

24. If Carlton is the same gender as Axelrod and plays in the round immediately following Axelrod's round, then which one of the following must be true?

(A) Benton plays in the first round.
(B) Benton is the same gender as Elliott.
(C) Benton is female.
(D) Dexter plays in the first round.
(E) Dexter is male.

25. Which one of the following could be an accurate list of the male and female players listed in the round in which they will play?

	Round 1	Round 2	Round 3
(A) Male:	Benton	Axelrod	Carlton
Female:	Dexter	Elliott	Fellows
(B) Male:	Carlton	Dexter	Axelrod
Female:	Elliott	Benton	Fellows

(C) Male: Carlton   Elliott   Dexter
Female: Axelrod   Fellows   Benton

(D) Male: Dexter   Carlton   Benton
Female: Axelrod   Elliott   Fellows

(E) Male: Dexter   Carlton   Fellows
Female: Benton   Elliott   Axelrod

26. If Benton and Dexter are on the same team, then which of the following statements must be true?

(A) Axelrod and Carlton are on the same team.
(B) Axelrod and Fellows are on the same team.
(C) Carlton and Fellows are on the same team.
(D) Elliott is male.
(E) Fellows plays in a later round than Axelrod.

Questions 27–34

Four men, A, B, C, and D, and three women, E, F, and G, are auditioning for a new TV pilot. The director is deciding the order in which they should audition. Since many of the actors have other auditions to attend at different locations, the director must observe the following restrictions:

A must audition first or last.
D and E must audition consecutively, but not necessarily in that order.
Neither F nor G can audition last.
E cannot audition until B has auditioned.

27. Which one of the following must be true?

(A) F cannot audition first.
(B) D cannot audition first.
(C) B cannot audition first or second.
(D) A must audition before D auditions.
(E) G must audition second.

28. If A auditions first, which one of the following CANNOT be true?

(A) G auditions second.
(B) F auditions before B auditions.
(C) D auditions second.
(D) B auditions fifth.
(E) G auditions before B auditions.

29. If F and G audition first and second respectively, then which one of the following must be false?

(A) C auditions fourth.
(B) B auditions fourth.
(C) E auditions sixth.
(D) D auditions fifth.
(E) B auditions fifth.

30. Assume that B auditions first, and that F and G audition second and third respectively. Which one of the following must be false?

(A) E auditions sixth.
(B) C auditions fifth.
(C) D auditions fourth.
(D) C auditions sixth.
(E) E auditions fifth.

31. Suppose that D auditions ahead of E. If A auditions first and B auditions fifth, who must audition sixth?

(A) D
(B) E
(C) F
(D) G
(E) C

32. Which one of the following is a possible order of auditions?

(A) A, E, B, D, F, G, C
(B) A, B, D, E, C, F, G
(C) C, B, G, F, E, A, D
(D) B, F, G, D, E, C, A
(E) F, B, E, G, D, A, C

33. If the director decides NOT to audition two men consecutively, and if C auditions first, which one of the following must be true?

    (A) F auditions second.
    (B) G auditions second.
    (C) E auditions fifth.
    (D) D auditions fourth.
    (E) B auditions third.

34. Assume that all the women must audition consecutively. If F auditions third and G does NOT audition second, then which one of the following must be true?

    (A) A auditions first.
    (B) B auditions second.
    (C) C auditions seventh.
    (D) G auditions fifth.
    (E) D auditions sixth.

Questions 35–40

Eight weight lifters, Aaron, Bryan, Clifford, David, Ellen, Jason, Logan, and Prescott, have joined a local gym. No two of these lifters lift the same weight. The following statements describe the relative strength of the lifters:

   Ellen lifts more than Aaron.
   Bryan lifts less than Logan but more than Prescott.
   David lifts more than Logan.
   Jason lifts less than Aaron but more than Clifford.
   Logan lifts more than Jason.

35. Which one of the following statements must be true?

    (A) David lifts more than Jason.
    (B) Jason lifts more than Prescott.
    (C) Ellen lifts more than Bryan.
    (D) Clifford lifts more than Ellen.
    (E) Bryan lifts more than David.

36. If Prescott lifts more than Aaron, then which one of the following must be true?

    (A) Logan lifts more than Aaron.
    (B) Aaron lifts more than Bryan.
    (C) Ellen lifts more than Bryan.
    (D) David lifts more than Ellen.
    (E) Clifford lifts more than Logan.

37. If Aaron lifts more than David, what is the maximum number that can lift more than Logan?

    (A) 0
    (B) 1
    (C) 2
    (D) 3
    (E) 4

38. If five people lift less than Logan, then which one of the following must be true?

    (A) Bryan lifts more than Aaron.
    (B) Prescott lifts more than Aaron.
    (C) Clifford lifts more than Prescott.
    (D) Jason lifts more than David.
    (E) David lifts more than Aaron.

39. If Bryan lifts more than Aaron and Jason lifts more than Prescott, then who can lift more than Ellen?

    (A) Prescott, Bryan, Logan.
    (B) David, Prescott, Clifford.
    (C) Logan, Bryan, Prescott.
    (D) David, Logan, Jason.
    (E) Logan, David, Bryan.

40. If Prescott lifts more than Jason, then which one of the following must be false?

    (A) Bryan lifts more than Aaron.
    (B) Prescott lifts more than Ellen.
    (C) Ellen lifts more than David.
    (D) Aaron lifts more than Logan.
    (E) Bryan lifts more than David.

Questions 41–46

There are nine cans of soft drinks lined up on a shelf. The cans are numbered from 1 to 9, from left to right.

> The first and fourth are different brands of cola.
> The sixth and eighth are different brands of root beer.
> The second, fifth, sixth, seventh, and ninth are the only caffeine-free soft drinks.
> The second, third, fifth, seventh, and ninth cans contain sugar-free beverages.

41. How many of the cans of sugar-free beverages contain caffeine?

    (A) 0
    (B) 1
    (C) 2
    (D) 3
    (E) 4

42. In which one of the following places is a beverage that contains caffeine?

    (A) second
    (B) fourth
    (C) fifth
    (D) sixth
    (E) ninth

43. Which place contains a caffeine-free beverage that is not sugar free?

    (A) first
    (B) third
    (C) fourth
    (D) sixth
    (E) seventh

44. If someone randomly chose two cans of caffeine-free beverage, which places could they be?

    (A) second and third
    (B) fourth and fifth
    (C) third and seventh
    (D) sixth and ninth
    (E) eighth and ninth

45. How many cans of sweetened beverage are next to at least one can of caffeine-free beverage?

    (A) 0
    (B) 1
    (C) 2
    (D) 3
    (E) 4

46. If the two root beers were replaced with two cans of orange-flavored beverage containing caffeine, how many cans would contain either cola or caffeine but not both?

    (A) 0
    (B) 1
    (C) 2
    (D) 3
    (E) 4

Questions 47–50

Eight people—A, B, C, D, E, F, G, H—are to be seated at a square table, two people on each side.

> B must sit directly across from H.
> A must sit between and next to F and G.
> C cannot sit next to F.

47. Which one of the following must be true?

    (A) C sits next to either B or H.
    (B) H must sit next to G.
    (C) F sits next to D or E.

(D) A sits directly across from B.
(E) F sits directly across from C or D.

48. If B does not sit next to G, then which one of the following is NOT possible?

(A) If C sits next to B, then D could sit directly across from F.
(B) If C sits next to D, then E could sit directly across from G.
(C) C could sit next to G.
(D) If C sits next to H, then B could sit between D and E.
(E) If C sits next to B, then A could sit next to H.

49. If C sits directly across from F, who could NOT sit next to H?

(A) C
(B) D
(C) E
(D) G
(E) A

50. How many different people could be seated directly across from A?

(A) 1
(B) 2
(C) 3
(D) 4
(E) 5

Questions 51–56

The math department has three part-time instructors (Stephens, Walters, and York) and six full-time instructors (Enriquez, Fink, Hilmer, Nguyen, Petrello, and Roberts). Each full-time instructor evaluates at least one part-time instructor. The following conditions must apply:

Enriquez does not evaluate any part-time instructor evaluated by Fink.
Fink does not evaluate any part-time instructor evaluated by Nguyen.

Nguyen evaluates more part-time instructors than Petrello.
Enriquez evaluates fewer part-time instructors than Nguyen.
Stephens is evaluated by both Hilmer and Petrello.
Roberts does not evaluate Stephens or York.
No part-time instructor is evaluated by more than four full-time instructors.

51. Which one of the following statements must be true?

(A) Enriquez evaluates a part-time instructor evaluated by Hilmer.
(B) Fink evaluates a part-time instructor evaluated by Petrello.
(C) Hilmer evaluates a part-time instructor evaluated by Fink.
(D) Nguyen evaluates a part-time instructor evaluated by Enriquez.
(E) Nguyen evaluates a part-time instructor evaluated by Petrello.

52. Which one of the following could be a complete and accurate list of the full-time instructors who evaluate Stephens?

(A) Fink and Petrello
(B) Hilmer and Petrello
(C) Hilmer, Nguyen, and Roberts
(D) Hilmer, Nguyen, and Petrello
(E) Enriquez, Hilmer, and Petrello

53. Which one of the following could be a complete and accurate list of the full-time instructors who could evaluate York?

(A) Enriquez
(B) Hilmer
(C) Enriquez and Nguyen
(D) Enriquez and Fink
(E) Petrello and Roberts

54. If Fink does not evaluate Stephens, then which one of the following must be true?

(A) Enriquez evaluates Walters.
(B) Fink evaluates York.
(C) Hilmer evaluates Walters.
(D) Nguyen evaluates Stephens.
(E) Nguyen evaluates Walters.

55. If exactly four of the full-time instructors evaluate Walters, which one of the following could be true?

(A) Enriquez evaluates Stephens.
(B) Fink evaluates Walters.
(C) Hilmer does not evaluate Walters.
(D) Hilmer evaluates York.
(E) Nguyen does not evaluate Walters.

56. If the conditions are changed so that Roberts does not evaluate a part-time instructor, then which one of the following is a list of the full-time instructors, any one of whom could be the only evaluator of Walters?

(A) Enriquez and Fink
(B) Enriquez and Nguyen
(C) Fink and Hilmer
(D) Fink and Nguyen
(E) Hilmer and Nguyen

Questions 57–63

During a trip to a museum, Jilian and Mark each attend three historical lectures (D, E, and F) and three scientific lectures (R, S, and T). They do not attend the same lecture at the same time, although they both attend all six one-hour lectures. The lecture schedule must conform to the following conditions:

Mark must attend each scientific lecture prior to Jilian attending that same lecture.

Jilian must attend each historical lecture prior to Mark attending that same lecture.

Mark cannot attend two historical lectures consecutively.

Jilian must attend lecture T third.

57. Which one of the following could be true?

(A) Mark attends R fourth.
(B) Mark attends D fifth.
(C) Mark attends E first.
(D) Jilian attends T fifth.
(E) Jilian attends F fourth.

58. If Jilian attends E second and Mark attends D second, which one of the following must be true?

(A) Mark attends E fourth.
(B) Jilian attends F fourth.
(C) Mark attends S fifth.
(D) Mark attends F fourth.
(E) Jilian attends R sixth.

59. Which one of the following is an acceptable lecture schedule ordered from first to sixth?

(A) Jilian: D, E, T, R, S, F
    Mark: T, D, R, E, F, S
(B) Jilian: D, E, T, F, R, S
    Mark: R, T, E, S, D, F
(C) Jilian: E, S, D, T, F, R
    Mark: S, E, T, D, R, F
(D) Jilian: D, E, T, R, F, S
    Mark: T, D, R, F, S, E
(E) Jilian: D, E, T, F, R, S
    Mark: T, D, R, E, S, F

60. Which one of the following is a complete and accurate list of when Jilian must attend a historical lecture?

(A) first, second
(B) second, third
(C) first, second, fifth

(D) first, third, fourth
(E) first, fourth, fifth

61. If Mark attends lecture F fourth and Jilian attends lecture D first, which one of the following CANNOT be true?

(A) Mark attends lecture R before lecture F.
(B) Jilian attends lecture E after lecture R.
(C) Lecture R is the fifth lecture attended by Jilian.
(D) Lecture E is the second lecture attended by Mark.
(E) Lecture D is the second lecture attended by Mark.

62. Which one of the following must be true?

(A) Mark must attend lecture S fifth.
(B) Jilian cannot attend lectures D and E consecutively.
(C) Mark must attend lecture T first.
(D) Jilian must attend lecture R before Mark attends lecture F.
(E) Mark attends lecture S sixth.

63. If Mark attends lecture R third, then Jilian must attend which lecture sixth?

(A) D
(B) E
(C) F
(D) R
(E) S

Questions 64–69

Kevin, famous hairdresser to the stars, has scheduled eight one-hour appointments, one for each of his best customers: Arnie, Betah, Coco, Dodi, Elvis, Fetina, Greg, and Hector. Scheduling of appointments must conform to the following conditions:

Elvis is scheduled immediately before Dodi.
Fetina's appointment must be scheduled before Arnie's but after Greg's.
Fetina's appointment must be scheduled either 3rd or 7th.
Betah is scheduled 2nd only if Coco is scheduled 3rd or Arnie is scheduled 8th.

64. Which one of the following is an acceptable appointment schedule?

(A) B C G F E D A H
(B) E D B G C H F A
(C) H B C G E A F D
(D) H B F C G E D A
(E) G B F C E D A H

65. It would NOT be possible for Arnie to be scheduled

(A) 3rd
(B) 4th
(C) 5th
(D) 6th
(E) 7th

66. If Arnie is scheduled 6th and Hector is scheduled after Dodi, which one of the following could be true?

(A) Greg is scheduled 5th.
(B) Hector is scheduled 2nd.
(C) Betah is scheduled 7th.
(D) Dodi is scheduled 2nd.
(E) Coco is scheduled 4th.

67. If Hector is scheduled 8th and Coco is scheduled 7th, which one of the following must be true?

(A) Betah is scheduled 1st.
(B) Dodi is scheduled 5th.
(C) Greg is scheduled 1st.

(D) Elvis is scheduled 6th.
(E) Arnie is scheduled 6th.

68. If Betah is scheduled 2nd and Arnie is scheduled immediately after Coco, Hector could be scheduled

(A) 1st
(B) 3rd
(C) 4th
(D) 5th
(E) 7th

69. Which one of the following is NOT an acceptable schedule of appointments from 1st to 8th?

(A) G C F E D A B H
(B) H G F A B C E D
(C) B H C G E D F A
(D) G B F H A E D C
(E) H B C E D G F A

Questions 70–75

The eight members of the Political Action Club (numbered 1–8) are either Lawyers or Accountants. Each member is either a Democrat or a Republican. The club members are arranging the seating for a group portrait. The arrangement will be two rows with four in each row. The front row will consist of numbers 1–4 and the back row will consist of numbers 5–8 as follows:

1 2 3 4
5 6 7 8

Each Lawyer must sit adjacent to, in front of, or in back of another Lawyer.
Each Accountant must sit adjacent to, in front of, or in back of another Accountant.
Each Republican must sit adjacent to, in front of, or in back of another Republican.

Each Democrat must sit adjacent to, in front of, or in back of another Democrat.
Members 2 and 8 are Republicans.
Member 3 is an Accountant.
Member 5 is a Democrat.
Member 7 is a Lawyer.

70. If all the Lawyers are Democrats, which one of the following must be true?

(A) Member 3 is a Republican.
(B) Member 4 is a Lawyer.
(C) Member 5 is a Lawyer.
(D) Member 6 is a Democrat.
(E) Member 7 is a Republican.

71. In addition to member 5, it is possible that the only two Democrats among the remaining seven members are

(A) Members 1 and 7
(B) Members 3 and 6
(C) Members 3 and 7
(D) Members 4 and 6
(E) Members 6 and 7

72. If there are exactly three Accountants and five Lawyers, which one of the following must be true?

(A) Member 1 is a Lawyer.
(B) Member 2 is a Lawyer.
(C) Member 4 is a Lawyer.
(D) Member 5 is a Lawyer.
(E) Member 6 is a Lawyer.

73. Which one of the following could be true?

(A) Members 1 and 4 are two of exactly four Lawyers.
(B) Members 1 and 6 are two of exactly four Republicans.
(C) Members 4 and 6 are two of exactly four Accountants.

(D) Members 4 and 7 are two of
exactly four Democrats.
(E) Members 5 and 7 are two of
exactly four Republicans.

74. What is the maximum number of
Democrats in the club?

(A) two
(B) three
(C) four
(D) five
(E) six

75. If there are four Republicans and four
Democrats in the club and exactly one
of the four Republicans is an
Accountant, which one of the
following CANNOT be true?

(A) Member 2 is a Lawyer.
(B) Member 3 is a Republican.
(C) Member 4 is an Accountant.
(D) Member 6 is a Republican.
(E) Member 6 is a Democrat.

Questions 76–80

In the Game of Bobcat, a player must
assign his eight pieces to either the left
flank or the right flank. The eight pieces are
named the King, the Queen, the Squire, the
Cornerman, the Runner, the Goalie, the
Boxman, and the Pawn. Assignment to
each flank must satisfy the following
conditions:

The right flank requires at least four
pieces.
The Pawn is always placed on the left
flank.
The King and the Boxman cannot be
placed on the same flank.
The Runner and the Squire cannot be
placed on the same flank.
The King and the Cornerman must be
placed on the same flank.

76. Which one of the following could be a
complete and accurate list of the
pieces placed on the right flank?

(A) Goalie, King, Runner, Squire
(B) Cornerman, King, Queen, Squire
(C) Cornerman, Runner, King, Queen,
Squire
(D) Boxman, Cornerman, King, Squire
(E) Boxman, Goalie, Runner

77. Which one of the following is a list of
all the pieces that could be placed on
the left flank at the same time?

(A) Cornerman, King, Pawn
(B) Boxman, King, Pawn, Squire
(C) Goalie, King, Pawn, Runner
(D) Boxman, Runner, Pawn
(E) Boxman, Goalie, Queen, Squire

78. If the Boxman is placed on the right
flank, then which one of the following
pieces must be placed on the left
flank?

(A) Squire
(B) Runner
(C) Queen
(D) Goalie
(E) Cornerman

79. If the Goalie and the Queen are placed
on the same flank, which one of the
following pieces must be placed on
the right flank?

(A) Cornerman
(B) Goalie
(C) King
(D) Runner
(E) Squire

80. If the King and the Cornerman do NOT have to be placed on the same flank, then which one of the following could be a list of all pieces placed on the right flank?

(A) Boxman, Cornerman, Goalie, Queen, Runner
(B) Boxman, Cornerman, Goalie, Runner, Squire
(C) Boxman, Goalie, King, Queen, Runner
(D) Cornerman, Goalie, King, Queen
(E) Cornerman, Goalie, Queen, Squire

Questions 81–86

Larry's exercise program consists of three aerobic dances, two free weight exercises, and two treadmill routines. Larry performs the aerobic dances (the Bounce, the Glide, the Hop) consecutively, but not necessarily in order; the free weight exercises (the Press, the Curl) consecutively, but not necessarily in order; and the treadmill routines (Speed, Endurance) consecutively, but not necessarily in order. The seven-exercise program is performed subject to the following conditions:

The free weight exercises are not performed first.
The free weight exercises are not performed last.
In the aerobic dances, Larry does the Glide before the Hop.
On the treadmill, Larry does the Speed routine before the Endurance routine.

81. Which one of the following CANNOT be an acceptable list of the exercises Larry performed second, third, and fourth, respectively?

(A) Bounce, Hop, Press
(B) Endurance, Press, Curl

(C) Glide, Bounce, Curl
(D) Glide, Hop, Curl
(E) Glide, Hop, Press

82. It is NOT possible that Larry performs the Glide dance

(A) first
(B) second
(C) third
(D) fifth
(E) sixth

83. Which one of the following statements CANNOT be true?

(A) Larry does the Bounce dance first.
(B) Larry does the Bounce dance second.
(C) Larry does the Endurance routine second.
(D) Larry does the Endurance routine third.
(E) Larry does the Speed routine first.

84. If Larry performed a free weight exercise and performed the Glide dance consecutively, but not necessarily in that order, then which one of the following statements must be false?

(A) He performed the Bounce dance before the Endurance routine.
(B) He performed the Bounce dance before the Hop dance.
(C) He performed the Curl exercise before the Glide dance.
(D) He performed the Endurance routine before the Press exercise.
(E) He performed the Hop dance before the Bounce dance.

85. If Larry does the Bounce dance immediately after the Hop dance, then which one of the following statements could be true?

    (A) Larry does the Endurance routine third.
    (B) Larry does the Endurance routine sixth.
    (C) Larry does the Endurance routine seventh.
    (D) Larry does the Glide dance second.
    (E) Larry does the Glide dance third.

86. Which one of the following statements could be true?

    (A) Larry does the Glide dance second.
    (B) Larry does the Glide dance seventh.
    (C) Larry does the Speed routine second.
    (D) Larry does the Speed routine third.
    (E) Larry does the Speed routine fourth.

Questions 87–91

State College offers the following courses for first-year students: languages (French, German, Italian), sciences (biology, chemistry, physics), and mathematics (algebra, statistics, trigonometry). Each student must enroll in exactly five of the courses, subject to the following conditions:

    Not more than two math classes may be taken.
    If physics is taken, then algebra cannot be taken.
    If algebra is taken, then Italian must be taken.
    Chemistry may be taken only if both trigonometry and French are taken.
    If both German and biology are taken, then statistics cannot be taken.
    Exactly one language must be taken.

87. Which one of the following could be a list of the five courses taken by a first-year student at State College?

    (A) algebra, trigonometry, French, Italian, physics
    (B) statistics, trigonometry, Italian, biology, physics
    (C) algebra, statistics, French, Italian, chemistry
    (D) algebra, statistics, trigonometry, French, chemistry
    (E) statistics, trigonometry, German, biology, physics

88. If a first-year student at State College takes statistics, which one of the following pairs of courses may also be taken?

    (A) Italian, chemistry
    (B) algebra, German
    (C) German, chemistry
    (D) algebra, French
    (E) chemistry, physics

89. Which of the following could be a list of three of the courses taken by a first-year student at State College?

    (A) algebra, French, biology
    (B) algebra, Italian, physics
    (C) statistics, German, chemistry
    (D) statistics, chemistry, physics
    (E) trigonometry, German, chemistry

90. Other than the language course, which of the following could be a list of the courses taken by a first-year student at State College?

    (A) algebra, statistics, biology, chemistry
    (B) algebra, biology, chemistry, physics

(C) algebra, statistics, trigonometry, physics

(D) trigonometry, biology, chemistry, physics

(E) statistics, biology, chemistry, physics

91. If a first-year student at State College takes Italian, which of the following pairs of courses must also be taken?

(A) German, biology

(B) biology, physics

(C) statistics, chemistry

(D) biology, chemistry

(E) algebra, French

Questions 92–97

On the sixth floor of an office building there are eight offices in a row, numbered from 1 to 8. Five custodians are employed to clean these eight offices. They are Alisa, Bart, Clyde, Drew, and Ethel. The maximum number of offices that can be cleaned by one custodian is two. Each office is cleaned by only one custodian. The following conditions govern the cleaning assignments:

Bart and Clyde are the only two custodians assigned to clean only one office each.

Alisa does not clean the office at either end of the row of offices.

One of the offices cleaned by Ethel is adjacent to both of the offices cleaned by Alisa.

The lower numbered office cleaned by Ethel is numbered higher than the office cleaned by Bart.

Office 7 has been assigned to Ethel.

92. If Drew cleans office 2, which one of the following CANNOT be true?

(A) Bart cleans office 1.

(B) Clyde cleans office 3.

(C) Alisa cleans office 6.

(D) Ethel cleans office 4.

(E) Drew cleans office 4.

93. Which one of the following is true about the cleaning assignment for office 4?

(A) The office is not cleaned by Alisa or Clyde.

(B) The office is not cleaned by Clyde or Ethel.

(C) The office is not cleaned by Bart or Drew.

(D) The office is not cleaned by Alisa or Drew.

(E) The office is not cleaned by Drew or Ethel.

94. Which one of the following represents a complete and accurate list of the offices that could be cleaned by Drew?

(A) 1, 2, 3, 5, 6

(B) 1, 2, 3, 5, 6, 8

(C) 1, 2, 4, 8

(D) 1, 2, 4, 6, 8

(E) 2, 3, 4, 5, 6, 8

95. Consecutive offices could be cleaned by which one of the following custodians?

(A) Alisa

(B) Bart

(C) Clyde

(D) Drew

(E) Ethel

96. Which one of the following represents a complete and accurate list of custodians who could clean office 6?

(A) Alisa, Clyde, Drew

(B) Bart, Clyde, Ethel

(C) Alisa, Bart, Clyde, Ethel

(D) Clyde, Drew, Ethel

(E) Alisa, Clyde, Drew, Ethel

97. If both end offices are cleaned by Drew, and Alisa and Clyde clean consecutive offices, which one of the following must be true?

    (A) Alisa cleans office 6.
    (B) Bart and Clyde clean consecutive offices.
    (C) Clyde cleans an even-numbered office.
    (D) Both of Alisa's offices are numbered lower than Clyde's.
    (E) Bart cleans office 2.

Questions 98–104

The Raxmeyers have seven daughters, each born two years apart. Their ages are 7, 9, 11, 13, 15, 17, and 19. Their names are Hilda, Ida, Joy, Kim, Loren, Marsha, and Nicole. The following conditions must be met:

> Joy is older than Marsha.
> Hilda is older than Loren but younger than Ida.
> Either Ida or Loren is 13 years old.
> Nicole is younger than Joy.
> The difference in ages between Marsha and Nicole is at least three years.

98. Which one of the following must be true?

    (A) Hilda is the oldest.
    (B) Kim is older than Joy.
    (C) Hilda is younger than Joy.
    (D) Ida is older than Loren.
    (E) Marsha is older than Loren.

99. If Loren is four years younger than Ida, then which one of the following could be true?

    (A) Marsha is 9 years old.
    (B) Hilda is 17 years old.
    (C) Joy is 15 years old.

    (D) Hilda is 9 years old.
    (E) Joy is 19 years old.

100. Which one of the following could be the order of the ages of the seven daughters from youngest to oldest?

    (A) L, H, K, I, M, N, J
    (B) M, H, N, L, J, I, K
    (C) N, K, M, L, H, I, J
    (D) M, L, N, H, I, J, K
    (E) L, M, H, I, J, N, K

101. If Ida is older than Joy, then how many different possible orders are there for the ages of the seven daughters?

    (A) three
    (B) four
    (C) five
    (D) six
    (E) seven

102. Which one of the following could be true?

    (A) Kim is two years older than Hilda.
    (B) Joy is two years younger than Marsha.
    (C) Loren is two years younger than Kim.
    (D) Joy is two years older than Hilda.
    (E) Hilda is two years older than Kim.

103. All of the following could be true EXCEPT:

    (A) If Loren is 13 years old, then Marsha is 7 years old.
    (B) If Hilda is 15 years old, then Nicole is 7 years old.
    (C) If Ida is 13 years old, then Kim is 7 years old.
    (D) If Ida is 17 years old, then Kim is 9 years old.
    (E) If Hilda is 11 years old, then Marsha is 7 years old.

104. If Kim is older than Joy, then Ida must be

(A) 9 years old
(B) 11 years old
(C) 13 years old
(D) 15 years old
(E) 17 years old

Questions 105–109

Seven friends—Paul, Ron, Sam, Tom, Victor, Willard, and Zack—are having dinner together. Each orders one of two possible starters, soup or salad, but not both. The following conditions must be satisfied:

If Tom orders salad, then Willard orders soup.
If Tom orders soup, then Ron orders salad.
If Zack orders soup, then Paul orders salad.
If Paul orders salad, then Willard orders salad.
If Victor orders salad, then Willard orders soup.
If Sam orders soup, then Tom orders soup.
If Zack orders soup, then Victor orders salad.
If Victor orders salad, then Ron orders soup.

105. If Victor orders salad, then which one of the following must be true?

(A) Willard orders salad.
(B) Sam orders soup.
(C) Zack orders soup.
(D) Paul orders salad.
(E) Tom orders salad.

106. If Paul and Tom have the same starter, each of the following could be true EXCEPT:

(A) Zack and Victor order different starters.
(B) Victor and Willard order different starters.
(C) Tom and Victor order different starters.
(D) Willard and Sam order different starters.
(E) Sam and Ron order different starters.

107. Which one of the following pairs of friends together must order at least one soup?

(A) Sam and Tom
(B) Paul and Victor
(C) Tom and Zack
(D) Sam and Ron
(E) Paul and Willard

108. If Ron orders soup, then which one of the following must be true?

(A) Tom orders soup.
(B) Victor orders salad.
(C) Zack orders soup.
(D) Paul orders soup
(E) Willard orders salad.

109. What is the maximum number of friends who could order soup?

(A) two
(B) three
(C) four
(D) five
(E) six

ANSWER KEY

1. E	29. E	57. E	85. C
2. D	30. B	58. A	86. A
3. B	31. A	59. E	87. B
4. B	32. D	60. A	88. E
5. D	33. E	61. D	89. D
6. D	34. E	62. C	90. D
7. A	35. A	63. E	91. B
8. C	36. A	64. B	92. E
9. B	37. D	65. A	93. C
10. D	38. E	66. C	94. B
11. C	39. E	67. A	95. D
12. D	40. E	68. C	96. A
13. C	41. B	69. D	97. E
14. B	42. B	70. D	98. D
15. A	43. D	71. E	99. E
16. D	44. D	72. D	100. C
17. B	45. E	73. C	101. B
18. D	46. D	74. C	102. C
19. E	47. A	75. B	103. C
20. B	48. E	76. B	104. C
21. E	49. E	77. D	105. E
22. B	50. C	78. E	106. C
23. A	51. D	79. B	107. B
24. D	52. D	80. A	108. D
25. D	53. C	81. C	109. D
26. B	54. D	82. C	
27. B	55. D	83. D	
28. C	56. D	84. A	

ANSWER EXPLANATIONS

Answers 1–4

By following statements 1–3, you could have made these two possible orders:

Y R B O or O B R Y

but statement 4 eliminates the first order, Y R B O.

1. **E** From statements 2 and 3, the red and blue books are between other books; thus, they cannot be first or fourth. Therefore, they are second and third. This leaves first and fourth positions for the orange and yellow books.

2. **D** Orange, blue, red, yellow, white is a possible order. Notice that each of the other orders could have been eliminated because each broke an initial statement:
   (A) Orange and blue are switched.
   (B) Blue and red are switched.
   (C) White must be on an end since the other four must be next to each other.
   (E) Blue cannot be on an end.

3. **B** This follows the order discovered from the initial conditions, YRBO.

4. **B** Because the blue book was in the second position, it will move to the third position, and the green book will take the second.

Answers 5–13

Drawing the simple diagram, below, will help answer the questions.

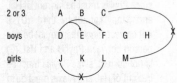

5. **D** If camper D is chosen, then campers E and F are also chosen. Thus three boys have been picked to go on the hike. Note that three girls, at most, can go on the hike. Since boys cannot outnumber girls, no other boys can be chosen.

6. **D** If camper K is not chosen, the maximum number of girls chosen can be two. Therefore, since boys cannot outnumber girls, D cannot be chosen, since selecting D means also selecting two more boys, E and F.

7. **A** If camper D is chosen, then boys E and F are also chosen. Since the maximum number of girls chosen can be three, no other boys may be chosen, since boys may not outnumber girls.

8. **C** Choices (A) and (E) include both C and M, which is not permitted. Choice (B) includes J and L, who will not hike together. In choice (D), boys outnumber girls, which is not permitted. Only choice (C) is an acceptable combination of campers and counselors.

9. **B** If counselor A is not chosen for the hike, then counselors B and C are chosen as there must be at least two counselors on the hike. Since counselor C is chosen, camper M (a girl) cannot be chosen. Therefore, the maximum number of girls on the hike can be two. Since boys cannot outnumber girls, D cannot be chosen, since selecting D would mean also selecting E and F, a total of three boys.

10. **D** If counselor A is not chosen, then counselors B and C will be chosen as there must be at least two counselors on the hike. If counselor C is chosen, camper M cannot be chosen, leaving the maximum number of girls possible on the hike at two. Therefore, since boys may not outnumber girls, D cannot be chosen

as choosing D would mean also selecting E and F, thus outnumbering the girls.

11. **C** Choices (A) and (E) included both C and M, which is not permitted. Choices (B) and (D) do not include camper E, who must accompany camper D. Only choice (C) includes acceptable companions for a hike with camper D.

12. **D** The largest number of hikers that can go on the hike is eight, as follows: three boys, three girls, and counselors A and B. (Example: A, B, D, E, F, J, K, M)

13. **C** The maximum number of girls possible for the hike is three. Therefore, since choosing camper D means also choosing campers E and F, no other boys (for instance, G) can be chosen, as boys would then outnumber girls.

Answers 14–19

The conditions are summarized as follows:

	1	A	P
S?	2	*	*
	3	* (2 or more)	H
S?	4	B	
	5		
S?	6		

14. **B** If Brady is behind Phyllis, then there are only two possible arrangements for Phyllis, Brady, and Hal.

1	Alexis	Alexis
2	Sandy	Sandy or Len
3	Len	Phyllis
4	Phyllis	Brady
5	Brady	Hal
6	Hal	Len or Sandy

The possible candidates for the fifth person in line are Brady and Hal. Since Brady is not one of the choices, it must be Hal.

15. **A** If Len is second, Alexis must be first. If Alexis was third, then Brady would be sixth, Phyllis and Hal would be second and fourth, and there would be no place for Sandy. Hal cannot be sixth because Phyllis would then be fourth, and there would be no place for Sandy. Phyllis cannot be fifth because there would be no place for Hal. The other choices MAY be true, but they do not have to be, as shown in the following arrangement.

1	Alexis
2	Len
3	Phyllis
4	Brady/Sandy
5	Hal
6	Sandy/Brady

16. **D** Sandy must be either second, fourth, or sixth. If Len were immediately in front of Sandy, there would not be enough spaces left to accommodate the other people properly as shown:

1	Len	*	Alexis
2	Sandy	*	*
3	Alexis	Len	*
4	*	Sandy	Brady
5	*	*	Len
6	Brady	*	Sandy

17. **B** (A) is not correct, since there must be at least two people between Alexis and Brady. (C) is not correct, since Phyllis must be in front of Hal, and Sandy cannot be third. (D) is not correct, since there must be one person between Phyllis and Hal. (E) is not correct, since Phyllis must be in front of Hal, and Alexis must be in front of Brady. (B) is a possible ordering of the people.

18. **D** If Sandy is the next person in line behind Phyllis, then Sandy is be-

tween Phyllis and Hal. This means Sandy cannot be sixth. Remember, Sandy must be second, fourth, or sixth. If Sandy were second, then Phyllis would be first, and Hal would be third. This would result in only one person between Alexis and Brady. Therefore, Sandy must be fourth. This implies that Phyllis is the third person in line.

1	Alexis or Len
2	Len or Alexis
3	Phyllis
4	Sandy
5	Hal
6	Brady

19. **E** (A) is a true statement. If Alexis were third, then Brady would have to be sixth. Since Sandy must then be second or fourth, this leaves no room for Phyllis and Hal. (B) is a true statement. If Phyllis is second, Hal would be fourth, and Sandy would be sixth. Also, Alexis would have to be first, and Brady would have to be fifth. This implies that Len must be third. (C) is a true statement. If Hal is sixth, then Phyllis must be fourth. This implies that Sandy must be second. Then Alexis must be first and Brady fifth. This leaves Len third. (D) is a true statement. If Phyllis is first, then Hal is third and Alexis is second. Len can be either fourth, fifth, or sixth. (E) is NOT a true statement. If Sandy is sixth, Len MAY be second or fourth, but Len COULD be third.

1	Alexis	Alexis	Phyllis	Alexis
2	Phyllis	Sandy	Alexis	Phyllis
3	Len	Len	Hal	Len
4	Hal	Phyllis	Len or Sandy or Brady	Hal
5	Brady	Brady	Sandy or Brady or Len	Brady
6	Sandy	Hal	Sandy or Len or Brady	Sandy

Answers 20–26

The conditions lead to the following:

"Fellows, who is female, will play in a later round than Carlton, who is male" can be illustrated as:

$$\text{Male—C} \qquad \text{C} \leftarrow \text{F}$$
$$\text{Female—F}$$

So C can play in round 1 or 2, and F can play in round 2 or 3. But if C plays in 2, then F plays in 3.

"Dexter will not play in a later round than Axelrod" can be illustrated as:

$$\leftarrow \text{D}$$
$$\text{A}$$

"Elliott will not play in the first or third rounds," so Elliott plays in round 2 and can be illustrated in the complete display as follows:

				F̶		C̶
				E̶	E	E̶
Male—C	C ← F			1	2	3
Female—F		Male		_	_	_
← D		Female		_	_	_
A						

Notice that since Fellows plays in a later round than Carlton, Fellows cannot play in round 1, and Carlton cannot play in round 3.

20. **B** If Elliott is female and plays in the second round, then Fellows, who is female and plays in the second or third round, must play in the third round. If Fellows plays in the third round, then Carlton must play in the second round. If Axelrod plays in an earlier round than Carlton, then Axelrod and Dexter must play in the first round. Thus, Benton must be male and plays in the third round. Axelrod could be male, and Dexter could be female, or vice versa.

	1	2	3
Male:	A/D	C	B
Female:	D/A	E	F

21. **E** If Fellows, who is female, plays in the second round, then Elliott, who also plays in the second round, must be male. If Fellows plays in the second round, then Carlton, who plays in an earlier round than Fellows, must play in the first round. If someone follows Dexter, then Dexter cannot play in the third round. Therefore, Dexter must be female and play in the first round. Thus, Fellows is the same gender as Dexter and plays in the round immediately following Dexter.

	1	2	3
Male:	C	E	A/B
Female:	D	F	B/A

22. **B** The right answer cannot include Elliott, since Elliott plays in round 2. Eliminate (E). The right answer cannot include Carlton because he is a male and cannot play in the third round. Eliminate (A). Each of the other players (Axelrod, Benton, Dexter, and Fellows) could be female and play in the third round as illustrated in the following four possible diagrams:

	1	2	3
Male:	C	E	B
Female:	D	F	**A**

	1	2	3
Male:	C	E	A
Female:	D	F	**B**

	1	2	3
Male:	C	E	A
Female:	B	F	**D**

	1	2	3
Male:	A	C	B
Female:	D	E	**F**

23. **A** The answer cannot be (B), (C), or (E), since Carlton is male. If Fellows, who is female, plays in round 2, then Elliot, who also plays in round 2, must be male. Therefore, (D) cannot be correct. Both Axelrod and Benton could be female.

24. **D** Carlton, who is male, can only play in round 1 or 2. If Axelrod is the same gender as Carlton and plays in a round preceding Carlton, then Axelrod is male and plays in round 1, with Carlton playing in round 2. Since Elliott plays in round 2, Elliot must be female. If Carlton is playing in round 2, then Fellows, who follows Carlton, is female and plays in round 3. If Axelrod plays in round 1, so must Dexter. Benton must then be male playing in round 3. (D) is the only accurate choice.

	1	2	3
Male:	A	C	B
Female:	D	E	F

25. **D** (A) is not correct, since Carlton must play in an earlier round than Fellows. (B) is not correct, since Elliott plays in round 2. (C) is not correct, since Axelrod, playing in round 1, would imply that Dexter plays in round 1 also. (E) is not correct, since Fellows is female.

26. **B** If Benton and Dexter play on the same team, then they cannot play in the second round, since Elliott is playing in the second round. Benton and Dexter cannot play in the third round, since that would imply that Fellows must play in round 2, forcing Axelrod into round 1. If Axelrod plays in round 1, then so must Dexter. Therefore, Benton and Dexter must play in round 1. Carlton, who cannot play in round 3, must play in round 2. Thus, Elliott is female. Since Fellows must play in round 2 or 3, Fellows must play in round 3. Therefore, Axelrod is male and plays in round 3. Thus, (B) is correct.

	1	2	3
Male:	B/D	C	A
Female:	D/B	E	F

Answers 27–34

From the information given, you could have constructed a diagram similar to this:

Notice the information listed off to the side of the diagram.

27. **B** D cannot audition first since D and E have to audition consecutively, and B must audition before E.

28. **C** If A auditions first, then D cannot audition second because B must audition before E, and therefore also before D.

29. **E** If F and G audition first and second respectively, then A must audition last and the diagram for this question would look like this:

```
F  G                    A
1  2  3  4  5  6  7
```

Therefore, A must audition last and B cannot audition fifth (no room for D and E to follow B). C could possibly audition fourth.

30. **B** If B auditions first, and F and G audition second and third respectively, then A must audition last and the diagram for this question would look like this:

```
B  F  G              A
1  2  3  4  5  6  7
```

Therefore, E auditions sixth could be true. C auditions fifth must be false because D and E must be next to each other. If C was fifth, he would split D and E. D auditions fourth could be true.

31. **A** If D auditions ahead of E, and if A auditions first and B fifth, then the diagram for this question would look like this:

```
A              B  D  E
1  2  3  4  5  6  7
```

Since B auditions fifth, then D must be sixth and E seventh.

32. **D** This question is most easily answered by eliminating the orders that are not possible. Choice (A) can be eliminated because E is ahead of B and not next to D. Choice (B) can be eliminated because G cannot audition last. Choices (C) and (A) can be eliminated because A is not first or last.

33. **E** From the new information given, men cannot audition consecutively; the diagram for this question would now look like this:

```
C     B     D     A
1  2  3  4  5  6  7
```

Therefore, B must audition third.

34. **E** If F auditions third and all the women must audition consecutively, then G must audition next to

F, since E must be next to D. The diagram for this question would now look like this:

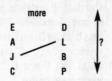

```
        F  G  E  D
1  2   3  4  5  6  7
   X
   X
```

Therefore, D must audition sixth.

Answers 35–40

The following diagram may prove helpful:

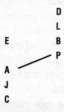

```
      more
   E        D        ↑
   A        L        ?
   J        B
   C        P        ↓
```

35. **A** Because David lifts more than Logan and Logan lifts more than Jason, David lifts more than Jason. Prescott and Bryan lift less than Logan, but we cannot say anything about their relationship to Jason. It is possible for Prescott to lift more than Ellen.

36. **A** Logan lifts more than Prescott. If Prescott lifts more than Aaron, so must Logan.

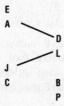

```
         D
         L
   E     B
         P
   A
   J
   C
```

37. **D** If Aaron lifts more than David, then Aaron, Ellen, and David each lift more than Logan.

```
   E
   A
         D
         L
   J
   C     B
         P
```

38. **E** If five people lift less than Logan, they must be Bryan, Prescott, Clifford, Jason, and Aaron. Thus, David and Ellen lift more than Logan, therefore, David lifts more than Aaron. Answer (C) may be true, but doesn't have to be.

```
         D
   E     L
   A     B
   J     P
   C
```

39. **E** Given these additional facts, we can redraw the diagram as follows:

```
         D     ↑
   E     L
         B
   A
   J
   C     P     ↓
```

You know that Aaron, Jason, and Clifford must lift less than Ellen. Since Prescott lifts less than Jason (and Jason lifts less than Ellen), Prescott must lift less than Ellen as well. That leaves only Bryan, David, and Logan as lifters who could lift more than Ellen.

40. **E** From the diagram, all of the following could be true:

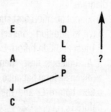

```
   E     D     ↑
         L
   A     B     ?
         P
   J
   C
```

From the diagram, you know that D > L > B > P > J > C and E > A > J > C. The question asks for an answer that must be false, so you can eliminate answers that could be true. Choice (A) could be either true or false since you cannot connect the two different sequences. Similarly, choices (B), (C), and (D) ask you to make connections between the two different sequences. However, choice (E) is false, since you know for certain that David lifts more than Bryan.

Answers 41–46
Use this organizer to show these relationships:

	1	2	3	4	5	6	7	8	9
Flavor	C		C		RB		RB		
Caffeinated		CF			CF	CF	CF		CF
Sweetened		SF	SF		SF		SF		SF

41. **B** It can be inferred from condition 3 that the drinks are either caffeinated or caffeine free. The sugar-free drinks are in positions 2, 3, 5, 7, and 9. Of those drinks, since positions 2, 5, 7, and 9 are caffeine free, the remaining drink in position 3 contains caffeine, answer choice (B).

42. **B** Since the beverages in positions 2, 5, 6, 7, and 9 are caffeine free (condition 3), the remaining positions 1, 3, 4, and 8 contain caffeine. The only answer choice that matches the caffeine-free positions is (B), the fourth position.

43. **D** The caffeine-free beverages are in positions 2, 5, 6, 7, and 9. By referring to the organizer, it can be seen that they are all sugar free except the sixth position, answer choice (D).

44. **D** The only drinks that are caffeine free are in positions 2, 5, 6, 7, and 9. The only answer choice that includes only these choices is the sixth and ninth positions, answer choice (D).

45. **E** The sweetened drinks are the cola, positions 1 and 4, and root beer, positions 6 and 8. The drinks that are caffeine free are positions 2, 5, 6, 7, and 9. Each of the sweetened drinks are next to at least one caffeine-free drink. 1 is next to 2, 4 is next to 5, 6

is next to both 5 and 7, and 8 is next to both 7 and 9. The correct answer is four drinks, answer choice (E).

46. **D** For this question, change the RBs to Os and delete the CF from position 6:

	1	2	3	4	5	6	7	8	9
Flavor	C			C		O		O	
Caffeinated		CF			CF		CF		CF
Sweetened		SF	SF		SF		SF		SF

From the new table, the drinks that are colas are positions 1 and 4. The drinks that contain caffeine are positions 1, 3, 4, 6, and 8. Since drinks 1 and 4 are both cola and contain caffeine, they will not meet the conditions. This leaves positions 3, 6, and 8, or three drinks, answer choice (D).

Answers 47–50
From the information given, it would be helpful to construct a diagram to answer the questions.
NOTE: When more than one letter appears at a seat, those letters represent all the possible occupants of that seat.

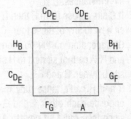

47. **A** From the diagram, C must sit next to B or H; therefore (A) is true. Taking a second look at the diagram, we can see that H doesn't have to sit next to G, and F doesn't have to sit next to D or E. Therefore, (B) and (C) are not necessarily true. Also, (D) is false since H sits directly across from B. Statement (E) is false since F could sit across from E.

48. **E** If B does not sit next to G, then we should adjust the diagram as follows:

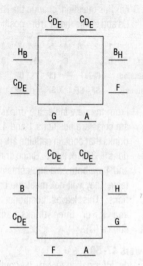

From these diagrams, we see that all statements are possible except (E). Since A sits between G and F, A cannot sit next to H under any circumstances.

49. **E** If C sits across from F, then H could sit next to any of these four (C, D, E, G) depending on the positions of B and H. A cannot sit next to H since A sits between G and F.

50. **C** B and H can't, since they must sit opposite each other. F and G can't, since they must sit next to A. That leaves only C, D, and E.

Answers 51–56

The five conditions may be summarized as follows:

E̶F̶   Enriquez does not evaluate any part-time instructor evaluated by Fink.

N̶F̶   Fink does not evaluate any part-time instructor evaluated by Nguyen.

N > P   Nguyen evaluates more part-time instructors than Petrello.

N > E   Enriquez evaluates fewer part-time instructors than Nguyen.

S   W   Y
P   R   Stephens is evaluated by both
H   Hilmer and Petrello.
            Roberts does not evaluate Stephens or York, so Roberts must evaluate Walters.

Nguyen cannot evaluate all three part-time instructors since Fink must evaluate at least one and does not evaluate any part-time instructor evaluated by Nguyen. Since Nguyen evaluates more part-time instructors than Petrello and Enriquez, Nguyen evaluates two part-time instructors and Petrello, Enriquez, and Fink each evaluate one part-time instructor. Hilmer evaluates at least one part-time instructor. Since Roberts does not evaluate Stephens or York, Roberts must evaluate only Walters. This information may be summarized as follows:

$N = 2$ $E = 1$ $F = 1$ $P = 1$ $H = 1, 2,$ or 3 $R = 1$

With the information above in mind, your working display would look like this:

S   W   Y
P   R   E̶F̶   N̶F̶
H

51. **D** Nguyen evaluates two part-time instructors ($N = 2$). Since Fink and Enriquez do not evaluate the same part-time instructor ($E \neq F$), Nguyen must evaluate the same part-time instructor as either Enriquez or Fink. Since Nguyen and Fink do not evaluate the same part-time instructor ($N \neq F$), Nguyen must evaluate a part-time instructor evaluated by Enriquez. The correct choice is (D). The following two diagrams illustrate possible arrangements show-

ing that the other choices do not have to be true.

S	W	Y		S	W	Y
P	R	E		P	R	N
H	F	N		H	N	E
N					F	

52. **D** (A) is not correct, since Hilmer is not included in the list. (B) is not correct, since if Hilmer and Petrello are the only two full-time instructors that evaluate Stephens, then Nguyen must evaluate the other two part-time instructors. Fink must also evaluate one of the other two part-time instructors, and Nguyen and Fink do not evaluate the same part-time instructor; therefore, there is a contradiction. (C) is not correct, since Petrello is not included in the list and Roberts is. (E) is not correct, since if only Hilmer, Petrello, and Enriquez evaluate Stephens, then Nguyen must evaluate the other two part-time instructors. This leaves Fink to evaluate the same part-time instructor as Nguyen, which contradicts the original conditions. (D) is the correct choice.

S	W	Y
P	R	F
H	E	
N	N	

53. **C** (A) is accurate but not complete. (B) is not correct, since Hilmer evaluates Stephens. (D) is not correct, since Enriquez and Fink do not evaluate the same part-time instructor. (E) is not correct, since Petrello evaluates Stephens, and Roberts only evaluates Walter. The correct answer is (C). The fact that Nguyen also evaluates Stephens does not affect the result.

S	W	Y
P	R	E
H	F	N
N		

54. **D** Nguyen must evaluate the two part-time instructors not evaluated by Fink. Since Fink does not evaluate Stephens, Nguyen must evaluate Stephens.

S	W	Y
P	R	E
H	F	N
N		

55. **D** Since Petrello evaluates only Stephens, Petrello cannot evaluate Walters. Fink cannot evaluate Walters, since that would eliminate Enriquez and Nguyen, resulting in only three evaluators for Walters. Therefore, Roberts, Enriquez, Hilmer, and Nguyen evaluate Walters. The following two arrangements could result:

S	W	Y		S	W	Y
P	R	F		H	R	N
H	E	H		F	E	H
	H				H	
	N				N	

(A) is not correct, since Enriquez evaluates only Walters. (B) is not correct, since Fink does not evaluate Walters. (C) is not correct, since Hilmer evaluates Walters. (E) is not correct, since Hilmer could evaluate York.

56. **D** Since Nguyen evaluates the two part-time instructors whom Fink does not evaluate, any list that contains anyone other than Nguyen or Fink is incorrect. (D) is the only correct list. In this situation, it is not possible for either Enriquez, Hilmer, or Petrello to be the only evaluator of any part-time instructor.

S	W	Y	S	W	Y
P	F	E	P	N	F
H		N	H		
N			N		
			E		

Answers 57–63

57. **E** From the initial conditions, the following chart can be drawn:

	1	2	3	4	5	6
Jilian	D, E, F		T			R, S
Mark		D, E, F		D, E, F		D, E, F

Not (D), since Jilian attends T third. Not (A), (B), or (C), since Mark must attend historical lectures second, fourth, and sixth so that no two historical lectures are attended consecutively.

58. **A** Filling in Mark's possible schedule gives:

	1	2	3	4	5	6
Jilian	D, E, F		T			R, S
Mark	T	D, E, F	R, S	D, E, F	R, S	D, E, F

If Jilian attends E second and Mark attends D second, we get:

	1	2	3	4	5	6
Jilian	D	E	T	F, R, S	F, R, S	R, S
Mark	T	D	R, S	E	R, S	F

Notice that Mark must attend F sixth, after it is attended by Jilian. E must, therefore, be attended fourth by Mark. Now choices can be eliminated. Not (B), since Jilian could attend F fourth or fifth. Not (C), since Mark could attend S third or fifth. Not (D), since Mark attends F sixth. Not (E), since Jilian could attend R fourth, fifth, or sixth.

59. **E** Referring to the initial chart and conditions, the unacceptable choices can be eliminated.

Not (A), since Mark must attend S prior to Jilian and Jilian must attend F prior to Mark. Also, Mark attends two historical lectures in a row. Not (B), since Mark attends two historical lectures in a row. Not (C), since Jilian attends T fourth. Not (D), since Mark attends F before Jilian.

60. **A** Using the initial chart and the conditions will give the following:
Jilian cannot attend a scientific lecture first since Mark must attend all scientific lectures first. Thus, Jilian must attend a historical lecture first. Not (D), since Jilian must attend T third. Not (C) or (E), since both Jilian and Mark can attend a scientific lecture fifth: Jilian—D, E, T, F, R, S and Mark—T D, R, E, S, F.

61. **D** Using and filling in the initial conditions chart will give the insight needed for this question.

	1	2	3	4	5	6
Jilian	D, E, F		T			R, S
Mark		D, E, F		D, E, F		D, E, F

If Mark attends lecture F fourth and Jilian attends lecture D first:

	1	2	3	4	5	6
Jilian	D	F	T	E, R, S	E, R, S	R, S
Mark	T	D	R, S	F	R, S	E

Lecture E is the sixth lecture attended by Mark; therefore, choice (D) is false. Each of the other four choices is possible.

62. **C** Not (A), (B), or (D) as the following counter example illustrates:
Jilian: D, E, T, S, F, R and
Mark: T, D, S, E, R, F.
Not (E), since Mark must attend a historical lecture sixth. The answer must be (C), since Mark must attend scientific lectures first, third, and fifth, and must attend T prior to

Jilian. Thus, first is the only possibility for T.

63. **E** Using the initial conditions chart, the following information can be included:

	1	2	3	4	5	6
Jilian	D, E, F		T			R, S
Mark	T	D, E, F	R	D, E, F	S	D, E, F

Mark attends lecture T first, since he must attend it prior to Jilian. If he attends lecture R third, he must attend lecture S fifth. Since he must attend S prior to Jilian, Jilian must attend S sixth.

Answers 64–69

From the initial conditions, a simple display could have been drawn.

```
        F?         F?       ED
   1  2  3  4  5  6  7  8   G - F - A
      B? C?           A?
```

64. **B** Using the simple display and the initial conditions makes eliminating the wrong answers much easier to do.

Not (A), since F is 4th and must be either 3rd or 7th. Not (C), since D does not immediately follow E. Also, GFA is not in the correct order. Not (D), since GFA is not in the correct order. Not (E), since C is not 3rd and A is not 8th, but B is 2nd.

65. **A** Using the initial conditions: Since Fetina's appointment must be before Arnie's and Fetina must be either 3rd or 7th, it is not possible for Arnie to be scheduled 3rd.

66. **C** Using the simple display and the initial conditions: Since Arnie is 6th, Fetina must be 3rd. Since Greg's appointment is before Fetina's, it must be either 1st or 2nd. Since Hector's appointment is after Dodi's, it must

be either 7th or 8th. Therefore, the answer is not (A), since Greg must be 1st or 2nd. Not (B), since Hector is either 7th or 8th. Not (D), since Dodi is 5th. Not (E), since Coco must be either 7th or 8th.

1	2	3	4	5	6	7	8
B,C,G	B,C,G	F	E	D	A	B,C,H	B,C,H

67. **A** Using the simple display and the initial conditions: If Coco is 7th, then Fetina must be 3rd. Since Greg must be scheduled before Fetina, the only appointments open for Elvis and Dodi are 4th, 5th, and 6th, with Arnie taking the remaining slot. This leaves 1st and 2nd available for Betah. Betah cannot be 2nd, since Coco is not 3rd and Arnie is not 8th. Thus, Betah must be 1st. The display would look like this:

1	2	3	4	5	6	7	8
B	G	F	A,E	D,E	A,D	C	H

68. **C** Using the simple display and the initial conditions: Since Arnie is scheduled after Coco, Arnie must be 8th and Coco must be 7th and Fetina 3rd. Since Betah is 2nd, Greg must be 1st. Since Dodi must immediately follow Elvis, Elvis is 4th and Dodi is 5th, or Elvis is 5th and Dodi is 6th. Therefore, Hector must be either 4th or 6th. The display would look like this:

1	2	3	4	5	6	7	8
G	B	F	E,H	E,D	D,H	C	A

69. **D** Using the initial conditions and simple display: Answer choice (D) is not valid since if Betah is 2nd, we must have either Coco 3rd or Arnie 8th.

Answers 70–75

70. **D** From the given information:

$$1 \quad 2_R \quad 3^A \quad 4$$
$$5_D \quad 6 \quad 7^L \quad 8_R$$

Since member 8 is a Republican and all of the Lawyers are Democrats, then member 8 must be an Accountant. This means that member 6 must be a Lawyer and, therefore, a Democrat. The following arrangement is required:

$$1 \quad 2_R^A \quad 3^A \quad 4_R^A$$
$$5_D \quad 6_D^L \quad 7_D^L \quad 8_R^A$$

71. **E** From the given information:

$$1 \quad 2_R \quad 3^A \quad 4$$
$$5_D \quad 6 \quad 7^L \quad 8_R$$

If there is a total of exactly three Democrats, members 6 and 7 along with 5 are possible. All other choices leave at least one Democrat isolated.

72. **D** From the given information:

$$1 \quad 2_R \quad 3^A \quad 4$$
$$5_D \quad 6 \quad 7^L \quad 8_R$$

If there are exactly three Accountants and member 5 is an Accountant, either member 3 or 5 would be isolated. Therefore, member 5 must be a Lawyer. Possible pairs of the other two Accountants are 1 and 2, 2 and 6, 2 and 4, 4 and 8.

73. **C** From the given information:

$$1 \quad 2_R \quad 3^A \quad 4$$
$$5_D \quad 6 \quad 7^L \quad 8_R$$

Not (A), since if members 1, 4, and 7 were Lawyers, either member 1 or member 4 would remain isolated with the addition of the 4th Lawyer. Not (B), since if members 1, 2, 6, and 8 are Republicans, member 8 would be isolated. Not (D), since if members 4, 5, and 7 were Demo-crats, either member 4 or 5 would be isolated. Not (E), since if members 2, 5, 7, and 8 are Republicans, member 2 would be isolated. More-over, the original set of conditions mandates that member 5 is a De-mocrat. Choice (C) is possible, since if member 2 is the fourth Ac-countant, none would be isolated.

74. **C** Two additional Republicans are needed (either members 3 and 4, 3 and 7, or 6 and 7) so that none are isolated. This leaves four members to be Democrats.

75. **B** From the given information:

$$1 \quad 2_R \quad 3^A \quad 4$$
$$5_D \quad 6 \quad 7^L \quad 8_R$$

If there are four Republicans, four Democrats, and exactly one of the Republicans is an Accountant, then the additional Republicans must be either members 3 and 4, 3 and 7, or 6 and 7. If members 3 and 4 are the Republicans, then members 2 and 4 must be Lawyers. This would isolate member 3. If members 3 and 7 were the Republicans, then member 4 must be a Democrat and would be isolated. Therefore, members 6 and 7 must be the other Republicans. Thus, member 3 cannot be a Re-publican. The following configura-tion results:

$$1_D \quad 2_R \quad 3_D^A \quad 4_D$$
$$5_D \quad 6_R \quad 7_R^L \quad 8_R$$

Answers 76–80

From the initial conditions, the following display could have been drawn:

Left P ? ? ?   Right _ _ _ _ ? ? ?

K̶B̶ R̶S̶ | KC |

76. **B** From the display and initial conditions, the elimination strategy can be applied as follows: Not (A) or (C), since the Runner and the Squire cannot be on the same flank. Not (D), since the Boxman and the King cannot be on the same flank. Not (E), since the right flank must have at least four pieces.

77. **D** Using the display and the initial conditions, the elimination strategy can again be applied: Not (A), since this would require the Runner and the Squire to be on the same flank, and that is not permitted. Not (B), since the King and the Boxman cannot be on the same flank. Not (C), since the King and the Cornerman must be on the same flank. Not (E), since the left flank must have the Pawn.

78. **E** Filling in the display with the information given in the question makes the reasoning processes easier to follow:

Left P ? ? ?   Right B̲ _ _ _ ? ? ?

K̶B̶ R̶S̶ | KC |

The King cannot be on the same flank as the Boxman, so therefore the King must be on the left flank.

Left P K ? ?   Right B̲ _ _ _ _ ? ?

K̶B̶ R̶S̶ | KC |

Since the King and the Cornerman must be on the same flank, the Cornerman must also be on the left flank.

79. **B** If the Queen and the Goalie were placed on the left flank, then the King and the Cornerman would have to be placed on the right flank since they must be together and at most three pieces can be placed on the left flank. The display would now look like this:

Left P Q G ?   Right K̲ C̲ _ _ ?

K̶B̶ R̶S̶ | KC |

This would require the Boxman and either the Runner or the Squire to be placed on the left flank. That would make five pieces on the left flank, which is not permitted. Therefore, the Queen and the Goalie must be on the right flank. So the display above is not possible.

80. **A** The information with the display would now look like this:

Left P ? ? ?   Right _ _ _ _ ? ? ?

K̶B̶ R̶S̶

Now use the elimination strategy. Not (B) or (D), since the Runner and the Squire would be on the same flank. Not (C) or (E), since the King and the Boxman would be on the same flank.

Answers 81–86

From the information given, you could set up the following display:

G → H   ✗ ✗   S → E
Dance Free Weight Treadmill
B G H   P C   S E

___ ___ ___ ___ ___ ___ ___

A closer look at the information gives two basic possible setups:

1	2	3	4	5	6	7
Tread	Tread	Free	Free	Dance	Dance	Dance
Dance	Dance	Dance	Free	Free	Tread	Tread

81. **C** Using the display and initial conditions: The Glide must be performed before the Hop. If the Glide is second and the Bounce is third, then the Hop must be fourth. Thus, the Curl cannot be fourth. Also, the dances cannot be second, third, and fourth. They could be first, second, and third, or fifth, sixth, and seventh.

82. **C** Since the free weight exercises cannot be performed first or last, they must be either third and fourth or fourth and fifth. If the Glide is third, then the Hop (which comes after the Glide) is either fourth or fifth. This conflicts with the possible positions of the free weight exercises.

83. **D** If Larry does the Endurance routine third, the Speed routine must be done second. This leaves first vacant. This is not permitted. The treadmill routines must be done either first and second or sixth and seventh.

84. **A** Work from the two possible setups and the conditions given in the question:

1	2	3 ✗	4	5	6	7 ✗
Tread	Tread	Free	Free	Dance	Dance	Dance
Dance	Dance	Dance	Free	Free	Tread	Tread

The Glide dance cannot be the last dance performed since the Hop is performed after the Glide. Therefore, if the Glide dance and a free weight exercise are performed consecutively, the dances must be performed fifth, sixth, and seventh, with the Glide being fifth. It follows that the treadmill routines must be done first and second. Thus, the Bounce dance is performed after the Endurance routine, not before.

85. **C** If Larry does the Bounce dance after the Hop, then these two setups are possible (remember the Glide is before the Hop):

1	2	3	4	G 5	H 6	B 7
Tread	Tread	Free	Free	Dance	Dance	Dance

or

G 1	H 2	B 3	4	5	6	7
Dance	Dance	Dance	Free	Free	Tread	Tread

If the Bounce dance is done immediately after the Hop, then the Glide/Hop/Bounce must be first/second/third or fifth/sixth/seventh. Thus, Speed/Endurance must be either first/second or sixth/seventh. Therefore, Larry could do the Endurance routine seventh.

86. **A** Using the initial conditions and the display, you can see that the Glide is performed before the Hop. Thus, the Glide could be performed first, second, fifth, or sixth. The Speed routine could be done first or sixth.

Answers 87–91

The initial conditions can be summarized as follows:

> Total = 5
>
> Languages   F, G, I ← 1
> Sciences   B, C, P
> Math   A, S, T ← 0, 1, 2

> P̶A̶
> A → I
> C → only if T and F
> G and B → S̶
> Languages = 1
> Math ≤ 2

87. **B** Not (A) or (C), since only one language may be taken. Not (D), because if algebra is taken, Italian must be taken. Not (E), because statistics cannot be taken if both German and biology are taken.

88. **E** Not (A), because chemistry may be taken only if French is taken. If French is taken, then Italian cannot be taken, since only one language may be taken. Not (B), because if algebra is taken, Italian must be taken, and thus German cannot be taken. Not (C), because chemistry may be taken only if French is taken; and therefore German cannot be taken. Not (D), because if algebra is taken, Italian must be taken and thus French cannot be taken.

89. **D** Not (A), because if algebra is taken, Italian must be taken. If Italian is taken, then French cannot be taken. Not (B), since physics cannot be taken with algebra. Not (C) or (E), because if chemistry is taken, French must also be taken; and therefore German cannot be taken.

90. **D** Not (A), (B), or (E), because if chemistry is taken, trigonometry must be taken. Not (C), since a maximum of two math classes may be

taken; and if physics is taken, algebra cannot be taken.

91. **B** Not (A) or (E) because a second language may not be taken. Not (C) or (D), because if chemistry is taken, French must be taken; and that would be a second language. Since Italian is taken, French is not, thus chemistry is not taken either. One math class must be eliminated, since all three cannot be taken. This leaves both biology and physics that must be taken.

Answers 92–97

From the information given, you could have constructed the following display:

```
A̶            E  A̶      1B   2A
1 2 3 4 5 6 7 8        1C   2D
                            2E
           B? AEA
```

92. **E** Office 4 can be cleaned only by A or E. Therefore, answer choice (E) is incorrect. The other choices are possible as follows.

	1	2	3	4	5	6	7	8
(A)	B	A	E	A	D	D	E	C
(B) & (C)	B	D	C	A	E	A	E	D
(D)	B	D	A	E	A	C	E	D

93. **C** Office 4 can be cleaned only by A or E. Therefore, choice (C) is the only correct one.

94. **B** Office 4 can be cleaned only by A or E. Therefore, choices (C), (D), and (E) are incorrect. Choice (A) is incorrect because D can clean office 8, so this choice is accurate but not complete. Choice (B) is correct.

95. **D** Choices (B) and (C) are incorrect since they each clean only one office. Choice (A) is incorrect since the conditions state that A's offices are separated by one of E's offices. Answer (E) is incorrect since one

of E's offices is between A's offices. Only choice (D) is possible as follows.

1	2	3	4	5	6	7	8
B	A	E	A	D	D	E	C

96. **A** Bart cannot clean office 6 since his office must be numbered lower than E's lowest. Also, Ethel cannot clean office 6 since E must be between A's and E is already cleaning office 7.

97. **E** There are two possible arrangements of rooms, as follows.

1	2	3	4	5	6	7	8
D	B	A	E	A	C	E	D
D	B	C	A	E	A	E	D

Choice (A) is incorrect since A may clean office 6. Choice (B) is incorrect since B and C may clean consecutive offices. Choice (C) is incorrect since C may or may not clean an even-numbered office. Choice (D) is incorrect since this may or may not be true. The only one that *must* be true is choice (E), Bart cleans office 2.

Answers 98–104

The six conditions could give the following display:

```
        L/I              MN or NM
7  9  11  13  15  17  19  N—J
                          M—J
                               L—H—I
```

You may have been able to deduce additional information.

98. **D** Choice (A) is incorrect since H is between L and I. Choice (B) is incorrect since Kim could be younger than Joy, as follows:

7	9	11	13	15	17	19
N	K	M	L	H	J	I

Choice (C) is incorrect since Hilda could be older than Joy, as follows:

7	9	11	13	15	17	19
N	K	M	L	J	H	I

Choice (E) is incorrect because Marsha could be younger than Loren, as illustrated above. Choice (D) is correct, since Hilda is older than Loren but younger than Ida.

99. **E** The correct answer is (E). Because there are only two possible basic setups, this could be true as follows:

7	9	11	13	15	17	19
M?	K	N?	L	H	I	J
M?	L	H	I	N?	K	J

Choice (A) is incorrect since if M were 9, it would be consecutive with N. Choice (B) is incorrect since if H was 17, L would be 15, which violates a condition. Choice (C) is incorrect since if J were 15, there would not be enough slots to the left of J for five daughters. Choice (D) is incorrect since if H were 9, I would be 11, which violates a condition.

100. **C** Choice (A) is incorrect since M and N are consecutive. Choice (B) is incorrect since H is not between L and I. Choice (D) is incorrect since I or L must be 13. Choice (E) is incorrect since N is older than J. Only choice (C) meets all the conditions.

101. **B** The correct choice is four (B). These four possibilities are shown below. If I is 19, L is 13, so H must be 15 or 17. Remember, M and N can't be next to each other.

7	9	11	13	15	17	19
N	K	M	L	H	J	I
M	K	N	L	H	J	I
N	K	M	L	J	H	I
M	K	N	L	J	H	I

102. **D** Choices (A) and (E) are incorrect. If Kim were two years older than Hilda, or Hilda were two years older than Kim, the following arrangements would result. In either case, M and N would be consecutive.

7	9	11	13	15	17	19
M	N	J	L	H?	K?	I
L	H?	K?	I	M	N	J

Choice (B) is incorrect since Joy is older than Marsha. Choice (C) is incorrect since M and N would be consecutive as follows:

7	9	11	13	15	17	19
M	N	J	L	K	H	I
L	K	H	I	M	N	J

Choice (D) is the correct choice as follows:

7	9	11	13	15	17	19
M	K	N	L	H	J	I

103. **C** Choice (C) is correct since if I is 13 and K is 7, you end up with M and N consecutive, as follows:

7	9	11	13	15	17	19
K	L	H	I	M	N	J

The other four choices are all possible, as follows:

	7	9	11	13	15	17	19
(A) & (D)	M	K	N	L	H	I	J
(B)	N	K	M	L	H	I	J
(E)	M	L	H	I	N	K	J

104. **C** Choice (C) is correct because, from the conditions, I must always be either 13, 17, or 19. If I was 17 or 19, M and N would be 7 and 9, and therefore consecutive. Thus, I must be 13. If I is 13, we could get the following:

7	9	11	13	15	17	19
M	L	H	I	N	J	K

Answers 105–109

The following display can be constructed from the conditions:

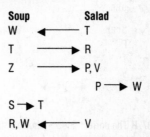

105. **E** If Victor orders salad, then the following ordering arrangement results:

Soup	Salad
R	V
W	T
P	Z
	S

If Victor orders salad, then both Ron and Willard order soup. Since Ron orders soup, Tom must order salad. We know that Zack must order salad; otherwise, Paul, Victor, and Willard would have to order salad. Since Tom orders salad, so must Sam. Since Willard orders soup, so must Paul. From this diagram, it is clear that choice (E) is the correct choice.

106. **C** If Paul and Tom have the same starter, it must be soup. It cannot be salad because if Paul has salad, so must Willard, and if Tom has salad, Willard must have soup. This is a contradiction. Thus, Paul and Tom have soup. Ron has salad since Tom has soup. Victor must have soup since Ron has salad. From the following diagram we can see that Zack and Victor do have different starters, Victor and Willard could have different starters, Willard and

Sam could have different starters, and Sam and Ron could have different starters. Only choice (C) is not true.

Soup	Salad
P	Z
T	R
V	

←W→
←S→

107. **B** The correct answer choice is (B). If Victor orders salad, then Willard orders soup. If Paul orders salad, then Willard orders salad. Willard cannot order both soup and salad. Each of the other choices is possible, as seen in the following two possible arrangements:

Soup	Salad	Soup	Salad
	Z	T	R
W	T	V	W
P	V		S
R	S		P
			Z

108. **D** If Ron orders soup, then Tom must order salad. If Tom orders salad, then Willard must order soup. Paul must order soup since Willard ordered soup. Sam must order salad since Tom ordered salad. Only Victor has a choice. Choice (A) is incorrect since Tom orders salad. Choice (B) is incorrect since Victor may or may not order salad. Choice (C) is incorrect since Zack must order salad. Choice (E) is incorrect since Willard orders soup.

Soup	Salad
R	T
W	Z
P	S

←V→

109. **D** The following arrangement results in a maximum of five friends ordering soup:

Soup	Salad
T	R
V	Z
P	
W	
S	

4

READING COMPREHENSION

INTRODUCTION TO QUESTION TYPE

The entire LSAT is, generally speaking, a test of reading and reasoning skills. However, the Reading Comprehension section itself is a test of general reading skills rather than the more particular analytical skills stressed in the Analytical Reasoning section.

Each Reading Comprehension section consists of four sets of passages and questions. Three of the four sets have passages that range in length from 400 to 500 words. The fourth set is called Comparative Reading and has two shorter passages (Passage A and Passage B). Each passage or comparative reading will be followed by 5 to 8 questions relating to the passage or passages. These 26 to 28 questions are to be answered in 35 minutes.

The comparative reading will be similar to the traditional reading; however, the questions will be based on the two shorter passages and will contain questions comparing the passages and items in the passages. Most questions should be about both passages and how they compare to each other.

The passages are drawn from the humanities, the natural sciences, the social sciences, and law. No specialized knowledge is necessary to answer any of the questions. All questions can be answered by referring to the passage or passages.

READING COMPREHENSION QUESTIONS

Types	Approx. Frequency
Main Point or Primary Purpose	27–28%
Meaning of Words or Phrases in Context	6–8%
Explicitly Stated	10–15%
Inferences or Implications	20–25%
Agree or Disagree (Support, Weaken)	20–25%
Author's Tone or Attitude	3–6%
Function of Part of the Passage	4–7%
Organization of Passage	3–6%

COMMON READING COMPREHENSION QUESTION STEMS

- Which one of the following most accurately states the main point of the passage?
- The author states which one of the following about . . . ?
- Which one of the following most accurately describes the organization of the passage?
- Based on the passage, with which one of the following statements would the author be most likely to agree?
- Which one of the following titles most completely and accurately describes the contents of the passage?
- The author's primary purpose in the passage is to . . .
- The passage provides the most support for which one of the following inferences?
- Which one of the following most accurately expresses what the author means by " . . . ." (line 20)?
- Which one of the following most accurately describes the author's attitude toward . . . ?
- Which one of the following could most logically be appended to the end of the final paragraph?
- The passage most strongly supports which one of the following inferences about . . . ?
- The passage provides the most support for which one of the following statements?
- The passage contains information sufficient to justify inferring which one of the following?

OVERVIEW OF THE FOUR (4) KEY STRATEGIES
YOUR ACTIONS AND . . . REACTIONS

Actions	Reactions
1. Skim the questions	Mark the key word or words (main point, purpose, strengthens, weakens, assumes)
2. Skim the passage (optional)	Some students like to skim the passage quickly, reading the first sentence in each paragraph to see the structure of the passage as a whole
3. Read the passage actively	Mark the main point, important points and support, and note the structure, tone, and purpose of the passage
4. Look for key words in choices	Spot and mark the essence of the choice, know what each choice means and how the choices differ

ACTIVE READING

The Reading Comprehension section presents long passages demanding your steady concentration. Because such passages are complex, you must approach them actively, focusing on a specific plan of attack.

Suppose that midway through the first paragraph of a passage you encounter a sentence like this:

> Ordinarily, of course, we are invited only to criticize the current neglect of government programs; politicians cling to their own fringe benefits while the strife in our inner cities is only nominally contained with a plethora of half-baked local projects whose actual effect is the gradual erosion of trust in the beneficence of the republic.

Different students may respond in different ways:

"What? Let me read that again" (and again and again).
"I used to know what beneficence meant; uh. . . ."
"Boy, am I tired."
"I should have eaten a better breakfast; my head aches."
"I wonder what I'll do tonight. . . ."
"This writer is screwy; I was a senator's aide and I know he's wrong."
"How can I read this!? It's written so poorly; that word *plethora* is a terrible choice."

These typical responses—getting stuck, getting distracted, getting angry—all work against your purpose: understanding the information given in the passage to answer the questions that follow. The techniques described below should help you avoid some common reading test pitfalls.

Essentially, active reading consists of marking as you read. But the marking you do must be strategic and efficient. To present some effective active reading techniques, we will consider seven typical LSAT questions and a sample reading passage that is shorter and less complex than those in the exam.

EXAMPLE

With the possible exception of equal rights, perhaps the most controversial issue across the United States today is the death penalty. Many argue that it is an effective deterrent to murder, while others maintain there is no conclusive evidence that the death penalty reduces the number of murders, and go
(5)
on to contend that it is cruel and inhuman punishment, that it is the mark of a brutal society, and finally, that it is of questionable effectiveness as a deterrent to crime anyway.

But, the death penalty is a necessary evil. Throughout
(10)
recorded history there have always been those extreme individuals who were capable of terribly violent crimes such as

murder. But some are more extreme, more diabolical than others. It is one thing to take the life of another in a momentary fit of blind rage, but quite another to coldly plot and carry
(15) out the murder of one or more people in the style of an executioner. Thus, murder, like all other crimes, is a matter of relative degree. While it could be argued with some conviction that the criminal in the first instance should be merely isolated from society, such should not be the fate of the latter type
(20) murderer. To quote Moshe Dayan, "Unfortunately, we must kill them." The value of the death penalty as a deterrent to crime may be open to debate, but there remains one irrefutable fact: Gary Gilmore will never commit another murder. Charles Manson and his followers, were they to escape, or—God
(25) forbid—be paroled, very well might.

The overwhelming majority of citizens believe that the death penalty protects them. Their belief is reinforced by evidence that shows that the death penalty deters murder. For example, the Attorney General points out that from 1954 to
(30) 1963, when the death penalty was consistently imposed in California, the murder rate remained between three and four murders for each 100,000 population. Since 1964 the death penalty has been imposed only once (in 1967), and the murder rate has skyrocketed to 10.4 murders for each 100,000 popu-
(35) lation. The sharp climb in the state's murder rate, which commenced when executions stopped, is no coincidence. It is convincing evidence that the death penalty does deter many murderers. If the governor were to veto a bill reestablishing the death penalty, an initiative would surely follow. However,
(40) an initiative cannot restore the death penalty for six months. In the interim, innocent people will be murdered—some whose lives may have been saved if the death penalty were in effect.

1. The primary purpose of the passage is to

   (A) criticize the governor
   (B) argue for the value of the death penalty
   (C) initiate a veto
   (D) speak for the majority
   (E) impose a six-month moratorium on the death penalty

2. The passage attempts to establish a relationship between

   (A) Gary Gilmore and Charles Manson
   (B) the importance of both equal rights and the death penalty
   (C) the murder rate and the imposition of the death penalty
   (D) executions and murders
   (E) the effects of parole and the effects of isolation

3. It can be inferred that the author assumes which one of the following about a governor's veto of the death penalty legislation?

(A) It might be upheld.
(B) It will certainly be overridden.
(C) It represents consultation with a majority of citizens.
(D) The veto is important, but not crucial.
(E) It is based on the principle of equal protection for accused murderers.

4. The author's response to those who urge the death penalty for all degrees of murder would most likely be

(A) strongly supportive
(B) noncommittal
(C) negative
(D) supportive
(E) uncomprehending

5. In the passage the author is primarily concerned with

(A) supporting a position
(B) describing an occurrence
(C) citing authorities
(D) analyzing a problem objectively
(E) settling a dispute

6. In lines 39–40 "initiative" refers to

(A) a demonstration against the governor's action
(B) a rise in the murder rate
(C) a more vocal response by the majority of citizens
(D) the introduction of legislation to reinstate the death penalty
(E) overriding the governor's veto

7. The passage provides answers to all of the following questions EXCEPT:

(A) Are all murders equally diabolical?
(B) Does the public believe the death penalty deters murder?
(C) What happened to Gary Gilmore?
(D) Will Charles Manson be paroled?
(E) Should the governor support the death penalty?

FOUR-STEP APPROACH

STEP ONE: SKIM THE QUESTIONS

Before reading the passage, spend a short time familiarizing yourself with the questions. You should preread or "skim" the questions for two reasons: (1) to learn what *types* of questions are being asked; and (2) to learn what specific *information* to look for when you do read the passage. In order to skim efficiently and effectively, you should read over only the portion of each question that *precedes* the multiple choices, and you should mark *key words* as you do so.

A *key word* or phrase is any segment that suggests what you should look for when you read the passage. Marking these key words will help you remember them as you read (luckily, the questions will be printed directly below and alongside the passage, so that as you read the passage you will be able to glance at the questions and remind yourself about what you've marked). In order to further explain and clarify these tips on skimming, let's examine the questions that follow the preceding passage.

The key words for each of them are circled.

1. The primary purpose of the passage is to. . . .

This is a "main idea" or "primary purpose" question; most LSAT reading passages are followed by at least one of these. You are asked what the passage is trying to *do* or *express,* as a whole. Here is a list of possible purposes that may be embodied in a reading passage:

to inform	to criticize	to show
to persuade	to argue for or against	to question
to analyze	to illustrate	to explain
to change	to represent	to prove
to restore	to parody	to describe

This list is by no means exhaustive; the possible purposes are almost endless, and you might try thinking of some yourself.

The main idea or primary purpose of a passage is usually stated or implied in the *thesis sentence* of one or more of the paragraphs. A thesis sentence tells what the paragraph as a whole is about; it states a main idea or primary purpose. For example, the second sentence of paragraph 3 in the passage is the thesis sentence; it sums up the evidence of that paragraph into a single statement.

A primary purpose or main idea question should direct your attention to the thesis sentences in the passage, that is, the *general statements* that sum up the specific details.

2. The passage attempts to establish a relationship between. . . .

This question requires that you locate *explicit* (established) *information* in the passage, information that defines a relationship. The question allows you to anticipate the mention of at least one relationship in the passage, and warns you through its wording that the relationship is not "hidden," but is instead one that the author deliberately attempts to establish.

3. It can be (inferred) that the author assumes which one of the following about the (veto of a governor's death penalty legislation?)

This question requires that you locate *implicit,* rather than explicit, information; you are asked to draw an *inference* (a conclusion based on reasoning), not just to locate obvious material. It is more difficult than question 2. When you read about the governor's veto in the passage, you should take mental note of any unstated assumptions that seem to lie behind the author's commentary.

4. The (author's response) to those who urge the (death penalty for all degrees of murder) would most likely be. . . .

This question type, usually more difficult than the types previously discussed, requires you to *apply* the information in the passage itself. As you read the passage, you should pay special attention to the author's attitude toward types, or degrees, of murder; applying this attitude to the situation described in the question should lead to the answer.

5. In the passage the author is (primarily concerned) with. . . .

This is another variety of the "primary purpose" or "main idea" question.

6. In lines 39–40, "initiative" refers to. . . .

The question requires you to focus on specific language in the passage and define it in context. Such a question is relatively easy insofar as it specifies just where to look for an answer; its difficulty varies according to the difficulty of the word or phrase you are asked to consider.

7. The passage provides answers to all of the following questions EXCEPT: . . .

Although many questions that you skim will lead you to useful information in the passage, some like this one, do not. It is still important, however, to circle key words in the question to avoid the misread.

In general, spend only a few seconds skimming the questions. Read each question, mark key words, and move on.

DO NOT:

• dwell on a question and analyze it extensively.
• be concerned with whether you are marking the "right" words (trust your intuition).
• read the multiple choices (this wastes time).

STEP TWO (OPTIONAL): SKIM THE PASSAGE

Some students find skimming the passage helpful. Skimming the passage consists of quickly reading the first sentence of each paragraph, and marking key words and phrases. This will give you an idea of what the paragraph as a whole is about. The first sentence is often a general statement or thesis sentence that gives the gist of the paragraph.

Consider the passage given above. Reading the first sentence of each paragraph, we mark the key words and phrases, and may draw the following conclusions:

Paragraph 1: "With the possible exception of equal rights, perhaps the most controversial issue across the United States today is the death penalty." This sentence suggests that the passage will be about the death penalty, and the word "controversial" suggests that the author is about to take a stand on the controversy.

". . . that it is cruel and inhuman punishment, that it is the mark of a brutal society, and finally that it is of questionable effectiveness as a deterrent to crime anyway." This sentence presents opposition arguments, and because those arguments are presented as the views of others, not the views of the author, we begin to suspect that he does not align himself with the opposition.

Paragraph 2: "But, the death penalty is a necessary evil." This confirms our suspicion; the author is beginning an argument *in favor* of the death penalty.

"For example, it is one thing to take the life of another in a momentary fit of blind rage but quite another to coldly plot and carry out the murder of one or more people in the style of an executioner." Here the author is distinguishing between *degrees* of murder, and you may at this point recall question 4; this information seems relevant to that question.

"The value of the death penalty as a deterrent to crime may be open to debate, but there remains one irrefutable fact: Gary Gilmore will never commit another murder." The most significant feature of this sentence is that the author's tone is so absolute, indicating his strong belief in his own position.

Paragraph 3: "The overwhelming majority of citizens believe that the death penalty protects them." This sentence points toward statistical evidence in favor of the author's view.

"If the governor were to veto a bill reestablishing the death penalty, an initiative will surely follow." Coincidentally with the author's faith in the will of the majority, here he suggests that the death penalty will be upheld one way or another, by overriding a veto or through initiative.

Do not expect your own skimming of the passage to necessarily yield a series of conclusions such as those expressed above. Most of the knowledge you gather as you skim will "happen" without a deliberate effort on your part to translate your intuitions into sentences. Just read and mark the sentences, without slowing yourself down by analyzing each sentence. The preceding analysis suggests some possible conclusions that may occur to a reader, but drawing such full conclusions from sentence clues will take both practice and a relaxed attitude; don't push yourself to make sense out of everything and don't reread sentences (skimming the passage should take only a few seconds). Some sentences you read may be too difficult to make sense of immediately; just leave these alone and move along. Remember that getting stuck wastes time and raises anxiety.

STEP THREE: READ AND MARK THE PASSAGE

Now you are ready to read the entire passage. To read quickly, carefully, and efficiently, you must be *marking* important words and phrases while you read. At least such marking will keep you alert and focused. At most it will locate the answers to many questions.

Skimming the questions will have helped you decide what to mark. If a question refers to a specific line, sentence, or quotation from the passage, you will want to mark this reference and pay special attention to it. Whenever a key word from a question corresponds with a spot in the passage, mark the spot. In the scheme for marking a passage, these spots are called, simply, ANSWER SPOTS. There are two other kinds of "spots" that you should mark as you read: REPEAT SPOTS and INTUITION SPOTS. Repeat spots are sections of the passage in which the same type of information is repeated.

As you read and mark the passage, you may also wish to paraphrase the main idea of each paragraph. This enables some students to better comprehend the organization and main idea of the passage.

Consider the following excerpt from a passage:

Proposed cutbacks in the Human Resources Agency are scheduled for hearing 9 A.M. on the 17th. Included in possible program reductions are cutbacks in the veterans' affairs program, including closure of the local office; in potential support for the county's Commission on the Status of Women; and in payments provided by the county for foster home care, which are not being adjusted for cost-of-living increases this year.

Programs in the Environmental Improvement Agency will be examined by the board beginning 9 A.M. Friday, August 18. The milk and dairy inspection program has been recommended by County Administrative Officer Fred Higgins for transfer to state administration. In addition, budget recommendations do not include funds for numerous community general plans which have been discussed previously by the board of supervisors. Such areas as Joshua Tree, Crestline, Lytle Creek, and Yucaipa are not included in the Planning Department's program for the upcoming year.

A special session to discuss proposed budget cuts in the county's General Services Agency will be conducted at 9 A.M. Saturday, August 19. A number of county branch libraries have been proposed for closure next year, including the Adelanto, Bloomington, Crestline, Joshua Tree, Mentone, Morongo, Muscoy, and Running Springs locations. A rollback in hours of operation will also be considered. Branches now open 60 hours a week will be cut to 52 hours. Other 50-hour-a-week

> branches will be reduced to 32 hours a week. Testimony will be heard on cutbacks in various agricultural service programs, including the county trapper program in the Yucaipa region and support for 4-H activities.

Generally, this excerpt stresses information about times, dates, and locations; we are conscious of repeated numbers and repeated place names. Marking the spots in which such information is found will help you to sort out the information, and also to answer more efficiently a question that addresses such information, a question such as "Which of the following cities are (is) *not* included in the Planning Department's program and *are* (is) liable to lose a branch library?" Having marked the REPEAT SPOTS that contain location names, you may be better able to focus on the appropriate information quickly.

INTUITION SPOTS are any spots that strike you as significant, for whatever reason. As we read, we tend to pay special attention to certain information; marking those spots that your intuition perceives as important will help increase your comprehension and will therefore contribute to correct answers.

You may notice that ANSWER SPOTS, REPEAT SPOTS, and INTUITION SPOTS are not necessarily different spots. An answer spot may also be a spot that contains repeat information AND appeals to your intuition.

Don't overmark. Some students, fearing that they will miss an important point, underline everything. Such misplaced thoroughness makes it impossible to find any specific word or phrase. Just mark the main idea of each paragraph and several important words or phrases. And vary your marks. You may want to underline main ideas, use circles or brackets or stars to indicate other important spots, and jot some notes to yourself in the margin. Here is how you might mark the death penalty passage:

> With the possible exception of equal rights, perhaps the most controversial issue across the United States today is the death penalty. Many argue that it is an effective deterrent to murder, while others maintain there is no conclusive evidence
> (5) that the death penalty reduces the number of murders, and go on to contend that it is cruel and inhuman punishment, that it is the mark of a brutal society, and finally that it is of questionable effectiveness as a deterrent to crime anyway.
>
> But, the death penalty is a necessary evil. Throughout
> (10) recorded history there have always been those extreme individuals who were capable of terribly violent crimes such as murder. But some are more extreme, more diabolical than others. It is one thing to take the life of another in a momentary fit of blind rage, but quite another to coldly plot and carry out the murder of
> (15) one or more people in the style of an executioner. Thus, murder, like all other crimes, is a matter of relative degree. While it could be argued with some conviction that the criminal in the first instance should be merely isolated from society, such should not

[margin notes: Contrast, Opposition points, degrees of murder, penalty]

be the fate of the latter type murderer. To quote Moshe Dayan,
(20) "Unfortunately, we must kill them." The value of the death
penalty as a deterrent to crime may be open to debate, but there
remains one irrefutable fact: Gary Gilmore will never commit
another murder. Charles Manson and his followers, were they to
escape, or—God forbid—be paroled, very well might.

(25) [The overwhelming majority of citizens believe that the
death penalty protects them.] Their belief is reinforced by evidence that shows that the death penalty deters murder. For example, the Attorney General points out that from 1954 to 1963,
when the death penalty was consistently imposed in Califor-
(30) nia, the murder rate remained between three and four murders
for each 100,000 population. Since 1964 the death penalty has
been imposed only once (in 1967), and the murder rate has
skyrocketed to 10.4 murders for each 100,000 population. The
sharp climb in the state's murder rate, which commenced
(35) when executions stopped, is no coincidence. It is convincing
evidence that the death penalty does deter many murderers. If
the governor were to veto a bill reestablishing the death
penalty, an initiative would surely follow. However, an initiative cannot restore the death penalty for six months. In the in-
(40) terim, innocent people will be murdered—some whose lives
may have been saved if the death penalty were in effect.

STATS (handwritten margin note)

veto effects (handwritten margin note)

Your marking method should be active, playful, and personal. While you are marking, don't worry about whether you are doing it correctly. You may notice that, in the discussion of skimming the passage, some sentences are marked differently than they are
here, in order to stress that there is no single, "correct" method.

Remember not to react subjectively to the passage, or add to it. Your own background may have you disagreeing with the passage, or you may be tempted to supply
information from your own experience in order to answer a question. You must use only
the information you are given, and you must accept it as true.

Avoid wasting time with very difficult or technical sentences. Concentrating on the
sentences and ideas you do understand will often supply you with enough material to
answer the questions. Rereading difficult sentences takes time, and usually does not
bring greater clarity.

STEP FOUR: ANSWER THE QUESTIONS

As you attempt to answer each question, follow these steps:

1. Focus on the key words.
2. Eliminate unreasonable and incorrect answer choices.
3. Make certain that information in the passage supports your answer.
4. Don't get stuck; assess the level of difficulty, and skip the question if necessary.

We will follow this procedure, using the questions on the "death penalty" passage as examples.

Question 1

The primary purpose of the passage is to

(A) criticize the governor
(B) argue for the value of the death penalty
(C) initiate a veto
(D) speak for the majority
(E) impose a six-month moratorium on the death penalty

Analysis

The correct answer is B. Remember that this sort of question asks for the *primary* purpose, not a subsidiary purpose. Often the incorrect answer choices will express minor or subsidiary purposes; this is true of (A) and (D). Another type of incorrect answer choice *contradicts* the information in the passage. So it is with (C) and (E). Both contradict the author's expressed support of the death penalty. Having marked thesis sentences in the passage, you should be aware of the author's repeated arguments for the value of the death penalty, and choose (B).

Question 2

The passage attempts to establish a relationship between

(A) Gary Gilmore and Charles Manson
(B) the importance of both equal rights and the death penalty
(C) the murder rate and the imposition of the death penalty
(D) executions and murders
(E) the effects of parole and the effects of isolation

Analysis

The correct answer is C. "Equal rights" is mentioned only in passing, and a relationship between parole and isolation is scarcely even implied; therefore (B) and (E) should be eliminated. (A) is not a good answer because, strictly speaking, Gary Gilmore and Charles Manson are not compared; their *sentences* are. (D) is a true answer, but not the best one because it is more vague and general than the best choice, (C); paragraph 3 makes this specific comparison.

Question 3

It can be inferred that the author assumes which of the following about a governor's veto of the death penalty legislation?

(A) It might be upheld.
(B) It will certainly be overridden.
(C) It represents consultation with a majority of citizens.
(D) The veto is important, but not crucial.
(E) It is based on the principle of equal protection for accused murderers.

Analysis

The correct answer is A. We are looking for information that is (1) assumed but not explicit, and (2) relevant to the governor's veto. Having marked the appropriate section of the passage, you are able to return immediately to the final two paragraphs, which discuss the veto. (B), (C), and (D) contradict passage information. (C) contradicts the author's earlier explanations that most citizens approve of the death penalty, and (D) contradicts the author's final statement. (B) contradicts the author's assumption that the veto might be upheld. (E) is irrelevant to the veto issue. (A) is correct because the assumption that the veto might be upheld would certainly underlie an argument against it.

Question 4

The author's response to those who urge the death penalty for all degrees of murder would most likely be

(A) strongly supportive
(B) noncommittal
(C) negative
(D) supportive
(E) uncomprehending

Analysis

The correct answer is C. Having marked the section that refers to different degrees of murder, you are once again able to focus on the appropriate section. In paragraph 2 the author argues that unpremeditated murder may not warrant the death penalty. This argument suggests his negative attitude toward someone who urges the death penalty for all murderers.

Question 5

In the passage the author is primarily concerned with

(A) supporting a position
(B) describing an occurrence
(C) citing authorities
(D) analyzing a problem objectively
(E) settling a dispute

Analysis

The correct answer is A. With your general knowledge of the passage, you should immediately eliminate (B) and (D), because the author is *argumentative* throughout, never merely descriptive or objective. Citing authorities (C) is a *subsidiary* rather than a primary concern; the author does so in paragraph 3. (E) is incorrect because it is the author himself who is *creating* a dispute over the death penalty. A review of the thesis sentences alone shows that the author is consistently supporting a position; (A) is certainly the best answer.

Question 6

In lines 39–40 "initiative" refers to

(A) a demonstration against the governor's action
(B) a rise in the murder rate
(C) a more vocal response by the majority of citizens
(D) the introduction of legislation to reinstate the death penalty
(E) overriding the governor's veto

Analysis
The correct answer is D. Skimming this question has allowed you to pay special attention to "initiative" as you read the passage. The sentence suggests that the initiative is a response to a governor's veto of the death penalty; and it is a *certain* response, as indicated by "surely." It is also an action that can eventually restore the death penalty; this fact especially signals (D) as the answer. (B) states information mentioned apart from the initiative; the murder rate will rise "in the interim." Demonstrations (A) or vocal responses (C) are not suggested as possibilities anywhere. (E) is eliminated because the last sentence of the passage urges an override, thus distinguishing this action from an initiative.

Question 7

The passage provides answers to all of the following questions EXCEPT:

(A) Are all murders equally diabolical?
(B) Does the public believe the death penalty deters murder?
(C) What happened to Gary Gilmore?
(D) Will Charles Manson be paroled?
(E) Should the governor support the death penalty?

Analysis
The correct answer is D. The passage answers all of these questions except the question of Manson's parole, which remains a possibility.

COMPARATIVE READING

As mentioned earlier, the comparative reading will be similar to the traditional reading; however, the questions will be based on the two shorter passages and will contain questions comparing the passages and items in the passages. Most questions should be about both passages and how they compare to each other.

The passages will be labeled "Passage A" and "Passage B" and will be numbered continuously. The passages will be on the same topic and will have a case in common or have some sort of commonality. There may be a short introduction to the passages. The following is a sample of a comparative reading set.

Tuna Fishing
These passages cover events before an international agreement to limit dolphin mortality during tuna fishing was reached. By 1994, only dolphin-safe tuna could be sold in the United States.

Passage A

Just as the members of the Inter-American Tropical Tuna Commission have subscribed to annual quotas on the tuna harvest, they are agreed that cooperation is essential in limiting the dolphin kill. The common interest is preservation of
(5) the tuna industry, and since modern fishing methods exploit the cozy relationship between the yellowfin tuna and the dolphin, tuna fishing would become less profitable if the number of dolphins decreased. Tuna and dolphin are often found together at sea, and the fishermen have learned to cast their
(10) nets where they see the dolphin, using them to locate the tuna. The problem is that many dolphins die in the nets.

The commission deliberations acknowledged the environmental pressures that have led to strict regulation of U.S. tuna crews under federal law. Delegates also recognized that
(15) dolphin protection goals are relatively meaningless unless conservation procedures are adopted and followed on an international basis. Commission supervision of survey, observer, and research programs won general agreement at the eight-nation conference. The method and timetable for im-
(20) plementing the program, however, remain uncertain.

Thus the federal regulation that leaves U.S. crews at a disadvantage in the tuna-harvest competition remains a threat to the survival of the tuna fleet. Still, the commission meetings have focused on the workable solution. All vessels
(25) should be equipped with the best dolphin-saving gear devised; crews should be trained and motivated to save the dolphin; a system must be instituted to assure that rules are enforced. Above all, the response must be international. Dolphin conservation could well be another element in an
(30) envisioned treaty that remains unhappily elusive at the continuing Law-of-the-Sea Conference.

The tuna industry's interest in saving dolphins is bothersome to many who also want to save the dolphin but object to the industry's motivation for doing so. For fishermen, sav-
(35) ing the dolphin is valuable only because the dolphins lead them to tuna. For more compassionate souls, however, the dolphin is not just a tuna finder but, more important, the sea creature that seems most human.

Passage B

(40)   At one time, tropical tuna were caught with poles and
fishing lines. Then, in the 1950s, a synthetic netting was developed that wouldn't rot in tropical waters. A hydraulically
driven power block could haul the large synthetic nets and
deploy them around entire schools of tuna, which resulted in
(45) being able to catch many tons of fish at one time. This
method of tuna fishing is called "purse seining," and the
ships that are equipped to do it are "purse seiners."

During "porpoise fishing" (the fishermen's term for purse
seining), schools of tuna are located by spotting dolphins or
(50) seabird flocks, often by a helicopter that takes off from the
purse seiner's upper deck. Tuna and the dolphin travel
together—usually accompanied by sea birds—for reasons
that are not completely understood but that are probably
associated with areas of food supply. Once the dolphin are
(55) spotted, speedboats are used by the fishermen to chase them
down, herd them into a group, and set the net around them.
The chase takes place over many miles of ocean and can
take as long as several hours. Once the dolphins have been
herded, cables draw the net taut at the bottom, like draw-
(60) strings on a purse. The purse seiner's powerful hydraulic
system then pulls the net upward. Once the net is hauled
back on board, the captain puts the seiner into reverse,
which is called the "backdown" procedure. As the slack of
the net eases, a panel of webbing designed to not snag the
(65) dolphins drops them back into the ocean. Back on deck the
tuna are scooped out of the net and put into storage wells on
a lower deck.

The backdown procedure to release the dolphins doesn't
always go smoothly, sometimes because of human error and
(70) sometimes because of strong rip tides and currents. The
dolphins, caught in a canopy of netting, can suffocate.
Because of their struggle in the net, they can be badly injured
and will die later. It is estimated that since the introduction of
the purse-seining method of catching tuna, over six million
(75) dolphins have been killed. This is by far the largest documented cetacean kill in the world. In comparison, the total
number of whales of all species killed during commercial
whaling in the twentieth century is about two million.

Efforts first in the United States and then internationally
(80) have reduced the dolphin kill substantially in the last thirty
years. Since 1993, reported dolphin mortality has been a
small fraction of the population size, so that recovery of the
dolphin population has been expected. But by 2002, this
hadn't occurred. There are several hypotheses, among which

(85) **are the negative effects of repeated chases on dolphin survival or reproduction, the separation of suckling calves from
their mothers during the fishing process, environmental
changes, and unobserved or unreported mortality.**

Question 1

Which of the following best contrasts the main ideas of Passage A and Passage B?

(A) Passage A presents the reasons an international agreement to protect dolphins is needed while Passage B details the fishing methods that endanger
dolphins.

(B) While Passage A focuses on the effects of U.S. dolphin legislation on the tuna
fishing industry, Passage B focuses on the reasons dolphins are valuable.

(C) Passage A presents two sides of the dolphin legislation controversy, while
Passage B presents only one side.

(D) Passage A explains the international program for protecting dolphins, while
Passage B explains the program's failure.

(E) While Passage A criticizes the U.S. dolphin protection legislation because it
negatively affects the tuna fishing industry Passage B criticizes it for failing to
protect dolphins.

Analysis

The correct answer is (A). Passage A is concerned primarily with the importance
of an international agreement about dolphin protection, and the main subject in Passage B is the method of tuna fishing that endangers dolphins. Choice (D) may seem
like a good answer because Passage A does outline ideas for an international program and Passage B indicates that the dolphin population has not recovered in spite
of a reduction in dolphin mortality. But this answer is not as good as (A) because it
covers only parts of each passage.

Question 2

The author of Passage A, unlike the author of Passage B,

(A) believes that international laws will help reduce dolphin mortality

(B) states that U.S. laws covering dolphin protection have been unsuccessful

(C) mentions a noncommercial motivation for protecting dolphins

(D) criticizes the Inter-American Tropical Tuna Commission

(E) insists on a timetable for international supervision of the tuna industry

Analysis

The correct answer is (C). In the last paragraph of Passage A, the author mentions that some "compassionate souls" are interested in saving the dolphin for reasons having nothing to do with commerce, making (C) the best answer, since
Passage B doesn't consider motivations for saving dolphins. Neither passage claims

that U.S. laws have been unsuccessful (B), and Passage A doesn't criticize the Inter-American Tropical Tuna Commission or "insist" on a timetable (D and E). Both passages see international laws as beneficial.

Question 3

The author presents the information in Passage A

(A) angrily
(B) cynically
(C) ironically
(D) indifferently
(E) objectively

Analysis

The correct answer is (E). The information is presented objectively, even though the author in the last paragraph suggests that some people are bothered by the tuna industry's commercial motivations. This fact is presented in a straightforward, not emotional, manner.

Question 4

The author of Passage A implies that the government and industry representatives concerned with dolphin conservation may lack which one of the following?

(A) knowledge
(B) altruism
(C) influence
(D) compassion
(E) efficiency

Analysis

The correct answer is (D). The author uses this word in line 29, and implies that although some people's interest in saving dolphins is based on an appreciation for the animals, the tuna industry's motivations have nothing to do with compassion.

Question 5

Which one of the following is NOT described in Passage A?

(A) the relationship between dolphins and tuna
(B) the requirements that must be met for tuna to be labeled dolphin-safe
(C) why dolphin protection is of international concern
(D) elements of a solution to the dolphin conservation problem
(E) the items that won general agreement at the Law-of-the-Sea Conference

Analysis

The correct answer is (B). All of the statements are items considered in Passage A except for (B), making this the correct answer. The relationship between dolphins and tuna is mentioned in lines 6–7, the importance of an international agreement is stated in lines 15–17, elements of a solution are touched on in lines 24–28, and the items that won general agreement are mentioned in lines 17–18.

Question 6

In Passage B, the "backdown" procedure is described as a way to

(A) protect dolphins from injury
(B) separate dolphin calves from their mothers
(C) return dolphins to the ocean
(D) ensure the safety of the tuna catch
(E) meet requirements of U.S. legislation

Analysis
The correct answer is (C). The backdown procedure is explained in lines 61–65, and its purpose is clearly to return the dolphins to the sea, making (C) the best answer. The procedure doesn't protect the dolphins from injury (A), as is made clear in the third paragraph. Nothing in the passage suggests either (D) or (E).

Question 7

According to Passage B, dolphin mortality became a major problem after

(A) tuna fishermen recognized that tuna and dolphin swam together
(B) the purse-seining method of tuna fishing was introduced
(C) tuna fishing became an international industry
(D) poor netting was used to catch tuna
(E) it became more economical to destroy dolphins rather than to save them

Analysis
The correct answer is (B). The passage shows that it was the introduction of purse seining, not tuna fishing itself, that presented a problem because it involved actually trapping the dolphins in netting, not merely using them as a means to spot tuna (A). Synthetic netting, not poor netting (D), allowed purse seining and, therefore, led to increases in dolphin mortality.

Question 8

Which of the following can be inferred from the last paragraph of Passage B?

(A) Improved fishing methods to reduce dolphin kill haven't succeeded.
(B) International agreements have not been effective in protecting dolphins.
(C) The fact that the dolphin population hasn't recovered needs further study.
(D) A large percentage of the dolphin population has been destroyed.
(E) Observers on purse seiners are often bribed to under-report the number of dead dolphins.

Analysis

The correct answer is (C). Lines 84–88 suggest several hypotheses that might explain why the dolphin population hasn't recovered even though dolphin mortality figures have been significantly reduced. The inference can be made from these hypotheses that further study is required, making (C) the best answer. (A), (B), and (D) are contradicted in the passage, and bribery (E), while possibly true, is not implied.

Active Reading, A Summary Chart

```
      SKIM THE QUESTIONS
      (Mark the key words
        and phrases.)
```

```
      SKIM THE PASSAGE
        —OPTIONAL—
   (Quickly read and mark the first
    sentence of each paragraph.)
```

```
  READ AND MARK THE PASSAGE
      • Answer Spots
      • Repeat Spots
      • Intuition Spots
      • Paraphrase
```

```
    ANSWER THE QUESTIONS
      • Focus on key words.
      • Eliminate weak choices.
      • Don't "read into" the passage.
      • Don't get stuck.
      • Skip if necessary.
```

AN ALTERNATIVE GENERAL APPROACH

Some students, regardless of how much they review, analyze, and practice, cannot seem to finish the Reading Comprehension section. They simply cannot work fast enough and continue to maintain a high level of comprehension. If you find that you consistently have a problem getting to or into the fourth passage, you may wish to try this alternative approach: Focus your time on three of the four passages. That is, try to do well on the three passages and the questions that follow, and simply guess at the questions for the remaining passage. You can skip a passage and still receive a good score. The idea is to significantly raise your percentage of correct answers on the passages and questions you are completing. Remember, this is an alternative approach that you may wish to try if you are having a real problem getting to all four passages and maintaining a good level of comprehension.

BASIC TRAINING: EXTRA, EFFECTIVE PRACTICE

The following procedure, *practiced daily,* should strengthen precisely the kinds of skills that you will need for the Reading Comprehension section of the LSAT:

1. Locate the editorial page in your daily newspaper. There you will probably find three or four editorials on different subjects.
2. Read several editorials at your normal reading speed, marking them, if possible.
3. Set the editorials aside, and try to write a summary sentence describing each editorial. Make your summary as precise as possible. Do not write, "This editorial was about the economy." Instead, try to write something like this: "This editorial argued against the value of supply-side economics by referring to rising unemployment and interest rates."

   You may not be able to write so precise a summary right away, but after a few days of practicing this technique, you will find yourself better able to spot and remember main ideas and specific details, and to anticipate and understand the author's point of view.

   It is most important that you *write down* your summary statements. This takes more time and effort than silently "telling" yourself what the editorial means, but the time and effort pay off.
4. Every few days, create some of your own multiple-choice questions about an editorial. What would you ask if you were a test maker? Putting yourself in the test maker's shoes can be very instructive. You will realize, for instance, how weak or incorrect answer choices are constructed, and that realization will help you to eliminate such choices when you take the LSAT.

ANSWER SHEET
EXTRA PRACTICE: READING COMPREHENSION

1. ⒶⒷⒸⒹⒺ
2. ⒶⒷⒸⒹⒺ
3. ⒶⒷⒸⒹⒺ
4. ⒶⒷⒸⒹⒺ
5. ⒶⒷⒸⒹⒺ
6. ⒶⒷⒸⒹⒺ
7. ⒶⒷⒸⒹⒺ
8. ⒶⒷⒸⒹⒺ
9. ⒶⒷⒸⒹⒺ
10. ⒶⒷⒸⒹⒺ
11. ⒶⒷⒸⒹⒺ
12. ⒶⒷⒸⒹⒺ
13. ⒶⒷⒸⒹⒺ

14. ⒶⒷⒸⒹⒺ
15. ⒶⒷⒸⒹⒺ
16. ⒶⒷⒸⒹⒺ
17. ⒶⒷⒸⒹⒺ
18. ⒶⒷⒸⒹⒺ
19. ⒶⒷⒸⒹⒺ
20. ⒶⒷⒸⒹⒺ
21. ⒶⒷⒸⒹⒺ
22. ⒶⒷⒸⒹⒺ
23. ⒶⒷⒸⒹⒺ
24. ⒶⒷⒸⒹⒺ
25. ⒶⒷⒸⒹⒺ

26. ⒶⒷⒸⒹⒺ
27. ⒶⒷⒸⒹⒺ
28. ⒶⒷⒸⒹⒺ
29. ⒶⒷⒸⒹⒺ
30. ⒶⒷⒸⒹⒺ
31. ⒶⒷⒸⒹⒺ
32. ⒶⒷⒸⒹⒺ
33. ⒶⒷⒸⒹⒺ
34. ⒶⒷⒸⒹⒺ
35. ⒶⒷⒸⒹⒺ
36. ⒶⒷⒸⒹⒺ
37. ⒶⒷⒸⒹⒺ

✂ To remove, cut along dotted rule.

EXTRA PRACTICE: READING COMPREHENSION

Directions: Read the passages and answer the questions following each passage by blackening the appropriate space on the answer sheet. You may refer back to the passages when answering the questions. Answer all questions on the basis of what is stated or implied.

Passage 1

In 1957, Congress passed the Price-Anderson Act, which provides a current limitation of $665 million on the liability of nuclear power companies in the
(5) event of a "nuclear incident." The dual purpose of the Act is to "protect the public and encourage the development of the atomic energy industry." While the objective of encouraging the
(10) development of atomic energy has been achieved, it is not yet known if Price-Anderson would fully compensate the public in the event of a serious nuclear accident.

(15)   In the event that a major accident does occur in this country, would the victims be adequately compensated for their injuries? The nuclear industry is promoted under Price-Anderson by
(20) having a limit on potential liability even if the accident was the result of gross negligence or willful misconduct. Victims are protected by having an asset pool of at least $665 million in
(25) which to recover for damages. This amount will undoubtedly be raised when Price-Anderson is renewed. Victims are also protected if an accident is deemed to be an
(30) "extraordinary nuclear occurrence" by the requirement that certain defenses be waived by the utility company. However, the victims would still substantially bear the risk because of

(35) the uncertainty of recovery for radiation injuries. This is contrary to the tort (wrongful act) concept that "he who breaks must pay."
    The Price-Anderson Act does not
(40) disturb the common law rule of causation. A person injured in a nuclear incident has the burden of proving a causal relationship between the incident and his alleged injury. While
(45) the plaintiff does not have to show that the conduct of the defendant was the sole cause of the injury, the plaintiff must prove that it is more likely than not that the conduct of the defendant
(50) was a substantial factor in bringing about the injury. The plaintiff has the burden of showing that there is a high probability (i.e., 51 percent or more) that the defendant's conduct caused
(55) his alleged injury. A mere possibility of such causation is not enough; and when the matter remains one of pure speculation or conjecture, or the probabilities are at least evenly
(60) balanced, it becomes the duty of the court to direct a verdict for the defendant. In the event of a nuclear incident involving a large release of radioactive material, such as
(65) Chernobyl, it would probably not be difficult for immediate victims to demonstrate a causal link between the accident and their injuries. Scientists are able to detect approximately how
(70) much radiation was released into the

atmosphere, and how surrounding areas are affected by it.

An argument in favor of Price-Anderson is that it ensures that (75) claimants have an asset pool of at least $665 million in which to recover for damages. Without Price-Anderson, the possibility is very real that the utility company would be unable to pay (80) claims arising out of a major accident. If the claims were sufficiently large or numerous, a private company could well choose bankruptcy over paying the claims. For example, the (85) Planex Corporation, a defendant in thousands of asbestos cases, filed for reorganization under Chapter 11 of the Bankruptcy Code in 1982.

1. The primary purpose of the passage is to

    (A) describe the Price-Anderson Act
    (B) criticize the Price-Anderson Act
    (C) support the Price-Anderson Act
    (D) analyze and then condemn the Price-Anderson Act
    (E) present the advantages and disadvantages of the Price-Anderson Act

2. The advantages to the nuclear industry in the United States of the Price-Anderson Act include all of the following EXCEPT:

    (A) the limitation of the liability to $665 million
    (B) some injuries may not be apparent until after the statute of limitations has expired
    (C) the potential liability far exceeds the limit fixed
    (D) the plaintiff must show the high probability that the defendant's conduct caused the injury

(E) the ceiling on liability will probably be raised when Price-Anderson is renewed

3. If there were a major nuclear accident in the United States equal in size to the Chernobyl incident, we can infer that under the rules of the Price-Anderson Act

    (A) there would be difficulty in proving causation
    (B) the asset pool would be exhausted
    (C) victims with latent injuries would be able to collect damages
    (D) the liability would not apply if the accident was caused by provable negligence
    (E) the concept of "he who breaks must pay" would be applied

4. Which one of the following is an advantage of the Price-Anderson Act to the general public?

    (A) The liability pool of $665 million would pay many victims of a nuclear accident.
    (B) A utility company responsible for a nuclear accident would not need to file for bankruptcy if the claim exceeded the $665 million in the asset pool.
    (C) A claim against a company responsible for a nuclear accident could be filed under relaxed common law rules of causation.
    (D) Injuries caused by nuclear exposure might not be apparent for many years.
    (E) Victims of an accident could collect punitive damages if an accident is caused by industry negligence.

5. Under the terms of the Price-Anderson Act, in the case of a minor nuclear accident a successful plaintiff would

have to show that the defendant's conduct was the

(A) sole cause of his or her injury
(B) probable cause of his or her injury
(C) possible cause of his or her injury
(D) contributing cause of his or her injury
(E) cause of his or her injury through negligence

6. According to the passage, the Planex Corporation (line 85) filed for bankruptcy

(A) after paying damages in a nuclear accident case
(B) after paying damages in a toxic waste case
(C) after paying damages in an asbestos case
(D) to avoid paying damages in a toxic waste case
(E) to avoid paying damages in an asbestos case

7. With which one of the following statements would the author of the passage be most likely to disagree?

(A) Attitudes toward nuclear energy have changed dramatically since the incidents at Three Mile Island and Chernobyl.
(B) The radioactive contamination from Chernobyl may result in thousands of cancer deaths in the next 50 years.
(C) Congress should disallow any expansion of the nuclear power industry.
(D) The size of the asset pool under Price-Anderson should be increased.
(E) The 20-year statute of limitations under the Price-Anderson Act is too short.

Passage 2

A recent study surveyed 3,576 trials in two reporting samples. Over 500 judges cooperated in the study. The survey was conducted using judges as
(5) reporters for jury trials. Two major questions were explored in the survey, "First, what is the magnitude and direction of the disagreement between judge and jury? And, second, what are
(10) the sources and explanations of such disagreement?"

The study found that judges and juries agree (would decide the same case the same way) in 75.4 percent of
(15) the cases. If cases resulting in a hung jury are eliminated, the overall agreement rate rises to 78 percent. Thus at the outset, whatever the defects of the jury system, it can be
(20) seen that the jury at least arrives at the same result as the judge in over three-fourths of the cases.

The direction of disagreement is clearly toward a more lenient jury than
(25) judge. The trend was not isolated to any particular type of offense but was spread throughout crime categories. Additionally, the pattern found was that in convictions, juries tended to be more
(30) lenient as far as counts, degrees, and sentencing.

For civil cases the percentage of agreement and disagreement was about the same except that there did
(35) not appear to be any strong sentiment in favor of plaintiff over defendant (or vice versa) by the jury.

In cases decided differently because the judge had facts the jury did not,
(40) generally, these facts related to suppressed evidence, personal knowledge of the defendant's prior record, etc. The factors that made the difference between judge and jury in

(45) these cases, then, were all facts that we as a society purposefully keep from juries because the information is irrelevant or because it is highly prejudicial. From the study it can be (50) assumed that the judge, hearing the information, did not disregard it but, quite the contrary, used it in reaching his (harsher) judgment.

The overwhelming number of cases (55) in which judge and jury agree argue for the jury's understanding of the evidence because it is not to be expected that a jury deciding cases it does not understand and a judge (60) deciding cases he does understand (we presume) would not agree in their results so often. Also, judges themselves generally did not identify "jury misunderstood the facts" as the (65) reason for disagreement.

The level of sympathy that the jury had with the defendant did make some difference. Although generally the jury was neutral, in about 36 percent of the (70) cases the jury had some reaction (positive or negative) because of the personal characteristics, occupation, family, or court appearance. These factors affected juries differently (75) depending on the age, race, or sex of the defendant. Through various statistical evaluations the study is able to state that "the sympathetic defendant causes disagreement in . . . (80) 4 percent of all cases." Similar figures apply for the unsympathetic defendant.

8. This passage was probably written in response to an argument for

   (A) the appointment rather than the election of judges
   (B) the election rather than the appointment of judges
   (C) the wider use of the trial by jury

   (D) the reduced use of the trial by jury
   (E) the increased use of statistics in the courts

9. According to the passage, judge and jury are likely to reach the same verdict in

   (A) criminal cases rather than in civil cases
   (B) civil cases rather than in criminal cases
   (C) cases where the judge has facts denied to the jury
   (D) cases resulting in a hung jury
   (E) roughly three-quarters of the cases

10. The results of this study suggest that, when there is disagreement between a judge and a jury, the judgments of the judge are

   (A) harsher than those of juries
   (B) less harsh than those of juries
   (C) very nearly the same as those of juries
   (D) less likely to be influenced by irrelevant or prejudicial information
   (E) less harsh than those of juries in criminal cases only

11. From the results of the study we can infer that withholding from a jury information that is irrelevant or prejudicial to a defendant

   (A) has no significant effect on the results of a trial
   (B) works to the disadvantage of most defendants
   (C) works to the advantage of most defendants
   (D) works to increase the objectivity of the judge
   (E) works to decrease the objectivity of the jury

12. The author's argument for the jury's understanding of the evidence presented in trial is based upon

(A) his assumption that the judge understands the evidence
(B) his assumption that evidence too complex for the jury to understand would not be admitted
(C) the fact that evidence is rarely complex
(D) the fact that juries are able to reach verdicts
(E) the fact that no judges have accused juries of misunderstanding

13. With which one of the following statements would the author be most likely to disagree?

(A) Juries are likely to be influenced by the personal characteristics, occupation, family, or court appearance of defendants.
(B) Juries are influenced by the age, race, or sex of the defendant.
(C) The judge's misunderstanding the evidence is not a likely cause of judge-jury disagreements.
(D) The jury's misunderstanding the evidence is not a likely cause of judge-jury disagreements.
(E) The jury's sympathy with a defendant is a major cause of judge-jury disagreements.

14. By including the information in the final paragraph about the effect of sympathy with the defendant upon the jury, the author of the passage

(A) unfairly denigrates the opposing argument
(B) undermines the case he has presented
(C) suggests that his arguments are objective

(D) conceals a weakness in his case
(E) underscores the lack of objectivity in judges

15. The author includes statistical information in the passage chiefly in order to

(A) demonstrate his familiarity with social science research methods
(B) support his case for the use of juries
(C) make what is really a hypothesis appear to be factual
(D) give an appearance of objectivity to a subjective view
(E) support a case against the use of juries

Passage 3-A

By the 1960s, some of the optimism of the postwar era began to fade. A series of recessions started in 1948: 1948–1949, 1953–1954, 1957–1958, and
(5) 1961–1963. A renewed and growing concern with unemployment developed when unemployment rates approached 7 percent in 1958 and again in 1961. After each recession, the economy
(10) bounced back but with less than full vigor. Indeed, each period of recovery was less energetic than that which preceded it, and definitions of full employment moved from the
(15) 2 percent of the 1940s to where some considered 4 percent as unrealistically low.

Despite this, the general view of the 1950s as the era of the affluent society
(20) held. What had changed was the view of poverty and of the poor. Kenneth Galbraith, writing in 1958, implied that poverty was spotty and scattered, not systemic. He identified two types of
(25) poverty: "insular" and "case." Insular

poverty covered problems that arose from structural unemployment and differential unemployment rates as were being experienced by the special
(30) problems of the Appalachian region. Case poverty denoted poverty arising from a personal deficiency, such as ill health, lack of education, or even racial or sexual discrimination.

(35)   Whether insular or case in nature, the problem was considered one of employability rather than of poverty per se. In fact, the United States rediscovered poverty as a serious
(40) social problem in the early 1960s, when a series of studies and publications made reality unavoidable. The Social Security Administration, using 1959 data, established a poverty
(45) index and, for the first time, provided an official statistical measure of individuals and groups in poverty. Increased attention came with the publication of Michael Harrington's
(50) *The Other America: Poverty in the United States* in 1962 and Dwight MacDonald's *Our Invisible Poor* in 1963. The 1964 Annual Report of the Council of Economic Advisors dealt
(55) with the situation at length and was transmitted to the Congress along with the Economic Report of the President.

Slowly, the response to poverty emerged, shaped by three factors:
(60) (1) the identification of depressed geographical areas, (2) the civil rights revolution, and (3) the shift in the composition of public assistance rolls that began early in the 1960s. Overall,
(65) there was a programmatic emphasis on employment: the opening up of employment opportunities and the upgrading of labor market skills of the poor.

Passage 3-B

(70)   As the country's efforts to eliminate poverty ground to a halt in the late 1960s and early 1970s, researchers and government officials alike began to ask why the government's war on
(75) poverty had been such a failure. But the initial soul-searching among poverty researchers over the lack of success in this war was often limited in scope and confined to policy issues.
(80) Instead of questioning the government's diagnosis of poverty, many researchers maintained that the government needed to be more creative in improving the training
(85) available to indigents. Other scholars, such as Michael Harrington, also stressed the underfunding of many welfare programs. In his mind, the battle against poverty had failed
(90) because the country was unwilling to spend enough resources to solve the problem.

To test these propositions, the field of policy evaluation was born in the
(95) 1960s and 1970s. By studying variations in either the delivery of government services or resources devoted to particular government activities, a variety of scholars hoped to
(100) identify policies that successfully reduced poverty. Unfortunately, most policy researchers came up empty-handed: they could identify few government programs in the
(105) educational and manpower field that seemed to work unequivocally.

In light of these inconclusive findings, both liberals and conservatives argued in the 1980s that efforts to eliminate
(110) poverty had failed because public officials had misdiagnosed its causes. It stood to reason that even the best-designed programs or ample resources

would prove to be ineffectual if they (115) were based on a faulty reading of the problem. In order for the government to understand why the fight against poverty began to lose steam by the late 1960s, it needed to go back to square (120) one and ask why people became poor in the first place. If critics from the Right and Left were finally in agreement that this question was a priority, they were hopelessly divided (125) about whom to blame for the persistence of poverty. The resolution of these issues was important because it would dictate what types of government programs would be (130) adopted. The increasing divergence between liberals and conservatives was a reflection of their different explanations as to why so many individuals had become hopelessly (135) trapped in poverty.

16. Which one of the following best describes the relationship between Passage A and Passage B?

    (A) Passage A and Passage B both argue that the causes of poverty were misdiagnosed.
    (B) Passage A addresses the period preceding the period addressed by Passage B.
    (C) Each of the passages focuses on social programs to alleviate poverty in the United States.
    (D) Passage A presents a general picture of poverty in America, whereas Passage B provides statistics.
    (E) Both passages question the wisdom of government intervention in solving the problem of poverty.

17. Passage A differs from Passage B in which one of the following ways?

    (A) Passage A presents an overview of poverty in the late 1950s and early 1960s, whereas Passage B details poverty's resolution by the federal government.
    (B) Passage A addresses how the view of poverty changed in the late 1950s and early 1960s, whereas Passage B addresses how the causes of poverty were misdiagnosed.
    (C) Passage A enumerates programs designed to eliminate poverty in the early 1960s, whereas Passage B identifies the ways those programs failed.
    (D) Passage A presents definitions of poverty in the late 1950s and early 1960s, whereas Passage B presents alternative definitions about the poor.
    (E) Passage A discusses the response to addressing poverty in the late 1950s and early 1960s, whereas Passage B discusses its redefinition.

18. According to Passage A, which one of the following best describes how poverty was viewed in the late 1950s and early 1960s?

    (A) The underlying issue of poverty was seen as intrinsic to the system.
    (B) Programs to address poverty were seen as ineffectual responses.
    (C) The generally affluent society considered poverty a minor issue.
    (D) Poverty was eventually considered a problem of employability.
    (E) Personal deficiency, not structural unemployment, was the cause of poverty.

19. According to the author of Passage B, the response to poverty described in Passage A was flawed for which one of the following reasons?

(A) The underlying causes of poverty were not correctly understood.
(B) Federal programs had been based on Galbraith's untested theories.
(C) The voting public did not support government poverty programs.
(D) Government underfunding made poverty programs ineffectual.
(E) Liberals and conservatives could not agree on programs.

20. Which one of the following can be inferred from Passage B about information in Passage A?

(A) The emphasis on improving skills of the poor was effectual.
(B) Galbraith was biased in his identification of two different types of poverty.
(C) A shift in the composition of public assistance rolls caused problems rather than solved them.
(D) Researchers and government officials ignored statistics about the extent of poverty.
(E) More research should have been directed at understanding the causes of poverty.

21. Michael Harrington is cited in both passages for which one of the following reasons?

(A) To indicate the new attention being given to American poverty
(B) To provide a strong contrasting view to popular opinion at that time
(C) To stress the government's unwillingness to examine the causes of poverty

(D) To be a representative of advocacy for full employment
(E) To show the shallowness of scholars who addressed the problem of poverty

22. Which one of the following can be inferred from information in Passage A?

(A) "Structural" poverty was a more critical problem than was "case" poverty.
(B) The poverty index readings in the 1960s were inaccurate.
(C) The 1964 Economic Report precipitated immediate action.
(D) Unemployment problems were particularly severe in Appalachia.
(E) Public assistance rolls were an unreliable measurement of poverty.

23. The author of Passage B cites which one of the following as evidence that the government's war on poverty had been a failure?

(A) A rising unemployment rate throughout the United States
(B) The rate increase of people being added to welfare rolls
(C) The mismanagement of poverty programs and misappropriation of funds
(D) The inability of most evaluators to identify many poverty programs that worked
(E) The unwillingness of Washington to fund any additional poverty programs

Passage 4

In the nineteenth century, anthropologists cheerfully asserted that race, language, and culture (ways of thinking and doing, moral values,

(5) and so forth) were essentially coterminous. Thus, there seemed to be adequate criteria to define ethnic identity in a straightforward and concrete manner. Any ethnic group

(10) would be recognizable by its unique racial, linguistic, and cultural profile. By the middle of the twentieth century, field studies had shown that ethnic identity was not so easy to define, but

(15) it was still regarded as an objective category. It could be measured in concrete ways. Research at this point concentrated on assembling a checklist of concrete categories: biological self-

(20) perpetuation, fundamental social values, interaction and communication, self-identification, and identification by others. The underlying assumption was that when examined under such

(25) headings, a particular social group would display a unique set of objective cultural features, the component parts of ethnic identity, that would distinguish it absolutely from

(30) surrounding groups. Each surrounding group would likewise have its own distinctive profile. The approach also implied that if you started with two distinct social groups—A and B—and,

(35) over time, they exchanged concrete cultural features to such an extent that A came to resemble B closely, then the two groups would be found to have amalgamated.

(40)   When identity was understood in such a way, it was only natural to write about groups of the past, such as the Goths, as though they too were entities of a very concrete and coherent kind.

(45) But since World War II, understandings of identity have been transformed by two separate lines of research. The first originated with Leach's study of North Burmese hill tribes in 1954. His

(50) conclusions explicitly challenged the assumption that social groups and observable cultural features coincide sufficiently for the latter to be a guide to the former. His study showed that,

(55) on occasion, people with little or nothing in common (when investigated under the traditional, objectively measurable categories) would claim to belong to the same social group.

(60) Similarly, those with much, if not everything, in common might claim to belong to different social groups. Exchanging cultural features, then, did not necessarily lead to the

(65) amalgamation of groups.

   The classic document of this revisionary approach came in 1969, with the publication of *Ethnic Groups and Boundaries,* a collection of essays

(70) assembled by the Norwegian anthropologist Frederick Barth. Because perceptions of identity do not always coincide with measurable cultural traits, Barth's collection

(75) switched the emphasis of research to subjective assessment as the basis of identity. What identity did individuals claim, and what identity was recognized in them by others? For

(80) Barth, the different cultural traits that ethnic groups tend to (but do not always) display were the result and not the cause of erecting a social boundary. Groups do not erect

(85) boundaries against one another because they are already different, but they become different because of the original decision to erect a boundary. Diverging cultural traits are thus

(90) symbols of identity, not its substance.

24. Which of the following best expresses the main point of the passage?

 (A) Ethnic groups are primarily distinguished by language, moral, and cultural values.
 (B) Determination of ethnic identity has changed from objective measurements to subjective assessment.
 (C) An individual's ethnic identity has become confused because of amalgamation and globalization.
 (D) A person's membership in an ethnic group is determined by that group's acceptance of the person.
 (E) Current theories suggest that the exchange of cultural features results in an amalgamation of ethnic groups.

25. The passage indicates that Leach's study of North Burmese hill tribes provides evidence *against* which one of the following views?

 (A) Common cultural values are the main determiner of an ethnic group.
 (B) People with the same language and many beliefs in common may belong to different ethnic groups.
 (C) Ethnic groups are not concrete, coherent entities.
 (D) Two groups that exchange cultural values are not always amalgamated.
 (E) Ethnic identity can develop as a result of creating boundaries between groups.

26. Which of the following most accurately describes the organization of the passage?

 (A) The first and second paragraphs present historical views of ethnic identity, and the third paragraph suggests that those views are not borne out by recent research.
 (B) The first paragraph defines the factors that constitute ethnic identity, and the second and third paragraphs give examples of ethnic groups.
 (C) The first two paragraphs present different views of ethnic identity, and the third paragraph presents the author's opinion of both views.
 (D) Paragraph 1 introduces the concept of ethnic identity, paragraph 2 describes current research, and paragraph 3 summarizes the main ideas in the passage.
 (E) The first paragraph presents the nineteenth-century views about ethnic identity, and the second and third paragraphs describe how those views have changed.

27. By describing distinct cultural traits as the "symbols" rather than the "substance" of different ethnic groups, the author of the passage is suggesting which one of the following?

 (A) Different cultural traits are of little importance in an ethnic group.
 (B) Divisions between ethnic groups are symbolic rather than real.
 (C) Specific cultural traits may signify an ethnic group, but they do not define its membership.
 (D) Identifying with a particular ethnic group is based on a person's history with that group.
 (E) Ethnic groups are artificially created and not based on substantial factors.

28. According to the passage, Barth's *Ethnic Groups and Boundaries* was of importance in the study of ethnic identity for which one of the following reasons?

(A) Rather than emphasizing differences, the essays stressed similarities among groups living close to each other.

(B) His work shifted the emphasis of ethnic identification from cultural similarities to linguistic similarities.

(C) Barth's work proved that the previous view of ethnicity was naive and deeply flawed.

(D) Barth shifted the view of identifying an ethnic group based on measurable traits to a view emphasizing individuals' subjective assessment of their ethnicity.

(E) Barth proved that groups previously assigned a particular ethnic identity were most likely incorrectly classified.

29. It can be inferred from the passage that the author would be most likely to agree with which of the following?

(A) Recent research has shown that ethnic identity is meaningless.

(B) The Goths cannot be seen as a concrete, coherent entity.

(C) Groups of people living in close proximity most likely share a common ethnic identity.

(D) The North Burmese hill tribes do not recognize themselves as an ethnic group.

(E) Disagreements between different ethnic groups have been a major cause of global unrest.

30. According to the passage, the concept of ethnic groups "amalgamating" (line 39) has been called into question because

(A) individuals with almost all objective ethnic measurements in common can claim to belong to different groups

(B) no two ethnic groups are identical

(C) an ethnic group will always create a boundary to separate it from other similar groups

(D) individuals will ultimately identify with the ethnic group that originally accepts them

(E) modern research has been unable to uncover any definitive evidence of ethnic groups amalgamating

Passage 5

The right to an unbiased jury is an inseparable part of the right to trial by jury as guaranteed by the Seventh Amendment of the United States
(5) Constitution. This right guarantees that twelve impartial jurors will hear and "truly try" the cause before them.

In September 1982, the California Supreme Court upheld a lower court's
(10) $9.2 million verdict against Ford Motor Company despite the fact that three jurors had been working crossword puzzles and one juror had been reading a novel during the presentation of
(15) testimony. Four of the twelve jurors hearing the case were admittedly participating in the activities charged and were clearly guilty of misconduct, yet the California Supreme Court found
(20) no resultant prejudice against Ford's position.

In the United States, citizens are called upon by the government to serve as jurors. Only under

(25) extraordinary circumstances may a
citizen be excused from such service.
Juries are therefore not necessarily
composed of willing volunteers, but
instead, are sometimes made up of
(30) individuals who are serving against
their will, and justice is adversely
affected when citizens are "forced" to
serve on juries. In "Reflections of a
Juror," the author, who served as a
(35) juror himself, recognized two distinct
perspectives shared among jurors.
Some jurors have a very positive
attitude about their being asked to
serve on a jury. Their perspective is
(40) that of rendering a public service by
fulfilling their jury duties. On the other
hand, some jurors view their obligation
as just that, a burdensome obligation,
and nothing more. Their attitude is one
(45) of getting through with the ordeal as
soon as possible, a let's-get-out-of-
here-by-this-afternoon approach.

A study conducted with mock juries,
concerned specifically with the issue of
(50) juror prejudgment, revealed that
25 percent of the jurors polled reached
their decision early in the trial. The
jurors in the study who admitted to
having made up their minds before
(55) having heard all the evidence also
stated that they generally held to their
first-impression assessments. By
prejudging the outcome of the case the
jurors had, in effect, breached their
(60) sworn duty.

From a reading of the California
Supreme Court's opinion, it appears
that the Court itself has committed the
one form of conduct universally
(65) prohibited, that of prejudgment. Ford's
battle was lost before it had even
begun to present its case. In the first
place, Ford is a multibillion-dollar
international corporation with
(70) "pockets" deeper than most. Secondly,

Ford had experienced a great deal of
negative publicity resulting from recent
jury verdicts awarding large sums of
money to victims of Pinto automobile
(75) accidents wherein it was determined
that Ford had defectively designed the
Pinto's gasoline tank so that it was
prone to explode upon rear end
impacts. Finally, the plaintiff was a
(80) nineteen-year-old college freshman
whose pursuit of a medical career was
abruptly ended when he suffered
extensive brain damage after the
brakes on his 1966 Lincoln failed,
(85) causing him to crash into a fountain
after careening down a steeply curving
hillside street. Ford presented a
considerable amount of evidence in an
attempt to prove that the cause of the
(90) accident was driver error and faulty
maintenance and not defective design.
The Supreme Court responded to
Ford's arguments by stating that the
jury was responsible for judging the
(95) credibility of witnesses and it would be
wholly improper for the Court to usurp
that function by reweighing the
evidence. How ironic that the Court
should so gallantly refuse to upset the
(100) decision of the jury, a jury wherein four
members admittedly were engaging in
extraneous activities when they were
supposed to be "judging the credibility
of witnesses." It would appear from the
(105) misconduct of the jury and the
conclusionary statements of the
California Supreme Court that Ford's
liability was indeed a predetermined,
prejudged fact.
(110) If the decision has any impact upon
our present system of justice, it will
regretfully be a negative one. The
California Supreme Court has, in effect,
approved a standard of jury conduct so
(115) unconscionable as to, in the words of
dissenting Justice Richardson,

"countenance such a complete erosion of a constitutional command," namely, the right to a fair and impartial jury
(120) trial.

31. Which one of the following best states the central idea of the passage?

(A) By not questioning the decision in the Ford case, the California Supreme Court, like the jury, was guilty of prejudgment.

(B) There are serious defects in the system of trial by jury.

(C) The jury in the Ford case was guilty of prejudging the case.

(D) The Supreme Court's handling of the Ford case may lead to an erosion of the constitutional right to a fair and impartial jury trial.

(E) Studies suggest that a large number of the men and women serving on juries fail to "truly try" the cases they hear.

32. All of the following data from the passage could be used to argue against the jury system EXCEPT:

(A) in the Ford case, three jurors were working crossword puzzles and one was reading a novel during the presentation of testimony

(B) juries are likely to include individuals who are serving against their will

(C) in a study of mock jurors, 25 percent reached a decision early in the trial

(D) pretrial publicity about Ford Pintos resulting in large jury verdicts to victims influenced the Supreme Court's decision

(E) some jurors view their service as an ordeal to be ended as quickly as possible

33. The author's belief that Ford was denied a fair trial in the lower court is best supported by the fact that

(A) the jury was unduly sympathetic to the nineteen-year-old accident victim who suffered extensive brain damage

(B) the jury was influenced by unfavorable publicity about the defective gas tanks on the Ford Pinto

(C) three of the jurors were admittedly working crossword puzzles during the testimony

(D) the California Supreme Court refused to reverse the decision of the jury

(E) the California Supreme Court refused to judge the credibility of the witnesses

34. An argument in favor of the Supreme Court decision in the Ford case might include all of the following EXCEPT:

(A) if the case were retried, the jury would probably include jurors who were serving against their will

(B) it is probable that the jurors working puzzles and reading were also paying attention to the testimony

(C) if the case were retried, some members of the jury are likely to come to a decision early in the trial

(D) if the case were retried, those jurors who made up their minds early would be unlikely to alter their verdicts later in the trial

(E) the jury at the original trial is in a better position to judge the credibility of the witnesses than the Supreme Court

35. The author suggests that the California Supreme Court reached its decision in the Ford case for all of the following reasons EXCEPT:

    (A) a prejudice against Ford because of its wealth
    (B) a prejudice against Ford because of recent negative publicity
    (C) an agreement with the lower court's evaluation of the credibility of the witnesses
    (D) a bias in favor of the young accident victim
    (E) a refusal to find fault with deplorable jury conduct

36. In the next to last paragraph of the passage, the author uses irony when he writes

    (A) "Ford's battle was lost before it had even begun to present its case."
    (B) "Ford is a multibillion-dollar international corporation with 'pockets' deeper than most."
    (C) The plaintiff's "pursuit of a medical career was abruptly ended when he suffered extensive brain damage . . ."
    (D) ". . . the Court should so gallantly refuse to upset the decision of the jury. . . ."
    (E) ". . . Ford's liability was indeed a predetermined, prejudged fact."

37. From information given in lines 110–120, it is clear that the Supreme Court decision

    (A) was unanimous
    (B) was not unanimous
    (C) will have a significant impact on the justice system
    (D) reverses that of the lower court
    (E) will be appealed

ANSWER KEY

1. E	20. E
2. E	21. A
3. B	22. D
4. A	23. D
5. B	24. B
6. E	25. A
7. C	26. E
8. D	27. C
9. E	28. D
10. A	29. B
11. C	30. A
12. A	31. A
13. E	32. D
14. C	33. C
15. B	34. B
16. B	35. C
17. B	36. D
18. D	37. B
19. A	

ANSWER EXPLANATIONS

Passage 1

1. **E** The primary purpose of the passage is to present both the advantages (lines 23–32) and disadvantages (lines 33–38) of the Price-Anderson Act. By providing more details, the author does describe the Price-Anderson Act (A), but only to further the purpose of the passage. To clarify the advantages and disadvantages, the author is both supportive (C) and critical (B). Not only does the author not condemn the Act (D), the last paragraph supports the legislation.

2. **E** It could be argued that $665 million is a large sum of money, but the fact that it is a maximum amount becomes an advantage to the nuclear power companies (A). In addition, the latent effects of radiation exposure (B), and the resulting possibility of further liability exceeding the fixed amount (C), are distinct advantages for the companies. The Act retains the logical concept of causation that requires the injured person to prove that the nuclear incident caused his or her injuries (D). The only disadvantage to the companies is the likelihood that the limit of liability will be raised (E), the correct answer.

3. **B** In all probability if a major nuclear incident occurred, it would not be difficult to prove immediate injuries (lines 62–68), and causation (A). Victims with latent injuries would still have to prove causation (C). Liability would most certainly apply if the accident was caused by negligence (D). What the author seems surprised by is that even if there was negligence, the ceiling on compensation would remain intact. According to the passage (lines 33–38), the Act is contrary to the concept of "he who breaks must pay" (E). While it is not absolute, it seems very likely that the number of deaths, injuries, and damages caused by an accident the size of Chernobyl would far exceed the asset pool (B), the correct answer.

4. **A** Only (A) is true and an advantage to the public. (B) is an advantage to the nuclear power companies, not to the public. The common law rules of causation (lines 39–41) would not be relaxed under the Act (C). Punitive damages (E) would be limited even if the accident was the result of gross negligence (lines 20–22). (D) is true, but because it may take time to identify the injuries, the victim may not be able to qualify for reparations before the statute of limitations expires.

5. **B** The plaintiff under common law rules of causation would have to show a probability of 51 percent or more that the defendant's conduct caused his or her injuries (lines 51–55). The defendant's conduct does not have to be the sole cause (lines 44–47) of the injury (A), nor the possibility (lines 55–56) that it caused the injury (C). It is not enough that the defendant's conduct contributed (D) to the injury. It must be the probable or reasonable cause of the injury (B), the correct answer. For the plaintiff to be successful, he or she does not need to prove negligence (E) by the defendant (lines 20–22), only a causal relationship (lines 41–44).

6. **E** The passage asserts that the Planex Corporation declared bankruptcy to avoid paying damages in a large number of suits involving asbestos.

7. **C** Though the author points to faults in Price-Anderson, he or she never suggests that the nuclear power industry's growth should be restricted. The author would agree that attitudes toward nuclear power have been focusing on more protections for victims (A) and the contamination from Chernobyl (B) will have far-reaching effects (lines 62–72). In (D) the author would probably feel that the asset pool should be increased (lines 23–27). The author alludes to the statute of limitations (lines 28–38), and the requirements that certain statutes be waived by the utility company and the uncertainty of recovery by the victims (E).

Passage 2

8. **D** The passage is part of a longer essay written to refute the arguments of Judge Jerome Frank, who holds that a judge alone is likely to be more reliable than a jury.

9. **E** The second paragraph says that judges and juries agree in 75.4 percent of the cases, according to the study.

10. **A** The third paragraph discusses the greater harshness of judges in all categories of crime—in counts, degrees, and sentencing.

11. **C** Because the effect of this information upon judges is to make their judgments harsher, we can infer it would have the same effect on juries and the withholding of this information is, predictably, to the defendant's advantage.

12. **A** The author assumes the judge understands the evidence and because the juries agree with the judge so often, he argues the juries must also have understood the evidence to come to the same conclusion as the judge.

13. **E** The passage supports each of the first four statements, but the jury's sympathy with a defendant according to the last paragraph leads to judge-jury differences in only 4 percent of all the cases studied and so could not be called a "major" cause of disagreement.

14. **C** By admitting frankly that juries are not always fully objective the author demonstrates a willingness to discuss facts that may not advance his case. All of the four other options are false.

15. **B** The statistics are used to support the author's case for the use of juries. Because the statistics are the result of other writers' research, and are based upon a large sample, they give more than an "appearance" of objectivity.

Passage 3

16. **B** Passage A addresses events from the late 1950s to the early 1960s. Passage B begins with "As the country's efforts to eliminate poverty ground to a halt in the late 1960s and early 1970s," and it then explores issues of the 1960s and 1970s. While Passage B states that both liberals and conservatives believed that the causes of poverty had been misdiagnosed, nothing in Passage A argues that poverty was misdiagnosed (A). Passage B addresses social programs to alleviate poverty, whereas Passage A focuses on identifying the *problem* of poverty, not its programmatic solutions (D). Lines 38–40 indicate that social programs came

later. No statistics (D) are provided in Passage B. Finally, while Passage B discusses criticism that government may have misdiagnosed the causes of poverty and thus the wisdom of its intervention (E), Passage A focuses on the government coming to identify poverty as a problem, never addressing its subsequent intervention.

17. **B** Indeed, the view of American poverty changed in the 1950s and 1960s, and this is a focus of Passage A, whereas Passage B addresses the problem of diagnosing correctly the causes of poverty. In (A), Passage A may be viewed as an overview, but Passage B does not detail poverty's resolution, as poverty was not resolved. (C) is incorrect, as Passage A identifies the problem of poverty but does *not* "enumerate programs" intended to resolve it. (D) is incorrect because Passage B does not "present alternative definitions of the poor." (E) is incorrect because Passage A's main focus is on the identification and redefinition of poverty, not on the response to addressing the problem; the correct order here is reversed.

18. **D** Lines 35–38 and 64–69 indicate that the view in Passage A is that poverty was a problem of employability. The economic system (A) is not addressed in Passage A, nor is the effect of poverty programs (B). The passage states that the generally affluent society was beginning to be disturbed by rising unemployment rates, and thus (C) is inaccurate. (E) refers to Galbraith's theory but states it incorrectly.

19. **A** Passage B addresses how the causes of poverty were misdiagnosed. The basis of federal programs (B) is not addressed by the passage, and (C) is never addressed at all. (D), the opinion of Michael Harrington, is mentioned in the passage as a possible cause, but it is not what the author finally discusses as its underlying flaw in the government's response. The disagreement between liberals and conservatives was not about programs (E) but about the causes of poverty.

20. **E** In Passage B the author implies that during the period covered by Passage A more attention should have been paid to understanding the factors that cause poverty. No indication is made that emphasis on improving skills was "effectual" (A); in fact, if it was effective, it might have helped to successfully diminish poverty. Galbraith distinguished two different types of poverty, but whether or not he was biased (B) in his judgment is never addressed or implied. While lines 62–63 indicate a "shift in public assistance roles," there is no indication that it caused problems or solved them (C). And the passage never addressed whether or not researchers and government officials ignored statistics.

21. **A** Lines 48–53 and 85–88 attest to Michael Harrington's *The Other America* bringing to attention the problem of poverty in America. Both (B) and (D) may possibly be true, according to the passage: (B) because Harrington's view may well have been different from the popular notion that had no realization that poverty existed in America at that time, and (D) because Harrington may well have argued in his book for full employment. However, the reason he is *cited in both passages*

is that he called to attention the problem of poverty. (E) is neither addressed nor implied by the passage.

22. **D** Lines 28–30 and lines 61–63 indicate that unemployment was particularly severe in Appalachia. Although structural poverty and case poverty were mentioned in citing differences, no distinction was made about which was the more critically important (A). While the 1960s poverty index was mentioned, one cannot infer from the passage that it was inaccurate (B), nor were the public assistance rolls an unreliable measurement of poverty. Lines 58–69 indicate that *immediate* action (C) was not, in fact, what had occurred.

23. **D** Lines 103–106 state that policy researchers could "identify few government programs in the educational and manpower field that seemed to work unequivocally." While (A) and (B) may have been mentioned initially as evidence of poverty, they were not cited as why the government's war on poverty had been a failure. Nor were (C) and (E) funding issues cited as the reason for government's failure to successfully address poverty.

Passage 4

24. **B** The main point of the passage is the change in the way ethnic identity has been regarded (lines 77–84). (A) describes how the nineteenth century determined ethnic identity, which is not the main point. (D) is partially accurate but also not the main point. (C) is irrelevant, and (E) represents a past theory, not a current theory.

25. **A** Leach's study showed that people who shared common cultural values did not always belong to the same ethnic group (lines 54–59). All of the other views were in keeping with Leach's findings.

26. **E** The first paragraph presents the previous view of how ethnic identity was determined, whereas the second and third paragraphs demonstrate the changes from that view because of the work of Leach and Barth.

27. **C** The word *symbol* here is most closely related to the concept of "signifying" as opposed to "defining." The substance of ethnic groups, according to the passage, has to do with how people identify themselves, not with the cultural traits they share with a group. (A), (D), and (E) are not suggested by the passage. (B) uses the idea of a symbol in a way not supported by the context.

28. **D** Barth's key point was that objective measurements of ethnicity are less important than subjective assessments because of the number of exceptions in an ethnic group when measured by the traditional method. (A), (B), and (E) are not covered in the passage. (C) is too strong a statement ("deeply flawed," "naive").

29. **B** Lines 40–44 indicate that using the nineteenth-century method, Goths would be considered a concrete, coherent group. The rest of the passage suggests that the nineteenth-century method is questionable. (C) and (E) may be true, but nothing in the passage implies these points. (A) is simply inaccurate; the passage does not imply that research into ethnicity is "meaningless."

30. **A** See lines 63–65. None of the other choices are indicated in the passage. *Amalgamation* is defined in the passage as occurring when two groups exchange many concrete cultural features and therefore become one group. Leach's study of the North Burmese hill tribes showed that exchanging cultural features didn't necessarily lead to the amalgamation of groups.

Passage 5

31. **A** The author wishes to criticize both the jury, which was inattentive, and the Supreme Court, which allowed the jury's decision to stand. Some of the other options are stated or implied ideas of the passage but not its central idea.

32. **D** (D) is relevant to the Supreme Court decision but not to the jury system. (A), (B), (C), and (E) all expose deficiencies in the jury system.

33. **C** The inattentiveness of four jurors is explicit support for a charge that Ford's case was not fairly heard. We don't know for certain if (A) or (B) is true. (D) and (E) are true but do not support the author's belief in the unfairness of the trial.

34. **B** The limitations of all juries discussed in the passage would apply as well to the jury retrying the case as to the jury who reached a decision already. The Supreme Court's argument that the original jury was in a better position to judge the credibility of the witnesses is surely correct; the Supreme Court did not see the witnesses who testified. Though (B) is remotely possible, it is not a point one would wish to use in support of the Supreme Court decision.

35. **C** Though the Supreme Court agreed with the lower court jury, it specifically asserted the impropriety of its attempting to reweigh the evidence and the credibility of the witnesses.

36. **D** A case could be made that (B), an understatement, is ironic but a clearer instance is the sarcasm of "gallantly"; the author does not believe the Supreme Court acted gallantly.

37. **B** Because Justice Richardson dissented, the decision cannot have been unanimous.

5

WRITING SAMPLE

INTRODUCTION

The LSAT will include a 35-minute writing sample. You will be asked to respond to one kind of writing prompt—the decision prompt.

The decision prompt requires that you write an argument for selecting between two people, positions, items, or courses of action based on the given criteria. No specialized knowledge is required for the writing prompt, but you should express yourself clearly and effectively.

You will write the essay on the lined area on the front and back of the separate writing sample response sheet. Anything you write outside the restricted space will not be reproduced. Space will be provided below the general directions and topic for scratch work, such as organizing and/or outlining your ideas. For practice purposes, restrict yourself to about two lined pages so that you will be more comfortable writing under the exam conditions.

Following are general directions for the writing sample, a careful analysis of the writing prompt, and a short review of the writing process as it applies to the prompt. Next, you will examine completed essays and then be given topics for writing your own essays.

GENERAL DIRECTIONS

You have 35 minutes to plan and write an essay on the topic given. Take a few minutes to consider the topic and organize your thoughts before you begin to write your essay. As you write your essay, be sure to develop your ideas fully. Try to leave time to review your essay. DO NOT WRITE ON A TOPIC OF YOUR OWN CHOICE. ESSAYS THAT DO NOT ADDRESS THE GIVEN TOPIC ARE UNACCEPTABLE.

You will not be expected to display any specialized knowledge in your essay. Law schools are interested in the reasoning, clarity, organization, language use, and writing mechanics that you display. The quality of your writing is more important than the length of your response.

Only the lined area on your response sheets will be reproduced for the law schools, so do not write outside this space. Make sure that your handwriting is legible.

THE APPROACH

ANALYZING THE WRITING SAMPLE TOPICS

THE DECISION PROMPT

You will be asked to write an argument for hiring, promoting, selecting, and so on, one of two candidates or items based on two criteria and two descriptions of the choices or courses of action.

Either one of the two choices can be supported based on the information given. You should consider both choices and argue *for* one and *against* the other, based on the two specific criteria and the facts provided. There is no "right" or "wrong" selection.

Some recent topics have included writing arguments in support of:

- Purchasing one of two films for a public television station
- Selecting one of two designs submitted for a commemorative sculpture
- Selecting one of two retirement communities for a retiree
- Selecting one of two ways of investing money inherited from an uncle
- Deciding which one of two schools to enter for an undergraduate business degree
- Selecting one of two proposals for an introductory course in computer training
- Selecting one of two athletes for a team

In each case the initial introductory statement or statements were followed by two criteria, and then the background of each candidate, or a description of each film, or a description of each school, or a description of each option.

Let's take a closer look. A recent topic gave us its two criteria for hiring a mathematics teacher: (1) the high school's increased concern with computers and (2) its wish to develop the mathematics program at the school to incorporate work-study projects in the business community. The first candidate had a solid educational background, high school teaching and minor administrative experience, good references, and recent training in computers. The second candidate had a slightly different but equally good educational background and no high school teaching experience, but had worked as a teaching assistant in college and a tutor in community programs, as well as having solid credentials in computers and experience as an employee in financial work for a retail store and a bank.

What should be apparent is that it does *NOT* matter which candidate you choose. The principles and qualifications will be written in such a way that you can write in favor of *EITHER* candidate. Make your choice, and stick to it. You should mention the other candidate to show either some of his or her weaknesses or how the candidate you selected is more qualified. What your readers will be looking for are clarity, consistency, relevance, and correctness of grammar and usage. Since you have only 35 minutes to read the topic and to plan and write your essay, you will not be expected to produce a long or a subtle essay. But you must write on the topic clearly and correctly.

The questions will make clear the sort of audience you are writing for, and you can be sure that this audience is literate and informed about the issues in your paper. In the math teacher topic, for example, the assumed audience is whoever is to hire the math teacher. You do not need to tell this audience what she already knows, but you do want to make her focus upon the issues that support your case. Let us assume you are making the case for the experienced teacher with some computer training. Your essay should stress the obvious qualifications—his teaching experience and computer training. Where you have no direct evidence of expertise, you can invent, so long as you do so plausibly and work from details that are given in the question. You could, for example, argue that, although there are two criteria, the computer issue is really the more important since the students will not be able to find good work-study projects in the community until they have a greater knowledge of computers.

Assume you have chosen the second candidate. Your essay should focus upon her strengths (for example, her experience in business will help her in setting up a business-related program for the students). Where her qualifications are weaker (her lack of high school teaching experience), your essay can emphasize the other kind of teaching experience she has had. Do not be afraid to introduce details to support your argument that are your own ideas. Just be sure that, when you do present additional information, it is consistent with and arises plausibly from the information on the test.

So far, the writing topics have used two slightly different forms. The first (the math teachers) used two sentences, one for each of two equally weighted criteria, and then described the two equally qualified candidates. Another sample topic type also uses two sentences to describe the principles, but the first contains the two criteria, and the second sentence elaborates on one of them. For example, the two principles might be (1) lifeguards are promoted on the basis of years of service and community activities; and (2) community activities include lifesaving clinics, talks to school children, waterfront safety seminars, and high school swimming-team coaching. The biographies would then describe two candidates whose years of service differ slightly, and each of whom has some strength in the areas listed under (2). Since you are not told which of the two criteria is the more important, or which of the various sorts of community service is most important, you can decide for yourself how to weigh these factors, as long as you do so plausibly. You cannot contradict the question—for example, by saying length of service is not important—but you can argue that, although your candidate's length of service is slightly less than that of her competition, her overwhelming superiority in community service is more important.

Here is a suggested plan for approaching any writing sample of this sort.

THE PHASES OF WRITING

Phase 1—Prewriting

1. Read the introductory statements carefully as they lay out the argument that follows. Circle or underline key words.
2. Read the two statements of policy or criteria at least twice, *actively*. (Circle or mark the essential points of the topic.) Are they equally weighted? If not, clarify the difference.
3. Read the biographies or descriptions at least twice, *actively*. Test them carefully against the policy or criteria statements.

4. Choose your candidate or item. Again set the qualifications or qualities beside those of the statements. Decide exactly what your choice's greatest strengths are. What are the limitations? Think about how these limitations can be invalidated or turned into strengths. You should list some of the weaknesses of the other candidate. Which of these do you want to mention to strengthen your position?

5. Outline your essay. Your essay should be four or five paragraphs long. Paragraph 1 should begin with a short introductory paragraph that lays out the argument that follows. If you are selecting a candidate, paragraph 2 might focus on his or her obvious strengths that meet the given criteria. Paragraph 3 might deal with how the candidate also shows promise of fulfilling the other requirements. Paragraph 4 might discuss some of the weaknesses of the other candidate or might compare the two candidates. Paragraph 5 might pull together and amplify the reasons for your selection.

Phase 2—Writing

1. Do *not* waste time with a fancy opening paragraph on an irrelevant topic like the importance of math teachers or lifeguards in this complex modern world.

2. Start with a direction. Your first sentence should serve a purpose.

3. Support your argument with examples or other specifics.

4. Do *not* write a closing paragraph that simply repeats what you have already said.

5. Write legibly. Write clearly. Write naturally. Do *not* use big words for their own sake. Do not try to be cute or ironic or funny.

6. Remember that the assumed purpose of this paper is to convince a reader to prefer one candidate or item to another. Your real purpose, of course, is to show a law school that you can follow instructions and write an essay that is well organized, adheres to the point, and is grammatically correct.

Phase 3—Proofreading

1. Allow sufficient time to proofread your essay. At this point, add any information that is vital, and delete any information that seems confusing or out of place.

2. Don't make extensive changes that will make your writing less readable.

3. Check each sentence for mechanical errors (spelling, punctuation, grammar). Some common types of errors are these:

- Using pronouns with no clear antecedents
- Lack of agreement between subject and verb
- Using the wrong verb tense
- Faulty parallelism in a series of items
- Misplaced or dangling modifiers
- Adjective-adverb confusion
- Misuse of comparative terms or comparisons

TWO COMPLETED DECISION WRITING SAMPLES

Following are two "model" essays. Notice that each of the two sample essays is written from a different perspective.

Sample Topic

Read the following descriptions of Bergquist and Kretchmer, applicants for the job of Assistant Director on a major motion picture. Then, in the space provided, write an argument for hiring one over the other. The following criteria are relevant to your decision:

- In addition to working closely with and advising the Director on creative decisions, the Assistant Director must work with all types of individuals—from stars to Teamster truck drivers—and elicit the best from every cast and crew member for the good of the motion picture.
- The Assistant Director is responsible for all the planning and organization—including paperwork, travel itinerary, meals, etc.—of the entire film project. He/she lays the groundwork for a successful "shoot."

BERGQUIST began her career in films as an Administrative Assistant to the president of a major film studio. As such, she often accompanied her employer in his wining and dining of stars, or to the set when problems arose. She double-checked contracts, shooting schedules, cast and crew checks, and kept a close eye on the budget of several multimillion-dollar films. When her boss was subsequently fired due to a poor season of films, Bergquist was able to secure a position as Assistant Editor at the studio, helping several highly respected film editors "cut" feature films. It was here that she learned about the creative end of the business, and soon after became the chief editor of an hour-long studio documentary, which won several awards. After two years, Bergquist was accepted into the Assistant Directors Training Program, and is presently a candidate for Assistant Director of this new $15,000,000 motion picture.

KRETCHMER was a principal/teacher for 12 years before embarking on a film career. She taught math at the New York School for the Creative Arts, and also worked with parents in the community, the board of education, and local government representatives in securing financing for the $20,000,000 school building. As Chairperson of the New Building Committee, she worked closely with architects, townspeople, contractors, and even children to understand their needs for the building. Today the building stands as a model for such schools everywhere. Eight years ago Kretchmer came to Hollywood and, through persistence and charm, secured a studio position and worked her way up to Chief Auditor, where she oversaw budgets on several multimillion-dollar films. She enrolled in the Assistant Directors Training Program, which she recently completed, and is now a candidate for the position of Assistant Director of this new film.

(On the actual exam, there will be space for scratch work below the topic.)

Sample Essay 1

What sets Bergquist apart from Kretchmer is her understanding of, and experience in, the creative elements of filmmaking.

An Assistant Director (AD) advises the Director in key creative decisions: how to best structure and order the shooting schedule, how to begin and end scenes, and how best to shoot a scene or sequence. Even though the ultimate decision rests with the Director, the AD's input is vital. Like a caddy advising a golfer of the distance and terrain of the course, the AD's knowledge of the creative elements of filmmaking enhances her abilities in these tasks. Since a film's success often hinges on these creative decisions, the AD's contributions can be critical.

As an editor, Bergquist learned how a film is cut together and how the pieces must fit coherently. She cut her own films and won numerous awards, thus reflecting her understanding of good creative choices. This special knowledge of film (which Kretchmer lacks)— how shots must match, how moods and sequences build upon each other—is essential to the final success of any film.

This is not to say that Kretchmer has no special talents to bring to this job. She does, in fact, have considerable organizational experience, an important area of expertise for an AD in that the AD must consistently deal effectively with complex schedules and budget concerns. And without that organizational ability, schedules and shoots can end in chaos, no matter how creatively planned. But the fact remains that Kretchmer's experience is primarily in areas far removed from the world of filmmaking—education and financing. Even in her Hollywood career, her responsibilities have centered on financial rather than creative matters.

Bergquist, however, while having excellent creative experience in her editing work, does not lack organizational expertise. In fact, her organizational experience is more likely to mesh with the requirements of the Assistant Director's job than Kretchmer's because that experience has been within the filmmaking community rather than in an area far removed from these specific concerns.

Sample Essay 2

Kretchmer has what Bergquist seriously lacks: the experience and ability to work well with all kinds of people—a crucial skill in the collaborative art/business of filmmaking.

Any film's lengthy end-credits attest to the huge number of people contributing talent—technicians, laborers, performing artists, and others. As the director's right-hand person, the Assistant Director (AD) must help orchestrate that effort. She must "read" the personalities of different individuals and know how to appeal to each ego to garner the best from each.

As chairperson of a building committee, Kretchmer worked successfully with dozens of different personalities in pursuit of a common goal, not unlike a film project. In working with diverse personalities (parents, administrators, children, teachers, architects, and builders, each with different goals), Kretchmer had to have a keen understanding of people and be able to know their strengths and limitations. This is precisely her most important task as a motion picture AD.

On first glance, it might seem that Bergquist's background is overall more suited to the job of AD. She has, in fact, been involved in aspects of filmmaking for much of her career. A closer look, however, would suggest that the specific responsibilities of her previous positions do not translate well to the requirements of the AD's work. Her resume emphasizes her background as Administrative Assistant to a film studio president. But a studio president's work is quite unlike that of a Director. It is an overseeing position rather than one that requires active and knowledgeable decisions before the fact. Similarly, film editing experience, while it certainly helps in understanding the elements of filmmaking, is generally accomplished in relative isolation and has little to do with the ability to work effectively in the diverse and sometimes chaotic world of a film set.

Kretchmer's background indicates not only the hard-headed business sense to effectively plan and organize a film project but also the essential ability to do so in the midst of the various, and sometimes competing, goals and beliefs of the hundreds of personalities involved in the film project.

REVIEW OF GENERAL TIPS

1. Read the topic question at least twice, *actively:* circle or mark the essential points of the question. Note the main question or parts to be discussed, the audience you are addressing, and the persona or position from which you are writing.

2. Remember to *prewrite,* or plan before you write. Spend at least five minutes organizing your thoughts by jotting notes, outlining, brainstorming, clustering, etc.

3. As you write, keep the flow of your writing going. Don't stop your train of thought to worry about the spelling of a word. You can fix little things later.

4. Leave a few minutes to reread and edit your paper after you finish writing. A careful rereading will often catch careless mistakes and errors in punctuation, spelling, etc., that you didn't have time to worry about as you wrote.

5. Remember that a good essay will be

   - on topic;
   - well organized;
   - well developed with examples;
   - grammatically sound with few errors;
   - interesting to read, with a variety of sentence types;
   - clear, neat, and easy to read.

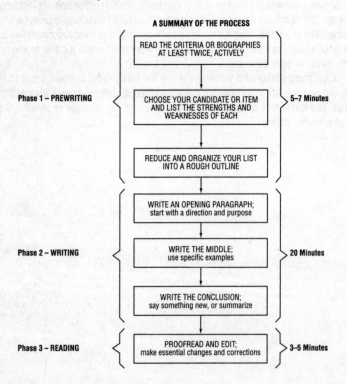

A SUMMARY OF THE PROCESS

READ THE CRITERIA OR BIOGRAPHIES
AT LEAST TWICE, ACTIVELY

Phase 1 – PREWRITING

CHOOSE YOUR CANDIDATE OR ITEM
AND LIST THE STRENGTHS AND
WEAKNESSES OF EACH   5–7 Minutes

REDUCE AND ORGANIZE YOUR LIST
INTO A ROUGH OUTLINE

Phase 2 – WRITING

WRITE AN OPENING PARAGRAPH;
start with a direction and purpose

WRITE THE MIDDLE;
use specific examples   20 Minutes

WRITE THE CONCLUSION;
say something new, or summarize

Phase 3 – READING

PROOFREAD AND EDIT;
make essential changes and corrections   3–5 Minutes

PRACTICE: WRITING SAMPLES

After reviewing the completed essays, try some practice on your own. We have provided sample questions.

Try following the steps we have suggested, varying them slightly, if necessary, to suit your personal style. Have an honest critic read and respond to each practice essay you complete.

You will be given special sheets of paper to write your essay. It will have the essay topic on the top followed by room for scratch work. For practice, write your essay on two sides of an 8½" by 11" college-ruled lined sheet of paper.

Writing Sample Topic 1

Read the following description of Arbit and Blatas, candidates for your party's nomination to the city council. *Then, in the space provided, write an argument for nominating one candidate over the other.* Use the information in this description and assume that two general policies guide your party's decision on nomination:

- Nominations are based upon a combination of the probable success in the election and party service.
- Party service includes seniority, committee work, and fund-raising.

Arbit, a Rumanian-American, has lived in the district and worked for the party for fifteen years. He is chairman of two key party committees and a member of two others. His fund-raising picnic, begun ten years ago, now raises at least $10,000 every year. Arbit is 47, a trial lawyer, with no prior experience in elective office. Twenty percent of the district is Rumanian-American, almost all of whom support the party in every election.

Blatas, of Hungarian background, moved to the district seven years ago. She has worked for the party for seven years as a member of several party committees, and as Arbit's assistant in arranging the fund-raising picnic. A graduate of law school, she is 35, and was recently promoted to director of the city's real estate research office. She narrowly lost an election for city assessor two years ago. Thirty-five percent of the voters in the district are Hungarian-American.

Writing Sample Topic 2

The *Times-Herald*, a large metropolitan newspaper, is about to add a new strip to its comic page. The editorial board must decide between two features that do not now appear in any of the city's other newspapers. *In the space provided, write an argument to be presented to the editorial board in support of one of the comic strips over the other.* Two considerations should guide your decision:

- The newspaper wishes to improve its reputation for serious journalism.
- The newspaper wishes to increase its circulation.

Described by *Time* magazine as "America's most beloved comic strip," *Tom Jordan, M.D.* is a serial that depicts the life of a handsome young doctor at a large New York hospital. It appears in more newspapers in the United States than any other comic. Its stories combine medical information, romance, and moral uplift. Each story takes thirty-two weeks to complete. An especially popular recent episode dealt with Tom Jordan's saving the life of an orphaned leukemia victim; others in the recent past have dealt with drug addiction among the very rich, kidney transplants, and anorexia. *Tom Jordan, M.D.* is the work of a group of four cartoonists.

Bart Pollard's comic, *D.C.,* was the first strip cartoon to win a Pulitzer Prize. Its satiric treatment of Democrats and Republicans, of clergymen, doctors, lawyers, and athletes, has at one time or another given such offense that a number of newspapers that had contracted to run the feature have refused to print it. In Washington, Pollard's *D.C.* is called the "comic strip that everyone hates, but everyone reads." A cabinet officer who closely resembled a character pilloried in the comic has recently filed a libel suit against Pollard. Readership of the strip is especially high on college campuses.

Writing Sample Topic 3

The Animal Protection Society must decide on a speaker to address its annual fund-raising dinner. *In the space provided, write an argument in support of one of the two following choices over the other.* Two considerations guide your decision:

- The society must immediately raise as much money as possible to support an emergency airlift to save an endangered species of crane.
- The society wishes to increase the number of life members, subscribers who can be counted on to give money every year.

Jan Gilbert is a comedienne and the star of a popular television talk show. On her program, she frequently invites keepers from the San Diego Zoo, who bring with them lion cubs, talking mynah birds, lemurs, and other small animals that appeal to large audiences. A dog lover, she often appears in public and on television with her miniature poodle, which travels with her wherever she goes. She is an active fund-raiser for conservative political causes. Because of her love of animals, she has agreed to waive half of her usual personal appearance fee of $12,000.

Katrina Nelson is a distinguished zoologist. She is an adjunct research professor at Cambridge University and has spent fourteen years in Africa observing the behavior of packs of Cape hunting dogs, jackals, and hyenas. A film she made on the scavengers and predators of Africa has been shown on educational television stations. She is the author of five books, including one on the animals of Africa that have become extinct in this century. She is an experienced and skillful public speaker. Her lecture fee is $500.

6

A SUMMARY OF STRATEGIES

DIRECTIONS AND STRATEGIES

GENERAL TIPS

- Use the "one-check, two-check" system, doing the easier questions first, and saving the time-consuming and difficult questions for later.
- Don't leave any blank answer spaces. At least guess on your unanswered questions.
- Eliminate unreasonable or irrelevant answers immediately, marking them out on your question booklet.
- Highlight key words and phrases by marking right in your question booklet. Use the margins to draw diagrams, set up charts, and so on.
- Watch out for the common mistake—the MISREAD.
- Spend some extra time reviewing Logical Reasoning problems. Remember, Logical Reasoning will comprise two of the four scored sections of your exam.

REVIEW OF LSAT AREAS

Logical Reasoning

Directions: **In this section you will be given brief statements or passages and will be required to evaluate the reasoning involved. In some instances, more than one choice will appear to be a possible answer. You are to choose the *best* answer. Use common sense and reasonableness in making your selection; then mark the proper space on the answer sheet.**

Strategies:

- Read the question first; then go back and read the argument or statement. This will give insight into what is going to be asked.
- Watch for items in the answer choices that are irrelevant or not addressed in the given information. Eliminate these immediately.
- Notice the overall tone of the question: Positive or negative? Agreeing with and strengthening the author's argument or criticizing and weakening the statement?
- Watch for key words: *some, all, none, only, one, few, no, could, must, each, except.*

Analytical Reasoning

Directions: In this section you will be given groups of questions based on different sets of conditions. Drawing a simple diagram may be helpful in answering some of the questions. You are to choose the *best* answer and mark the corresponding space on your answer sheet.

Strategies:

- No formal logic is required.
- Make simple charts or diagrams.
- Fill in as much of the diagram as possible, but don't worry if you cannot complete it.
- Look for the framework of the diagram that would be most effective.
- Apply evidence in both directions, that is, also use what you know is *not* true.
- Use question marks for information that is variable.
- Sometimes looking at the questions can tip off the framework of the diagram that would be most helpful.
- If no standard applies, simply pull out information or use simple notes.

Reading Comprehension

<u>*Directions:*</u> Read the passages and answer the questions following each passage by blackening the appropriate space on the answer sheet. You may refer to the passages when answering the questions.

Strategies:

- Skim the questions first, marking key words and phrases. (Don't read the answer choices.)
- Skim the passage (optional). Read and mark the first sentence of each paragraph.
- Read actively, marking the passage. In particular, look for answer spots, repeat spots, intuition spots.
- Answer the questions. Skip if necessary. Eliminate weak choices. Don't "read into" the passage.

Writing Sample

Directions: You have 35 minutes to write an essay in response to a given topic. Take a few minutes to plan your work before you begin writing. DO NOT WRITE ON A TOPIC OF YOUR OWN CHOICE. ESSAYS THAT DO NOT ADDRESS THE GIVEN TOPIC ARE UNACCEPTABLE.

The quality of your writing is more important than the length of your response or the content. Pay attention to organization, appropriate diction, and correct usage. You will not be expected to display any specialized knowledge in your response, nor will you be expected to write a "perfect" essay; law schools understand that you are writing under a time constraint, and will allow for the minor lapses in writing ability that might occur under this circumstance.

Only the lined area in your booklet will be reproduced for the law schools, so do not write outside this space. *Do not* skip lines or use wide margins. These precautions, along with careful planning and legible handwriting that is not unduly large, will keep you within the allowed space.

Strategies:

- Read statements and biographies or descriptions at least twice, actively.
- Choose your candidate or item.
- Outline your essay.
- Start with a direction. Your first sentence should serve a purpose.
- Support your decision with examples or other specifics.
- Do *not* write a closing paragraph that simply repeats what you have already said.
- Write legibly. Write clearly. Write naturally.
- Proofread and edit your essay.

PART THREE

PRACTICE

Mastering Problem Types and Time Pressures

7

MODEL TEST ONE

This chapter contains full-length Model Test One. It is geared to the format of the LSAT, and it is complete with answers and explanations. It is equivalent to the LSAT in question structure, number of questions, level of difficulty, and time allotments. (The questions used are not taken directly from the LSAT, as those questions are copyrighted and may not be reproduced.)

Model Test One should be taken under strict test conditions. The test ends with a 35-minute Writing Sample, which is not scored.

Section	Description	Number of Questions	Time Allowed
I.	Reading Comprehension	28	35 minutes
II.	Analytical Reasoning	24	35 minutes
III.	Logical Reasoning	26	35 minutes
IV.	Analytical Reasoning	24	35 minutes
V.	Logical Reasoning	25	35 minutes
	Writing Sample		35 minutes
TOTALS:		127	3 hours 30 minutes

Now please turn to the next page, remove your answer sheet, and begin Model Test One.

ANSWER SHEET—MODEL TEST ONE

Section 1	Section 2	Section 3	Section 4	Section 5
1. Ⓐ Ⓑ Ⓒ Ⓓ Ⓔ	1. Ⓐ Ⓑ Ⓒ Ⓓ Ⓔ	1. Ⓐ Ⓑ Ⓒ Ⓓ Ⓔ	1. Ⓐ Ⓑ Ⓒ Ⓓ Ⓔ	1. Ⓐ Ⓑ Ⓒ Ⓓ Ⓔ
2. Ⓐ Ⓑ Ⓒ Ⓓ Ⓔ	2. Ⓐ Ⓑ Ⓒ Ⓓ Ⓔ	2. Ⓐ Ⓑ Ⓒ Ⓓ Ⓔ	2. Ⓐ Ⓑ Ⓒ Ⓓ Ⓔ	2. Ⓐ Ⓑ Ⓒ Ⓓ Ⓔ
3. Ⓐ Ⓑ Ⓒ Ⓓ Ⓔ	3. Ⓐ Ⓑ Ⓒ Ⓓ Ⓔ	3. Ⓐ Ⓑ Ⓒ Ⓓ Ⓔ	3. Ⓐ Ⓑ Ⓒ Ⓓ Ⓔ	3. Ⓐ Ⓑ Ⓒ Ⓓ Ⓔ
4. Ⓐ Ⓑ Ⓒ Ⓓ Ⓔ	4. Ⓐ Ⓑ Ⓒ Ⓓ Ⓔ	4. Ⓐ Ⓑ Ⓒ Ⓓ Ⓔ	4. Ⓐ Ⓑ Ⓒ Ⓓ Ⓔ	4. Ⓐ Ⓑ Ⓒ Ⓓ Ⓔ
5. Ⓐ Ⓑ Ⓒ Ⓓ Ⓔ	5. Ⓐ Ⓑ Ⓒ Ⓓ Ⓔ	5. Ⓐ Ⓑ Ⓒ Ⓓ Ⓔ	5. Ⓐ Ⓑ Ⓒ Ⓓ Ⓔ	5. Ⓐ Ⓑ Ⓒ Ⓓ Ⓔ
6. Ⓐ Ⓑ Ⓒ Ⓓ Ⓔ	6. Ⓐ Ⓑ Ⓒ Ⓓ Ⓔ	6. Ⓐ Ⓑ Ⓒ Ⓓ Ⓔ	6. Ⓐ Ⓑ Ⓒ Ⓓ Ⓔ	6. Ⓐ Ⓑ Ⓒ Ⓓ Ⓔ
7. Ⓐ Ⓑ Ⓒ Ⓓ Ⓔ	7. Ⓐ Ⓑ Ⓒ Ⓓ Ⓔ	7. Ⓐ Ⓑ Ⓒ Ⓓ Ⓔ	7. Ⓐ Ⓑ Ⓒ Ⓓ Ⓔ	7. Ⓐ Ⓑ Ⓒ Ⓓ Ⓔ
8. Ⓐ Ⓑ Ⓒ Ⓓ Ⓔ	8. Ⓐ Ⓑ Ⓒ Ⓓ Ⓔ	8. Ⓐ Ⓑ Ⓒ Ⓓ Ⓔ	8. Ⓐ Ⓑ Ⓒ Ⓓ Ⓔ	8. Ⓐ Ⓑ Ⓒ Ⓓ Ⓔ
9. Ⓐ Ⓑ Ⓒ Ⓓ Ⓔ	9. Ⓐ Ⓑ Ⓒ Ⓓ Ⓔ	9. Ⓐ Ⓑ Ⓒ Ⓓ Ⓔ	9. Ⓐ Ⓑ Ⓒ Ⓓ Ⓔ	9. Ⓐ Ⓑ Ⓒ Ⓓ Ⓔ
10. Ⓐ Ⓑ Ⓒ Ⓓ Ⓔ	10. Ⓐ Ⓑ Ⓒ Ⓓ Ⓔ	10. Ⓐ Ⓑ Ⓒ Ⓓ Ⓔ	10. Ⓐ Ⓑ Ⓒ Ⓓ Ⓔ	10. Ⓐ Ⓑ Ⓒ Ⓓ Ⓔ
11. Ⓐ Ⓑ Ⓒ Ⓓ Ⓔ	11. Ⓐ Ⓑ Ⓒ Ⓓ Ⓔ	11. Ⓐ Ⓑ Ⓒ Ⓓ Ⓔ	11. Ⓐ Ⓑ Ⓒ Ⓓ Ⓔ	11. Ⓐ Ⓑ Ⓒ Ⓓ Ⓔ
12. Ⓐ Ⓑ Ⓒ Ⓓ Ⓔ	12. Ⓐ Ⓑ Ⓒ Ⓓ Ⓔ	12. Ⓐ Ⓑ Ⓒ Ⓓ Ⓔ	12. Ⓐ Ⓑ Ⓒ Ⓓ Ⓔ	12. Ⓐ Ⓑ Ⓒ Ⓓ Ⓔ
13. Ⓐ Ⓑ Ⓒ Ⓓ Ⓔ	13. Ⓐ Ⓑ Ⓒ Ⓓ Ⓔ	13. Ⓐ Ⓑ Ⓒ Ⓓ Ⓔ	13. Ⓐ Ⓑ Ⓒ Ⓓ Ⓔ	13. Ⓐ Ⓑ Ⓒ Ⓓ Ⓔ
14. Ⓐ Ⓑ Ⓒ Ⓓ Ⓔ	14. Ⓐ Ⓑ Ⓒ Ⓓ Ⓔ	14. Ⓐ Ⓑ Ⓒ Ⓓ Ⓔ	14. Ⓐ Ⓑ Ⓒ Ⓓ Ⓔ	14. Ⓐ Ⓑ Ⓒ Ⓓ Ⓔ
15. Ⓐ Ⓑ Ⓒ Ⓓ Ⓔ	15. Ⓐ Ⓑ Ⓒ Ⓓ Ⓔ	15. Ⓐ Ⓑ Ⓒ Ⓓ Ⓔ	15. Ⓐ Ⓑ Ⓒ Ⓓ Ⓔ	15. Ⓐ Ⓑ Ⓒ Ⓓ Ⓔ
16. Ⓐ Ⓑ Ⓒ Ⓓ Ⓔ	16. Ⓐ Ⓑ Ⓒ Ⓓ Ⓔ	16. Ⓐ Ⓑ Ⓒ Ⓓ Ⓔ	16. Ⓐ Ⓑ Ⓒ Ⓓ Ⓔ	16. Ⓐ Ⓑ Ⓒ Ⓓ Ⓔ
17. Ⓐ Ⓑ Ⓒ Ⓓ Ⓔ	17. Ⓐ Ⓑ Ⓒ Ⓓ Ⓔ	17. Ⓐ Ⓑ Ⓒ Ⓓ Ⓔ	17. Ⓐ Ⓑ Ⓒ Ⓓ Ⓔ	17. Ⓐ Ⓑ Ⓒ Ⓓ Ⓔ
18. Ⓐ Ⓑ Ⓒ Ⓓ Ⓔ	18. Ⓐ Ⓑ Ⓒ Ⓓ Ⓔ	18. Ⓐ Ⓑ Ⓒ Ⓓ Ⓔ	18. Ⓐ Ⓑ Ⓒ Ⓓ Ⓔ	18. Ⓐ Ⓑ Ⓒ Ⓓ Ⓔ
19. Ⓐ Ⓑ Ⓒ Ⓓ Ⓔ	19. Ⓐ Ⓑ Ⓒ Ⓓ Ⓔ	19. Ⓐ Ⓑ Ⓒ Ⓓ Ⓔ	19. Ⓐ Ⓑ Ⓒ Ⓓ Ⓔ	19. Ⓐ Ⓑ Ⓒ Ⓓ Ⓔ
20. Ⓐ Ⓑ Ⓒ Ⓓ Ⓔ	20. Ⓐ Ⓑ Ⓒ Ⓓ Ⓔ	20. Ⓐ Ⓑ Ⓒ Ⓓ Ⓔ	20. Ⓐ Ⓑ Ⓒ Ⓓ Ⓔ	20. Ⓐ Ⓑ Ⓒ Ⓓ Ⓔ
21. Ⓐ Ⓑ Ⓒ Ⓓ Ⓔ	21. Ⓐ Ⓑ Ⓒ Ⓓ Ⓔ	21. Ⓐ Ⓑ Ⓒ Ⓓ Ⓔ	21. Ⓐ Ⓑ Ⓒ Ⓓ Ⓔ	21. Ⓐ Ⓑ Ⓒ Ⓓ Ⓔ
22. Ⓐ Ⓑ Ⓒ Ⓓ Ⓔ	22. Ⓐ Ⓑ Ⓒ Ⓓ Ⓔ	22. Ⓐ Ⓑ Ⓒ Ⓓ Ⓔ	22. Ⓐ Ⓑ Ⓒ Ⓓ Ⓔ	22. Ⓐ Ⓑ Ⓒ Ⓓ Ⓔ
23. Ⓐ Ⓑ Ⓒ Ⓓ Ⓔ	23. Ⓐ Ⓑ Ⓒ Ⓓ Ⓔ	23. Ⓐ Ⓑ Ⓒ Ⓓ Ⓔ	23. Ⓐ Ⓑ Ⓒ Ⓓ Ⓔ	23. Ⓐ Ⓑ Ⓒ Ⓓ Ⓔ
24. Ⓐ Ⓑ Ⓒ Ⓓ Ⓔ	24. Ⓐ Ⓑ Ⓒ Ⓓ Ⓔ	24. Ⓐ Ⓑ Ⓒ Ⓓ Ⓔ	24. Ⓐ Ⓑ Ⓒ Ⓓ Ⓔ	24. Ⓐ Ⓑ Ⓒ Ⓓ Ⓔ
25. Ⓐ Ⓑ Ⓒ Ⓓ Ⓔ	25. Ⓐ Ⓑ Ⓒ Ⓓ Ⓔ	25. Ⓐ Ⓑ Ⓒ Ⓓ Ⓔ	25. Ⓐ Ⓑ Ⓒ Ⓓ Ⓔ	25. Ⓐ Ⓑ Ⓒ Ⓓ Ⓔ
26. Ⓐ Ⓑ Ⓒ Ⓓ Ⓔ	26. Ⓐ Ⓑ Ⓒ Ⓓ Ⓔ	26. Ⓐ Ⓑ Ⓒ Ⓓ Ⓔ	26. Ⓐ Ⓑ Ⓒ Ⓓ Ⓔ	26. Ⓐ Ⓑ Ⓒ Ⓓ Ⓔ
27. Ⓐ Ⓑ Ⓒ Ⓓ Ⓔ	27. Ⓐ Ⓑ Ⓒ Ⓓ Ⓔ	27. Ⓐ Ⓑ Ⓒ Ⓓ Ⓔ	27. Ⓐ Ⓑ Ⓒ Ⓓ Ⓔ	27. Ⓐ Ⓑ Ⓒ Ⓓ Ⓔ
28. Ⓐ Ⓑ Ⓒ Ⓓ Ⓔ	28. Ⓐ Ⓑ Ⓒ Ⓓ Ⓔ	28. Ⓐ Ⓑ Ⓒ Ⓓ Ⓔ	28. Ⓐ Ⓑ Ⓒ Ⓓ Ⓔ	28. Ⓐ Ⓑ Ⓒ Ⓓ Ⓔ
29. Ⓐ Ⓑ Ⓒ Ⓓ Ⓔ	29. Ⓐ Ⓑ Ⓒ Ⓓ Ⓔ	29. Ⓐ Ⓑ Ⓒ Ⓓ Ⓔ	29. Ⓐ Ⓑ Ⓒ Ⓓ Ⓔ	29. Ⓐ Ⓑ Ⓒ Ⓓ Ⓔ
30. Ⓐ Ⓑ Ⓒ Ⓓ Ⓔ	30. Ⓐ Ⓑ Ⓒ Ⓓ Ⓔ	30. Ⓐ Ⓑ Ⓒ Ⓓ Ⓔ	30. Ⓐ Ⓑ Ⓒ Ⓓ Ⓔ	30. Ⓐ Ⓑ Ⓒ Ⓓ Ⓔ

✂ To remove, cut along dotted rule.

SECTION I

Directions: Read the passages and answer the questions following each passage by blackening the appropriate space on the answer sheet. You may refer back to the passages when answering the questions. Answer all questions on the basis of what is stated or implied.

Although statutory law (a law enacted by the legislature) expressly forbids strikes by government workers, the constitutional validity of these laws as
(5) well as their interpretative applications have been under attack in various cases, the most publicized case being that of the federal government air traffic controllers.
(10)   The First Amendment to the United States Constitution guarantees the right of free speech. The constitutional issue to be resolved therefore is whether strikes are a form of "symbolic
(15) speech" or "symbolic conduct" that should be accorded the same degree of First Amendment protection as verbal communications. In a case that involved private rather than public
(20) employees, a Texas Court held that picketing as an incident to a labor dispute is a proper exercise of freedom of speech. The court went on to say that only a "clear and present danger of
(25) substantive evil will justify an abridgement of the right to picket." Later, the New Jersey state court concluded that even though picketing is protected by freedom of speech, this
(30) does not mean that statutes prohibiting strikes are constitutionally invalid. This case involved a constitutional interpretation of the New Jersey statute. The court stated that the
(35) justification of this statute is based on the ground of "clear and present

danger" that would result to the state if the performance of functions of a public utility was ceased or impaired by
(40) a strike. Those in favor of no-strike clauses seem to concede that strikes are a form of symbolic speech that should be accorded the same degree of First Amendment protection as verbal
(45) speech. Their justification for upholding these clauses is the "clear and present danger" doctrine. They tend to believe that strikes by government employees automatically
(50) present a "clear and present danger of substantive evil." However, according to the U.S. Supreme Court, legislatures cannot be relied upon to make a determination of what constitutes a
(55) "clear and present danger." In effect this is what happened when President Reagan ordered the firing of the air traffic controllers, based on the antistrike clause pronounced by
(60) Congress. The Supreme Court held that courts themselves must determine what constitutes a clear and present danger. The Supreme Court went on to say that mere public inconvenience or
(65) annoyance is not enough to constitute a clear and present danger. Thus, the public inconvenience and annoyance created by the curtailment of air traffic as a result of the controllers' strike may
(70) not be sufficient to constitute such a danger. The argument that a clear and present danger resulted from the

emergency staffing of control towers by military and supervisory personnel (75) is invalidated by the fact that the airlines have run safely since the strike.

This is not to suggest that every employee should automatically have the right to strike. However, (80) constitutional consideration of due process and freedom of speech should bar denying government workers, as a class, the right to strike. A close look should be taken at what actually (85) constitutes a "clear and present danger of substantive evil." It is an evasion for courts to allow legislatures to prejudge all government services to be different for "strike" purposes than those (90) provided by the private sector. The court itself should look at such factors as the nature of the service in determining whether particular no-strike clauses are constitutionally valid. (95) The nature of the provider of the service (i.e., government v. private) is not a compelling justification for upholding no-strike clauses.

1. According to the passage, strikes by government workers are

   (A) constitutionally invalid
   (B) forbidden by statutory law
   (C) permissible when there is no danger of substantial evil
   (D) permissible when there is no public inconvenience or annoyance
   (E) permissible when there is no danger to national security and safety

2. If government workers as a class are denied the right to strike, it can be argued that they have been denied all of the following EXCEPT:

   (A) due process
   (B) freedom of speech

   (C) the clear and present danger doctrine
   (D) redress from abnormally dangerous working conditions
   (E) an abridgment of the right to picket

3. According to the passage, the "clear and present danger" justification of forbidding a strike has been misapplied for all of the following reasons EXCEPT:

   (A) the dangers were determined by the executive branch
   (B) the dangers are often merely inconveniences
   (C) the dangers were determined by the courts
   (D) strikes by government workers do not automatically present dangers
   (E) the inconvenience caused by the air traffic controllers may not have been a danger

4. The fact that there was no rise in the number of airline accidents in the first six months after the firing and replacement of the striking air traffic controllers undermines the

   (A) government's argument that a strike would present a danger to the public
   (B) argument that the no-strike clause violates first amendment rights
   (C) argument that a strike is a form of symbolic speech
   (D) air traffic controllers' argument that they left their jobs because of dangerous working conditions
   (E) argument that no-strike clauses discourage more highly qualified individuals from applying for positions

5. The author of the passage objects to the current situation in which

(A) all employees equally have the right to strike
(B) the government regards national security more important than an individual's freedom
(C) the Supreme Court avoids taking a position in its dealing with regret-to-strike cases
(D) an unfair burden of proof is placed upon workers who leave jobs they believe to have unsafe working conditions
(E) a false distinction is made between workers doing similar jobs for the government and private employees

6. Which one of the following might the author cite to exemplify another of the harmful effects of the no-strike rule?

(A) It deters the highly skilled from taking government jobs.
(B) It can be used as a precedent in the private sector.
(C) It places too much power in the hands of the judicial branch of the government.
(D) It encourages the courts to determine whether or not particular no-strike clauses are valid.
(E) It protects some workers from abnormally dangerous working conditions.

The following paired passages discuss the confusion and controversy surrounding copyright law.

Passage A

Understanding copyright law is a little like wandering in a maze and hoping that you find the right outlet. As of 1976, the basic copyright law
(5) (and there are many qualifications and exceptions) is that an original work is the property of the author from the time of its creation to 70 years after the author's death, at
(10) which time it becomes part of the public domain and may be used by others. For over two hundred years, copyright has protected intellectual property from unauthorized use. This
(15) encourages creators because it ensures that they control the use of their works and the profits that may accrue from those works.

Then came the Internet. Is it a
(20) whole new ball game? Some people believe that anything on the Internet is in the public domain. Not true. Congress passed the Digital Millennium Copyright Act (DMCA) in
(25) 1998, and this act set standards for protecting software, written works, and music on the Internet. It also made illegal any technology used to break copyright-protection devices.
(30) (One provision of the act, however, exempts Internet service providers— America Online and Earthlink are just two examples—from lawsuits based on copyright violations that occur on
(35) their networks.)

Copyright protection of material on the Internet hasn't been completely successful. For example, book publishers complained that
(40) professors cost their industry at least $20 million a year by posting long excerpts of texts on the Internet, making material free to students rather than having them buy
(45) textbooks. Cornell University was the first school to respond to textbook publishers by agreeing that legal guidelines for copyright should apply to Web use. But faculty members
(50) from some schools complain that this restricts the free flow of ideas. Publishers, on the other hand, say

that they must protect $3.35 billion in college textbook sales.

(55) Copyright protection on the Internet is justified. The Internet is an impressive tool for distributing ideas, publications, music, art, and so on. But should it allow stealing? Instead,
(60) copyright laws should protect intellectual property wherever it is published and distributed. These laws encourage creative thinkers, and creative thinkers help drive the United
(65) States economy. If intellectual property is protected, the Internet's commercial possibilities will be fully realized.

Passage B
The idea that the Internet should be subject to increasingly rigid copyright
(70) laws is a bad one. It's true that not having copyright apply to the Internet means less profit for some including entities such as the motion picture and recording industries, who lobbied
(75) furiously for new copyright legislation in 1998. But the profit motive shouldn't be the sole consideration.
    The world is a different place in the twenty-first century. Accessibility and
(80) instant communication are the attributes that make the Internet such a powerful new force, and we shouldn't interfere with this means of passing information, ideas, movies,
(85) art, and music from person to person around the world. Traditional barriers such as copyright laws don't belong. If copyright laws are strictly enforced on the Internet—and it is doubtful
(90) whether they even can be—we could end up being unable to send a copy of our favorite poem or short story to a friend without risking a lawsuit.
    What about the concept of "fair
(95) use," which is part of the existing copyright laws? "Fair use" is meant to protect the financial stake of creators and publishers while allowing a limited use of material for primarily
(100) educational or artistic purposes, as for example, when reviewers quote passages from works they review. Unfortunately, according to Kenneth D. Crews, a law professor at Indiana
(105) University and director of its Copyright Management Center, fair use is an "inherently flexible doctrine. It can be interpreted differently by different courts under the same
(110) circumstances." Copyright law doesn't state where fair use ends and where copyright infringement begins. It isn't hard to imagine an endless stream of lawsuits.
(115) Recently the Australian government announced that it was planning to update their copyright law to keep up with the changing digital landscape. The head of public policy at Google,
(120) the giant Internet search engine, took issue with the proposed changes. If proposed new Australian copyright laws were to be adopted, Google warned, copyright owners could take
(125) action against search engines for caching and archiving material. This would "condemn the Australian public to the pre-Internet era." "Given the vast size of the Internet it is impossible
(130) for a search engine to contact personally each owner of a web page to determine whether the owner desires its web page to be searched, indexed or cached," Google wrote in
(135) its submission to the Senate Legal and Constitutional Affairs Committee.
    Google's point about the proposed Australian update illustrates only one of many problems with stricter
(140) copyright laws on the Internet. Exclusive ownership of intellectual property is inimical to the Internet.

7. The authors of Passage A and Passage B would most likely agree with which of the following statements?

(A) Without copyright protection, creators of material on the Internet will be unable to fully profit from their creations.
(B) Copyrights are cumbersome tools for protecting intellectual property.
(C) Traditional copyright laws are too rigid.
(D) Strict copyright laws will negatively affect the commercial possibilities of the Internet.
(E) The use of "stealing" as a term for unauthorized use of materials on the Internet is misleading.

8. Which of the following statements best characterizes the main difference between the arguments in Passage A and B?

(A) Passage A argues that copyright protection on the Internet is a necessary evil, while Passage B argues that the copyright laws need to be changed.
(B) The author of Passage A believes copyright laws are outdated, while the author of Passage B believes they are adequate.
(C) The author of Passage A believes copyright laws encourage creators of original material, while the author of Passage B believes they limit the free flow of ideas.
(D) The author of Passage A believes that current enforcement of copyright laws on the Internet is successful, while the author of passage B believes that enforcement has been impossible.

(E) Passage A supports copyright laws because they favor business, while Passage B argues against them for the same reason.

9. The author of Passage B would be most likely to identify which of the following as the basis for the argument set forth in Passage A?

(A) tradition
(B) rejection of "fair use"
(C) regulation of the Internet
(D) the profit motive
(E) practicality

10. According to Passage A, the Digital Millennium Copyright Act

(A) protects material on the Internet for an indefinite period of time.
(B) solves the copyright issue for all materials on the Internet.
(C) has proved to be ineffective for Internet services such as AOL and Earthlink.
(D) is considerably more limiting than the copyright law of 1976.
(E) forbids breaking copyright-protection devices.

11. In line 134, which is the best meaning for the word *cached*?

(A) placed in a hidden file
(B) accessed by password only
(C) stored in memory
(D) deleted from memory
(E) integrated into existing files

12. In line 142, the word "inimical" probably means

(A) illegal
(B) unfriendly
(C) opposite
(D) synonymous
(E) related

13. According to Passage B, Google's negative response to the Australian government's proposed changes to Internet copyright laws was in part based on the

(A) fear of censorship
(B) objections from other governments
(C) impossibility of compliance
(D) danger of misinterpretation
(E) belief in voluntary adherence to guidelines

Much as they may deplore the fact, historians have no monopoly on the past and no franchise as its privileged interpreters to the public. It may have
(5) been different once, but there can no longer be any doubt about the relegation of the historian to a back seat. Far surpassing works of history, as measured by the size of their public
(10) and the influence they exert, are the novel, works for the stage, the screen, and television. It is mainly from these sources that millions who never open a history book derive such conceptions,
(15) interpretations, convictions, or fantasies as they have about the past. Whatever gives shape to popular conceptions of the past is of concern to historians, and this surely includes
(20) fiction.

Broadly speaking, two types of fiction deal with the past—historical fiction and fictional history. The more common of the two is historical fiction,
(25) which places fictional characters and events in a more or less authentic historical background. Examples range from *War and Peace* to *Gone With the Wind*. Since all but a few novelists
(30) must place their fictional characters in some period, nearly all fiction can be thought of as in some degree

historical. But the term is applied as a rule only to novels in which historical
(35) events figure prominently. Fictional history, on the other hand, portrays and focuses attention upon real historical figures and events, but with the license of the novelist to imagine
(40) and invent. It has yet to produce anything approaching Tolstoy's masterpiece. Some fictional history makes use of invented characters and events, and historical fiction at times
(45) mixes up fictional and nonfictional characters. As a result the two genres overlap sometimes, but not often enough to make the distinction unimportant.
(50) Of the two, it is fictional history that is the greater source of mischief, for it is here that fabrication and fact, fiction and nonfiction, are most likely to be mixed and confused. Of course,
(55) historians themselves sometimes mix fact with fancy, but it is a rare one who does it consciously or deliberately, and he knows very well that if discovered he stands convicted of betraying his
(60) calling. The writer of fictional history, on the other hand, does this as a matter of course and with no compunction whatever. The production and consumption of fictional history
(65) appear to be growing of late. Part of the explanation of this is probably the fragmentation of history by professionals, their retreat into specializations, their abandonment of
(70) the narrative style, and with it the traditional patronage of lay readers. Fictional history has expanded to fill the gap thus created but has at the same time gone further to create a
(75) much larger readership than history books ever had.

14. We can infer from the passage that the author is probably

    (A) a historian
    (B) a historical novelist
    (C) a literary critic
    (D) a social commentator
    (E) a literary historian

15. According to the passage, which one of the following is likely to have contributed to the increasing popularity of fictional history?

    (A) a change in the demographics of lay readers of history
    (B) an increase in the audience for movies and television
    (C) a decline in historians' use of a storytelling style
    (D) an increase in historians' mixing fact and fancy
    (E) a decline in the writing ability of professional historians

16. The author's attitude toward fictional history can best be summarized in which one of the following statements?

    (A) Masterpieces such as *War and Peace* and *Gone With the Wind* could not be created in the fictional history genre.
    (B) Fictional history is responsible for leading the reading public away from traditional historical works.
    (C) Fictional history provides a useful service by filling the gap for readers not interested in traditional history.
    (D) Writers of fictional history should not mix historical figures with fictional characters.
    (E) Fictional history can mislead readers about actual historical events.

17. Of the following, which one would the author consider most likely to cause a reader to confuse fact and fiction?

    (A) a book about the Watergate scandal with fictionalized dialogue between President Nixon and his attorney general, John Mitchell
    (B) a book about a fictional platoon in Vietnam during the last days of the war
    (C) a fictional account of the adventures of a group of servants in the White House under Eisenhower, Kennedy, Johnson, and Nixon
    (D) an account of the assassination of President Kennedy as viewed by a Texas adolescent on the parade route
    (E) a book based on newspaper accounts about the reaction to the Cuban missile crisis in the United States, the U.S.S.R., and Western Europe

18. The function of the second paragraph of the passage is to

    (A) reinforce the argument about fictionalized history presented in the first paragraph
    (B) define and contrast fictional history and historical fiction
    (C) emphasize the superiority of historical fiction to fictional history
    (D) provide context for the analysis in the third paragraph
    (E) clarify the difference between history and fiction

19. According to the passage, the author would agree with all of the following statements EXCEPT:

    (A) historical fiction and fictional history are of concern to the professional historian
    (B) the works of today's professional historians tend to be more specialized than historical works of the past
    (C) professional historians understand that they should not mix fact and fiction in their works
    (D) a historical event presented as a TV miniseries is likely to be accepted as true by many people
    (E) fictional history has succeeded because of a failure of the academic history curriculum

20. The author's attitude about the issue of fiction and history is presented most clearly in

    (A) paragraph 1, lines 1–8
    (B) paragraph 1, lines 17–20
    (C) paragraph 2, lines 35–42
    (D) paragraph 3, lines 50–54
    (E) paragraph 3, lines 63–65

21. The tone of this passage could best be described as

    (A) hostile and didactic
    (B) moderate and concerned
    (C) pedantic and detached
    (D) ironic and condescending
    (E) philosophical and enlightened

Most of our knowledge about how the brain links memory and emotion has been gleaned through the study of so-called classical fear conditioning. In (5) this process the subject, usually a rat, hears a noise or sees a flashing light that is paired with a brief, mild electric shock to its feet. After a few such experiences, the rat responds (10) automatically to the sound or light even in the absence of the shock. Its reactions are typical to any threatening situation: the animal freezes, its blood pressure and heart rate increase, and it (15) startles easily. In the language of such experiments, the noise or flash is a conditioned stimulus, the foot shock is an unconditioned stimulus, and the rat's reaction is a conditioned (20) response, which consists of readily measured behavioral and physiological changes.

Conditioning of this kind happens quickly in rats—indeed, it takes place (25) as rapidly as it does in humans. A single pairing of the shock to the sound or sight can bring on the conditioned effect. Once established, the fearful reaction is relatively permanent. If the (30) noise or light is administered many times without an accompanying electric shock, the rat's response diminishes. This change is called extinction. But considerable evidence (35) suggests that this behavioral alteration is the result of the brain's controlling the fear response rather than the elimination of the emotional memory. For example, an apparently (40) extinguished fear response can recover spontaneously or can be reinstated by an irrelevant stressful experience. Similarly, stress can cause the reappearance of phobias in people who

(45) have been successfully treated. This resurrection demonstrates that the emotional memory underlying the phobia was rendered dormant rather than erased by treatment.

(50)   Fear conditioning has proved an ideal starting point for studies of emotional memory for several reasons. First, it occurs in nearly every animal group in which it has been examined: fruit flies,

(55) snails, birds, lizards, fish, rabbits, rats, monkeys, and people. Although no one claims that the mechanisms are precisely the same in all these creatures, it seems clear from studies

(60) to date that the pathways are very similar in mammals and possibly in all vertebrates. We therefore are confident in believing that many of the findings in animals apply to humans. In addition,

(65) the kinds of stimuli most commonly used in this type of conditioning are not signals that rats—or humans, for that matter—encounter in their daily lives. The novelty and irrelevance of

(70) these lights and sounds help to ensure that the animals have not already developed strong emotional reactions to them. So researchers are clearly observing learning and memory at

(75) work. At the same time, such cues do not require complicated cognitive processing from the brain. Consequently, the stimuli permit us to study emotional mechanisms relatively

(80) directly. Finally, our extensive knowledge of the neural pathways involved in processing acoustic and visual information serves as an excellent starting point for examining

(85) the neurological foundations of fear elicited by such stimuli.

22. Which one of the following best states the main idea of the passage?

(A) Fear conditioning in animals and humans proves the direct link between emotion and memory.

(B) The mechanisms for linking memory and emotion are the same in mammals and possibly all vertebrates.

(C) Fear conditioning is a helpful starting point to use in studying emotional memory.

(D) Fearful reactions created by a conditioned stimulus are relatively permanent in both animals and humans.

(E) Fear conditioning in rats and other mammals is similar to the creation of phobias in humans.

23. Which one of the following statements is best supported by information presented in the passage?

(A) Fear conditioning requires that the conditioned and unconditioned stimuli are paired on many occasions.

(B) Emotional mechanisms in the brain are linked to complicated cognitive processing.

(C) The recurrence of human phobias under stress may be compared to the spontaneous recovery of the fear response in rats.

(D) A conditioned response is weakened in times of stress provided emotion and memory have been successfully linked.

(E) A rat's conditioned response to the pairing of conditioned and unconditioned stimuli diminishes over time.

24. A rat is exposed to a buzzer and an electric shock. After pairing the two stimuli 50 times, the rat exhibits a fear response when the buzzer alone is administered. The buzzer is then sounded *without* the shock an additional 200 times. According to the passage, the rat will probably

   (A) continue to exhibit the fear response to the buzzer alone
   (B) initially exhibit the fear response to the buzzer alone but then entirely lose the response
   (C) initially exhibit the fear response to the buzzer alone, then appear to lose the response, then after the buzzer and shock are paired one additional time, exhibit it again to the buzzer alone
   (D) initially exhibit the fear response to the buzzer alone, then appear to lose the response, then exhibit it again after a cat is introduced into the area
   (E) initially exhibit the fear response to the buzzer alone, then begin to exhibit the response erratically, then lose the response entirely

25. The author contends that an apparently extinguished fear response that is recovered under stress indicates

   (A) learning and memory
   (B) complex cognitive processing
   (C) previous strong emotional response to stimuli
   (D) inadequate pairing of conditioned/unconditioned stimuli
   (E) lack of control by the brain

26. The passage lists the nine specific animal groups for which fear conditioning studies have been performed in order to

   (A) suggest the neural basis of the fear response
   (B) show in how wide a range of animals fear conditioning is exhibited
   (C) show the developmental link from fruit flies to people
   (D) raise the question of the role of complex cognitive processes in fear conditioning
   (E) show that emotions are present in simple as well as complex creatures

27. We can infer that the immediate goal of research described in the passage is to understand

   (A) the neural basis of fear
   (B) the relationship between cognition and emotion
   (C) the mechanism of conditioning
   (D) the effects of acoustic and visual stimuli
   (E) the similarities among mammalian cognitive processes

28. Which one of the following best describes the relationship of the third paragraph to the passage as a whole?

   (A) It completes the definition of the method begun by the author in the first paragraph and elaborated upon in the second paragraph.
   (B) It presents qualifications to the points made in the first and second paragraphs and suggests other possible approaches.

(C) It summarizes the evidence and conclusions described in detail in the second paragraph.

(D) It presents further applications of the method explained in the first and second paragraphs.

(E) It justifies the use of the method explained in the first and second paragraphs.

STOP

IF YOU FINISH BEFORE TIME IS UP, CHECK YOUR WORK ON THIS SECTION OF THE TEST ONLY.
DO NOT GO ON TO THE NEXT SECTION OF THE TEST UNTIL TIME IS UP FOR THIS SECTION.

SECTION II

Time — 35 minutes
24 Questions

Directions: In this section you will be given groups of questions based on different sets of conditions. Drawing a simple diagram may be helpful in answering some of the questions. You are to choose the best answer and mark the corresponding space on your answer sheet.

Questions 1–6

The Bell Canyon Condominium is a four-story building with a single penthouse apartment on the fourth floor. There are two apartments on each of the three other floors. The apartments are owned by A, B, C, D, E, F, and G.

A's apartment is on one of the floors higher than B's.

C's apartment is on one of the floors lower than D's.

C's apartment is on one of the floors lower than E's.

F and G's apartments are on the same floor.

1. Which one of the following could be the owner of the penthouse?

   (A) B
   (B) C
   (C) E
   (D) F
   (E) G

2. If F's apartment is on the second floor, which one of the following must be true?

   (A) C's apartment is on the first floor.
   (B) D's apartment is on the third floor.
   (C) A's apartment is on the fourth floor.
   (D) G's apartment is on the first floor.
   (E) B's apartment is on the third floor.

3. If D owns the penthouse apartment, on which floor or floors could G's apartment be located?

   (A) the first floor only
   (B) the second floor only
   (C) the third floor only
   (D) the second or the third floor
   (E) the first, second, or third floor

4. If D's and E's apartments are on the same floor, which one of the following must be true?

   (A) D and E are on the third floor.
   (B) D and E are on the second floor.
   (C) A is on the fourth floor.
   (D) B and C are on the first floor.
   (E) F and G are on the second floor.

5. If C's apartment is on the first floor, and A is the owner of the penthouse, which one of the following must be true?

   (A) G's apartment is on the third floor.
   (B) D's apartment is on the second floor.
   (C) E's apartment is on the second floor.
   (D) B's apartment is on the first floor.
   (E) F's apartment is on the second floor.

6. Which one of the following is possible?

   (A) A and C are on the same floor.
   (B) A and E are on the same floor.
   (C) A is on the first floor.
   (D) D is on the first floor.
   (E) C is on the fourth floor.

Questions 7–12

A new bank has decided to stay open only on weekends—all day Saturday and Sunday—and no other days. The bank has hired two managers (U and V), four tellers (W, X, Y, and Z), and two operations officers (S and T), for a total of exactly eight full-time employees. No part-time employees are hired. Each employee works a complete day when working.

A manager must be on duty each day.
The managers cannot work on the same day.
At least two tellers must be working on the same day.
W and X will not work on the same day.
S and Z will only work on Saturday.
No employee can work on consecutive days, but each employee must work on Saturday or Sunday.

7. Which one of the following could be false?

   (A) If U works on Saturday, then V works on Sunday.
   (B) If X works on Saturday, then W works on Sunday.
   (C) T can work either day.
   (D) If W works on Saturday and Y works on Sunday, then X works on Sunday.
   (E) If U works on Sunday, then X works on Saturday.

8. Which one of the following is an acceptable group of employees that could work on Saturday?

   (A) ZWYST
   (B) UVWYZS
   (C) VWXZT
   (D) UZST
   (E) VWZS

9. What is the greatest number of employees that can work on Saturday?

   (A) 2
   (B) 3
   (C) 4
   (D) 5
   (E) 6

10. If W works on Sunday, then which one of the following must be true?

   (A) X works on Saturday.
   (B) Y works on Saturday.
   (C) T works on Sunday.
   (D) Z works on Sunday.
   (E) U works on Saturday.

11. Which one of the following must be true?

   (A) T always works the same day as Y.
   (B) S never works the same day as U.
   (C) Z never works the same day as X.
   (D) If W works on Sunday, then Y always works on Saturday.
   (E) Only two tellers work on Saturday.

12. Which one of the following is a complete and accurate list of the employees who have the possibility of working on Sunday?

   (A) UWYZ
   (B) UWYS
   (C) UVWXT
   (D) UVWXYT
   (E) UVWXYTS

Questions 13–19

Three division office managers, Fred, Al, and Cynthia, draw office assistants each day from the clerical and typing pools available to them. The clerical pool consists of Lyndia, Jim, Dennis, and Sylvia. The typing pool consists of Edra, Gene, and Helen. The office assistants are selected according to the following conditions:

> Fred always needs at least one typist, but never more than two assistants.
> Al always needs at least two assistants, but never more than three.
> Sylvia or Gene and one other assistant always work for Cynthia.
> Gene and Lyndia always work together.
> Dennis and Edra will not work together.
> No more than two typists work for the same manager, but all three typists must work each day.

13. If Gene works for Fred and all of the assistants work, then which one of the following must be false?

(A) Jim works for Cynthia.
(B) Sylvia works for Cynthia.
(C) Lyndia works for Fred.
(D) Dennis works for Al.
(E) Edra works for Al.

14. If Sylvia doesn't work for Cynthia, then which one of the following must be true?

(A) Edra works for Fred.
(B) Gene works for Al.
(C) Lyndia works for Cynthia.
(D) Dennis works for Al.
(E) Helen works for Cynthia.

15. Assume that Lyndia and Jim work for Al. Which one of the following must be true?

(A) Gene works for Al.
(B) Edra works for Cynthia.
(C) Helen works for Fred.
(D) Edra works for Fred.
(E) Helen works for Cynthia.

16. Assume that Sylvia and Jim work for Al. If all of the assistants work, then which one of the following must be true?

(A) Edra works for Al.
(B) Gene works for Fred.
(C) Lyndia works for Al.
(D) Helen works for Fred.
(E) Dennis works for Fred.

17. Which one of the following must be false?

(A) Helen and Edra never work for Cynthia on the same day.
(B) Edra can work for Cynthia.
(C) Dennis and Gene never work for Fred on the same day.
(D) Jim and Sylvia never work for Fred on the same day.
(E) Lyndia and Sylvia can work for Al on the same day.

18. If Jim works for Cynthia and all of the assistants work, then

(A) Dennis works for Al.
(B) Edra works for Al.
(C) Helen works for Al.
(D) Lyndia works for Al.
(E) Sylvia works for Fred.

19. Assume that Al needs only two assistants and Fred needs only one assistant. If Helen works for Fred, then which one of the following must be true?

  (A) Jim works for Al.
  (B) Sylvia doesn't work.
  (C) Dennis doesn't work.
  (D) Edra works for Al.
  (E) Edra works for Cynthia.

Questions 20–24

Four teams (Red, Blue, Green, and Yellow) participate in the Junior Olympics, in which there are five events. In each event participants place either 1st, 2nd, 3rd, or 4th. First place is awarded a gold medal, 2nd place is awarded a silver medal, and 3rd place is awarded a bronze medal. There are no ties and each team enters one contestant in each event. All contestants finish each event.

The results of the Junior Olympics are:
  No team wins gold medals in two consecutive events.
  No team fails to win a medal within two consecutive events.
  The Blue team wins only two medals, neither of them gold.
  The Red team only wins three gold medals, and no other medals.

20. If the green team wins only one gold medal, then which one of the following must be true?

  (A) The yellow team wins two gold medals.
  (B) The red team wins only two bronze medals.
  (C) The yellow team wins only one gold medal.

(D) The yellow team wins only silver medals.
(E) The green team wins only bronze medals.

21. Which one of the following must be true?

  (A) The yellow team wins only bronze and gold medals.
  (B) The yellow team wins five medals.
  (C) The green team cannot win a silver medal.
  (D) The yellow team cannot win a bronze medal.
  (E) The green team wins exactly three medals.

22. If the yellow team wins five silver medals, then the green team must win

  (A) more silver than gold
  (B) more gold than bronze
  (C) two gold, two bronze, one silver
  (D) two gold, three bronze
  (E) six medals

23. All of the following must be true EXCEPT:

  (A) the green team wins five medals
  (B) the yellow team wins five medals
  (C) if the green team wins one gold medal, the yellow team wins one gold medal
  (D) if the green team wins only one silver medal, the yellow team wins only one silver medal
  (E) if the yellow team wins only silver medals, the green team cannot win a silver medal

24. If a fifth team, Orange, enters all events and wins only three consecutive silver medals, which one of the following must be true?

(A) If green wins a gold in the 2nd event, it also wins a bronze in the 3rd event.

(B) If green wins a gold in the 2nd event, it also wins a silver in the 4th event.

(C) If yellow wins a gold in the 2nd event, green wins a bronze in the 3rd event.

(D) If yellow wins a gold in the 2nd event, blue wins a silver in the 3rd event.

(E) If red wins a gold in the 1st event, orange wins a silver in the last event.

STOP

IF YOU FINISH BEFORE TIME IS UP, CHECK YOUR WORK ON THIS SECTION OF THE TEST ONLY.
DO NOT GO ON TO THE NEXT SECTION OF THE TEST UNTIL TIME IS UP FOR THIS SECTION.

SECTION III

Time — 35 minutes
26 Questions

<u>*Directions:*</u> In this section you will be given brief statements or passages and will be required to evaluate the reasoning involved. In some instances, more than one choice will appear to be a possible answer. You are to choose the *best* answer. Use common sense and reasonableness in making your selection; then mark the proper space on the answer sheet.

1. Though the benefits of the hot tub and the Jacuzzi have been well publicized by their manufacturers, there are also some less widely known dangers. Young children, of course, cannot be left unattended near a hot tub, and even adults have fallen asleep and drowned. Warm water can cause the blood vessels to dilate and the resulting drop in blood pressure can make people liable to fainting, especially when they stand up quickly to get out. Improperly maintained water can promote the growth of bacteria that can cause folliculitis.

The main point of this passage is that

(A) the benefits of the hot tub and the Jacuzzi have been overrated
(B) the dangers of the hot tub and Jacuzzi outweigh their potential publicized benefits
(C) users of hot tubs and Jacuzzis should be aware of the dangers connected with their use
(D) the hot tub and Jacuzzi are dangerous only when improperly maintained
(E) the hot tub is potentially beneficial in the treatment of high blood pressure

2. *Chariots of Fire* may have caught some professional critics off guard in 1982 as the Motion Picture Academy's choice for an Oscar as the year's best

film, but it won wide audience approval as superb entertainment.

Refreshingly, *Chariots of Fire* features an exciting story, enchanting English and Scottish scenery, a beautiful musical score, and appropriate costumes.

All of these attractions are added to a theme that extols traditional religious values—without a shred of offensive sex, violence, or profanity.

Too good to be true? See *Chariots of Fire* and judge for yourself.

Those who condemn the motion picture industry for producing so many objectionable films can do their part by patronizing wholesome ones, thereby encouraging future Academy Award judges to recognize and reward decency.

Which one of the following is a basic assumption underlying the final sentence of the passage?

(A) Academy judges are not decent people.
(B) The popularity of a film influences academy judges.
(C) Future academy judges will be better than past ones.
(D) There are those who condemn the motion picture industry.
(E) *Chariots of Fire* is a patronizing film.

3. *Andy:* All teachers are mean.
   Bob: That is not true. I know some doctors who are mean too.

   Bob's answer demonstrates that he thought Andy to mean that

   (A) all teachers are mean
   (B) some teachers are mean
   (C) doctors are meaner than teachers
   (D) teachers are meaner than doctors
   (E) only teachers are mean

4. *Essayist:* Theodore Roosevelt was a great hunter. He was the mighty Nimrod of his generation. He had the physical aptitude and adventurous spirit of the true frontiersman. "There is delight," he said, "in the hardy life of the open; in long rides, rifle in hand; in the thrill of the fight with dangerous game." But he was more than a marksman and tracker of beasts, for he brought to his sport the intellectual curiosity and patient observation of the natural scientist.

   Which one of the following would most weaken the author's concluding contention?

   (A) Theodore Roosevelt never studied natural science.
   (B) Actually, Theodore Roosevelt's sharpshooting prowess was highly exaggerated.
   (C) Theodore Roosevelt always used native guides when tracking game.
   (D) Theodore Roosevelt was known to become bored and leave safaris if their first few days were unproductive.
   (E) Theodore Roosevelt's powers of observation were significantly hampered by his nearsightedness.

5. The following is an excerpt from a letter sent to a law school applicant:
   "Thank you for considering our school to further your education. Your application for admission was received well before the deadline and was processed with your admission test score and undergraduate grade report.
   "We regret to inform you that you cannot be admitted for the fall semester. We have had to refuse admission to many outstanding candidates because of the recent cut in state funding of our program.
   "Thank you for your interest in our school and we wish you success in your future endeavors."

   Which one of the following can be deduced from the above letter?

   (A) The recipient of the letter did not have a sufficiently high grade point average to warrant admission to this graduate program.
   (B) The recipient of the letter was being seriously considered for a place in the evening class.
   (C) The law school sending the letter could not fill all the places in its entering class due to a funding problem.
   (D) Criteria other than test scores and grade reports were used in determining the size of the entering class.
   (E) The school sending the letter is suffering severe financial difficulties.

Questions 6–7

At birth we have no self-image. We cannot distinguish anything from the confusion of light and sound around us. From this beginning of no-dimension, we gradually begin to differentiate our body from our environment and develop a sense of identity, with the realization that we are a separate and independent human being. We then begin to develop a conscience, the sense of right and wrong. Further, we develop social consciousness, where we become aware that we live with other people. Finally, we develop a sense of values, which is our overall estimation of our worth in the world.

6. Which one of the following would be the best completion of this passage?

(A) The sum total of all these developments we call the self-image or the self-concept.
(B) This estimation of worth is only relative to our value system.
(C) Therefore, our social consciousness is dependent on our sense of values.
(D) Therefore, our conscience keeps our sense of values in perspective.
(E) The sum total of living with other people and developing a sense of values makes us a total person.

7. The author of this passage would most likely agree with which one of the following?

(A) Children have no self-dimension.
(B) Having a conscience necessitates the ability to differentiate between right and wrong.
(C) Social consciousness is our most important awareness.

(D) Heredity is predominant over environment in development.
(E) The ability to distinguish the difference between moral issues depends on the overall dimension of self-development.

---

8. Opportunity makes the thief. Without thieves there would be no crime. Without opportunity there would be no crime.

Which one of the following most weakens the statements above?

(A) Thieves wait for opportunities.
(B) Without crime there would be no opportunity.
(C) Thieves are not the only criminals.
(D) Some crimes carry greater penalties.
(E) Many thieves are not caught.

Questions 9–10

In a report released last week, a government-funded institute concluded that there is "overwhelming" evidence that violence on television leads to criminal behavior by children and teenagers.
The report based on an extensive review of several hundred research studies conducted during the 1970s, is an update of a 1972 Surgeon General's report that came to similar conclusions.

9. Which one of the following is the most convincing statement in support of the argument in the first paragraph above?

(A) A 50-state survey of the viewing habits of prison inmates concluded that every inmate watches at least 2 hours of violent programming each day.

(B) A 50-state survey of the viewing habits of convicted adolescents shows that each of them had watched at least 2 hours of violent programming daily since the age of 5.

(C) One juvenile committed a murder that closely resembled a crime portrayed on a network series.

(D) The 1972 Surgeon General's report was not nearly as extensive as this more recent study.

(E) Ghetto residents who are burglarized most often report the theft of a television set.

10. The argument above is most weakened by its vague use of the word

(A) violence
(B) government
(C) extensive
(D) update
(E) overwhelming

Questions 11–12

Violence against racial and religious minority groups increased sharply throughout the county last year, despite a slight decline in statewide figures. Compiling incidents from police departments and private watchdog groups, the County Human Relations Committee reported almost 500 hate crimes in the year, up from only 200 last year. It was the first increase since the committee began to report a yearly figure six years ago. The lower statewide figures are probably in error due to underreporting in other counties; underreporting is the major problem that state surveyors face each year.

11. All of the following, if true, would support the conclusion or the explanation of the discrepancy in the state and county figures EXCEPT:

(A) the number of hate crimes and those resulting in fatalities has increased in neighboring states

(B) anti-immigration sentiment was fanned this year by an anti-immigration ballot referendum

(C) funding for police departments throughout the state has decreased

(D) many law-abiding members of minority groups are fearful or distrustful of the police

(E) all of the counties in the state have active private watchdog groups that carefully monitor hate crimes

12. The author of this passage makes his case by

(A) establishing the likelihood of an event by ruling out several other possibilities

(B) combining several pieces of apparently unrelated evidence to build support for a conclusion

(C) contrasting a single certain case with several others with less evidence in their support

(D) assuming that what is only probable is certain

(E) using a general rule to explain a specific case

13. The study of village communities has become one of the fundamental methods of discussing the ancient history of institutions. It would be out of the question here to range over the whole field of human society in search for communal arrangements of rural life. It will be sufficient to confine the present inquiry to the varieties presented by nations of Aryan race, not because greater importance is to be attached to these nations than to other branches of humankind, although this view might also be reasonably urged, but principally because the Aryan race in its history has gone through all manner of experiences, and the data gathered from its historical life can be tolerably well ascertained. Should the road be sufficiently cleared in this particular direction, it will not be difficult to connect the results with similar researches in other racial surroundings.

Which one of the following, if true, most weakens the author's conclusion?

(A) Information about the Aryan race is no more conclusive than information about any other ethnic group.
(B) The experiences and lifestyle of Aryans are uniquely different from those of other cultures.
(C) The Aryans were originally herdsmen and therefore nomadic.
(D) The historical life of the Aryans dates back only 12 centuries.
(E) Aryans lived predominantly in villages, while today 90 percent of the world population live predominantly in or around major cities.

14. Although any reasonable modern citizen of the world must abhor war and condemn senseless killing, we must also agree that honor is more valuable than life. Life, after all, is transient, but honor is _____.

Which one of the following most logically completes the passage above?

(A) sensible
(B) real
(C) eternal
(D) of present value
(E) priceless

Questions 15–16

Bill said, "All dogs bark. This animal does not bark. Therefore it is not a dog."

15. Which one of the following most closely parallels the logic of this statement?

(A) All rocks are hard. This lump is hard. Therefore, it may be a rock.
(B) All foreign language tests are difficult. This is not a foreign language test. Therefore, it is not difficult.
(C) All Blunder automobiles are poorly built. Every auto sold by Joe was poorly built. Therefore, Joe sells Blunder automobiles.
(D) Rocks beat scissors, scissors beat paper, and paper beats rocks. Therefore, it is best to choose paper.
(E) All paint smells. This liquid does not smell. Therefore, it is not paint.

16. Which one of the following would weaken Bill's argument the most?

   (A) Animals other than dogs bark.
   (B) Some dogs cannot bark.
   (C) Dogs bark more than cockatiels.
   (D) You can train a dog not to bark.
   (E) You can train birds to bark.

17. In the last three years, the number of arrests for burglary and robbery in Sandy Beach has declined by more than 30 percent. At the same time, the city has reduced the size of its police force by 25 percent.

   Which one of the following helps to resolve an apparent discrepancy in the information above?

   (A) Neighborhood Watch programs have always been active in Sandy Beach.
   (B) The number of reported burglaries and robberies in Sandy Beach has increased in the last three years.
   (C) Compared to other cities in the state, Sandy Beach has one of the lowest crime rates.
   (D) By using motorcycles rather than foot patrols, the police are able to cover larger areas of the city using fewer officers.
   (E) Many of the residents of Sandy Beach have installed expensive security in their homes.

Questions 18–19

California and Nevada officials have questioned the impartiality of the board of scientists from the National Academy of Science who assess the safety of proposed nuclear dumping sites. They claim that the panels are heavily weighted in favor of the nuclear power companies that have been lobbying for the creation of nuclear dump sites in the deserts of the Southwest. At least ten members of the panels are or have been employees of the Department of Energy, but none is associated with any environmental organization. Environmentalists fear that long-lived nuclear wastes may leach into the groundwater and ultimately into the waters of the Colorado River. They also point out that 90 percent of the budget of the National Academy's Radioactive Waste Management Board is provided by the Department of Energy. The inventory of radioactive waste has been growing larger and larger in temporary storage places, but so far there has been virtually no agreement about a permanent dump site.

18. The officials who question the impartiality of the Management Board assume that the Department of Energy

   (A) supports the activities of the nuclear power industry
   (B) supports the activities of environmental groups
   (C) wishes to delay the selection of permanent nuclear waste dumping sites for as long as possible
   (D) is indifferent to the growing mass of nuclear wastes in temporary storage sites
   (E) has declined to take a stand for or against the use of nuclear power

19. The Nuclear Waste Management Board could best allay doubt of its impartiality if it were to

(A) publish the results of its studies of the feasibility of locating nuclear waste dumps in the deserts of the Southwest
(B) add one or two environmentalists to the panels that assess locations for nuclear dump sites
(C) make public the sources of all its funding
(D) recommend desert sites at a greater distance from the Colorado River
(E) base decisions on feasibility studies by scientists with no connection to the National Academy

20. The law of parsimony urges a strict economy upon us; it requires that we can never make a guess with two or three assumptions in it if we can make sense with one.

Which one of the following is the main point of the author's statement?

(A) Complications arise from economy.
(B) Simplify terminology whenever possible.
(C) Don't complicate a simple issue.
(D) Every assumption complicates the issue.
(E) Excess assumptions never clarify the situation.

21. Fifty of the 150 businesses in Cutbright Township have closed during the last calendar year. Since the number of businesses in a community is a sign of economic health, it is obvious that Cutbright Township has experienced serious economic decline.

Which of the following is an assumption upon which this argument depends?

(A) All of the businesses closed in the first quarter of the fiscal year.
(B) The businesses that closed were predominately small sole proprietorships.
(C) Fewer than fifty new businesses opened in Cutbright Township during the last calendar year.
(D) The sites formerly occupied by the closed businesses are now public buildings, parks, or recreational centers.
(E) Cutbright Township has experienced similar closings in previous years.

22. To be admitted to Bigshot University, you must have a 3.5 grade-point average (GPA) and a score of 800 on the admissions test, a 3.0 GPA and a score of 1000 on the admissions test, or a 2.5 GPA and a score of 1200 on the admissions test. A sliding scale exists for other scores and GPAs.

Which one of the following is inconsistent with the above?

(A) The higher the GPA, the lower the admissions test score needed for admission.
(B) Joe was admitted with a 2.7 GPA and a score of 1100 on the admissions test.

(C) No student with a score of less than 800 on the admissions test and a 3.4 GPA will be admitted.

(D) More applicants had a GPA of 3.5 than had a GPA of 2.5.

(E) Some students with a score of less than 1200 on the admissions test and a GPA of less than 2.5 were admitted.

23. The Census Bureau's family portrait of America may remind us of the problems we face as a nation, but it also gives us reason to take heart in our ability to solve them in an enlightened way. The 1980 census was the first in history to show that the majority of the population in every state has completed high school. And the percentage of our people with at least 4 years of college rose from 11 percent in 1970 to 16.3 percent in 1980. That's progress—where it really counts.

Which one of the following assumptions underlies the author's conclusion in the above passage?

(A) Greater numbers of high school and college degrees coincide with other firsts in the 1980 census.

(B) Greater numbers of high school and college degrees coincide with greater numbers of well-educated people.

(C) Greater numbers of high school and college degrees coincide with a great commitment to social progress.

(D) Greater numbers of high school and college degrees coincide with a better chance to avoid national catastrophe.

(E) Greater numbers of high school and college degrees coincide with the 1980 census.

24. *Advertisement:* Add No-NOCK to your car and watch its performance soar. No-NOCK will give it more get-up-and-go and keep it running longer. Ask for No-NOCK when you want better mileage!

According to the advertisement above, No-NOCK claims to do everything EXCEPT:

(A) improve your car's performance

(B) increase your car's life

(C) improve your car's miles per gallon

(D) cause fewer breakdowns

(E) stop the engine from knocking

25. So many arrogant and ill-tempered young men have dominated the tennis courts of late that we had begun to fear those characteristics were prerequisites for championship tennis.

Tennis used to be a gentleman's game. What is sad is not just that the game has changed. With so much importance placed on success, it may be that something has gone out of the American character—such things as gentleness and graciousness.

Which one of the following statements, if true, would most weaken the above argument?

(A) Arrogant and ill-tempered athletes are common in tennis today.

(B) Incompetent officiating has frustrated and angered many contemporary players.

(C) Some ill-tempered tennis players are unsuccessful.

(D) The "gentlemen" of early tennis often dueled to the death off the court.

(E) Some even-tempered tennis players are successful.

26. *Dolores:* To preserve the peace, we
     must be prepared to go to war
     with any nation at any time,
     using either conventional or
     nuclear weapons.

    Fran: Which shall it be, conventional
     weapons or nuclear weapons?

    Fran mistakenly concludes that the
    "either . . . or" phrase in Dolores's
    statement indicates

    (A) fear
    (B) indecision
    (C) a choice
    (D) a question
    (E) a refusal

STOP

IF YOU FINISH BEFORE TIME IS UP, CHECK YOUR WORK ON THIS SECTION OF THE TEST ONLY.
DO NOT GO ON TO THE NEXT SECTION OF THE TEST UNTIL TIME IS UP FOR THIS SECTION.

SECTION IV

Directions: In this section you will be given groups of questions based on different sets of conditions. Drawing a simple diagram may be helpful in answering some of the questions. You are to choose the best answer and mark the corresponding space on your answer sheet.

Questions 1–6

A group of tourists is planning to visit a cluster of islands—U, V, W, X, Y, and Z, connected by bridges. The tourists must stay on each island visited for exactly three days and three nights. Each bridge takes one hour to cross, may be crossed in either direction, and can be crossed only in the morning to give the tourists a full day on the island.

The islands are connected by bridges only as indicated below:

U is connected to W, X, and Y
V is connected to Y and Z
X is connected to Z and W
Y is connected to X and Z

1. If the group visits island W first, eight days later it could NOT be at which one of the following islands?

   (A) U
   (B) V
   (C) X
   (D) Y
   (E) Z

2. If the group stays on island X for three nights, it CANNOT spend the next three days and nights on island

   (A) U
   (B) V
   (C) W
   (D) Y
   (E) Z

3. Which one of the following is a possible order of islands visited in twelve days and nights?

   (A) UWYZ
   (B) UVYZ
   (C) UYVX
   (D) UXZV
   (E) UWYX

4. If the group visits island W first and can visit an island more than once, but does not use a bridge more than once, what is the greatest number of visits it can make?

   (A) five
   (B) six
   (C) seven
   (D) eight
   (E) nine

5. Assume the group visits island X first, and does not use a bridge more than once. Assume also that the group does stay at island Y twice. What is the greatest number of different islands the group can visit?

   (A) three
   (B) four
   (C) five
   (D) six
   (E) seven

6. Assume another island, T, is added to the tour. Assume also that T is connected only to U. Which one of the following statements must be true?

(A) On the eighth day of a tour, starting its visit at island T, the group could be on island V.
(B) On the fifth day of a tour, starting its visit at island T, the group could be on island X.
(C) On the seventh day of a tour, starting its visit at island T, the group could be on island U.
(D) On the eighth day of a tour, starting its visit at island V, the group could be on island T.
(E) On the tenth day of a tour, starting its visit at island Z, the tour group could be on island T.

Questions 7–13

Teams A and B play a series of nine games. To win the series, a team must win the most games, but must also win a minimum of three games.
There are no ties in the first three games.
Team A wins more of the last three games than team B.
Team B wins more of the last five games than team A.
The last game is a tie.
Games 1 and 3 are won by the same team.

7. Which one of the following must be true?

(A) One team must win five games to win the series.
(B) There are no ties.
(C) One team wins at least two of the first three games.
(D) The same team wins the last five games.
(E) The last three games are won by one team.

8. Considering all of the conditions mentioned above, game 6

(A) could be won by team A
(B) could be won by team B
(C) could be a tie
(D) must be won by team A
(E) must be won by team B

9. If game 7 is won by team A, then

(A) game 8 is a tie
(B) game 2 is a tie
(C) game 4 is won by team A
(D) game 5 is a tie
(E) game 6 is won by team A

10. Which one of the following must be true?

(A) There is only one tie in the last five games.
(B) Team A wins two of the first three games.
(C) Team B can win three of the last five games.
(D) Game 4 is a tie.
(E) Team A can win only one of the last five games.

11. If team A wins game 1 and game 4, then which one of the following must be false?

(A) Team A wins game 3.
(B) Team A wins game 2.
(C) Team B wins game 2.
(D) Team A wins the series.
(E) Team B wins the series.

12. Assume that game 4 is won by the winner of game 5. If game 2 is not won by the winner of game 3, then which one of the following must be true?

(A) Team A wins game 7.
(B) Team B is the winner of the series.
(C) Team A wins game 2.
(D) Team B wins game 1.
(E) Team A wins game 3.

13. Which one of the following must be true?

(A) For team A to win the series, team A must win exactly two of the first four games.
(B) For team B to win the series, team B must win exactly one of the first four games.
(C) For team A to win the series, team A must win only three of the first seven games.
(D) For team B to win the series, team B must win at least three of the first four games.
(E) For team A to win the series, team A must win two consecutive games.

Questions 14–18

Eight busts of American Presidents are to be arranged on two shelves, left to right. Each shelf accommodates exactly four busts. One shelf is directly above the other shelf. The busts are of John Adams, George Washington, Abraham Lincoln, Thomas Jefferson, James Monroe, John Kennedy, Theodore Roosevelt and Franklin Delano Roosevelt.

The Roosevelt busts may not be directly one above the other.

The bust of Kennedy must be adjacent to the bust of a Roosevelt.

The bust of Jefferson must be directly above the bust of John Adams.

The busts of Monroe, Adams, Kennedy and Franklin Delano Roosevelt must be on the bottom shelf.

The bust of Monroe must be third from the left.

14. If the bust of Theodore Roosevelt is second from the left on one shelf, which one of the following must be true?

(A) The bust of Adams must be first on a shelf.
(B) The bust of Adams must be third on a shelf.
(C) The bust of Kennedy must be first on a shelf.
(D) The bust of Kennedy must be second on a shelf.
(E) The bust of Kennedy must be third on a shelf.

15. Which one of the following must be true about the bust of Monroe?

(A) It is next to the bust of Adams.
(B) It is next to the bust of Kennedy.
(C) It is next to the bust of Franklin Delano Roosevelt.
(D) It is directly under the bust of Lincoln.
(E) It is directly under the bust of Theodore Roosevelt.

16. If the bust of Washington is first, directly above Kennedy's, all of the following must be true EXCEPT:

(A) the bust of Jefferson is fourth
(B) the bust of Theodore Roosevelt is third
(C) the bust of Franklin Delano Roosevelt is second
(D) the bust of Lincoln is third
(E) the bust of Adams is fourth

17. Which one of the following is NOT a possible order for the busts on either shelf?

(A) Washington, Lincoln, Theodore Roosevelt, Jefferson
(B) Franklin Delano Roosevelt, Kennedy, Monroe, Adams

(C) Theodore Roosevelt, Lincoln, Washington, Jefferson
(D) Lincoln, Theodore Roosevelt, Washington, Jefferson
(E) Kennedy, Adams, Monroe, Franklin Delano Roosevelt

18. If the bust of Lincoln is next to the bust of Jefferson, all of the following are true EXCEPT:

(A) if the bust of Kennedy is first, the bust of Theodore Roosevelt is also first
(B) if the bust of Washington is first, the bust of Franklin Delano Roosevelt is also first
(C) if the bust of Washington is second, the bust of Kennedy is also second
(D) if the bust of Kennedy is second, the bust of Theodore Roosevelt is also second
(E) if the bust of Washington is second, the bust of Franklin Delano Roosevelt is also second

Questions 19–24

Six houses are numbered from 1 to 6 in order from left to right. Each house is to be painted a different color. Each house is to be painted by a different painter. Each painter paints using only colors he or she likes. No two painters use the same color.

The first house is painted by a painter who likes only orange, white, and yellow.
The second house is painted by a painter who likes only blue, green, and yellow.
The third and fourth houses are painted by painters who each like only red and yellow.
The fifth house is painted by a painter who likes only blue, green, red, and yellow.

The sixth house is painted by a painter who likes only red, orange, violet, and white.

19. Which one of the following could be true?

(A) The first house is painted yellow.
(B) The second house is painted red.
(C) The fifth house is painted red.
(D) The fifth house is painted yellow.
(E) The sixth house is painted orange.

20. What is the maximum number of possible color combinations for the six houses if orange is not used?

(A) four
(B) five
(C) six
(D) seven
(E) eight

21. Which one of the following would provide sufficient information to determine the color of each of the six houses?

(A) The houses that are painted blue, white, and yellow
(B) The houses that are painted blue, red, violet, and yellow
(C) The houses that are painted green, orange, red, and white
(D) The houses that are painted blue, green, red, and yellow
(E) The houses that are painted blue, green, orange, and white

22. If the primary colors are red, blue, and yellow, and the secondary colors are green, orange, and violet, which one of the following could be true?

(A) The second and fifth houses are painted primary colors.
(B) The third and sixth houses are painted primary colors.

(C) The second and fifth houses are painted secondary colors.
(D) The first and fourth houses are painted secondary colors.
(E) The second and sixth houses are painted secondary colors.

23. If the violet house is next to the green house and the blue house is next to the yellow house, then which one of the following must be true?

(A) The first house is white.
(B) The first house is orange.
(C) The third house is red.
(D) The fourth house is red.
(E) The fifth house is blue.

24. Suppose that the painter of the third house also likes the color pink. If all the other conditions remain the same, then each of the following could be true EXCEPT:

(A) the fourth house is yellow and the sixth house is red
(B) the second house is green and the sixth house is white
(C) the second house is yellow and the third house is red
(D) the first house is yellow and the fifth house is blue
(E) the first house is white and the second house is yellow

STOP

IF YOU FINISH BEFORE TIME IS UP, CHECK YOUR WORK ON THIS SECTION OF THE TEST ONLY.
DO NOT GO ON TO THE NEXT SECTION OF THE TEST UNTIL TIME IS UP FOR THIS SECTION.

SECTION V

Directions: In this section you will be given brief statements or passages and will be required to evaluate the reasoning involved. In some instances, more than one choice will appear to be a possible answer. You are to choose the best answer. Use common sense and reasonableness in making your selection; then mark the proper space on the answer sheet.

1. Chrysanthemums that have not been fertilized in July will normally not blossom in October. In October, the chrysanthemums did not blossom.

   With the premises given above, which one of the following would logically complete an argument?

   (A) Therefore, the chrysanthemums were not fertilized in July.
   (B) Therefore, the chrysanthemums may not have been fertilized in July.
   (C) Therefore, the chrysanthemums may blossom later in the fall.
   (D) Therefore, the chrysanthemums will blossom in the fall.
   (E) Therefore, the chrysanthemums will not blossom later in the fall.

2. When asked about the danger to public health from the spraying of pesticides by helicopters throughout the county, the County Supervisor replied, "The real danger to the public is the possibility of an infestation of harmful fruit-flies, which this spraying will prevent. Such an infestation would drive up the cost of fruits and vegetables by 15 percent."

   Which one of the following is the most serious weakness in the Supervisor's reply to the question?

   (A) He depends upon the ambiguity in the word "danger."
   (B) His response contains a self-contradiction.
   (C) He fails to support his argument concretely.
   (D) He fails to answer the question that has been asked.
   (E) His chief concern is the economic consequences of spraying.

3. So far this year researchers have reported the following:

   > Heavy coffee consumption can increase the risk of heart attacks.
   > Drinking a cup of coffee in the morning increases feelings of well-being and alertness.
   > Boiled coffee increases blood cholesterol levels.
   > Coffee may protect against cancer of the colon.

   If all these statements are true, which one of the following conclusions can be drawn from this information?

   (A) Reducing coffee consumption will make people healthier.
   (B) Reducing coffee consumption will make people feel better.
   (C) People at risk for heart attack should limit their coffee drinking.
   (D) Percolated coffee will not affect cholesterol levels.
   (E) People at risk for cancer should reduce their coffee consumption.

4. *Governor:* Compared with children in other states, infants born in California weigh more, survive the first years in greater numbers, and live longer. The hysteria about the danger of pesticides in California has attracted attention simply because a few Hollywood stars have appeared on television talk shows. Pesticides are the responsibility of the California Department of Food and Agriculture, and we can be sure its members are doing their job.

The governor's argument would be weakened if all of the following were shown to be true EXCEPT:

(A) rates of melanoma and some forms of leukemia in California are above national norms

(B) the three highest positions at the California Department of Food and Agriculture are held by farm owners

(C) synthetic pesticide residues in food cause more cancer than do "natural pesticides" that the plants themselves produce

(D) more Californians suffer the consequences of air pollution than do the citizens in any other state

(E) children of farm workers are three times more likely to suffer childhood cancers than children of urban parents

5. Should we allow the Fire Department to continue to underpay its women officers by using policies of promotion that favor men?

The question above most closely resembles which one of the following in terms of its logical features?

(A) Should the excessive tax on cigarettes, liquor, and luxury goods be unfairly increased again this year?

(B) Should corrupt politicians be subject to the same sentencing laws as blue-collar felons?

(C) Should the police chief be chosen by examination score regardless of gender or seniority?

(D) Should the religious right be allowed to determine the censorship laws for all of society?

(E) Are liberal political values an appropriate basis for all of the social values in this state?

6. If airline fares have risen, then either the cost of fuel has risen or there are no fare wars among competing companies. If there are no fare wars among competing companies, the number of airline passengers is larger than it was last year.

According to the passage above, if there has been a rise in airline fares this month, which one of the following CANNOT be true?

(A) There are no fare wars among competing airlines.

(B) The cost of fuel has risen, and the number of passengers is the same as last year.

(C) The cost of fuel has risen, there are no fare wars, and the number of passengers is larger than it was last year.

(D) There are no fare wars, and the number of passengers is larger than it was last year.

(E) The cost of fuel has risen, there are no fare wars, and the number of passengers is smaller than it was last year.

7. Only 75 years ago, the best fishing in the world was the Grand Banks of the North Atlantic. But now overfishing and man's pollution have decimated the area. There will be no fishing industry in the Americas in a very few years. The waters off Newfoundland now yield less than half the catch of five years ago, and less than one quarter of the total of ten years ago. The cod has almost disappeared. The number of fishermen in Newfoundland and New England has declined, and their yearly earnings are now at an all-time low. Yet radar has made fishing methods more efficient than ever.

Which one of the following identifies most clearly a faulty assumption in the reasoning of this passage?

(A) Ten years is too short a time period to use to draw conclusions about the natural world.
(B) The argument assumes that the waters off Newfoundland are representative of all the American oceans.
(C) The pollution of the sea may have been caused by natural as well as by human forces.
(D) The argument does not allow for the possibility that the catch may increase in size in the next five years.
(E) The argument fails to consider that the decline in the catch may be due to factors other than pollution.

8. A cigarette advertisement in a magazine asks, "What do gremlins, the Loch Ness monster, and a filter cigarette claiming 'great taste' have in common?" The answer is "You've heard of all of them, but don't really believe they exist."
The advertisement contains no pictures, and no additional text except the words Gold Star Cigarettes and the Surgeon General's warning in a box in the lower corner.

Which one of the following conclusions can be drawn from the information given above?

(A) Cigarette advertising depends upon visual appeal to create images for specific brands.
(B) All cigarette advertising depends on praising a specific brand.
(C) Gold Star Cigarettes are non-filters.
(D) The writers of this advertisement do not believe in advertising.
(E) The writers of this advertisement do not believe the Surgeon General's warning is true.

9. The traffic on the Imperial Highway has always been slowed by the dangerous curves in the road. It was built when cars were much smaller and less powerful, and very few drivers traveled between Imperial City and Fremont. All this has changed. The cost of widening and straightening the road would now be many times greater than building the proposed new toll road on the borders of the Imperial Wetlands reserve. Environmentalists fear the construction noise and waste will harm the wildlife in the reserve, and have urged that the toll road not be constructed.

Which one of the following, if true, would most strengthen the case of the environmentalists?

(A) None of the animals living in the Imperial Wetlands is on the list of endangered species.

(B) The traffic congestion on the Imperial Highway increases each year.

(C) The cost of building the new road will be amortized in ten years by the tolls collected.

(D) There are several less direct routes the toll road could take between Fremont and Imperial City.

(E) The environmentalists threaten to bring a lawsuit in federal court to halt construction of the road.

10. Despite the very large increase in the federal tax on luxury items, the value of the stock of Harry Evans, Inc., seller of the world's most expensive jewelry, continues to rise. Six months after the introduction of the tax, Evans's stock is at an all-time high. Moreover, sales in the United States continue to increase. In other countries, where Evans does 30 percent of its business, there have been no rises in excise taxes and the company will open new stores in Tokyo, Monte Carlo, and Singapore. According to a company spokesperson, _____.

Which one of the following most logically completes this paragraph?

(A) American customers who can afford to shop at Evans are not likely to be deterred by a rise in luxury taxes

(B) American customers are expected to spend far less at Evans because of the tax rise

(C) American sales are not significant enough to affect the overall profits of the firm

(D) the company will probably be forced to close most of its stores in America

(E) state taxes are more likely to influence jewelry sales than federal taxes

11. *Speaker:* A recent study of cigarette smokers has shown that, of cancer patients who are heavy smokers of unfiltered cigarettes, 40 percent will die of the disease. For cancer patients who are light smokers of filter cigarettes, the percentage is 25 percent.

Which one of the following conclusions can be drawn from the information above?

(A) There are more heavy smokers of unfiltered cigarettes than light smokers of filter cigarettes.

(B) More heavy smokers of unfiltered cigarettes die of cancer than light smokers of filter cigarettes.

(C) A heavy smoker of unfiltered cigarettes who has cancer is more likely to die than a light smoker of unfiltered cigarettes.

(D) A heavy smoker of unfiltered cigarettes who has cancer may be more likely to die than a light smoker of unfiltered cigarettes.

(E) A heavy smoker of unfiltered cigarettes who has cancer is more likely to die than a light smoker of filtered cigarettes who has cancer.

Questions 12–13

Archeologists have come to the support of Arctic anthropologists. A small minority of anthropologists assert that Stone-Age tribes of the Arctic domesticated wolves and trained them to haul sleds. Excavations have recently found evidence to support this claim. Archeologists have found wolf bones near the site of a Stone-Age village. They have also found walrus bones that might have been used on primitive sleds. The small minority of anthropologists believe that their theories have been proved.

12. Which one of the following is true of the evidence cited in the paragraph above?

(A) It is not relevant to the anthropologists' conclusions.

(B) It conclusively contradicts the anthropologists' conclusions.

(C) It neither supports nor refutes the anthropologists' conclusions positively.

(D) It supports the anthropologists' conclusions authoritatively.

(E) It conclusively supports only a part of the anthropologists' conclusions.

13. Which one of the following, if true, would best support the theory of the anthropologists?

(A) Wolves are known to have fed upon the garbage of villages in northern Europe.

(B) Wolves as a species are easily domesticated and trained.

(C) Almost all Stone-Age Arctic tools were made of walrus bone.

(D) Stone-Age villages were located on the migration routes of the caribou herds upon which wolves preyed.

(E) The earliest sled part found in the Arctic was made one thousand years after the Stone Age.

Questions 14–15

The following criticism of a self-portrait by Vincent van Gogh appeared in a magazine in 1917:

"Here we have a work of art which is so self-evidently a degenerate work by a degenerate artist that we need not say anything about the inept creation. It is safe to say that if we were to meet in our dreams such a villainous looking jailbird with such a deformed Neanderthal skull, degenerate ears, hobo beard and insane glare, it would certainly give us a nightmare."

14. The author of this passage makes his point by using

    (A) invective
    (B) analogy
    (C) citation of authority
    (D) paradox
    (E) example

15. In relation to the first sentence of the quotation, the second sentence is

    (A) an example of an effect following a cause
    (B) a specific derived from a general principle
    (C) a logical conclusion
    (D) a contradiction
    (E) a personal experience in support of a generalization

---

16. A company called Popcorn Packaging is promoting the use of popcorn as a cushioning material in packing. Unlike the commonly used Styrofoam beads or chips, popcorn can be recycled as a food for birds or squirrels and can serve as a garden mulch. Used out of doors, popcorn disappears almost overnight, while the Styrofoam beads may be in the environment for centuries. Even before we became ecology conscious, popcorn was used in packing in the 1940s. Since it now costs less to produce than Styrofoam, there is every reason to return to wide-scale use of packaging by popcorn.

Which one of the following, if true, would most seriously weaken the author's argument?

    (A) A package using popcorn as a cushioning material will weigh less than a package using Styrofoam beads.
    (B) Popcorn may attract rodents and insects.
    (C) A large number of squirrels can damage a garden by consuming flowering bulbs.
    (D) Less than 1 percent of the material now used for package cushioning is recycled.
    (E) Styrofoam replaced popcorn in the early 1950s because it was cheaper to produce.

17. This produce stand sells fruits and vegetables. All fruits are delicious, and all vegetables are rich in vitamins. Every food that is vitamin-rich is delicious, so everything sold at this stand is delicious.

Which one of the following assumptions is necessary to make the conclusion in the argument above logically correct?

    (A) The stand sells many fruits and vegetables.
    (B) This produce stand sells only fruits and vegetables.
    (C) Something cannot be both vitamin-rich and delicious.
    (D) Some stands sell fruits that are not delicious.
    (E) Some vegetables are delicious.

18. Voter turnout in primary elections has declined steadily from 1982 to 1990. In 1990, more than 80 percent of the Americans eligible to vote failed to do so. Only 11.9 percent of the Democrats and 7.7 percent of the Republicans went to the polls. The largest number of voters turned out for elections in the District of Columbia (28 percent) and in Massachusetts, where the 32 percent total was the highest since 1962. In each of the twenty-four other states holding elections, the number of voters was smaller than it had been in 1986 and 1982.

Based on the information in this passage, which one of the following must be true?

(A) The turnout in the District of Columbia was affected by favorable weather conditions.
(B) Fewer than 20 percent of the eligible major-party voters voted in the 24 states other than Massachusetts.
(C) The voter turnout in Massachusetts is always higher than the turnouts in other states.
(D) The voter turnout decline is a signal of a nationwide voter rebellion.
(E) More voters cast their votes in general elections than in primary elections.

19. Each year the number of schools that no longer allow smoking on school property grows larger. Four states, New Jersey, Kansas, Utah, and New Hampshire, now require tobacco-free schools. The Tobacco Institute has fought against regulations restricting smoking everywhere from airlines to restaurants on the grounds that they trample on the rights of smokers, but is conspicuously absent from school board lobbyists. Tobacco industry spokesmen have denounced the rules treating teachers like children, but have said they will not go on record to defend policies that affect children.

Which one of the following, if true, best accounts for the Tobacco Institute's behavior?

(A) The tobacco industry is presently fighting the charge that it attempts to recruit new smokers among minors.
(B) The tobacco industry can depend on continued high profits from overseas operations, where restrictions do not exist.
(C) Most tobacco companies are highly diversified corporations whose profits no longer depend wholly on tobacco products.
(D) The tobacco industry believes the rights of children to be equal to the rights of adults.
(E) The tobacco industry agrees with the schools that have rules against tobacco.

Questions 20–21

A number of lawsuits have been brought against popular singing groups charging that suicidal themes in their songs have led to teenage suicides. So far, the courts have found that the lyrics are protected by the First Amendment. But what if this should change, and a court decides that suicidal themes in popular songs are dangerous? In fact, the songs that have been charged so far are antisuicide; they present sardonically the self-destructive behavior of drinking, drugs, and escape by death. They describe a pitiful state of mind, but they do not endorse it.

Blaming suicide on the arts is nothing new. In the late eighteenth century, Goethe's popular novel *Werther* was said to be the cause of a rash of suicides in imitation of the novel's hero. If we begin to hold suicide in books or music responsible for suicides in real life, the operas of Verdi and Puccini will have to go, and *Romeo and Juliet* and *Julius Caesar* will disappear from high school reading lists.

20. The author of this passage argues by

(A) providing examples to support two opposing positions
(B) using an observation to undermine a theoretical principle
(C) disputing an interpretation of evidence cited by those with an opposing view
(D) predicting personal experience from a general principle
(E) accusing the opposing side of using inaccurate statistical information

21. Which one of the following is an assumption necessary to the author's argument?

(A) A lyric presenting suicide in a favorable light should not have First Amendment protection.
(B) Literature or music cannot directly influence human behavior.
(C) Many record albums already carry labels warning purchasers of their dangerous contents.
(D) The audience, not the performer, is responsible for the audience's actions.
(E) Freedom of speech is the most threatened of our personal freedoms.

22. Haven't you at some time had a favorite song or book or film that was not well known but later became popular? And didn't you feel somehow betrayed and resentful when what you had thought was unique became commonplace? On a larger scale, the same thing happens to novelists or film makers who have enjoyed critical esteem without popular success. Let them become public sensations, and the critics who praised their work will attack them virulently.

This paragraph most likely introduces an article on a film maker who has made a

(A) series of commercially successful films
(B) series of commercially unsuccessful films
(C) single film, a commercial success
(D) single film, a commercial failure
(E) critical success and a commercial success

23. Studies of the effects of drinking four or more cups of coffee per day have shown that coffee consumption increases work efficiency by improving the ability to process information. People who drink two cups of coffee in the morning are more alert and feel better than those who do not. But there are other factors to be considered.

Which one of the following sentences would provide the most logical continuation of this paragraph?

(A) Contrary to popular belief, drinking coffee cannot erase the effect of alcohol.
(B) Some studies suggest that coffee drinking will protect against cancer of the colon.
(C) Combined with the stress of heavy exercise, coffee drinking may be the cause of higher blood pressure.
(D) Drinking two or more cups of coffee per day increases the risk of heart attacks in men.
(E) Many people cannot distinguish between the taste of decaffeinated and that of regular coffee.

24. All of the members of the chorus will sing in the performance of the oratorio *Messiah*. Some of these are highly trained professionals, some are gifted amateurs, and some are singers of mediocre ability.

If the statements above are true, which one of the following must also be true?

(A) *Messiah* will be performed by highly trained professionals, gifted amateurs, and some singers of mediocre ability.
(B) Some of the members of the chorus are not highly trained professionals, gifted amateurs, or singers of mediocre ability.
(C) *Messiah* will be performed by some highly trained professionals, but not all of them are in the chorus.
(D) Not all of those in the chorus who are gifted amateurs will perform in the oratorio.
(E) All of those who will perform *Messiah* are members of the chorus.

25. *Politician:* The passage of laws that limit elected officials to one or two terms in office is an admission that voters are civic fools, unable to tell good lawmakers from bad ones. To ban all the politicians when the real intention is to get rid of the corrupt ones is to burn the house down to get rid of the vermin.

The author of this passage makes his point chiefly by

(A) defining a key term
(B) exposing a self-contradiction
(C) drawing an analogy
(D) questioning the evidence of his opponents
(E) citing an example

STOP

IF YOU FINISH BEFORE TIME IS UP, CHECK YOUR WORK ON THIS SECTION OF THE TEST ONLY.
DO NOT GO ON TO THE NEXT SECTION OF THE TEST UNTIL TIME IS UP FOR THIS SECTION.

WRITING SAMPLE

Directions: You have 35 minutes to write an essay in response to a given topic. Take a few minutes to plan your work before you begin writing. DO NOT WRITE ON A TOPIC OF YOUR OWN CHOICE. ESSAYS THAT DO NOT ADDRESS THE GIVEN TOPIC ARE UNACCEPTABLE.

The quality of your writing is more important than the length of your response or the content. Pay attention to organization, appropriate diction, and correct usage. You will not be expected to display any specialized knowledge in your response, nor will you be expected to write a "perfect" essay; law schools understand that you are writing under a time constraint, and will allow for the minor lapses in writing ability that might occur under this circumstance.

Only the lined area in your booklet will be reproduced for the law schools, so do not write outside this space. _Do not_ skip lines or use wide margins. These precautions, along with careful planning and legible handwriting that is not unduly large, will keep you within the allowed space.

Sample Topic

Read the following descriptions of Thomas and Peters, candidates for the position of head coach of the Ventura Vultures professional football team. *Then, in the space provided, write an argument for appointing one over the other.* Use the information in this description and assume that the two general policies below equally guide the Vultures' decision on the appointment:

- The head coach should possess the ability to work with players and coaching staff toward achieving a championship season.
- The head coach should successfully manage the behind-the-scenes activities of recruiting, analyzing scouting reports, and handling the media and fans in order to enhance the public relations and image of the team.

THOMAS has been General Manager of the Vultures for the past ten years. A physical education major with a masters in psychology, he knows the player personnel as well as anyone, including the coaching staff. His on-target assessment of player skills and weaknesses has been instrumental in building a more balanced team over the past decade through his skillful trading and recruitment of college athletes. As the chief managing officer, he has also enhanced the team's image by his careful press relationship and understated approach when negotiations with star players reached an impasse. He rarely alienates players, coaches, press, or fans with his even-handed (though sometimes unemotional) attitude, and the Vultures' owners feel fortunate that they were able to entice him away from his high school coaching position, which he left ten years ago. He has never played either pro or college ball.

PETERS is presently a wide receiver and defensive end for the Vultures. A one-time star, Peters has played both offense and defense for the Vultures since their inception in the league fourteen years ago, a remarkable feat equaled by few in the game. He was elected captain of the team the past five years because of his charisma, although he occasionally angers management and fellow players with his strong comments about his philosophy of the game. His only experience in the front office was leading a player charity benefit for the Vultures, which raised more than $2,000,000 for abused Ventura County children. Although a high school dropout, Peters is a self-made man who firmly believes the key to life is having a strong educational background, even though he sometimes feels uncomfortable around college-educated athletes. The Vulture owners believe Peters may provide the emotional charge the team needs at its helm to win its first championship.

On the actual exam you will be given special sheets of paper to write your essay. It will have the essay topic on the top followed by room for scratch work. For practice, write your essay on two sides of an 8½" x 11" college-ruled lined sheet of paper.

ANSWER KEY

Section I: Reading Comprehension

1. B	6. A	11. C	16. E	21. B	26. B
2. C	7. A	12. B	17. A	22. C	27. A
3. C	8. C	13. C	18. B	23. C	28. E
4. A	9. D	14. A	19. E	24. D	
5. E	10. E	15. C	20. D	25. A	

Section II: Analytical Reasoning

1. C	5. D	9. D	13. A	17. E	21. B
2. A	6. B	10. A	14. C	18. D	22. D
3. E	7. E	11. E	15. A	19. C	23. D
4. C	8. E	12. D	16. D	20. C	24. C

Section III: Logical Reasoning

1. C	6. A	11. E	16. B	21. C	26. B
2. B	7. B	12. C	17. B	22. E	
3. E	8. C	13. B	18. A	23. B	
4. D	9. B	14. C	19. E	24. E	
5. D	10. E	15. E	20. C	25. D	

Section IV: Analytical Reasoning

1. B	5. D	9. A	13. E	17. E	21. C
2. B	6. E	10. E	14. D	18. C	22. E
3. D	7. C	11. E	15. A	19. E	23. D
4. E	8. E	12. B	16. D	20. A	24. C

Section V: Logical Reasoning

1. B	6. E	11. E	16. B	21. D	
2. D	7. B	12. C	17. B	22. E	
3. C	8. C	13. B	18. B	23. D	
4. D	9. D	14. A	19. A	24. A	
5. A	10. A	15. D	20. C	25. C	

MODEL TEST ANALYSIS

Doing model exams and understanding the explanations afterwards are of course important in acquainting you with typical LSAT question types and successful approaches to the questions. However, another benefit of carefully analyzing these model tests is to understand the kinds of errors you are making and thus work to minimize them. For instance, if a very high percentage of your incorrect answers is due to "careless error" or "misread problem" then perhaps you are working much too fast and should slow your pace accordingly. If your incorrect answers are due primarily to "lack of knowledge," then a careful rereading and reworking of the appropriate question-type chapter may be in order. Or if you find that you aren't completing a large number of questions because of lack of time, you may need to either increase your speed or learn to use the "one-check, two-check" technique more effectively.

This kind of analysis of the model tests will enable you to identify your particular weaknesses and thus remedy them.

MODEL TEST ONE ANALYSIS

Section	Total Number of Questions	Number Correct	Number Incorrect	Number Unanswered*
I. Reading Comprehension	28			
II. Analytical Reasoning	24			
III. Logical Reasoning	26			
IV. Analytical Reasoning	24			
V. Logical Reasoning	25			
TOTALS:	127			

*At this stage in your preparation, you should not be leaving any blank answer spaces. At least fill in a guess, as there is no penalty for a wrong answer.

REASONS FOR INCORRECT ANSWERS
You may wish to evaluate the explanations before completing this chart.

Section	Total Number Incorrect	Lack of Knowledge	Misread Problem	Careless Error	Unanswered or Wrong Guess
I. Reading Comprehension					
II. Analytical Reasoning					
III. Logical Reasoning					
IV. Analytical Reasoning					
V. Logical Reasoning					
TOTALS:					

ANSWER EXPLANATIONS

Section I

Passage 1

1. **B** The first sentence of the passage makes it clear that government workers are forbidden to strike by statutory law.

2. **C** If strikes are a form of symbolic speech, the denial of the right to strike is arguably a denial of free speech. It also can be argued that it denies due process, the right to picket, and the right to avoid abnormally dangerous working conditions.

3. **C** The courts, not the legislative or executive branches, must determine the "clear and present danger," according to the Supreme Court decision described in the second paragraph. (C) is correct, and therefore the exception.

4. **A** Because the firing of the controllers had the same effect as a strike, it appears that there was no danger to the public.

5. **E** The author points out that workers in government who do that same job as workers in private industry cannot strike. The passage argues that the nature of the service should determine the right to strike, not the employer.

6. **A** It is possible that the "highly qualified" may seek employment outside of government, because of the no-strike clause. Choices (B), (C), (D), (E) are not plausible weaknesses of the no-strike rule.

Passage 2

7. **A** Both passages agree that a lack of copyright laws on the Internet means less profit for creators, and therefore (A) is the best answer. This fact is a main point in Passage A, while the author of Passage B believes profit shouldn't be the "sole consideration" (line 78). The passages do not agree on the statements in any of the other choices. Both passages see that there are problems with current copyright laws on the Internet, but Passage A sees these problems as a matter of enforcement, not limiting the free flow of information.

8. **C** Choice (C) best summarizes the main idea in each passage. The argument throughout Passage A is that using material on the Internet without regard to copyright laws is stealing and will therefore discourage creators of original material, while the author of Passage B focuses on the Internet as a "powerful new force" for passing on ideas, and therefore it shouldn't be subject to barriers. (E) may seem like a good answer, but the author of Passage B isn't opposed to copyright laws because they may favor business; rather, the passage says that financial motives shouldn't be primary.

9. **D** The author of Passage B would be most likely to identify (D) as the basis of the arguments in Passage A. The author of Passage A in lines 16–18, 22–23, and 27–29 indicates that copyright laws ensure profits for creators. (A) is the second-best answer, since Passage A in lines 12–14 cites the fact that for over 200 years copyright laws have protected intellectual property. But it isn't this "tradition" that the author is using as a basis of argument but rather the financial considerations concerning copy-

right. (C) is too broad, and (B) and (E) are irrelevant.

10. **E** Choice (E) is the best answer. This is the only specific provision of the Act that is covered in Passage A (lines 27–29). (B) is contradicted in both passages, and although AOL and Earthlink are mentioned, the passage states they are exempted by the Act from copyright violations on their networks.

11. **C** The best meaning for "cached" here is (C). "Cached" is a commonly used term in the computer world. It is also, in context, the meaning that makes most sense.

12. **B** The best meaning for *inimical* in this context is (B). The author's point throughout the passage is that the Internet encourages the free flow of information, and the concept of exclusive ownership is "unfriendly" to such a technology. One dictionary definition of inimical is "reflecting or indicating hostility." This clearly rules out (D) and (E), and neither (A) nor (C) makes sense in context.

13. **C** Choice (C) is the best answer (lines 122–127). Although Google undoubtedly had many objections, it is the virtually impossible task of compliance that is cited in the submission. Beyond the issue of compliance, Google stated that the law would condemn Australia to a "pre-Internet era," but this is not one of the choices given.

Passage 3

14. **A** The author is obviously most concerned with the work of historians and the current state of written history, which is what prompts his discussion of fiction in relation to history. See lines 4–8, 17–20,

54–60, 65–71. Literature and literary concerns (answer C) are secondary.

15. **C** See lines 69–70: "... their abandonment of the narrative style. ..." A decline in the writing *ability* of historians (E) is not implied. And although the author does mention the movies and television, he does not attribute the growth of fictional history to an increase in their audiences (B).

16. **E** This attitude is clearly stated in lines 50–54. (B) may seem correct, but the author does not say that fictional history on its own has won the audience away from traditional history. On the contrary, he suggests that professional historians themselves may be partly responsible for the growth of fictional history (lines 65–69).

17. **A** This book would most clearly fit the definition of fictional history given in lines 35–40. According to the author, it is fictional history that causes the greatest confusion (lines 50–54). (B) and (C) would be classified as historical fiction according to the author's definitions, and (D) and (E) as nonfiction.

18. **B** The second paragraph is devoted to defining and contrasting the two terms. (D) might be considered a possible answer but is less clear and specific. The other answers are simply inaccurate.

19. **E** Nothing in the passage suggests a judgment of history taught in the schools. The other statements are all supported in the passage: (A)—lines 17–20; (B)—lines 65–69; (C)—lines 54–60; (D)—lines 12–16.

20. **D** Throughout the passage the author is most concerned with the growth of fictional history and its effects.

None of the other answers present his *attitude* as clearly, though (C) does define fictional history.

21. **B** The author is obviously concerned with the "mischief" that the mixture of history with fiction can cause. However, he presents his concern in a moderate fashion. He is not hostile, he does not preach, he is not pedantic, nor does he display irony. (E) suggests an elevated tone not present in the passage.

Passage 4

22. **C** (C) is the best answer because the author explains fear conditioning in order to show how it is a good method for studying emotional memory. (A) is incorrect; the passage "proves" nothing. (B) is also incorrect. The fact that the mechanisms in mammals and vertebrates may be similar is not the main point of the passage; also, the passage does not state that the mechanisms are "the same." (D) is only a supporting point—not the main point—of the passage. (E) is incorrect; the way that phobias are initially created in humans is not addressed in the passage.

23. **C** The passage makes this connection in lines 39–45. (A) is incorrect—see lines 28–29. (B) is also incorrect; lines 75–77 specifically state that cues to which subjects respond fearfully are not linked to complicated cognitive processing. (D) is incorrect because the passage states that stress, rather than *weakening* a response, may cause its recurrence. (E) is not the right choice. See lines 28–29. The rat's conditioned response diminishes only when the conditioned stimulus is administered many times without the unconditioned stimulus. As long as the shock and conditioned stimulus are paired, the rat's response to the conditioned stimulus will remain.

24. **D** The passage states than an extinguished fear response can recover spontaneously or can be reinstated by an irrelevant stressful experience (lines 39–42). We can assume that for a rat, introduction of a cat could be an "irrelevant stressful experience." (A) and (B) are incorrect; both are contradicted by information in the passage (lines 29–34 and lines 34–38). (C) and (E) are not supported by information in the passage.

25. **A** This answer is directly supported in lines 73–75. According to lines 28–29, the response is not related to complex cognitive processing. Therefore, (B) is incorrect. (C) and (D) are not supported by any information presented in the passage. (E) is incorrect; in lines 34–38, the brain's control, rather than lack of control, is cited.

26. **B** The author cites the nine animals to show the wide range of animal groups in which fear conditioning occurs. This supports his point that fear conditioning is an ideal starting point for studies of emotional memory. Although fear conditioning occurring in so many animal groups may support (A) (that the fear response is neural), this is not the primary reason for citing them. See lines 50–54. There is no suggestion of a developmental link between the animal groups listed, making (C) an incorrect choice. (D) and (E) are also incorrect; the author's listing of the nine animals is not connected in the passage to the role of the brain, nor

is any point made about the emotions of fruit flies, snails, and so on.

27. **A** The last line of the passage states that the object of the research is to examine the "neurological foundations of fear." (B) and (E) are incorrect; the primary object of the research is not "cognition" nor how mammals are similar. (C) is also incorrect; conditioning is the *method* to be used to study the neurological basis of fear, not the object of the research itself. (D) should be ruled out because the effects of acoustic and visual stimuli are a small part of the research, not its main object.

28. **E** The third paragraph is devoted to reasons that fear conditioning is an "ideal starting point" for research of emotional memory, i.e., it occurs in many animal groups, the signals are not the type to which subjects have preexisting strong emotional reactions, and so on. (A) is incorrect because the definition is completed in paragraphs 1 and 2. (B) is incorrect because the author presents no qualifications or reservations about fear conditioning. (C) is not a good choice because the passage adds new information (i.e., reasons or justifications) and does not summarize. Finally, (D) is not correct because the passage does not present any applications other than the study of emotion and memory for the fear conditioning method.

Section II

Answers 1–6

From the information given, you could have made the following diagram:

Higher	A	D	E		Pent.	4	___	
	?	?	?	FG		3	___	___
						2	___	___
Lower	B	C	C			1	___	___

1. **C** Since F and G are on the same floor, they can't be on 4. Since B and C are below A or D/E, they can't be on 4; therefore only A, D, or E can be on 4.

2. **A** If F is on the second floor, so is G. You also know that C is on a lower floor than both D and E. If one of them (D or E) is in the penthouse, then the other would be on the third floor. Therefore, C could only be on the first floor (A). D could be on the third or fourth floor (B). A could also be on the third or fourth floor (C). G must be on the same floor as F, the second floor (D). B must be on the first floor (E).

3. **E** If D is on 4, G (and F) *can* be on 3, 2, or 1.

D	D	D
FG	AE	AE
AE	FG	BC
BC	BC	FG

4. **C** If D and E are on the same floor, it cannot be on the fourth floor (only one apartment) or the first floor (C must be on a lower floor). If you put them on the second floor, the arrangement could be

```
A
FG
CE
CB
```

If you put them on the third floor, the arrangement would be

```
A              A
DE    or       DE
FG             CB
CB             FG
```

Regardless of the arrangement, A would be on the fourth floor—the answer is (C). All of the other answers are possible but do not have to be true.

5. **D** If A is on the fourth floor and C is on the first floor, then F and G will be together on either the second or third floor:

A		A
Vacant	or	FG
FG		Vacant
BC		BC

Since D and E both need to be on a higher floor than C, they will be together on the vacant floor:

A		A
DE	or	FG
FG		DE
BC		BC

Therefore, the only open position for B is on the first floor. The answer is (D). All other answers are possible but not absolutely true.

6. **B** A and E can be on the same floor if D is on the fourth floor. A cannot be on the first floor (C) because B must be below A. D cannot be on the first floor (D) because C must be below D. C cannot be on the fourth floor (E) because D and E must be above C. For A and C to be on the same floor (A), they would have to be below D and E and above B on floor 2 or 3. If A and C were on floor 3, there would not be room for both D and E on floor 4. If A and C were on floor 2, either D or E would be on floor 3 or 4, and B would have to be on floor 1. There would not be an open floor for F and G to stay together. The remaining choice is answer (B), A and E on the same floor. There are three possibilities, which satisfy the original conditions:

D	D	D
AE	AE	FG
BC	FG	AE
FG	BC	BC

Answers 7–12

From the information given, you may have constructed a simple grouping display of information similar to this:

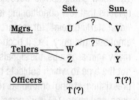

Another possible display might look like this:

	Sat.	Sun.
Mgrs.	U ⌒ ? ⌒	V
Tellers	W ⌒ ? ⌒	X
	Z	Y
Officers	S	T(?)
	T(?)	

7. **E** From the original information, a manager must be on duty each day and the managers cannot work on the same day. Therefore (A) must be true. (E) does not have to be true, since U's schedule has no bearing on X's schedule. Since W and X will not work on the same day, (B) must also be true. There is no restriction placed on T.

8. **E** V, W, Z, S can work on Saturday without breaking any of the conditions given. Choice (A) is missing a manager. Choice (B) has two managers working on the same day. Choices (C) and (D) have W and X working on the same day.

9. **D** Five employees, U or V, X or W, Z, S, and T are the greatest number to work on Saturday.

10. **A** Since W and X will not work on the same day, (A) must be true. (B) is false since Y must work on Sunday. (C) could be true. Since W's schedule has no effect on Z and U, (D) and (E) may be true or false.

11. **E** Since no employee can work on consecutive days, and there are four tellers, then two must work on Saturday.

12. **D** U, V, W, X, Y, Z, and T have the possibility of working on Sunday; S and Z do not.

Answers 13–19

From the information given, you could have constructed the following simple diagram and display of information:

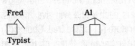

13. **A** From the diagram and information above, if Gene works for Fred, then Lyndia also works for Fred, and Sylvia must work for Cynthia. Since Dennis and Edra will not work together, one of them must work for Cynthia; therefore choice (A) must be false. Jim cannot work for Cynthia.

14. **C** Using the diagram, if Sylvia doesn't work for Cynthia, then Gene must work for Cynthia. If Gene works for Cynthia, then Lyndia must also work for Cynthia, since Gene and Lyndia always work together.

15. **A** If Lyndia and Jim work for Al, then Gene must also work for Al, and Sylvia must work for Cynthia. The diagram would look like this:

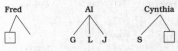

First, (A) is true since Gene and Lyndia always work together. Stop there. Go no further. Edra could work for Cynthia or Fred, and also Helen could work for Cynthia or Fred.

16. **D** If Sylvia and Jim work for Al, then Gene and Lyndia must work for Cynthia. Since Dennis and Edra cannot work together, one of them must work for Fred and the other for Al. The diagram would now look like this:

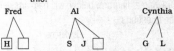

Therefore, only (D) is true.

17. **E** From the diagram, if Lyndia and Sylvia work for Al, then Gene also must work for Al. But either Sylvia or Gene must work for Cynthia. Therefore (E) must be false.

18. **D** From the diagram, if Jim works for Cynthia, then Sylvia must also work for Cynthia, since Gene and Lyndia must work together. Gene and Lyndia cannot work for Fred, because then Dennis and Edra (who cannot work together) would work for Al. Therefore, Lyndia must work for Al. The diagram would look like this:

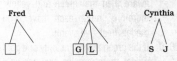

19. **C** If Al needs only two assistants and Fred needs only one, and if Helen works for Fred, then the diagram would look like this:

Fred

Al

Cynthia

S or G

Since Gene and Lyndia must work together, they can work for either Al or Cynthia. Since Edra (typist) must work and Dennis and Edra cannot work together, then Dennis doesn't work. Otherwise, Dennis and Edra would work together. Statements A, B, D, and E *could* be true.

Answers 20–24

Drawing a diagram, below, will help answer the questions.

EVENTS

	1	2	3	4	5
RED	G	—	G	—	G
BLUE	—	B/S	—	B/S	—
GREEN					
YELLOW					

Since the red team wins only three gold medals, it must win gold medals in events 1, 3, and 5, since no team wins gold medals in consecutive events. Also, note that since blue wins only two medals (neither of them gold), it must have won medals in events 2 and 4, so that it didn't fail to win a medal within two consecutive events. Be aware then that green and yellow, therefore, must each have won medals in all five events.

20. **C** If the green team wins only one gold medal, there remains only one gold medal, which the yellow team must win.

21. **B** Since three medals are given for each event, and, according to our diagram from the facts, red and blue already account for their total awards with one medal in each event, the other two medals in each event must go to yellow and green. Thus, yellow and green will each be awarded five medals.

22. **D** By completing the chart such that the yellow team wins five silver medals, we can see that green must win two gold and three bronze medals.

	1	2	3	4	5
RED	G	—	G	—	G
BLUE	—	B/S	—	B/S	—
GREEN					
YELLOW	S	S	S	S	S

23. **D** We know choices (A) and (B) are both true: both the green and yellow teams each must win five medals. Therefore (E) is also true. Choice (C) is true because three of the gold medals are already won by the red team; since blue doesn't win gold, if green wins one gold, yellow wins the remaining gold medal. Choice (D) is not true: if the green team wins only one silver medal, the yellow team must win at least two silver medals.

24. **C** If a fifth team enters all events and wins only three consecutive silver medals, it must win the silver in events 2, 3, and 4, so that it does not fail to win a medal within two consecutive events. Therefore our diagram would look like this:

	1	2	3	4	5
RED	G	—	G	—	G
BLUE	—	B	—	B	—
GREEN					
YELLOW					
ORANGE	—	S	S	S	—

Therefore, if yellow wins a gold in the 2nd event, green must win a medal in the 3rd event (since no team fails to win a medal within two consecutive events). Thus, green must win a bronze in the 3rd event.

Section III

1. **C** The passage is more restrained in its criticism than (A) or (B), while (D) and (E) are only elements of the paragraph, not its main point.

2. **B** By urging moviegoers to patronize films *in order to* influence academy judges, the author reveals his assumption that the academy will be influenced by the number of people paying to see a movie.

3. **E** Bob's answer shows that he thinks that people other than teachers are mean. His thought was that Andy meant otherwise.

4. **D** The author's concluding contention is that Roosevelt was not only a good marksman, but also an intellectually curious and patient man. If Roosevelt was known to leave safaris which were not immediately productive, this fact would substantially weaken the author's contention about Roosevelt's "patient observation."

5. **D** The words "because of a recent cut in state funding of our program" indicate that another criterion was used in determining entering class size besides candidates' scores and grades, namely, the financial situation of the college. The words *seriously* in choice (B) and *severe* in choice (E) are not necessarily supported by the passage, and thus make those choices incorrect. Since grade point average is only one of several criteria for admission, we cannot deduce (A) with certainty.

6. **A** This sentence not only fits well stylistically but completes the thought of the passage by tying it into the opening statement.

7. **B** The author of this passage actually defines conscience as the ability to sense right and wrong.

8. **C** "Without opportunity there would be no crime" fails to consider that thievery is not the only type of crime.

9. **B** This choice offers the most thorough and comprehensive evidence that the viewing of violent television precedes criminal behavior. (A) is not the best choice because it describes viewing habits that follow rather than precede criminal behavior.

10. **E** The use of "overwhelming" leaves the evidence unspecified, thus opening to challenge the extent and nature of the report's data.

11. **E** All of the first four statements can be used to explain the underreporting. In D, for example, if the size of police departments has declined, they would have less manpower available to gather and report information. E is a reason against underreporting rather than an explanation for it.

12. **C** The argument uses the case of the county to call the state figures into question. The underreported figures are "less evidence."

13. **B** If the experiences and lifestyle of the Aryan race are uniquely different from those of other cultures, it would seriously weaken the author's conclusion that studying the Aryan race will be helpful in understanding the experiences and life styles of other races. That its communal arrangements are *unique* would make comparison between the

Aryan race and other cultures impossible.

14. **C** The author presents a *contrast* between life and honor: in particular, the final sentence suggests that life and honor have opposite qualities. Of the choices, the only opposite of *transient* is *eternal*.

15. **E** The logic of this statement goes from the general absolute ("all") to the specific ("this animal"), concluding with specific to specific. Symbolically, if P implies Q, then *not Q* implies *not P*. (E) goes from general absolute ("all") to specific ("this liquid"), concluding with specific to specific. Notice how and where the inverse ("not") is inserted. Using symbols, we have that, if P implies Q, then *not Q* implies *not P*.

16. **B** This is a close one. (B) and (D) both weaken the argument by pointing out that all dogs do not always bark, but (B) is absolute. (D) is tentative, since a dog trained not to bark might do so by accident.

17. **B** The apparent discrepancy in the paragraph, is "Why should arrests decline when there are fewer policemen to arrest the criminals?" One explanation is that though the number of arrests has declined, the number of crimes has risen, and because there are fewer police officers, more crimes are unsolved.

18. **A** The complaint about ex-employees of the Department of Energy on the board, and the financial tie of the National Academy Board to the Energy Department indicate the officials' belief that the Department of Energy supports the nuclear power industry against the views of environmentalists.

19. **E** Though adding one or two environmentalists might help, they would still be outnumbered by the ten panel members with ties to the Department of Energy. Of the five choices, E offers the best hope of impartiality.

20. **C** (A) contradicts the statement's urging of economy. (B) introduces an irrelevant word, "terminology." (D) and (E) are *absolute* statements about assumptions, but the statement itself is *relative*, urging us only to simplify our assumptions *if one such simplification is possible; in other words, "If an issue is simple, don't complicate it."*

21. **C** If, for example, fifty businesses closed but sixty had opened, you would have a net gain of ten new businesses and presumably a healthier economy. It is immaterial at what point in the year the businesses closed, only that they did close (A). The addition of public buildings (D) could be interpreted as a sign of increased economic health, but (C) is the best answer since the number of businesses is the sign of economic health. (E) only suggests that the township may have experienced economic declines before.

22. **E** (A) is obviously true. (B) also satisfies the conditions. (C) is correct, since 3.5 was required with a score of 800. (D) is correct, since we do not know anything about numbers of applicants. (E) is inconsistent, since a score of 1200 is required with a GPA of 2.5. (E) specifies a score *less than* 1200. Therefore, a GPA greater than (*not less than*) 2.5 would be required for admittance.

23. **B** To speak in positive terms about the increase in school degrees, the author must assume that the degrees indicate what they are supposed to indicate, that is, well-educated individuals. (A) and (E) are empty statements; (C) and (D) are altogether unsubstantiated by either expressed or implied information.

24. **E** Although the brand name is No-NOCK, the advertisement makes no claim to stop the engine from knocking. All the other claims are contained in the advertisement.

25. **D** The choice repudiates the suggestion that gentleness and graciousness were once part of the American character. (B) offers an excuse for ill-tempered athletes, but (D) clearly undermines the contention that tennis was once a gentleman's sport.

26. **B** By asking Dolores to choose between conventional and nuclear weapons, Fran has concluded that Dolores's statement calls for a decision. (C), worth considering, is not best because Fran supposes that Dolores has *not* made a choice—hence her question.

Section IV

Answers 1–6

From the information given, you should have constructed a diagram similar to this:

1. **B** From the diagram, if the group begins on island W, it could not reach island V in the eight days. Remember three days would have to be spent on W and three on X.

2. **B** From the diagram, if the group stays on island X for three nights, then the group cannot get to island V on the next visit.

3. **D** To answer this question, you must try each answer choice and eliminate the ones that do not connect. From the diagram, the only possible order listed would be U X Z V.

4. **E** From the diagram, if the group visits island W first, it could go to X to Y to Z, back to X, to U back to Y, to V and back to Z. A total of nine visits. You could work from the choices, but remember to start from the highest number.

5. **D** From the diagram, the group could go from X to W to U to Y to V to Z to Y. This would be six different islands.

6. **E** Adding island T to the diagram connected only to U could look like this:

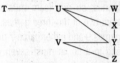

From this revised diagram, only (E) must be true. On the tenth day of a tour starting on Z, the tour group could be on island T. It would go from Z to Y to U to T or Z to X to U to T.

Answers 7–13

From the information given, you could have constructed the following diagram:

Notice the simple markings to show: There are no ties in the first three games.
Team A wins more of the last three games than team B.
Team B wins more of the last five games than team A.

The last game is a tie.

Games 1 and 3 are won by the same team.

From this information you could deduce that team A wins either game 7 or 8, but not both, and team B cannot win any of the last three games. (If team A won both, team B could not win more of the last five games.) If team A wins game 7, then game 8 is a tie, and if team A wins game 8, then game 7 is a tie.

You could also deduce that team B must win games 5 and 6. Your diagram now looks like this:

```
No Ties                    B > A
┌──────────────┐    ┌───┬───┬───┬───┬───┐
                    │ B │ B │ A │ T │ T │
  1    2    3    4  │ 5 │ 6 │ 7 │ 8 │ 9 │
       ﹀                │   │ T │ A │
```

7. C   There are no ties in the first three games, so one team must win at least two of the three games. Since games 9 and either game 7 or 8 will end in a tie, at most seven games will not be ties. That means that the winning team would need to win at most four games, not five (A). Game 9 is a tie (B). Since game 9 is a tie, the same team cannot win all of the last five games (D). Since game 9 is a tie, the last three games cannot be won by the same team (E).

8. E   Of the last three games, A wins more than B, and game 9 ends in a tie. That means that either A wins two games to none, or one game to none. Since B wins more of the last five games than A, B must win games 5 and 6.

9. A   From the answer to the previous question, you know that of the last five games, B wins more than A, and the only games B wins are games 5 and 6.

```
5    6    7    8    9
B    B    A    ?    Tie
```

If A wins game 8, then it would not be possible for B to have more wins over the last five games. If B wins game 8, then it would not be possible for A to have more wins than B over the last three games. Therefore, game 8 ends in a tie (A).

10. E   According to the last problem, there are two ties in the last five games, not one tie (A). It is possible that team A could win two of the last three games, but it does not have to be true (B). According to the last problem, B will win only two of the last five games (C). There is no information given about game 4; it may be possible but does not necessarily have to be true (D). Team A wins either game 7 or 8, but none of the rest of the last five games (E).

11. E   If team A wins games 1 and 4, then it must also win game 3. This would give team A four wins total, and team B could only win three, therefore team B could not win the series. For this question, the diagram would now look like this:

```
A         A    A    B    B       A      T
1    2    3    4    5    6      ﹀       9
                               7    8
```

12. B   If game 4 is won by the winner of game 5, then team B wins game 4. If game 2 is not won by the winner of game 3, then team B wins either game 2 or 3. This gives team B at least four wins and team A only a possible three wins, therefore B is the winner of the series.

13. E   From the original diagram, team A must win either games 1, 2, and 3, or games 1, 3, and 4 to win the series. [This also eliminates choice (A).] If team B wins exactly one of the first four games [choice (B)], then team B cannot win the series as team A will win at least three games. If team A wins only three of the first seven games [choice (C)], then team A could still lose the series as team B could win games 2, 4, 5, and 6, with team A winning only games 1, 3, and 7. Team B could win the series by winning two of the first four games, eliminating choice (D).

Answers 14–18
Drawing a simple diagram, below, will help answer the questions.

```
                              TR
                               *
            __ __ __  J      FDR
M, A, K, FDR→ __ __  M  A    K – FDR or
                              FDR – K
```

Note that, once Madison is placed in position 3 on the bottom, Adams must go in position 4 in order to leave spots for Kennedy to be adjacent to Franklin Delano Roosevelt.

14. **D** If Theodore Roosevelt is second from the left (on top), then Franklin Delano Roosevelt must be first on the bottom since one Roosevelt may not be above the other. Therefore, Kennedy must be second on the bottom.

15. **A** Adams must go to the far right on the bottom to allow Kennedy to be adjacent to Franklin Delano Roosevelt.

16. **D** If Washington and Kennedy are both first on their shelves, then Franklin Delano Roosevelt must be second on the lower shelf. Therefore, Theodore Roosevelt cannot be second on the top shelf and therefore must be third. Thus, statement (D) cannot be true.

17. **E** Since Adams must be on the right in the second row, only (E) is not possible.

18. **C** If Lincoln is next to Jefferson, that leaves Theodore Roosevelt and Washington for the first two positions on the top shelf. All of the choices are therefore true except (C) because that choice would place one Roosevelt above the other, which is not permitted.

Answers 19–24
The following display can be drawn from the information given:

1	2	3	4	5	6
O	B	R	R	B	R
W	G	Y	Y	G	O
Y	Y			R	V
				Y	W

19. **E** The only two color choices for houses 3 and 4 are R and Y. Therefore, houses 3 and 4 must be the two houses painted R and Y. Therefore, no other house is painted R or Y. Thus, choice (A) is incorrect. Choices (B), (C), and (D) are incorrect for the same reason.

20. **A** If orange is not used, the color choices reduce to the following possibilities:

1	2	3	4	5	6
W	B	R	R	B	W
	G	Y	Y	G	V

There is one way to paint houses 1 and 6. Since house 1 must be W, house 6 must be V. There are two ways to paint houses 2 and 5: BG or GB. There are two ways to paint houses 3 and 4: RY or YR. Therefore, there are $1 \times 2 \times 2$ ways, or four ways to paint the houses.

21. **C** Since houses 3 and 4 are the R and Y houses, the possible color combinations reduce to the following:

1	2	3	4	5	6
O	B	R	R	B	O
W	G	Y	Y	G	V
					W

Choice (A) is incorrect since, if house 1 is painted W, we still do not know the color of house 6. Choice (B) is incorrect since, if house 6 is painted V, we still do not know the color of house 1. Choice (D) is incorrect since we do not know the colors of houses 1 or 6. Choice (E) is incorrect since we do not know the colors of houses 3 and 4. Choice (C) is correct since all colors are determined. If you know G you know B, if you know R you know Y, and if you know W you know O.

22. **E** Since houses 3 and 4 are the R and Y houses, the possible color combinations reduces to the following (p = primary, s = secondary):

1	2	3	4	5	6
Os	Bp	Rp	Rp	Bp	Os
W	Gs	Yp	Yp	Gs	Vs
					W

Choice (A) is incorrect since it is not possible for both the second and sixth house to be Bp. Choice (B) is incorrect since the sixth house cannot be painted a primary color. Choice (C) is incorrect since it is not possible for both the second and fifth house to be Gs. Choice (D) is incorrect since the fourth house must be painted a primary color.

Choice (E) is the only possible combination.

23. **D** Since houses 3 and 4 are the R and Y houses, the possible color combinations reduce to the following:

1	2	3	4	5	6
O	B	R	R	B	O
W	G	Y	Y	G	V
					W

If the V house is next to the G house, the possible combinations reduce to the following:

1	2	3	4	5	6
O	B	R	R	G	V
W		Y	Y		

If the B house is next to the Y house, the possible combinations reduce to the following:

1	2	3	4	5	6
O	B	Y	R	G	V
W					

Choices (A) and (B) are incorrect since the first house could be either O or W. Choice (C) is incorrect since the third house is not R. Choice (E) is incorrect since the fifth house is not B. Choice (D) is correct.

24. **C** If the painter of the third house also likes pink, then the possible color combinations are as follows:

1	2	3	4	5	6
O	B	R	R	B	R
W	G	Y	Y	G	O
Y	Y	P		R	V
				Y	W

Choices (A), (B), (D), and (E) are possible as follows:

1	2	3	4	5	6	
O	B	P	Y	G	R	(A)
O	G	R	Y	B	W	(B)
Y	G	P	R	B	W	(D)
W	Y	P	R	G	V	(E)

Choice (C) is correct, since if the second house is yellow, the fourth house not the third house, must be red.

Section V

1. **B**   The correct answer must use both premises. The first qualifies the assertion with "normally," so (A) will not follow, but (B) (with the qualifier "may") will. (C) may or may not be true, but it is not a logical conclusion based on the two premises. (D) and (E), like (A), do not use both premises.

2. **D**   The question asked concerns the danger to public health, but the reply does not deal with this issue at all. It changes the subject.

3. **C**   Reducing coffee consumption in general will not guarantee a healthier population (A) if "heavy" consumers do not reduce their coffee intake. Reducing coffee consumption would make those who drink a morning cup of coffee feel less well (B). (C) is a logical conclusion since heavy consumption increases heart attack risk. There is no information in the passage to justify the assertion about percolated coffee (D). If coffee may protect against colon cancer, (E) is not true.

4. **D**   The issue of the danger of pesticides is addressed by (A), (C), and (E), while (B) calls into question the objectivity of the Food and Agriculture Department. But (D) deals with a different issue: air pollution. And if air pollution is a cause of illness, pesticides may be less to blame.

5. **A**   The question contains its own prior judgment (underpay, unfair promotion policies) on what it asks, regardless of a "yes" or "no" answer. Similarly, the adjective "excessive" and the adverb "unfairly" prejudge any answer in choice (A).

6. **E**   Since fares have risen, the cost of fuel has risen or there are no fare wars. And if there are no fare wars, the number of passengers is larger. Only (E) cannot be true. (B) is possible if fuel costs have risen, and there are fare wars.

7. **B**   Though the argument for a decline in fishing off Newfoundland is convincing, the generalization that the "fishing industry in the Americas" will disappear is here based only on information about the Atlantic waters off Canada. It is possible that other areas have not been so affected.

8. **C**   The advertisement asserts filter cigarettes cannot have great taste. A reasonable inference is that Gold Star is not a filter cigarette. (A) is contradicted by this ad without visual appeal. (B) is contradicted by this ad, which does not specifically praise a brand. (D) is illogical given the existence of this ad. Nothing in the ad supports (E).

9. **D**   Choices (A), (B), and (C) strengthen the case for building the toll road. The environmentalists may be able to make their case for one of the other possible routes that, if less direct, would not disturb the reserve. With the information we have, the value of (E) is indeterminable.

10. **A**   There is nothing in the paragraph to support (E), and there are details that contradict (B), (C), and (D). That "sales in the United States continue to increase" supports (A).

11. **E** The passage does not give the information that would lead to the conclusion in (A), (B), or (C). (E) is a better answer than (D), the odds against the heavy smoker being 40 in 100 as opposed to 25 in 100 for the light smoker.

12. **C** The presence of wolf bones and walrus bones near a village is not evidence that wolves were trained to haul sleds; it does not disprove the theory, however.

13. **B** Choices (A), (C), (D), and (E) would undermine the theory. But if wolves were easily domesticated and trained, it would make the theory of their domestication by Stone Age tribes more plausible.

14. **A** The author makes his point by invective, an abrasive verbal attack.

15. **D** The first sentence asserts the needlessness of commenting on the picture; the second nonetheless makes a detailed criticism.

16. **B** If popcorn attracts rodents and insects, warehouses where packages using popcorn are stored would have vermin problems.

17. **B** Only (B) is a necessary assumption. It must be assumed that no other items (for example dressings, recipes, spices, etc.) are sold at the stand in order to conclude definitively that everything sold there is delicious.

18. **B** Though (E) is probably true, it is not a conclusion based on the information in the passage. But the passage does assert that only 19.6 percent (11.9 plus 7.7) of the eligible voters in the Democratic and Republican parties went to the polls.

19. **A** Choices (B) and (C), although true, are not relevant, while (D) and (E) are probably untrue. That it is only in the schools that the tobacco spokesmen are silent supports the inference of (A).

20. **C** In both paragraphs, the author disputes the interpretations of his opponents.

21. **D** The author assumes that an audience is able to evaluate a work and determine its own course of action.

22. **E** The opening lines describe esteem without popularity, later followed by popular success.

23. **D** The "But" introducing the last sentence suggests that a contrast, a disadvantage of coffee, is to follow. Either (C) or (D) is possible, but since exercise has not been an issue, (D) is the better choice.

24. **A** Only choice (A) must be true. There may be other performers as well as the chorus members (the orchestra, for example) in the performance, so (E) is incorrect.

25. **C** The passage draws an analogy comparing corrupt politicians to vermin.

8

MODEL TEST TWO

This chapter contains full-length Model Test Two. It is geared to the format of the LSAT, and it is complete with answers and explanations. It is equivalent to the LSAT in question structure, number of questions, level of difficulty, and time allotments. (The questions used are not taken directly from the LSAT, as those questions are copyrighted and may not be reproduced.)

Model Test Two should be taken under strict test conditions. The test ends with a 35-minute Writing Sample, which is not scored.

Section	Description	Number of Questions	Time Allowed
I.	Logical Reasoning	26	35 minutes
II.	Reading Comprehension	28	35 minutes
III.	Analytical Reasoning	25	35 minutes
IV.	Logical Reasoning	26	35 minutes
V.	Reading Comprehension	28	35 minutes
	Writing Sample		35 minutes
TOTALS:		133	3 hours 30 minutes

Now please turn to the next page, remove your answer sheet, and begin Model Test Two.

ANSWER SHEET—MODEL TEST TWO

Section 1	Section 2	Section 3	Section 4	Section 5
1. Ⓐ Ⓑ Ⓒ Ⓓ Ⓔ	1. Ⓐ Ⓑ Ⓒ Ⓓ Ⓔ	1. Ⓐ Ⓑ Ⓒ Ⓓ Ⓔ	1. Ⓐ Ⓑ Ⓒ Ⓓ Ⓔ	1. Ⓐ Ⓑ Ⓒ Ⓓ Ⓔ
2. Ⓐ Ⓑ Ⓒ Ⓓ Ⓔ	2. Ⓐ Ⓑ Ⓒ Ⓓ Ⓔ	2. Ⓐ Ⓑ Ⓒ Ⓓ Ⓔ	2. Ⓐ Ⓑ Ⓒ Ⓓ Ⓔ	2. Ⓐ Ⓑ Ⓒ Ⓓ Ⓔ
3. Ⓐ Ⓑ Ⓒ Ⓓ Ⓔ	3. Ⓐ Ⓑ Ⓒ Ⓓ Ⓔ	3. Ⓐ Ⓑ Ⓒ Ⓓ Ⓔ	3. Ⓐ Ⓑ Ⓒ Ⓓ Ⓔ	3. Ⓐ Ⓑ Ⓒ Ⓓ Ⓔ
4. Ⓐ Ⓑ Ⓒ Ⓓ Ⓔ	4. Ⓐ Ⓑ Ⓒ Ⓓ Ⓔ	4. Ⓐ Ⓑ Ⓒ Ⓓ Ⓔ	4. Ⓐ Ⓑ Ⓒ Ⓓ Ⓔ	4. Ⓐ Ⓑ Ⓒ Ⓓ Ⓔ
5. Ⓐ Ⓑ Ⓒ Ⓓ Ⓔ	5. Ⓐ Ⓑ Ⓒ Ⓓ Ⓔ	5. Ⓐ Ⓑ Ⓒ Ⓓ Ⓔ	5. Ⓐ Ⓑ Ⓒ Ⓓ Ⓔ	5. Ⓐ Ⓑ Ⓒ Ⓓ Ⓔ
6. Ⓐ Ⓑ Ⓒ Ⓓ Ⓔ	6. Ⓐ Ⓑ Ⓒ Ⓓ Ⓔ	6. Ⓐ Ⓑ Ⓒ Ⓓ Ⓔ	6. Ⓐ Ⓑ Ⓒ Ⓓ Ⓔ	6. Ⓐ Ⓑ Ⓒ Ⓓ Ⓔ
7. Ⓐ Ⓑ Ⓒ Ⓓ Ⓔ	7. Ⓐ Ⓑ Ⓒ Ⓓ Ⓔ	7. Ⓐ Ⓑ Ⓒ Ⓓ Ⓔ	7. Ⓐ Ⓑ Ⓒ Ⓓ Ⓔ	7. Ⓐ Ⓑ Ⓒ Ⓓ Ⓔ
8. Ⓐ Ⓑ Ⓒ Ⓓ Ⓔ	8. Ⓐ Ⓑ Ⓒ Ⓓ Ⓔ	8. Ⓐ Ⓑ Ⓒ Ⓓ Ⓔ	8. Ⓐ Ⓑ Ⓒ Ⓓ Ⓔ	8. Ⓐ Ⓑ Ⓒ Ⓓ Ⓔ
9. Ⓐ Ⓑ Ⓒ Ⓓ Ⓔ	9. Ⓐ Ⓑ Ⓒ Ⓓ Ⓔ	9. Ⓐ Ⓑ Ⓒ Ⓓ Ⓔ	9. Ⓐ Ⓑ Ⓒ Ⓓ Ⓔ	9. Ⓐ Ⓑ Ⓒ Ⓓ Ⓔ
10. Ⓐ Ⓑ Ⓒ Ⓓ Ⓔ	10. Ⓐ Ⓑ Ⓒ Ⓓ Ⓔ	10. Ⓐ Ⓑ Ⓒ Ⓓ Ⓔ	10. Ⓐ Ⓑ Ⓒ Ⓓ Ⓔ	10. Ⓐ Ⓑ Ⓒ Ⓓ Ⓔ
11. Ⓐ Ⓑ Ⓒ Ⓓ Ⓔ	11. Ⓐ Ⓑ Ⓒ Ⓓ Ⓔ	11. Ⓐ Ⓑ Ⓒ Ⓓ Ⓔ	11. Ⓐ Ⓑ Ⓒ Ⓓ Ⓔ	11. Ⓐ Ⓑ Ⓒ Ⓓ Ⓔ
12. Ⓐ Ⓑ Ⓒ Ⓓ Ⓔ	12. Ⓐ Ⓑ Ⓒ Ⓓ Ⓔ	12. Ⓐ Ⓑ Ⓒ Ⓓ Ⓔ	12. Ⓐ Ⓑ Ⓒ Ⓓ Ⓔ	12. Ⓐ Ⓑ Ⓒ Ⓓ Ⓔ
13. Ⓐ Ⓑ Ⓒ Ⓓ Ⓔ	13. Ⓐ Ⓑ Ⓒ Ⓓ Ⓔ	13. Ⓐ Ⓑ Ⓒ Ⓓ Ⓔ	13. Ⓐ Ⓑ Ⓒ Ⓓ Ⓔ	13. Ⓐ Ⓑ Ⓒ Ⓓ Ⓔ
14. Ⓐ Ⓑ Ⓒ Ⓓ Ⓔ	14. Ⓐ Ⓑ Ⓒ Ⓓ Ⓔ	14. Ⓐ Ⓑ Ⓒ Ⓓ Ⓔ	14. Ⓐ Ⓑ Ⓒ Ⓓ Ⓔ	14. Ⓐ Ⓑ Ⓒ Ⓓ Ⓔ
15. Ⓐ Ⓑ Ⓒ Ⓓ Ⓔ	15. Ⓐ Ⓑ Ⓒ Ⓓ Ⓔ	15. Ⓐ Ⓑ Ⓒ Ⓓ Ⓔ	15. Ⓐ Ⓑ Ⓒ Ⓓ Ⓔ	15. Ⓐ Ⓑ Ⓒ Ⓓ Ⓔ
16. Ⓐ Ⓑ Ⓒ Ⓓ Ⓔ	16. Ⓐ Ⓑ Ⓒ Ⓓ Ⓔ	16. Ⓐ Ⓑ Ⓒ Ⓓ Ⓔ	16. Ⓐ Ⓑ Ⓒ Ⓓ Ⓔ	16. Ⓐ Ⓑ Ⓒ Ⓓ Ⓔ
17. Ⓐ Ⓑ Ⓒ Ⓓ Ⓔ	17. Ⓐ Ⓑ Ⓒ Ⓓ Ⓔ	17. Ⓐ Ⓑ Ⓒ Ⓓ Ⓔ	17. Ⓐ Ⓑ Ⓒ Ⓓ Ⓔ	17. Ⓐ Ⓑ Ⓒ Ⓓ Ⓔ
18. Ⓐ Ⓑ Ⓒ Ⓓ Ⓔ	18. Ⓐ Ⓑ Ⓒ Ⓓ Ⓔ	18. Ⓐ Ⓑ Ⓒ Ⓓ Ⓔ	18. Ⓐ Ⓑ Ⓒ Ⓓ Ⓔ	18. Ⓐ Ⓑ Ⓒ Ⓓ Ⓔ
19. Ⓐ Ⓑ Ⓒ Ⓓ Ⓔ	19. Ⓐ Ⓑ Ⓒ Ⓓ Ⓔ	19. Ⓐ Ⓑ Ⓒ Ⓓ Ⓔ	19. Ⓐ Ⓑ Ⓒ Ⓓ Ⓔ	19. Ⓐ Ⓑ Ⓒ Ⓓ Ⓔ
20. Ⓐ Ⓑ Ⓒ Ⓓ Ⓔ	20. Ⓐ Ⓑ Ⓒ Ⓓ Ⓔ	20. Ⓐ Ⓑ Ⓒ Ⓓ Ⓔ	20. Ⓐ Ⓑ Ⓒ Ⓓ Ⓔ	20. Ⓐ Ⓑ Ⓒ Ⓓ Ⓔ
21. Ⓐ Ⓑ Ⓒ Ⓓ Ⓔ	21. Ⓐ Ⓑ Ⓒ Ⓓ Ⓔ	21. Ⓐ Ⓑ Ⓒ Ⓓ Ⓔ	21. Ⓐ Ⓑ Ⓒ Ⓓ Ⓔ	21. Ⓐ Ⓑ Ⓒ Ⓓ Ⓔ
22. Ⓐ Ⓑ Ⓒ Ⓓ Ⓔ	22. Ⓐ Ⓑ Ⓒ Ⓓ Ⓔ	22. Ⓐ Ⓑ Ⓒ Ⓓ Ⓔ	22. Ⓐ Ⓑ Ⓒ Ⓓ Ⓔ	22. Ⓐ Ⓑ Ⓒ Ⓓ Ⓔ
23. Ⓐ Ⓑ Ⓒ Ⓓ Ⓔ	23. Ⓐ Ⓑ Ⓒ Ⓓ Ⓔ	23. Ⓐ Ⓑ Ⓒ Ⓓ Ⓔ	23. Ⓐ Ⓑ Ⓒ Ⓓ Ⓔ	23. Ⓐ Ⓑ Ⓒ Ⓓ Ⓔ
24. Ⓐ Ⓑ Ⓒ Ⓓ Ⓔ	24. Ⓐ Ⓑ Ⓒ Ⓓ Ⓔ	24. Ⓐ Ⓑ Ⓒ Ⓓ Ⓔ	24. Ⓐ Ⓑ Ⓒ Ⓓ Ⓔ	24. Ⓐ Ⓑ Ⓒ Ⓓ Ⓔ
25. Ⓐ Ⓑ Ⓒ Ⓓ Ⓔ	25. Ⓐ Ⓑ Ⓒ Ⓓ Ⓔ	25. Ⓐ Ⓑ Ⓒ Ⓓ Ⓔ	25. Ⓐ Ⓑ Ⓒ Ⓓ Ⓔ	25. Ⓐ Ⓑ Ⓒ Ⓓ Ⓔ
26. Ⓐ Ⓑ Ⓒ Ⓓ Ⓔ	26. Ⓐ Ⓑ Ⓒ Ⓓ Ⓔ	26. Ⓐ Ⓑ Ⓒ Ⓓ Ⓔ	26. Ⓐ Ⓑ Ⓒ Ⓓ Ⓔ	26. Ⓐ Ⓑ Ⓒ Ⓓ Ⓔ
27. Ⓐ Ⓑ Ⓒ Ⓓ Ⓔ	27. Ⓐ Ⓑ Ⓒ Ⓓ Ⓔ	27. Ⓐ Ⓑ Ⓒ Ⓓ Ⓔ	27. Ⓐ Ⓑ Ⓒ Ⓓ Ⓔ	27. Ⓐ Ⓑ Ⓒ Ⓓ Ⓔ
28. Ⓐ Ⓑ Ⓒ Ⓓ Ⓔ	28. Ⓐ Ⓑ Ⓒ Ⓓ Ⓔ	28. Ⓐ Ⓑ Ⓒ Ⓓ Ⓔ	28. Ⓐ Ⓑ Ⓒ Ⓓ Ⓔ	28. Ⓐ Ⓑ Ⓒ Ⓓ Ⓔ
29. Ⓐ Ⓑ Ⓒ Ⓓ Ⓔ	29. Ⓐ Ⓑ Ⓒ Ⓓ Ⓔ	29. Ⓐ Ⓑ Ⓒ Ⓓ Ⓔ	29. Ⓐ Ⓑ Ⓒ Ⓓ Ⓔ	29. Ⓐ Ⓑ Ⓒ Ⓓ Ⓔ
30. Ⓐ Ⓑ Ⓒ Ⓓ Ⓔ	30. Ⓐ Ⓑ Ⓒ Ⓓ Ⓔ	30. Ⓐ Ⓑ Ⓒ Ⓓ Ⓔ	30. Ⓐ Ⓑ Ⓒ Ⓓ Ⓔ	30. Ⓐ Ⓑ Ⓒ Ⓓ Ⓔ

To remove, cut along dotted rule.

SECTION I

Directions: In this section you will be given brief statements or passages and will be required to evaluate the reasoning involved. In some instances, more than one choice will appear to be a possible answer. You are to choose the *best* answer. Use common sense and reasonableness in making your selection; then mark the proper space on the answer sheet.

Questions 1–2

Professor: Probability is a curiously unstable concept. Semantically speaking, it is an assumption, a pure artifice, a concept that may or may not be true, but nevertheless facilitates a logical process. It is not a hypothesis because, by its very nature, it cannot be proved. Suppose we flip a coin that has a distinguishable head and tail. In our ignorance of the coming result we say that the coin has one chance in two of falling heads up, or that the probability of a head turning up is one-to-two. Here it must be understood that the one-to-two is not "true" but is merely a species of the genus probability.

1. The professor assumes that

    (A) nothing about our coin influences its fall in favor of either side or that all influences are counterbalanced by equal and opposite influences
    (B) probability can be dealt with without the use of logic
    (C) an assumption must be plausible
    (D) the probability of the coin's landing on an edge is counterbalanced by the probability of its not landing on an edge
    (E) probability can be precisely calculated

2. The last sentence implies that

    (A) probability is not absolute
    (B) one-to-two is merely a guess
    (C) one-to-two is a worthless ratio
    (D) truth is not important
    (E) genus is a category of species

3. Self-confidence is a big factor in success. The person who thinks he can, will master most of the things he attempts. The person who thinks he can't, may not try.

    The author of these statements would agree that

    (A) nothing is impossible
    (B) no task is too large
    (C) success relies on effort
    (D) self-confidence is of most importance
    (E) trying is half the battle

4. People who risk riding on roller coasters are more likely to take risks in other areas of their lives than those who avoid roller coasters. So roller coaster riders are more likely than others to be successful in situations in which taking risks can result in benefit to them.

If the above comments are true, they most strongly support which of the following statements?

(A) No roller coaster riders avoid taking risks in other areas of their lives, but some may take more risks than others.
(B) Risk taking in life decisions is important not only because of the possible financial gain but because of the psychological benefits produced.
(C) Some people who are not roller coaster riders may take more risks in other areas of their lives than do roller coaster riders.
(D) Mountain climbing is riskier than riding on roller coasters, so people who climb mountains will be more successful in other areas of their lives than are roller coaster riders.
(E) Risk taking in one type of activity indicates a likelihood of risk taking in other types of activities.

5. *Anthropologist:* For many years, anthropologists believed that the unusually long lives of the men of the island of Zobu were the result of their active lives and their eating only fish from the lagoon and fruits and vegetables grown on the island. However, recent studies of the inhabitants of nearby Luku, where the way of life and diet are virtually identical with Zobu's, have revealed that the men there rarely survive beyond early middle age.

If the information in this paragraph is correct, it best supports which one of the following?

(A) There are important differences in the lagoons of the two islands of which scientists are unaware.
(B) The inhabitants of Luku and Zobu probably have many ancestors in common.
(C) The longevity of the natives of Zobu is not due simply to their diet and way of life.
(D) Some, though not all, of the residents of Luku live as long as some of the residents of Zobu.
(E) Because longevity depends on so many different factors, it is useless to compare longevity in one area with that in another.

Questions 6–7

Because college-educated men and women as a group earn more than those without college educations, and because in Eastern Europe and Latin America, 105 women are enrolled in colleges for every 100 men, the total earnings of college women in these areas should be equal to, if not greater than, the earnings of college men. But college women in Eastern Europe and in Latin America earn only 65 percent of what college men in these countries earn.

6. Which one of the following, if true, is most useful in explaining this discrepancy?

(A) The earning power of both men and women rises sharply in accord with their level of education.

(B) In some countries of Western Europe, the earning power of college-educated women is higher than that of men in Eastern Europe and Latin America.

(C) In Eastern Europe, more men than women who enter college fail to complete their educations.

(D) The largest percentage of women in Eastern European and Latin American universities study to become teachers; the largest percentage of men study engineering.

(E) In Eastern Europe and Latin America, about 60 percent of the total workforce is college educated.

7. Which of the following is a faulty assumption based on the statistics of the passage?

(A) The passage assumes all of the college women enter the workforce.

(B) The passage assumes conditions in Eastern Europe and in Latin America are the same.

(C) The passage assumes that men and women should be paid equally.

(D) The passage assumes that college-educated women outnumber women who have not attended college in Eastern Europe and Latin America.

(E) The passage assumes that all college-educated workers will be paid more than workers who do not have college educations.

8. *Economist:* When consumers are in a buying mood, and the cost of money is low, a shrewd retailer with a popular product will reduce prices of items that are selling slowly and make up for any loss by raising prices on the product or products that are popular.

In which one of the following situations are these recommendations observed?

(A) At Easter, John's Markets offered one dozen eggs at half their usual price, hams and turkeys at a 40 percent discount, but because of heavy rains, raised the price of many green vegetables.

(B) This Christmas Arrow Clothiers is offering six-month interest free charge accounts to any customers who purchase $50 or more of merchandise from their stock of discontinued summer wear and the fashionable new op-art neckwear.

(C) Since interest rates have reached a yearly low, the price of tax-free bonds is near an all-time high. Discount Brokerage has launched a campaign to sell off all of its holding in precious metals mutual funds that are now at a their lowest price in years.

(D) Angus Jewelry is offering special savings for customers who make purchases in May. With graduations coming soon, they are offering engraved gold Swiss watches, as well as lower prices on heart-shaped jewelry items that were featured on Valentine's Day.

(E) Travel agents in Orlando are capitalizing on the lowered airfares to lure tourists by offering special rates on hotel accommodations and discounted admission tickets to two of the large theme parks in the area.

9. While some cities impose tough, clear restrictions on demolitions of older buildings, our city has no protection for cultural landmarks. Designation as a landmark by the Cultural Heritage Commission can delay a demolition for only one year. This delay can be

avoided easily by an owner's demonstrating an economic hardship. Developers who simply ignore designations and tear down buildings receive only small fines. Therefore, _____.

Which one of the following best completes the passage above?

(A) the number of buildings protected by Cultural Heritage Commission designation must be increased

(B) developers must be encouraged to help preserve our older buildings

(C) the designation as landmark must be changed to delay demolition for more than one year

(D) developers who ignore designations to protect buildings must be subject to higher fines

(E) if our older buildings are to be saved, we need clearer and more rigorously enforced laws

10. Michael claimed that the large dent in the fender of the company-owned vehicle he had borrowed was caused by the careless act of another motorist, who backed into the car when it was parked in a public garage. Yet Michael's own car has several similar dents in its fenders, all of which he acknowledges as having been caused by his own careless driving. Therefore, Michael's contention that the dent in the formerly undented company-owned vehicle was caused by the careless act of another person is not true.

The reasoning in this argument is vulnerable because it

(A) fails to recognize that Michael could be lying about the dents in his own vehicle.

(B) fails to recognize that the motorist who backed into him simply did not see him.

(C) fails to acknowledge that many such accidents occur in parking garages.

(D) presumes, without justification, that because Michael has caused similar dents to his own car, he caused the dent in the company car.

(E) fails to take into consideration that Michael was recently named Employee of the Month.

Questions 11–12

Sixty percent of the American people, according to the latest polls, now believe that inflation is the nation's most important problem. This problem of inflation is closely related to rising prices. The inflation rate has been 10 percent or more most of this year. Undoubtedly, our gluttonous appetite for high-priced foreign oil has been a major factor. We have been shipping billions of dollars overseas, more than foreigners can spend or invest here. Dollars are selling cheaply and this has forced the value of the dollar down. Government programs now being inaugurated to slow this trend are at best weak, but deserve our support, as they appear to be the best our government can produce. Hopefully, they won't fail as they have in the past.

11. The author of this passage implies that

(A) inflation cannot be stopped or slowed, because of a weak government

(B) the fear of inflation is not only unwarranted, but also detrimental

(C) 40 percent of non-Americans believe inflation is not the most important problem

(D) foreign oil is the sole reason for the sudden increase in inflation

(E) the present programs will probably not slow inflation

12. Which one of the following contradicts something in the preceding passage?

(A) Foreign oil is actually underpriced.

(B) The inflation rate has not risen for most of this year.

(C) Overseas investors are few and far between.

(D) Our government is trying a new approach to end inflation.

(E) The weakness of the programs stems from lack of support.

---

13. Sales of new homes in Arizona fell almost 20 percent in the month of February, compared to last year. Analysts attribute the decline to several factors. Record rainfalls kept both builders and buyers indoors for most of the month. The rise in the interest rates have brought mortgage rates to a ten-month high. Both the sales of new homes and housing starts have reached new lows. With every indication that mortgage rates will remain high for the rest of the year, Arizona home builders foresee a very grim year ahead.

Which one of the following would add support to the conclusion of this passage?

(A) Last year's sales increased in the second half of the year, despite some increase in interest rates.

(B) Last year's sales were accelerated by good weather in January and February.

(C) Widespread advertising and incentives to attract buyers this February were ineffective.

(D) Rain in Arizona usually ends late in February.

(E) Home sales and building starts throughout the country are about the same this year as last year.

14. No one reads *Weight-Off* magazine unless he is fat. Everyone reads *Weight-Off* magazine unless he eats chocolate.

Which one of the following is inconsistent with the above?

(A) No one is fat and only some people eat chocolate.

(B) Some people are fat and no one eats chocolate.

(C) Everyone is fat.

(D) No one is fat and no one reads *Weight-Off.*

(E) No one who is fat eats chocolate.

15. *Jerry:* Every meal my wife cooks is fantastic.
    Dave: I disagree. Most of my wife's meals are fantastic, too.

Dave's response shows that he understood Jerry to mean that

(A) Dave's wife does not cook fantastic meals

(B) only Jerry's wife cooks fantastic meals

(C) every one of Jerry's wife's meals is fantastic

(D) not every one of Jerry's wife's meals is fantastic

(E) no one cooks fantastic meals all the time

<u>Questions 16–17</u>

Commentators and politicians are given to enlisting the rest of America as allies, sprinkling such phrases as "Americans believe" or "Americans will simply not put up with" into their pronouncements on whatever issue currently claims their attentions. They cite polls showing 60 or 80 or 90 percent support for their views. There may (or may not) have been such polls, but even if the polls are real, their finer points will not be reported because they usually contradict the speaker's point. The alleged 80 percent support for a balanced budget amendment, for example, plummets to less than 30 percent if the pollster so much as mentions an entitlement program like social security. People do have opinions, but they are rarely so specific or so unequivocal as your news broadcaster or your senator would lead you to believe.

16. The argument of this passage would be less convincing if it could be shown that

(A) In a recent poll, 80 percent of the Americans responding supported a balanced budget amendment.
(B) Most polls used by television commentators are conducted by telephone calls lasting less than 35 seconds.
(C) Far more Americans are indifferent to or badly informed about current affairs than are well informed.
(D) The polls' predictions of who will be elected president have been correct about every presidential election since Truman defeated Dewey.
(E) Many polls are based on samples that do not accurately represent the demographics of an area.

17. The argument of this passage proceeds by using all of the following EXCEPT:

(A) supporting a general point with a specific example
(B) questioning the honesty of politicians and commentators
(C) reinterpreting evidence presented as supporting a position being rejected
(D) pointing out inherent inconsistencies in the claims of the politicians and commentators
(E) exposing the limitations of arguments based on statistics

18. The most often heard complaint about flights on Scorpio Airlines is that there is insufficient room in the cabin of the plane to accommodate all of the passengers' carry-on baggage. The number of passengers who carry on all of their luggage rather than checking it at the ticket counter has increased so much that on more than half of the flights on Scorpio Airlines passengers have difficulty finding space for their bags in the cabin of the plane. The company is considering ways to alleviate this problem.

All of the following are plausible ways of dealing with the problem EXCEPT:

(A) Reducing the allowable size of carry-on luggage.
(B) Charging passengers who carry on more than one bag a fee.
(C) Increasing the fares of flights on lightly traveled routes.
(D) Reducing the seating capacity of the cabins to provide more space for luggage.
(E) Offering a price reduction to ticket buyers who check their bags.

19. X: "We discover new knowledge by the syllogistic process when we say, for example, 'All men are mortal; Socrates is a man; therefore Socrates is mortal.'"

Y: "Yes, but the fact is that if all men are mortal we cannot tell whether Socrates is a man until we have determined his mortality—in other words, until we find him dead. Of course, it's a great convenience to assume that Socrates is a man because he looks like one, but that's just a deduction. If we examine its formulation—'Objects that resemble men in most respects are men; Socrates resembles men in most respects; therefore Socrates is a man'—it's obvious that if he is a man, he resembles men in *all* necessary respects. So it's obvious we're right back where we started."

X: "Yes, we must know all the characteristics of men, and that Socrates has all of them, before we can be sure."

Which one of the following best expresses X's concluding observation?

(A) In deductive thinking we are simply reminding ourselves of the implications of our generalizations.
(B) It is often too convenient to arrive at conclusions simply by deduction instead of induction.
(C) Socrates' mortality is not the issue; the issue is critical thinking.
(D) Socrates' characteristics do not necessarily define his mortality.
(E) The key to the syllogistic process is using theoretical, rather than practical, issues of logic.

20. It takes a good telescope to see the moons of Neptune. I can't see the moons of Neptune with my telescope. Therefore, I do not have a good telescope.

Which one of the following most closely parallels the logic of this statement?

(A) It takes two to tango. You are doing the tango. Therefore, you have a partner.
(B) If you have a surfboard, you can surf. You do not have a surfboard. Therefore, you cannot surf.
(C) You need gin and vermouth to make a martini. You do not have any gin. Therefore, you cannot make a martini.
(D) If you know the area of a circle, you can find its circumference. You cannot figure out the circumference. Therefore, you do not know the area.
(E) You can write a letter to your friend with a pencil. You do not have a pencil. Therefore, you cannot write the letter.

Questions 21–22

Over 90 percent of our waking life depends on habits which for the most part we are unconscious of, from brushing our teeth in the morning, to the time and manner in which we go to sleep at night. Habits are tools which serve the important function of relieving the conscious mind for more important activities. Habits are stored patterns of behavior which are found to serve the needs of the individual that has them and are formed from what once was conscious behavior which over years of repetition can become an automatic behavior pattern of the unconscious mind.

21. It can be inferred that the author bases his beliefs on

(A) the testimony of a controlled group of students
(B) biblical passages referring to the unconscious state
(C) an intense psychological research
(D) extensive psychological research
(E) recent findings of clinical psychologists

22. The last sentence implies that

(A) all repetitious patterns become unconscious behavior
(B) conscious behavior eventually becomes habit
(C) the unconscious mind causes repetitive behavior
(D) automatic behavior patterns of the conscious mind are not possible
(E) habits can be good or bad

Questions 23–24

It should be emphasized that only one person in a thousand who is bitten by a disease-carrying mosquito develops symptoms that require hospitalization, according to Dr. Reeves. But it is a potentially serious disease that requires close collaboration by citizens and local government to prevent it from reaching epidemic proportions.

Citizens should fill or drain puddles where mosquitoes breed. They should repair leaking swamp coolers and be sure swimming pools have a good circulating system. Make sure drain gutters aren't clogged and holding rainwater. Keep barrels and other water-storage containers tightly covered. Use good window screens.

23. Which one of the following statements, if true, would most strengthen the advice given in the second paragraph above?

(A) Leaking swamp coolers are the primary cause of mosquito infestation.
(B) It is possible to completely eliminate mosquitoes from a neighborhood.
(C) No one can completely protect herself from being bitten by a mosquito.
(D) Tightly covered water containers do not ensure the purity of the water in all cases.
(E) Window screens seldom need to be replaced.

24. What additional information would strengthen the clarity of the second sentence above?

(A) The names of some local governments that have fought against disease.

(B) The name of the disease under discussion.

(C) The names of those bitten by disease-carrying mosquitoes.

(D) The full name of Dr. Reeves.

(E) A description of the symptoms that a bitten person might develop.

---

25. That which is rare is always more valuable than that which is abundant. And so we are continually frustrated in our attempts to teach young people how to use time wisely; they have too much of it to appreciate its value.

Which one of the following statements, if true, would most weaken the argument above?

(A) Appreciation is not the same as obedience.

(B) Teaching something as abstract as the appreciation of time is difficult.

(C) Currency that is based on rare metals is more valuable than currency that is not.

(D) Many young people possess an intuitive knowledge of what time is, a knowledge they lose around middle age.

(E) The leisure time of people ages 18 to 24 has decreased significantly over the last ten years.

26. Many theorists now believe that people cannot learn to write if they are constantly worrying about whether or not their prose is correct. When a would-be writer worries about correctness, his ability for fluency is frozen.

With which one of the following statements would the author of the above passage probably agree?

(A) Writing theorists are probably wrong.

(B) Writing prose is different from writing poetry.

(C) Literacy is a function of relaxation.

(D) Fear blocks action.

(E) Most good writers are careless.

STOP

IF YOU FINISH BEFORE TIME IS UP, CHECK YOUR WORK ON THIS SECTION OF THE TEST ONLY.
DO NOT GO ON TO THE NEXT SECTION OF THE TEST UNTIL TIME IS UP FOR THIS SECTION.

SECTION II

Time — 35 minutes
28 Questions

Directions: Read the passages and answer the questions following each passage by blackening the appropriate space on the answer sheet. You may refer back to the passages when answering the questions. Answer all questions on the basis of what is stated or implied.

The Sixth Amendment's right to the "assistance of counsel" has been the subject of considerable litigation in twentieth-century American courts. (5) The emphasis has traditionally centered on the degree to which a criminal defendant can demand the assistance of counsel in various courts and at different hierarchical stages of (10) the criminal proceeding. Although past courts have alluded to the idea that a defendant has a converse right to proceed without counsel, the issue had not been squarely addressed by the (15) United States Supreme Court until late in its 1974–75 term. At that time, the Court held that within the Sixth Amendment rests an implied right of self-representation.

(20) As early as 1964, Justice Hugo Black wrote that "the Sixth Amendment withholds from federal courts, in all criminal proceedings, the power and authority to deprive an accused of his (25) life or liberty unless he has or waives the assistance of counsel." However, recognizing that the Sixth Amendment does not require representation by counsel, it is quite another thing to say (30) that the defendant has a constitutional right to reject professional assistance and proceed on his own. Notwithstanding such a logical and legal fallacy, the Court has, by way of (35) opinion, spoken of a Sixth Amendment "correlative right" to dispense with a lawyer's help. Many lower federal courts have seized upon this and supported their holdings on it, in whole (40) or in part.

The basic motivation behind this proffered right of self-representation is that "respect for individual autonomy requires that (the defendant) be (45) allowed to go to jail under his own banner if he so desires" and that he should not be forced to accept counsel in whom he has no confidence. Courts have ruled that neither due process nor (50) progressive standards of criminal justice require that the defendant be represented at trial by counsel. The Supreme Court, in its 1975 decision, held that a defendant in a state criminal (55) trial has a constitutional right to waive counsel and carry on his own case *in propria persona.* In raising this obscure privilege to a constitutional level, the Court stated that, so long as the (60) defendant is made aware of the dangers and disadvantages of self-representation, his lack of technical legal knowledge will not deprive him of the right to defend himself personally.

(65) The Court conceded that the long line of right to counsel cases have alluded to the idea that the assistance of counsel is a prerequisite to the realization of a fair trial. However, the (70) Court noted that the presence of counsel is of minor significance when a stubborn, self-reliant defendant

prohibits the lawyer from employing his knowledge and skills. This line of
(75) reasoning is concluded with the observation that "the defendant and not his lawyer or the state, will bear the personal consequences of a conviction." The logical extension of
(80) this premise brings the Court to its decision that, recognizing the traditional American respect for the individual, the defendant "must be free personally to decide whether in his
(85) particular case counsel is to his advantage."

1. According to the passage, the chief purpose of the Sixth Amendment is to

  (A) assure a defendant the assistance of counsel in capital cases
  (B) assure a defendant the assistance of counsel in civil cases
  (C) assure a defendant the assistance of counsel in criminal cases
  (D) allow a defendant to represent himself in a criminal trial
  (E) allow a defendant to represent himself in a civil trial

2. The "logical and legal fallacy" referred to in lines 33–34 is probably

  (A) the ability to waive a right does not automatically give rise to a replacement of that right
  (B) the right to reject implies a correlative right to refuse to reject
  (C) the right to dispense with a lawyer's help
  (D) the right to legal assistance
  (E) the defendant who chooses to go to jail is free to do so

3. From the passage, the phrase *"in propria persona"* in lines 56–57 means

  (A) in his own person
  (B) by an appropriate person

  (C) in place of another person
  (D) improperly
  (E) by using a stand-in

4. In allowing a defendant to refuse counsel, the Supreme Court may have reasoned all of the following EXCEPT:

  (A) a defendant who objected to a court-appointed attorney would prevent the lawyer from defending him effectively
  (B) the assistance of counsel is necessary to the realization of a fair trial
  (C) in the event of an unfavorable verdict, the defendant will suffer the consequences
  (D) American tradition recognizes the individual's freedom to make decisions that will affect him
  (E) it is possible that a defendant might defend himself more effectively than a court-appointed lawyer

5. A defendant who is acting as counsel in his own defense must be

  (A) given additional legal assistance
  (B) allowed to give up his own defense if he chooses to do so before the trial has concluded
  (C) warned of the disadvantages of self-representation
  (D) assisted by the judge in areas where the defendant's lack of knowledge of technical legal terms is deficient
  (E) tried before a jury

6. All of the following are objections that might be raised to self-representation EXCEPT:

  (A) by accepting the right to self-representation, a defendant must waive his right to assistance of counsel

(B) a defendant determined to convict himself can do so more easily

(C) if the right to self-representation is not asserted before the trial begins, it is lost

(D) self-representation has a tradition in American law that dates back to the colonial period

(E) a self-representation defendant may be unruly or disruptive

The colonial powers followed a policy of mercantilism, which required their colonies to buy and sell only to them, thus enabling the colonial powers to (5) export more than they imported and build up economic profit. As a result, although some of Africa's resources were developed, the profits went outside the country. Since Africans (10) were encouraged to raise cash crops and forced to buy more expensive finished products from the mother country, most African nations did not accumulate any capital reserves.

(15)   When the African nations became independent, they needed capital to continue development of their resources and to build industries and modernize. They were therefore forced (20) to borrow heavily from the superpowers and from their former colonial rulers. They also turned to international organizations such as the World Bank. However, they have (25) borrowed so heavily from such organizations that, with their current economic problems, these organizations are reluctant to lend them more.

(30)   Africa's economic problems are a result of many factors. With the capital from international loans, some gains were made, but often local conditions were not considered. Factories have (35) been built in areas where the climate makes work difficult, both for people and machines. Dams that were built to supply hydroelectric power sometimes ruin the ecological balance of a region (40) and are therefore harmful to farmers. Also, capital investment in most African countries has been concentrated in the industrial sectors, and since most of Africa is still rural, (45) these investments haven't given Africans greater purchasing power. Therefore, there is little domestic market for manufactured products.

Africa also lacks skilled workers. (50) Colonial education was designed to provide lower-level government workers, and those who can afford higher education today are more interested in law, medicine, and so (55) on—education that provides prestige or entry into politics and government. In addition, transportation and communication systems in Africa are still inadequate. Roads are difficult to (60) build and maintain in the tropical climates, and transporting resources to the sites of manufacturing plants presents a problem.

To achieve progress, people must (65) work together, and this is difficult in African nations where ethnic rivalries are prevalent. Much of the money from international loans and foreign aid has been squandered in schemes designed (70) to promote national pride (such as huge government buildings, statues, and so on) or has simply been confiscated by corrupt leaders.

World economic conditions have also (75) affected Africa. During the 1970s many African nations were forced to pay high prices for petroleum. On the other hand, countries like Nigeria, which export oil, suffered from low oil prices (80) in the 1980s. Prices for many of

Africa's cash crops have dropped in the world market. Africa's heavy debt burden and the export of cash crops create an economic dependency for (85) trade, capital, and food, which is deeply resented by many African peoples and interpreted as neo-colonialism. The presence of multinational corporations has been encouraged by African (90) nations, even though many Africans resent the foreign ownership and fear a loss of control.

Various attempts at economic development have included the (95) introduction of socialism or mixed economic activities. For example, when Julius Nyerere became president of Tanzania in the 1960s, he introduced a socialist system called ujamaa, and in (100) 1967 a program of nationalizing industries and plantations and creating cooperative farms began. Villages in rural areas were formed into cooperatives, schools and clinics were (105) established and new farm machinery and techniques were introduced. But in the 1970s the rising costs of petroleum products hurt Tanzania, and there were problems with ujamaa. Hit by drought (110) in 1980 to 1984, Tanzania had to appeal for international aid. Nyerere himself was replaced in 1985.

In Nigeria, as well as in several other African nations, a mixed economy is (115) in place. Major Nigerian industries and oil production are nationalized, while small industries and agriculture remain in private hands. Multinational corporations are required to serve local (120) needs as well as their own interests. While Nigeria has experienced success in industrial and petroleum output, agricultural production still lags, and food must be imported.

7. Which one of the following would be the best title for this passage?

(A) African Governments since Independence
(B) The African Dilemma
(C) Africa: Moving Forward or Moving Backward?
(D) Economic Problems in Post-Colonial Africa
(E) Africa in the World Market

8. According to the passage, economic development in Africa has been hindered by all of the following EXCEPT:

(A) limited natural resources
(B) lack of capital reserves
(C) poor utilization of available capital
(D) limited purchasing power of the majority of Africans
(E) low prices in the world market for many African exports

9. The author of this passage uses which one of the following methods to present information?

(A) comparison and contrast
(B) general statements followed by examples
(C) specific examples leading to a general conclusion
(D) presentation of case histories
(E) analysis of statistics

10. According to the passage, African achievements in economic development

(A) sometimes resulted in new ethnic rivalries.
(B) led to the need for more doctors, lawyers, and teachers.
(C) sometimes created environmental problems.

(D) significantly reduced the burden of debt.

(E) adversely affected the market for African exports.

11. To understand why Julius Nyerere was replaced as president of Tanzania, which additional information would probably be most helpful?

(A) Nyerere's educational background

(B) the number of cooperatives created in rural vs. urban areas

(C) specific statistics, such as changes in Tanzania's mortality rate

(D) more details about the problems with ujamaa

(E) details about Tanzania's exports vs. imports

12. The main purpose of the last two paragraphs of the passage is to

(A) provide examples of African attempts to encourage economic development

(B) describe the results of neo-colonialism in Africa

(C) illustrate the failure of two African countries to deal with economic problems

(D) summarize the problems addressed in the rest of the passage

(E) personalize the general problems in post-colonial Africa

13. Which one of the following words or phrases in the passage suggests a negative judgment?

(A) "lower-level government workers" (lines 51–52)

(B) "deeply resented" (lines 85–86)

(C) "borrow heavily" (line 20)

(D) "prestige" (line 55)

(E) "squandered" (line 69)

14. The best definition of "neo-colonialism" as it is used in this passage (line 87) is

(A) relying on foreigners to perform high-level jobs and hold political offices

(B) being controlled economically and politically by powerful outside countries

(C) permitting foreign control of branches of multinational corporations

(D) basing economic and political systems on Western models

(E) exporting cash crops while importing manufactured goods from major powers

In the competitive model—the economy of many sellers each with a small share of the total market—the restraint on the private exercise of
(5) economic power was provided by other firms on the same side of the market. It was the eagerness of competitors to sell, not the complaints of buyers, that saved the latter from spoliation. It was
(10) assumed, no doubt accurately, that the nineteenth-century textile manufacturer who overcharged for his product would promptly lose his market to another manufacturer who did not. If all
(15) manufacturers found themselves in a position where they could exploit a strong demand, and mark up their prices accordingly, there would soon be an inflow of new competitors. The
(20) resulting increase in supply would bring prices and profits back to normal.

As with the seller who was tempted to use his economic power against the
(25) customer, so with the buyer who was tempted to use it against his labor or suppliers. The man who paid less than the prevailing wage would lose his

labor force to those who paid the
(30) worker his full (marginal) contribution
to the earnings of the firm. In all cases
the incentive to socially desirable
behavior was provided by the
competitor. It was to the same side of
(35) the market—the restraint of sellers by
other sellers and of buyers by other
buyers, in other words to
competition—that economists came to
look for the self-regulatory
(40) mechanisms of the economy.

They also came to look to
competition exclusively and in formal
theory still do. The notion that there
might be another regulatory
(45) mechanism in the economy had been
almost completely excluded from
economic thought. Thus, with the
widespread disappearance of
competition in its classical form and its
(50) replacement by the small group of
firms if not in overt, at least in
conventional or tacit, collusion, it was
easy to suppose that since competition
had disappeared, all effective restraint
(55) on private power had disappeared.
Indeed, this conclusion was all but
inevitable if no search was made for
other restraints, and so complete was
the preoccupation with competition
(60) that none was made.

In fact, new restraints on private
power did appear to replace
competition. They were nurtured by the
same process of concentration which
(65) impaired or destroyed competition. But
they appeared not on the same side of
the market but on the opposite side,
not with competitors but with
customers or suppliers. It will be
(70) convenient to have a name for this
counterpart of competition and I shall
call it countervailing power.

To begin with a broad and somewhat
too dogmatically stated proposition,
(75) private economic power is held in
check by the countervailing power of
those who are subject to it. The first
begets the second. The long trend
toward concentration of industrial
(80) enterprise in the hands of a relatively
few firms has brought into existence
not only strong sellers, as economists
have supposed, but also strong buyers,
a fact they have failed to see. The two
(85) develop together, not in precise step,
but in such manner that there can be
no doubt that the one is in response to
the other.

15. Which one of the following would be
the best title for this passage?

(A) Capitalism and the Competitive
Model
(B) Competition and the Concept of
"Countervailing Power"
(C) Problems in American Capitalism
(D) The Importance of Economic
Regulatory Mechanisms
(E) The Failure of the Classic
Competition Model

16. In the classic competition model, when
competitive manufacturers marked up
prices because of strong demand, a
return to normal was provided by

(A) new manufacturers entering the
market
(B) refusal to buy on the part of
customers
(C) governmental intervention in the
form of regulation
(D) repositioning of the labor force
(E) failure of weaker manufacturers

17. In the classic competition model, the
incentive for manufacturers to behave
in a socially desirable way toward
workers was provided by

(A) competition for the labor supply
(B) competition for the customer

(C) imbalance between supply and demand

(D) self-regulation among competitors

(E) humanistic economic theory

18. According to the author, which one of the following statements is true?

(A) The classic model of competition was inadequate because it ignored the role of labor and rewarded individual greed.

(B) The classic model of competition provided self-regulation prior to, but not after, the Industrial Revolution.

(C) The classic model of competition was undermined by the "restraint of sellers by other sellers and of buyers by other buyers."

(D) The classic model of competition was replaced by concentration of industrial enterprise and collusion among manufacturers.

(E) The classic model of competition was destroyed by the growth of "countervailing power."

19. Examples of "countervailing power" in the regulation of the economic power of manufacturers could include all of the following EXCEPT:

(A) organized customer boycotts

(B) cooperative buying organizations

(C) large retail chains

(D) retailers developing their own sources of supply

(E) organizations that network manufacturers

20. According to the author, a weakness of economic thought has been

(A) a preoccupation with competition

(B) a failure to recognize the need for reasonable government regulation

(C) a belief in the "trickle-down" theory

(D) a failure to recognize concentration of industrial enterprise

(E) a bias toward unregulated capitalism

21. Which one of the following best describes the structure of this passage?

(A) The first three paragraphs describe the strengths of economic competition and the fourth and fifth paragraph describe its weaknesses.

(B) The first paragraph presents the historical perspective on competition, the second and third present examples of its effect on the economy, and the fourth and fifth paragraphs set forth the idea of "countervailing power."

(C) The first two paragraphs describe how competition is thought to work, the third paragraph provides a transition, and the fourth and fifth paragraphs describe "countervailing power."

(D) The first three paragraphs describe the classic model of competition, while the fourth and fifth paragraphs describe "countervailing power."

(E) The first three paragraphs present a view of competition in opposition to the author's, while the fourth and fifth paragraphs present the author's view.

Passage A

Antoine-Laurent Lavoisier (1743–1794) can justly be called the father of modern chemistry, not because of earth-shaking discoveries (5) or experiments but because he introduced a new approach to the understanding of chemical reactions. Some of his conclusions were later called into question or improved upon,

(10) but his relentless pursuit of knowledge and logical reasoning led to hundreds of experiments, all of which challenged the preconceived scientific notions of his day.

(15)   Lavoisier at twenty-five was elected to France's Academy of Sciences, in large part because of his work in geology, not chemistry. In 1775, he was appointed to the Royal Gunpowder (20) and Saltpeter Administration, and in his laboratory he produced better gunpowder, in part by focusing on the purity of its ingredients and improved methods of granulating the powder.

(25)   An important aspect of Lavoisier's work was his determination of the weights of reagents and products, including gaseous components, involved in chemical reactions. He (30) believed that matter, identified by weight, would always be conserved through these reactions. Lavoisier's methods led to, among other things, his definitive proof that water was (35) made up of oxygen and hydrogen.

His methods also led him to challenge the phlogistic theory of combustion, which initially had been proposed by the German alchemist (40) Johann Joachim Becher in the late 1600s and which was still widely accepted well into the eighteenth century. According to that theory, something called "phlogiston," named (45) by Georg Ernst Stahl, existed in all materials and was released during combustion, the resulting ash being the remaining material, but "dephlogisticated." Since phlogiston (50) wasn't—according to its proponents— a material substance, it was unweighable and without color or odor. Also according to the theory, acids produced by combustion were (55) elementary substances, not the

products of a chemical reaction. Lavoisier, through his experiments, came to recognize that a chemical reaction with oxygen, not a vague (60) principle called phlogiston, caused combustion.

At first, Lavoisier referred to oxygen as "air in its purest form," but he later called it oxygen, from the Greek words (65) *oxus*, meaning sharp, acidic, and *ginomai*, meaning to become or cause to be. He believed that oxygen caused the acids produced by combustion. Later, however, Sir Humphry Davy, (70) Louis Joseph Gay-Lussac, and Louis-Jacques Thenard showed in their experiments with hydrochloric acid, chlorine, and hydrocyanic acid that acid could be produced without (75) oxygen.

But Lavoisier, even though some of his ideas were later proved wrong, succeeded in turning away from alchemy and the theory of phlogiston. (80) In the words of Justus von Liebig, Lavoisier's immortal glory "consists in this—that he infused into the body of the science a new spirit."

Passage B

(85)   Among the definitions of *theory* is "the analysis of a set of facts in their relation to one another." That definition doesn't take us very far, however, because almost any set of facts can be (90) analyzed in a dozen or more ways. In science, theories are set forth and later discarded, or modified, all the time.

For example, in the seventeenth century, heat was erroneously (95) explained through theories of combustion. Johann Joachim Becher and George Ernst Stahl introduced the theory that phlogiston, present in all matter, was released during (100) combustion. It was thought to be the source of heat. Phlogiston couldn't be weighed and, in fact, wasn't considered a material at all but rather a principle. Such notable scientists as Joseph (105) Priestley (1733–1804), who conducted extensive research on the nature and property of gases, interpreted his results in terms of phlogiston. Priestley's experiments isolated and (110) characterized eight gases, including oxygen, which he described as "dephlogisticated air."

Antoine Lavoisier, a French scientist who rightly explained combustion in (115) terms of oxygen and not the principle of phlogiston, introduced another theory of heat. In his *Reflexions sur le phlogistique* (1783), he argued that the phlogiston theory was inconsistent (120) with his experimental results. Ironically, however, Lavoisier proposed a substance called *caloric* (which he considered an "element"—one of 33 substances that couldn't be broken (125) down into simpler entities) as the source of heat. Like phlogiston, caloric couldn't be weighed, and Lavoisier called it "a subtle fluid." The quantity of caloric, according to Lavoisier, was (130) constant throughout the universe and flowed from warmer to colder bodies.

Not surprisingly, observable facts could be explained by the caloric theory. For instance, a hot bowl of (135) soup cools at room temperature. Why? Because caloric slowly flows from regions dense with it (the hot soup) to regions less dense with it (the cooler air in the room). Another example is (140) that air expands when heated. According to the caloric theory, this would be because caloric is absorbed by air molecules, thereby increasing the volume of the air.

(145)   Ultimately, the caloric theory as posited by Lavoisier was discarded.

The calorists' principle of the conservation of heat was replaced by a principle of conservation of energy. (150)   Modern thermodynamics defines heat not as a result of a "subtle fluid" but as a result of the kinetic energy of molecules.

22. Which of the following characterizes the main difference between Passage A and Passage B?

(A) Passage A praises Antoine Lavoisier, whereas Passage B discredits him.
(B) The focus in Passage A is on a scientist's work, while the focus in Passage B is on a particular theory.
(C) Passage A explains the phlogiston theory, whereas Passage B does not.
(D) In Passage A, the emphasis is on chemical reactions, while in Passage B the emphasis is on the scientific method.
(E) The author of Passage A is objective toward science, while the author of Passage B is skeptical.

23. The author of Passage B uses the term "ironically" in line 120 to

(A) emphasize how fallible scientists can be in interpreting their own results and the results of their predecessors
(B) undermine Lavoisier's designation as the "father of modern chemistry"
(C) note that while Lavoisier proved that phlogiston didn't exist, he introduced another nonexistent substance

(D) suggest the absurdity of scientific debates

(E) lighten the tone of the passage as a whole

24. According to Passage A, among Lavoisier's accomplishments was

(A) proving the chemical composition of water

(B) explaining the cause of heat

(C) changing the composition of gunpowder

(D) identifying caloric as a fluid

(E) isolating and characterizing eight gases

25. Which of the following best illustrates that facts can be explained by more than one theory (paragraph one of Passage B)?

(A) Hydrochloric acid cannot be produced without oxygen.

(B) The agent of combustion is weightless and odorless.

(C) Boiling water will cool at room temperature.

(D) Combustion results in ash made up of "dephlogisticated" material.

(E) Acids produced by combustion are elementary substances.

26. The author of Passage B would most likely agree with which of the following statements?

(A) Alchemy contributed nothing to science.

(B) Joseph Priestley was not as important as Antoine Lavoisier in the study of gases.

(C) Thermodynamics is an inexact science.

(D) A theory is a possible, but not necessarily the only, explanation of facts.

(E) The scientific method is seriously flawed and cannot be counted on to prove a fact.

27. According to information in Passage A and Passage B, Lavoisier believed that

(A) matter was not destroyed during a chemical reaction

(B) the acids produced during combustion were elementary substances

(C) molecular movement was responsible for the production of heat

(D) matter was converted to energy in chemical reactions

(E) a fluid called "caloric" caused combustion

28. In Passage B, Joseph Priestley is used as an example of

(A) a scientist who relied heavily on alchemy

(B) the importance of an open exchange of ideas between scientists

(C) a scientist who made a major discovery, as distinguished from Lavoisier

(D) a precursor to Lavoisier's experiments with gases

(E) the persistence of the phlogistic theory well into the eighteenth century

STOP

IF YOU FINISH BEFORE TIME IS UP, CHECK YOUR WORK ON THIS SECTION OF THE TEST ONLY.
DO NOT GO ON TO THE NEXT SECTION OF THE TEST UNTIL TIME IS UP FOR THIS SECTION.

SECTION III

Directions: **In this section you will be given groups of questions based on different sets of conditions. Drawing a simple diagram may be helpful in answering some of the questions. You are to choose the best answer and mark the corresponding space on your answer sheet.**

Questions 1–6

There are five flagpoles lined up next to each other in a straight row in front of a school. Each flagpole flies one flag (red, white, or blue) and one pennant (green, white, or blue). The following are conditions that affect the placement of flags and pennants on the poles:

On a given flagpole, the pennant, and the flag cannot be the same color.
Two adjacent flagpoles cannot fly the same color flags.
Two adjacent flagpoles cannot fly the same color pennants.
No more than two of any color flag or pennant may fly at one time.

1. If the 2nd and 5th pennants are blue, the 2nd and 5th flags are red, and the 3rd flag is white, then which one of the following must be true?

(A) Two of the flags are white.
(B) Two of the pennants are white.
(C) The 4th pennant is green.
(D) If the 1st pennant is green, then the 1st flag is blue.
(E) If the 1st flag is white, then the 1st pennant is green.

2. If the 1st flag is red and the 2nd pennant is blue, then which one of the following is NOT necessarily true?

(A) The 2nd flag is white.
(B) If the 5th flag is red, then the 3rd flag is blue.
(C) If the 4th pennant is green, then the 1st pennant is white.
(D) If the 1st and 5th flags are the same color, then the 3rd flag is blue.
(E) If the 4th pennant is green and the 5th pennant is white, then the 1st and 3rd pennants are different colors.

3. If the 1st and 3rd flags are white and the 2nd and 4th pennants are blue, then which one of the following is FALSE?

(A) The 4th flag is red.
(B) The 1st pennant is green.
(C) The 3rd pennant is not red.
(D) The 5th pennant is green.
(E) There is one blue flag.

4. If the 1st and 4th flags are blue and the 3rd pennant is white, then which one of the following must be true?

(A) If the 1st pennant is green, then the 5th pennant is white.
(B) If the 5th pennant is white, then the 1st pennant is green.
(C) The 2nd flag is red.
(D) The 5th flag is red.
(E) The 1st pennant is green.

5. If the 2nd flag is red and the 3rd flag is white, and the 4th pennant is blue, then which one of the following must be true?

(A) If the 5th flag is white, then two of the pennants are blue.
(B) If the 1st flag is white, then the 2nd flag is white.
(C) If the 1st pennant is blue, then the 5th pennant is green.
(D) If the 1st pennant is green, then the 5th flag is not blue.
(E) If the 1st and 5th flags are the same color, then the 1st and 5th pennants are not the same color.

6. If the 1st flag and the 2nd pennant are the same color, the 2nd flag and the 3rd pennant are the same color, the 3rd flag and the 4th pennant are the same color, and the 4th flag and the 5th pennant are the same color, then which one of the following must be true?

(A) The 1st pennant is white.
(B) The 2nd flag is not white.
(C) The 5th flag is red.
(D) The 3rd pennant is blue.
(E) The 4th flag is white.

Questions 7–13

In the Norfolk Library returned book section there are ten books standing next to each other on a shelf. There are two math books, two science books, three English books, and three poetry books. The books are arranged as follows:

There is a math book on one end and an English book on the other end.
The two math books are never next to each other.
The two science books are always next to each other.
The three English books are always next to each other.

7. If the 8th book is a math book, then which one of the following must be true?

(A) The 5th book is a science book.
(B) The 7th book is an English book.
(C) The 6th book is not a poetry book.
(D) The 4th book is next to an English book.
(E) The 9th book is a science book.

8. If the 9th book is an English book and the 5th and 6th books are poetry books, then which one of the following must be true?

(A) There is a math book next to a poetry book.
(B) The 2nd book is a science book.
(C) The three poetry books are all next to one another.
(D) The 7th book is a math book.
(E) The 4th book is not a poetry book.

9. If the 1st book is a math book and the 7th book is a science book, then which one of the following could be false?

(A) Both math books are next to poetry books.
(B) All three poetry books are next to each other.
(C) The 2nd book is a poetry book.
(D) The 10th book is an English book.
(E) The 6th book is a science book.

10. If the 4th book is a math book and the 5th book is a science book, then which one of the following must be true?

(A) An English book is next to a science book.
(B) If the 7th book is a poetry book, then the 3rd book is an English book.
(C) If the 8th book is an English book, then the 2nd book is a poetry book.

(D) If the 10th book is a math book, then a poetry book is next to an English book.

(E) The three poetry books are next to each other.

11. If no two poetry books are next to each other, then which one of the following must be true?

(A) A science book is next to a math book.

(B) The 7th book is a poetry book.

(C) The 8th book is an English book.

(D) An English book is next to a science book.

(E) A poetry book is next to an English book.

12. If a science book is next to an English book, but not next to a poetry book, then which one of the following must be true?

(A) The 7th book is a poetry book.

(B) The 3rd book is an English book or a math book.

(C) The 5th or the 6th book is a math book.

(D) The three poetry books are not next to each other.

(E) The 7th or the 10th book is a math book.

13. If the 7th and 8th books are poetry books, how many different arrangements are there for the ten books?

(A) one

(B) two

(C) three

(D) four

(E) five

Questions 14–20

A homeowner has purchased six paintings, one each from six local artists. The artists' first names are Diego, Frank, Glenda, Rich, Tina, and Yolanda. The six paintings will be positioned in a straight row, numbered left to right as one through six. The following restrictions will apply:

Rich's painting is positioned to the right of Tina's painting.

Glenda's painting is positioned to the left of Tina's painting.

Tina's painting is positioned to the right of Frank's painting.

Diego's painting is positioned to the left of both Frank's painting and Yolanda's painting.

14. If Glenda's painting is hanging in position #4, then each of the following could be true EXCEPT:

(A) Diego's painting is hanging to the left of and next to Frank's painting.

(B Glenda's painting is hanging to the right of and next to Frank's painting.

(C) Tina's painting is hanging to the left of and next to Yolanda's painting.

(D) Yolanda's painting is hanging to the right of and next to Diego's painting.

(E) Yolanda's painting is hanging to the left of and next to Frank's painting.

15. What is the maximum number of paintings that can be placed between Glenda's painting and Yolanda's painting?

(A) none

(B) one

(C) two

(D) three

(E) four

16. If Frank's painting is in position 2, then which one of the following must be true?

   (A) Tina's painting is in position 5.
   (B) Glenda's painting is in position 3.
   (C) Rich's painting is in position 6.
   (D) Diego's painting is in position 1.
   (E) Yolanda's painting is in position 4.

17. If Yolanda's painting is hanging to the left of Frank's painting, then which one of the following must be true?

   (A) Frank's painting is hanging to the left of and next to Glenda's painting.
   (B) Glenda's painting is hanging to the left of and next to Tina's painting.
   (C) Rich's painting is hanging to the right of and next to Tina's painting.
   (D) Tina's painting is hanging to the right of and next to Frank's painting.
   (E) Yolanda's painting is hanging to the right of and next to Diego's painting.

18. Which one of the following conditions would NOT result in only one possible arrangement of the six paintings?

   (A) Diego's painting is between and next to Yolanda's painting and Glenda's painting.
   (B) Diego's painting is next to Yolanda's painting and Glenda's painting is next to Tina's painting.
   (C) Frank's painting is between and next to Glenda's painting and Yolanda's painting.
   (D) Tina's painting is between and next to Yolanda's painting and Glenda's painting.
   (E) Yolanda's painting is next to Glenda's painting and Tina's painting is next to Glenda's painting.

19. If Glenda's painting is hanging next to Yolanda's painting, then how many possible arrangements are there for the six paintings?

   (A) one
   (B) two
   (C) three
   (D) four
   (E) five

20. Which one of the following CANNOT be a true statement?

   (A) Frank's painting is hanging to the left of Glenda's painting.
   (B) Glenda's painting is hanging to the left of Frank's painting.
   (C) Tina's painting is hanging to the left of Diego's painting.
   (D) Tina's painting is hanging to the right of Yolanda's painting.
   (E) Yolanda's painting is hanging to the right of Rich's painting.

Questions 21–25

Seven track and field coaches, A, B, C, D, E, F, and G, are each assigned to coach exactly one of four activities—sprints, distance, jumpers, and throwers. Coaching assignments are made subject to the following conditions:

   Each sport is coached by one or two of the seven coaches.
   B coaches jumpers.
   Neither E nor F is a distance coach.
   If C coaches sprints, F and G coach throwers.
   If D coaches distance or throwers, A and G do not coach either distance or throwers.

21. If C and E coach sprints, which one of the following must be true?

   (A) Distance has two coaches.
   (B) G coaches jumping.
   (C) A coaches jumping or throwing.
   (D) D coaches jumping.
   (E) Jumping has one coach.

22. If G coaches jumping and A coaches distance, which one of the following must be true?

   (A) D coaches sprints.
   (B) F coaches throwing.
   (C) E coaches sprints.
   (D) C coaches distance.
   (E) F coaches sprints.

23. If D coaches throwing, which one of the following CANNOT be true?

   (A) G coaches sprints.
   (B) A coaches jumping.
   (C) E coaches sprints.
   (D) F coaches throwing.
   (E) C coaches jumping.

24. If G is the only throwing coach, which one of the following could be true?

   (A) D coaches distance.
   (B) If F coaches sprints, D coaches sprints.
   (C) A coaches jumping.
   (D) If F coaches jumping, D coaches jumping.
   (E) C and D coach the same sport.

25. If A does not coach sprints and D coaches distance, which one of the following CANNOT be true?

   (A) C coaches distance.
   (B) E coaches throwing.
   (C) G coaches jumping.
   (D) F coaches sprints.
   (E) E coaches sprints.

STOP

IF YOU FINISH BEFORE TIME IS UP, CHECK YOUR WORK ON THIS SECTION OF THE TEST ONLY.
DO NOT GO ON TO THE NEXT SECTION OF THE TEST UNTIL TIME IS UP FOR THIS SECTION.

SECTION IV

Time — 35 minutes
26 Questions

Directions: In this section you will be given brief statements or passages and will be required to evaluate the reasoning involved. In some instances, more than one choice will appear to be a possible answer. You are to choose the *best* answer. Use common sense and reasonableness in making your selection; then mark the proper space on the answer sheet.

Questions 1–2

The spate of bills in the legislature dealing with utility regulation shows that our lawmakers recognize a good political issue when they see one. Among the least worthy is a proposal to establish a new "Consumers Utility Board" to fight proposed increases in gas and electric rates.

It is hardly a novel idea that consumers need representation when rates are set for utilities which operate as monopolies in their communities. That's exactly why we have a state Public Utilities Commission.

Supporters of the proposed consumer board point out that utility companies have the benefit of lawyers and accountants on their payrolls to argue the case for rate increases before the PUC. That's true. Well, the PUC has the benefit of a $40 million annual budget and a staff of 900—all paid at taxpayer expense—to find fault with these rate proposals if there is fault to be found.

1. Which one of the following is the best example to offer in support of this argument against a Consumers Utility Board?

   (A) the percentage of taxpayer dollars supporting the PUC
   (B) the number of lawyers working for the Consumers Utility Board
   (C) the number of concerned consumers

   (D) a PUC readjustment of rates downward
   (E) the voting record of lawmakers supporting the board

2. Which one of the following would most seriously weaken the above argument?

   (A) Private firms are taking an increasing share of the energy business.
   (B) Water rates are also increasing.
   (C) The PUC budget will be cut slightly, along with other state agencies.
   (D) Half of the PUC lawyers and accountants are also retained by utilities.
   (E) More tax money goes to education than to the PUC.

3. Most of those who enjoy music play a musical instrument; therefore, if Maria enjoys music, she probably plays a musical instrument.

   Which one of the following most closely parallels the reasoning in the statement above?

   (A) The majority of those who voted for Smith in the last election oppose abortion; therefore, if the residents of University City all voted for Smith, they probably oppose abortion.

(B) If you appreciate portrait painting you are probably a painter yourself; therefore, your own experience is probably the cause of your appreciation.

(C) Most of those who join the army are male; therefore, if Jones did not join the army, Jones is probably female.

(D) Over 50 percent of the high school students polled admitted hating homework; therefore, a majority of high school students do not like homework.

(E) If most workers drive to work, and Sam drives to work, then Sam must be a worker.

4. "To be a good teacher, one must be patient. Some good teachers are good administrators."

Which one of the following can be concluded from the above statement?

(A) Some good teachers are not patient.

(B) All good administrators are patient.

(C) Some good administrators are patient.

(D) Only good administrators are patient.

(E) Many good administrators are patient.

5. "Good personnel relations of an organization depend upon mutual confidence, trust, and goodwill. The basis of confidence is understanding. Most troubles start with people who do not understand each other. When the organization's intentions or motives are misunderstood, or when reasons for actions, practices, or policies are misconstrued, complete cooperation from individuals is not forthcoming. If management expects full cooperation from employees, it has a responsibility of sharing with them the information which is the foundation of proper understanding, confidence, and trust. Personnel management has long since outgrown the days when it was the vogue to 'treat them rough and tell them nothing.' Up-to-date personnel management provides all possible information about the activities, aims, and purposes of the organization. It seems altogether creditable that a desire should exist among employees for such information which the best-intentioned executive might think would not interest them and which the worst-intentioned would think was none of their business."

The above paragraph implies that one of the causes of the difficulty that an organization might have with its personnel relations is that its employees

(A) have not expressed interest in the activities, aims, and purposes of the organization

(B) do not believe in the good faith of the organization

(C) have not been able to give full cooperation to the organization

(D) do not recommend improvements in the practices and policies of the organization

(E) can afford little time to establish good relations with their organization

6. Of all psychiatric disorders, depression is the most common; yet, research on its causes and cures is still far from complete. As a matter of fact, very few facilities offer assistance to those suffering from this disorder.

The author would probably agree that

(A) depression needs further study
(B) further research will make possible further assistance to those suffering from depression
(C) most facilities are staffed by psychiatrists whose specialty is not depression
(D) those suffering from depression need to know its causes and cures
(E) depression and ignorance go hand in hand

7. *Editorial:* The politicians who wish to see the schools run like businesses will have some trouble establishing a standard of accountability. In the business world, profits provide a clear standard, measurable in numbers. But in public education, standards are culturally derived, and differ very widely among age, ethnic, and political groups. We can evaluate a school's record keeping or its facilities, but there is no way to use the standards of quality control that are used to judge the profitability of a business and apply them to the academic performance of students throughout a public school system.

To which one of the following is the writer of this passage objecting?

(A) the assumption that a school and a business are analogous
(B) the belief that profitability is a universal standard

(C) the assumption that schools, like businesses, can show a financial profit
(D) the belief that school vouchers are undemocratic
(E) the assumption that record keeping and facilities are adequate gauges of business success

8. *Ivan:* What the Church says is true because the Church is an authority.
   Mike: What grounds do you have for holding that the Church is a genuine authority?
   Ivan: The authority of the Church is implied in the Bible.
   Mike: And why do you hold that the Bible is true?
   Ivan: Because the Church holds that it is true.

Which one of the following is the best description of the reasoning involved in the argument presented in the foregoing dialogue?

(A) deductive
(B) inductive
(C) vague
(D) pointed
(E) circular

9. *Mary:* All Italians are great lovers.
   Kathy: That is not so. I have met some Spaniards who were magnificent lovers.

   Kathy's reply to Mary indicates that she has misunderstood Mary's remark to mean that

   (A) every great lover is an Italian
   (B) Italians are best at the art of love
   (C) Spaniards are inferior to Italians
   (D) Italians are more likely to be great lovers than are Spaniards
   (E) there is a relationship between nationality and love

Questions 10–11

Mr. Dimple: Mrs. Wilson's qualifications are ideal for the position. She is intelligent, forceful, determined, and trustworthy. I suggest we hire her immediately.

10. Which one of the following, if true, would most weaken Mr. Dimple's statement?

    (A) Mrs. Wilson is not interested in being hired.
    (B) There are two other applicants whose qualifications are identical to Mrs. Wilson's.
    (C) Mrs. Wilson is currently working for a rival company.
    (D) Mr. Dimple is not speaking directly to the hiring committee.
    (E) Mrs. Wilson is older than many of the other applicants.

11. Which one of the following, if true, offers the strongest support of Mr. Dimple's statement?

    (A) All the members of the hiring committee have agreed that intelligence, trustworthiness, determination, and forcefulness are important qualifications for the job.
    (B) Mr. Dimple holds exclusive responsibility for hiring new employees.
    (C) Mr. Dimple has known Mrs. Wilson longer than he has known any of the other applicants.
    (D) Mrs. Wilson is a member of Mr. Dimple's family.
    (E) Mrs. Dimple is intelligent, forceful, determined, and trustworthy.

12. All of the candidates for the spring track team must have participated in fall cross-country and winter track. Some runners, however, find cross-country tedious, and refuse to run in the fall. Thus, some winter track runners who would like to be members of the spring track teams are not permitted to try out.

    In which one of the following is the reasoning most like that of this passage?

    (A) Mice become aggressive if confined in close quarters for an extended period of time, or if they are deprived of protein-rich foods. Therefore, highly aggressive mice have been closely confined and denied high-protein foods.
    (B) Roses grown in full sun are less susceptible to mildew than roses grown in partial shade. Roses grown in partial shade are also more susceptible to black spot.

Thus, roses should be grown in full sun.

(C) To qualify for the June primary, a candidate for office must reside in the district for six months and gather 500 signatures of district residents who support the candidate. Thus, a longtime district resident would not qualify for the June primary if she gathered only 300 signatures.

(D) A convenience store sells three chocolate bars for a dollar, and a large soft drink for 50 cents. A competitor sells four chocolate bars for a dollar, and a medium-size soft drink for 50 cents. Therefore, neither of the two stores offers more for the same price.

(E) The City Council has passed an ordinance that allows cyclists to use the city bike paths only if they are over 12 years old and are wearing bicycle helmets. Thus, parents with children under 12 will be unable to cycle with their families on the city bike paths unless they wear helmets.

13. When a dental hygienist cleans your teeth, you may not see much evidence that she is supervised by a dentist. Hygienists often work pretty much on their own, even though they are employed by dentists. Then why can't hygienists practice independently, perhaps saving patients a lot of money in the process? The patients would not have to pay the steep profit that many dentists make on the hygienists' labors.

Which one of the following statements weakens the argument above?

(A) Some patients might get their teeth cleaned more often if it costs less.

(B) Some dentists do not employ dental hygienists.

(C) Hygienists must be certified by state examinations.

(D) A dentist should be on hand to inspect a hygienist's work to make sure the patient has no problems that the hygienist is unable to detect.

(E) In some states, there are more female hygienists than male.

14. There are those of us who, determined to be happy, are discouraged repeatedly by social and economic forces that cause us nothing but trouble. And there are those of us who are blessed with health and wealth and still grumble and complain about almost everything.

To which one of the following points can the author be leading?

(A) Happiness is both a state of mind and a state of affairs.

(B) Both personal and public conditions can make happiness difficult to attain.

(C) Happiness may be influenced by economic forces and by health considerations.

(D) No one can be truly happy.

(E) Exterior forces and personal views determine happiness.

15. "Keep true, never be ashamed of doing right; decide on what you think is right and stick to it."—*George Eliot*

If one were to follow Eliot's advice, one

(A) would never change one's mind

(B) would do what is right
(C) might never know what is right
(D) would never be tempted to do wrong
(E) would not discriminate between right and wrong

16. To paraphrase Oliver Wendell Holmes, taxes keep us civilized. Just look around you, at well-paved superhighways, air-conditioned schools, and modernized prisons, and you cannot help but agree with Holmes.

Which one of the following is the strongest criticism of the statement above?

(A) The author never actually met Holmes.
(B) The author does not acknowledge those of us who do not live near highways, schools, and prisons.
(C) The author does not assure us that he has been in a modernized prison.
(D) The author does not offer a biographical sketch of Holmes.
(E) The author does not define "civilized."

Questions 17–18

Information that is published is part of the public record. But information that a reporter collects, and sources that he contacts, must be protected in order for our free press to function free of fear.

17. The above argument is most severely weakened by which one of the following statements?

(A) Public information is usually reliable.
(B) Undocumented evidence may be used to convict an innocent person.

(C) Members of the press act ethically in most cases.
(D) The sources that a reporter contacts are usually willing to divulge their identity.
(E) Our press has never been altogether free.

18. Which one of the following statements is consistent with the argument above?

(A) Privileged information has long been an important and necessary aspect of investigative reporting.
(B) Not all the information a reporter collects becomes part of the public record.
(C) Tape-recorded information is not always reliable.
(D) The victim of a crime must be protected at all costs.
(E) The perpetrator of a crime must be protected at all costs.

Questions 19–21

A federal court ruling that San Diego County can't sue the government for the cost of medical care of illegal aliens is based upon a legal technicality that ducks the larger moral question. But the U.S. Supreme Court's refusal to review this decision has closed the last avenue of legal appeal.

The medical expenses of indigent citizens or legally resident aliens are covered by state and federal assistance programs. The question of who is to pay when an undocumented alien falls ill remains unresolved, however, leaving California counties to bear this unfair and growing burden.

19. The author implies that

(A) the U.S. Supreme Court has refused to review the federal court ruling

(B) the burden of medical expenses for aliens is growing

(C) the larger moral question involves no legal technicalities

(D) San Diego should find another avenue of appeal

(E) the federal government is dodging the moral issue

20. Which one of the following arguments, if true, would most seriously weaken the argument above?

(A) There are many cases of undocumented aliens being denied medical aid at state hospitals.

(B) A private philanthropic organization has funded medical aid programs that have so far provided adequate assistance to illegal aliens nationwide.

(C) Illegal aliens do not wish federal or state aid, because those accepting aid risk detection of their illegal status and deportation.

(D) Undocumented aliens stay in California only a short time before moving east.

(E) Judges on the Supreme Court have pledged privately to assist illegal aliens with a favorable ruling once immigration laws are strengthened.

21. Which one of the following changes in the above passage could strengthen the author's argument?

(A) adding interviews with illegal aliens

(B) a description of the stages that led to a rejection by the Supreme Court

(C) a clarification with numbers of the rate at which the burden of medical expenses is growing

(D) the naming of those state and federal assistance programs that aid indigent citizens

(E) the naming of those California counties that do not participate in medical aid to illegal aliens

22. *Historian:* History is strewn with the wreckage of experiments in communal living, often organized around farms and inspired by religious or philosophical ideals. To the more noble failures can now be added Mao Tse-tung's notorious Chinese communes. The current rulers of China, still undoing the mistakes of the late Chairman, are quietly allowing their agricultural communes to _____.

Which one of the following is the most logical completion of the passage above?

(A) evolve

(B) increase

(C) recycle

(D) disintegrate

(E) organize

23. *Sal:* Herb is my financial planner.
    Keith: I'm sure he's good; he's my cousin.

Which one of the following facts is Keith ignoring in his response?

(A) Financial planning is a professional, not a personal, matter.

(B) Sal is probably flattering Keith.

(C) Professional competence is not necessarily a family trait.

(D) "Good" is a term with many meanings.

(E) Sal's financial planner is no one's cousin.

24. Many very effective prescription drugs are available to patients on a "one time only" basis. Suspicious of drug abuse, physicians will not renew a prescription for a medicine that has worked effectively for a patient. This practice denies a patient's right to health.

Which one of the following is a basic assumption made by the author?

(A) A new type of medicine is likely to be more expensive.
(B) Physicians are not concerned with a patient's health.
(C) Most of the patients who need prescription renewals are female.
(D) Most physicians prescribe inadequate amounts of medicine.
(E) Patients are liable to suffer the same ailment repeatedly.

Questions 25–26

Forty years ago, hardly anybody thought about going to court to sue somebody. A person could bump a pedestrian with his Chrysler Airflow and the victim would say something like, "No harm done," and walk away. Ipso facto. No filing of codicils, taking of depositions or polling the jury. Attorneys need not apply.

25. Which one of the following sentences most logically continues the above passage?

(A) The Chrysler Airflow is no longer the harmless machine it used to be.
(B) Fortunately, this is still the case.
(C) Unfortunately, times have changed.
(D) New legislation affecting the necessity for codicils is a sign of the times.
(E) But now, as we know, law schools are full of eager young people.

26. Which one of the following details, if true, would most strengthen the above statement?

(A) There were fewer courthouses then than now.
(B) The marked increase in pedestrian accidents is a relatively recent occurrence.
(C) Most citizens of 40 years ago were not familiar with their legal rights.
(D) The number of lawsuits filed during World War II was extremely low.
(E) Most young attorneys were in the armed forces 40 years ago.

STOP

IF YOU FINISH BEFORE TIME IS UP, CHECK YOUR WORK ON THIS SECTION OF THE TEST ONLY.
DO NOT GO ON TO THE NEXT SECTION OF THE TEST UNTIL TIME IS UP FOR THIS SECTION.

SECTION V

Directions: **Read the passages and answer the questions following each passage by blackening the appropriate space on the answer sheet. You may refer back to the passages when answering the questions. Answer all questions on the basis of what is stated or implied.**

In the negotiation of tax treaties, developing nations, as a group, share two objectives somewhat at odds with those of developed-nation treaty
(5) partners. One such goal, attracting foreign investment, is in the broader context of foreign policy objectives. In the narrower realm of tax policy a common developing-country objective
(10) is to maximize the public capture of revenues from foreign investment activities.

Unfortunately for potential Third World treaty partners, this latter goal
(15) can conflict directly with the desires of both First World governments and individual investors. The preference of First World authorities for restricted source-based taxation is due to
(20) considerations of administrative feasibility. Such restrictions, though formally reciprocal, only produce equitable revenue effects when investment flows between treaty
(25) partners are relatively equal. However, when investment flows primarily in one direction, as it generally does from industrial to developing countries, the seemingly reciprocal source-based
(30) restrictions produce revenue sacrifices primarily by the state receiving most of the foreign investment and producing most of the income—namely, the developing country partner. The benefit
(35) is captured either by the taxpayer in the form of reduced excess credits, or by

the treasury of the residence (First World) state as the taxpayer's domestically creditable foreign tax
(40) liabilities decrease. The potential public revenue gain to the residence state further bolsters the industrial nations' preference for restrictions on source-based taxation—at the direct expense
(45) of the treaty partner's revenue goals.

The facilitation of foreign investment by tax treaties, whereas potentially serving the tax-policy goal of maximizing public revenue, also (or
(50) even instead) may serve broader economic objectives of developing countries. Foreign investments may be seen as essential sources of technical and managerial knowledge, capital,
(55) jobs, and foreign exchange. As such, the significance of foreign investments as an immediate source of public revenue could pale next to their longer-term "ripple effect" on development. In
(60) the negotiation of tax treaties, then, a developing country might be expected to ignore revenue goals and accept substantial limitations on source-based taxation, at least insofar as such
(65) limitations could be expected to encourage investment.

Frequently, however, Third World nations take a considerably more aggressive approach, seeking treaty
(70) terms that, in effect, provide subsidies to private investors at the expense of First World treaty partners. The United

States traditionally has followed a strict policy of "capital export neutrality," (75) providing no tax incentives for investment in the Third World through either the Internal Revenue Code or tax treaty provisions.

1. Normally, a developing country will negotiate a tax treaty for the purpose of

   (A) attracting foreign workers
   (B) decreasing tax revenues
   (C) attracting international investment and reducing tax revenues
   (D) attracting foreign investment and increasing tax revenues
   (E) decreasing dependence on special interest local investors

2. We can infer that a reciprocal source-based taxation treaty between a First World and a developing nation will produce

   (A) greater revenues for the First World nation
   (B) greater revenues for the developing nation
   (C) equal revenues for each country
   (D) no revenues for either country
   (E) losses to the economy of the First World nation

3. In negotiated treaties with developing countries, a First World country is likely to prefer

   (A) unrestricted source-based taxation
   (B) reciprocal restricted source-based taxation
   (C) nonreciprocal source-based taxation
   (D) equal investment flow between the partners
   (E) limited investment flow between the partners

4. In a treaty with a developing country that generates an excess of foreign tax credits, all of the following are likely EXCEPT:

   (A) the treaty will require some reduction of at-source taxation
   (B) the treaty will discourage private investors
   (C) the treaty will not produce what is perceived as the optimal revenue-producing balance
   (D) the treaty will require some expansion of at-source taxation
   (E) the excess of tax credits will be larger if the source country reserves more taxing jurisdiction

5. According to the passage, all of the following are potential advantages of foreign investment to developing countries EXCEPT:

   (A) increased managerial expertise
   (B) increased capital
   (C) increased availability of new materials
   (D) increased foreign exchange
   (E) increased employment

6. A developing country that did not insist upon immediate higher public revenues might be expected to

   (A) deter foreign investment
   (B) increase foreign investment
   (C) avoid the "ripple effect"
   (D) decrease employment
   (E) decrease the availability of raw materials

The following paired passages discuss twentieth-century Mexican artists' interpretations of the pre-Columbian world.

Passage A

The pre-Columbian past is everywhere evident in Mexico. Material remains are abundant. Indigenous people make up a great majority of the
(5) population. Twentieth-century artists have been cognizant of this past, with Diego Rivera at the forefront of those who champion it and José Clemente Orozco equally forceful in denouncing
(10) it. But regardless of their attitudes toward this past, Mexican artists have not been able to ignore it. All muralists used various aspects of the pre-Columbian world in their mural
(15) programs. Rivera presented it as an ideal world in his National Palace murals and the conquest as a heroic struggle against all odds. David Alfaro Siqueiros developed a thematic
(20) program in his murals at Chillan, Chile, and in Mexico City, in which Cuauhtémoc personifies the successful fight against the oppressor, symbolized by the centaur—half man, half beast.
(25) To Orozco, this world was inhabited by inhospitable gods, who appear to have more in common with the vengeful god in the Judaic tradition than with the pre-Columbian world. He, of course,
(30) overwhelms the opposition with a massive satirical brush, as he occasionally did in his murals. In fact, it is when this part of his personality was allowed to go unchecked that we have
(35) caricature rather than painting.

At any rate, whatever the attitudes toward their pre-Columbian past, negative or positive, all used a European pictorial language. Even the techniques
(40) are European. The muralists' use of fresco and the thematic and formal programs fit into a European tradition that was initiated in Florence, Italy, during the fifteenth century by Masaccio
(45) and others. The content is Mexican, the expression is Mexican, but the language is European.

Passage B

It must be kept in mind that Mexico was a colonized nation from the
(50) sixteenth to the nineteenth centuries and, despite the 1810 War of Independence that freed Mexico politically from Spain, the colonized mentality of the ruling classes
(55) maintained a position of imitation vis-à-vis European culture and a contempt for indigenous culture.

In Mexico, as in Latin America generally, nationalism has been one of
(60) the greatest forces impelling change. It has been deeply entwined with a necessary sense of dignity, pride, and affirmation. To counter engendered feelings of inferiority, intellectuals have
(65) reconstructed the past, and in so doing have created a mythology of ancient utopias. The Mexican painter who epitomized this tendency was Diego Rivera who, within a framework of
(70) Marxism, dialectically compared the positive and negative forces operating in a historical period, with an emphasis on the positive. In his vast epic of Mexican history on the staircase of the
(75) Palacio Nacional, Mexico City, he created a golden age, where Quetzalcoatl is the prophet. Cultural reaffirmation alone, however, is not the full substance of Rivera's mural.
(80) Mexico's Indian population composed the largest and most exploited class of the country, the rural base on which the entire economic structure rested. To revitalize this class, to set before it,

(85) in a mural, not only its ancient tradition idealized but also its power to reconstruct the present and control the future, was to continue the work that the military phase of the revolution had (90) started. This is the true significance of Rivera's murals, which rest on a twin construct of nationalism and indigenism.

Nationalism and indigenism were (95) also elements in the work of both Siqueiros and Orozco, but serving different purposes. Siqueiros's 1944 mural *Cuauhtémoc Against the Myth* used the Aztec emperor as a symbol of (100) the possibility of a struggle against seemingly overwhelming forces. On the surface, Orozco disdained the use of nationalism, partly because of his scorn for romanticized visions of (105) Indian life "fit to flatter the tourist" and partly because of a middle-class snobbery directed at "hateful and degenerate types of the lower classes" that caused him to eschew the painting (110) of "Indian sandals and dirty clothes." Nevertheless, his treatment of the positive aspects of the human condition often present Quetzalcoatl and the revolutionary heroes Hidalgo (115) and Zapata in heroic and grandiose terms.

7. Which one of the following is the best description of the subject of both passages?

(A) The reaction to colonialism by twentieth-century Mexican muralists
(B) The techniques dominating the work of Mexican muralists
(C) Pre-Columbian mysticism in the works of the muralists

(D) The differences among the three main Mexican muralists
(E) Pre-Columbian influence on three Mexican muralists

8. From information in both Passage A and Passage B, which of the following can be inferred?

(A) Diego Rivera most successfully captured pre-Columbian history in his murals.
(B) The three major muralists rejected European painting techniques.
(C) Of the three major muralists, Orozco's attitude toward the pre-Columbian past was the most ambivalent.
(D) Siqueiros primarily produced murals depicting life during the period of colonialism.
(E) Only Rivera used his art for political purposes.

9. Which one of the following statements illustrates a contrast between Passage A and Passage B?

(A) Passage A mentions the technique used by the muralists, whereas Passage B does not.
(B) Passage B praises the work of Rivera, Orozco, and Siqueiros, whereas Passage A is neutral toward Siqueiros.
(C) Passage A places the works of the muralists in historical context, whereas Passage B places them in a sociopolitical context.
(D) Passage B describes the public's reaction to the works of the muralists, whereas Passage A does not.
(E) Passage A identifies Rivera as the most important of the Mexican muralists, whereas Passage B makes no judgment.

10. According to Passage A and Passage B, all of the following characterize Orozco EXCEPT his

(A) tendency to use caricature in his works
(B) portrayal of the gods as unfriendly
(C) snobbery toward the lower-class Indian population
(D) romanticized picture of the indigenous population
(E) use of satire

11. The term "Cultural reaffirmation" (lines 77–78) in Passage B refers to which one of the following?

(A) The use of indigenous art and culture in the muralists' works
(B) Antagonism toward European domination of art
(C) The public's interest in and acceptance of pre-Columbian art
(D) The insistence on a nationalistic spirit in modern Mexican art
(E) Attempts by the muralists to glorify the accomplishments of pre-Columbian artists

12. According to Passage B, Diego Rivera's primary political intention in his mural of Mexican history was to

(A) show his feelings about Karl Marx
(B) depict the heroic battles of the revolution
(C) energize the Indian population and direct it to the future
(D) create an artistic language for modern Mexico
(E) preserve pre-Columbian symbolism and mythology

13. According to both passages, all of the following are mentioned or implied as characterizing the Mexican muralists EXCEPT:

(A) the use of Mexican subject matter
(B) disdain for European art
(C) recognition of the indigenous population
(D) appreciation for pre-Columbian works of art
(E) reference to Mexican heroes

War and change—political and economic foremost, but social and cultural not far behind—have been linked in America from the beginning.
(5) War was the necessary factor in the birth of the new American republic, as it has been in the birth of every political state known to us in history. War, chiefly the Civil War, in U.S. history has
(10) been a vital force in the rise of industrial capitalism, in the change of America from a dominantly agrarian and pastoral country to one chiefly manufacturing in nature. War, in
(15) focusing the mind of a country, stimulates inventions, discoveries, and fresh adaptations. Despite its manifest illth*, war, by the simple fact of the intellectual and social changes it
(20) instigates, yields results which are tonics to advancement.

By all odds, the most important war in U.S. history, the war that released the greatest number and diversity of
(25) changes in American life, was the Great War, the war that began in Europe in August 1914 and engulfed the United States in April 1917. Great changes in America were immediate.
(30) In large measure these changes reflected a release from the sense of isolation, insularity, and exceptionalism that had suffused so much of the American mind during the nineteenth
(35) century. The early Puritans had seen

*illth = ill effects (word coined by the author earlier in the full selection)

their new land as a "city upon a hill" with the eyes of the world on it. It was not proper for the New World to go to the Old for its edification; what was
(40) proper was for the Old World, grown feeble and hidebound, to come to America for inspiration. A great deal of that state of mind entered into what Tocqueville called the "American
(45) Religion," a religion compounded of Puritanism and ecstatic nationalism.

What we think of today as modernity—in manners and morals as well as ideas and mechanical things—
(50) came into full-blown existence in Europe in the final part of the nineteenth century, its centers such cities as London, Paris, and Vienna. In contrast America was a "closed"
(55) society, one steeped in conventionality and also in a struggle for identity. This was how many Europeans saw America and it was emphatically how certain somewhat more sophisticated
(60) Americans saw themselves. The grand tour was a veritable obligation of better-off, ambitious, and educated Americans—the tour being, of course, of Europe.

(65)   Possibly the passage of American values, ideas, and styles from "closed" to "open," from the isolated to the cosmopolitan society, would have taken place, albeit more slowly, had
(70) there been no transatlantic war of 1914–1918. We can't be sure. What we do know is that the war, and America's entrance into it, gave dynamic impact to the processes of secularization,
(75) individualization, and other kinds of social-psychological change which so drastically changed this country from the America of the turn of the century to the America of the 1920s.

14. In the passage the author makes all of the following points about war EXCEPT:

(A) war increases the pace of changes that might occur anyway
(B) war stimulates new inventions and discoveries
(C) war causes social and intellectual changes
(D) war in a capitalistic society is inevitable
(E) war sometimes stimulates a closed society toward greater openness

15. If true, which one of the following best illustrates the author's point about the effects of war on American society?

(A) During World War II, the Germans developed a variety of lethal nerve gas to use in the field.
(B) The development of radioactive isotopes used in treating cancer grew out of research to build the atomic bomb used in World War II.
(C) The American influenza epidemic of 1919 in all likelihood was a result of the return of infected soldiers from the battlefields of World War I.
(D) After the Civil War and the abolition of slavery in the South, racial intolerance across America grew in bitterness.
(E) A significant drain on America's material resources was a result of relaxed immigration policies occurring after World War II.

16. According to the author, World War I was the most important war in U.S. history because it

(A) ended the notion of a war to end all wars
(B) resulted in a weakened Germany that in turn led to Hitler's appeal

(C) changed America from a dominantly agrarian country to a manufacturing country

(D) led to more changes and a wider diversity of changes than any other American war

(E) made Americans more aware of advances made in European centers such as London, Paris, and Vienna

17. The main purpose of paragraph three is to

(A) characterize the American mind in the nineteenth century

(B) define Tocqueville's concept of American religion

(C) indicate the main cause of America's entrance into World War I

(D) contrast Civil War America with World War I America

(E) indicate the areas of America's strength at the start of World War I

18. According to the author, which one of the following contributed to America's insularity before World War I?

(A) The inability of all but the most wealthy, educated Americans to travel abroad

(B) The nationalistic view that the New World (America) shouldn't turn to the Old World (Europe) for ideas

(C) The emphasis on agrarian pursuits as opposed to belief in industry and technology

(D) The puritanical idea that traveling widely in the world exposed one to sin and corruption

(E) The superiority of the New World (America) to a feeble, decadent Old World (Europe)

19. Which one of the following best describes the main subject of this passage?

(A) a comparison of wars in America

(B) the benefits of war to society

(C) the importance of World War I to changes in America

(D) the contrast between the New World (America) and the Old World (Europe)

(E) secularization and individualization in American society

20. The relationship of paragraph one to the rest of the passage is best described by which one of the following?

(A) It presents a popular view that is proved inadequate by the rest of the passage.

(B) It introduces a philosophical question that is then answered in the rest of the passage.

(C) It outlines the contents of each of the other four paragraphs in the passage.

(D) It sets up the first of four examples developed in the rest of the passage.

(E) It presents a general idea that introduces the specific topic developed in the rest of the passage.

21. According to information in the passage, all of the following inferences can be made EXCEPT:

(A) well-to-do nineteenth-century American parents would be more likely to send their son to Europe than to California

(B) European "ecstatic nationalism" would be greater after World War I than before it

(C) religious influence in the daily workings of American society would be less evident in 1920 than 1900

(D) a census in America twenty years after the Civil War would indicate more manufacturing operations than before the war

(E) in the nineteenth century, avant garde movements in art and literature would be more likely to originate in Europe than in the U.S.

At a particular moment roughly 15 billion years ago, all the matter and energy we can observe, concentrated in a region smaller than a dime, began
(5) to expand and cool at an incredibly rapid rate. By the time the temperature had dropped to 100 million times that of the sun's core, the forces of nature assumed their present properties, and
(10) the elementary particles known as quarks roamed freely in a sea of energy. When the universe had expanded an additional 1,000 times, all the matter we can measure filled a
(15) region the size of the solar system.

At that time, the free quarks became confined in neutrons and protons. After the universe had grown by another factor of 1,000, protons and neutrons
(20) combined to form atomic nuclei, including most of the helium and deuterium present today. All of this occurred within the first minute of the expansion. Conditions were still too
(25) hot, however, for atomic nuclei to capture electrons. Neutral atoms appeared in abundance only after the expansion had continued for 300,000 years and the universe was 1,000
(30) times smaller than it is now. The neutral atoms then began to coalesce into gas clouds, which later evolved into stars. By the time the universe had

expanded to one-fifth its present size,
(35) the stars had formed groups recognizable as young galaxies.

When the universe was half its present size, nuclear reactions in stars had produced most of the heavy
(40) elements from which terrestrial planets were made. Our solar system is relatively young: It formed five billion years ago, when the universe was two-thirds its present size. Over time the
(45) formation of stars has consumed the supply of gas in galaxies, and hence the population of stars is waning. Fifteen billion years from now stars like our sun will be relatively rare, making
(50) the universe a far less hospitable place for observers like us.

Our understanding of the genesis and evolution of the universe is one of the great achievements of twentieth-
(55) century science. This knowledge comes from decades of innovative experiments and theories. Modern telescopes on the ground and in space detect the light from galaxies billions of
(60) light years away, showing us what the universe looked like when it was young. Particle accelerators probe the basic physics of the high-energy environment of the early universe.
(65) Satellites detect the cosmic background radiation left over from the early stages of expansion, providing an image of the universe on the largest scales we can observe.
(70) Our best efforts to explain this wealth of data are embodied in a theory known as the standard cosmological model or the big bang cosmology. The major claim of the theory is that in the
(75) large scale average the universe is expanding in a nearly homogeneous way from a dense early state. At present, there are no fundamental challenges to the big bang theory,

(80) although there are certainly unresolved
    issues within the theory itself.
    Astronomers are not sure, for example,
    how the galaxies were formed, but
    there is no reason to think the process
(85) did not occur within the framework of
    the big bang. Indeed, the predictions of
    the theory have survived all tests to
    date.

22. Which one of the following best
    expresses the main idea of the
    passage?

    (A) Twentieth-century technological
        achievements, such as particle
        accelerators, have made it possible
        for us to understand how the
        universe evolved.
    (B) Over the past 15 billion years the
        universe has evolved through a
        process of expansion and cooling,
        as explained by the big bang
        theory.
    (C) Because in the next 15 billion years
        the population of stars will greatly
        diminish, life in the universe will be
        precarious at best.
    (D) Although the big bang theory is
        widely accepted by astronomers,
        there are a number of questions
        and issues that remain unresolved.
    (E) Our solar system, formed 5 billion
        years ago, is relatively young
        viewed against the 15-billion-year
        evolution of the universe.

23. Which one of the following statements
    regarding the formation of the universe
    is best supported by information in the
    passage?

    (A) Stars were formed only after the
        universe cooled enough for atomic
        nuclei to capture electrons.
    (B) Helium and deuterium coalesced
        into gas clouds that gave birth to
        stars.

    (C) Quarks became confined in atomic
        nuclei at about the same time that
        our solar system was formed.
    (D) Planets came into being when
        neutral atoms formed gas clouds
        and heavy elements.
    (E) Galaxies were formed as a result of
        a series of nuclear reactions in
        stars.

24. According to the passage, which one of
    the following is a correct sequence of
    events in the evolution of the universe?

    (A) quarks; neutral atoms; stars; gas
        clouds; galaxies; planets
    (B) quarks; neutral atoms; gas clouds;
        stars; heavy elements; planets
    (C) atomic nuclei; helium; gas clouds;
        electrons; stars; planets
    (D) atomic nuclei; gas clouds;
        electrons; stars; galaxies; planets
    (E) quarks; atomic nuclei; electrons;
        gas clouds; planets; heavy
        elements

25. At what point does the passage
    markedly shift in direction?

    (A) Lines 16–17: "At that time the free
        quarks became confined in
        neutrons and protons."
    (B) Lines 41–44: "Our solar system is
        relatively young: It formed 5 billion
        years ago, when the universe was
        two-thirds its present size."
    (C) Lines 48–51: "Fifteen billion years
        from now stars like our sun will be
        relatively rare, making the universe
        a far less hospitable place for
        observers like us."
    (D) Lines 52–55: "Our understanding
        of the genesis and evolution of the
        universe is one of the great
        achievements of twentieth-century
        science."

(E) Lines 77–81: "At present, there are no fundamental challenges to the big bang theory, although there are certainly unresolved issues within the theory itself."

26. According to the passage, all of the following statements are true EXCEPT:

(A) the formation of planets was possible because of nuclear reactions in stars
(B) helium and deuterium atoms do not include electrons
(C) we are able to know what the universe looked like billions of years ago
(D) without the cooling that accompanied expansion, the evolution of the universe as we know it would have been impossible
(E) according to the big bang theory, it is not possible that other solar systems developed during the same period as ours

27. The information in the first three paragraphs of the passage is presented as if it is

(A) theoretical
(B) factual
(C) hypothetical
(D) evidentiary
(E) axiomatic

28. Which one of the following can be inferred about the future from the information in the passage?

(A) Because the predictions of the big bang theory have so far proved accurate, the theory will soon be accepted as fact.
(B) Although the expansion of the universe will continue, it will slow down over the next 15 billion years.
(C) Because the supply of gas in the galaxies will have been consumed, there will be less chance of a sun being formed 15 billion years from now.
(D) Although the process by which the universe was formed will continue to be studied, the "first cause" will never be determined by scientific means.
(E) Although the universe will continue to expand in the same way it has been expanding, cooling will not accompany the expansion.

STOP

IF YOU FINISH BEFORE TIME IS UP, CHECK YOUR WORK ON THIS SECTION OF THE TEST ONLY.
DO NOT GO ON TO THE NEXT SECTION OF THE TEST UNTIL TIME IS UP FOR THIS SECTION.

WRITING SAMPLE

Directions: You have 35 minutes to write an essay in response to a given topic. Take a few minutes to plan your work before you begin writing. DO NOT WRITE ON A TOPIC OF YOUR OWN CHOICE. ESSAYS THAT DO NOT ADDRESS THE GIVEN TOPIC ARE UNACCEPTABLE.

The quality of your writing is more important than the length of your response or the content. Pay attention to organization, appropriate diction, and correct usage. You will not be expected to display any specialized knowledge in your response, nor will you be expected to write a "perfect" essay; law schools understand that you are writing under a time constraint, and will allow for the minor lapses in writing ability that might occur under this circumstance.

Only the lined area in your booklet will be reproduced for the law schools, so do not write outside this space. _Do not_ skip lines or use wide margins. These precautions, along with careful planning and legible handwriting that is not unduly large, will keep you within the allowed space.

Sample Topic

The Black Hills County Art Museum, a small, well-run institution, must decide how to spend a large state grant. The money was given with the understanding that the museum would accomplish two objectives. *In the space provided, write an argument in favor of Plan A or Plan B.* Keep these objectives in mind:

- The museum will open an area for the display of Native American artifacts.
- The museum will substantially increase its revenues from memberships, contributions, and sales.

Plan A: The museum will use all of the money to construct a display space large and secure enough to attract several of the major popular traveling art exhibits each year. At present, the display space at the museum is too small to be used to present the art exhibits that attract attention in the national media. With the large university population in the area, there is a local audience for such shows, and with the new galleries, the museum could become the most important exhibition space in a six-state area. A leading modern architect has expressed interest in designing the new gallery at a greatly reduced fee. By selling some of the museum's permanent collection, space could be made available for Native American art exhibits.

Plan B: The museum will use the money to construct a new, small gallery for the display of Native American art, and to construct classrooms, a sculpture garden, a museum shop, and a restaurant. The museum has never sponsored a program of art education for either its adult supporters or local schoolchildren, but the many college teachers, along with the museum staff, would provide a fine core of instructors. The museum has never had a shop or a restaurant, though many of its wealthiest supporters have encouraged these additions. The sculpture garden would also serve as an ideal place to display the large Native American carvings that are too tall to be shown inside the buildings.

On the actual exam you will be given special sheets of paper to write your essay. It will have the essay topic on the top followed by room for scratch work. For practice, write your essay on two sides of an 8½" x 11" college-ruled lined sheet of paper.

ANSWER KEY

Section I: Logical Reasoning

1. A	6. D	11. E	16. D	21. D	26. D
2. A	7. A	12. D	17. D	22. B	
3. D	8. B	13. C	18. C	23. C	
4. E	9. E	14. A	19. A	24. B	
5. C	10. D	15. B	20. D	25. E	

Section II: Reading Comprehension

1. C	6. D	11. D	16. A	21. C	26. D
2. A	7. D	12. A	17. A	22. B	27. A
3. A	8. A	13. E	18. D	23. C	28. E
4. B	9. B	14. B	19. E	24. A	
5. C	10. C	15. B	20. A	25. C	

Section III: Analytical Reasoning

1. E	6. C	11. E	16. D	21. D
2. C	7. D	12. C	17. C	22. A
3. D	8. A	13. B	18. C	23. E
4. B	9. B	14. C	19. D	24. B
5. A	10. C	15. E	20. C	25. C

Section IV: Logical Reasoning

1. D	6. B	11. A	16. E	21. C	26. D
2. D	7. A	12. C	17. B	22. D	
3. A	8. E	13. D	18. A	23. C	
4. C	9. A	14. D	19. E	24. E	
5. B	10. B	15. B	20. B	25. C	

Section V: Reading Comprehension

1. D	6. B	11. A	16. D	21. B	26. E
2. A	7. E	12. C	17. A	22. B	27. B
3. B	8. C	13. B	18. B	23. A	28. C
4. D	9. A	14. D	19. C	24. B	
5. C	10. D	15. B	20. E	25. D	

MODEL TEST ANALYSIS

Doing model exams and understanding the explanations afterwards are of course important in acquainting you with typical LSAT question types and successful approaches to the questions. However, another benefit of carefully analyzing these model tests is to understand the kinds of errors you are making and thus work to minimize them. For instance, if a very high percentage of your incorrect answers is due to "careless error" or "misread problem," then perhaps you are working much too fast and should slow your pace accordingly. If your incorrect answers are due primarily to "lack of knowledge," then a careful rereading and reworking of the appropriate question-type chapter may be in order. Or if you find that you aren't completing a large number of questions because of lack of time, you may need to either increase your speed or learn to use the "one-check, two-check" technique more effectively.

This kind of analysis of the model tests will enable you to identify your particular weaknesses and thus remedy them.

MODEL TEST TWO ANALYSIS

Section	Total Number of Questions	Number Correct	Number Incorrect	Number Unanswered*
I. Logical Reasoning	26			
II. Reading Comprehension	28			
III. Analytical Reasoning	25			
IV. Logical Reasoning	26			
V. Reading Comprehension	28			
TOTALS:	133			

*At this stage in your preparation, you should not be leaving any blank answer spaces. At least fill in a guess, as there is no penalty for a wrong answer.

REASONS FOR INCORRECT ANSWERS

You may wish to evaluate the explanations before completing this chart.

Section	Total Number Incorrect	Lack of Knowledge	Misread Problem	Careless Error	Unanswered or Wrong Guess
I. Logical Reasoning					
II. Reading Comprehension					
III. Analytical Reasoning					
IV. Logical Reasoning					
V. Reading Comprehension					
TOTALS:					

ANSWER EXPLANATIONS

Section I

1. **A** The author must assume that "nothing about our coin influences its fall in favor of either side or that all influences are counterbalanced by equal and opposite influences"; otherwise "our ignorance of the coming result" is untrue. Also, he mentions that the chances are one out of two that the coin will fall heads up; this could not be correct if the coin had been weighted or tampered with.

2. **A** (A) is implied by the author's statement that one-to-two is not "true." (B), (C), (D), and (E) are not implied and would not follow from the passage.

3. **D** The author is actually pointing out that self-confidence is of most importance. (C) and (E) focus on behavior, while the author is focusing on mental attitude.

4. **E** Only choice (E) is supported by these comments. The comments suggest that riding on roller coasters is taking a risk and that this risk translates to a proclivity to taking other risks in life. The passage doesn't suggest, however, that *no* roller coaster riders avoid taking risks elsewhere (A), nor does it have any bearing on the importance of taking risks (B). Choice (C) is a difficult one to eliminate because the passage certainly doesn't rule out this possibility (the passage says "than others," not "than *all* others")—but it doesn't directly support it, either. The comments have nothing to do with varying levels or types of risk taking (D).

5. **C** If the diet and way of life of the men of the two islands are alike, but the life expectancies are very different, the cause of the difference is probably something other than diet and the way of life. Some of the other answers are reasonable inferences, but they do not follow so clearly from the paragraph as (C).

6. **D** None of the other four choices offer information that explains the discrepancy. If the women in college are preparing for a profession that pays less (teaching) than the profession the men will enter (engineering), the discrepancy is explained.

7. **A** To conclude that the women should earn as much or more than the men, the passage must assume that all of the men and all of the women, or at least an equal number, enter the workforce. It also assumes that all of them, or at least an equal number, graduate from college, though the passage says only "are enrolled."

8. **B** The six-month interest-free charge is the money at a low cost; the stock of discontinued summer wear is the slow selling product, and the fashionable new neck wear is the popular product. None of the other choices covers all three conditions.

9. **E** Though all of the choices are plausible, (E) deals with all three of the problems mentioned in the paragraph. Each of the other choices deals only with one.

10. **D** Although Michael may be lying, there is no factual evidence to that effect. Michael is truthful and readily admits to the previous dents to his own vehicle (A). (B) and (C) reinforce Michael's contention that the dents were caused by someone else. Even (E) reflects positively on Michael's character, though it is not mentioned in the original set of conditions.

11. **E**   The author states that the present programs are at best weak and hopefully won't fail as they have in the past.

12. **D**   The statement that "Hopefully, they won't fail as they have in the past" tells us that our government is *not* trying a new approach to end inflation. (A) is close, but the passage states that foreign oil is "high-priced," not "overpriced." "High-priced" tells us the relative cost, not the actual comparative value.

13. **C**   The conclusion is the prediction of a grim year for home builders. Choices (A), (B), (D), and (E) do not point to continued bad sales, but (C), revealing that sales fell even with advertising and incentives, supports the prediction of a bad year ahead.

14. **A**   Three possibilities exist:
   (a) You read *Weight-Off* magazine, are fat, and do not eat chocolate.
   (b) You are fat, eat chocolate, but do not read *Weight-Off* magazine.
   (c) You eat chocolate, are not fat, and do not read *Weight-Off* magazine.
   Thus,
   (A) is inconsistent by (a) and (b). (B) is not inconsistent if (b) and (c) are void of people. (C) is not inconsistent if (c) is void of people. (D) and (E) are not inconsistent by (c) and (a).

15. **B**   Dave felt that Jerry implied that no one except Jerry's wife cooks fantastic meals.

16. **D**   Only (D) offers an instance of success in the polls. (A) simply repeats a point of the passage without including the qualification that comes later. Choices (B), (C), and (E) would support rather than undermine the viewpoint of the passage.

17. **D**   The passage does not point inherent inconsistencies. It does support a point with a specific example (the two figures on the balanced budget poll), question the honesty of politicians (the phrase "or may not"), reinterprets the 80 percent support figure, and shows how statistics can be used to mislead.

18. **C**   Decreasing the fares on lightly traveled routes might attract some passengers away from the over-crowded more popular flights, but increasing the fares would not help to solve the luggage problem. The four other suggestions are plausible ways of dealing with the lack of space.

19. **A**   X's new realization is expressed in his final sentence: "We must know all the characteristics of men, and that Socrates has all of them, before we can be sure." The "characteristics of men" are what is implied by the generalization "man," in "Socrates is a man." Therefore, deductive thinking is simply reminding ourselves of the particular specifics implied by generalizations.

20. **D**   Symbolically, A is necessary to have B (a good telescope to see moons of Neptune). You do not have B (can't see moons with my telescope). Therefore, you cannot have A (a good telescope). (D) is the only choice that follows this line of reasoning. Symbolically, A is necessary to have B (knowing area of circle to find circumference). You do not have B (can't figure out circumference). Therefore, you cannot have A (area of circle).

21. **D** Extensive psychological research would most likely give the information that the author discusses. (E) limits the research to clinical psychologists and to recent findings.

22. **B** "Conscious behavior eventually becomes habit" is indirectly stated in the last sentence. (A) is a close answer, but that absolute word "all" is inconsistent with the words "can become" in the last sentence. This does not imply that they *must* become unconscious behavior.

23. **B** The given advice would be strengthened by the assurance that such measures are effective. Each of the other choices either weakens the advice, or addresses only a portion of the paragraph.

24. **B** The disease under discussion is termed "it," and thus its identity is unclear. The other choices either are not applicable to the second sentence or refer to terms that require no further definition.

25. **E** (E) weakens the argument that young people have abundant time. The other choices are only tangentially relevant to the argument.

26. **D** The passage says that worrying about writing unfortunately keeps one from writing at all; (D) summarizes this viewpoint. (B) and (C) are irrelevant notions; (A) contradicts the author's implied support for writing theorists; and (E) is an unreasonable, unsupported conclusion.

Section II

Passage 1

1. **C** The chief purpose of the Sixth Amendment was to assure the assistance of counsel in criminal cases. The guarantee to the right to self-representation was not the chief purpose of the amendment though the amendment has been used to support it.

2. **A** The phrase refers to the end of the second paragraph. The author regards the waiving of the right to counsel as a choice, which should not be seen as a guarantee of the right of self-representation.

3. **A** The phrase *"in propria persona"* means "in his own person," "by himself," or "by herself."

4. **B** If the Court had believed a fair trial was impossible without the assistance of counsel, it would not have allowed self-representation.

5. **C** The passage emphasizes the importance of warning a defendant of the risks of self-representation.

6. **D** Though true, the tradition of self-representation is not a valid objection to the practice. In fact, it might be cited as an argument in favor of self-representing defendants.

Passage 2

7. **D** This title addresses the main subject of the paragraph and is more specific than (B). (A) suggests that the passage deals more with governments than with economic problems, while in fact only the last two paragraphs address governmental systems. The passage does not examine the rhetorical question presented in (C), and (E) covers only a minor point.

8. **A** Nowhere in the passage are Africa's limited natural resources cited as a reason for its economic problems; therefore, this is the best answer. Lines 13–14 cite a lack of capital reserves (B); lines 30–40 indicate poor utilization of capital (C); lines 41–46 address the limited purchasing power of the majority of Africans;

and lines 74–82 describe Africa's problems in the world market.

9. **B** Paragraphs 3 through 6 provide specific examples of the causes of Africa's economic problems; the first sentence of paragraph 3 is the topic sentence. The author does not present case histories (D) or include any statistics (E). The passage does not end with a general conclusion (C), and nowhere does the author use comparison and contrast to make a point (A).

10. **C** Lines 30–40 cite examples of how local conditions were often not considered when steps were taken to improve Africa's economic potential, and lines 37–40 specifically refer to ecological damage. Although ethnic rivalries are mentioned as hindering development, there is no suggestion that attempts at development caused new rivalries (A). According to the passage, more skilled workers (as opposed to professionals) are needed to support economic development (B). Nothing suggests that achievements have significantly reduced the debt burden, which is cited as a continuing problem (D), and nothing indicates that the market has been adversely affected (E).

11. **D** Lines 108–109 state "there were problems with ujamaa," but no details are provided. Understanding what these problems were and how they affected Tanzanian life would probably be most helpful in understanding why Nyerere was replaced. The second best answer would be (C), but nothing in the passage suggests changes in mortality rate, literacy rate, and so on, whereas problems with ujamaa are specifically mentioned. Both Nyerere's

educational background and details about Tanzania's exports are minor points (A and E). (B) is unclear and irrelevant.

12. **A** These two paragraphs briefly mention two countries' attempts to provide a governmental system that encourages economic development. (C) is incorrect, because although both countries encounter setbacks, they attempt to deal with economic problems. (B) doesn't make sense; neither paragraph is concerned with the results of neocolonialism. Rather than summarizing the problems covered in the rest of the passage (D), these paragraphs provide two examples of attempts to deal with the problems. (E) overstates the purpose of the last two paragraphs; there is no attempt to "personalize" issues or address general problems.

13. **E** *To squander* by definition means *to waste foolishly*, which is a negative judgment. (A), (C), and (B) are descriptive, but they are not in themselves judgmental. (D) is not a negative word.

14. **B** Economic dependency on powerful countries suggests that these countries will exert political and economic control reminiscent of true colonialism; therefore, this is the best definition. (C) and (D) are not related to colonial systems, and (A) and (E) are incomplete.

Passage 3

15. **B** (B) is the best choice because the passage first describes the classic model of competition and then introduces what the author refers to as the concept of "countervailing power." Although the ideas in (D) and (E) are both present in the pas-

sage, these titles are too restrictive. (A) is incomplete, and (C) is clearly wrong, in that the passage doesn't specifically address "American capitalism."

16. **A** (A) is directly from the passage (lines 18–22). Although (B) and (C) might occur, these are not part of the classic competition model described by the author. (E) would certainly not provide a return to normal prices; although it might offer a change in *supply,* it would not alter *demand.* Answer (D) is simply unclear.

17. **A** (A) is the best choice. See lines 27–34. (D) and (E) are clearly wrong. (C) is unclear. The second-best answer is (B), since the behavior of manufacturers is ultimately related to competition for the customer. However, (A) is the more specific answer provided by the passage.

18. **D** (D) is the best choice. See lines 47–55. (A) is incorrect because the classic model of competition does *not* ignore the role of labor (lines 27–31). Also, although the author might agree that greed undermined the classic model, this is not an issue addressed in the passage. (B) is incorrect because the author does not relate change in self-regulation of competition to any particular event, nor does he place it in a specific time frame. (C) is clearly the opposite of the point made in the passage. The restraint of "sellers by other sellers and buyers by other buyers" is part of the classic model of competition. (E) is incorrect because, according to the author, "countervailing power" did not destroy competition but grew as a result of a change in the classic

model, i.e., the reduction of the number of competitors and resulting concentration of power among a small group of firms.

19. **E** Organizations that network manufacturers would not provide a customer- or supplier-generated restraint on them, which is the way the author defines "countervailing power." All of the other choices are possible wielders of "countervailing power."

20. **A** In lines 34–47 and lines 55–60, the author makes it clear that economists have almost exclusively focused on the classic model of competition in considering restraints on manufacturers. (B) is incorrect because the author does not discuss government regulation or the lack of it as part of economic theory. Similarly, (C) is incorrect; the "trickle-down" theory (i.e., that what is good for those at the top will ultimately benefit those at the bottom) is also not mentioned in the passage. (D) is contradicted in the passage; according to the author, economists did recognize the trend toward concentration (lines 47–55, 78–84). Finally, although the author might agree with (E), the passage suggests that economists have been preoccupied with the classic model of competition (including its built-in restraints) rather than biased toward "unregulated" capitalism. The preoccupation with the classic models led them to ignore other types of restraint in the economy.

21. **C** The passage sets up the classic model of competition in paragraphs one and two. Paragraph 3 is a shift in the discussion to the idea that there might be a restraining

mechanism exclusive of the competitive model that economists haven't recognized. Paragraphs 4 and 5 describe this restraining mechanism. The second-best answer is (D); however, paragraph 3 does provide a transition, which makes (C) the better choice.

Passage 4

22. B Although Passage B includes Lavoisier, its focus is on the caloric theory of heat, while Passage A covers other aspects of the scientist, not just one theory. Passage B, while showing how Lavoisier's theory of heat was later disproved, does not "discredit" him (A). (E) is also inaccurate; while showing how theories can be supplanted by new theories, the author's tone toward science is not skeptical.

23. C The use of the term follows the statement that Lavoisier disproved the theory of phlogiston, a nonexistent substance (or "flammability principle"). It is ironic that he then posits another substance, caloric, that cannot be weighed or measured.

24. A In lines 32–35, the passage states that Lavoisier's methods led to his proof that oxygen and hydrogen made up water, and therefore (A) is the best answer. Lavoisier's caloric theory was incorrect in explaining heat (B) and (D), and it was Priestley (mentioned in Passage B), not Lavoisier, who isolated eight gases (E). Although Passage A says that Lavoisier produced better gunpowder, there is no indication that he changed its composition (C).

25. C (C) is the best example of the author's point in the first paragraph. In lines 134–144, two specific examples are given of how observable

facts can be explained by Lavoisier's caloric theory, a theory that was later proved wrong. None of the other choices are observable facts explained by the caloric theory.

26. D The best answer is (D), a point the author makes in the first paragraph. The passage doesn't imply either that alchemy "contributed nothing to science" (A) or that thermodynamics is an inexact science (C). Although (E) may seem like a possible answer, the author doesn't criticize the scientific method but merely suggests that theories can be disproved or modified in time.

27. A (A) is the best answer (lines 30–32). Although Lavoisier did believe in a fluid called caloric, he thought it caused heat, not combustion (E). (B) was part of the phlogiston theory, not Lavoisier's theory, and (C) and (D) are related to theories after Lavoisier.

28. E Passage B refers to Priestley as an important eighteenth century scientist who firmly believed in the phlogiston theory, making (E) the best answer.

Section III

Answers 1–6

UPPER-case letters denote colors given in the problem, and lower-case letters denote deduced colors.

1. E	1	2	3	4	5	
	b/w	R	W	b	R	(flag)
	w/g	B	g	w	B	(pennant)

The 3rd pennant cannot be blue or white, so therefore it is green. The 4th flag cannot be white or red, so it must be blue. The 4th pennant cannot be green or blue, so it must be white. The 1st flag cannot be red, so it is either blue or white. The 1st pennant cannot be blue, so it must be green or white.

2. **C**

	1	2	3	4	5	
	R	w	r/b			(flag)
	g/w	B	g/w			(pennant)

(A) is clearly true. If the 5th flag is red, then the 3rd flag cannot be, since the 1st flag is red and we can have only two of any one color. Thus, (B) is true. If the 4th pennant is green, then the 3rd pennant must be white. But that does not determine the color of the 1st pennant. Thus, (C) is not necessarily true. (D) is the same as (A) and is also true. If the 4th pennant is green, this implies that the 3rd pennant must be white. If the 5th pennant is white, then the 1st pennant cannot be. Therefore (E) is true.

3. **D**   Here is what you start with:

	1	2	3	4	5
Flag	W		W		
Pennant		B		B	

The 2nd and 4th flags cannot be white because they are adjacent to white flags and they cannot be blue because they would be the same colors as the pennants on the same flagpoles. Therefore, they must be red (A).

	1	2	3	4	5
Flag	W	r	W	r	
Pennant		B		B	

For the same reasons, the 1st and 3rd pennants cannot be white or blue, so they must be green (B) and (C).

	1	2	3	4	5
Flag	W	r	W	r	
Pennant	g	B	G	b	

Since no more than two flags or pennants of the same color can be flying at the same time, the 5th flagpole must have a blue flag and a white pennant (E). The 5th pennant could not be green because there are already two green pennants flying (D). (D) is therefore false.

	1	2	3	4	5
Flag	W	r	W	r	b
Pennant	g	B	g	B	w

4. **B**

	1	2	3	4	5	
	B	w	r	B		(flag)
		W	g			(pennant)

Statement (B) is true since the 1st pennant cannot be blue or white. Statement A is false since the 5th pennant could be blue or white. Statement (C) is false since it is white. Statements (D) and (E) are false since they could be white.

5. **A**

	1	2	3	4	5	
		R	W	r		(flag)
			g	B		(pennant)

If the 5th flag is white, then the 5th pennant must be green. Thus the 1st and 2nd pennants cannot be green and cannot be the same color, so one of them is blue. Therefore, (A) is true. All the other statements are false.

6. **C**

	1	2	3	4	5	
	W	B	W	B	r	(flag)
	g	W	B	W	B	(pennant)

	1	2	3	4	5	
	B	W	B	W	r	(flag)
	g	B	W	B	W	(pennant)

Since blue and white are the two common colors between flags and pennants, the above are the only two arrangements possible. In both cases, the 5th flag is red and the 1st pennant is green.

Answers 7–13

7. **D**

1	2	3	4	5	6	7	8	9	10
E	E	E					M		M

If the 8th book is a math book, then the three English books must be in positions 1, 2, and 3, since they cannot be in positions 8, 9, and 10. Thus, the other math book is in position 10. The 4th book must be next to the English book in position 3.

8. **A**

1	2	3	4	5	6	7	8	9	10
M				P	P		E	E	E

If the 9th book is an English book, then so are the 8th and 10th books. Thus there is a math book in position 1. The science books must be in positions 2 and 3 *or* 3 and 4. This leaves only positions 4 and 7 for the other math book. Thus (A) is always true. (C) could be true, but does not have to be true. The 3rd poetry book could be in position 2.

9. **B**

1	2	3	4	5	6	7	8	9	10
M						S	S	E	E

If the 1st book is a math book, then the 8th, 9th, and 10th books must be the English books. If the 7th book is a science book, so must be the 6th book. This means that the other math book must be either the 3rd, the 4th, or the 5th book. The remainder of the books are poetry books, including the 2nd book.

10. **C**

1	2	3	4	5	6	7	8	9	10
M	P	P	M	S	S	P	E	E	E

or

E	E	E	M	S	S	P	P	P	M

If the 4th book is a math book and the 5th book is a science book, then the 6th book is also a science book. This leaves two possible arrangements for the remaining books, as shown above. Statement (C) is the only correct one.

11. **E**

1	2	3	4	5	6	7	8	9	10
E	E	E	P					P	M

or

M	P					P	E	E	E

The poetry books must be in positions 4 and 9 *or* 2 and 7, depending on whether the math book is in position 1 or 10. See diagrams above. For example, let us assume that the math book is the 10th book. In order for no two poetry books to be next to each other, the 4th and 9th books must be poetry books, with the 3rd poetry book in either position 6 or 7, depending on the positions of the science books. The same argument holds if the 1st book is a math book.

12. **C**

1	2	3	4	5	6	7	8	9	10
E	E	E	S	S	M	P	P	P	M

and

M	P	P	P	M	S	S	E	E	E

These are the two possible arrangements. We see that (A) is false, (B) could be false, (D) is false, and (E) could be false. Only (C) is always true.

13. **B**

1	2	3	4	5	6	7	8	9	10
E	E	E	M	S	S	P	P	P	M

and

E	E	E	S	S	M	P	P	P	M

These are the only two possible combinations; thus, (B) is the correct answer.

Answers 14–20

The conditions lead to the following diagram that shows the positional relationship between the paintings, illustrated from left to right.

```
|——Y→            1 2 3 4 5 6
D   F   T   R
←G——|
```

It is clear that the four paintings by Diego, Frank, Tina, and Rich, must be placed in that order from left to right. Yolanda's painting is to the right of Diego's painting, and Glenda's painting is to the left of Tina's painting. Some immediate conclusions can be drawn, such as, Diego's painting must be in position 1 or 2.

Although you probably wouldn't have the time to do a complete analysis at the beginning of the set, some other conclusions that you could draw include: Tina's painting must be in position 4 (if Yolanda's painting is to the right of Tina's painting) or 5 (if only Rich's painting is to its right). Yolanda's painting could be in positions 2–6, and Glenda's painting could be in positions 1–4.

14. **C**   (C) cannot be true since there are only two positions to the right of Glenda's position, positions 5 and 6, and they must be occupied by Tina's and Rich's paintings. There is no room for Yolanda's painting. The other four choices are possible as shown below:

	1	2	3	4	5	6
(A)	D	F	Y	G	T	R
(B)	D	Y	F	G	T	R
(C)			G	T	R	Y?
(D)	D	Y	F	G	T	R
(E)	D	Y	F	G	T	R

15. **E**   Glenda's painting must hang to the left of Tina's painting, and Yolanda's painting must hang to the right of Diego's painting. Therefore, Glenda's painting could be in position 1, and Yolanda's painting could be in position 6. Therefore, four paintings could hang between them.

1	2	3	4	5	6
G	D	F	T	R	Y

16. **D**   Diego's painting must hang to the left of Frank's painting. Since Frank's painting is in position 2, Diego's painting must be in position 1. At this point you should scan the answers looking for Diego. (D) is correct. Go on to the next question. But for your information, (A) is not correct, since Tina's painting could be in position 4 with Yolanda's painting in position 5. (B) is not correct, since Glenda's painting could be in position 4. (C) is not correct, since Rich's painting could be in position 5 with Yolanda's painting in position 6. (E) is not correct, since Yolanda's painting could be in positions 3–6.

17. **C**   If Yolanda's painting is hanging to the left of Frank's painting, then there are four paintings to the left of Tina's painting. This implies that Tina's painting must be in position 5 and Rich's painting must be in position 6. Therefore, (C) is correct. Since Glenda's painting can be positioned anywhere to the left of Tina's painting, it could be between any of the other pairs. Thus, (A), (B), (D),

and (E), could be true, but they do not have to be true. For your information, the following four possibilities exist:

1	2	3	4	5	6
G	D	F	Y	T	R
D	G	F	Y	T	R
D	F	G	Y	T	R
D	F	Y	G	T	R

18. **C**   Choice C results in two possible arrangements. Choices A, B, D, and E, result in only one possible arrangement.

	1	2	3	4	5	6
(A)	G	D	Y	F	T	R
(B)	D	Y	F	G	T	R
(C)	D	Y	F	G	T	R
(C)	D	G	F	Y	T	R
(D)	D	F	G	T	Y	R
(E)	D	F	Y	G	T	R

19. **D**   Since Glenda's painting is hanging to the left of Tina's painting, and Yolanda's painting is hanging to the right of Diego's painting, there are four possible arrangements:

1	2	3	4	5	6
D	F	Y	G	T	R
D	F	G	Y	T	R
D	Y	G	F	T	R
D	G	Y	F	T	R

20. **C**   (C) cannot be true since the only painting that can hang to the left of Diego's painting is Glenda's painting. The other choices are possible as illustrated.

	1	2	3	4	5	6
(A)	D	Y	F	G	T	R
(B)	D	Y	G	F	T	R
(D)	D	G	F	Y	T	R
(E)	D	G	F	T	R	Y

Answers 21–25

From the information given, you could have constructed the following display:

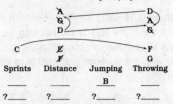

Sprints	Distance	Jumping	Throwing
		B	
?___	?___	?___	?___

21. **D**   If C and E are both sprint coaches, then from the original conditions F and G coach throwers. Since G coaches throwers, D cannot coach distance, so D must coach jumping.

Sprints	Distance	Jumping	Throwing
C		B	F
? E	?___	? D	? G

22. **A**   If G coaches jumping and A coaches distance we have:

Sprints	Distance	Jumping	Throwing
	A	B	
?___	?___	? G	?___

If D coaches distance or throwing, A must coach sprints or jumping. Since A coaches distance, D cannot coach distance or throwing. This means D must coach sprints. The other choices are possible, but not necessarily true.

Sprints	Distance	Jumping	Throwing
D	A	B	
?___	?___	? G	?___

23. **E**   If D coaches throwing, A and G cannot coach distance or throwing. This leaves only C to be the distance coach. So C CANNOT coach jumping.

| | E̶ F̶ | | |
Sprints	Distance	Jumping	Throwing
___	C	B	D
?___	?___	?___	?___
	A̶		A̶
	G̶		G̶

| | E̶ F̶ | | |
Sprints	Distance	Jumping	Throwing
A̶	D	B	___
?___	?___	? A	?___
	A̶		A̶
	G̶		G̶

24. **B** If G is the only throwing coach, we have the following:

| | E̶ F̶ | | |
Sprints	Distance	Jumping	Throwing
___	___	B	G
?___	?___	?___	? X

If D coaches distance or throwers, G must coach sprints or jumping. Since G coaches throwing, D does not coach distance or throwers. Thus, A and C must coach distance giving the following arrangement:

| | E̶ F̶ | | |
Sprints	Distance	Jumping	Throwing
___	A	B	G
?___	? C	?___	? X
	D̶		D̶

Choice (A) is incorrect since D doesn't coach distance.

Choice (C) is incorrect since A coaches distance.

Choice (D) is incorrect since, if F coaches jumping, D and E must coach sprints.

Choice (E) is incorrect since C and D coach different sports.

25. **C** If D coaches distance, A and G do not coach distance or throwing.

| | E̶ F̶ | | |
Sprints	Distance	Jumping	Throwing
A̶	D	B	___
?___	?___	?___	?___
	A̶		A̶
	G̶		G̶

Since A does not coach sprints, then A must coach jumping. So A and B coach jumping; therefore, G CANNOT coach jumping.

Section IV

1. **D** This choice provides the most direct evidence of the effectiveness of the PUC consumer action. Each of the other choices is only tangentially related to the argument.

2. **D** This choice most seriously weakens the author's contention that the PUC acts in the public interest. (C) is a weaker choice, especially because "slightly" softens the statement.

3. **A** This choice parallels both the reasoning and the structure of the original. The original reasoning may be summarized as follows: most $X \rightarrow Y$; therefore $X \rightarrow Y$ (probably).

4. **C** The reasoning goes as follows: All good teachers are patient (rephrasing of the first statement); some good teachers (patient) are good administrators; therefore, some good administrators are patient. To use a term of degree other than some requires assumptions beyond the information given.

5. **B** Since good personnel relations of an organization, according to the passage, rely upon "mutual confidence, trust and goodwill," one of the causes of personnel difficulties would most certainly be the employees' not believing in the good faith of the organization.

6. **B** In the second sentence, the author implies that the lack of facilities is related to the lack of research mentioned in the first sentence. In any case, the passage reveals the author's concern with both research

and assistance, and therefore agrees more fully with (B) than with (A), which mentions research only.

7. **A** The "But" that begins the third sentence marks a contrast between the business world and the schools. The writer's point is that they are not alike and, therefore, cannot be run using the same standards of judgment.

8. **E** The correct answer is "circular." The argument that what the Church says is true is ultimately based upon this same assertion.

9. **A** Kathy believes Mary to have meant that *only Italians* are great lovers. Therefore, Kathy takes issue with this and points out in her reply that there are non-Italians who are great lovers. (A), if replaced for Mary's statement, would make Kathy's reply a reasonable one.

10. **B** Only (B) addresses Dimple's assumption that Mrs. Wilson is the *only* applicant whose qualifications are ideal. Other choices are irrelevant to the *argument,* although some may be relevant to the implied situation.

11. **A** Only (A) addresses the substance of Dimple's argument.

12. **C** The passage offers a pattern in which failure to meet one of two specific requirements results in a failure to qualify for something. In (C), the fall and winter track seasons become the residence requirement and the collecting of signatures. Failure to complete both leads to disqualification (for the spring team, for the June primary).

13. **D** The author of the argument avoids the issue of *quality.* The statement that stresses the incompleteness of the pro-hygienist position weakens it. (B) and (E) are irrelevant.

14. **D** The passage describes two types of obstacles to happiness: exterior forces and personal attitude. Both these factors are mentioned in (A), (B), (C), and (E). (D) requires the assumption that the two categories discussed by the author are the only categories.

15. **B** (A) may be eliminated because changing one's mind need not involve issues of right and wrong (in the moral sense that Eliot implies). (C) and (E) may be eliminated because they refute the underlying assumption of Eliot's words, that one can tell what is right. The passage does not address the issue of temptation (D).

16. **E** Without an implied or explicit definition of "civilized," the relevance of the examples is vague, at best. (A) and (D) are irrelevant considerations, and (B) and (C), although possibly relevant, do not address the most apparent weakness of the passage.

17. **B** (A) and (C) strengthen the argument. Although (D) and (E) partially weaken certain aspects of the argument, only (B) introduces a situation which suggests that freedom of the press may have harmful consequences.

18. **A** (B) and (C) are irrelevant to the argument. (D) and (E) contradict the implied assertion that a free press must be protected at all costs. Only (A) offers a statement both favorable to the concept of a free press and directly relevant to the subject discussed: the use of privileged information.

19. **E** By stating that "a legal technicality … ducks the … moral question," the author is implying that the federal government which benefits from the technicality is associated

with dodging the issue. (A) and (B) restate explicit information; (C) is implausible; and (D) contradicts information in the passage.

20. **B** Private medical aid would render the author's argument unnecessary. (C), a choice worth considering, is not the best one because the author's focus is less on the aliens' needs than on the monetary burden borne by the counties.

21. **C** By documenting the rate at which the medical expense burden grows, the author could strengthen the argument that the situation he describes is indeed a burden.

22. **D** The passage talks about communes as failures. Therefore, the most logical completion must be a negative term consistent with failure. The only negative choice is (D).

23. **C** By linking Herb's ability with his "cousinhood," Herb is assuming that the latter determines the former; therefore, he is ignoring (C). (B) is irrelevant. (A) is too vague to be the best answer. (D) is inapplicable, because Keith uses "good" in a context that makes its meaning clear. Finally, (E) refers to contradictory information.

24. **E** In order to argue for the value of renewable prescriptions, the author must first assume that more medicine may be necessary, or, in other words, that the patient may suffer a relapse. Without the possibility of relapse, a call for more medicine that has already effected a cure ("worked effectively") is illogical.

25. **C** The passage consistently implies a difference between the past and the present, and (C) makes this contrast explicit. (B) contradicts the implication of the passage, while (A) and

(D) narrow the focus unnecessarily, and (E) is irrelevant.

26. **D** This fact would strengthen the merely impressionistic evidence that lawsuits were less prevalent 40 years ago. It is the only choice dealing directly with the implied subject of the passage—lawsuits.

Section V

Passage 1

1. **D** According to the first paragraph, a developing country hopes to attract foreign investment and increase its revenues from taxation ("maximize the public capture of revenues").

2. **A** Unless the investment flow is equal in each direction, the First World nation from which the greater revenue is likely to come is more likely to benefit.

3. **B** According to the second paragraph, reciprocal source-based taxation produces revenue sacrifices by the state receiving most of the foreign investment, that is, the developing country.

4. **D** Excess foreign tax credits are a disincentive to private investors. If the at-source taxation is reduced, there will be fewer excess foreign credits.

5. **C** The passage makes no reference to the availability of raw materials. The four other options are cited.

6. **B** A country that reduced its revenue expectations would be expected to increase foreign investment.

Passage 2

7. **E** Both passages show how the pre-Columbian past affected Mexico's most prominent muralists. Answers (A) through (D), although perhaps true, are too narrow to define the subject of the passages.

8. **C** According to Passage A, Orozco denounced the pre-Columbian past (see lines 10, 26–29) and according to Passage B, he treated "the positive aspects of the human condition" in the person of Quetzalcoatl (lines 111–116). This suggests ambivalence. Although Passage B states that Rivera "epitomized" the creation of a mythology of ancient Mexico, it does not imply that he "most successfully" captured history in his murals (A). (B) and (D) are simply inaccurate. (E), which may seem a good answer, is not implied; although Passage B makes it clear that Rivera did use his art for political purposes (e.g., "within a Marxist framework" to inspire the indigenous population to "reconstruct the present and control the future"), it does not imply that the other muralists did *not* have political purposes.

9. **A** Passage A, in the last paragraph, states that the muralists' "pictorial language" and techniques—for example, the use of fresco—fit into the European tradition. Passage B makes no references to techniques. (B) through (E) are inaccurate.

10. **D** Orozco scorned romanticized visions of Indian life (lines 104–105). (A) through (E) are all mentioned in either Passage A or Passage B (and sometimes both). Note the word "EXCEPT" in the question.

11. **A** To counter the "colonized mentality" of Mexico, the muralists reaffirmed their national heritage by turning to pre-Columbian history and art. This does not indicate, however, that they were antagonistic to Europe's role in art history (B) nor does it indicate the public's reaction (C). (D) and (E), which may seem possible answers, are not as accurate as (A). "Insistence" on a nationalistic spirit (D) is not mentioned, nor do the muralists "glorify" pre-Columbian artists, although they may glorify pre-Columbian deeds.

12. **C** See lines 84–93. Although (A), (B), (D), and (E) may be interests of Rivera, the passage makes it clear that revitalizing the Indian population was one of his primary "political" intentions.

13. **B** Neither passage indicates that the muralists disdained European art; in fact, Passage A states that the muralists used traditional European techniques. Both passages include or imply (A), (C), (D), and (E).

Passage 3

14. **D** The author says that war and change have been inevitably linked in America, and that war has been a vital force in the rise of capitalism, but he does *not* say that war is inevitable. All of the other answers are supported by the passage: (A)—lines 65–79; (B)—lines 14–16; (C)—lines 17–29; (E)—lines 65–71.

15. **B** See lines 14–21. Radioactive isotopes used in treating cancer are an example of a positive advance caused by preparations for war. On the other hand, lethal nerve gases (A), in addition to being a German and not an American development, did not lead to positive peacetime uses. (C), (D), and (E), while possibly effects of wars that have changed America, did not "yield results which are tonic to advancement."

16. **D** See lines 22–28. (C) is incorrect; the author states that this is a result of the Civil War. (E) is a statement supported by the passage, but is not the

primary reason for World War I's importance. (A) and (B) are not supported by information in the passage.

17. **A** In this paragraph the author paints a picture of, and indicates some of the reasons for, the "isolation, insularity, and exceptionalism" of America before World War I. The paragraph does define "American Religion" (B), but this is too limited an answer to describe the paragraph's main point. (C) and (E) are not covered in this paragraph. There is no contrast drawn between Civil War America and World War I America (D).

18. **B** See lines 35–46. (A) is incorrect; the grand tour is cited as an example that sophisticated Americans saw a trip to Europe as necessary to overcome insularity and complete an education. No social comment is made about its availability only to the rich. (D) is also incorrect; Puritanism is cited in paragraph four, but not in the context indicated in this answer, i.e., the sin and corruption of the world. (E) might seem correct at first, but the passage does not state that America was in fact superior to Europe; it comments on the *view* that Americans had of their country. (C) is irrelevant; this point is not made in relation to America's insularity.

19. **C** After the first paragraph introduces the idea of war as a force of change, the passage is devoted to the importance of World War I in changing American society. (B) is incorrect; paragraph one concerns some of the benefits of war, but this is not the main topic of the passage; it is an underlying idea. (A) is also incorrect; the passage mentions the Civil War briefly but is mostly concerned with World War I. (D) and (E) are

points touched on in the passage, but neither is the main subject.

20. **E** War as a force for change (the topic of paragraph one) is a general idea that introduces the passage's main subject of World War I. It is not a "popular view" that is refuted in the passage (A), nor does the passage ask a question (B). The first paragraph doesn't outline the contents of the passage (C), nor does it set up the first of four examples (D).

21. **B** "Ecstatic nationalism" is part of what Tocqueville called "American Religion." It would not increase in Europe after World War I. (A) can be inferred because Europe was seen as a necessity in a young man's education. (California would have been considered the Wild West.) The inference in (C) is supported by lines 71–79; (D), by lines 8–14, (E), by lines 47–56.

Passage 4

22. **B** (B) is the best answer because most of the passage is devoted to this description of the development of the universe; the description is then explicitly identified as the big bang theory. (A), (D), and (E) are all accurate statements according to the passage, but they are each a secondary point, not the main idea.

23. **A** See lines 22–33. All the other answers are factually inaccurate according to the passage.

24. **B** This sequence is presented in lines 16–41. (A) and (E) are closest to the correct answer, but each reverses two items in the sequence. (A) reverses stars and gas clouds; (E) reverses planets and heavy metals.

25. **D** Up until lines 52–55 the passage presents a narrative of the evolution of the universe. Lines 52–55 change

the direction of the passage because they summarize the methods by which data have been gathered. The second-best answer is (C), because these lines make a future prediction. However, the shift is not as notable as it is in (D), and the future prediction is not developed.

26. **E** There is no indication in the passage that only our solar system could have evolved as the universe expanded. All the other answers are supported by information in the passage. For (A), see lines 37–41; nuclear reactions in stars produced the heavy metals that formed planets. For (B), see lines 16–26. The passage states that helium and deuterium formed early, before the universe had cooled enough for atomic nuclei to capture electrons. For (C), see lines 55–61. Since modern telescopes give us a view of galaxies billions of light years away, we are now seeing the universe in its early stages. For (D), see lines 22–33. Atomic nuclei were unable to capture electrons until the universe had cooled; without electrons, neutral atoms could not have been formed, and the stars as we know them would not have evolved.

27. **B** Although the big bang *theory* is being described, the information in paragraphs one through three is presented as fact. No mention of theory (A) is made until paragraph five.

28. **C** See lines 47–51. Although (A) may appear to be correct, the author indicates only that up until now the big bang theory seems to be borne out by the data. There is no indication that absolute proof will soon be available. (B), (D), and (E) are not supported by any information in the passage.

9

MODEL TEST THREE

This chapter contains full-length Model Test Three. It is geared to the format of the LSAT, and it is complete with answers and explanations. It is equivalent to the LSAT in question structure, number of questions, level of difficulty, and time allotments. (The questions used are not taken directly from the LSAT, as those questions are copyrighted and may not be reproduced.)

Model Test Three should be taken under strict test conditions. The test ends with a 35-minute Writing Sample, which is not scored.

Section	Description	Number of Questions	Time Allowed
I.	Reading Comprehension	28	35 minutes
II.	Analytical Reasoning	24	35 minutes
III.	Logical Reasoning	26	35 minutes
IV.	Reading Comprehension	28	35 minutes
V.	Logical Reasoning	25	35 minutes
	Writing Sample		35 minutes
TOTALS:		131	3 hours 30 minutes

Now please turn to the next page, remove your answer sheet, and begin Model Test Three.

ANSWER SHEET—MODEL TEST THREE

Section 1	Section 2	Section 3	Section 4	Section 5
1. Ⓐ Ⓑ Ⓒ Ⓓ Ⓔ	1. Ⓐ Ⓑ Ⓒ Ⓓ Ⓔ	1. Ⓐ Ⓑ Ⓒ Ⓓ Ⓔ	1. Ⓐ Ⓑ Ⓒ Ⓓ Ⓔ	1. Ⓐ Ⓑ Ⓒ Ⓓ Ⓔ
2. Ⓐ Ⓑ Ⓒ Ⓓ Ⓔ	2. Ⓐ Ⓑ Ⓒ Ⓓ Ⓔ	2. Ⓐ Ⓑ Ⓒ Ⓓ Ⓔ	2. Ⓐ Ⓑ Ⓒ Ⓓ Ⓔ	2. Ⓐ Ⓑ Ⓒ Ⓓ Ⓔ
3. Ⓐ Ⓑ Ⓒ Ⓓ Ⓔ	3. Ⓐ Ⓑ Ⓒ Ⓓ Ⓔ	3. Ⓐ Ⓑ Ⓒ Ⓓ Ⓔ	3. Ⓐ Ⓑ Ⓒ Ⓓ Ⓔ	3. Ⓐ Ⓑ Ⓒ Ⓓ Ⓔ
4. Ⓐ Ⓑ Ⓒ Ⓓ Ⓔ	4. Ⓐ Ⓑ Ⓒ Ⓓ Ⓔ	4. Ⓐ Ⓑ Ⓒ Ⓓ Ⓔ	4. Ⓐ Ⓑ Ⓒ Ⓓ Ⓔ	4. Ⓐ Ⓑ Ⓒ Ⓓ Ⓔ
5. Ⓐ Ⓑ Ⓒ Ⓓ Ⓔ	5. Ⓐ Ⓑ Ⓒ Ⓓ Ⓔ	5. Ⓐ Ⓑ Ⓒ Ⓓ Ⓔ	5. Ⓐ Ⓑ Ⓒ Ⓓ Ⓔ	5. Ⓐ Ⓑ Ⓒ Ⓓ Ⓔ
6. Ⓐ Ⓑ Ⓒ Ⓓ Ⓔ	6. Ⓐ Ⓑ Ⓒ Ⓓ Ⓔ	6. Ⓐ Ⓑ Ⓒ Ⓓ Ⓔ	6. Ⓐ Ⓑ Ⓒ Ⓓ Ⓔ	6. Ⓐ Ⓑ Ⓒ Ⓓ Ⓔ
7. Ⓐ Ⓑ Ⓒ Ⓓ Ⓔ	7. Ⓐ Ⓑ Ⓒ Ⓓ Ⓔ	7. Ⓐ Ⓑ Ⓒ Ⓓ Ⓔ	7. Ⓐ Ⓑ Ⓒ Ⓓ Ⓔ	7. Ⓐ Ⓑ Ⓒ Ⓓ Ⓔ
8. Ⓐ Ⓑ Ⓒ Ⓓ Ⓔ	8. Ⓐ Ⓑ Ⓒ Ⓓ Ⓔ	8. Ⓐ Ⓑ Ⓒ Ⓓ Ⓔ	8. Ⓐ Ⓑ Ⓒ Ⓓ Ⓔ	8. Ⓐ Ⓑ Ⓒ Ⓓ Ⓔ
9. Ⓐ Ⓑ Ⓒ Ⓓ Ⓔ	9. Ⓐ Ⓑ Ⓒ Ⓓ Ⓔ	9. Ⓐ Ⓑ Ⓒ Ⓓ Ⓔ	9. Ⓐ Ⓑ Ⓒ Ⓓ Ⓔ	9. Ⓐ Ⓑ Ⓒ Ⓓ Ⓔ
10. Ⓐ Ⓑ Ⓒ Ⓓ Ⓔ	10. Ⓐ Ⓑ Ⓒ Ⓓ Ⓔ	10. Ⓐ Ⓑ Ⓒ Ⓓ Ⓔ	10. Ⓐ Ⓑ Ⓒ Ⓓ Ⓔ	10. Ⓐ Ⓑ Ⓒ Ⓓ Ⓔ
11. Ⓐ Ⓑ Ⓒ Ⓓ Ⓔ	11. Ⓐ Ⓑ Ⓒ Ⓓ Ⓔ	11. Ⓐ Ⓑ Ⓒ Ⓓ Ⓔ	11. Ⓐ Ⓑ Ⓒ Ⓓ Ⓔ	11. Ⓐ Ⓑ Ⓒ Ⓓ Ⓔ
12. Ⓐ Ⓑ Ⓒ Ⓓ Ⓔ	12. Ⓐ Ⓑ Ⓒ Ⓓ Ⓔ	12. Ⓐ Ⓑ Ⓒ Ⓓ Ⓔ	12. Ⓐ Ⓑ Ⓒ Ⓓ Ⓔ	12. Ⓐ Ⓑ Ⓒ Ⓓ Ⓔ
13. Ⓐ Ⓑ Ⓒ Ⓓ Ⓔ	13. Ⓐ Ⓑ Ⓒ Ⓓ Ⓔ	13. Ⓐ Ⓑ Ⓒ Ⓓ Ⓔ	13. Ⓐ Ⓑ Ⓒ Ⓓ Ⓔ	13. Ⓐ Ⓑ Ⓒ Ⓓ Ⓔ
14. Ⓐ Ⓑ Ⓒ Ⓓ Ⓔ	14. Ⓐ Ⓑ Ⓒ Ⓓ Ⓔ	14. Ⓐ Ⓑ Ⓒ Ⓓ Ⓔ	14. Ⓐ Ⓑ Ⓒ Ⓓ Ⓔ	14. Ⓐ Ⓑ Ⓒ Ⓓ Ⓔ
15. Ⓐ Ⓑ Ⓒ Ⓓ Ⓔ	15. Ⓐ Ⓑ Ⓒ Ⓓ Ⓔ	15. Ⓐ Ⓑ Ⓒ Ⓓ Ⓔ	15. Ⓐ Ⓑ Ⓒ Ⓓ Ⓔ	15. Ⓐ Ⓑ Ⓒ Ⓓ Ⓔ
16. Ⓐ Ⓑ Ⓒ Ⓓ Ⓔ	16. Ⓐ Ⓑ Ⓒ Ⓓ Ⓔ	16. Ⓐ Ⓑ Ⓒ Ⓓ Ⓔ	16. Ⓐ Ⓑ Ⓒ Ⓓ Ⓔ	16. Ⓐ Ⓑ Ⓒ Ⓓ Ⓔ
17. Ⓐ Ⓑ Ⓒ Ⓓ Ⓔ	17. Ⓐ Ⓑ Ⓒ Ⓓ Ⓔ	17. Ⓐ Ⓑ Ⓒ Ⓓ Ⓔ	17. Ⓐ Ⓑ Ⓒ Ⓓ Ⓔ	17. Ⓐ Ⓑ Ⓒ Ⓓ Ⓔ
18. Ⓐ Ⓑ Ⓒ Ⓓ Ⓔ	18. Ⓐ Ⓑ Ⓒ Ⓓ Ⓔ	18. Ⓐ Ⓑ Ⓒ Ⓓ Ⓔ	18. Ⓐ Ⓑ Ⓒ Ⓓ Ⓔ	18. Ⓐ Ⓑ Ⓒ Ⓓ Ⓔ
19. Ⓐ Ⓑ Ⓒ Ⓓ Ⓔ	19. Ⓐ Ⓑ Ⓒ Ⓓ Ⓔ	19. Ⓐ Ⓑ Ⓒ Ⓓ Ⓔ	19. Ⓐ Ⓑ Ⓒ Ⓓ Ⓔ	19. Ⓐ Ⓑ Ⓒ Ⓓ Ⓔ
20. Ⓐ Ⓑ Ⓒ Ⓓ Ⓔ	20. Ⓐ Ⓑ Ⓒ Ⓓ Ⓔ	20. Ⓐ Ⓑ Ⓒ Ⓓ Ⓔ	20. Ⓐ Ⓑ Ⓒ Ⓓ Ⓔ	20. Ⓐ Ⓑ Ⓒ Ⓓ Ⓔ
21. Ⓐ Ⓑ Ⓒ Ⓓ Ⓔ	21. Ⓐ Ⓑ Ⓒ Ⓓ Ⓔ	21. Ⓐ Ⓑ Ⓒ Ⓓ Ⓔ	21. Ⓐ Ⓑ Ⓒ Ⓓ Ⓔ	21. Ⓐ Ⓑ Ⓒ Ⓓ Ⓔ
22. Ⓐ Ⓑ Ⓒ Ⓓ Ⓔ	22. Ⓐ Ⓑ Ⓒ Ⓓ Ⓔ	22. Ⓐ Ⓑ Ⓒ Ⓓ Ⓔ	22. Ⓐ Ⓑ Ⓒ Ⓓ Ⓔ	22. Ⓐ Ⓑ Ⓒ Ⓓ Ⓔ
23. Ⓐ Ⓑ Ⓒ Ⓓ Ⓔ	23. Ⓐ Ⓑ Ⓒ Ⓓ Ⓔ	23. Ⓐ Ⓑ Ⓒ Ⓓ Ⓔ	23. Ⓐ Ⓑ Ⓒ Ⓓ Ⓔ	23. Ⓐ Ⓑ Ⓒ Ⓓ Ⓔ
24. Ⓐ Ⓑ Ⓒ Ⓓ Ⓔ	24. Ⓐ Ⓑ Ⓒ Ⓓ Ⓔ	24. Ⓐ Ⓑ Ⓒ Ⓓ Ⓔ	24. Ⓐ Ⓑ Ⓒ Ⓓ Ⓔ	24. Ⓐ Ⓑ Ⓒ Ⓓ Ⓔ
25. Ⓐ Ⓑ Ⓒ Ⓓ Ⓔ	25. Ⓐ Ⓑ Ⓒ Ⓓ Ⓔ	25. Ⓐ Ⓑ Ⓒ Ⓓ Ⓔ	25. Ⓐ Ⓑ Ⓒ Ⓓ Ⓔ	25. Ⓐ Ⓑ Ⓒ Ⓓ Ⓔ
26. Ⓐ Ⓑ Ⓒ Ⓓ Ⓔ	26. Ⓐ Ⓑ Ⓒ Ⓓ Ⓔ	26. Ⓐ Ⓑ Ⓒ Ⓓ Ⓔ	26. Ⓐ Ⓑ Ⓒ Ⓓ Ⓔ	26. Ⓐ Ⓑ Ⓒ Ⓓ Ⓔ
27. Ⓐ Ⓑ Ⓒ Ⓓ Ⓔ	27. Ⓐ Ⓑ Ⓒ Ⓓ Ⓔ	27. Ⓐ Ⓑ Ⓒ Ⓓ Ⓔ	27. Ⓐ Ⓑ Ⓒ Ⓓ Ⓔ	27. Ⓐ Ⓑ Ⓒ Ⓓ Ⓔ
28. Ⓐ Ⓑ Ⓒ Ⓓ Ⓔ	28. Ⓐ Ⓑ Ⓒ Ⓓ Ⓔ	28. Ⓐ Ⓑ Ⓒ Ⓓ Ⓔ	28. Ⓐ Ⓑ Ⓒ Ⓓ Ⓔ	28. Ⓐ Ⓑ Ⓒ Ⓓ Ⓔ
29. Ⓐ Ⓑ Ⓒ Ⓓ Ⓔ	29. Ⓐ Ⓑ Ⓒ Ⓓ Ⓔ	29. Ⓐ Ⓑ Ⓒ Ⓓ Ⓔ	29. Ⓐ Ⓑ Ⓒ Ⓓ Ⓔ	29. Ⓐ Ⓑ Ⓒ Ⓓ Ⓔ
30. Ⓐ Ⓑ Ⓒ Ⓓ Ⓔ	30. Ⓐ Ⓑ Ⓒ Ⓓ Ⓔ	30. Ⓐ Ⓑ Ⓒ Ⓓ Ⓔ	30. Ⓐ Ⓑ Ⓒ Ⓓ Ⓔ	30. Ⓐ Ⓑ Ⓒ Ⓓ Ⓔ

✂ To remove, cut along dotted rule.

SECTION I

Directions: Read the passages and answer the questions following each passage by blackening the appropriate space on the answer sheet. You may refer back to the passages when answering the questions. Answer all questions on the basis of what is stated or implied.

The Constitution of the United States protects both property rights and freedom of speech. At times these rights conflict. Resolution then requires
(5) a determination as to the type of property involved. If the property is private and not open to the general public, the owner may absolutely deny the exercise of the right of free speech
(10) thereon. On the other hand, if public land is at issue, the First Amendment protections of expression are applicable. However, the exercise of free speech thereon is not absolute.
(15) Rather it is necessary to determine the appropriateness of the forum. This requires that consideration be given to a number of factors including: character and normal use of the
(20) property, the extent to which it is open to the public, and the number and types of persons who frequent it. If the forum is clearly public or clearly private, the resolution of the greater of
(25) rights is relatively straightforward.

In the area of quasi-public property, balancing these rights has produced a dilemma. This is the situation when a private owner permits the general
(30) public to use his property. When persons seek to use the land for passing out handbills or picketing, how is a conflict between property rights and freedom of expression resolved?
(35)   The precept that a private property owner surrenders his rights in

proportion to the extent to which he opens up his property to the public is not new. In 1675, Lord Chief Justice
(40) Hale wrote that when private property is "affected with a public interest, it ceases to be private." Throughout the development of Anglo-American law, the individual has never possessed
(45) absolute dominion over property. Land becomes clothed with a public interest when the owner devotes his property to a use in which the public has an interest. In support of this position the
(50) chairman of the board of the Wilde Lake Shopping Center in Columbia, Maryland said:

> The only real purpose and justification of any of these centers
> (55) is to serve the people in the area— not the merchants, not the architects, not the developers. The success or failure of a regional shopping center will be measured
> (60) by what it does for the people it seeks to serve.

These doctrines should be applied when accommodation must be made between a shopping center owner's
(65) private property rights and the public's right to free expression. It is hoped that when the Court is asked to balance these conflicting rights it will keep in mind what Justice Black said in 1945:
(70) "When we balance the Constitutional rights of owners of property against

those of the people to enjoy (First Amendment) freedom(s) . . . we remain mindful of the fact that the
(75) latter occupy a preferred position."

1. In which one of the following cases would the owner of the property probably be most free to restrict the freedom of speech?

    (A) an amusement park attended by five million people each year owned by a multinational company
    (B) a small grocery store owned by a husband and wife
    (C) an enclosed shopping mall owned by a single woman
    (D) a fenced public garden and park owned by a small town
    (E) an eight-unit residential apartment building owned by a large real estate company

2. A conflict between property rights and freedom of speech might arise in all of the following situations, EXCEPT:

    (A) protesters carrying signs outside a cinema in an enclosed shopping mall
    (B) a disgruntled employee passing out leaflets in front of a hairdresser's salon
    (C) a religious order soliciting funds and converts in the swimming pool area of a condominium
    (D) a candidate for mayor handing out flyers in front of his opponent's headquarters
    (E) environmentalists carrying signs at the entrance to an oil refinery

3. According to the passage, an owner's freedom to deny freedom of speech on his property is determined by all of the following EXCEPT:

    (A) whether or not the land is open to the public
    (B) the nature of and the usual use of the property
    (C) the type of person who frequents the land
    (D) the nature of character of the owner
    (E) how many people use the property

4. We can infer from the passage that the author believes that shopping malls in America

    (A) should be in the service of the people who frequent them
    (B) have a right to prohibit distribution of advertising handbills
    (C) have a right to prohibit the distribution of religious printed matter
    (D) have a right to control any distributed materials
    (E) should permit any charitable solicitations

5. According to the passage, the idea that a property owner's rights decline as the property is more used by the general public

    (A) is peculiar to recent Supreme Court decisions
    (B) is attested to by a 300-year-old opinion
    (C) conflicts with the idea that property affected with a public interest ceases to be private
    (D) is in accord with the idea that ownership confers absolute dominion
    (E) is now universally accepted in Great Britain and in Canada

6. All other things being equal, the courts must favor

(A) First Amendment rights over property rights
(B) Fourth Amendment rights over property rights
(C) property rights over First Amendment rights
(D) property rights and First Amendment rights equally
(E) property rights and Fourth Amendment rights equally

When completing *David Copperfield,* Dickens experienced a powerful aftereffect that left him confused about "whether to laugh or to cry . . .
(5) strangely divided . . . between sorrow and joy." He felt that he had been turned inside out, his inner life now visible, in partly disguised forms, in the shadowy world of ordinary daylight.
(10) The story he had written was so deeply personal that "no one can believe [it] in the reading, more than I have believed it in the writing." Having transformed his private memories and his emotional
(15) life into a public myth about himself, particularly his development from an abandoned child into a great popular artist surrounded by love and success, he felt the excitement both of exposure
(20) and catharsis. Exorcising the wounds of childhood and young adulthood, he also dramatized the unresolved problems of his personality and his marriage, anticipating the turmoil that
(25) was to come. Though energized by the process of writing, he was also exhausted by "heaps of Copperfieldian blots," by that "tremendous paroxysm of Copperfield." Towards the end, he
(30) felt "rigid with Copperfield . . . from head to foot." When he finally put down his pen in October 1850, he took

up his "idea of wandering somewhere for a day or two." Almost inevitably, he
(35) went back "to Rochester . . . where I was a small boy."

In *David Copperfield* he re-created in mythic terms his relationship with his mother, his father, his siblings,
(40) particularly Fanny, and with his wife and his wife's sisters. The novel was more precious to him than his own children because the favorite child was himself. Soon after beginning, he
(45) confessed that he had stuck to that fictional name through the exploration of alternative titles because he had, even at the earliest stage, recognized that he was writing a book about
(50) himself.

His passion for names also expressed his need to pattern and control. After the birth of Katie in 1839, he assumed the right to name all his
(55) children (Catherine had "little or nothing to say" about that). The elaborate christening of Alfred D'Orsay Tennyson Dickens provides the representative example of the novelist
(60) imposing his literary constructs on other people's lives as well as his own. When it came to his family, he did not admit of any distinction. When it came to his novels, the distinction between
(65) self and other was subordinated to the dramatization of the many varieties of the single self. Changing Charles Dickens into David Copperfield had the force both of unconscious reversal and
(70) of minimal autobiographical distancing. At the heart of the novel was a partly mediated version of himself that represented his effort to claim that he had come through, that all was well
(75) with him as he approached the age of forty.

7. Which one of the following best expresses the main idea of the passage?

(A) The creation of *David Copperfield* was, for Dickens, a painful, wrenching experience.

(B) While writing *David Copperfield*, Dickens put his novel above everything else, including his children.

(C) In creating *David Copperfield*, Dickens transformed his memories and feelings into a public myth about himself.

(D) In addition to being auto-biographical, *David Copperfield* is a prophetic novel.

(E) *David Copperfield*, in addition to being Dickens' most auto-biographical novel, is also his greatest masterpiece.

8. The author's primary intention in this passage is to

(A) provide a psychological study of Dickens' motivations for writing *David Copperfield* and suggest a basis for evaluating the novel

(B) create a picture of Dickens as a writer burdened by childhood memories and contrast this with his public image

(C) show the connection between Dickens as a self-centered husband and father and as a literary genius

(D) present Dickens' reactions to writing *David Copperfield* and comment on the novel's relationship to his life and personality

(E) describe Dickens as he finished *David Copperfield* and show how that novel became a turning point in his career

9. The purpose of the last sentence of paragraph one (lines 34–36) is to

(A) show Dickens' complete exhaustion after finishing *David Copperfield*

(B) emphasize the connection between Dickens' writing of *David Copperfield* and his own childhood memories

(C) indicate Dickens' emotional response to writing *David Copperfield* and his inability to separate reality from fiction

(D) inform the reader of Dickens' actual origins as opposed to the fictional origins created in *David Copperfield*

(E) show that in finishing *David Copperfield* Dickens had finally exorcised the traumas of his childhood

10. Which one of the following can be inferred about Charles Dickens' life from information presented in the passage?

(A) His marriage would end badly.

(B) His most successful works were heavily autobiographical.

(C) He was a distant, uncaring father.

(D) His relationship with his sister Fanny had been significant to him.

(E) Because of the problems in his childhood, he was a man driven by the need for public success.

11. According to the passage, the title of *David Copperfield* is most significant because it

(A) demonstrates Dickens' view of the protagonist as a version of himself

(B) with the unconscious reversal of initials, shows Dickens' inability to come to terms with his life

(C) demonstrates Dickens' need to pattern and control his experience

(D) is a prime example of Dickens' passion for names

(E) represents both Dickens seeing the protagonist as himself and playing a game with the reader

12. The primary effect of lines 53–56—"After the birth of Katie in 1839, he assumed the right to name all his children (Catherine had 'little to say' about that")—is to

(A) suggest that Catherine Dickens was an inadequate mother

(B) indicate that Dickens' creativity with names extended to his family

(C) show that Dickens tended to confuse art with life

(D) suggest the relationship between Dickens and Catherine

(E) indicate that Dickens put his work over his family life

13. Which one of the following best describes the author's tone in the passage?

(A) cool and ironic

(B) argumentative and sarcastic

(C) detached and condescending

(D) intimate and persuasive

(E) objective and analytical

14. Which one of the following best describes the structure of the passage?

(A) Paragraph 1 focuses on Dickens' reactions to writing *David Copperfield,* while paragraph 2 includes more of the author's comments and ties in related points.

(B) Paragraph 1 recounts Dickens' problems in writing *David Copperfield,* while paragraph 2 describes his creative solutions and his reactions to the work.

(C) Paragraph 1 presents Dickens' opinions of *David Copperfield,* while paragraph 2 provides the author's critique and relates the book to Dickens' other works.

(D) Paragraph 1 describes Dickens' relationship to his novels, while paragraph 2 describes his relationship to his family.

(E) Paragraph 1 shows the effect of his childhood on Dickens, while paragraph 2 describes his later life and its effect on his novels.

Passage A

The Corporation for Public Broadcasting (CPB) was created by the U.S. Congress in 1967 as part of President Lyndon B. Johnson's
(5) mission to create a "Great Society." Johnson said, as he signed the bill into law, "Public television will help make our nation a replica of the old Greek marketplace, where public affairs took
(10) place in view of all citizens."

After the creation of the CPB, existing educational stations and their umbrella organization, National Educational Television, were affiliated
(15) into a membership organization, the Public Broadcasting System (PBS). To clarify, the Corporation for Public Broadcasting, as distinguished from the Public Broadcasting System, is a
(20) private corporation, funded by the federal government, that does not produce or distribute programs itself. PBS, on the other hand, is a private, nonprofit media enterprise owned and
(25) operated by member stations. Currently, there are about 350 PBS stations in the United States.

Congress appropriates funds for the CPB, which uses 95 percent of the
(30) money to strengthen PBS's technical infrastructure and develop

programming. The 1967 Public Broadcasting Act called for public broadcasting to take "creative risks," (35) "address the needs of unserved and underserved audiences," and "encourage the growth of non-broadcast telecommunications technologies." The biggest single (40) source of funds for PBS is individual membership (thus, the many pledge drives on PBS) and contributions by "Friends of..." groups.

The United States was actually late (45) in establishing public broadcasting. It was already well established in other countries. In England, the British Broadcasting Corporation (BBC) took control of television in 1932. It is still (50) supported primarily by television household license fees. Other countries, such as Denmark, France, Japan, the Netherlands, Sweden, and Switzerland support their public (55) broadcasting similarly. In Germany, commercial broadcasters underwrite public broadcasting by paying special fees. It should be noted that federal governments in Australia, Canada, (60) and Britain provide generous subsidies for their public broadcasting—a much greater percentage of their gross national product (GNP) than the United States (65) provides of its GNP.

A few of the many goals of public broadcasting are programming that is available throughout the country; programming that caters to a wide (70) variety of interests and tastes and addresses all citizens, including minorities; and programming that is free from commercialism, vested interests, and government control. In (75) addition, quality and impartiality are prime concerns of public broadcasting.

Passage B

Public television in the United States is in trouble. Between 1993 and 2003, PBS memberships declined by (80) 20 percent, and fewer members means fewer viewers. The question is "Why?" One obvious reason is that viewers have more and more choices. In the 1980s, cable television (85) blossomed, which meant more diversified and specialized programming than had been available on the major commercial networks. Cable news networks cut into the PBS (90) news and public affairs franchise, certain "niche" networks offered competition to PBS's cultural and performance programming, and PBS's well-received children's programming (95) went up against competitors such as the Disney Channel, Nickelodeon, and the Cartoon Network. The public, since the advent of cable, has been flooded with viewing opportunities. According (100) to some critics, the quality and innovation on some cable channels are noteworthy. Generally, PBS has been unable to keep up.

Part of the reason is that PBS, which (105) receives funding from viewers but also from the federal government, has been under attack by both conservatives and liberals. In 2005, $100 million was slashed from the PBS budget. PBS's (110) programming was deemed to be slanted to the left by many of those voting for the cut. The money was later restored, but the criticism continued. Actions by the chairman of (115) the Corporation for Public Broadcasting then angered the liberals. The issue of PBS's neutrality, or lack of it, has become a hot button among both conservatives and liberals. (120) Because of funding problems and loss of members, PBS has been

unable to create many new, different programs, which further erodes viewership. To avoid cuts and
(125) shortfalls, it has also been forced to accept what amounts to watered-down commercials from corporate interests, and endless pledge drives that tend to feature bland
(130) programming or "specials" that have been shown too many times. According to polls, most people agree that we need public television, that it is a good thing in a free society. There
(135) is less agreement, however, on how to cure the patient without sacrificing the original noble intentions of its founders.

15. The main purpose of Passage A is to

(A) briefly explain the government's role in U.S. public television
(B) contrast public broadcasting in the United States with public broadcasting in England
(C) emphasize the importance of public television in the United States.
(D) criticize the method of funding PBS
(E) briefly explain the origin and organization of public television in the United States.

16. The main purpose of Passage B is to

(A) set forth some reasons for the problems facing PBS
(B) criticize the method of funding PBS
(C) explain why PBS is accepting commercial messages
(D) predict the demise of public television in the United States.
(E) answer the arguments of politicians who criticize PBS

17. The author of Passage B would be most likely to argue that the goals for public television set forth in the last paragraph of Passage A have been most hindered by

(A) PBS's lack of creativity
(B) programming that focuses on children more than adults
(C) the effect of political controversy on funding
(D) limited distribution of programs
(E) management issues at the Corporation for Public Broadcasting

18. Which of the following most accurately states the tone of Passage A and the tone of Passage B?

(A) Passage A is generally objective, whereas Passage B includes some negative judgments.
(B) Passage A is optimistic about public television, whereas Passage B is pessimistic.
(C) While the author of Passage A is mildly critical, the author of Passage B is harshly critical.
(D) Both authors are neutral and objective.
(E) Passage A praises public television, while Passage B questions its importance.

19. According to Passage A, the Corporation for Public Broadcasting (CPB)

(A) is the main source of funding for PBS
(B) is based on the model of the British Broadcasting Corporation
(C) distributes programs created for PBS
(D) is funded by Congress

(E) uses 95 percent of its money to promote public broadcasting

20. In Passage B, which of the following is cited as an obvious reason for declining membership in PBS?

(A) a conservative bias
(B) a liberal bias
(C) more choices for viewers
(D) bland programming
(E) too many pledge drives

21. In line 91 of Passage B, the best definition of the word "niche" is

(A) small
(B) specialized
(C) non-profit
(D) recessed
(E) restricted

22. In Passage A, all of the following are mentioned as ways that countries fund public broadcasting EXCEPT:

(A) government subsidies
(B) government trust funds
(C) viewer membership
(D) household license fees
(E) fees from commercial broadcasters

Taxonomy, the science of classifying and ordering organisms, has an undeserved reputation as a harmless, and mindless, activity of listing,
(5) cataloguing, and describing—consider the common idea of a birdwatcher, up at 5:30 in the morning with binoculars, short pants, and "life list" of every bird he has seen. Even among scientists,
(10) taxonomy is often treated as "stamp collecting." It was not always so. During the eighteenth and early nineteenth centuries, taxonomy was in the forefront of the sciences. The

(15) greatest biologists of Europe were professional taxonomists—Linnaeus, Cuvier, Lamarck. Darwin's major activity during the twenty years separating his Malthusian insights
(20) from the publication of his evolutionary theory was a three-volume work on the taxonomy of barnacles. Thomas Jefferson took time out from the affairs of state to publish one of the great
(25) taxonomic errors in the history of paleontology—he described a giant sloth claw as a lion's three times the size of Africa's version. These heady days were marked by discovery as
(30) naturalists collected the fauna and flora of previously uncharted regions. They were also marked by the emergence of intellectual structure, as coherent classifications seemed to mirror the
(35) order of God's thought.
    America played its part in this great epoch of natural history. We often forget that 150 years ago much of our continent was as unknown and
(40) potentially hazardous as any place on earth. During the eighteenth century, when most naturalists denied the possibility of extinction, explorers expected to find mammoths and other
(45) formidable fossil creatures alive in the American West. There are a number of passionate, single-minded iconoclasts who fought the hostility of the wilderness, and often of urban literary
(50) people, to disclose the rich fauna and flora of America. For the most part, they worked alone, with small support from patrons or government. The Lewis and Clark expedition is an
(55) exception—and its primary purpose was not natural history. We may now look upon tales of frontier toughness and perseverance as the necessary mythology of a nation too young to
(60) have real legends. But there is often a

residue of truth in such tales, and
naturalists are among the genuine
pioneers.

   Alexander Wilson walked from New
(65) England to Charleston peddling
subscriptions to his *American
Ornithology.* Thomas Nuttall—
oblivious to danger, a Parsifal under a
lucky star, vanquishing every Klingsor
(70) in the woods, discovered some of the
rarest, most beautiful, and most useful
of American plants. J. J. Audubon
drank his way across Europe selling his
beautiful pictures of birds to lords and
(75) kings. John Lawson, captured by
Tuscarora Indians, met the following
fate according to an eyewitness: "They
struck him full of fine small, splinters
or torchwoods like hog's bristles and
(80) so set them gradually afire." David
Douglas fell into a pit trap for wild
cattle and was stomped to death by
a bull.

23. According to the passage, taxonomy
was considered to be an important
science from about

   (A) 1700 to 1800
   (B) 1700 to 1830
   (C) 1700 to 1950
   (D) 1800 to 1930
   (E) 1818 to 1918

24. As they are used in the first paragraph
(line 30), "flora and fauna" refer to

   (A) lands and waters
   (B) botanists and zoologists
   (C) plants and animals
   (D) cataloging and describing
   (E) mythology and folklore

25. We can infer from the passage that

   (A) taxonomy was favorably regarded
   in the sixteenth and seventeenth
   centuries
   (B) taxonomy was invented in the
   eighteenth century
   (C) the number of kinds of barnacles is
   very large
   (D) Lamarck and Linnaeus were
   amateur scientists
   (E) most of the world's plants have
   already been classified

26. The relation of the third paragraph to
the rest of the passage may be best
described as

   (A) a comic contrast to the seriousness
   of the first two paragraphs
   (B) specific examples of the pioneers
   mentioned in the second paragraph
   (C) examples of American taxonomists
   to set against the exclusively
   European names of the first
   paragraph
   (D) real taxonomists of the western
   United States as opposed to the
   legendary figures of the second
   paragraph
   (E) examples of the tall tales of the
   frontier days

27. In the third paragraph, Parsifal and
Klingsor were probably a

   (A) hunter and his prey
   (B) German taxonomist and his subject
   of study
   (C) knight and his enemy
   (D) a colonizer and the colonized
   (E) a mythical animal and its master

28. This passage is best described as a(n)

    (A) description of the modern bias
        against taxonomy
    (B) comparison of nineteenth-century
        and twentieth-century scientists
    (C) account of famous American
        naturalists
    (D) history and defense of taxonomy
    (E) argument for the renewed study of
        the classification of organisms

STOP

IF YOU FINISH BEFORE TIME IS UP, CHECK YOUR WORK ON THIS SECTION OF THE TEST ONLY.
DO NOT GO ON TO THE NEXT SECTION OF THE TEST UNTIL TIME IS UP FOR THIS SECTION.

SECTION II

Time — 35 minutes
24 Questions

Directions: In this section you will be given groups of questions based on different sets of conditions. Drawing a simple diagram may be helpful in answering some of the questions. You are to choose the best answer and mark the corresponding space on your answer sheet.

Questions 1–6

A radio station will play eight songs during its "Winners" hour. Each song will be played once. The eight songs represent the following types of music: Jazz, Rock, and Country, with at least two songs of each type. The following restrictions are placed on the order and type of songs:

> All the jazz songs are played consecutively.
> No two rock songs are played consecutively.
> No two country songs are played consecutively.
> A rock song must be played before a jazz song is played.
> There are more jazz songs than country songs.

1. If four jazz songs are played and the first and last songs are of the same type, which one of the following must be true?

   (A) A jazz song is played second.
   (B) A jazz song is played third.
   (C) A rock song is played seventh.
   (D) A rock song is played eighth.
   (E) A country song is played first.

2. If three rock songs are played and a country song is played sixth, which one of the following CANNOT be true?

   (A) A jazz song is played second.
   (B) A rock song is played fifth.
   (C) A rock song is played first.
   (D) A country song is played last.
   (E) A country song is played first.

3. If a jazz song is played third, and the first and last songs are of the same type, which one of the following CANNOT be true?

   (A) A jazz song is sixth.
   (B) A country song is sixth.
   (C) A country song is first.
   (D) A rock song is second.
   (E) A rock song is seventh.

4. If all the jazz songs are played last, how many different arrangements of song types are possible?

   (A) one
   (B) two
   (C) three
   (D) four
   (E) five

5. If a country song is played first and seventh, which one of the following must be true?

   (A) A country song is sixth.
   (B) A jazz song is sixth.
   (C) A country song is third.
   (D) A jazz song is second.
   (E) A jazz song is third.

6. If a single classical song is added to the play list (making nine songs in all) and it is to be played fourth and a country song is to be played fifth, which one of the following must be true?

   (A) A jazz song is sixth.
   (B) A jazz song is last.
   (C) A rock song is second.
   (D) A rock song is third.
   (E) A country song is last.

Questions 7–13

Seven students—George, Hal, Ken, Jon, Neil, Lynn, and Melanie—are playing a game involving play money. The only bills used are play dollar bills. No coins are used.

   Jon has more bills than Lynn, Melanie, and Neil combined.
   The total of Lynn's and Melanie's bills are equal to Neil's bills.
   Melanie has more bills than Ken and George combined.
   Hal has fewer bills than George.
   Ken and George have the same number of bills.

7. Which one of the following students has the most bills?

   (A) Ken
   (B) George
   (C) Jon
   (D) Lynn
   (E) Melanie

8. Which one of the following students has the fewest bills?

   (A) Melanie
   (B) Neil
   (C) George
   (D) Ken
   (E) Hal

9. Which one of the following must be true?

   (A) Melanie has fewer bills than Ken.
   (B) Neil has more bills than Lynn.
   (C) Lynn has fewer bills than Melanie.
   (D) Lynn has more bills than George.
   (E) George has more bills than Melanie.

10. Assume that Ken is given one bill from Hal. Assume also that Melanie has more bills than Ken, George, and Lynn combined. If none of the students has the same number of bills, which one of the following is a possible order from highest to lowest of students who have the most bills?

   (A) Jon, Melanie, Lynn, Neil, Ken, George, Hal
   (B) Jon, Neil, Melanie, Lynn, George, Ken, Hal
   (C) Neil, Jon, Melanie, George, Ken, Hal, Lynn
   (D) Jon, Neil, Ken, Melanie, George, Lynn, Hal
   (E) Jon, Neil, Melanie, Ken, George, Hal, Lynn

11. Assume that Lynn does not have the same number of bills as Ken. Which one of the following must be false?

   (A) Lynn has the same number of bills as Hal.
   (B) Neil has twice as many bills as Melanie.
   (C) George has more bills than Hal and Lynn combined.
   (D) George does not have the same number of bills as Lynn.
   (E) Jon has fewer than twice the number of Lynn's and Melanie's bills combined.

12. If Lynn and Melanie have the same number of bills, then which one of the following must be false?

   (A) Neil has more bills than Melanie.
   (B) Melanie has more bills than Ken, George, and Hal combined.
   (C) George has fewer bills than Hal and Ken combined.
   (D) Neil has fewer bills than Lynn, George, and Hal combined.
   (E) Jon has more bills than Lynn, Ken, George, and Hal combined.

13. Assume that Tom decides to join the game. Assume also that he is given bills from the bank. If his total number of bills are more than Ken's and fewer than Lynn's, which one of the following must be true?

   (A) Melanie has fewer bills than Tom.
   (B) Tom has fewer bills than George.
   (C) Lynn has fewer bills than Melanie.
   (D) Melanie and Lynn have the same number of bills.
   (E) Lynn has more bills than Hal.

Questions 14–20

At the snack bar at a party, Alli, Boris, Cisco, and Dan are eating cookies. There are five kinds of cookies to choose from—chocolate chip cookies, oatmeal cookies, sugar cookies, peanut butter cookies, and raisin cookies. Each of these four people eat at least two kinds of cookies. Their choices are governed by the following rules:

   At most two of them eat oatmeal cookies.
   At least two of them eat sugar cookies.
   Alli does not eat any sugar cookies.
   Boris and Cisco do not eat the same type of cookie.
   Boris eats chocolate chip cookies.
   Cisco eats sugar cookies.
   No one eats both raisin cookies and sugar cookies.
   If someone eats raisin cookies, they also eat peanut butter cookies.

14. Which one of the following must be true?

   (A) Cisco eats chocolate chip cookies.
   (B) Alli eats chocolate chip cookies.
   (C) Boris does not eat peanut butter cookies.
   (D) Dan does not eat raisin cookies.
   (E) Alli does not eat peanut butter cookies.

15. If Boris eats exactly three kinds of cookies, which one of the following must be true?

   (A) Cisco eats exactly three kinds of cookies.
   (B) Dan eats only sugar cookies.
   (C) If Alli eats oatmeal cookies, Dan eats oatmeal cookies.
   (D) Boris eats oatmeal cookies.
   (E) Cisco eats oatmeal cookies.

16. Which one of the following CANNOT be true?

   (A) No one eats raisin cookies.
   (B) Alli and Dan both eat oatmeal cookies.
   (C) Alli and Dan both eat chocolate chip cookies.
   (D) Boris and Cisco eat the same number of kinds of cookies.
   (E) Dan does not eat raisin cookies.

17. Which pair of cookie types could each be eaten by at least three different people?

(A) chocolate chip and oatmeal
(B) oatmeal and peanut butter
(C) chocolate chip and peanut butter
(D) oatmeal and sugar
(E) sugar and raisin

18. Which pair of cookie types contains a cookie type eaten by exactly two different people?

    (A) chocolate chip and oatmeal
    (B) oatmeal and peanut butter
    (C) chocolate chip and peanut butter
    (D) oatmeal and raisin
    (E) sugar and raisin

19. If Alli does not eat chocolate chip or raisin cookies, which one of the following could be true?

    (A) Dan eats oatmeal cookies.
    (B) More people eat chocolate chip cookies than sugar cookies.
    (C) Only one person eats peanut butter cookies.
    (D) Cisco does not eat peanut butter cookies.
    (E) Boris eats sugar cookies.

20. Which cookie type could be eaten by none of the people?

    (A) chocolate chip
    (B) oatmeal
    (C) sugar
    (D) peanut butter
    (E) raisin

Questions 21–24

The National Domino League is planning to expand by adding one more team. All of the players for the new team will be chosen from the existing teams. Each team must make three players eligible to be chosen for the new team.

(1) The players eligible to be chosen from Team 1 are A, B, and C.
(2) The players eligible to be chosen from Team 2 are D, E, and F.
(3) The players eligible to be chosen from Team 3 are G, H, and K.
(4) The new team must choose two players from each of the three teams.
(5) B refuses to play with D.
(6) If C is chosen, then K must be chosen.
(7) G and H refuse to play together.

21. If A is not chosen, then how many members of the new team are determined?

    (A) two
    (B) three
    (C) four
    (D) five
    (E) six

22. If D is chosen, then which one of the following groups of three players could NOT be chosen?

    (A) A, G, K
    (B) B, C, G
    (C) C, E, K
    (D) A, E, G
    (E) E, H, K

23. Which one of the following is (are) true?

    (A) C must be chosen.
    (B) If A is chosen, then F must be chosen.
    (C) If B is chosen, then E must be chosen.
    (D) E must be chosen.
    (E) If G is chosen, then K is not chosen.

24. In addition to facts (1), (2), (3), and
(4), which of the facts lead(s) to the
conclusion that K must be chosen?

(A) (5)
(B) (6)
(C) (7)
(D) (6) and (7)
(E) (5), (6), and (7)

STOP

IF YOU FINISH BEFORE TIME IS UP, CHECK YOUR WORK ON THIS SECTION OF THE TEST ONLY.
DO NOT GO ON TO THE NEXT SECTION OF THE TEST UNTIL TIME IS UP FOR THIS SECTION.

SECTION III

Directions: In this section you will be given brief statements or passages and will be required to evaluate the reasoning involved. In some instances, more than one choice will appear to be a possible answer. You are to choose the *best* answer. Use common sense and reasonableness in making your selection; then mark the proper space on the answer sheet.

1. *Mr. Kent:* Recent studies show that reduction in the maximum speed limit from 65 mph to 55 mph substantially reduces the number of highway fatalities.

   The preceding statement would be most weakened by establishing that

   (A) most fatal car accidents occur at night
   (B) most accidents occurring at speeds between 45 and 55 mph are nonfatal
   (C) few fatal accidents involve only one vehicle
   (D) prior to this reduction, 97 percent of fatal accidents occurred below 45 mph
   (E) prior to the reduction, 97 percent of fatal accidents occurred between 55 and 65 mph

2. A recent poll indicates that 75 percent of all investors have lost money in their brokerage accounts since the beginning of the year. However, when asked whether they were motivated to switch accounts to another brokerage, more than 85 percent of those polled responded that they would be staying with their present brokerage.

   Each of the following, if true, helps to resolve the paradox mentioned above EXCEPT:

   (A) the recent downturn in the economy explains many of the economic losses
   (B) investors are generally a conservative lot who are reluctant to change
   (C) the costs of switching brokerages are nominal
   (D) that, although many have lost money in this fiscal year, the losses have not been as extreme as losses incurred in previous years
   (E) most investors who were polled make their own investment decisions rather than relying on the advice of their brokers

3. Daniel Webster said, "Falsehoods not only disagree with truths, but usually quarrel among themselves."

   Which one of these would follow from Webster's statement?

   (A) Quarreling is endemic to American political life.
   (B) Truth and falsehood can be distinguished from one another.
   (C) Liars often quarrel with each other.
   (D) Those who know the truth are normally silent.
   (E) Truth and falsehood are emotional, rather than intellectual, phenomena.

4. A recording industry celebrity observed: "I am not a star because all my songs are hits; all my songs are hits because I am a star."

Which one of the following most nearly parallels this reasoning?

(A) A college professor noted: "I am the final word in the classroom not because my judgment is always correct, but my judgment in the classroom is always correct because I am the instructor."

(B) A nurse observed: "I am not competent in my duties because I am a nurse, but I am competent in my duties because of my training in nursing."

(C) A dance instructor noted: "I am not the instructor because I know all there is about dance; rather I am an instructor because of my ability to teach dancing."

(D) A recording industry celebrity observed: "I am not wealthy because I am a star; I am wealthy because so many people buy my recordings."

(E) A recording industry celebrity observed: "I am not a star because my every song is enjoyed; I am a star because people pay to watch me perform."

5. *Economist:* As a rule, the price of gasoline at the pump increases when the oil refineries in the United States are operating at below 75 percent of capacity. If the unrest in the Middle East continues, the shipment of oil to the United States will decline and refineries here will have to operate at 60 percent of capacity for at least six months.

If the statements above are correct, which one of the following is the most likely conclusion?

(A) Imports from oil-producing areas other than the Middle East are likely to increase next year.

(B) A sudden resolution of tensions in the Middle East will have little or no effect on the price of gasoline.

(C) Oil prices decline only when refineries in the United States operate at more than 75 percent of their capacity.

(D) The rise or fall in gasoline prices is determined by supply and demand and not by political events.

(E) It is likely that prices of gasoline in the United States will increase in the next year.

6. If a speaker were highly credible, would an objectively irrelevant personal characteristic of the speaker influence the effectiveness of her communication? For example, if a Nobel prize-winning chemist were speaking on inorganic chemistry, would she induce a lesser change in the opinions of an audience if she were known to be a poor cook? Would the speaker's effectiveness be different if she were obese rather than trim, sloppy rather than neat, ugly rather than attractive?

By failing to consider irrelevant aspects of communicator credibility, studies in communication science have unknowingly implied that audiences are composed of individuals who are responsive only to objectively relevant aspects of a speaker.

Which one of the following represent(s) assumptions upon which the foregoing passage is based?

(A) Audiences are composed of people who are responsive only to objectively relevant aspects of a communicator.
(B) Objectively irrelevant personal characteristics have a bearing on a speaker's effectiveness.
(C) Some characteristics of a communicator are of greater relevance than others.
(D) A trim speaker is likely to be more persuasive than an obese one.
(E) Irrelevant aspects of a communication have more effect on an audience than the content of a speech.

Questions 7–8

I read with interest the statements of eminent archaeologists that the presence of a crude snare in an early Neolithic grave indicates that man of this period subsisted by snaring small mammals. I find this assertion open to question. How do I know the companions of the deceased did not toss the snare into the grave with the corpse because it had proved to be totally useless?

7. The author employs which one of the following as a method of questioning the archaeologists' claims?

(A) evidence that contradicts the conclusion drawn by the archaeologists
(B) a doubtful tone about the motives of the archaeologists
(C) a body of knowledge inconsistent with that employed by the archaeologists

(D) an alternative to the conclusion drawn by the archaeologists
(E) the suggestion that archaeological studies are of little use

8. Which one of the following best expresses the author's criticism of the archaeologists whose statements he questions?

(A) They have not subjected their conclusions to scientific verification.
(B) They have stressed one explanation and ignored others.
(C) They have drawn a conclusion that does not fit the evidence upon which it was based.
(D) They failed to employ proper scientific methods in arriving at their conclusion.
(E) They have based their conclusion on behaviors exhibited by more modern humans.

9. *Editorial:* A previously undisclosed transcript has revealed that Richard Nixon's secret White House slush fund that was used to silence the Watergate burglars came from illegally donated campaign money. After Nixon resigned, his successor, Gerald Ford, pardoned him. The same Gerald Ford has joined Presidents Carter and Bush in urging campaign funding reforms. Recent hearings have shown all too clearly that both parties have been guilty of highly questionable fund-raising practices. Unless the laws are changed, the shoddy practices of the last thirty years will undoubtedly continue.

Which one of the following most accurately states the main point of the argument?

(A) It is hypocritical of Gerald Ford to urge campaign reform after his pardon of Richard Nixon.
(B) Both the Democrats and the Republicans have been guilty of unethical campaign fund-raising practices.
(C) The laws governing campaign fund-raising must be reformed.
(D) Reform of campaign fund-raising has been supported by former presidents of both parties.
(E) We cannot expect that those who benefit from a problem will wish to take steps to solve it.

10. *Bill:* Professor Smith has been late for class almost every morning.
   Dave: That can't be true; he was on time yesterday.

   Dave apparently believes that Bill has said which one of the following?

   (A) Professor Smith is seldom late.
   (B) Professor Smith does not enjoy teaching.
   (C) Professor Smith has been late every day without exception.
   (D) Professor Smith was late yesterday.
   (E) Professor Smith informs Bill of his whereabouts.

11. Sunbathers do not usually spend much time in the shade. Shade prevails during most of June in La Jolla. It is June 14.

   Which one of the following conclusions would be logically defensible, based upon the foregoing premises?

(A) La Jolla is the site of frequent sunbathing.
(B) The sun is not shining today.
(C) There are sunbathers in La Jolla today.
(D) There may be sunbathers in La Jolla today.
(E) There are more sunbathers in La Jolla in July than in June.

12. *Political Theorist:* Although American politicians disagree about many things, none of them disagrees with Wendell Willkie's assertion that "the Constitution does not provide for first- and second-class citizens."

   Willkie's statement implies that

(A) the Constitution provides for third- and fourth-class citizens
(B) first-class citizens don't need to be provided for
(C) there is no such thing as a second-class citizen
(D) the Constitution makes no class distinctions
(E) no citizens can be first and second class simultaneously

13. There are 500 students in the school. In the fall semester, 30 were in the glee club, 30 were members of the debating society, and 40 were on the staff of the school newspaper. In the spring semester, all three of these activities had twice as many participants. Thus, in the course of the school year, all but 200 of the 500 students in the school participated in these extracurricular activities.

All of the following can be used to question the conclusion of this passage EXCEPT:

(A) some students participated in more than one activity in the fall semester

(B) some students participated in an activity in more than one semester

(C) some students participated in activities in only the fall semester

(D) some students never participated in activities

(E) some students participated in more than one activity in both semesters

14. Nothing can come of nothing; nothing can go back to nothing.

Which one of the following follows most logically from the above statement?

(A) Something can come out of something; something can go back to something.

(B) Something can come out of nothing; something can go back to nothing.

(C) Nothing can come out of something; nothing can go back to something.

(D) Something must come out of something; something must go back to something.

(E) Something must come out of something; nothing can go back to nothing.

15. The president has vowed in speeches across the country that there will be no increase in taxes and no reduction in defense; he has repeatedly challenged Congress to narrow the deficit through deeper spending cuts. Congressional critics have responded with labored comparisons between a bloated Pentagon and the nation's poor being lacerated by merciless budget cutters. In Democratic cloakrooms, laments about the "intolerable deficit" are code words for higher taxes.

Which one of the following additions to the passage would make clear the author's position on the budget issue?

(A) Everyone agrees that the president's budget deficit of around 100 billion is highly undesirable, to say the least.

(B) Everyone agrees that the president's budget deficit is both undesirable and unavoidable.

(C) Everyone agrees that this will be a summer of hot debate in Congress over the president's budget proposal.

(D) Everyone agrees that the partisan disagreement over the president's budget proposal will be won by those who create the most persuasive terminology.

(E) Everyone agrees that the president's budget proposal is a product of careful, honest, but sometimes misguided analysis.

16. *The average wage in this plant comes to exactly $7.87 per working day.* In this statement *average* has the strict mathematical sense. It is the quotient obtained by dividing the sum of all wages for a given period by the product of the number of workers and the number of days in the period.

Which one of the following is the most logical implication of the passage above?

(A) More workers in the plant earn $7.87 per day than those who do not earn $7.87 per day.

(B) Any particular worker in the plant receives $7.87 per day.

(C) There must be workers in the plant who earn far more than $7.87 per day.

(D) If some workers in the plant earn more than $7.87 per day, there must be others in the plant who earn less than $7.87 per day.

(E) There must be workers in the plant who earn exactly $7.87 per day.

17. *Magazine article:* Davy "Sugar" Jinkins is one of the finest boxers to have ever fought. Last week Davy announced his retirement from the ring, but not from the sport. Davy will continue in boxing as the trainer of "Boom Boom" Jones. With Jinkins handling him, we are sure that Boom Boom will become a title contender in no time.

The foregoing article is based upon all of the following assumptions EXCEPT:

(A) boxers who have a good trainer can do well

(B) those who were good boxers can be fine trainers

(C) Jones is capable of being trained

(D) title contenders should be well trained

(E) Jinkins did well as a boxer

18. You can solve a problem. You cannot solve a dilemma, for it requires a choice between two disagreeable alternatives.

All of the following exemplify a dilemma EXCEPT:

(A) Amleth must avenge his father's death by killing his assassins. He must also protect his mother who was one of the murderers.

(B) the zoo has one vacant enclosure that is suitable for the exhibition of hyenas or lesser kudus. Hyenas prey upon kudus. The zoo will lose a federal grant if it fails to exhibit both kinds of animals.

(C) Ames must relocate his business in Belmont or Arlington. Office rentals are much more expensive in Belmont; office locations in Arlington are inconvenient for customers.

(D) to have enough meat to feed the four guests I must buy two pounds of beef. But one pound of beef costs two dollars and I have only three dollars.

(E) I must park my car on Ash or Maple Street and go to the market. If I park on Ash Street, I will probably get a parking ticket; if I park on Maple Street, my radio will probably be stolen.

19. The stores are always crowded on holidays. The stores are not crowded; therefore, it must not be a holiday.

Which one of the following most closely parallels the kind of reasoning used in the above sentences?

(A) The stores are always crowded on Christmas. The stores are crowded; therefore, it must be Christmas.

(B) Reptiles are present on a hot day in the desert. Reptiles are absent in this desert area; therefore, this cannot be a hot desert day.

(C) There is a causal relationship between the occurrence of holidays and the number of people in stores.

(D) The voting places are empty; therefore, it is not an election day.

(E) The stores are always empty on Tuesdays. It is Tuesday; therefore, the stores will be empty.

Questions 20–21

For one to be assured of success in politics, one must have a sound experiential background, be a polished orator, and possess great wealth. Should an individual lack any one of these attributes, he most certainly will be considered a dark horse in any campaign for public office. Should an individual be without any two of these attributes, he cannot win an election. If Nelson Nerd is to win the presidency, he must greatly improve his ability as a public speaker. His extraordinary wealth is not enough.

20. The author of the above passage appears to believe that

   (A) Nerd is the wealthiest candidate
   (B) Nerd is a sufficiently experienced politician
   (C) being a good public speaker alone can win one a high public office
   (D) if Nerd's public speaking improves, he will win the presidency
   (E) Nerd is not a dark horse now

21. Which one of the following would most weaken the speaker's claims?

   (A) Many successful politicians are born into poor families.
   (B) The incumbent president had little relevant experience before coming into office and has always been a poor public speaker.
   (C) Of the individuals elected to public office, 0.001 percent have lacked either oratory skill, experience, or money.
   (D) Nerd failed in his last bid for the presidency.
   (E) The incumbent president, who is running for reelection, is as wealthy as Nerd.

22. Tom is test driving a blue car. After driving for a short while he comes to the following conclusion: Since this car is blue, it must not accelerate quickly.

   The foregoing conclusion can be properly drawn if it is also known that

   (A) all red cars accelerate quickly
   (B) there are some slow blue cars
   (C) all blue cars may not accelerate slowly
   (D) all cars that accelerate quickly are red
   (E) all slow cars are red

Questions 23–24

As almost everyone is painfully aware, the federal government has butted into almost every sector of human existence in recent years. But this manic intrusiveness isn't always the government's fault. Sometimes there is a compulsion to enlist Uncle Sam as a "superbusybody."

23. Which one of the following is one of the author's basic assumptions?

   (A) Most of his readers have suffered government intrusion.
   (B) All government intrusion is unwarranted.
   (C) Government intrusion is always government-initiated.
   (D) All memories of government intrusion are painful memories.
   (E) At no time has the federal government practiced nonintrusiveness.

24. Which one of the following most nearly restates the final sentence?

   (A) Most of the time government is responsible for government intrusion.

(B) Sometimes government does more than intrude; it compels intrusion.

(C) Sometimes Uncle Sam himself enlists in the ranks of the intruders.

(D) Uncle Sam has a compulsion to intervene because he is a super-busybody.

(E) Sometimes the government itself is not responsible for government intrusion.

---

25. Those who dictate what we can and cannot see on television are guilty of falsely equating knowledge with action. They would have us believe that to view violent behavior is to commit it.

On the basis of the content of the above passage, we may infer that the author would believe which one of the following?

(A) Knowing how to manufacture nuclear weapons leads to nuclear war.

(B) Those guilty of committing a crime were not necessarily influenced by an awareness that similar crimes had occurred.

(C) Media censorship is based upon logical justification.

(D) Knowledge of an act compels a person to perform that act.

(E) Knowledge is the basis of all action.

26. In 1975, the U.S. Supreme Court ruled that the federal government has exclusive rights to any oil and gas resources on the Atlantic Outer Shelf beyond the three-mile limit.

Which one of the following must be true in order for this ruling to be logical?

(A) The U.S. Supreme Court has met recently.

(B) The Atlantic Outer Shelf may possibly contain oil and gas resources.

(C) No oil and gas resources exist within the three-mile limit.

(D) In 1977, the Court reversed this ruling.

(E) Oil and gas on the Atlantic Shelf has not been explored for in the past three years.

STOP

IF YOU FINISH BEFORE TIME IS UP, CHECK YOUR WORK ON THIS SECTION OF THE TEST ONLY.
DO NOT GO ON TO THE NEXT SECTION OF THE TEST UNTIL TIME IS UP FOR THIS SECTION.

SECTION IV

Time — 35 minutes
28 Questions

Directions: Read the passages and answer the questions following each passage by blackening the appropriate space on the answer sheet. You may refer back to the passages when answering the questions. Answer all questions on the basis of what is stated or implied.

The Constitution gives the Congress power to make the laws that determine the election of senators and representatives. At first Congress (5) exercised its power to supervise apportionment by simply specifying in the statutes how many representatives each state was to have. From 1842 until the 1920s, it went further and (10) required that the districts be relatively compact (not scattered areas) and relatively equal in voting population.

Major shifts in population occurred in the twentieth century: large numbers of (15) farmers could no longer maintain small farms and moved to the cities to find employment; rapidly growing industries, organized in factory systems, attracted rural workers; and (20) many blacks who could no longer find work in southern agriculture moved to the North to get better jobs and get away from strict Jim Crow living conditions. The rural areas of the (25) country became more sparsely populated while the city populations swelled.

As these changes were occurring, Congress took less interest in its (30) reapportionment power, and after 1929 did not reenact the requirements. In 1946, voters in Illinois asked the Supreme Court to remedy the serious malapportionment of their state (35) congressional districts. Justice Frankfurter, writing for the Court,

said the federal courts should stay out of "this political thicket." Reapportionment was a "political (40) question" outside the jurisdiction of these courts. Following this holding, malapportionment grew more severe and widespread in the United States.

In the Warren Court era, voters again (45) asked the Court to pass on issues concerning the size and shape of electoral districts, partly out of desperation because no other branch of government offered relief, and partly (50) out of hope that the Court would reexamine old decisions in this area as it had in others, looking at basic constitutional principles in the light of modern living conditions. Once again (55) the Court had to work through the problem of separation of powers, which had stood in the way of court action concerning representation. In this area, too, the Court's rulings were (60) greeted by some as shockingly radical departures from "the American way," while others saw them as a reversion to the democratic processes established by the Constitution, applied (65) to an urbanized setting.

1. The primary purpose of the passage is to

   (A) criticize public apathy concerning apportionment
   (B) describe in general the history of political apportionment

(C) argue for the power of the Supreme Court

(D) describe the role of the Warren Court in political apportionment

(E) stress that reapportionment is essentially a congressional concern

2. The author implies which one of the following opinions about federal supervision of apportionment?

(A) Federal supervision is unnecessary.

(B) Federal supervision is necessary.

(C) Apportionment should be regulated by the Court.

(D) Apportionment should be regulated by Congress.

(E) Court rulings on apportionment violate "the American way."

3. In the third paragraph, "malapportionment" refers to the

(A) influx of farmers into the city

(B) Jim Crow phenomenon

(C) shift from rural to urban populations

(D) distribution of voters in Illinois

(E) unfair size and shape of congressional districts

4. We may infer that during the Warren Court era

(A) the most dissatisfied voters lived in cities

(B) the constituency was dissatisfied

(C) the separation of powers became important for the first time

(D) the public turned its attention away from issues of apportionment

(E) a ballot issue concerning electoral apportionment passed

5. The passage answers which one of the following questions?

(A) Does the Constitution delegate authority for supervising apportionment?

(B) Do population shifts intensify racism?

(C) Should the Constitution still be consulted, even though times have changed?

(D) Why did the Warren Court agree to undertake the issue of representation?

(E) How did the Warren Court rule on the separation of powers issue?

6. We may conclude that Justice Frankfurter was

(A) a member of the Warren Court

(B) not a member of the Warren Court

(C) opposed to reapportionment

(D) skeptical about the separation of powers

(E) too attached to outmoded interpretations of the Constitution

7. In the passage the author is primarily concerned with

(A) summarizing history

(B) provoking a controversy

(C) suggesting a new attitude

(D) reevaluating old decisions

(E) challenging constitutional principles

Primitive humans knew intuitively that there was a world of the spirit, and that intuitive knowledge progressed and expanded into the history of many (5) religious movements. While the majority of humans probably have never given up their belief in a world of the spirit, the success of scientific materialism encouraged the claim to a (10) universe that excluded everything but that which could be weighed, measured, or dissected. As children, not yet plagued by the knowledge of science, we all shared a common (15) heritage of humankind in the belief in the world that we could not see. But in time, the harshness of rational day's spotlight changed our "childlike" beliefs into the pejorative "childish," (20) and we ceased to believe or rather could no longer admit to ourselves that we did.

Not so with the young Irish poet, dramatist, and essayist William Butler (25) Yeats. Somehow he escaped the "rationalistic" strictures to which most thoroughly civilized people succumb. Born into a nation whose people were steeped in the traditions of prehistory, (30) in the lore of the faeries and the Druids, he remained free to believe. Much of his younger life, spent with his mother's people in Sligo, tended to enhance this belief. In his (35) autobiography, he recalls instances of supernatural forces at work upon his imagination. He awoke screaming from a dream one night insisting that his grandfather had been in a shipwreck, (40) which proved the next day to have been true. In his first close brush with death, when his brother Robert died, he said, "Next day at breakfast I heard people telling how my mother and the (45) servant had heard the banshee crying the night before he died."

It was during this period that many of the symbols of Irish mythology took hold of his mind, symbols that were to (50) recur throughout his poetic career, refined and enlarged, but in some measure the same. Such is the symbol of the tree, which perhaps had its genesis in the folktale of the Island of (55) Innisfree and was repeated over and over throughout his poems. The study of magic and the occult became a primary force in Yeats's life and such a part of him that to read his poetry we (60) must at least have an understanding of its meaning to him and the depth to which it affected everything he wrote.

For the reader, rather than becoming lost in the intricacies of Yeats's occult (65) practices, it may be more to the point to realize that all of the rituals involved are calling to a deep-seated capacity for reaction in all of us. Yeats sees the poet as a supernatural artist who enchants (70) his own mind when he would enchant the minds of others. He is conjuring up the imagination, but the imagination far more enlarged than that which we normally conceive, and he does this by (75) means of symbols. He says of them, "I cannot now think symbols less than the greatest of all powers whether they are used consciously by the masters of magic or half unconsciously by their (80) successors the poet, the musician, and the artist. . . . Whatever the passions of man have gathered about, becomes a symbol in the great memory." It is this great mind, and great memory, to (85) which Yeats is calling and which he insists can be evoked by symbols, whether from Celtic lore, the Upanishads, or the Noh plays, if they be appropriate. Yeats calls to us to (90) remember what we have not forgotten, an elemental force, a reality outside that of materialistic science. His hidden things embrace all that humans have forgotten to open their minds to, not in (95) past time or future time, but in that reality that knows no time.

8. The passage best supports which one of the following statements?

   (A) The great memory arises from the cultural history of individual nations.
   (B) To understand Yeats's writing, one is obliged to understand the specific occult and magic rituals he practiced in the context of the times.
   (C) One's acceptance of and belief in the lore of faeries and Druids is enhanced if one's environment is also accepting.
   (D) Imagination in writing is rationalistic, relying also on symbol and nonscientific reality.
   (E) Yeats's writing is rooted in mythology and consequently calls to the child in the adult and the adult in the child.

9. The organization of the passage is best described by which one of the following?

   (A) An author is introduced; the author's titles are discussed; generalities about humankind are drawn; suggestions are made concerning extrapolating an understanding of one kind of writing to aid in the understanding of other kinds of writing.
   (B) Symbols are defined; the use of symbols in a particular work is investigated; the great memory is connected to other authors' works; generalizations are made concerning the concept of time and the ideal.
   (C) Concepts about humanity are introduced; the same concepts are connected with an author's works and life; the author's attitude toward those concepts is explored.
   (D) Humanity's understanding of literary symbolism is defined; the author's understanding of such symbolism is discussed; symbolism in other works is investigated.
   (E) The history of mythological beliefs is outlined; the similarities of one mythology to other mythologies is considered; these mythologies are connected to the concept of the great memory.

10. Of the following statements, the passage best supports which one as compatible with Yeats's beliefs?

   (A) Although the rationalistic approach of science is essential in the modern world, it can be used only marginally in art, whereas mythology can be combined with it to produce a viable synthesis.
   (B) The symbolism of the tree is likely to evoke similar effects in readers from different areas of the world.
   (C) The Upanishads, Celtic lore, and the Noh plays were written in times when childlike beliefs were the norm among adults, not the exception as they are now.
   (D) The cry of the banshees is inevitably connected with the death of someone close to the person who hears them.
   (E) Magic and the occult have a place in materialistic science and could enhance people's understanding of and belief in that science.

11. Of the following titles, which one best describes the passage's content?

   (A) "Irish Mythology in the Writing of William Butler Yeats"
   (B) "Rationalism vs. Symbolic Reality"
   (C) "Childhood Belief and Adult Pragmatism: A Loss of Innocence"
   (D) "Mythology and the Occult in the Folktale of the Island of Innisfree"
   (E) "Yeats's Use of Mythology and Symbolism"

12. The author most likely mentions Celtic lore, the Upanishads, and the Noh plays for which one of the following reasons?

   (A) The three examples suggest that symbolism may be found in all cultures and that Yeats believed these symbols to be common to them.
   (B) Celtic lore is part of Yeats's literary base, while the Upanishads and the Noh plays come from other cultures, which would not use Celtic lore as part of their system of symbols.
   (C) Celtic lore is an example of a nonliterary tradition; the Upanishads illustrate religious writing; and the Noh plays combine both forms.
   (D) The three examples illustrate the "strictures to which most thoroughly civilized people succumb."
   (E) All three examples involve use of magic and the occult.

13. Of the following, according to the information in the passage, which statement is LEAST consistent with Yeats's life and beliefs?

   (A) Dreams involve symbols common to humankind.

   (B) Artists, poets, and musicians are aware of the power and magic of the symbols they use.
   (C) Childhood beliefs remain in the subconscious minds of adults.
   (D) Symbolism is based on emotion, not rational thought.
   (E) Civilized societies focus on the rational rather than the symbolic.

14. Which one of the following sentences would most logically begin a new paragraph following the third paragraph of the passage as given?

   (A) The innocuous ghosts and goblins of modern Halloween are much less threatening than those they are historically derived from.
   (B) Yeats became increasingly disillusioned with Irish politics.
   (C) Yeats died in 1939 in France, but he is buried in Ireland, in the land of his childhood, the land of the banshees and the faeries.
   (D) Yeats's interest in the occult survived into adulthood and affected even his choice of a marriage partner, Georgie Hyde-Lees, who was herself interested in automatic writing through what she called her "communicators."
   (E) If you are ten years old, you are alone, and it is night, you feel you are the only person in the world, and you believe in the world of the unseen.

Passage A

   The biting Dadaist critique of modern life cut across the whole development of formalizing abstract sculpture, bringing with it a new permissiveness.
(5) Objects out of the ordinary environment of modern man were selected and exhibited in the Dada

shows as works of art. Duchamp, with serene impudence, mocked serious
(10) artistic intention with chance selection of objects such as a bicycle wheel, bottle washer, urinal, corkscrew, and other ready-made commonplace things. These, André Breton called
(15) "manufactured objects promoted to the dignity of objects of art through the choice of the artist." For Duchamp, as for a generation of artists after him who were profoundly influenced by his
(20) art and especially his attitude, life and art were a matter of chance and arbitrary choice; the essence of the artistic act is willful selection, each act individual and unique. He said, "Your
(25) chance is not the same as mine, just as your throw of the dice will rarely be the same as mine." This philosophy of utter freedom for the artist is fundamental to the history of art in the
(30) twentieth century, and Duchamp can stand as perhaps the shrewdest and most perceptive theorist of the modern movement. The freedom he granted himself to set up a bicycle wheel (with
(35) its fork) on a kitchen stool, he granted to visitors in allowing them to spin the wheel as they chose.

The "ready-mades" of Duchamp led to "found objects" such as the random
(40) junk that Schwitters used in his *Merz Pictures;* the collages of cubism had pointed the way. Interest in found objects spread to the public, who began to collect oddments such as
(45) rocks, driftwood, and fragments of manufactured objects. A happy junction of two ordinary objects, never before appearing together in this way, makes up Picasso's *Bull's Head.* The
(50) never-failing ingenuity of this modern master turns the handle bars and seat of a bicycle into an image of a bull, beautifully stylized. The work, which

might seem only a clever trick,
(55) illustrates an important method in modern art—the unexpected unity that two objects can make when taken out of their usual context and brought into a radically new relationship. We have
(60) seen this phenomenon of new meanings arising out of uncommon juxtapositions in the case of the seemingly opposed caption and image in painting. Much of the pungency and
(65) surprise in modern painting and sculpture, its impact, is the result of such strenuous feats of conjunctive imagination.

Passage B
Dadaism was the product of the
(70) disillusionment, defeatism, and insane butchery of World War I. Anguished artists felt that the civilization that had brought about such horrors should be swept away and a new beginning
(75) made. To christen their movement, they chose at random a childish word out of the French dictionary—*dada*, a hobbyhorse.

Dadaism, consequently, was a
(80) nihilistic movement, particularly distrustful of order and reason, a challenge to polite society, a protest against all prevailing styles in art; it was, in fact, anti-art. Dada artists
(85) worked out an *ism* to end all isms, painted nonpictures compounded of the contents of wastebaskets, concocted nonsense for the sake of nonsense, wrote manifestos against
(90) manifestos, and their political expression was anarchy. Their bitter humor and iconoclasm, however, helped to explode hypocritical pomposities and, by reducing the role
(95) of art to absurdity, cleared the air of the postwar period.

The original Dadaism did not last long. It was soon absorbed into surrealism, which has aptly been (100) described as the "Dadaism of the successful." After half a century in limbo, however, the vocabulary was revived in the 1960s with a vengeance. The paraphernalia of Neodadaism still (105) comprises the same combinations of banality and the commonplace, the same assemblages of debris from attics and junkyards. Although Dadaism grew out of the disillusionment and despair (110) of a bankrupt society during World War I, Neodadaism is nurtured by a joyous acceptance of modern materialism and the techniques of mass media; whereas the former was a (115) desperately and deadly serious movement, the latter revels in nonsense for the sake of nonsense and laughs with the world, not at it.

As Robert Rauschenberg has (120) disarmingly remarked, he just wants to live in the world, not reform it. His pictures—*Tracer*, for example—are what he calls "combines" of trash objects placed in incongruous (125) juxtapositions. Because he uses actual automobile tires, umbrellas, bicycle wheels, and stuffed birds, his combines are often as much sculpture as paintings. Other Neodadaists of the (130) pop art persuasion who share Rauschenberg's enthusiasm for the trivia of everyday experience have worked up a passion for packaging, and found their poetry in the (135) supermarket by using soup cans, cola bottles, and the bright, crisp containers for detergents.

15. The purpose of both Passage A and Passage B can best be described as

(A) praising the artistic accomplishments of the Dada artists
(B) disputing the claim that the Dada movement is anti-art
(C) describing the horrors of the society that gave birth to Dada
(D) defining characteristics of Dada and noting its role in art history
(E) contrasting Dadaism with surrealism.

16. The authors of both passages would be most likely to agree with all of the following characteristics of Dada EXCEPT:

(A) the role of chance as opposed to serious intention
(B) a belief in art as a motivation for social reform
(C) an ability to join seemingly different objects imaginatively
(D) the validity of using manufactured objects in works of art
(E) a rejection of traditional approaches to art

17. From the tone and information in each passage, which of the following best expresses the authors' attitudes toward their subject?

(A) Although both authors agree that Dadaism cleared the air after World War I, the author of Passage A emphasizes more strongly how its concept of "utter freedom" is central to modern art.
(B) The author of Passage B views Dadaism as a minor artistic movement, whereas the author of Passage A sees it as the most

significant artistic movement in the first half of the twentieth century.

(C) The author of Passage A believes the work of Duchamp elevates Dadaism to a position above surrealism, but the author of Passage B sees Dadaism as ultimately a failed movement and surrealism as "Dadaism of the successful."

(D) Both artists recognize the achievements of individual artists such as Duchamp and Rauschenberg, but both believe the movement as a whole was a failure.

(E) Whereas the author of Passage A applauds the iconoclasm of Dada artists, the author of Passage B views it as bitter, shortsighted, and ultimately unproductive.

18. The most significant difference between Passage A and Passage B is described most accurately in which of the following statements?

(A) Passage A is more positive than Passage B.

(B) Passage B covers particular artists, whereas Passage A is a general overview.

(C) Passage B, unlike Passage A, covers the original Dada movement as well as the period that followed it.

(D) The author of Passage B favors Neodadaism, whereas the author of Passage A favors the earlier movement.

(E) Passage A describes the techniques the Dada artists used, whereas Passage B describes completed works.

19. In Passage A, Duchamp's allowing a visitor to spin the bicycle wheel of an artwork is an example of his

(A) nihilism
(B) rejection of conventional politeness
(C) belief in artistic freedom
(D) contempt for society
(E) elevation of ordinary objects

20. According to Passage B, which one of the following is the most significant difference between Dadaism and Neodadaism?

(A) Dadaism grew out of disillusionment, and Neodadaism grew out of optimism.

(B) Dada artists saw their movement as darkly serious and iconoclastic, whereas Neodadaist artists celebrated nonsense and materialism.

(C) Dadaism attracted classically trained artists, whereas Neodadaism was the result of amateurs who raided junk shops and attics.

(D) The artists of the Dada movement were active anarchists, whereas the Neodadaist artists were social reformers.

(E) Dadaism had a prominent spokesman in Duchamp, but no one was a spokesperson for Neodadaism.

21. According to the author of Passage B, surrealism as an artistic movement

(A) was less nihilistic than Dadaism and produced greater works of art

(B) absorbed elements of Dada and became more important than Dadaism

(C) was more influential but lasted for a shorter time than Dadaism

(D) was the predominant artistic movement of the 1960s

(E) championed materialism and mass media

22. The author of Passage B uses Robert Rauschenberg as an example of

(A) a surrealist

(B) a more important artist than Schwitters in Passage A

(C) the originator of the concept of found objects

(D) a descendant of Duchamp

(E) a pop art Neodadaist

The theory of natural selection cites the fact that every organism produces more gametes and/or organisms than can possibly survive. If every gamete
(5) produced by a given species united in fertilization and developed into offspring, the world would become so overcrowded in a short period of time that there would be no room for
(10) successive generations. This does not happen. There is a balance that is maintained in the reproduction of all species and therefore natural populations remain fairly stable, unless
(15) upset by a change in conditions. In the struggle for existence, some organisms die and the more hardy survive.

The differences that exist between
(20) organisms of the same species, making one more fit to survive than another, can be explained in terms of variations. Variations exist in every species and in every trait in members
(25) of a species. Therefore some organisms can compete more successfully than others for the available food or space in which to grow, or they can elude their enemies
(30) better. These variations are said to add

survival value to an organism. Survival value traits are passed on to the offspring by those individuals that live long enough to reproduce. As time
(35) goes on, these special adaptations for survival are perpetuated and new species evolve from a common ancestral species. The environment is the selecting agent in natural selection
(40) because it determines which variations are satisfactory for survival and which are not.

The major weakness in Darwin's theory of natural selection is that he did
(45) not explain the source, or genetic basis, for variations. He did not distinguish between variations that are hereditary and those that are nonhereditary, making the assumption
(50) that all variations that have survival value are passed on to the progeny. Like Jean Baptiste Lamarck, Darwin believed in the inheritance of even acquired characteristics.

(55)   Hugo De Vries (1845–1935), a Dutch botanist, explained variations in terms of mutations. His study of 50,000 plants belonging to the evening primrose species enabled him to
(60) identify changes in the plants that were passed on from parent to offspring. In 1901 De Vries offered his mutation theory to explain organic evolution. Today, we know that mutations are
(65) changes in genes that can come about spontaneously or can be induced by some mutagenic agent. Spontaneous mutation rates are very low, and mutations alone do not affect major
(70) changes in the frequencies of alleles, which are alternative forms of genes that occupy a given place on a chromosome.

An important cause of variation
(75) within species is genetic recombination that results from sexual reproduction.

The genes of two individuals are sorted out and recombined into a new combination, producing new traits—
(80) and thus variation.

Gene flow is also responsible for the development of variations. It is the movement of new genes into a population. Gene flow often acts
(85) against the effects of natural selection. Genetic drift is a change in a gene pool that takes place in a population as a result of chance. If a mutation occurs in a gene of one person, and that
(90) person does not reproduce, the gene is lost to the population. Sometimes a small population breaks off from a larger one. Within that population is a mutant gene, and because the mating
(95) within the small population is very close, the frequencies of the mutant gene will increase. In the Amish population, for example, where there is little or no outbreeding, an increase in
(100) the homozygosity of the genes in the gene pool is evinced in the high frequencies of genetic dwarfism and polydactyly (six fingers). The isolated smaller population has a different gene
(105) frequency than the larger population from which it came. This is known as the "founder principle." Genetic drift and the random mutations that increase or decrease as the result of
(110) genetic drift are known as non-Darwinian evolution.

Another cause of variation is speciation, or the forming of new species from a species already in
(115) existence. This can happen when a population becomes geographically divided and part of the original species continues life in a new habitat. The separated populations cannot
(120) interbreed. Over evolutionary time, different environments present different selective pressures, and the

change in gene pools will eventually produce new species.

23. The passage supports which one of the following statements?

(A) Spontaneous mutations cause the most significant evolutionary changes.
(B) Darwin's theory of evolution depends on rejecting the idea that acquired characteristics can be inherited.
(C) Variations among individual members of a species occur only when new genes move into an established population of that species.
(D) It is possible for a survival value trait to be eliminated from a species.
(E) New species are generally the result of genetic recombination.

24. Which one of the following, if true, would support the idea that acquired characteristics can be inherited?

(A) A spontaneous mutation causes some members of a rodent population to develop webbed feet. This segment of the population becomes isolated and is unable to breed with the original group. An exceptionally high frequency of webbed feet occurs in the successive generations of the isolated segment.
(B) A gene from a virus is experimentally transmitted to a fruit fly, making it vulnerable to carbon dioxide poison. This vulnerability is then passed on to the fruit fly's offspring.
(C) Antelopes raised in captivity are released into the wild. They run significantly more slowly than the

wild antelope. After a year, the released antelopes' speed equals that of the wild antelopes.

(D) A population of long-haired dogs is shaved and bred with a population of hairless dogs. Their offspring include more hairless than long-haired pups.

(E) Fourteen different species of finches live on the Galapagos Islands. It is determined that all descended from a single species of finch found on mainland Peru.

25. The passage provides explanations for each of the following EXCEPT:

(A) genetic drift
(B) the founder principle
(C) survival value
(D) speciation
(E) homozygosity

26. Random mutations are known as non-Darwinian evolution because they

(A) are not necessarily related to the survival value of an organism
(B) are more infrequent than spontaneous mutations
(C) tend to refute Darwin's theories about the formation of species
(D) occur only in small populations that have been isolated
(E) were first described by Hugo De Vries, not Charles Darwin

27. Based on the passage, which one of the following can be inferred about Charles Darwin?

(A) Darwin did not believe the theory of genetic inheritance.
(B) Darwin did not believe that genetic theories were relevant to evolution.
(C) Darwin's work was more concerned with the survival value of traits than with the mechanics of how they were inherited.
(D) Darwin's theories did not include a recognition that variation within members of a species was crucial to evolution.
(E) Darwin was more interested in traits that were acquired and passed on than he was in genetically inherited traits.

28. In the passage, the author's primary concern is to

(A) address briefly the history of evolutionary theory.
(B) provide a brief overview of the concept of variation.
(C) expose the weakness inherent in Darwin's evolutionary theory.
(D) differentiate between genetic and evolutionary theories.
(E) describe one of the ways in which nonadaptive traits can be inherited.

STOP

IF YOU FINISH BEFORE TIME IS UP, CHECK YOUR WORK ON THIS SECTION OF THE TEST ONLY.
DO NOT GO ON TO THE NEXT SECTION OF THE TEST UNTIL TIME IS UP FOR THIS SECTION.

SECTION V

Time — 35 minutes
25 Questions

Directions: In this section you will be given brief statements or passages and will be required to evaluate the reasoning involved. In some instances, more than one choice will appear to be a possible answer. You are to choose the _best_ answer. Use common sense and reasonableness in making your selection; then mark the proper space on the answer sheet.

Questions 1–2

By passing more and more regulations allegedly to protect the environment, the state is driving the manufacturing industry away. And when the employers leave, the workers will follow. The number of new no-growth or environmental rules passed each year is increasing by leaps and bounds. Rich environmentalists who think they are sympathetic to workers have no real sympathy for the blue-collar employees who are injured by their activities. One major manufacturer has been fined for failing to establish a car-pool plan. Another is accused of polluting the air with industrial emissions, although everyone knows that two thirds of the pollutants come from cars and trucks. No wonder the large manufacturers are moving to states with fewer restrictive laws. And as the manufacturers go, unemployment and the number of workers leaving the state will rise more rapidly than ever before.

1. The author's argument that strict environmental laws will eventually lead to loss of workers in the state will be most weakened if it can be shown that

(A) so far, the number of manufacturers who have left the state is small
(B) the unemployment rate has climbed steadily in the last three years

(C) most workers who leave the state give as their reason for leaving the poor environmental quality
(D) several other manufacturing states have strict environmental laws
(E) rich environmentalists are more powerful in many other states

2. Which one of the following is NOT an argument of this passage?

(A) Environmentalists are responsible for depriving workers of their jobs.
(B) When workers leave a state, it is a sign that manufacturers will follow.
(C) A car-pool law should not be enforced, as cars and trucks are responsible for most air pollution.
(D) Large manufacturers prefer states with fewer restrictions.
(E) A rise in unemployment will lead to an increase in workers leaving the state.

3. _Dick:_ There will be a disastrous rise in the temperatures on Earth unless we are able to reduce the carbon dioxide content of the atmosphere to the levels of the 1980s. The only way to do this is to reduce drastically our use of carboniferous fuels.

Harry: The fear of too much carbon dioxide in the atmosphere is unwarranted. Throughout geological time, the oceans have absorbed carbon dioxide from the atmosphere and precipitated it as limestone. Since the ocean waters are alkaline and contain large amounts of calcium and magnesium, they can control any excessive carbon dioxide in the atmosphere.

In replying to Dick, Harry does which one of the following?

(A) questions Dick's assumption that reducing the use of carboniferous fuels will reduce the amount of carbon dioxide in the atmosphere

(B) denies that the reduction of the use of carbon-producing fuel will reduce the likelihood of global warming

(C) asserts that the reduction of carbon dioxide in the atmosphere is not the only way to avoid global warming

(D) suggests that reducing the use of fuels that produce carbon dioxide is economically unfeasible

(E) challenges Dick's belief that the increasing amounts of carbon dioxide in the atmosphere are dangerous

4. Unlike most graduates of American high schools, all graduates of high schools in Bermuda have completed four years of advanced mathematics.

Which one of the following, if true, would best explain the situation described above?

(A) Math anxiety is higher in the United States than in Bermuda.

(B) There are far more high schools and high school students in the United States than in Bermuda.

(C) More students in America take full-time jobs without completing high school.

(D) Math programs in American high schools are frequently understaffed.

(E) High schools in Bermuda require four years of advanced mathematics for graduation.

5. Psychological novels are superior to novels of adventure. Immature readers prefer novels of adventure to novels with less action and greater psychological depth. The immature reader, who prefers James Bond's exploits to the subtleties of Henry James, can be identified easily by his choice of inferior reading matter.

A criticism of the logic of this argument would be likely to find fault with the author's

(A) presupposing the conclusion he wishes to prove

(B) failure to define "adventure" clearly

(C) failure to cite possible exceptions to this rule

(D) hasty generalization on the basis of a limited specific case

(E) inaccurate definitions of key terms

6. *Literary critic:* A good mystery novel should have three strengths: an interesting location, complex and engaging characters, and a plot that is unpredictable, but observes probability. If two of the three are especially good, the book may please many readers. In Kate Rudman's latest mystery story, the detective and the suspects are original and entertaining and the plot is full of surprises, but the book will probably disappoint most readers.

If the above is true, we can infer that

(A) it is too easy for a reader to solve the mystery before the detective can do so
(B) the setting is unrealized and the events of the book are hard to believe
(C) the solution depends on information that is unfairly concealed from the reader, and the setting is the same as that of Rudman's last novel
(D) the language of the book is unsuitable for children and, at the end, evil wins out over good
(E) most mystery readers are satisfied if a story has an interesting detective and a plot that is full of surprises

7. In professional athletics, the small number of record-setting performers in each thirty-year span is remarkably consistent. In hockey, for example, 5 percent of all the professional players were responsible for more than half of the new records, and 95 percent of the new records were set by only 8 percent of the players. Similar percentages were found in baseball, football, and basketball records, where the numbers of participants are much higher.

If the statements above are true, which one of the following conclusions may be most reasonably inferred?

(A) An increase in the number of athletic teams playing hockey, football, or baseball would significantly increase the number of record-setting performances.
(B) Reducing the number of athletic teams playing hockey, football, or baseball would not necessarily cause a decrease in the number of record-setting performances.
(C) Record-setting performances would increase if the number of amateur teams were increased.
(D) Many record-setting performances are not recorded by statisticians.
(E) As records become higher with the passage of time, fewer and fewer records will be broken.

8. By refusing to ban smoking in restaurants, the city council has put the financial well-being of restaurant owners above the health of the citizens of this city. No doubt the council would support the restaurateurs if they decided to use asbestos tablecloths and to barbecue using radioactivity. These devices would be no more risky.

The author of this paragraph makes her case by arguing

(A) from experience
(B) from example
(C) by authority
(D) from observation
(E) from analogy

9. The GOP's attempt to win the South has, however indirectly, played on the racial anxiety of white voters. It has produced a vocabulary of civility to conceal their opposition to school integration ("forced busing") and affirmative action ("quotas"). And, to the horror of regular Republicans, the party's candidate for senator in Louisiana is a neo-Nazi and Ku Klux Klan alumnus. The ease with which this candidate has merged his bigotry with a respectable conservative social agenda is frightening. There is, however, a ray of hope. The candidate is sup-ported by about 30 percent of the voters.

The passage above is structured to lead to which one of the following conclusions?

(A) If the candidate disavows his views, he will lose his support; but if he does not disavow them, he cannot gain any new supporters.
(B) And that 30 percent has grown from only 15 percent three weeks ago.
(C) We cannot predict now whether that percentage will increase or decrease before the election.
(D) Two opponents also have about 30 percent of voters with another 10 percent undecided.
(E) There is still a possibility that Louisiana, with its unmatched history of corrupt, demagogic, and ineffectual state politics, will support his candidacy.

Questions 10–11

The gill-net is used to catch halibut and sea bass, but up to 72 percent of what it ensnares is not marketable and is thrown back dead. Gill-nets are often called "walls of death" because they entangle and painfully kill mammals such as dolphins, whales, and sea otters. To use the gill-net at sea is like strip mining or clear-cutting on land.

Powerful lobbyists representing the commercial fishing industry have prevented the legislature from passing a ban on the use of gill-nets within the three-mile limit. They claim that the banning of gill-nets will raise the price of fish. They also charge that the law would benefit rich sport fishermen who want the ocean for their yachts.

10. In the first paragraph, the case against gill-nets is made by using

(A) statistical analysis
(B) ambiguity and indirection
(C) biased definitions
(D) simile and metaphor
(E) understatement

11. Which one of the following, if true, would support the argument in favor of a ban on gill-nets within the three-mile limit?

(A) Less than one percent of the fish sold in this country is imported from abroad.
(B) Gill-net users catch all but two percent of their fish within the three-mile limit.
(C) The halibut population has fallen to a near extinction level.
(D) There is a serious overpopulation of the coastal sea otter.
(E) Coastal sea otters have nearly destroyed the abalone beds along the coast.

12. According to the Supreme Court, the First Amendment does not protect "obscene" speech. To the "obscene," the Court explained, speech must appeal to a "prurient" interest, describe conduct in a way "patently offensive to contemporary community standards," and lack serious literary, artistic or scientific value.

All of the following arguments can be used to question the validity of the Court's definition of "obscene" EXCEPT:

(A) there is no certain way of knowing just what an "appeal" to "prurient interest" is

(B) the phrase "patently offensive" is impossible to define precisely

(C) no two communities are likely to have the same standards of decency

(D) most juries are incapable of determining what is "serious" artistic or literary value

(E) there is no writing that is without some "scientific value"

13. There are no edible fish in the streams of this county because there are no pesticide controls.

Which one of the following assumptions must be made before the conclusion above can be reached?

(A) Edible fish cannot be found in areas where there are no pesticide controls.

(B) If there are pesticide controls, there will be many edible fish.

(C) Without adequate pesticide controls, the fish population will rapidly decline.

(D) If there are pesticide controls, there will be some edible fish.

(E) With pesticide controls, the fish population will rapidly increase.

14. For eighteen years, a state has had three conservative congressmen, all representing the agricultural counties in the northern parts of the state. It also has three liberal congressmen from the large capital city in the south. One of the two senators is a liberal from the south, and the other is a conservative from the north.

Which one of the following can be inferred from this passage?

(A) Voters in the southern parts of the state will always vote liberal.

(B) Voters in the northern part of the state are likely to vote liberal in the next election.

(C) Voters in the state are influenced more by a candidate's political leanings than by where the candidate lives.

(D) The population of the three northern counties is about equal to the population of the capital city.

(E) The governor of the state is probably a liberal.

15. In the United States, people can get their medications. Those who say they can't are being vocal about it just to get another free ride. HMOs offer drug coverage at only a minimal copay; other private policies have many drug options; state programs offer discounted prescriptions for low income families; and drug companies make free medications available to those who cannot afford them.

All of the following, if true, would weaken the argument above EXCEPT:

(A) drug companies change the types of medications they offer free from month to month

(B) incomes may vary considerably from month to month and year to year

(C) the definition of what is a "minimal" copay varies depending on the income of the individual paying it

(D) private insurers set rates based on previous prescription usage of an individual

(E) drug companies sell drugs in other countries for less than they do in the United States, so people are forced to order their medications by mail from those countries or go there to purchase them

16. *Political Analyst:* Over the last three decades, the President's party has lost an average of twenty-two House of Representatives seats and two Senate seats in the midterm elections. This year, with a popular Republican President in the White House, GOP strategists had hoped to pick up seats in the House and the Senate. But the polls show these expectations are unrealistic. This should be an election with results much like those of the recent past.

According to information in this passage, the election should

(A) produce large Republican gains in the House and the Senate
(B) produce about twenty-five new House and Senate seats for the Democrats
(C) result in virtually no change in the balance of Republican and Democratic members of the House
(D) produce small Republican gains in the House and even smaller gains in the Senate
(E) produce two new Republican seats in the Senate

17. Ten percent of the state lottery winners interviewed by researchers of the paranormal have reported that they had visions or other signs instructing them to select the winning numbers. On the basis of these results, the researchers claim to have proved the existence of paranormal gifts.

Which one of the following pieces of additional information would be most relevant in assessing the logical validity of the researcher's claim?

(A) the total sum of money these men and women win on the lottery

(B) the percentage of lottery players who win money
(C) the percentage of contestants interviewed who were not lottery winners
(D) the percentage of lottery players who had visions or signs but did not win money
(E) the amount of money the lottery winners spend each year on lottery tickets

18. By spraying with pesticides like malathion, we can eradicate dangerous pests like the fruit-fly. But malathion spraying also destroys the ladybug, the best natural predator of aphids. Areas that have been sprayed with malathion are now free of the fruit-fly, but infested with aphids. This is the price we must pay to protect our citrus crop.

The argument above assumes all of the following EXCEPT:

(A) pesticide spraying is the only way to eradicate the fruit-fly
(B) the aphid infestation is caused by the lack of ladybugs
(C) a pesticide that would kill fruit-flies and spare ladybugs cannot be made
(D) the use of pesticides has disadvantages
(E) the aphid infestation could be prevented by introducing a natural predator other than the ladybug

19. The Superintendent of Education complains that the share of the total state budget for education has decreased in each of the last four years; he blames the fall-off on the steady rise in the cost of law enforcement. Organizations opposing increased spending on education point out that the amount of money the state

has spent on education has increased by at least three million dollars in each of the last four years.

Which one of the following, if true, best resolves the apparent contradiction in the passage above?

(A) The total state budget has increased more rapidly than the expenditure for education.

(B) Both the pro- and con-educational-spending spokesmen have failed to take inflation into account.

(C) Law-enforcement costs have not risen as rapidly as the superintendent claims.

(D) Some educational expenses are not included in the state budget, but are paid by local taxes.

(E) School construction is paid for by funds from bonds, not by funds from the state budget.

20. How can I write any of the essays when there are so many essays to be written?

In terms of its logical structure, the remark above most closely resembles which one of the following?

(A) How can he buy a new car when he is already deeply in debt?

(B) How can she increase her collection of books when it is already so large?

(C) How can he iron any of his shirts when he has so many shirts that need ironing?

(D) How can she visit London and Paris when she has not yet visited New York and Washington?

(E) How can they raise horses when they already raise so many cows?

21. Great playwrights do not develop in countries where there is no freedom of opinion. Repressive countries are likely to produce great satiric writers.

If both of these statements are true, which one of the following is the most logical continuation?

(A) Therefore, countries with no restrictions on expression will produce great satiric playwrights.

(B) Therefore, great satirists in repressive countries will use forms other than the play.

(C) Therefore, playwrights in repressive countries will not write satire.

(D) Therefore, great satiric writers will not develop in countries where there is freedom of speech.

(E) Therefore, no great satire is likely to be written in dramatic forms.

22. Contrary to the expectations of the Canadian government, a majority of the Mohawk population in Quebec is calling for native sovereignty. The Mohawk separatists cite a written agreement from colonial times in which Great Britain recognized the Mohawks' separateness from Canada. Unfortunately, the various Mohawk factions, each with its own agenda, have made it difficult to reach lasting agreements. What satisfies one group displeases another. The bleak outlook is for _____.

Which one of the following most logically concludes this paragraph?

(A) continued struggle within the tribe and between the tribe and the Canadian government

(B) some kind of compromise which recognizes the rights of both the

Indians and the government of Canada

(C) some sort of agreement among the divided groups within the Mohawk tribe

(D) the establishment of a separate Mohawk state with its sovereignty recognized by the Canadian government

(E) a decline in Mohawk militarism and a series of fence-mending conferences

23. A new law will require labels giving consumers more nutritional information on all prepackaged foods manufactured in the United States. Food sold by restaurants or grocers with annual sales of less than $500,000 will be exempt. The required labels will reveal the number of servings, the serving size, the number of calories per serving, and the amount of fat, cholesterol, sodium, and dietary fiber.

The effectiveness of the new labels in improving overall U.S. nutrition could be seriously questioned if which one of the following were shown to be true?

(A) More than 80 percent of the food sold in this country is not prepackaged.

(B) More than 80 percent of the prepackaged food sold in this country is marketed by the eight major food corporations.

(C) The amount of money Americans spend on prepackaged foods for microwaving has more than tripled every year for the last five years, and the trend is expected to continue.

(D) An increasingly large number of consumers now read the nutritional information on food packages.

(E) Small retailers who manufacture packaged foods sell to only a tiny percentage of American food buyers.

24. A year ago the presidential science advisor announced prematurely that the United States would reveal its plan for combating global warming at the World Climate Conference in Geneva, Switzerland. Five European countries have already announced plans to make reductions in carbon dioxide emissions, and five others have committed themselves to goals of stabilizing their emissions. But the United States is still unprepared to announce targets or a schedule for reducing carbon dioxide emissions.

Which one of the following sentences would provide the most logical continuation of this paragraph?

(A) The Geneva Conference will be the last international meeting before negotiations on a global-warming convention begin next year.

(B) The United States accounts for about 22 percent of the carbon dioxide pumped into the atmosphere, while the former Soviet Union accounts for 18 percent.

(C) By adopting renewable energy strategies that would permit stabilization of carbon dioxide emissions, the United States could save millions of dollars.

(D) The British Prime Minister and top environmental officials of many nations will attend the conference in Geneva.

(E) Anticipating a debate in which the Europeans will criticize the United States for failing to act, the administration is downplaying the importance of the conference.

25. There is increasing reason to believe that Americans are talking themselves into a recession. Consumers are becoming more and more pessimistic, and the index of consumer confidence has plunged to its lowest level in years. What bothers analysts is fear that consumer pessimism about the economy will lead to spending cuts and become a self-fulfilling prophecy, speeding the onset of a recession.

Widespread predictions in the media of a coming recession may be one reason for the pessimistic attitudes of consumers. They may be bracing for a recession by cutting back on spending plans for new cars, vacations, and restaurant meals—the very behavior pattern that analysts say will intensify the slump. Real estate values have been in decline for a year and a half, and the stock market has declined for four months in a row.

When the economy is on the ropes, waning consumer confidence can deliver the knock-out punch.

The argument in the passage above would be weakened if it were shown that

(A) in the 1955 recession, the widespread concern over the President's health precipitated an economic downturn

(B) although consumer spending in the last fiscal quarter was the same as last year's, most of that strength stemmed from unusual government military spending

(C) the steady rise in car sales has continued, despite the phasing out of discount prices and low-interest car loans

(D) the predicted recession after the steep fall in stock prices two years ago did not lead to recession

(E) some consumers are more eager than ever to maintain the living standards they have enjoyed for the last two years

STOP

IF YOU FINISH BEFORE TIME IS UP, CHECK YOUR WORK ON THIS SECTION OF THE TEST ONLY.
DO NOT GO ON TO THE NEXT SECTION OF THE TEST UNTIL TIME IS UP FOR THIS SECTION.

WRITING SAMPLE

Directions: You have 35 minutes to write an essay in response to a given topic. Take a few minutes to plan your work before you begin writing. DO NOT WRITE ON A TOPIC OF YOUR OWN CHOICE. ESSAYS THAT DO NOT ADDRESS THE GIVEN TOPIC ARE UNACCEPTABLE.

The quality of your writing is more important than the length of your response or the content. Pay attention to organization, appropriate diction, and correct usage. You will not be expected to display any specialized knowledge in your response, nor will you be expected to write a "perfect" essay; law schools understand that you are writing under a time constraint, and will allow for the minor lapses in writing ability that might occur under this circumstance.

Only the lined area in your booklet will be reproduced for the law schools, so do not write outside this space. *Do not* skip lines or use wide margins. These precautions, along with careful planning and legible handwriting that is not unduly large, will keep you within the allowed space.

Sample Topic

The State Legislature has appropriated funds to build a new maximum security prison somewhere in Metropolis County. The prison is to house one hundred prisoners convicted of serious crimes and also the two hundred prisoners awaiting trial or being tried in Metropolis City. These prisoners are now held at the overcrowded and antiquated Metropolis City Jail. Two locations have been proposed.

As an aide to the state senator who represents Metropolis County, you have been asked to write an argument to be presented to the Legislature in support of one site over the other. Two considerations guide your decision:

- The state funds for building and maintaining the prison and for transporting the prisoners to the courts are limited.
- The senator is eager to increase his popular support in anticipation of the upcoming election.

The Metropolis City site is located ten minutes from the court buildings near the downtown district. This area of the city is densely populated and has a high, slowly declining, crime rate. Residents of the district strongly oppose the building of the prison in their neighborhood, especially since a number of prisoners have recently escaped from the old Metropolis City Jail. Art preservation groups also oppose the proposed location since it would require the destruction of two buildings with unique architectural features. The estimated cost for the land and the construction of the prison on the Metropolis City site is eight million dollars.

The Deer Valley site is located in the sparsely populated Metropolis County, seventy-five miles from the court buildings. Deer Valley is a small town in a depressed rural area. Many of the residents of Deer Valley favor the construction of the prison, since they believe it will bring new jobs to the area. The roads between Deer Valley and Metropolis are narrow, and in a winter when the rains or snows are heavy, they may be impassable. The cost of utilities in Deer Valley is about twice the cost of utilities in Metropolis City. The estimated building cost in Deer Valley is seven million dollars.

On the actual exam you will be given special sheets of paper to write your essay. It will have the essay topic on the top followed by room for scratch work. For practice, write your essay on two sides of an 8½" x 11" college-ruled lined sheet of paper.

ANSWER KEY

Section I: Reading Comprehension

1. E	6. A	11. A	16. A	21. B	26. B
2. C	7. C	12. D	17. C	22. B	27. C
3. D	8. D	13. E	18. A	23. B	28. D
4. A	9. B	14. A	19. D	24. C	
5. B	10. D	15. E	20. C	25. C	

Section II: Analytical Reasoning

1. B	5. E	9. B	13. E	17. C	21. D
2. E	6. D	10. E	14. D	18. E	22. B
3. B	7. C	11. E	15. E	19. D	23. C
4. C	8. E	12. D	16. B	20. E	24. C

Section III: Logical Reasoning

1. D	6. C	11. D	16. D	21. B	26. B
2. C	7. D	12. D	17. E	22. D	
3. C	8. B	13. D	18. D	23. A	
4. A	9. C	14. D	19. B	24. E	
5. E	10. C	15. A	20. B	25. B	

Section IV: Reading Comprehension

1. B	6. B	11. E	16. B	21. B	26. A
2. B	7. A	12. A	17. A	22. E	27. C
3. E	8. C	13. B	18. C	23. D	28. B
4. E	9. C	14. D	19. C	24. B	
5. A	10. B	15. D	20. B	25. E	

Section V: Logical Reasoning

1. C	6. B	11. C	16. B	21. B
2. B	7. B	12. E	17. D	22. A
3. E	8. E	13. A	18. E	23. A
4. E	9. A	14. D	19. A	24. E
5. A	10. D	15. E	20. C	25. C

MODEL TEST ANALYSIS

Doing model exams and understanding the explanations afterwards are of course important in acquainting you with typical LSAT question types and successful approaches to the questions. However, another benefit of carefully analyzing these model tests is to understand the kinds of errors you are making and thus work to minimize them. For instance, if a very high percentage of your incorrect answers is due to "careless error" or "misread problem," then perhaps you are working much too fast and should slow your pace accordingly. If your incorrect answers are due primarily to "lack of knowledge," then a careful rereading and reworking of the appropriate question-type chapter may be in order. Or if you find that you aren't completing a large number of questions because of lack of time, you may need to either increase your speed or learn to use the "one-check, two-check" technique more effectively.

This kind of analysis of the model tests will enable you to identify your particular weaknesses and thus remedy them.

MODEL TEST THREE ANALYSIS

Section	Total Number of Questions	Number Correct	Number Incorrect	Number Unanswered*
I. Reading Comprehension	28			
II. Analytical Reasoning	24			
III. Logical Reasoning	26			
IV. Reading Comprehension	28			
V. Logical Reasoning	25			
TOTALS:	131			

*At this stage in your preparation, you should not be leaving any blank answer spaces. At least fill in a guess, as there is no penalty for a wrong answer.

REASONS FOR INCORRECT ANSWERS

You may wish to evaluate the explanations before completing this chart.

Section	Total Number Incorrect	Lack of Knowledge	Misread Problem	Careless Error	Unanswered or Wrong Guess
I. Reading Comprehension					
II. Analytical Reasoning					
III. Logical Reasoning					
IV. Reading Comprehension					
V. Logical Reasoning					
TOTALS:					

ANSWER EXPLANATIONS

Section I

Passage 1

1. **E** Each of the first four cases is public or quasi-public land. The last is private, not likely to be open to the general public and therefore the owner may deny free speech on the property.

2. **C** In this instance, the property is clearly private; in the other cases, it is not always clear whether the property is public or private.

3. **D** The nature or character of the owner of the property is not a factor mentioned by the passage. All of the four other options are alluded to in the opening paragraphs of the passage.

4. **A** The author approvingly quotes the words of a mall chairman in support of this position. Choice (E) may not be true if the charity seekers are offensive.

5. **B** The passage cites Lord Chief Justice Hale's remarks of 1675. (C) and (D) are false and the passage does not discuss current practice in Canada and Great Britain (E).

6. **A** The passage concludes with Justice Black's remarks on the "preferred position" of First Amendment freedoms.

Passage 2

7. **C** This is the best answer because the passage recounts both Dickens' realization that the novel, based on his memories, was deeply personal and also his recognition that he was creating a "mediated version" of himself. See lines 13–20, 67–76. (A) covers only paragraph 1 of the passage; (B) is a secondary point, not the main idea. The novel can hardly be called prophetic (C), although one line suggests it "anticipated" turmoil in his marriage. However, this is not a main idea. (E) is an opinion not presented or suggested in the passage.

8. **D** This answer is supported by the main points in both paragraphs 1 and 2. The author does not present a "psychological study of motivations" (A) nor does he primarily contrast two aspects of Dickens (B), (C). (E) is inaccurate; the passage does not show that the novel became a turning point in his life.

9. **B** The line indicates that writing the book has called up his childhood memories and therefore "almost inevitably" led him back to the place where he was a small boy. The line does not indicate complete exhaustion (A) nor does it suggest that he was unable to separate reality and fiction (C). (D) is simply inaccurate. It is too far a leap to infer that because he returns to Rochester, he has overcome the trauma of his childhood (E), particularly because of the inclusion of the words "almost inevitably."

10. **D** This is the best of the answers because Fanny's significance is clearly suggested in lines 37–41. Although (A) might seem correct because future turmoil in his marriage is indicated (lines 22–25), an end to the marriage is not implied. (C) is incorrect because although it is suggested that he sometimes put his work and his own ego above his family, coolness and distance are not implied. (B) and (E) are not supported by information in the passage.

11. **A** Although (C) and (D) are accurate statements, they are not the *most significant* reasons for Dickens' choice of the name. Lines 67–76 suggest that (A) is the correct answer. (B) and (E) are not supported by information in the passage.

12. **D** This is the best answer because the parenthetical phrase concerning Catherine indicates her reaction to her husband's assumption of the right to name the children, which in turn suggests something about their relationship. Failing to insist on naming her children does not indicate that she is an inadequate mother (A). (B), (C), and (E) are simply not suggested in this line.

13. **E** The author is primarily objective and analytical in the passage. (A) is incorrect because although there is perhaps some irony (e.g., lines 41–44), it is minor. (B), (C), and (D) are simply incorrect; the author is neither argumentative, condescending, nor persuasive, for example.

14. **A** The first paragraph includes an account of Dickens' reactions to writing the novel, using many of his own quotations. The second paragraph relies on more commentary from the author, and also introduces related points, such as Dickens' choice of the novel's title and his interest in names. (E) is incorrect because paragraph 1 doesn't show the *effect* of Dickens' childhood on him, nor does the second paragraph connect his later life with his novels. Similarly, (B), (C), and (D) all include inadequate (or inaccurate) descriptions of the two paragraphs of the passage.

Passage 3

15. **E** Choice (E) best describes the purpose of Passage A. Although the passage does briefly explain the government's role (A), that is only part of its main idea.

16. **A** In Passage B, line 81, the author asks a question ("Why has public broadcasting declined in the United States?") and then proceeds in the rest of the passage to cite some reasons, making (A) the best answer. (B) may be implied in the passage, but criticism of funding is not its main purpose, and (C) is a secondary point.

17. **C** Choice (C) is the best answer. The last paragraph of Passage B cites funding issues as being responsible for many of PBS's problems, and the federal government's role in funding is emphasized in the second paragraph. The author of Passage B states that because of the lack of sufficient funding, PBS has been unable to create many new, different programs, but the author does not imply that PBS "lacks creativity" (A).

18. **A** Both passages are generally neutral (D), but Passage B includes mild criticism (i.e., "endless pledge drives that tend to feature bland programming or 'specials' that have been shown too many times," "watered-down commercials"). This makes (A) the best answer. Although perhaps Passage B is somewhat pessimistic, Passage A is neither pessimistic nor optimistic (B). (C) and (E) are too extreme: Passage B isn't "harshly" critical, nor does Passage A "praise" public television.

19. **D** Choice (D) is the best answer. PBS's primary funding comes from viewers (lines 39–41), but CPB is directly funded by Congress (lines 28–29). (E) is not accurate; CPB uses 95 percent of its funds to "strengthen PBS's techni-

cal infrastructure and develop programming," but it does not use funds to promote PBS.

20. **C** In lines 81–83, the author of Passage B cites one "obvious reason" for fewer PBS viewers: more choices since the advent of cable.(C) is therefore correct. (A), (B), (D), and (E) may also be responsible for the decline in viewership, but they are not the "obvious reason."

21. **B** One of the definitions of "niche" is "a specialized market," making (B) the best answer in this context. (The Disney Channel, Nickelodeon, and the Cartoon Network are networks that specialize in children's programming.)

22. **B** Choice (B) is the correct answer. Government subsidies (line 61), viewer membership (lines 40–41), household license fees (line 51), and fees from commercial broadcasters (line 56) are all mentioned.

Passage 4

23. **B** The first paragraph says that taxonomy was "in the forefront of the sciences" in "the eighteenth and early nineteenth centuries."

24. **C** The terms refer to plants and animals.

25. **C** The passage gives us no information to support (A), (B), or (E). (D) is untrue (they were among the "greatest biologists of Europe"). That Darwin spent many years and wrote three volumes about the taxonomy of barnacles suggest that there are a large number of kinds to describe.

26. **B** The third paragraph gives examples of the "genuine pioneers" mentioned at the end of the second paragraph. The scientists of the first paragraph are not "exclusively European," (Jefferson).

27. **C** Parsifal was a naive knight of German legend and Klingsor was his enemy, a magician with an enchanted garden. The reference to Parsifal's bravery and the use of the word "vanquished" should suggest this answer.

28. **D** Though the passage does include (A), (B), and (C), the best choice here is (D), which describes all three paragraphs in the passage.

Section II

Answers 1–6

From the information given you should pull out information and list the two possibilities:

```
          1  2  3  4  5  6  7  8

 JJJJ or JJJ
 ̶R̶R̶
 ̶C̶C̶

  R ? J
```

Two Possibilities:

```
 JJJJ                 JJJ
 R R        or        R R R
 C C                  C C
```

1. **B** If four jazz songs are played and the first and last song are of the same type, there are two possible arrangements. Remember, at least two of each type of song are required. Start by placing the first and last song; for example, two rock songs. It is apparent that there is only one place for the four jazz songs, since, other than jazz, no two songs of the same type can be consecutive.

```
 R  C  J  J  J  J  C  R
 C  R  J  J  J  J  R  C
```

In both arrangements a jazz song is played third. For each of the other answer choices, there are two types of songs played.

C	R	J	J	J	R	C	R
C	R	J	J	J	J	C	R

2. E If three rock songs are played, the remaining five songs must be made up of two country songs and three jazz songs, since there must be more jazz songs than country songs. Since a rock song must precede the first jazz song, there is only one arrangement where a country song is played sixth.

R	J	J	J	R	C	R	C

3. B There are four possible arrangements where a jazz song is played third and the first and last songs of the same type.

R	J	J	J	C	R	C	R
R	C	J	J	J	R	C	R
R	C	J	J	J	J	C	R
C	R	J	J	J	J	R	C

In none of the arrangements is the sixth song a country song.

4. C There is only one arrangement containing three jazz songs where all three jazz songs are last. There are two arrangements containing four jazz songs. The songs at the beginning of the play list must alternate.

R	C	R	C	R	J	J	J
R	C	R	C	J	J	J	J
C	R	C	R	J	J	J	J

5. E If a country song is played first and seventh, there is only one possible arrangement using three jazz songs and one arrangement using four jazz songs. In both cases, a jazz song is being played third.

6. D Since a country song was fifth, the first three songs must be rock-country-rock. This leaves only three arrangements for the remaining songs.

R	C	R	K	C	J	J	J	J
R	C	R	K	C	J	J	J	R
R	C	R	K	C	R	J	J	J

In all three arrangements, there is a rock song played third.

Answers 7–13

From the information given, you could have made the following relationships:

$$J > L + M + N$$
$$N = L + M$$
$$M > K + G$$
$$G > H$$
$$K = G$$

7. C From the diagram above, since Jon has more bills than Lynn, Melanie, and Neil combined and since Melanie has more bills than Ken and George combined, then Jon has the most bills.

8. E Since Hal has fewer bills than George, and George has fewer bills than Melanie, and Melanie has fewer bills than Neil, and Neil has fewer bills than Jon, then Hal has the fewest number of bills. At this point you may have deduced most of the order of students:

Jon
Neil
Melanie   **Lynn?**
Ken—George
Hal

If you realized these relationships immediately from the initial conditions, you should have made this part of your first diagram.

9. **B** Refer to the chart for the last problem. George has an equal amount of bills as Ken and Melanie has more bills than both of them combined (A). From the set of conditions, it is only possible to determine for certain that Lynn has fewer bills than Jon and Neil. Beyond that, Lynn is a variable. She could have more or less than Melanie (C) or George (D). We do know that Ken and George combined have fewer than Melanie (E). Since Neil is equal to Lynn and Melanie combined, he must have more than Lynn (B), the correct answer.

10. **E** Using this new information with the order chart, we have the following chart:

Jon
Neil
Melanie
―――――――――――――
Ken　　　　　　　Lynn?
George
Hal

You may have approached this problem by eliminating the incorrect choices.

11. **E** Since Neil has the same number of bills as Lynn and Melanie combined, and Jon has more bills than Lynn, Melanie, and Neil combined, therefore Jon has more bills than twice the number of Lynn's and Melanie's bills. Choice (E) is false.

12. **D** If Lynn and Melanie have the same number of bills, then Lynn has more bills than Ken and George combined. Since George has more bills than Hal and since Neil has the same number of bills as Lynn and Melanie combined, then Neil has more bills than Lynn, George, and Hal combined.

13. **E** If Tom has more bills than Ken and fewer than Lynn, the order of students would now be as follows:

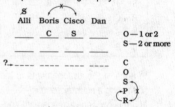

Jon
Neil
Melanie
Lynn
Tom
Ken　　　　　　George
Hal

Therefore, Lynn having more bills than Hal is the only one that must be true.

Answers 14–20

From the information given, you may have set up the following display:

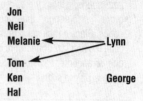

Since Boris eats chocolate chip cookies, Cisco does not. Since Cisco eats sugar cookies, Boris does not. We are given that Alli does not eat sugar cookies and at least two people must eat sugar cookies, so Dan must eat sugar cookies. Anyone who eats sugar cookies does not eat raisin cookies, thus Dan does not eat raisin cookies. Your display should now look like this:

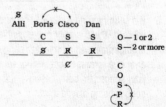

Model Test Three 477

14. D From the display you can see that Dan does not eat raisin cookies.

15. E If Boris eats exactly three kinds of cookies they must be chocolate chip, peanut butter, and raisin. Since Boris eats chocolate chip cookies but does not eat sugar cookies, he must eat two of the remaining three—peanut butter, raisin, oatmeal. But Cisco cannot eat raisin, so if Boris eats raisin, he must eat peanut butter. Since Cisco must eat at least two types, he must eat sugar cookies and oatmeal cookies. The display should look like this:

```
        S̸   ⌒x⌒
      Alli  Boris Cisco Dan
      ____   C     S     S
      ____   P     O     ____
             R     K̸     K̸
                   C̸
```

16. B At most, two people eat oatmeal cookies, thus, if Alli and Dan eat oatmeal cookies, Boris and Cisco cannot. Thus, Boris must eat at least one more type of cookie. Either Boris eats peanut butter cookies, or raisin and peanut butter cookies. Either way, Boris eats peanut butter cookies. Thus, Cisco cannot eat peanut butter cookies. This is not a possible arrangement since Cisco must eat at least two types of cookies. The display would look like this:

```
        S̸   ⌒x⌒
      Alli  Boris Cisco Dan
      ____   C     S     S
       O     S̸    ____   O
             P     K̸     K̸
                   C̸
                   P̸
```

17. C The general conditions state that oatmeal cookies can only be eaten by a maximum of two people, thus, choices (A), (B), and (D) are incor-

rect. Choice (E) can be eliminated since Alli cannot eat sugar cookies and Boris does not eat them either. Therefore, by process of elimination, choice (C) must be correct.

18. E From the diagram shown, you know that sugar cookies are eaten by Cisco and Dan but not Alli or Boris. You also know that raisin cookies are eaten by Alli and Boris but not Cisco or Dan. Therefore, both sugar and raisin cookies are eaten by exactly two different people.

19. D If Alli does not eat chocolate chip or raisin cookies (or sugar cookies), she must eat oatmeal and peanut butter cookies, since those are the only ones left.

```
        S̸   ⌒x⌒
      Alli  Boris Cisco Dan
       O     C     S     S
       O     R     K̸     K̸
       C̸     P     C̸
       K̸
```

It is possible for Boris to eat raisin and peanut butter cookies, which would preclude Cisco from eating peanut butter cookies.

Choice (A) is not possible. If Dan eats oatmeal cookies, Boris and Cisco cannot, since at most two people eat oatmeal cookies. In order for Cisco to eat two kinds of cookies, he must eat peanut butter cookies. If Cisco eats peanut butter cookies, Boris cannot. But this is not possible, since Boris needs to eat two types of cookies too, and he cannot eat raisin cookies without peanut butter cookies.

Choice (B) is incorrect, since two people eat sugar cookies and at most two can eat chocolate chip cookies.

Choice (C) is incorrect. If only Alli eats peanut butter cookies, Boris does not eat peanut butter or raisin cookies. Thus Boris would have to eat oatmeal cookies in order to eat two types. But Cisco would also have to eat oatmeal cookies in order to eat two types. Boris and Cisco cannot both eat oatmeal cookies. Choice (E) is incorrect because the initial conditions state that Cisco eats sugar cookies, so Boris could not.

20. **E**   Raisin cookies cannot be eaten by Cisco and Dan, and they do not have to be eaten by Alli or Boris. We can also eliminate the other choices. From initial conditions, chocolate chip cookies are eaten by at least one person and sugar cookies are eaten by two people. This eliminates choices (A) and (C). If no one eats peanut butter cookies, no one can eat raisin cookies either. This would force Boris and Cisco to eat oatmeal cookies, but they can't eat the same cookie. This eliminates choice (D). If no one eats oatmeal cookies, Cisco must eat peanut butter cookies, since he must eat two kinds of cookies. Boris must eat raisin cookies in order to eat at least two kinds of cookies, but if he eats raisin cookies, he must eat peanut butter cookies as well. This is not possible, since Cisco is already eating peanut butter cookies. This eliminates choice (B).

Answers 21–24

From the information given, it would be helpful to construct the following chart to answer the questions:

A ╲ B   C*┐
D ╳ E   F ◄── Two from each row
G ─╳─ H   K ◄── │ must be chosen.

*If C, then also K.

21. **D**   If A is not chosen, then B and C are chosen. Since C is chosen, K is chosen too. Since B is chosen, D is not chosen. Thus, E and F are chosen. So, if A is not chosen, B, C, E, F, and K must be chosen.

22. **B**   If D is chosen, then B is not chosen. Therefore, (B) could NOT be chosen. Also, A and C must be chosen. If C is chosen, then so is K. E or F is chosen. G or H is chosen.

23. **C**   If B is chosen, then D is not chosen. Thus, E and F are chosen. Notice that statement 6 is not two-directional.

24. **C**   Since G and H do not play together, only one will be chosen. Thus, K must be chosen.

Section III

1. **D**   If 97 percent of fatalities occurred *below 45 mph,* then a reduction in the maximum speed from 65 to 55 mph would have little impact, no more than a 3 percent reduction (if we assume that all other fatalities occurred between 55 and 65 mph). (A) and (C) are not relevant, (B) provides no conclusive data, and (E) *strengthens* the argument.

2. **C**   If the financial cost of switching to another brokerage were indeed minimal, it may encourage a switch to another brokerage. (A) and (E) do not blame the brokerage for their losses. Presumably, a reluctance to change (B), and having experienced more extreme losses in the past (D), would imply that a person would resist change and continue with their current brokerage.

3. **C**   Webster is stating that not only do lies disagree with truth, but they usually also disagree with other lies. Thus, it would follow that liars often quarrel with other liars.

4. **A** The given argument can be reduced to:

is not	S (star)	because	H (hit)
is	H	because	S

(A) exhibits the structure closest to that of the given argument:

is not	F	because	C
	(final		(correct)
	word)		
is	C	because	F ("Instructor"
	(correct)		is the final
			word.)

5. **E** The logic here is straightforward. If the refineries are operating at 60 percent, not 75 percent of their capacity, then oil prices will probably rise.

6. **C** The discussion points out that (A) is an implication (rather than an assumption) of the studies. (B) is also not an assumption but is a restatement of the discussion's central issue. In order to consider speaker characteristics as either relevant or irrelevant, the author must assume that such a distinction exists; that assumption is expressed by (C). The passage does not assume a trim speaker will be "more persuasive" (D) or that irrelevant aspects are more influential than content (E), though it does suggest that these are issues worth examining.

7. **D** The final sentence of the passage offers an alternative explanation of the phenomenon introduced in the first sentence.

8. **B** The author, by offering an alternative explanation, stresses the scientists' unwillingness to consider such alternatives. (A), a choice worth considering, should be eliminated because the alternative suggested by the author is no more verifiable than the assertion he criticizes.

9. **C** The main point of the paragraph is the need for campaign reform. Choice (D) supports the argument, whereas the other three choices are assumptions that might arise, but not the main point of the paragraph.

10. **C** The misunderstanding arises from Dave's assumption that Bill has said *every* morning, not *almost* every morning. (D), although worth considering, is not best because it does not address the scope of Bill's remark.

11. **D** Because the first two statements are not absolute, we may conclude sunbathing is unlikely but still possible. It is not known how frequently people visit La Jolla to sunbathe (A), whether the sun is shining (B), or if July would attract more sunbathers than the month of June (E). While there may be sunbathers there today (D), we do not know it for a certainty (C).

12. **D** (A) and (B) are, by commonsense standards, implausible. (C) might be a valid statement, but it is not implied by Wilkie's assertion, which makes no distinction between first- and second-class citizens, and so implies (D).

13. **D** Since the passage does not say that the 200 students in spring activities were all different and all different from the 100 in fall activities, the total number of students could be much lower than 300. A single student could participate in all three activities in both semesters. (C) could apply if there were more than one activity, but (D) is a correct assumption in any case.

14. **D** If *nothing* produces only nothing, then the production of something *must* require something. (A) makes the production of something from

something a possibility; however, the original statement implies that the something/something relationship is imperative.

15. **A** Only (A) makes an unqualified negative assessment; each of the other choices is either a neutral statement or one that attempts to balance positive and negative terms.

16. **D** The term *average* in the passage implies that if some workers earned more than $7.87 per day, others must have earned less. In choice (C) the words *far more than* make that choice not necessarily true.

17. **E** The magazine is sure that Jones will be a contender soon, and all that is offered to support this is the fact that Jinkins will train him. Therefore, (A) and (B) are the assumptions motivating the passage. (E) is not an assumption, but rather a statement made explicitly in the article.

18. **D** All the other examples are dilemmas. Amleth must choose between failure to avenge or failure to protect his mother; the zoo must choose between the loss of the grant and the loss of a kudu. Ames must choose between higher rent and customer inconvenience. The driver must choose between a parking ticket and losing a radio. In (D), there is no choice between disagreeable alternatives. If you don't have enough money, you can't buy enough meat.

19. **B** The structure of question 19 may be simplified as follows:

C (crowded) <u>whenever</u> H (holiday)
<u>Not C</u>; <u>therefore</u>, <u>not H</u>

(B) is most nearly parallel to the relationships presented in the question:

R (reptiles) <u>whenever</u> D (hot desert day)
<u>Not R</u> (absent); <u>therefore</u>, not <u>D</u>.

20. **B** (A) is not a strong choice; the author indicates only that Nerd is *very* wealthy. The author does not compare Nerd's wealth to that of the other candidates. (C) contradicts the third sentence of the author's statement. Since the author tells us that Nerd has the necessary wealth and should acquire skill as a speaker, the author must believe that the third attribute (experience) is not an issue. In other words, the author believes that Nerd has satisfactory experience. The passage does not assert that an improvement in Nerd's public speaking will guarantee a win (D). Since Nerd has wealth and experience but inadequate speaking skills, he is a dark horse (E).

21. **B** The author does not address the financial origins of successful politicians, only that they must possess great wealth to successfully run for office (A). (D) attests to the fact that Nerd must be lacking a prerequisite for office, because he has failed before. (E) is consistent with the passage. (C) contradicts the author's assertions, but the extremely low percentage virtually invalidates the statistic. (B) directly contradicts two of the three requirements for being politically successful.

22. **D** The given statement tells us only that the car is blue. For us to be *assured* that it is slow we must know either that every blue car is slow *or* that no blue car accelerates quickly. (D) restricts quick acceleration to red cars.

23. **A** The argument obviously avoids absolute terms, relying instead on

words such as "almost" and "sometimes." Therefore, it would seem consistent that a basic assumption would also avoid absolute terms; only (A) does so. In addition, (A) makes explicit the assumption underlying the first sentence of the passage.

24. **E** The second sentence diminishes the government's "fault," and the final sentence continues this idea. The need for government intervention is not the same as a compulsion to enlist Uncle Sam as a "superbusybody." The difference in tone from the original would by itself be a strong point that (D) is not the correct answer. The only restatement that takes into account extra governmental responsibility for intrusion is (E).

25. **B** The key phrase in the author's remarks is "falsely equating knowledgé [viewing] with action [crime]." (A) is poor because it links knowledge with action. (C) is poor because the author indicates that those who dictate what we see (in other words, the censors) are guilty of drawing false (illogical) relationships. (D) introduces the idea of compulsion, which is not implied in the original. (E) is clearly false. Many actions are performed without prior knowledge. (B) is consistent with the author's position that knowledge and action do not necessarily go hand in hand.

26. **B** A ruling on resources must at least presume the possibility that such resources exist; otherwise it is absurd. All other choices are irrelevant to the ruling.

Section IV

Passage 1

1. **B** Each of the other choices is too specific and/or not indicative of the *neutral* rather than argumentative *tone* of the passage.

2. **B** In the fourth paragraph, the author notes that after Congress had stopped enacting its reapportionment power, "serious malapportionment" problems ensued; the author thus implies that federal supervision is necessary. (C), (D), and (E) are issues on which the author does not imply an opinion.

3. **E** A clue to this answer occurs in paragraph 5, in which "malapportionment" is replaced by "the size and shape of electoral districts." Each of the other choices *may contribute* to malapportionment, but each is too specific to be the best choice.

4. **E** In the fifth paragraph we learn that the *voters* asked the Warren Court to rule on apportionment issues; therefore, we must assume that a ballot was taken that expressed the voters' opinions.

5. **A** Question 1 is answered in the first paragraph. The other questions, although they may be implied as *issues* in the passage, are not answered.

6. **B** Justice Frankfurter did not declare his opinion about reapportionment per se, but did declare that the Supreme Court should not address the issue; the Warren Court, on the other hand, did deliberate over the reapportionment issue. Therefore, we may conclude that Frankfurter was not a member of the Warren Court.

7. **A** The passage is a summary of events that occurred through the century,

relative to apportionment. Each of the other choices has the author writing a passage calculated to persuade rather than to inform.

Passage 2

8. **C** The passage says, "Born into a nation whose people were steeped in the traditions of prehistory, in the lore of the faeries and the Druids, he remained free to believe." Choice (C) reiterates this idea, that the environment of the believer enhances the belief. The great memory (A), however, is not confined to a single environment, but rather exists for all humans. Choice (B) is incorrect because the passage suggests the opposite: The reader need not know the specific occult practices in order to understand Yeats's writing. Choice (D) is incorrect because, according to the passage, imagination, as Yeats understands it, is *not* rationalistic, and (E) is incorrect because although the writing may call to the child, it does not call to the adult, who has lost belief.

9. **C** Choice (C) directly follows the progression of the passage's paragraphs. The first paragraph discusses the primitive and childhood belief in "the world that we could not see," that is, certain concepts about humanity. The second and third paragraphs connect that belief with Yeats's belief and background. The final paragraph deals with Yeats's use of that belief in his writing, that is, his attitudes toward these concepts. None of the other choices follows the development of the passage.

10. **B** The passage states that Yeats conjures up the imagination by the use of symbols, which are in the "great memory." It's appropriate to think, then, that Yeats would agree that the symbol of the tree is also part of the "great memory" and that it would evoke similar responses in readers not only in a particular environment but throughout the world.

11. **E** Choice (E) is the most straightforward and complete title for the passage. The other choices describe only a portion of the passage.

12. **A** The passage says, "It is this great mind, and great memory, to which Yeats is calling and which he insists can be evoked by symbols, whether from Celtic lore, the Upanishads, or the Noh plays." The sentence illustrates the commonality of symbols, even in works from different cultures—Celtic lore (Ireland, Scotland, Wales), the Upanishads (Hindu religious writing), and Noh plays (Japan).

13. **B** If, as Yeats suggests, the successors of "the masters of magic," the "poet, the musician, and the artist," may use symbols "half unconsciously," then he would most likely not agree that they are "aware of the power and magic of the symbols they use."

14. **D** The second paragraph deals with the young Yeats living in Sligo. The third paragraph extends this time into the near future, a time in which Yeats became fascinated with symbols, and the final sentence says, "we must at least have an understanding of its [the occult's] meaning to him and the depth to which it affected everything he wrote." The final paragraph changes focus to comment on the reader and on Yeats's general attitudes toward symbolism. The only choice given that could logically fit between these

two paragraphs is (D), which follows the discussion of Yeats's early interest in the occult with a paragraph that would probably go on to detail his involvement with the study of the occult in later life. All the other choices disrupt the flow and organization of the passage.

Passage 3

15. **D** Neither Passage A nor Passage B is most concerned with praising the accomplishments of particular artists (A), but both are interested in presenting the main characteristics of the movement and indicating its place in twentieth-century art history. The authors do not dispute anything (B). Although both, particularly Passage B, address the society that gave birth to Dadaism (C), this is not the purpose of either. (E) is a secondary point in Passage B.

16. **B** Using art to motivate social reform is not a characteristic of Dadaism, which tends to be anarchic and nihilistic. All the other choices are mentioned in one or both of the passages.

17. **A** The author of Passage A mentions in lines 27–35 how central to modern art is a belief in the artist's utter freedom. However, Passage A does not make a claim that Dadaism is the most significant movement in the first half of the twentieth century (B), nor does it cite Duchamp as elevating Dada above surrealism (C). (D) is inaccurate; the author of Passage A states the importance of the movement, although the author of Passage B does describe surrealism as the "Dadaism of the successful." (E) is also inaccurate; the author of Passage B cites the movement's bitter humor and iconoclasm as helping to "clear the air" of the postwar period.

18. **C** The second and third paragraphs of Passage B cover the post-Dada era. (A) is too vague and general. Both passages cite particular artists (B). Neodadaism isn't mentioned in Passage A (D), and neither passage goes into the artists' techniques (E).

19. **C** (C) is the best answer, as stated in lines 14–17.

20. **B** See lines 119–137. (A) may seem a good answer, but it is much broader (and more vague) than (B). (C) and (D) are not supported in the passage, and (E) is irrelevant.

21. **B** See lines 97–118. Nothing supports the inference that surrealism was the predominant artistic movement of the 1960s (D) or that it was less nihilistic than Dadaism and produced greater works (A). Passage B cites Neodadaism, not surrealism, as championing materialism and mass media (E). And nothing in the passage indicates that surrealism lasted a shorter time than Dadaism (C).

22. **E** Passage B identifies Rauschenberg as a "Neodadaist of the pop art" persuasion.

Passage 4

23. **D** In lines 88–91 the passage describes genetic drift, a change in the gene pool that occurs by chance. If an organism with a survival trait gene doesn't reproduce, the gene is lost. (A) is incorrect; the passage does not indicate which mutations are most "significant." (B) is contrary to fact; see lines 52–54. (C) is contradicted by several examples in the passage of the ways variations occur, and genetic recombination (E) is not cited as the cause of the formation of new species.

24. **B** The vulnerability to carbon dioxide was a trait from a gene that was transmitted to the fruit fly by an outside agent; it is therefore an acquired characteristic. That the fruit fly's offspring exhibit the same vulnerability supports the theory that acquired characteristics can be inherited. In (A), the webbed feet are not an acquired characteristic but a result of mutation and were perpetuated by inbreeding. (C) has no relevance to the question of inheritance, and in (D), the shaving of the dogs has nothing to do with the number of hairless offspring; genetic inheritance (dominant and recessive genes) account for that. (E) does not address the issue of how characteristics were transmitted.

25. **E** (A), (B), (C), and (D) are all explained (however briefly) in the passage. Although (E) is mentioned in line 100, it is not defined or explained.

26. **A** By definition, random mutations occur by chance and are therefore not necessarily related to any survival trait. Darwin's theory states that natural selection accounts for the perpetuation of traits. (B) is incorrect; although spontaneous mutations are said to be infrequent, the frequency of random mutations is not addressed. That random mutations occur doesn't refute or replace Darwin's evolutionary concept; it is simply another possibility for explaining the inheritance of certain traits (C). Both (D) and (E) are factually incorrect.

27. **C** Darwin was more concerned with why certain traits were passed on (survival of the fittest) than with the mechanics of inheritance. (A) and

(B) are incorrect; the passage doesn't imply that Darwin had any opinion about genetics. (In fact, the concept of the gene was developed after Darwin's work.) (D) is incorrect because Darwin recognized that variation among members of a species was central to the idea of natural selection. Although the passage states that he believed acquired characteristics could be inherited, it does not imply that he felt acquired traits were more important than hereditary ones (E).

28. **B** Most of the passage deals briefly with how variation occurs, not with the history of a theory (A) or the differences between genetic and evolutionary theories (D). (C) may seem to be a good answer because the author mentions that Darwin's failure to address the source of variations is "a major weakness." "Expose," however, is too strong a word; the passage is focused not on Darwin's weakness but rather on brief explanations of variation. (E) is a minor, not the primary, concern of the passage.

Section V

1. **C** The passage argues that environmental restrictions will lead to losses of jobs and hence workers, but if workers are already leaving because the environmental quality is poor, the argument is seriously weakened.

2. **B** The passage makes no comment on workers leaving before a manufacturer. It argues that the loss of manufacturers leads to a loss of workers (E).

3. **E** Harry does not need to deal with the connection between excessive carbon dioxide and global warming,

because he does not believe that there is too much carbon dioxide in the atmosphere. He argues that the oceans take care of the gas, so there is no danger.

4. **E** Though choices (A), (B), (C), and (D) might contribute to increased study of math in Bermuda, (E) leaves no doubt. High schools in Bermuda require four years of advanced math for graduation; high schools in the United States do not.

5. **A** Though all of the choices are plausible here, (A) is the best choice. The first sentence asserts the conclusion ("superior"), and the second asserts a consequence ("immature . . . prefer"). The last repeats what has already been insisted upon.

6. **B** The critic requires a good mystery to have "an interesting location" and "a plot that observes probability." If the book in question is disappointing, it may well have "an unrealized setting" and events that "are hard to believe."

7. **B** The passage suggests that records are set only by rare, superior performers, and an increase or decrease in the number of participants would not significantly change the number of record-setting performances.

8. **E** The passage makes its point by analogy, comparing the dangers of smoking to the dangers of asbestos and radioactivity.

9. **A** The passage is clearly hostile to the racist candidate, and has found a "ray of hope." The conclusion should logically predict his defeat. Choice (A) also draws a conclusion related to the part of the paragraph that refers to "regular Republicans."

10. **D** The argument uses both simile ("like strip mining or clear-cutting") and metaphor ("walls of death").

11. **C** If the halibut population is endangered, the banning of gill-nets would improve the fish's chance for survival. If (A) and (B) are true, the fisheries' argument about the price rise has more merit. If (D) and (E) are true, the reduction of the sea otter population would be more defensible.

12. **E** Choices (A), (B), (C), and (D) are reasonable objections, but the argument that *no* writing is without some scientific value is an overstatement.

13. **A** The assumption is that where there are no pesticide controls, no edible fish can be found, not the reverse as in (B), (D), and (E).

14. **D** The results of the elections and the fact that there are three congressmen from the north and three from the south suggest that the populations are nearly equal. Choice (A) would be a likely choice if "always" were changed to "usually." Choice (B) is unlikely, and the passage gives us no reason either to believe in or to disbelieve (C) and (E).

15. **E** The argument is that, one way or another, people can afford to buy their medications. Choice (E), in some measure, supports that argument or at the least is irrelevant to it. People who travel to buy their prescriptions or order them by mail *are*, it would seem, able to afford them somehow. All the other choices weaken the argument, with choices (B), (C), and (D) each suggesting reasons people couldn't afford the drugs and (A) indicating that the type of drug needed may

not be available free from the drug companies.

16. **B**   If the results are like those of the "recent past," the total should approximate "an average of twenty-two House" and "two Senate seats."

17. **D**   The conclusion could be more reasonably assessed if we knew how often the paranormal signs had been false. The issue is not how many contestants win money or how much money they win. The issue is the paranormal aid.

18. **E**   The words "this is the price we must pay" (that is, we must suffer aphid infestation because the rutabagas have been destroyed) indicated that the author makes all of the assumptions of (A), (B), (C), and (D). The idea of (E) may be true, but it is not an assumption of the passage.

19. **A**   The apparent contradiction disappears if the total state budget has increased enough so that the *expenditure* on education has been raised by three million each year while at the same time the *percentage* spent on education is a smaller part of the whole budget.

20. **C**   In each case, the verb ("iron" . . . "need ironing"; "write" . . . "to be written") is repeated, while the adjective ("many") modifies the repeated noun.

21. **B**   The first statement asserts that great playwrights will not develop in repressive countries. Therefore, the great satirists which repressive countries will produce (the second statement) will not write plays.

22. **A**   The details of the paragraph and the phrase "bleak outlook" suggest that a settlement is not likely.

23. **A**   If the new labels will appear on less than 20 percent of the food sold, they will not be very effective.

24. **E**   As the United States is still unwilling to act, its downplaying the conference is a predictable response. Though several of the other choices are plausible, none follows so clearly from what the paragraph has already said.

25. **C**   If there has been a steady rise in car sales, consumers cannot be "cutting back on spending plans for new cars," as the predictions assert.

PART FOUR

FINAL TOUCHES

10

A FINAL CHECKLIST

A Few Days Before the Test

- Review the test directions and strategies for each area.
- Become familiar with the test site; visit it if necessary.
- Follow your normal daily routine; don't make drastic changes.

The Night Before the Test

- Review briefly, but don't cram.
- Get a normal night's sleep; don't go to bed too early or too late.

On the Day of the Test

- Arrive on time, equipped with three or four sharpened No. 2 pencils, a good eraser, proper identification, your admission ticket, and a watch.
- Dress comfortably. (You may wish to dress in "layers" so that you can add or remove a sweater or jacket if the room temperature changes.)
- Read the test directions carefully.
- Use the "one-check, two-check" system.
- Read *actively*.
- In Reading Comprehension and Logical Reasoning, remember to look at all choices before marking your answer.
- In Analytical Reasoning, be aware that you may not always need to review all of the choices before marking your answer.
- Before you leave a problem, be sure to take a guess. Try to make it an educated guess by eliminating some choices.
- If there are only a few minutes left for a section, fill in the remaining problems with guesses before time is called.
- Remember: look for problems that you CAN DO and SHOULD GET RIGHT, and DON'T GET STUCK on any one problem.

NOTES

NOTES

NOTES

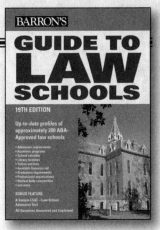

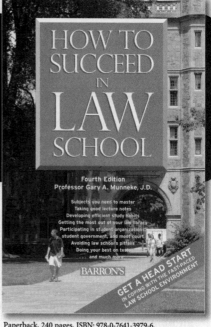

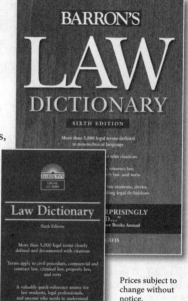

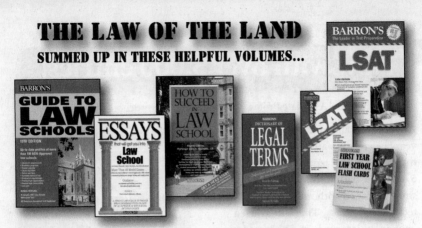